JOHN

C000185265

AN EXAMINATION

OF

SIR WILLIAM HAMILTON'S

PHILOSOPHY

AND OF

THE PRINCIPAL PHILOSOPHICAL QUESTIONS
DISCUSSED IN HIS WRITINGS

Elibron Classics
www.elibron.com

Elibron Classics series.

© 2005 Adamant Media Corporation.

ISBN 1-4212-6400-5 (paperback)
ISBN 1-4212-0841-5 (hardcover)

This Elibron Classics Replica Edition is an unabridged facsimile
of the edition published in 1889 by Longmans, Green, and Co., London and
New York.

AN EXAMINATION

OF

SIR WILLIAM HAMILTON'S PHILOSOPHY.

AN EXAMINATION

OF

SIR WILLIAM HAMILTON'S PHILOSOPHY

AND OF

THE PRINCIPAL PHILOSOPHICAL QUESTIONS DISCUSSED IN HIS WRITINGS

BY

JOHN STUART MILL

SIXTH EDITION

LONDON
LONGMANS, GREEN, AND CO.
AND NEW YORK: 15 EAST 16th STREET
1889

PREFACE TO THE THIRD EDITION.

In former writings I have perhaps seemed to go in search
of objectors, whom I might have disregarded, but who
enabled me to bring out my opinions into greater clearness and relief. My present condition is far different;
for a host of writers, whose mode of philosophic thought
was either directly or indirectly implicated in the
criticisms made by this volume on Sir W. Hamilton,
have taken up arms against it, and fought as *pro aris et
focis*. Among these are included, not solely friends or
followers of Sir W. Hamilton, who were under some
obligation to say whatever could fairly be said in his
defence, but many who stand almost as widely apart
from him as I do, though mostly on the reverse side.
To leave these attacks unanswered, would be to desert
the principles which as a speculative thinker I have
maintained all my life, and which the progress of my
thoughts has constantly strengthened. The criticisms
which have come under my notice (omitting the daily
and weekly journals) are the following; there may be
others :—

Mr. Mansel: "The Philosophy of the Conditioned;
comprising some remarks on Sir William Hamilton's
Philosophy, and on Mr. J. S. Mill's Examination of that
Philosophy." (First published in Nos. 1 and 2 of the
Contemporary Review.)

"The Battle of the Two Philosophies; by an Inquirer."

Dr. M'Cosh : "An Examination of Mr. J. S. Mill's Philosophy, being a Defence of Fundamental Truth."

Dr. Calderwood : "The Sensational Philosophy—Mr. J. S. Mill and Dr. M'Cosh;" in the *British and Foreign Evangelical Review* for April 1866.

Dr. Henry B. Smith : "Mill *v.* Hamilton," in the American *Presbyterian and Theological Review* for January 1866.

Mr. H. F. O'Hanlon : "A Criticism of John Stuart Mill's Pure Idealism ; and an Attempt to show that, if logically carried out, it is Pure Nihilism."

Review of this work in *Blackwood's Magazine* for January 1866.

(The two last mentioned are confined to the doctrine of Permanent Possibilities of Sensation.)

Mr. J. P. Mahaffy, in the Introduction to his translation of Professor Kuno Fischer's account of Kant's Kritik.   (Confined to the doctrine of Permanent Possibilities, and the subject of Necessary Truths.)

Mr. Patrick Proctor Alexander : "An Examination of Mr. John Stuart Mill's Doctrine of Causation in Relation to Moral Freedom ; " forming the greater part of a volume entitled " Mill and Carlyle."

Reviews of this work in the *Dublin Review* for October 1865 (with the signature R. E. G.), and in the *Edinburgh Review* for July 1866.

And, earlier than all these, the able and interesting volume of my friend Professor Masson, entitled " Recent British Philosophy: a Review, with Criticisms ; including some Comments on Mr. Mill's Answer to Sir William Hamilton."

All these, in regard to such of the main questions as they severally discuss, are unqualifiedly hostile : though some of the writers are, in a personal point of view, most courteous, and even over-complimentary; and the last eminently friendly as well as flattering.

The following are only partially adverse:—

Review of the present work in the *North British Review* for September 1865, attributed to Professor Fraser, and bearing the strongest internal marks of that origin. This able thinker, though he considers me to have often misunderstood Sir W. Hamilton, is, on the substantive philosophic doctrines principally concerned, a most valuable ally; to whom I might almost have left the defence of our common opinions.

Mr. Herbert Spencer: "Mill *v.* Hamilton—The Test of Truth;" in the *Fortnightly Review* for July 15, 1865.

Review of the present work in the *North American Review* for July 1866.

The only important criticism, in all essentials favourable, to which I am able to refer, is that in the *Westminster Review* for January 1866, by an illustrious historian and philosopher, who, of all men now living, is the one by whom I should most wish that any writing of mine, on a subject in speculative philosophy, should be approved. There have also been published since the first edition of the present work, two remarkable books, which, if they do not give me direct support, effect a powerful diversion in my favour. One is Mr. Bolton's ' Inquisitio Philosophica; an Examination of the Principles of Kant and Hamilton;" which, along with much other valuable matter, contains a vigorous assault upon my most conspicuous assailant, Mr. Mansel. The other is Mr. Stirling's "Sir William Hamilton, being the Philosophy of Perception; an Analysis:" an able and most severe criticism on Sir W. Hamilton's inconsistencies, and on his general character as a philosopher, taken from a different point of view from mine, and expressed with far greater asperity than I should myself think justifiable; legitimated, no doubt, to the writer's mind by "a certain vein of disingenuousness" which he finds in Sir W. Hamilton, but which I have not found, and shall not believe until I see it proved.

I must have been quite incapable of profiting by criticism, if I had learned nothing from assailants so numerous, all of more or less, and some of very considerable, ability. They have detected not a few inadvertences of expression, as well as some of thought: and partly by their help, partly without it, I have discovered others. They have not shaken any statement or opinion of real moment; but I am sincerely indebted to them, both for the errors they have corrected, and for compelling me to strengthen my defences. The point in which it was to be expected that they would oftenest prevail, was in showing me to have erroneously interpreted Sir W. Hamilton. The difficulty to any thinker is so great, in these high regions of speculation, of placing himself completely at the point of view of a different philosophy, and even of thoroughly understanding its language, that it would be very presumptuous in me to imagine that I had always overcome that difficulty; and that too with the warning before me, of the absolute failure of able and accomplished minds on the other side in philosophy, to accomplish this in regard to the modes of thinking with which I am most familiar. I have been surprised, therefore, to find in how few instances, and those how little important, the defenders of Sir W. Hamilton have been able to show that I have misunderstood or incorrectly stated his opinions or arguments. I cannot doubt that more such mistakes remain to be pointed out: and I regret that the greater part of the volume has not yet, in its relation to Sir W. Hamilton, had the benefit of a sufficiently minute scrutiny. Had the unsparing criticism of Mr. Mansel on the first few chapters been continued to the remainder, he would doubtless have pointed out real mistakes; he might perhaps have thrown light on some of the topics from his own thoughts; and I should at least have had to thank him for additional confidence in the statements and opinions which had passed unharmed through the ordeal of his attacks.

Where criticism or reconsideration has convinced me that anything in the book was erroneous, or that any improvement was required in the mode of stating and setting forth the truth, I have made the requisite alterations. When the case seemed to require that I should call the reader's attention to the change, I have done so; but I have not made this an invariable rule. Mere answers to objectors I have generally relegated to notes. With so many volumes to deal with, I could not take express notice of every criticism which they contained. When any of my critics finds that he, or some of his objections, are not individually referred to, let him be assured that it is from no disrespect, but either because I consider them to have been answered by the reply made to some one else, or because their best confutation is to remand the objector to the work itself, or because the edge of the objection has been turned by some, perhaps quite unapparent, correction of the text. A slight modification in a sentence, or even in a phrase, which a person acquainted with the former editions might read without observing it, and of which, even if he observed it, he would most likely not perceive the purpose, has sometimes effaced many pages of hostile criticism.

Of the assailants to whom I replied, two only have published a rejoinder; Dean Mansel, in the *Contemporary Review* for September 1867, and Dr. M'Cosh, in the *British and Foreign Evangelical Review* for April 1868. Neither of them appears to me to have added much of value to what he had previously advanced; and so far as concerns Dean Mansel, his regretted death has put a final termination to the controversy between us. I am not, however, thereby exempted from taking notice, however briefly, of such points in his rejoinder as appear to require it. Dr. M'Cosh seems to think it a great triumph of his assaults upon me, that many of them were not noticed in my replies to critics. It is a little unreasonable in Dr. M'Cosh to suppose that in a work, the subject of which is the philosophy of Sir William Hamilton, I was bound to fight a pitched battle with Dr. M'Cosh on the whole line. His book was an attack directed against the whole of my philosophical opinions. I answered such parts of it as had reference to the present work, when they seemed to require an answer, and not to have received it sufficiently in what I had already written. And I have done the same, in the present edition, with his rejoinder.

Besides several unpublished criticisms which I owe to the kindness of correspondence, and which have helped me to correct or otherwise improve some of the details of the work; two more attacks have been made upon it subsequently to the third edition. Professor Veitch, in the Appendices to his interesting Memoir of Sir W. Hamilton, has commented sharply on what I have said respecting Sir W. Hamilton's mode of understanding the Relativity of human knowledge, and respecting his failure to apprehend correctly the general character of Hume and Leibnitz as philosophers, as well as some particular passages of Aristotle. On the first subject, that of Relativity, I find so much difficulty in reducing Professor Veitch's statement to distinct propositions, and, so far as I understand his meaning, it differs so little, and that little not to its advantage, from what I have already commented on in answering Mr. Mansel, that I do not think it necessary to burthen this volume with an express reply to him. With regard to Hume and Leibnitz I am content that they who have a competent knowledge of those philosophers should form their own opinion. As regards Sir W. Hamilton's interpretation of Aristotle, Professor Veitch has convicted me of a mistake in treating a citation made by his editors as if it had been made by himself, and of an overstatement of one of Sir W. Hamilton's opinions which I only noticed incidentally. These errors I have corrected, in their places, and it will be found that they do not affect anything of importance in the criticism there made upon Sir W. Hamilton.

Professor Veitch * considers it unfair that I should press against Sir W. Hamilton anything contained in his Lectures, these having been hastily written under pressure from time, and not being the most matured expression of some of his opinions. But though thus written, it is admitted that they continued to be delivered by Sir W. Hamilton as long as he performed the duties of Professor; which would not have been the case if he had no longer considered them as a fair representation of his philosophy. A complete representation I never pretended that they were; a correct representation I am bound to think them; for it cannot be believed that he would have gone on delivering to his pupils matter which he judged to be inconsistent with the subsequent developments of his philosophy.

The other thinker who has taken the field against my psychological opinions is Dr. Ward, who, in the *Dublin*

* Memoir of Sir William Hamilton, pp. 212, 213.

Review for October 1871, has made an able attack on
the views I have expressed in this and other writings on
the subject of what is called Necessary Truth.   Some of
Dr. Ward's observations are more particularly directed
against a portion of my System of Logic, and the fittest
place for their discussion is in connection with that
treatise.   But the greater part of his article principally
regards the chapter of the present work which relates
to Inseparable Association, and a reply to it will be
found in a note which I have added at the end of that
chapter.

CONTENTS.

———

AN EXAMINATION

OF

SIR WILLIAM HAMILTON'S PHILOSOPHY.

CHAPTER I.

INTRODUCTORY REMARKS.

AMONG the philosophical writers of the present century in these islands, no one occupies a higher position than Sir William Hamilton. He alone, of our metaphysicians of this and the preceding generation, has acquired, merely as such, an European celebrity : while, in our own country, he has not only had power to produce a revival of interest in a study which had ceased to be popular, but has made himself, in some sense, the founder of a school of thought. The school, indeed, is not essentially new; for its fundamental doctrines are those of the philosophy which has everywhere been in the ascendant since the setting in of the reaction against Locke and Hume, which dates from Reid among ourselves and from Kant for the rest of Europe. But that general scheme of philosophy is split into many divisions, and the Hamiltonian form of it is distinguished by as marked peculiarities as belong to any other of its acknowledged varieties. From the later German and French developments of the common doctrine, it is separated by differences great in reality, and still greater in appearance ; while it stands superior to the earlier Scottish and English forms by the whole

A

difference of level which has been gained to philosophy
through the powerful negative criticism of Kant. It
thus unites to the *prestige* of independent originality, the recommendation of a general harmony with
the prevailing tone of thought. These advantages,
combined with an intellect highly trained and in many
respects highly fitted for the subject, and a knowledge
probably never equalled in extent and accuracy of
whatever had been previously thought and written in
his department, have caused Sir William Hamilton to
be justly recognised as, in the province of abstract
speculation, one of the important figures of the age.

The acknowledged position of Sir W. Hamilton at
the head, so far as regards this country, of the school
of philosophy to which he belongs, has principally
determined me to connect with his name and writings
the speculations and criticisms contained in the present work. The justification of the work itself lies in
the importance of the questions, to the discussion of
which it is a contribution. England is often reproached
by Continental thinkers, with indifference to the higher
philosophy. But England did not always deserve this
reproach, and is already showing, by no doubtful symp-
toms, that she will not deserve it much longer. Her
thinkers are again beginning to see, what they had
only temporarily forgotten, that a true Psychology is
the indispensable scientific basis of Morals, of Politics,
of the science and art of Education; that the difficulties of Metaphysics lie at the root of all science;
that those difficulties can only be quieted by being
resolved, and that until they are resolved, positively
whenever possible, but at any rate negatively, we are
never assured that any human knowledge, even physical, stands on solid foundations.

My subject, therefore, is less Sir W. Hamilton, than
the questions which Sir W. Hamilton discussed. It is,
however, impossible to write on those questions in our
own country and in our own time, without incessant
reference, express or tacit, to his treatment of them. On

all the subjects on which he touched, he is either one of the most powerful allies of what I deem a sound philosophy, or (more frequently) by far its most formidable antagonist; both because he came the latest, and wrote with a full knowledge of the flaws which had been detected in his predecessors, and because he was one of the ablest, the most far-sighted, and the most candid. Whenever any opinion which he deliberately expressed is contended against, his form of the opinion, and his arguments for it, are those which especially require to be faced and carefully appreciated : and it being thus impossible that any fit discussion of his topics should not involve an estimate of his doctrines, it seems worth while that the estimate should be rendered as complete as practicable, by being extended to all the subjects on which he has made, or on which he is believed to have made, any important contribution to thought.

In thus attempting to anticipate, as far as is yet possible, the judgment of posterity on Sir W. Hamilton's labours, I sincerely lament that on the many points on which I am at issue with him, I have the unfair advantage possessed by one whose opponent is no longer in a condition to reply. Personally I might have had small cause to congratulate myself on the reply which I might have received, for though a strictly honourable, he was a most unsparing controversialist, and whoever assailed even the most unimportant of his opinions, might look for hard blows in return. But it would have been worth far more, even to myself, than any polemical success, to have known with certainty in what manner he would have met the objections raised in the present volume. I feel keenly, with Plato, how much more is to be learnt by discussing with a man, who can question and answer, than with a book, which cannot. But it was not possible to take a general review of Sir W. Hamilton's doctrines while they were only known to the world in the fragmentary state in which they were published during his life. His Lectures, the fullest and the only consecutive exposition (as far as it

goes) of his philosophy, are a posthumous publication ;
while the latest and most matured expression of many
of his opinions, the Dissertations on Reid, left off,
scarcely half finished, in the middle of a sentence ;
and so long as he lived, his readers were still hoping
for the remainder. The Lectures, it is true, have
added less than might have been expected to the knowledge we already possessed of the author's doctrines ;
but it is something to know that we have now all that
is to be had ; and though we should have been glad to
have his opinions on more subjects, we could scarcely
have known more thoroughly than we are now at last
enabled to do, what his thoughts were on the points
to which he attached the greatest importance, and
which are most identified with his name and fame.

CHAPTER II.

THE RELATIVITY OF HUMAN KNOWLEDGE.

THE doctrine which is thought to belong in the most especial manner to Sir W. Hamilton, and which was the ground of his opposition to the transcendentalism of the later French and German metaphysicians, is that which he and others have called the Relativity of Human Knowledge. It is the subject of the most generally known, and most impressive, of all his writings, the one which first revealed to the English metaphysical reader that a new power had arisen in philosophy; and, together with its developments, it composes the "Philosophy of the Conditioned," which he opposed to the German and French philosophies of the Absolute, and which is regarded by most of his admirers as the greatest of his titles to a permanent place in the history of metaphysical thought.

But the "relativity of human knowledge," like most other phrases into which the words relative or relation enter, is vague, and admits of a great variety of meanings. In one of its senses, it stands for a proposition respecting the nature and limits of our knowledge, in my judgment true, fundamental, and full of important consequences in philosophy. From this amplitude of meaning its significance shades down through a number of gradations, successively more thin and unsubstantial, till it fades into a truism leading to no consequences, and hardly worth enunciating in words. When, therefore, a philosopher lays great stress upon the relativity of our knowledge, it is necessary to cross-examine his writings, and compel them to disclose in which of its many degrees of meaning he understands the phrase.

There is one of its acceptations, which, for the purpose now in view, may be put aside, though in itself
defensible, and though, when thus employed, it expresses
a real and important law of our mental nature.   This is,
that we only know anything, by knowing it as distinguished from something else ; that all consciousness is
of difference ; that two objects are the smallest number
required to constitute consciousness; that a thing is only
seen to be what it is, by contrast with what it is not.
The employment of the proposition, that all human
knowledge is relative, to express this meaning, is sanc-
tioned by high authorities,* and I have no fault to find
with that use of the phrase.   But we are not concerned
with it in the present case ; for it is not in this sense,
that the expression is ordinarily or intentionally used
by Sir W. Hamilton ; though he fully recognises the
truth which, when thus used, it serves to express.   In
general, when he says that all our knowledge is relative,
the relation he has in view is not between the thing
known and other objects compared with it, but between
the thing known and the mind knowing.

All language recognises a distinction between myself
—the Ego—and a world, either material, or spiritual,
or both, external to me, but of which I can, in some
mode and measure, take cognisance.   The most fundamental questions in philosophy are those which seek to
determine what we are able to know of these external
objects, and by what evidence we know it.

In examining the different opinions which are or
may be entertained on this subject, it will simplify the
exposition very much, if we at first limit ourselves to
the case of physical, or what are commonly called
material objects.   These objects are of course known
to us through the senses.   By those channels and no
otherwise do we learn whatever we do learn concerning
them.   Without the senses we should not know nor
suspect that such things existed.   We know no more

* In particular by Mr. Bain, who habitually uses the phrase "relativity
of knowledge" in this sense.

of what they are, than the senses tell us, nor does nature afford us any means of knowing more. Thus much, in the obvious meaning of the terms, is denied by no one, though there are thinkers who prefer to express the meaning in other language.

There are, however, conflicting opinions as to *what it is* that the senses tell us concerning objects. About one part of the information they give, there is no dispute. They tell us our sensations. The objects excite, or awaken in us, certain states of feeling. A part, at least, of what we know of the objects, is the feelings to which they give rise. What we term the properties of an object, are the powers it exerts of producing sensations in our consciousness. Take any familiar object, such as an orange. It is yellow; that is, it affects us, through our sense of sight, with a particular sensation of colour. It is soft; in other words it produces a sensation, through our muscular feelings, of resistance overcome by a slight effort. It is sweet; for it causes a peculiar kind of pleasurable sensation through our organ of taste. It is of a globular figure, somewhat flattened at the ends: we affirm this on account of sensations that it causes in us, respecting which it is still in dispute among psychologists whether they originally came to us solely through touch and the muscles, or also through the organ of sight. When it is cut open, we discover a certain arrangement of parts, distinguishable as being, in certain respects, unlike one another; but of their unlikeness we have no measure or proof except that they give us different sensations. The rind, the pulp, the juice, differ from one another in colour, in taste, in smell, in degree of consistency (that is, of resistance to pressure) all of which are differences in our feelings. The parts are, moreover, outside one another, occupying different portions of space: and even this distinction, it is maintained (though the doctrine is vehemently protested against by some) may be resolved into a difference in our sensations. When thus analysed, it is affirmed that all the attributes which we ascribe to objects, consist in their having the

power of exciting one or another variety of sensation in
our mind; that to us the properties of an object have
this and no other meaning; that an object is to us nothing else than that which affects our senses in a certain
manner; that we are incapable of attaching to the word
object, any other meaning; that even an imaginary object is but a conception, such as we are able to form, of
something which would affect our senses in some new
way; so that our knowledge of objects, and even our
fancies about objects, consist of nothing but the sensations which they excite, or which we imagine them
exciting in ourselves.

This is the doctrine of the Relativity of Knowledge
to the knowing mind, in the simplest, purest, and, as I
think, the most proper acceptation of the words.   There
are, however, two forms of this doctrine, which differ
materially from one another.

According to one of the forms, the sensations which,
in common parlance, we are said to receive from objects,
are not only all that we can possibly know of the objects,
but are all that we have any ground for believing to
exist.   What we term an object is but a complex conception made up by the laws of association, out of the
ideas of various sensations which we are accustomed to
receive simultaneously.   There is nothing real in the
process but these sensations.   They do not, indeed, accompany or succeed one another at random; they are
held together by a law, that is, they occur in fixed groups,
and a fixed order of succession : but we have no evidence
of anything which, not being itself a sensation, is a substratum or hidden cause of sensations.   The idea of such
a substratum is a purely mental creation, to which we
have no reason to think that there is any corresponding
reality exterior to our minds.   Those who hold this
opinion are said to doubt or deny the existence of matter.
They are sometimes called by the name Idealists, sometimes by that of Sceptics, according to the other opinions
which they hold.   They include the followers of Berkeley
and those of Hume.   Among recent thinkers, the acute

and accomplished Professor Ferrier, though by a circuitous path, and expressing himself in a very different phraseology, seems to have arrived at essentially the same point of view.   These philosophers maintain the Relativity of our knowledge in the most extreme form in which the doctrine can be understood, since they contend, not merely that all we can possibly know of anything is the manner in which it affects the human faculties, but that there is nothing else to be known; that affections of human or of some other minds are all that we can know to exist.

This, however, is far from being the shape in which the doctrine of the Relativity of our knowledge is usually held.   To most of those who hold it, the difference between the Ego and the Non-Ego is not one of language only, nor a formal distinction between two aspects of the same reality, but denotes two realities, each having a separate existence, and neither dependent on the other.   In the phraseology borrowed from the Schoolmen by the German Transcendentalists, they regard the Noumenon as in itself a different thing from the Phenomenon, and equally real; many of them would say, much more real, being the permanent Reality, of which the other is but the passing manifestation.   They believe that there is a real universe of "Things in Themselves," and that whenever there is an impression on our senses, there is a "Thing in itself," which is behind the phenomenon, and is the cause of it.   But as to what this Thing *is* "in itself," we, having no organs except our senses for communicating with it, can only know what our senses tell us; and as they tell us nothing but the impression which the thing makes upon *us*, we do not know what it is *in itself* at all.   We suppose (at least these philosophers suppose) that it must be something "in itself," but all that we know it to be is merely relative to us, consisting in the power of affecting us in certain ways, or, as it is technically called, of producing Phenomena.   External things exist, and have an inmost nature, but their inmost nature is inaccessible to our faculties. We know it not, and can assert nothing of it with a meaning. Of the ultimate Realities, as such, we know the existence, and nothing more. But the impressions which these Realities make on us—the sensations they excite, the similitudes, groupings, and successions of those sensations, or, to sum up all this in a common though improper expression, the *representations* generated in our minds by the action of the Things themselves—these we may know, and these are all that we can know respecting them. In some future state of existence it is conceivable that we may know more, and more may be known by intelligences superior to us. Yet even this can only be true in the same sense in which a person with the use of his eyes knows more than is known to one born blind, or in which we should know more than we do if we were endowed with two or three additional senses. We should have more sensations ; phenomena would exist to us of which we have at present no conception ; and we might know better than we now do, many of those which are within our present experience ; for if the new impressions were linked with the old, as the old are with one another, by uniformities of succession and co-existence, we should now have new marks indicating to us known phenomena in cases in which we should otherwise have been unaware of them. But all this additional knowledge would be, like that which we now possess, merely phenomenal. We should not, any more than at present, know things as they are in themselves, but merely an increased number of relations between them and us. And in the only meaning which we are able to attach to the term, all knowledge, by however exalted an Intelligence, can only be relative to the knowing Mind. If Things have an inmost nature, apart not only from the impressions which they produce, but from all those which they are fitted to produce, on any sentient being, this inmost nature is unknowable, inscrutable, and inconceivable, not to us merely, but to every other creature. To say that even the Creator could know it, is

to use language which to us has no meaning, because
we have no faculties by which to apprehend that there
is any such thing for him to know.

It is in this form that the doctrine of the Relativity
of Knowledge is held by the greater number of those
who profess to hold it, attaching any definite idea to the
term.   These again are divided into several distinct
schools of thinkers, by some of whom the doctrine is
held with a modification of considerable 'importance.

Agreeing in the opinion that what we know of Noumena, or Things in themselves, is but their bare existence, all our other knowledge of Things being but a
knowledge of something in ourselves which derives its
origin from them ; there is a class of thinkers who hold
that our mere sensations, and an outward cause which
produces them, do not compose the whole of this relative
knowledge.   The Attributes which we ascribe to outward things, or such at least as are inseparable from
them in thought, contain, it is affirmed, other elements,
over and above sensations *plus* an unknowable cause.
These additional elements are still only relative, for they
are not in the objects themselves, nor have we evidence
of anything in the objects that answers to them.   They
are added by the mind itself, and belong, not to the
Things, but to our perceptions and conceptions of them.
Such properties as the objects can be conceived divested
of, such as sweetness or sourness, hardness or softness,
hotness or coldness, whiteness, redness, or blackness—
these, it is sometimes admitted, exist in our sensations
only.   But the attributes of filling space, and occupying
a portion of time, are not properties of our sensations
in their crude state, neither, again, are they properties
of the objects, nor is there in the objects any prototype
of them.   They result from the nature and structure of
the Mind itself: which is so constituted that it cannot
take any impressions from objects except in those particular modes.   We see a thing in a place, not because
the Noumenon, the Thing in itself, is in any place, but
because it is the law of our perceptive faculty that we

must see as in some place, whatever we see at all.   Place
is not a property of the Thing, but a mode in which the
mind is compelled to represent it.   Time and Space are
only modes of our perceptions, not modes of existence,
and higher Intelligences are possibly not bound by
them.   Things, in themselves, are neither in time nor
in space, though we cannot represent them to ourselves
except under that twofold condition.   Again, when we
predicate of a thing that it is one or many, a whole or a
part of a whole, a Substance possessing Accidents, or an
Accident inhering in a Substance—when we think of it
as producing Effects, or as produced by a Cause (I omit
other attributes not necessary to be here enumerated),
we are ascribing to it properties which do not exist in
the Thing itself, but with which it is clothed by the
laws of our conceptive faculty—properties not of the
Things, but of our mode of conceiving them.   We are
compelled by our nature to construe things to ourselves
under these forms, but they are not forms of the Things.
The attributes exist only in relation to us, and as inherent laws of the human faculties; but differ from
Succession and Duration in being laws of our intellectual, not our sensitive faculty; technically termed
Categories of the Understanding.   This is the doctrine
of the Relativity of our knowledge as held by Kant,
who has been followed in it by many subsequent
thinkers, German, English, and French.

By the side of this there is another philosophy, older
in date, which, though temporarily eclipsed and often
contemptuously treated by it, is, according to present
appearances, likely to survive it.   Taking the same view
with Kant of the unknowableness of Things in themselves, and also agreeing with him that we mentally
invest the objects of our perceptions with attributes
which do not all point, like whiteness and sweetness, to
specific sensations, but are in some cases constructed by
the mind's own laws; this philosophy, however, does
not think it necessary to ascribe to the mind certain
innate forms, in which the objects are (as it were)

moulded into these appearances, but holds that Place, Extension, Substance, Cause, and the rest, are conceptions put together out of ideas of sensation by the known laws of association. This, the doctrine of Hartley, of James Mill, of Professor Bain, and other eminent thinkers, and which is compatible with either the acceptance or the rejection of the Berkeleian theory, is the extreme form of one mode of the doctrine of Relativity, as Kant's is of another. Both schemes accept the doctrine in its widest sense—the entire inaccessibility to our faculties of any other knowledge of Things than that of the impressions which they produce in our mental consciousness.

Between these there are many intermediate systems, according as different thinkers have assigned more or less to the original furniture of the mind on the one hand, or to the associations generated by experience on the other. Brown, for example, regards our notion of Space or Extension as a product of association, while many of our intellectual ideas are regarded by him as ultimate and undecomposable facts. But he accepts, in its full extent, the doctrine of the Relativity of our knowledge, being of opinion that though we are assured of the objective existence of a world external to the mind, our knowledge of that world is absolutely limited to the modes in which we are affected by it. The same doctrine is very impressively taught by one of the acutest metaphysicians of recent times, Mr. Herbert Spencer, who, in his " First Principles," insists with equal force upon the certainty of the existence of Things in Themselves, and upon their absolute and eternal relegation to the region of the Unknowable.* This is also, apparently, the doctrine of Auguste Comte : though while maintaining with great emphasis the unknowableness of Noumena by our faculties, his aversion to metaphysics prevented him from giving any definite opinion as to their real existence, which, however, his language always by implication assumes.

It is obvious that what has been said respecting the

* See, however, below, a note near the end of chap. ix.

unknowableness of Things "in themselves," forms no
obstacle to our ascribing attributes or properties to them,
provided these are always conceived as relative to us.
If a thing produces effects of which our sight, hearing,
or touch can take cognisance, it follows, and indeed is
but the same statement in other words, that the thing
has *power* to produce those effects. These various powers
are its properties, and of such, an indefinite multitude is
open to our knowledge. But this knowledge is merely
phenomenal. The object is known to us only in one
special relation, namely, as that which produces, or is
capable of producing, certain impressions on our senses ;
and all that we really know is these impressions. This
negative meaning is all that should be understood by
the assertion, that we cannot know the Thing in itself ;
that we cannot know its inmost nature or essence. The
inmost nature or essence of a Thing is apt to be
regarded as something unknown, which, if we knew it,
would explain and account for all the phenomena which
the thing exhibits to us. But this unknown something
is a supposition without evidence. We have no ground
for supposing that there is anything which if known to
us would afford to our intellect this satisfaction ; would
sum up, as it were, the knowable attributes of the object
in a single sentence. Moreover, if there were such a
central property, it would not answer to the idea of an
" inmost nature ; " for if knowable by any intelligence,
it must, like other properties, be relative to the intelligence which knows it, that is, it must solely consist in
producing in that intelligence some specifically definite
state of consciousness ; for this is the only idea we have
of knowing ; the only sense in which the verb " to
know " means anything.

It would, no doubt, be absurd to assume that our
words exhaust the possibilities of Being. There may be
innumerable modes of it which are inaccessible to our
faculties, and which consequently we are unable to name.
But we ought not to speak of these modes of Being by
any of the names we possess. These are all inapplicable,
because they all stand for known modes of Being. We

might invent new names for such unknown modes; but the new names would have no more meaning than the x, y, z, of Algebra. The only name we can give them which really expresses an attribute, is the word Unknowable.

The doctrine of the Relativity of our knowledge, in the sense which has now been explained, is one of great weight and significance, which impresses a character on the whole mode of philosophical thinking of whoever receives it, and is the key-stone of one of the only two possible systems of Metaphysics and Psychology. But the doctrine is capable of being, and is, understood in at least two other senses. In one of them, instead of a definite and important tenet, it means something quite insignificant, which no one ever did or could call in question. Suppose a philosopher to maintain that certain properties of objects are in the Thing, and not in our senses; in the thing itself, not as whiteness may be said to be in the thing (namely, that there is in the thing a power whereby it produces in us the sensation of white), but in quite another manner; and are known to us not indirectly, as the inferred causes of our sensations, but by direct perception of them in the outward object. Suppose the same philosopher nevertheless to affirm strenuously that all our knowledge is merely phenomenal, and relative to ourselves; that we do not and cannot know anything of outward objects, except relatively to our own faculties. I think our first feeling respecting a thinker who professed both these doctrines, would be to wonder what he could possibly mean by the latter of them. It would seem that he must mean one of two trivialities; either that we can only know what we have the power of knowing, or else that all our knowledge is relative to us inasmuch as it is we that know it.

There is another mode of understanding the doctrine of Relativity, intermediate between these insignificant truisms and the substantial doctrine previously expounded. The position taken may be, that perception of Things as they are in themselves is not entirely denied to us, but is so mixed and confounded with impressions derived from their action on us, as to give a relative character to the whole aggregate. Our absolute knowledge may be vitiated and disguised by the presence of a relative element. Our faculty (it may be said) of perceiving things as they are in themselves, though real, has its own laws, its own conditions, and necessary mode of operation: our cognitions subsequently depend, not solely on the nature of the things to be known, but also on that of the knowing faculty, as our sight depends not solely upon the object seen, but upon that together with the structure of the eye. If the eye were not achromatic, we should see all visible objects with colours derived from the organ, as well as with those truly emanating from the object. Supposing, therefore, that Things in themselves are the natural and proper object of our knowing faculty, and that this faculty carries to the mind a report of what is in the Thing itself, apart from its effects on us, there would still be a portion of uncertainty in these reports, inasmuch as we could not be sure that the eye of our mind is achromatic, and that the message it brings from the Noumenon does not arrive tinged and falsified, in an unknown degree, through an influence arising from the necessary conditions of the mind's action. We may, in short, be looking at Things in themselves, but through imperfect glasses: what we see may be the very Thing, but the colours and forms which the glass conveys to us may be partly an optical illusion. This is a possible opinion : and one who, holding this opinion, should speak of the Relativity of our knowledge, would not use the term wholly without meaning. But he could not, consistently, assert that *all* our knowledge is relative ; since his opinion would be that we have a capacity of Absolute knowledge, but that we are liable to mistake relative knowledge for it.

In which, if in any, of these various meanings, was the doctrine of Relativity held by Sir W. Hamilton? To this question, a more puzzling one than might have been expected, we shall endeavour in the succeeding chapter to find an answer.

9

17)

CHAPTER III.

THE DOCTRINE OF THE RELATIVITY OF HUMAN KNOW-
LEDGE, AS HELD BY SIR WILLIAM HAMILTON.

IT is hardly possible to affirm more strongly or more explicitly than Sir W. Hamilton has done, that Things in themselves are to us altogether unknowable, and that all we can know of anything is its relation to us, composed of, and limited to, the Phenomena which it exhibits to our organs. Let me cite a passage from one of the Appendices to the "Discussions."[*]

"Our whole knowledge of kind and of matter is re-
"lative, conditioned—relatively conditioned. Of things
"absolutely or in themselves, be they external, be they
"internal, we know nothing, or know them only as in-
"cognisable; and become aware of their incomprehen-
"sible existence, only as this is indirectly and accidentally
"revealed to us, through certain qualities related to our
"faculties of knowledge, and which qualities, again, we
"cannot think as unconditioned, irrelative, existent in
"and of themselves. All that we know is therefore
"phenomenal,—phenomenal of the unknown . . . .
"Nor is this denied; for it has been commonly con-
"fessed, that, as substances, we know not what is
"Matter, and are ignorant of what is Mind."

This passage might be matched by many others, equally emphatic, and in appearance equally decisive; several of which I shall have occasion to quote. Yet in the sense which the author's phrases seem to convey—in the only important meaning capable of being attached to them—the doctrine they assert was certainly not held

* "Discussions on Philosophy," p. 643.

B

by Sir W. Hamilton.   He by no means admits that we
know nothing of objects except their existence, and the
impressions produced by them upon the human mind.
He affirms this in regard to what have been called by
metaphysicians the Secondary Qualities of Matter, but
denies it of the Primary.

On this point his declarations are very explicit.   One
of the most elaborate of his Dissertations on Reid is
devoted to expounding the distinction.   The Dissertation begins thus : *

"The developed doctrine of Real Presentationism, the
" basis of Natural Realism " (the doctrine of the author
himself) " asserts the consciousness or immediate per-
" ception of certain essential attributes of Matter ob-
" jectively existing ; while it admits that other properties
" of body are unknown in themselves, and only inferred
" as causes to account for certain subjective affections of
" which we are cognisant in ourselves.   This discrimina-
" tion, which to other systems is contingent, superficial,
" extraneous, but to Natural Realism necessary, radical,
" intrinsic, coincides with what since the time of Locke
" has been generally known as the distinction of the
" Qualities of Matter or Body, using these terms as
" convertible, into Primary and Secondary."

Further on,† he states, in additional development of
so-called Natural Realism, " that we have not merely a
" notion, a conception, an imagination, a subjective re-
" presentation—of Extension, for example—called up or
" suggested in some incomprehensible manner to the
" mind, on occasion of an extended object being pre-
" sented to the sense ; but that in the perception of such
" an object we really have, as by nature we believe we
" have, an immediate knowledge of that external object
" *as extended*."

"If‡ we are not percipient of any extended reality,
" we are not percipient of body as existing ; for body

* Dissertations appended to Sir W. Hamilton's Edition of Reid's
Works, p. 825.
          † Dissertations, p 842.   ‡ Ibid.

" exists, and can only be known immediately, and in
" itself, *as extended.* The material world, on this sup-
" position, sinks into something unknown and proble-
" matical ; and its existence, if not denied, can, at least,
" be only precariously affirmed, as the occult cause, or in-
" comprehensible occasion, of certain subjective affections
" we experience in the form either of a sensation of the
" secondary quality or of a perception of the primary."

Not only, in Sir W. Hamilton's opinion, do we know,
by direct consciousness or perception, certain properties
of Things as they exist in the Things themselves, but
we may also know those properties as in the Things, by
demonstration *à priori.* " The notion* of body being
" given, every primary quality is to be evolved out of
" that notion, as necessarily involved in it, independently
" altogether of any experience of sense." " The† Pri-
" mary Qualities may be deduced *à priori,* the bare notion
" of matter being given ; they being, in fact, only evo-
" lutions of the conditions which that notion necessarily
" implies." He goes so far as to say, that our belief of
the Primary Qualities is, not merely necessary as involved in a fact of which we have a direct perception,
but necessary in itself, by our mental constitution. He
speaks‡ of "that absolute or insuperable resistance which
" we are compelled, independently of experience, to
" think that every part of matter would oppose to any
" attempt to deprive it of its space, by compressing it
" into an inextended."

The following is still more specific.§ " The Primary "
Qualities " are apprehended as they are in bodies ; the
Secondary, as they are in us : the Secundo-primary "
(a third class created by himself, comprising the mechanical as distinguished from the geometrical properties
of Body) "as they are in bodies and as they are in us. . . .
" We know the Primary qualities immediately as objects
" of perception ; the Secundo-primary both immediately
" as objects of perception and mediately as causes of sen-

* Dissertations, p. 844.
† Ibid. p. 846.   ‡ Ibid. p. 848.   § Ibid. pp. 857, 858.

" sation ; the Secondary only mediately as causes of sen-
" sation.   In other words : The Primary are known im-
" mediately in themselves ; the Secundo-primary, both
" immediately in themselves and mediately in their effects
" on us ; the Secondary, only mediately in their effects
" on us. . . . . . We are conscious, as objects, in the
" Primary Qualities, of the modes of a not-self ; in the
" Secondary, of the modes of self ; in the Secundo-pri-
" mary, of the modes of self and of a not-self at once."

There is nothing wonderful in Sir W. Hamilton's
entertaining these opinions ; they are held by perhaps a
majority of metaphysicians.   But it is surprising that,
entertaining them, he should have believed himself, and
been believed by others, to maintain the Relativity of all
our knowledge.   What he deems to be relative, in any
sense of the term that is not insignificant, is only our
knowledge of the Secondary Qualities of objects.   Extension and the other Primary Qualities he positively asserts
that we have an immediate intuition of, " as they are in
bodies"—"as modes of a not-self ; " in express contradistinction to being known merely as causes of certain
impressions on our senses or on our minds.   As there
cannot have been, in his own thoughts, a flat contradiction between what he would have admitted to be the two
cardinal doctrines of his philosophy, the only question
that can arise is, which of the two is to be taken in a
non-natural sense.   Is it the doctrine that we know
certain properties as they are in the Things ?   Were we
to judge from a foot-note to the same Dissertation, we
might suppose so.   He there observes *—" In saying
" that a thing is known in itself, I do not mean that this
" object is known in its absolute existence, that is, out
" of relation to us.   This is impossible : for our know-
" ledge is only of the relative.   To know a thing in itself
" or immediately, is an expression I use merely in con-
" trast to the knowledge of a thing in a representation,
" or mediately : " in other words, he merely means that
we perceive objects directly, and not through the *species*

* P. 866.

sensibiles of Lucretius, the Ideas of Locke, or the Mental Modifications of Brown. Let us suppose this granted, and that the knowledge we have of objects is gained by direct perception. Still, the question has to be answered whether the knowledge so acquired is of the objects as they are in themselves, or only as they are relatively to us. Now what, according to Sir W. Hamilton, *is* this knowledge? Is it a knowledge of the Thing, merely in its effects on us, or is it a knowledge of somewhat in the Thing, ulterior to any effect on us? He asserts in the plainest terms that it is the latter. Then it is not a knowledge wholly relative to us. If what we perceive in the Thing is something of which we are only aware as existing, and as causing impressions on us, our knowledge of the Thing is only relative. But if what we perceive and cognise is not merely a cause of our subjective impressions, but a Thing possessing, in its own nature and essence, a long list of properties, Extension, Impenetrability, Number, Magnitude, Figure, Mobility, Position, all perceived as " essential attributes ". of the Thing as " objectively existing "—all as " Modes of a Not-self" and by no means as an occult cause or causes of any Modes of Self—(and that such is the case Sir W. Hamilton asserts in every form of language, leaving no stone unturned to make us apprehend the breadth of the distinction) then I am willing to believe that in affirming this knowledge to be entirely relative to Self, such a thinker as Sir W. Hamilton had a meaning, but I have no small difficulty in discovering what it is.

The place where we should expect to find this difficulty cleared up, is the formal exposition of the Relativity of Human Knowledge, in the first volume of the Lectures.

He declares his intention * of "now stating and ex- " plaining the great axiom that all human knowledge, " consequently that all human philosophy, is only of the " relative or phenomenal. In this proposition, the term " *relative* is opposed to the term *absolute ;* and therefore, " in saying that we know only the relative, I virtually

* Lectures, i. 136–8.

" assert that we know nothing absolute,—nothing exist-
" ing absolutely, that is, in and for itself, and without rela-
" tion to us and our faculties.   I shall illustrate this by
" its application.   Our knowledge is either of matter or
" of mind.   Now, what is matter?   What do we know
" of matter?   Matter, or body, is to us the name either
" of something known, or of something unknown.   In so
" far as matter is a name for something known, it means
" that which appears to us under the forms of extension,
" solidity, divisibility, figure, motion, roughness, smooth-
" ness, colour, heat, cold, &c. ; in short, it is a common
" name for a certain series, or aggregate, or complement
" of appearances or phenomena manifested in coexistence.

" But as these phenomena appear only in conjunction,
" we are compelled by the constitution of our nature to
" think them conjoined in and by something ; and as they
" are phenomena, we cannot think them the phenomena
" of nothing, but must regard them as the properties or
" qualities of something that is extended, solid, figured,
" &c.   . But this something, absolutely and in itself,
" *i.e.* considered apart from its phenomena—is to us as
" zero.   It is only in its qualities, only in its effects, in
" its relative or phenomenal existence, that it is cognis-
" able or conceivable ; and it is only by a law of thought
" which compels us to think something absolute and un-
" known, as the basis or condition of the relative and
" known, that this something obtains a kind of incom-
" prehensible reality to us.   Now, that which manifests
" its qualities—in other words, that in which the appear-
" ing causes inhere, that to which they belong,—is called
" their *subject,* or *substance,* or *substratum.*   To this sub-
" ject of the phenomena of extension, solidity, &c., the
" term *matter* or *material substance* is commonly given ;
" and therefore, as contradistinguished from these quali-
" ties, it is the name of something unknown and incon-
" ceivable.

" The same is true in regard to the term *mind.*   In so
" far as mind is the common name for the states of
" knowing, willing, feeling, desiring, &c., of which I am

" conscious, it is only the name for a certain series of
" connected phenomena or qualities, and, consequently,
" expresses only what is known. But in so far as it
" denotes that subject or substance in which the pheno-
" mena of knowing, willing, &c., inhere—something be-
" hind or under these phenomena—it expresses what,
" in itself or in its absolute existence, is unknown.

  " Thus, mind and matter, as known or knowable, are
" only two different series of phenomena or qualities ;
" mind and matter, as unknown and unknowable, are
" the two substances in which these two different series
" of phenomena or qualities are supposed to inhere.
" The existence of an unknown substance is only an in-
" ference we are compelled to make from the existence
" of known phenomena ; and the distinction of two sub-
" stances is only inferred from the seeming incompati-
" bility of the two series of phenomena to coinhere in
" one.

  " Our whole knowledge of mind and matter is thus,
" as we have said, only relative ; of existence, absolutely
" and in itself, we know nothing : and we may say of
" man what Vigil said of Æneas, contemplating in the
" prophetic sculpture of his shield the future glories of
" Rome—

  " Rerumque ignarus, imagine gaudet."

Here is an exposition of the nature and limits of our
knowledge, which would have satisfied Hartley, Brown,
and even Comte. It cannot be more explicitly laid
down, that Matter, as known to us, is but the incomprehensible and incognisable basis or substratum of a
bundle of sensible qualities, appearances, phenomena ;
that we know it " only in its effects ; " that its very
existence is " only an inference we are compelled to
make " from those sensible appearances. On the subject
of Mind, again, could it have been more explicitly
affirmed, that all we know of Mind is its successive
states " of knowing, willing, feeling, desiring, &c.," and
that Mind, considered as " something behind or under
these phenomena," is to us unknowable ?

Subsequently he says, that not only all the knowledge we have of anything, but all which we could have
if we were a thousandfold better endowed than we are,
would still be only knowledge of the mode in which the
thing would affect us.   Had we as many senses (the
illustration is his own) as the inhabitants of Sirius, in
the "Micromegas" of Voltaire ; were there, as there
may well be, a thousand modes of real existence as
definitely distinguished from one another as are those
which manifest themselves to our present senses, and
" had we,* for each of these thousand modes, a separate
" organ competent to make it known to us,—still would
" our whole knowledge be, as it is at present, only of
" the relative.   Of existence, absolutely and in itself, we
" should then be as ignorant as we are now.   We should
" still apprehend existence only in certain special modes—
" only in certain relations to our faculties of knowledge."
Nothing can be truer or more clearly stated than all
this : but the clearer it is, the more irreconcileable does
it appear with our author's doctrine of the direct cognoscibility of the Primary Qualities.   If it be true that
Extension, Figure, and the other qualities enumerated,
are known "immediately in themselves," and not, like
Secondary qualities, " in their effects on us ; " if the
former are " apprehended as they are in bodies," and not,
like the Secondary, " as they are in us ; " if it is these
last exclusively that are " unknown in themselves, and
only "inferred as causes to account for certain subjective
" affections in ourselves : " while, of the former, we are
immediately conscious as "attributes of matter objectively existing ;" and if it is not to be endured that
matter should " sink into something unknown and
problematical," whose existence " can be only precari-
" ously affirmed as the occult cause or incomprehensible
" occasion of certain subjective affections we experience
"in the form either of a sensation of the secondary qua-
" lity or of a perception of the primary " (being precisely what Sir W. Hamilton, in the preceding quota-

* Lectures, i. 153.

tions, appeared to say that it is) ; if these things be so, our faculties, as far as the Primary Qualities are concerned, do cognise and know Matter as it is in itself, and not merely as an unknowable and incomprehensible substratum ; they do cognise and know it as it exists absolutely, and not merely in relation to us ; it is known to us directly, and not as a mere "inference" from Phenomena.

Will it be said that the attributes of extension, figure, number, magnitude, and the rest, though known as in the Things themselves, are yet known only relatively to us, because it is by our faculties that we know them, and because appropriate faculties are the necessary condition of knowledge? If so, the "great axiom" of Relativity is reduced to this, that we can know things as they are in themselves, but can know no more of them than our faculties are competent to inform us of. If such be the meaning of Relativity, our author might well maintain* that it is a truth "harmoniously re-echoed by every philosopher of every school ;" nor need he have added "with the exception of a few late Absolute theorisers in Germany ;" for certainly neither Schelling nor Hegel claims for us any other knowledge than such as our faculties are, in their opinion, competent to give.

Is it possible, that by knowledge of qualities "as they are in Bodies," no more was meant than knowing that the Body must have qualities whereby it produces the affection of which we are conscious in ourselves? But this is the very knowledge which our author predicates of Secondary Qualities, as contradistinguished from the Primary. Secondary he frankly acknowledges to be occult qualities : we really, in his opinion, have no knowledge, and no conception, what that is in an object, by virtue of which it has its specific smell or taste. But Primary qualities, according to him, we know all about : there is nothing occult or mysterious to us in these ; we perceive and conceive them as they are in

* Discussions, Appendix, p. 644.

themselves, and as they are in the body they belong to. They are manifested to us, not like the Secondary qualities, only in their effects, in the sensations they exite in us, but in their own nature and essence.

Perhaps it may be surmised, that in calling knowledge of this sort by the epithet Relative, Sir W. Hamilton meant that though we know those qualities as they are in themselves, we only discover them through their relation to certain effects in us; that in order that there may be Perception there must also be Sensation; and we thus know the Primary Qualities, in their effects on us and also in themselves. But neither will this explanation serve. This theory of Primary Qualities does not clash with the Secondary, but it runs against the Secundo-primary. It is this third class, which, as he told us, are known "both immediately in themselves and mediately in their effects on us." The Primary are only known "immediately in themselves." He has thus with his own hands deliberately extruded from our knowledge of the Primary qualities the element of relativity to us :—except, to be sure, in the acceptation in which knowing is itself a relation, inasmuch as it implies a knower; whereby instead of the doctrine that Things in themselves are not possible objects of knowledge, we obtain the "great axiom" that they cannot be known unless there is somebody to know them.

Can any light be derived from the statement that we do not know any qualities of things except those which are in connection with our faculties, or, as our author expresses it (surely by a very strained use of language), which are "analogous to our faculties"? * If, by "our faculties," is to be understood our knowing faculty, this proposition is but the trivial one already noticed, that we can know only what we can know. And this is what the author actually seems to mean; for in a sentence immediately following, † he paraphrases the expression "analogous to our faculties," by the phrase that we must "possess faculties accommodated to their apprehension."

* Lectures, i. 141, 153.   † P. 153.

To be able to see, we must have a faculty accommodated
to seeing. Is this what we are intended to understand
by the "great axiom"? But if "our faculties" does
not here mean our knowing faculty, it must mean our
sensitive faculties; and the statement is, that, to be
known by us, a quality must be "analogous" (meaning,
I suppose, related) to our senses. But what is meant by
being related to our senses? That it must be fitted to
give us sensations. We thus return as before to an
identical proposition.

There is still another possible supposition; that, in
calling our knowledge relative in contradistinction to
absolute, Sir W. Hamilton was not thinking of our
knowledge of qualities, but of substances—of Matter
and Mind; and meant that qualities might be cognised
absolutely, or as they are in themselves, but that, since
substances are only known through their qualities, the
knowledge of substances is not knowledge of them as
they are in themselves, but is merely relative. According to this interpretation, the relativity which Sir W.
Hamilton ascribes to our knowledge of substances is relativity not to us, but to their attributes: we "become
"aware of their incomprehensible existence only as this
"is revealed to us through certain qualities." And
when he adds, "which qualities, again, we cannot think
"as unconditioned, irrelative, existent in and of them-
"selves," thus predicating relativity of attributes also
(considered as known or conceived by us), he means relativity to a substance. We can only know a substance
through its qualities, but also, we can only know qualities as inhering in a substance. Substance and attribute are correlative, and can only be thought together:
the knowledge of each, therefore, is relative to the other;
but need not be, and indeed is not, relative to us. For
we know attributes as they are in themselves, and our
knowledge of them is only relative inasmuch as attributes have only a relative existence. It is relative
knowledge in a sense not contradictory to absolute. It
is an absolute knowledge, though of things which only

exist in a necessary relation to another thing called a substance.*

I am not disposed to deny that this interpretation of Sir W. Hamilton's doctrine is, to a certain point, correct. He did draw a distinction between our manner of knowing attributes and our manner of knowing substances; and did regard certain attributes (the primary qualities) as objects of direct and immediate knowledge; which, in his opinion, substances are not, but are merely assumed or inferred from phenomena, by a law of our nature which compels us to think phenomena as attributes of something beyond themselves.   I do not doubt that when he said that our knowledge of attributes is relative, the necessity of thinking every attribute as an attribute of a substance was present to his mind, and formed a part of his meaning.   There is, however, abundant evidence that the relativity which Sir W. Hamilton ascribed to our knowledge of attributes was not merely relativity to their substances, but also relativity to us.   He affirms of attributes as positively as of substances, that all our knowledge of them is relative to us.   The passages already quoted apply as much to attributes as to substances.   " In saying that we know only the relative, I "virtually assert that we know *nothing* absolute—nothing " existing absolutely, that is, in and for itself, and *without* " *relation to us and our faculties.*" †   " In saying that a " thing is known in itself, I do not mean that this object " is known in its absolute existence, that is, *out of rela-* " *tion to us.*   This is impossible, for *our knowledge is only* " *of the relative.*" ‡   In the following passages he is speaking solely of attributes.   " By the expression *what* " *they are in themselves,* in reference to the primary " qualities, and of *relative notion* in reference to the " secondary, Reid cannot mean that the former are " known to us absolutely and in themselves, that is, out

---

* This is essentially the interpretation put on Sir W. Hamilton's meaning by the ingenious reviewer of the present work in the *Edinburgh Review.*

    † Lectures, i. 137.   ‡ Dissertations, p. 866.

" of relation to our cognitive faculties ; for he elsewhere
" admits that all our knowledge is relative." *   " We
" can know, we can conceive, only what is relative.
" Our knowledge of qualities or phenomena is neces-
" sarily relative ; for these exist only as they exist in
" relation to our faculties." †   The distinction, therefore,
which Sir W. Hamilton recognises between our knowledge of substances and that of attributes, though
authentically a part of his philosophy, is quite irrelevant
here.   He affirms without reservation, that certain
attributes (extension, figure, &c.) are known to us as
they really exist out of ourselves ; and also that all our
knowledge of them is relative to us.   And these two
assertions are only reconcileable, if relativity to us is
understood in the altogether trivial sense, that we know
them only so far as our faculties permit. ‡

The conclusion I cannot help drawing from this col-
lation of passages is, that Sir W. Hamilton either never
held, or when he wrote the Dissertations had ceased to
hold (for his theory respecting knowledge of the Primary
Qualities does not occur in the Lectures) the doctrine
for which he has been so often praised and nearly as
often attacked—the Relativity of Human Knowledge.
He certainly did sincerely believe that he held it.   But
he repudiated it in every sense which makes it other
than a barren truism.   In the only meaning in which
he really maintained it, there is nothing to maintain.
It is an identical proposition, and nothing more.

And to this, or something next to this, he reduces it
in the first portion of the summary with which he concludes its exposition.   " From what has been said," he

* Footnote to Reid, p. 313.
† Ib. p. 320. I am indebted to Mr. Mansel (Philosophy of the Conditioned, p. 79) for reminding me of the last two passages. I should not
have failed to quote them in the first edition, if I had kept references to
them.
‡ I may add that even the Edinburgh Reviewer's supposition does not
save either the relativity of human knowledge *to us*, or its relativity in
the sense in which relative is opposed to absolute, as doctrines of Sir W.
Hamilton : for by the Reviewer's interpretation our knowledge of attributes
would be relative only to their substances ; absolute in their cognition by us.

observes,* "you will be able, I hope, to understand
" what is meant by the proposition, that all our know-
" ledge is only relative. It is relative, 1st. Because
" existence is not cognisable absolutely in itself, but
" only in special modes ; 2nd. Because these modes
" can be known only if they stand in a certain relation
" to our faculties." Whoever can find anything more
in these two statements, than that we do not know all
about a Thing, but only as much about it as we are
capable of knowing, is more ingenious or more fortunate
than myself.

He adds, however, to these reasons why our knowledge is only relative, a third reason. " 3rd. Because
" the modes, thus relative to our faculties, are assented
" to, and known by, the mind only under modifications
" determined by those faculties themselves." Of this
addition to the theory we took notice near the conclusion of the preceding chapter. It shall have the advantage of a fuller explanation in Sir W. Hamilton's words.

" In † the perception of an external object, the mind
" does not know it in immediate relation to itself, but
" mediately, in relation to the material organs of sense.
" If, therefore, we were to throw these organs out of
" consideration, and did not take into account what they
" contribute to, and how they modify, our knowledge of
" that object, it is evident that our conclusion in regard
" to the nature of external perception would be erroneous.
" Again, an object of perception may not even stand in
" immediate relation to the organ of sense, but may
" make its impression on that organ through an inter-
" vening medium. Now, if this medium be thrown out
" of account, and if it be not considered that the real
" external object is the sum of all that externally con-
" tributes to affect the sense, we shall, in like manner,
" run into error. For example, I see a book—I see that
" book through an external medium (what that medium
" is, we do not now inquire) and I see it through my
" organ of sight, the eye. Now, as the full object pre-

* Lectures, i. 148..   † Ibid. pp. 146–148.

" sented to the mind (observe that I say the mind) in
" perception, is an object compounded of the external
" object emitting or reflecting light, i.e., modifying the
" external medium—of this external medium—and of
" the living organ of sense, in their mutual relation,
" let us suppose, in the example I have taken, that the
" full or adequate object perceived is equal to twelve, and
" that this amount is made up of three several parts : of
" four, contributed by the book,—of four, contributed by
" all that intervenes between the book and the organ,—
" and of four, contributed by the living organ itself. I
" use this illustration to show that the phenomenon of
" the external object is not presented immediately to
" the mind, but is known by it only as modified through
" certain intermediate agencies ; and to show, that sense
" itself may be a source of error, if we do not analyse
" and distinguish what elements, in an act of perception,
" belong to the outward reality, what to the outward
" medium, and what to the action of sense itself. But
" this source of error is not limited to our perceptions ;
" and we are liable to be deceived, not merely by not
" distinguishing in an act of knowledge what is con-
" tributed by sense, but by not distinguishing what is
" contributed by the mind itself. This is the most diffi-
" cult and important function of philosophy; and the
" greater number of its higher problems arise in the
" attempt to determine the shares to which the knowing
" subject, and the object known, may pretend in the
" total act of cognition. For according as we attribute
" a larger or a smaller proportion to each, we either run
" into the extremes of Idealism and Materialism, or
" maintain an equilibrium between the two."

The proposition that our cognitions of objects are
only in part dependent on the objects themselves, and
in part on elements superadded by our organs or by our
minds, is not identical, nor *primâ facie* absurd. It cannot, however, warrant the assertion that all our knowledge, but only that the part so added, is relative. If
our author had gone as far as Kant, and had said that

all the primary qualities which we think we perceive in
bodies, are put in by the mind itself, he would have
really held, in one of its forms, the doctrine of the
Relativity of our knowledge.   But what he does say,
far from implying that the whole of our knowledge is
relative, distinctly imports that all of it which is real
and authentic is the reverse.   If any part of what we
fancy that we perceive in the objects themselves, originates in the perceiving organs or in the cognising mind,
thus much is purely relative ; but since, by supposition,
it does not all so originate, the part that does not, is as
much absolute as if it were not liable to be mixed up
with these delusive subjective impressions.   The ad-
mixture of the relative element not only does not take
away the absolute character of the remainder, but does
not even (if our author is right) prevent us from recognising it.   The confusion, according to him, is not inextricable.   It is for us to "analyse and distinguish what
elements " in an " act of knowledge " are contributed by
the object, and what by our organs, or by the mind.
We may neglect to do this, and as far as the mind's
share is concerned, can only do it by the help of philosophy ; but it is a task to which in his opinion philosophy
is equal.   By thus stripping off such of the elements in
our apparent cognitions of Things as are but cognitions
of something in us, and consequently relative, we may
succeed in uncovering the pure nucleus, the direct intuitions of Things in themselves ; as we correct the
observed positions of the heavenly bodies by allowing
for the error due to the refracting influence of the
atmospheric medium, an influence which does not alter
the facts, but only our perception of them.

    This last doctrine, however,—that the mind's own con-
stitution contributes along with the outward object, to
make up what is called our knowledge of the object,—
is what Mr. Mansel maintains Sir W. Hamilton to
have meant by the assertion that our whole knowledge
of the object is relative.   And this is the foundation of
all that Mr. Mansel presents as a refutation of the
present chapter.

If it be true (to use Mr. Mansel's words) * that, in the constitution of our knowledge, the mind " reacts on the " objects affecting it, so as to produce a result different "from that which would be produced, were it merely a "passive recipient," this modifying action of the mind must consist, as is affirmed by Kant and by all others who profess the doctrine, in making us ascribe to the object, and apprehend as in the object, properties which are not really in the object, but are merely lent to it by the constitution of our mental nature. Now, if the attributes which we perceive, or think we perceive, in objects, are partly given by the mind, but not wholly, being also partly given by the nature of the object itself (which is admitted to be Sir W. Hamilton's opinion); this joint agency of the object and of the mind's own laws in generating what we call our knowledge of the object, may be conceived in two ways.

First: The two factors may be jointly operative in every part of the effect. Every attribute with which we perceive the thing as invested, may be a joint product of the thing itself and of the modifying action of the mind. If this be the case, we do not really know any property as it is in the object: we have no reason to think that the object as we apprehend it, and as we figure to ourselves that we perceive and know it, agrees in any respect with the object that exists without us ; but only that it depends upon that outward object, as one of its joint causes. Such was the opinion of Kant; and whoever is of this opinion, holds, in one of its forms, as I have expressly admitted, the genuine doctrine of the Relativity of our knowledge. For all must agree with Mr. Mansel when he says, that an object of thought, into which the mind puts a positive element of its own, thereby making it different from what it otherwise would be, *is* that which it is, only relatively to the mind. This seems to be Mr. Mansel's own mode of representing to himself the combined action of the mind and the object

---

* Mansel, p. 64.

C

in perception.   For he compares it * to the action of an acid and an alkali in forming a neutral salt ; and † to a chemical fusion together of two elements, in contra-distinction to a mere mechanical juxtaposition.   If we had never seen, and could not get at, the acid or the alkali except as united in the salt, Mr. Mansel could not think that our knowledge of the salt gave us any knowledge of the acid or the alkali themselves.

But, secondly : there is another mode in which the co-operation of the object and the mind's own properties in producing our cognition of the object, may be con-ceived as taking place.   Instead of their being joint agents in producing our cognitions of all the attributes with which we mentally clothe the object, some of the attributes as cognised by us may come from the object only, and some from the mind only, or from both.   Now it is not open to a holder of this second opinion, as it is to one of the first, to affirm that all the attributes are only known relatively to us.   Such of them, indeed, as are made to be that which they are by what the mind puts into them, are on this theory, only known relatively to the mind : they have even no existence except rela-tively to the mind.   But those into which no positive element is introduced by the mind's laws (I say no posi-tive element, because a mere negative limitation by the mind's capacities is nothing to the purpose), these, as their cognition contains nothing but what is presented in the external object, must be held to be known not relatively, but absolutely.   The doubt how much of what we apprehend in them is due to our own constitu-tion, and how much to the external world, has no place here : they are, by supposition, wholly perceptions of something in the external world.

Now, this second view of the joint action of the mind and the outward thing, as the two factors in our cog-nition of the thing, is Sir W. Hamilton's.   The pas-sages in which he characterises our knowledge of the

* Mansel, p. 71.   † Ibid. p. 75.

PrimaryQualities place this beyond question.   Heaffirms clearly and consistently that extension, figure, and the other Primary Qualities are known by us " as they are in bodies,"and not " as they are in us;" that theyare known as " essential attributes of matter objectively existing; " as "modes of a not-self," not even combined, as in the Secundo-primary, with any "modes of self; " so that no element originating in our subjective constitution in-terferes with the purity of the apperception.   In this respect the physical phenomena which Mr. Mansel calls in as illustrations afford no parallel.   No one would say that the acid in a neutral salt is perceived and known by us in the salt as what it is as an acid. Indeed, the discrimination which Sir W. Hamilton thinks it possible for philosophy to make, between that in our knowledge which the object contributes and that which the mind contributes, almost requires as its con-dition that some attributes should be wholly contributed by the one and some by the other : for if every attri-bute was the joint product of both, it is difficult to see what means the case could afford of making the dis-crimination, any more than of discriminating between the acid and the alkali in Mr. Mansel's salt.   The question, how much of the salt is due to the acid and how much to the alkali, is not merely unresolvable, but intrinsically absurd.*

* Sir W. Hamilton has the appearance of disclaiming the opinion here attributed to him, and professing the alternative opinion that every attri-bute is a joint product of the object and the mind, in the following foot-note to Reid (p. 313) :

"The distinctions of perception and sensation, and of primary and " secondary qualities, may be reduced to one higher principle.   Knowledge " is partly objective, partly subjective ; both these elements are essential " to every cognition, but in every cognition they are always in the inverse " ratio of each other.   Now, in perception and the primary qualities, the " objective element preponderates ; whereas the subjective element pre-" ponderates in sensation and the secondary qualities.   See Notes D " and D*."

But a reference to the Notes in question will show, that in admitting a subjective element in the Primary Qualities, he only meant that a sub-jective element *accompanies* our apprehension of them ; that whenever we perceive the primary qualities we are conscious of a sensation also. "Sensation proper," he says, "is the *conditio sine qua non* of a Perception

Mr. Mansel's mode of reconciling Sir W. Hamilton's
emphatic declaration, that we know the Primary Qualities
as they are in objects, with his assertion of the entire
incognoscibility of Things in themselves, is by saying *
that " objects " are not identical with " things in themselves." "Objective existence,"he says,† "does not mean
" existence *per se;* and a phenomenon does not mean a
" mere mode of mind. Objective existence is existence as
" an object, in perception, and therefore in relation ; and
" a phenomenon may be material, as well as mental. The
" thing *per se* may be only the unknown cause of what
" we directly know ; but what we directly know is some-
" thing more than our own sensations. In other words,
" the phenomenal effect is material as well as the cause,
" and is, indeed, that from which our primary conceptions
" of matter are derived."

Now, this is a possible opinion ; it was really the
opinion of Kant. That philosopher did recognise a
direct object of our perceptions, different from the thing
itself, and intermediate between it and the perceiving
mind. And it was open to Kant to do so ; because he
held what Sir W. Hamilton calls a representative theory
of perception. He maintained that the object of our
perception, and of our knowledge, is a representation in
our own minds. In his philosophy, both object and subject are accommodated within the mind itself—the object
within the subject. The mind has no perception of the
external thing, nor comes into any contact with it in the

" proper of the Primary qualities." And again, "Every Perception proper
"has a Sensation proper as its condition." "The fact of Sensation proper
"and the fact of Perception proper imply each other:" they always coexist, though "in the degree or intensity of their existence they are always
"found in an inverse ratio to one another" (Reid, p. 886). This coexistence does not prevent the two from being entirely distinct. "The
"apprehensions of the Primary" qualities "are perceptions, not sensa-
"tions ; of the Secondary, sensations, not perceptions ; of the Secundo-
"primary, perceptions and sensations together" (p. 858). Perceptions,
the apprehensions of the Primary qualities, are themselves wholly
objective.

* Mansel, p. 79.   † Ibid. p. 82.

act of perception.* Was this Sir W. Hamilton's opinion?
On the contrary, if there be a doctrine of his philosophy
which he has laboured at beyond any other, against,
as he affirms, nearly all philosophers, it is, that the
thing we perceive is the real thing which exists outside
us, and that the preceiving mind is in direct contact with
it, without any intermediate link whatever. We never
hear from Sir W. Hamilton of three elements in our
cognition of the outward world, but of two only, the
mind, and the real object; which he sometimes calls
the external object, sometimes Body, sometimes Matter,
sometimes a Non-ego. Yet, according to Mr. Mansel, he
must have believed that this object, which he so strenuously contended to be the very thing itself, is not the
very thing *in* itself, but that behind it there is another
Thing in itself, the unknown cause of it. I can discover
no trace in Sir W. Hamilton's writings of any such
entity. The outward things which he believed to exist,
he believed that we perceive and know : not, indeed,
" absolutely or in themselves," because only in such of
their attributes as we have senses to reveal to us; but
yet as they really are. He did not believe in, or recognise, a Thing *per se*, itself unknowable, but engendering
another material object called a phenomenon, which is
knowable. The only distinction he recognised between
a phenomenon and a Thing *per se*, was that between
attributes and a substance. But he believed the primary attributes to be known by us as they exist in the
substance, and not in some intermediate object.†

* Such, at least, is the doctrine of Kant in the first edition of the
Kritik, though, in the so-called Refutation of Idealism introduced into
the second, he is sometimes supposed to have intended to explain it away ;
but Mr. Mahaffy (Introd. part iv. and notes to Appendix C) seems to
have explained away the explanation ; and Mr. Stirling, who holds (p. 30)
" the second edition of the Kritik of Pure Reason to supersede the first,"
still credits Kant with this doctrine, interpreting in a sense consistent
with it, the externality which Kant ascribes to objects in space. Kant's
external and internal were both internal to the mind. Nothing but the
noumenon was external to it.
    † If any doubt could remain that Mr. Mansel defends Sir W. Hamil-
ton by ascribing to him an opinion he never held, the following passage

The mark by which Mr. Mansel distinguishes between the object and the Thing in itself, is that the object is in space and time, but the Thing out of space and time ; space and time having merely a subjective existence, in us, not in external nature. This is Kantism, but it is not Hamiltonism. I do not believe that the expression "out of space and time" is to be found once in all Sir

---

would dispel it. "If, indeed," says Mr. Mansell (p. 83) "Hamilton had "said with Locke, that the primary qualities are in the bodies themselves, "whether we perceive them or no, he would have laid himself open to "Mr. Mill's criticism. But he expressly rejects this statement, and con- "trasts it with the more cautious language of Descartes, 'ut sunt, vel "saltem esse possunt.'" Sir W. Hamilton may never have said, *totidem verbis*, that the Primary Qualities are in the bodies even when we do not perceive them : but can any one who has read his writings doubt that this was his opinion? The passage which Mr. Mansel refers to as "reject- ing" it (Dissertations, p. 839) runs as follows :—"On the doctrine of "both philosophers" (Locke and Descartes) "we know nothing of material "existence in itself : we know it only as represented, or in idea. When "Locke, therefore, is asked, how he became aware that the known idea "truly represents the unknown reality, he can make no answer. On the "first principles of his philosophy, he is wholly and necessarily ignorant "whether the idea does or does not represent to his mind the attributes "of matter, as they exist in nature. His assertion is, therefore, con- "fessedly without a warrant ; it transcends, *ex hypothesi*, the sphere of "possible knowledge. Descartes is more cautious. He only says, that "our ideas of the qualities in question represent those qualities as they "are, or as they may exist ; 'ut sunt, vel saltem esse possunt.' The "Cosmothetic Idealist can only assert to them a problematical reality." Mr. Mansel actually thinks this an adoption of Descartes' opinion ; and does not see that Sir W. Hamilton merely pronounces Descartes to be right and Locke wrong from their own point of view, that of Cosmothetic Idealism. As Cosmothetic Idealists, they have, he says, no evidence that the qualities we perceive are in the object itself, and are as we perceive them. Not admitting that we directly perceive the qualities in the object, they cannot do more than assert problematically that the qualities are in the object ; and this Descartes saw, and Locke, more inconsistently, did not see. But what they as Cosmothetic Idealists could not affirm, Sir W. Hamilton, as a Natural Realist, could ; because, as a Natural Realist, he held that we directly perceive the qualities in the object. Mr. Mansel mistakes one of the thousand statements by Sir W. Hamilton of his difference with the Cosmothetic Idealists, for an adhesion to them. (Mr. Mansel, in his rejoinder, admits and withdraws this error.) Sir W. Hamilton, as Professor Fraser observes (p. 22), believed that "the "solid and extended percepts which our sensations reveal to us, exist, "whether we are conscious or not." He believed that bodies exist whether we perceive them or not, and that they always carry their "essential attributes," the Primary Qualities, with them : if, therefore, he had thought that the Primary Qualities only exist while we perceive them, he must have thought so of the bodies likewise, and must have believed that we create the bodies in the act of perceiving them ; which Kant, who

W. Hamilton's writings. It belongs to the Kantian, not to the Hamiltonian philosophy. Sir W. Hamilton does indeed hold with Kant, and on Kant's showing, that space and time are *à priori* forms of the mind, but he believes that they are also external realities, known empirically.* And it is worth notice, that he grounds the outward reality of Space, not on his favourite evidence, that of our Natural Beliefs, but on the specific reason, that (Extension being only another name for Space), if Space was not an outward thing cognisable

deemed the body we perceive to be really in the mind, did believe ; but if Sir W. Hamilton did, his whole philosophy of perception is without a meaning.

In the essay in his "Discussions," headed "Philosophy of Perception," Sir W. Hamilton speaks of the knowledge of external objects claimed by a Natural Realist, *ipsissimis verbis*, as knowledge of "things in themselves." (Discussions, p. 57, in the statement of the opinion of Hypothetical Realists.)

For a critical examination of the doctrine ascribed to Sir W. Hamilton by Mr. Mansel, that of an external object cognisable by us, and an uncognisable Noumenon besides, I may refer to Mr. Bolton's able work, pp. 218 et seqq.

Mr. Mansel, in his rejoinder, though he does not give up the theory of the *tertium quid*, does not further insist on it ; but attempts to show that when Sir W. Hamilton speaks of knowing the Primary qualities as they are in themselves, and as they are in the body, he means knowing them in immediate relation to the mind, in contradistinction to knowing them mediately through a mental representation, or merely inferring them as the hypothetical cause of a mental state. I admit, and have already admitted, that Sir W. Hamilton did mean this, and did say that he meant it. But the "immediate relation to the mind" which Sir W. Hamilton thus distinguished from the different modes of mediate relation, is no other than that between perceiver and perceived : and to say that all our knowledge is relative, meaning only *this* relation, is but to say, that we know of external things only what we perceive of them, and that in order that we may know an object of sense it must be presented to our senses. The knowledge, when we do get it, according to Sir W. Hamilton, is not (in the case of Primary Qualities) knowledge of an impression made on our own sensitive faculty, which would be really relative knowledge ; it is knowledge of the Thing as it exists in itself, independently of our perceptions. It is this which, as I have pointed out, reduces the pretended Relativity to a name.

It is a great confirmation of the unmeaningness of the Relativity Doctrine in Sir W. Hamilton's hands, that those who have most studied his philosophy, Dean Mansel and Professor Veitch, are reduced to such straits in the attempt to find a meaning for it, and do not always find the same meaning.

* See Lectures, ii. 113, 114 ; Discussions, p. 16 ; Dissertations, p. 882 ; and, in further illustration, foot-note to Reid, p. 126 ; passages strangely overlooked by Mr. Mansel (p. 138).

à posteriori, we could not, as he affirms that we do, cognise Extension as an external reality. He must therefore have thought, not that Space is a mere form in which our perceptions of objects are clothed by the laws of our perceiving faculty, but that we perceive real things in real space.*

Mr. Mansel is not the only one of my critics who has interpreted Sir W. Hamilton's doctrine of our direct knowledge of outward objects, as if those outward objects were a *tertium quid*, between the mind and the real outward, or if the expression may be permitted, the outer outward object. For irreconcilable as this supposition is with the evidence of his writings, it is the only one which can be thought of to give a substantial meaning to his doctrine of Relativity, consistent with the external reality of the Primary Qualities. Professor Mason consequently had already taken refuge in the same interpretation as Mr. Mansel; but propounded it in the modest form of an hypothesis, not a dogmatical assertion. The North American Reviewer in like manner says† : "An existence non-ego may be immediately cog- "nisable consistently with the doctrine of the relativity "of knowledge, provided this non-ego be phenomenal, "that is, necessarily dependent on some other incognis- "able existence among the real causes of things. . . . . "If the meaning of the word phenomenon which we "have attributed to Hamilton be a valid one, his philo- "sophy escapes from this criticism by affirming that the "primary qualities of matter, that is, the having exten- "sion, figure, &c., though not cognised as the effects of

---

* When Sir W. Hamilton says (Dissertations, p. 841) that although Space is a native, necessary, *à priori* form of imagination, we yet have an immediate perception of a really objective extended world, Mr. Mansel imagines that Sir W. Hamilton is maintaining at once the subjectivity of Space, and the objectivity of bodies as occupying space. But Sir W. Hamilton himself declares unequivocally that these two opinions contradict one another, unless reconciled by the supposition that Space is objective and external to us as well as subjective : not, therefore, properly a form of our mind, but an outward reality which has a form of our mind corresponding to it. See the whole of the passages referred to in the last note.

† Pp. 252, 253.

" matter on us, are yet modes of existence implying an
" unknown substance, and are hence phenomenal in
" Hamilton's meaning of the word." This explanation
might pass, if Sir W. Hamilton's assertion of the relativity of our knowledge to our mind were all contained
in the word phenomenal, and could be explained away
by supposing that word to mean relativity not to us,
but to an unknown cause. But I need not requote his
declaration that our knowledge of Qualities is all relative
to us, nor his assertion that nevertheless certain qualities
are in the object, and are perceived and known in the
object, and that the object perceived and known is no
other than the real Thing itself. Nowhere in his works
do I find any recognition of another real Thing, which
is not the Thing perceived by us through its attributes.
He does not tell us of a Body perceived, and an unperceived Substance in the background : the Body is the
Substance. He does indeed say that the Substance is
only an inference from the Attributes ; but he also says
that certain attributes are perceived as in the real external Thing ; and he never drops the smallest hint of
any real external thing *in* which the attributes can
be, except the Substance itself, which he expressly
defines as " that which manifests its qualities," that in
which " the phenomena or qualities are supposed to
" inhere."

Professor Fraser, in the (in many respects) profound
Essay of which he has done this work the honour of
making it the occasion, vindicates at once the consistency
of Sir W. Hamilton, and the substantial significance of
his doctrine of Relativity, by ascribing to him, in opposition to his incessant declarations, Mr. Fraser's own far
clearer views of the subject. Mr. Fraser, like myself,
believes the Primary Qualities to have no more existence
out of our own or other minds, than the Secondary
Qualities have, or than our pains and pleasures have ;
and he asks,* " Where does he " (Sir W. Hamilton) " say

* Fraser, p. 16.

"that we have an absolute knowledge of the primary
"qualities of matter, in any other sense than that in
"which he says that we have a like knowledge of a feel-
"ing of pain or pleasure in our minds while it is being
"felt, or of an act of consciousness while it is being
"acted?" To this "where," I answer, in every place
where he says that we know the Primary Qualities not
as they are in us, but as they are in the Body. That is
asserting an absolute knowledge of them, as distinguished
from relativity to us : and he would not have made a
similar assertion of our pains and pleasures, or of our
acts of internal consciousness. Again, asks Mr. Fraser,*
"How does the assertion that we are percipient directly,
"and not through a medium, of phenomena of solidity
"and extension, contradict the principle that all our
"knowledge is relative, when the assertion that we are
"percipient, directly and not through a medium, of the
"phenomena of sensation or emotion or intelligence
"does not?" Because the phenomena of sensation or
emotion or intelligence are admitted to be perceived or
felt as facts that have no reality out of us, and the facts
being only relative to us, the knowledge of the facts
partakes of the same relativity : but the phenomena of
solidity and extension are alleged by Sir W. Hamilton
to be perceived as facts whose reality is out of our
minds, and in the material object: which is indeed knowing them relatively to the outward object, but is the
diametrical opposite of knowing them relatively to us.†
It has now been shown, by accumulated proof, that

* Fraser, p. 15.
† Mr. Fraser affirms (p. 20) with me, and contrary to Mr. Mansel and
the North American Reviewer, that in Sir W. Hamilton's opinion "there
"is nothing *behind* the proper objects of sense-consciousness, these being
"the very things or realities themselves which we call material, external,
"extended, solid." Instead of recognising three elements, a Noumenal
real thing, a Phenomenal real thing, and the perceiving mind, the middle
one of the three being that which the mind cognises, Mr. Fraser sees that
Sir W. Hamilton recognised but one real Thing, the very Thing which we
perceive ; unknown to us in its essence, but perceived and known through
its attributes ; and by means of those attributes, actually brought into
what Sir W. Hamilton calls our consciousness. This Mr. Fraser regards
as "a distinct and important contribution by Sir W. Hamilton to the

Sir W. Hamilton did not hold any opinion in virtue of which it could rationally be asserted that all human knowledge is relative; but did hold, as one of the main elements of his philosophical creed, the opposite doctrine, of the cognoscibility of external Things, in certain of their aspects, as they are in themselves, absolutely.

But if this be true, what becomes of his dispute with

"theory of matter previously common in this country," because bringing matter into our consciousness is part of the way towards making it (what Mr. Fraser believes it to be) wholly a phenomenon of mind. But Sir W. Hamilton did not intend his doctrine to lead to this; he admits Matter into our consciousness because, contrary to the general opinion of philosophers, he thinks (see below, chap. viii.) that we can be conscious of what is outside our mind. Sir W. Hamilton, in short, was not a Berkeleian, as Mr. Fraser is, and as that philosopher almost admits (p. 26) that the interpretation which he would like to put on Sir W. Hamilton's doctrine would make Sir W. Hamilton.

Mr. Fraser seems to me, throughout his defence of Sir W. Hamilton, to have yielded to the natural tendency of a consistent thinker when standing up for an inconsistent one, to interpret ambiguous utterances which face two ways, as if they looked only one way; though the part of their author's philosophy towards which those expressions face on their other side, is thereby set at nought and abolished.

Since the publication of the third edition of this work, my attention has been drawn to a passage (unfortunately left unfinished) in the posthumous continuation of Sir W. Hamilton's Dissertations on Reid, which strikingly confirms the opinion I have expressed, that the relativity of human knowledge, as understood by him, is a mere identical proposition.

"That all knowledge consists in a certain relation of the object known "to the subject knowing, is self-evident. What is the nature of this "relation, and what are its conditions, is not, and never can be, known to "us; because we know only the qualities of our own faculties of know-"ledge, as relations to their objects, and we only know the qualities of "their objects, as relations to our minds. All qualities both of mind and "of matter are therefore only known to us as relations; we know nothing "in itself. We know not the cause of this relation, we know nothing of "its conditions, the fact is all. *The relation is the relation of knowledge.* "We know nothing consequently of the kind of the relation; we have no "consciousness and no possible knowledge whether the relation of know-"ledge has any analogy to the relations of similarity, contrariety, identity, "difference—we have no consciousness that it is like any other, or any "modification of any other: these are all relations of a different kind "between object and object; this between subject and object: we can "institute no point of comparison" (Reid, p. 965).

That is to say, we know nothing except in relation to us, but that relation is simply the relation of being known by us, and this is the only relation cognisable by us which exists between the knower and the known. Our knowledge is relative, but only in the sense that knowing is itself a relation. Would Cousin, or Hegel, or Schelling, have had the slightest objection to admit that our knowledge even of the Absolute is relative, in the sense that it is we that know it?

Cousin, and with Cousin's German predecessors and teachers? That celebrated controversy surely meant something. Where there was so much smoke there must have been some fire. Some difference of opinion must really have existed between Sir W. Hamilton and his antagonists.

Assuredly there was a difference, and one of great importance from the point of view of either disputant; not unimportant in the view of those who dissent from them both. In the succeeding chapter I shall endeavour to point out what the difference was.

CHAPTER IV.

IN WHAT RESPECT SIR WILLIAM HAMILTON REALLY DIFFERS FROM THE PHILOSOPHERS OF THE ABSOLUTE.

THE question really at issue in Sir W. Hamilton's celebrated and striking review of Cousin's philosophy, is
this : Have we, or have we not, an immediate intuition
of God. The name of God is veiled under two extremely abstract phrases, "The Infinite" and "The
Absolute," perhaps from a reverential feeling : such, at
least, is the reason given by Sir W. Hamilton's disciple,
Mr. Mansel,* for preferring the more vague expressions.
But it is one of the most unquestionable of all logical
maxims, that the meaning of the abstract must be sought
for in the concrete, and not conversely ; and we shall
see, both in the case of Sir W. Hamilton and of Mr.
Mansel, that the process cannot be reversed with im-
punity.†

---

* Bampton Lectures. (The Limits of Religious Thought.) Fourth
edition, p. 42.
† Mr. Mansel (pp. 90–98) denies the correctness of the representations
made in this paragraph ; and at least seems to assert, that the question
between M. Cousin and Sir W. Hamilton did not relate to the possibility
of knowing *the* Infinite Being, but to a "pseudo-concept of the Infinite,"
which Sir W. Hamilton believed to be not a proper predicate of God, but
a representation of a non-entity. And Mr Mansel affirms (p. 92) that to
substitute the name of God in the place of the Infinite and the Absolute,
is exactly to reverse Sir W. Hamilton's argument. We have here a direct
issue of fact, of which every one is a judge who will take the trouble to
read Sir W. Hamilton's Essay. I maintain that what M. Cousin affirms
and Sir W. Hamilton denies, is the cognoscibility not of an Infinite and
Absolute which is not God, but of the Infinite and Absolute which is God.
I might refer to almost any page of the Essay ; I will only quote the
application which Sir W. Hamilton himself makes of his own doctrine
(Disc. p. 15, note). " True, therefore, are the declarations of a pious philosophy :—'A God understood would be no God at all.' ' To think that
" God is, as we can think him to be, is blasphemy.' The Divinity, in a

I proceed to state, chiefly in the words of Sir W. Hamilton, the opinions of the two parties to the controversy. Both undertake to decide what are the facts which (in their own phraseology) are given in Consciousness; or, as others say, of which we have intuitive knowledge. According to Cousin, there are, in every act of consciousness, three elements; three things of which we are intuitively aware. There is a finite element; an element of plurality, compounded of a Self or Ego, and something different from Self, or Non-ego. There is also an infinite element; a consciousness of something infinite. "At * the same instant when we are

"certain sense, is revealed; in a certain sense, is concealed: he is at once "known and unknown. But the last and highest consecration of all true "religion, must be an altar 'Αγνώστῳ Θεῷ—'To the unknown and unknow- "able God.'" When this is what the author of the Essay presents as its practical result, it is too much to tell us that the Essay is not concerned about God but about a "Pseudo-Infinite," and that we are not entitled, when we find in it an assertion about the Infinite, to hold the author to the assertion as applicable to God. We shall next be told that Mr. Mansel himself, in his Bampton Lectures, is not treating the question of our knowledge of God. It is very true that the only Infinite about which either Sir W. Hamilton or Mr. Mansel proves anything, is a Pseudo-Infinite; but they are not in the least aware of this; they fancy that this Pseudo-Infinite is the real Infinite, and that in proving it to be unknowable by us, they prove the same thing of God.

The reader who desires further elucidation of this point, may consult the sixth chapter of Mr. Bolton's Inquisitio Philosophica. That acute thinker also points out various inconsistencies and other logical errors in Mr. Mansel's work, with which I am not here concerned, my object in answering him not being recrimination, but to maintain my original assertions against his denial.

Mr. Mansel, in his rejoinder, quotes from his Bampton Lectures some passages in which he says, and others in which he implies, that "our "human conception of the Infinite is not the true one," and that "the "infinite of philosophy is not the true Infinite:" and thinks it very unfair that, with these passages before me, I should accuse him of mistaking a pseudo-infinite for the real Infinite. But the mistake from which he clears himself is not that which I charged him with. I maintained, that the abstraction "The Infinite," in whatever manner understood, as distinguished from some particular attribute possessed in an infinite degree, has no existence, and is a pseudo-infinite. Mr. Mansel, on the contrary, affirmed throughout, and affirms in the very passages which he quotes, that "The Infinite" has a real existence, and is God: though when we attempt to conceive what it is, we only reach a mass of contradictions, which is a pseudo-infinite. Mr. Mansel did not suppose *his* pseudo-infinite to be the true Infinite; but my assertion, which stands unrefuted, is, that his "true Infinite" is a pseudo-infinite; and that in proving it to be unknowable by us, he mistakenly fancied that he had proved this of God.

* Discussions, p. 9.

"conscious of these [finite] existences, plural, relative,
"and contingent, we are conscious likewise of a superior
"unity in which they are contained, and by which they
"are explained; a unity absolute as they are conditioned,
"substantive as they are phenomenal, and an infinite
"cause as they are finite causes.   This unity is God."
The first two elements being the Finite and God, the
third element is the relation between the Finite and God,
which is that of cause and effect.   These three things
are immediately given in every act of consciousness, and
are, therefore, apprehended as real existences by direct
intuition.

Of these alleged elements of Consciousness, Sir W.
Hamilton only admits the first; the Finite element,
compounded of Self and a Not-self, "limiting and con-
ditioning one another."   He denies that God is given
in immediate consciousness—is apprehended by direct
intuition.   It is in no such way as this that God,
according to him, is known to us: and as an Infinite
and Absolute Being he is not, and cannot be, known
to us at all; for we have no faculties capable of apprehending the Infinite or the Absolute.   The second of
M. Cousin's elements being thus excluded, the third
(the Relation between the first and second) falls with
it; and Consciousness remains limited to the finite
element, compounded of an Ego and a Non-ego.

In this contest it is almost superfluous for me to say,
that I am entirely with Sir W. Hamilton.   The doctrine,
that we have an immediate or intuitive knowledge of
God, I consider to be bad metaphysics, involving a false
conception of the nature and limits of the human faculties, and grounded on a superficial and erroneous psychology.   Whatever relates to God I hold to be matter of
inference; I would add, of inference à posteriori.   And
in so far as Sir W. Hamilton has contributed, which
he has done very materially, towards discrediting the
opposite doctrine, he has rendered, in my estimation, a
valuable service to philosophy.   But though I assent to
his conclusion, his arguments seem to me very far from

inexpugnable : a sufficient answer, I conceive, might without difficulty be given to most of them, though I do not say that it was always competent to M. Cousin to give it. And the arguments, in the present case, are of as much importance as the conclusion : not only because they are quite as essential a part of Sir W. Hamilton's philosophy, but because they afford the premises from which some of his followers, if not himself, have drawn inferences which I venture to think extremely mischievous. While, therefore, I sincerely applaud the scope and purpose of this celebrated piece of philosophical criticism, I think it important to sift with some minuteness the reasonings it employs, and the general mode of thought which it exemplifies.

The question is, as already remarked, whether we have a direct intuition of "the Infinite" and "the Absolute:" M. Cousin maintaining that we have—Sir W. Hamilton that we have not ; that the Infinite and the Absolute are inconceivable to us, and, by consequence, unknowable.

It is proper to explain to any reader not familiar with these controversies, the meaning of the terms. Infinite requires no explanation. It is universally understood to signify that, to the magnitude of which there is no limit. If we speak of infinite duration, or infinite space, we are supposed to mean duration which never ceases, and extension which nowhere comes to an end. Absolute is much more obscure, being a word of several meanings ; but, in the sense in which it stands related to Infinite, it means (conformably to its etymology) that which is finished or completed. There are some things of which the utmost ideal amount is a limited quantity, though a quantity never actually reached. In this sense, the relation between the Absolute and the Infinite is (as Bentham would have said) a tolerably close one, namely a relation of contrariety. For example, to assert an absolute minimum of matter, is to deny its infinite divisibility. Again, we may speak of absolutely, but not of infinitely, pure water. The purity of water is not a fact of which, whatever degree we suppose attained, there remains a greater beyond. It has an absolute limit : it is capable of being finished or complete, in thought, if not in reality. The extraneous substances existing in any vessel of water cannot be of more than finite amount, and if we suppose them all withdrawn, the purity of the water cannot, even in idea, admit of further increase.

The idea of Absolute, in this sense of the term, being thus contrasted with that of Infinite, they cannot, both of them, be truly predicated of God ; or, if truly, not in respect of the same attributes. But the word Absolute, without losing the signification of perfect or complete, may drop that of limited. It may continue to mean the *whole* of that to which it is applied ; but without requiring that this whole should be finite. Granted (for instance) a being of infinite power, that Being's knowledge, if supposed perfect, must be infinite ; and may therefore, in an admissible sense of the term, be said to be both absolute and infinite.* In this acceptation there is no inconsistency or incongruity in predicating both these words of God.

* In the first edition of this work it was maintained, that though Power admits of being regarded as Infinite, Knowledge does not ; because "the "highest degree of knowledge that can be spoken of with a meaning, only "amounts to knowing all that there is to be known." But Mr. Mansel and the "Inquirer" (author of "The Battle of the Two Philosophies") have justly remarked, that on the supposition of an Infinite Being, "all "that there is to be known" includes all which a Being of infinite power can think or create ; consequently, the power being infinite, the knowledge, if supposed complete, must be infinite too. In regard to the moral attributes, it was said in the first edition, that Absolute is the proper word for them, and not Infinite, since those attributes "cannot be more "than perfect. There are not infinite degrees of right. The will is "either entirely right, or wrong in different degrees." In this I did not properly distinguish between moral rightness or justice as predicated of acts or mental states, and the same regarded as attributes of a person. Conformity to the standard of right has a positive limit, which can only be reached, not surpassed ; but persons, though all exactly conforming to the standard, may differ in the strength of their adherence to it: influences (temptations for example) might detach one of them from it, which would have no effect upon another. There are thus, consistently with complete observance of the rule of right, innumerable gradations of the attribute considered as in a person. But, on the other hand, there is an extreme limit to these gradations—the idea of a Person whom no influences or causes, either in or out of himself, can deflect in the minutest degree from the law of right. This I apprehend to be a conception of absolute, not of infinite, righteousness. The doctrine, therefore, of the first edition,

The word Absolute, however, has other meanings, which have nothing to do with perfection or completeness, though often mixed and confounded with it; the more readily as they are all habitually predicated of the Deity. By Absolute is often meant the opposite of Relative; and this is rather many meanings than one; for Relative also is a term used very indefinitely, and wherever it is employed, the word Absolute always accompanies it as its negative. In another of its senses, Absolute means that which is independent of anything else: which exists, and is what it is, by its own nature, and not because of any other thing. In this fourth sense as in the third, Absolute stands for the negation of a relation; not now of Relation in general, but of the specific relation expressed by the term Effect. In this signification it is synonymous with uncaused, and is therefore most naturally identified with the First Cause. The meaning of a First Cause is, that all other things exist, and are what they are, by reason of it and of its properties, but that it is not itself made to exist, nor to be what it is, by anything else. It does not depend, for its existence or attributes, on other things: there is nothing upon the existence of which its own is conditional: it exists absolutely.

In which of these meanings is the term used in the polemic with M. Cousin? M. Cousin makes no distinction at all between the Infinite and the Absolute. Sir W. Hamilton distinguishes them as two species of a higher genus, the Unconditioned; and defines the Infinite as "the unconditionally unlimited," the Absolute as "the unconditionally limited."* Here is a new word introduced, the word "unconditionally;" of which we look in vain for any direct explanation, but which needs it as much as either of the words which it is employed to explain. In the Essay itself, this is the only

---

that an Infinite being may have attributes which are absolute, but not infinite, still appears to me maintainable. But as it is immaterial to my argument, and was only the illustration nearest at hand of the meaning of the terms, I withdraw it from the discussion.

* Discussions, p. 13.

attempt made to define the Absolute : but in the reprint Sir W. Hamilton appends the following note : *

"The term Absolute is of a twofold (if not threefold) "ambiguity, corresponding to the double (or treble) sig- "nification of the word in Latin." The third applica- tion he, with reason, dismisses, as here irrelevant. The other two as are follows :

" 1. *Absolutum* means what is *freed* or *loosed :* in "which sense the Absolute will be what is aloof from "relation, comparison, limitation, condition, depend- "ence, &c., and thus is tantamount to τὸ ἀπόλυτον of "the lower Greeks. In this meaning the Absolute is "not opposed to the Infinite." This is an amplification of my third meaning.

" 2. *Absolutum* means *finished, perfected, completed ;* "in which sense the Absolute will be what is out of "relation, &c., as finished, perfect, complete, total, and "thus corresponds to τὸ ὅλον and τὸ τέλειον of Aristotle. "In this acceptation—and it is that in which for myself "I exclusively use it,—the Absolute is diametrically "opposed to, is contradictory of, the Infinite." This second meaning of Sir W. Hamilton, which I, in the first edition, by a blameable inadvertence, confounded with my own first meaning,† must be reckoned as a fifth, compounded of the first and third—of the idea of finished or completed, and the idea of being out of rela- tion. How to make an intelligible meaning out of the two combined, is the question. One can, with some difficulty, find a meaning in being " aloof from relation, "comparison, limitation, condition, dependence ;" but what is meant by being all this "as finished, perfect, "complete, total"? Does it mean, being *both* out o. relation and also complete? and must the Absolute in

---

* Discussions, p. 14, note.

† And, in consequence, erroneously charged Sir W. Hamilton with having, in one of his arguments against Cousin, departed from his own meaning of the term. I have freed the text from everything which de- pended on this error, the only serious misrepresentation of Sir W. Hamil- ton which has been established against me.

Sir W. Hamilton's second sense be also Absolute in his
first, and be out of all relation whatever ? or does the
particle " *as* " signify that it is out of relation only in
respect of its completeness, which (I suppose) means
that it does not depend for its completeness on anything
but itself? Mr. Mansel's comment, which otherwise
does not help us much, decides for the latter. "Out of
"relation as completed " means (he says) * " self-existent
"in its completeness, and not implying the existence of
"anything else." † Without further attempt to clear up
the obscurity, let it suffice that Sir W. Hamilton's
Absolute, though not synonymous with a "finished,
perfected, completed," but limited, whole, includes that
idea, and is therefore incompatible with Infinite.‡—

Having premised these verbal explanations, I proceed
to state, as far as possible in Sir W. Hamilton's own
words, the heads of his argumentation to prove that the
Absolute and Infinite are unknowable. His first summary statement of the doctrine is as follows : §—

"The unconditionally unlimited, or the Infinite, the
"unconditionally limited, or the Absolute, cannot posi-
"tively be construed to the mind : they can be conceived
"only by a thinking away from, or abstraction of, those
"very conditions under which thought itself is realised ;
"consequently, the notion of the Unconditioned is only
"negative ; negative of the conceivable itself. For
"example : On the one hand, we can positively conceive

---

* Mansel, p. 104.

† But the assimilation with τὸ ὅλον and τὸ τέλειον again throws us out ;
for τὸ ὅλον, with all Greek thinkers, meant either the completed aggregate
of all that exists, or an abstract entity which they conceived as the Principle of Wholeness—in virtue of which, and by participation in which,
that universal aggregate and all other wholes *are* wholes. Either of these
would be an additional meaning for the word Absolute, different from all
which have yet been mentioned.

‡ I demur, however, to Sir W. Hamilton's assertion, that for himself he
exclusively uses the term in this meaning. In the whole of the discussion
respecting the relativity of our knowledge, Absolute, with Sir W. Hamilton,
is simply the opposite of relative, and contains no implication of "finished,
perfected, completed." Moreover, in this very Essay, when arguing against
M. Cousin, who uses Absolute in a sense compatible with Infinite, Sir
W. Hamilton continually falls into M. Cousin's sense.

§ Discussions, p. 13.

"neither an absolute whole, that is, a whole so great
"that we cannot also conceive it as a relative part of a
"still greater whole; nor an absolute part, that is, a part
"so small that we cannot also conceive it as a relative
"whole divisible into smaller parts.   On the other hand,
"we cannot positively represent, or realise, or construe
"to the mind (as here Understanding and Imagination
"coincide) an infinite whole, for this could only be done
"by the infinite synthesis in thought of finite wholes,
"which would itself require an infinite time for its
"accomplishment; nor, for the same reason, can we
"follow out in thought an infinite divisibility of parts.
"The result is the same, whether we apply the process
"to limitation in space, in time, or in degree.   The un-
"conditional negation, and the unconditional affirmation
"of limitation; in other words, the Infinite and the
"Absolute properly so called, are thus equally incon-
"ceivable to us."

This argument, that the Infinite and the Absolute are
unknowable by us because the only conceptions we are
able to form of them are negative, is stated still more
emphatically a few pages later. *   "Kant has clearly
"shown, that the Idea of the Unconditioned can have
"no objective reality,—that it conveys no knowledge,—
"and that it involves the most insoluble contradictions.
"But he ought to have shown that the Unconditioned
"had no objective application, because it had, in fact, no
"subjective affirmation; that it afforded no real know-
"ledge, because it contained nothing even conceivable;
"and that it is self-contradictory, because it is not a
"notion, either simple or positive, but only *a fasciculus*
"*of negations*—negations of the Conditioned in its oppo-
"site extremes, and bound together merely by the aid
"of language, and their common character of incom-
"prehensibility."

Let us note, then, as the first and most fundamental
of Sir W. Hamilton's arguments, that our ideas of the
Infinite and the Absolute are purely negative, and the

* Discussions, p. 17.

Unconditioned which combines the two, "a fasciculus of negations." I reserve consideration of the validity of this and every other part of the argumentation, until we have the whole before us.   He proceeds : *—

"As the conditionally limited (which we may briefly " call the Conditioned) is thus the only possible object of " knowledge and of positive thought,—thought neces- " sarily supposes condition. *To think* is *to condition ;* and " conditional limitation is the fundamental law of the " possibility of thought.   For, as the greyhound cannot " outstrip his shadow, nor (by a more appropriate simile) " the eagle outsoar the atmosphere in which he floats, " and by which alone he is supported ; so the mind " cannot transcend that sphere of limitation, within and " through which exclusively the possibility of thought " is realised.   Thought is only of the conditioned ; be- " cause, as we have said, to think is simply to condition. " The *Absolute* is conceived merely by a negation of con- " ceivability ; and all that we know, is known as—

"Won from the cold and formless *Infinite*."

" How, indeed, it could ever be doubted that thought " is only of the conditioned, may well be deemed a " matter of the profoundest admiration.   Thought cannot " transcend consciousness ; consciousness is only possible " under the antithesis of a subject and object of thought " known only in correlation, and mutually limiting each " other ; while, independently of this, all that we know " either of subject or object, either of mind or matter, " is only a knowledge in each of the particular, of the " plural, of the different, of the modified, of the pheno- " menal.   We admit that the consequence of this doc- " trine is—that philosophy, if viewed as more than a " science of the conditioned, is impossible.   Departing " from the particular, we admit that we can never, in " our highest generalisations, rise above the Finite ; that " our knowledge, whether of mind or matter, can be " nothing more than a knowledge of the relative mani-

* Discussions, p. 13.

" festations of an existence which in itself it is our highest
" wisdom to recognise as beyond the reach of philosophy.
" This is what, in the language of St. Austin, *Cog-*
" *noscendo ignoratur, et ignoratione cognoscitur.*"

The dictum that "to think is to condition" (the
meaning of which will be examined hereafter) may be
noted as our author's second argument. And here ends
the positive part of his argumentation. There remains
his refutation of opponents. After an examination of
Schelling's opinion, into which I need not follow him, he
grapples with M. Cousin, against whom he undertakes to
show,* that " his argument to prove the correality of his
" three Ideas proves directly the reverse ;" "that the
" conditions under which alone he allows intelligence to
" be possible, necessarily exclude the possibility of a
" knowledge, not to say a conception, of the Absolute ;"
and " that the Absolute, as defined by him, is only a re-
" lative and a conditioned."   Of this argument in three
parts, if we pass over (or, as our author would say, dis-
count) as much as is only *ad hominem,* what is of general
application is as follows :—

First: M. Cousin and our author are agreed that
there can be no knowledge except " where there exists a
plurality of terms ; " there are at least a perceived and
a perceiver, a knower and a known. But this necessity
of " difference and plurality " as a condition of knowledge, is inconsistent with the meaning of the Absolute,
which " as absolutely universal, is absolutely one. Ab-
" solute unity is convertible with the absolute negation
" of plurality and difference. . . . . . . The condition
" of the Absolute as existing, and under which it must
" be known, and the condition of intelligence, as capable
" of knowing, are incompatible. For, if we suppose the
" Absolute cognisable : it must be identified either—1°,
" with the subject knowing : or, 2°, with the object
" known : or, 3°, with the indifference of both. The
" first hypothesis, and the second, are contradictory of
" the Absolute. For in these the Absolute is supposed

* Discussions, p. 25.

" to be known, either as contradistinguished from the
" knowing subject, or as contradistinguished from the
" object known : in other words, the Absolute is asserted
" to be known as absolute unity, *i.e.*, as the negation of
" all plurality, while the very act by which it is known,
" affirms plurality as the condition of its own possibility.
" The third hypothesis, on the other hand, is contradic-
" tory of the plurality of intelligence ; for if the subject
" and the object of consciousness be known as one, a
" plurality of terms is not the necessary condition of
" intelligence. The alternative is therefore necessary :
" either the Absolute cannot be known or conceived at
" all ; or our author is wrong in subjecting thought to
" the conditions of plurality and difference." *

Secondly : In order to make the Absolute knowable
by us, M. Cousin, says the author, is obliged to present
it in the light of an absolute cause : now causation is a
relation ; therefore M. Cousin's Absolute is but a relative.
Moreover, " what exists merely as a cause, exists merely
" for the sake of something else—is not final in itself,
" but simply a mean towards an end. . . . Abstractly
" considered, the effect is therefore superior to the cause."
Hence an absolute cause " is dependent on the effect for
" its perfection ; " and, indeed, " even for its reality. For
" to what extent a thing exists necessarily as a cause, to
" that extent it is not all-sufficient to itself ; since to that
" extent it is dependent on the effect, as on the condition
" through which it realises its existence ; and what
" exists absolutely as a cause, exists therefore in abso-
" lute dependence on the effect for the reality of its
" existence. An absolute cause, in truth, only exists in its
" effects : it never *is*, it always *becomes:* for it is an exist-
" ence *in potentia*, and not an existence *in actu*, except
" through and by its effects. The Absolute is thus, at
" best, something merely inchoative and imperfect." †

* Discussions, pp. 32, 33.
† Discussions, pp. 34, 35. In the first edition three points of our author's
argument were discussed, instead of two only : but I now perceive that
the remaining argument is *ad hominem* merely, and has reference to M.
Cousin's confusion of the Absolute with the Infinite.

Let me ask, *en passant*, why M. Cousin is under an obligation to think that if the Absolute, or, to speak plainly, if God, is only known to us in the character of a cause, he must therefore "exist merely as a cause," and be merely "a mean towards an end"? It is surely possible to maintain that the Deity is known to us only as he who feeds the ravens, without supposing that the Divine Intelligence exists solely in order that the ravens may be fed.*

* A passage follows, which being only directed against a special doctrine of M. Cousin, (that God is determined to create by the necessity of his own nature—that an absolute creative force cannot but pass into creative activity)—I should have left unmentioned, were it not worth notice as a specimen of the kind of arguments which Sir W. Hamilton can sometimes use. On M. Cousin's hypothesis, says our author, (p. 36)—"One of two "alternatives must be admitted. God, as necessarily determined to pass "from absolute essence to relative manifestation, is determined to pass "either from the better to the worse, or from the worse to the better. A "third possibility, that both states are equal, as contradictory in itself and "as contradicted by our. author, it is not necessary to consider. The *first* "supposition must be rejected. The necessity in this case determines "God to pass from the better to the worse, that is, operates to his partial "annihilation. The power which compels this must be external and hostile, "for nothing operates willingly to its own deterioration ; and as superior "to the pretended God, is either itself the real deity, if an intelligent and "free cause, or a negation of all deity, if a blind force or fate. The *second* "is equally inadmissible : that God, passing into the universe, passes from "a state of comparative imperfection into a state of comparative perfection. "The divine nature is identical with the *most perfect nature*, and is also "identical with the first cause. If the first cause be not identical with "the most perfect nature, there is no God, for the two essential conditions "of his existence are not in combination. Now, on the present supposition, "the most perfect nature is the derived ; nay, the universe, the creation, "the γινόμενον, is, in relation to its cause, the actual, the ὄντως ὄν. It would "also be the divine, but that divinity supposes also the notion of cause, "while the universe, *ex hypothesi*, is only an effect."
This curious subtlety, that creation must be either passing from the better to the worse or from the worse to the better (which, if true, would prove that God cannot have created anything unless from all eternity) can be likened to nothing but the Eleatic argument that motion is impossible, because if a body moves it must either move where it is or where it is not ; an argument, by the way, for which Sir W. Hamilton often expresses high respect ; and of which he has here produced a very successful imitation. If it were worth while expending serious argument upon such a curiosity of dialectics, one might say it assumes that whatever is now worse must always have been worse, and that whatever is now better must always have been better. For, on the opposite supposition, perfect wisdom would have begun to will the new state at the precise moment when it began to be better than the old. We may add that our author's argument though never so irrefragable, in no way avails him against M. Cousin ; for (as he has himself said only a sentence before) on M. Cousin's theory the uni-

In reviewing the series of arguments adduced by Sir W. Hamilton for the incognoscibility and inconceivability of the Absolute, the first remark that occurs is, that most of them lose their application by simply substituting for the metaphysical abstraction "The Absolute," the more intelligible concrete expression "Something Absolute." If the first phrase has any meaning, it must be capable of being expressed in terms of the other. When we are told of an "Absolute" in the abstract, or of an Absolute Being, even though called God, we are entitled, and if we would know what we are talking about, are bound to ask, absolute in *what?* Do you mean, for example, absolute in goodness, or absolute in knowledge? or do you, perchance, mean absolute in ignorance, or absolute in wickedness? for any one of these is as much an Absolute as any other. And when you talk of something in the abstract which is called the Absolute, does it mean one, or more than one, of these? or does it, peradventure, mean all of them? When (descending to a less lofty height of abstraction) we speak of The Horse, we mean to include every object of which the name horse can be predicated. Or, to take our examples from the same region of thought to which the controversy belongs—

verse can never have had a beginning, and God, therefore, never was in the dilemma supposed.

[On this Mr. Mansel remarks (p. 107), "Hamilton is not speaking of "states of things, but of states of the divine nature, as creative or not "creative : and Mr. Mill's argument to refute Hamilton, must suppose a "time when the new nature of God begins to be better than the old." This is not a happy specimen of Mr. Mansel's powers of confutation. If God made the universe at the precise moment when it was wisest and best to do so—and if the universe was made by a perfectly wise and good being, this must have been the case—who besides Mr. Mansel, or, according to him, Sir W. Hamilton, would assert that God, in doing so, acquired a new nature? or passed out of one state into another state of his own nature? Did he not simply remain in the state of perfect wisdom and goodness in which he was before?

Mr. Mansel makes the odd assertion, that this argument of Sir W. Hamilton is taken from Plato. There is very little in common between it and the passage in the Republic in which Socrates, to disprove the fabulous metamorphoses of the gods into the forms of men, animals, or inanimate things, argues that no being would voluntarily change itself from better to worse. I cannot be mistaken in the passage of Plato which Mr. Mansel has in view, for he had himself cited a part of it, with the same intention, in the notes to his Bampton Lectures (p. 209.)]

when The True or The Beautiful are spoken of, the phrase is meant to include all things whatever that are true, or all things whatever that are beautiful.* If this rule is good for other abstractions, it is good for the Absolute. The word is devoid of meaning unless in reference to predicates of some sort. What is absolute must be absolutely something; absolutely this or absolutely that. The Absolute, then, ought to be a genus comprehending whatever is absolutely anything—whatever possesses any predicate in finished completeness. If we are told therefore that there is some one Being who is, or which is, The Absolute—not something absolute, but the Absolute itself,—the proposition can be understood in no other sense than that the supposed Being possesses in absolute completeness *all* predicates ; is absolutely good, and absolutely bad; absolutely wise, and absolutely stupid; and so forth.† The conception of

---

* Mr. Mansel (pp. 108, 109) considers this sentence a curious specimen of my reading in philosophy, and informs me that "Plato expressly dis-"tinguishes between 'the beautiful' and 'things that are beautiful' as "the One in contrast to the Many—the Real in contrast to the Apparent." Mr. Mansel will doubtless be glad to hear that I already possessed the very elementary knowledge of Plato which he seeks to impart to me ; indeed (if it were of any consequence) I have elsewhere given an account of this theory of Plato, and made the excuses which may justly be made for such a doctrine in Plato's time. But to recognise it as a theory which it is necessary to take into consideration now, is to follow the example of the later German transcendentalists in putting philosophy back to its very *incunabula.*

† The "Inquirer" objects, that merely negative predicates should be excluded from the account ; and that many of those here mentioned are merely negative : absolute littleness being but the negation of greatness ; weakness, of strength ; folly, of wisdom ; evil, of good (p. 22). But (without meddling with the very disputable position, that all bad qualities are merely deficiency of good ones) the question is, not whether the qualities which the "Inquirer" enumerates are negative, but whether they are capable of being predicated as absolute. If they are, the general or abstract Absolute logically includes them. And, surely, negations are still more susceptible of being absolute than positive qualities. The "Inquirer" will hardly deny that "absolutely none" is as correct an employment of the word absolute as "absolutely all." With regard to Infinite, the same writer says, "To talk of infinite littleness—infinite non-"extension or non-duration—is to talk of infinite nothing. Which is "indeed to talk, we must not say infinite, but absolute nonsense." It is hardly fair to refer a pupil of Sir W. Hamilton to mathematics ; but the "Inquirer" might have learnt from Sir W. Hamilton himself that it is not nonsense to talk of infinitely small quantities.

such a being, I will not say of such a God, is worse than
a "fasciculus of negations;" it is a fasciculus of contradictions: and our author might have spared himself
the trouble of proving a thing to be unknowable, which
cannot be spoken of but in words implying the impossibility of its existence.   To insist on such a truism is
not superfluous, for there have been philosophers who
saw that this must be the meaning of "The Absolute,"
and yet accepted it as a reality.   "What kind of an
"Absolute Being is that," asked Hegel,* "which does
"not contain in itself all that is actual, even evil
"included?"   Undoubtedly: and it is therefore necessary to admit, either that there is no Absolute Being, or
that the law, that contradictory propositions cannot both
be true, does not apply to the Absolute.   Hegel chose
the latter side of the alternative; and by this, among
other things, has fairly earned the honour which will
probably be awarded to him by posterity, of having logically extinguished transcendental metaphysics by a series
of *reductiones ad absurdissimum*.

What I have said of the Absolute is true, *mutatis
mutandis*, of the Infinite.   This also is a phrase of no
meaning, except in reference to some particular predicate; it must mean the infinite in something—as in
size, in duration, or in power.   These are intelligible
conceptions.   But an abstract Infinite, a Being not
merely infinite in one or in several attributes, but which
is "The Infinite" itself, must be not only infinite in
greatness, but also in littleness; its duration is not only
infinitely long, but infinitely short; it is not only
infinitely awful, but infinitely contemptible; it is the
same mass of contradictions as its companion the Absolute.   There is no need to prove that neither of them
is knowable, since, if the universal law of Belief is of
objective validity, neither of them exists.

It is these unmeaning abstractions, however, these
muddles of self-contradiction, which alone our author has
proved, against Cousin and others, to be unknowable.

* Quoted by Mr. Mansel, "The Limits of Religious Thought," p. 30.

He has shown, without difficulty, that we cannot know The Infinite or The Absolute. He has not shown that we cannot know a concrete reality as infinite or as absolute. Applied to this latter thesis, his reasoning breaks down.

We have seen his principal argument, the one on which he substantially relies. It is, that the Infinite and the Absolute are unknowable because inconceivable, and inconceivable because the only notions we can have of them are purely negative. If he is right in his antecedent, the consequent follows. A conception made up of negations is a conception of Nothing. It is not a conception at all.

But *is* a conception, by the fact of its being a conception of something infinite, reduced to a negation? This is quite true of the senseless abstraction "The Infinite." That indeed is purely negative, being formed by excluding from the concrete conceptions classed under it, all their positive elements. But in place of "the Infinite," put the idea of Something infinite, and the argument collapses at once. "Something infinite" is a conception which, like most of our complex ideas, contains a negative element, but which contains positive elements also. Infinite space, for instance: is there nothing positive in that? The negative part of this conception is the absence of bounds. The positive are, the idea of space, and of space greater than any finite space. So of infinite duration: so far as it signifies "without end" it is only known or conceived negatively; but in so far as it means time, and time longer than any given time, the conception is positive. The existence of a negative element in a conception does not make the conception itself negative and a non-entity. It would surprise most people to be told that "the life eternal" is a purely negative conception; that immortality is inconceivable. Those who hope for it for themselves have a very positive conception of what they hope for. True, we cannot have an *adequate* conception of space or duration as infinite; but between a conception which though inadequate is real, and correct as far as it goes, and the impossibility of any conception, there is a wide difference. Sir W. Hamilton does not admit this difference. He thinks the distinction without meaning. " To say * that " the infinite can be thought, but only inadequately " thought, is a contradiction *in adjecto;* it is the same as " saying that the infinite can be known, but only known " as finite." I answer, that to know it as greater than anything finite is not to know it as finite. The conception of Infinite as that which is greater than any given quantity, is a conception we all possess, sufficient for all human purposes, and as genuine and good a positive conception as one need wish to have. It is not adequate ; our conception of a reality never is. But it is positive ; and the assertion that there is nothing positive in the idea of infinity can only be maintained by leaving out and ignoring, as Sir W. Hamilton invariably does, the very element which constitutes the idea. Considering how many recondite laws of physical nature, afterwards verified by experience, have been arrived at by trains of mathematical reasoning grounded on what, if Sir W. Hamilton's doctrine be correct, is a non-existent conception, one would be obliged to suppose that conjuring is a highly successful mode of the investigation of nature. If, indeed, we trifle by setting up an imaginary Infinite which is infinite in nothing in particular, our notion of it is truly nothing, and a " fasciculus of negations." But this is a good example of the bewildering effect of putting nonsensical abstractions in the place of concrete realities. Would Sir W. Hamilton have said that the idea of God is but a negation, or a fasciculus of negations? As having nothing greater than himself, he is indeed conceived negatively. But as himself greater than all other real or imaginable existences, the conception of him is positive.

Put Absolute instead of Infinite, and we come to the same result. "The Absolute," as already shown, is a heap of contradictions, but "absolute" in reference to

* Lectures, ii. 375.

any given attribute, signifies the possession of that attribute in finished perfection and completeness. A Being absolute in knowledge, for example, is one who knows, in the literal meaning of the term, everything. Who will pretend that this conception is negative, or unmeaning to us? We cannot, indeed, form an adequate conception of a being as knowing everything, since to do this we must have a conception, or mental representation, of all that he knows. But neither have we an adequate conception of any person's finite knowledge. I have no adequate conception of a shoemaker's knowledge, since I do not know how to make shoes : but my conception of a shoemaker and of his knowledge is a real conception ; it is not a fasciculus of negations. If I talk of an Absolute Being (in the sense in which we are now employing the term) I use words without meaning ; but if I talk of a Being who is absolute in wisdom and goodness, that is, who knows everything, and at all times intends what is best for every sentient creature, I understand perfectly what I mean : and however much the fact may transcend my conception, the shortcoming can only consist in my being ignorant of the details of which the reality is composed : as I have a positive, and may have a correct conception of the empire of China, though I know not the aspect of any of the places, nor the physiognomy of any of the human beings, comprehended therein.

It appears, then, that the leading argument of Sir W. Hamilton to prove the inconceivability and consequent unknowability of the Unconditioned, namely, that our conception of it is merely negative, holds good only of an abstract Unconditioned which cannot possibly exist, and not of a concrete Being, supposed infinite and absolute in certain definite attributes.* Let us now see if there be any greater value in his other arguments.

---

* The answer of Mr. Mansel and the "Inquirer" to the preceding argument, is, that it confounds the infinite with the indefinite. They could not have understood the argument worse if they had never read it. Indefinite, in its ordinary acceptation, is that which has a limit, but a limit either variable in itself, or unknown to us. Infinite is that which

The first of them is, that all knowledge is of things plural and different; that a thing is only known to us by being known as different from something else; from ourselves as knowing it, and also from other known things which are not it. Here we have at length something which the mind can rest on as a fundamental truth. It is one of the profound psychological observations which the world owes to Hobbes; it is fully recognised both by M. Cousin and by Sir W. Hamilton; and it has, more recently, been admirably illustrated and applied by Mr. Bain and by Mr. Herbert Spencer. That to know a thing is to distinguish it from other things, is, as I formerly remarked, one of the truths which the very ambiguous expression "the relativity of human knowledge" has been employed to denote. With this doctrine I have no quarrel. But Sir W. Hamilton proceeds to argue that the Absolute, being "absolutely One," cannot be known under the conditions of plurality and difference,

---

has no limit. In what Mr. Mansel calls the metaphysical use of the word indefinite, he affirms it (p. 114) to mean "indefinitely increasable." Elsewhere (p. 50) he says "An indefinite time is that which is capable of per-"petual addition: an infinite time is one so great as to admit of no "addition." I now ask, which of these is the correct expression for that which is greater than anything finite? Is this a property which can be affirmed of anything which has an undetermined limit? or of anything which is indefinitely increasable? or of anything which is capable of perpetual addition? Is a merely indefinite time greater than every finite time? Is a merely indefinite space greater than every finite space? Is a merely indefinite power greater than every finite power? The property of being greater than everything finite belongs, and can belong, only to what is in the strictest sense of the term, both popular and philosophical, Infinite.

Mr. Mansel, in his rejoinder, defends himself by saying that Descartes and Cudworth agree with him in giving the name indefinite to what I (and as he acknowledges, the mathematicians) understand by infinite. I cannot affirm that Descartes and Cudworth have nowhere done this; but they certainly have not done it in the passages which Mr. Mansel quoted, either in his first reply or in this. All that either Descartes or Cudworth says in those passages is that the indefiniteness, to our minds, of the possible extension of the physical universe, is not tantamount to, nor a proof of, its infinity; as of course it is not.

Mr. Mansel adds that even supposing me to be in the right, it would only follow, not that Sir W. Hamilton is wrong, but that he and I do not mean the same thing by the same term. Whoever has read the present note must, however, be aware, that I maintain my position to be true even in what Mr. Mansel affirms to be Sir W. Hamilton's meaning of the term.

and as these are the acknowledged conditions of all our
knowledge, cannot, therefore, be known at all.   There
is here, as it seems to me, a strange confusion of ideas.
Sir W. Hamilton seems to mean that, being absolutely
One, it cannot be known as plural.   But the proposition
that plurality is a condition of knowledge, does not
mean that the thing known must be known as itself
plural.   It means, that a thing is only known, by being
known as distinguished from something else.   The plurality required is not within the thing itself, but is made
up between itself and other things.   Again, even if we
concede that a thing cannot be known at all unless
known as plural, does it follow that it cannot be known
as plural because it is also One?   Are the One and the
Many, then, incompatible things, instead of different
aspects of the same thing?   Sir W. Hamilton surely
does not mean by Absolute Unity, an indivisible Unit;
the minimum, instead of the maximum of Being.   He
must mean, as M. Cousin certainly means, an absolute
Whole ; the Whole which comprehends all things.   If
this be so, does not this Whole not only admit of, but
necessitate, the supposition of parts?   Is not an Unity
which comprehends everything, *ex vi termini* known as
a plurality, and the most plural of all pluralities, plural
in an unsurpassable degree?   If there is any meaning
in the words, must not Absolute Unity be Absolute
Totality, which is the highest degree of Plurality?
There is no escape from the alternative : the Absolute either means a single atom or monad, or it means
Plurality in the extreme degree.

Though it is hardly needful, we will try this argument
by the test we applied to a previous one ; by substituting
the concrete, God, for the abstract Absolute.   Would
Sir W. Hamilton have said that God is not cognisable
under the condition of Plurality—is not known as distinguished from ourselves, and from the objects in
nature ?   Call any positive Thing by a name which
expresses only its negative predicates, and you may
easily prove it under that name to be incognisable and

E

a non-entity. Give it back its full name (if Mr. Mansel's reverential feelings will permit), its positive attributes reappear, and you find, to your surprise, that what *is* a reality can be known as one.*

The next argument is chiefly directed against the doctrine of M. Cousin, that we know the Absolute as Absolute Cause. This doctrine, says Sir W. Hamilton, destroys itself. The idea of a cause is irreconcilable with the Absolute, for a Cause is relative, and implies an Effect : this Absolute, therefore, is not an Absolute at all. This would be unanswerable, if by the Absolute we were obliged to understand something which is not only " out of " all relation, but incapable of ever passing into relation. But is this what any one can possibly mean by the Absolute, who identifies it with the Creator? Granting that the Absolute implies an existence in itself, standing in no relation to anything : the only Absolute with which we are concerned, or in which anybody

---

* Mr. Mansel, as I have mentioned, vehemently objects to testing what Sir W. Hamilton says of the Infinite by its applicability to God, affirming that the Infinite which Sir W. Hamilton is speaking of, namely the Infinite as we conceive it, is a "pseudo-infinite." This is a curious inversion of the parts of Sir W. Hamilton and of his critic. It is I who assert that Sir W. Hamilton's Infinite is a pseudo-infinite ; it is he who maintains that it is the real. At least he substitutes this pseudo-infinite which is really inconceivable, for an intelligible infinite, a concrete Deity, and proving the inconceivability of the one, thinks he has sufficiently proved the inconceivability of the other. It was his business, it is what he professes, to prove that God, considered as Infinite, is inconceivable by us. Instead of this, he proves the inconceivability of an Infinite which is not and cannot be God, and which does not and cannot exist, and leaves it to Mr. Mansel to discover (after others have pointed it out) that this is a pseudo-infinite.

Mr. Mansel is still more indignant that I should try what Sir W. Hamilton says of the Absolute, by the test of applicability to God, and says that this is actually inverting Sir W. Hamilton's meaning, since his definition of the Absolute, "the unconditionally limited," is contradictory to the nature of God. But Sir W. Hamilton is here arguing with M. Cousin, who does not mean by Absolute the limited, but the complete, and who does predicate it of God. As Mr. Bolton truly remarks (p. 159) " In discussing the doctrines of Schelling and Cousin, Hamilton uses the " word Absolute in conformity with their usage, according to which the " Infinite and the Absolute are not opposed, or contraries, as in Hamil- " ton's own terminology." Nor for this does he deserve any blame ; for if the Absolute which he affirms to be unknowable, because it cannot be known under the conditions of Plurality, is Absolute only in his own sense of the term, and not in M. Cousin's, he has not refuted M. Cousin.

believes, must not only be capable of entering into relation with things, but must be capable of entering into
any relation whatever, except that of dependence, with
anything.   May it not be known in some, at least, of
those relations, and particularly in the relation of a
cause?   And if it is a "finished, perfected, completed"
Cause, *i.e.* the most a cause that it is possible to be—
the cause of everything except itself—then, if known as
such, it is known as an Absolute Cause.   Has Sir W.
Hamilton shown that an Absolute Cause, thus understood, is inconceivable, or unknowable?   No: all he
shows is, that, though capable of being known, it is
known relatively to something else, namely to its effects;
and that such knowledge of God is not of God in himself, but of God in relation to his works.   The truth is,
M. Cousin's doctrine is too legitimate a product of the
metaphysics common to them both, to be capable of
being refuted by Sir W. Hamilton.   For this knowledge
of God in and by his effects, according to M. Cousin, *is*
knowing him as he is in himself: because the creative
power whereby he causes, is in himself, is inseparable
from him, and belongs to his essence.   And as far as I
can see, the principles common to the two philosophers
are as good a warrant to M. Cousin for saying this, as
to Sir W. Hamilton for maintaining that extension and
figure are "essential attributes" of matter, and perceived
as such by intuition.

I have now examined, with one exception, every
argument (which is not merely *ad hominem*) advanced
by Sir W. Hamilton to prove against M. Cousin the
unknowableness of the Unconditioned.   The argument
which I have reserved, is the emphatic and oracular one,
that the Unconditioned must be unthinkable, because
"to think is to condition."   I have kept this for the
last, because it will occupy us the longest time: for we
must begin by finding the meaning of the proposition;
which cannot be done very briefly, so little help is
afforded us by the author.

According to the best notion I can form of the meaning of "conditioned," either as a term of philosophy or of common life, it means that on which something else is contingent, or (more definitely) which being given, something else exists, or takes place. I promise to do something *on condition* that you do something else : that is, if you do this, I will do that ; if not, I will do as I please. A Conditional Proposition, in logic, is an assertion in this form : " If so and so, then so and so." The conditions of a phenomenon are the various antecedent circumstances which, when they exist simultaneously, are followed by its occurrence. As all these antecedent circumstances must coexist, each of them in relation to the others is a *conditio sine quâ non ; i.e.* without it the phenomenon will not follow from the remaining conditions, though it perhaps may from some set of conditions totally different.

If this be the meaning of Condition, the Unconditioned should mean, that which does not depend for its existence or its qualities on any antecedent ; in other words, it should be synonymous with Uncaused. This, however, cannot be the meaning intended by Sir W. Hamilton ; for, in a passage already quoted from his argument against Cousin, he speaks of the effect as a condition of its cause. The condition, therefore, as he understands it, needs not be an antecedent, and may be a subsequent fact to that which it conditions.

He appears, indeed, in his writings generally, to reckon as a condition of a thing, anything necessarily implied by it : and uses the word Conditioned almost interchangeably with Relative. For relatives are always in pairs : a term of relation implies the existence of two things, the one which it is affirmed of, and another : parent implies child, greater implies less, like implies another like, and *vice versâ.* Relation is an abstract name for all concrete facts, whch concern more than one object. Wherever, therefore, a relation is affirmed, or anything is spoken of under a relative name, the existence of the correlative may be called a condition of the relation, as well as of the truth of the assertion. When, accordingly, Sir W. Hamilton calls an effect a condition of its cause, he speaks intelligibly, and the received use of the term affords him a certain amount of justification for thus speaking.

But, if the Conditioned means the Relative, the Unconditioned must mean its opposite; and in this acceptation, the Unconditioned would mean all Noumena; Things in themselves, considered without reference to the effects they produce in us, which are called their phenomenal agencies or properties. Sir W. Hamilton does, very frequently, seem to use the term in this sense. In denying all knowledge of the Unconditioned, he often seems to be denying any other than phenomenal knowledge of Matter or of Mind. Not only, however, does he not consistently adhere to this meaning, but it directly conflicts with the only approach he ever makes to a definition or an explanation of the term. We have seen him declaring that the Unconditioned is the genus of which the Infinite and the Absolute are the two species. But Things in themselves are not all of them infinite and absolute. Matter and Mind, as such, are neither the one nor the other. It is evident that Sir W. Hamilton had never decided what extent he intended giving to the term Unconditioned. Sometimes he gives it one degree of amplitude, sometimes another. Between the meanings in which he uses it there is undoubtedly a link of connection; but this only makes the matter still worse than if there were none. The phrase has that most dangerous kind of ambiguity, in which the meanings, though essentially different, are so nearly allied that the thinker unconsciously interchanges them one with another.*

* In page 8 of the Discussions, speaking of the one of M. Cousin's three elements of Consciousness which that author "variously expresses "by the terms, *unity, identity, substance, absolute cause, the infinite, pur-* "*thought,* &c.," Sir W. Hamilton says, "we will briefly call it the Uncon- "ditioned." What M. Cousin denominates "*plurality, difference, pheno-* "*menon, relative cause, the finite, determined thought,* &c.," Sir W. Hamilton says, "we would style the Conditioned." This, I think, is as near as he ever comes to an explanation of what he means by these words. It is obviously no explanation at all. It tells us what (in logical language)

The probability is that when our author asserts that
" to think is to condition," he uses the word Condition
in neither of these senses, but in a third meaning,
equally familiar to him, and recurring constantly in
such phrases as " the conditions of our thinking faculty,"
" conditions of thought," and the like.   He means by
Conditions something similar to Kant's Forms of
Sense and Categories of Understanding ; a meaning
more correctly expressed by another of his phrases,
" Necessary Laws of Thought."   He is applying to the
mind the scholastic maxim, " Quicquid recipitur, recipitur ad modum recipientis."   He means that our
perceptive and conceptive faculties have their own laws,
which not only determine what we are capable of perceiving and conceiving, but put into our perceptions and
conceptions elements not derived from the thing perceived or conceived, but from the mind itself : That,
therefore, we cannot at once infer that whatever we find in
our perception or conception of an object, has necessarily
a prototype in the object itself : and that we must, in each
instance, determine this question by philosophic investigation.   According to this doctrine, which no fault
can be found with our author for maintaining, though
often for not carrying it far enough—the " conditions of
thought " would mean the attributes with which, it is
supposed, the mind cannot help investing every object
of thought—the elements which, derived from its own
structure, cannot but enter into every conception it is
able to form ; even if there should be nothing corresponding in the object which is the prototype of the
conception : though our author, in most cases (therein
differing from Kant), believes that there is this correspondence.

We have here an intelligible meaning for the doctrine

the terms denote, but not what they connote. An enumeration of the
things called by a name is not a definition. If the name, for instance,
were "dog," it would be no definition to say that what are variously
denominated spaniels, mastiffs, and so forth, "we would style" dogs. The
thing wanted is to know what attributes common to all these the word
signifies,—what is affirmed of a thing by calling it a dog.

that to think is to condition; and as Mr. Mansel, in his
reply, guarantees this as the true meaning of Sir W.
Hamilton, I will accept it as being so. If, then (which
I do not here discuss), the philosophical doctrine be
true, which was held partially by Sir W. Hamilton, and
in a more thorough-going manner by Kant, viz. that, in
the act of thought, the mind, by an *à priori* necessity,
invests the object of thought with attributes which are
not in itself, but are created by the mind's own laws;
and if we consent to call these necessities of thought
the conditions of thought; then evidently to think is to
condition, and to think the Unconditioned would be to
think the unthinkable. But the Unconditioned, in this
application of the term, is not identical with the Infinite
plus the Absolute.   The Infinite and the Absolute are
not necessarily, in this sense, unconditioned.   The
words infinite and absolute, as I have already said, have
no meaning save as expressing some concrete reality
or supposed reality, possessing infinitely or absolutely
attributes of some sort, which attributes, as finite and
limited, we are able to think.   In thinking these attributes, we are not able to divest ourselves of our mental
conditions, but we can think the attributes as surpassing
the conditions.   "To condition," and "to think under
conditions," are ambiguous phrases. An Infinite Being
may be thought, and is thought, *with reference* to the
conditions, but not as limited by them. The most
familiar examples of the alleged necessary conditions
of thought, are Time and Space: we cannot, it is
affirmed, think anything, except in time and space.
Now, an Infinite Being is not thought as *in* time and
space, if this means as occupying a portion of time or
a portion of space. But (substituting for Time the
word Duration, to get rid of the theological antithesis
of Time and Eternity) we do actually conceive God *in
reference* to Duration and Extension, namely, as occupying the whole of both; and these being conceived as
infinite, to conceive a Being as occupying the whole of
them is to conceive that Being as infinite.   If thinking

God as eternal and omnipresent is thinking him in
Space and Time, we do think God in Space and Time :
if thinking him as eternal and omnipresent is not thinking him in Space and Time, we are capable of thinking
something out of Space and Time.   Mr. Mansel may
make his choice between the two opinions.   I have
already shown that the ideas of infinite space and time
are real and positive conceptions : that of a Being who
is in all Space and in all Time is no less so.   To think
anything, must of course be to condition it by attributes
which are themselves thinkable ; but not necessarily
to condition it by a limited quantum of those attributes : on the contrary, we may think it under a
degree of them greater than all limited degrees, and
this is to think it as infinite.*

If we now ask ourselves, as the result of this long
discussion, what Sir W. Hamilton can be considered as
having accomplished in this celebrated Essay, our answer
must be : That he has established, more thoroughly
perhaps than he intended, the futility of all speculation
respecting those meaningless abstractions "The Infinite" and "The Absolute," notions contradictory in
themselves, and to which no corresponding realities do
or can exist.†   Respecting the unknowableness, not of

* "To be conceived as unconditioned," says Mr. Mansel (pp. 17, 18),
"God must be conceived as exempt from action in time : to be conceived
"as a person, if his personality resembles ours, he must be conceived as
"acting in time."   Exempt from action in time, as much as you please ;
in other words, not necessitated to it, nor restricted by its conditions ; but
did any one ever conceive the Deity as *not* acting in time ?   Nay, even if
he is not conceived as a person, but only as the first principle of the universe, "one absolutely first principle on which everything else depends,"
a belief which is held by Mr. Mansel along with the Christian doctrine of
the Divine Personality (pp. 7 to 18) ; even so, the first principle of everything which takes place in Time, must, from the very meaning of the
words, not only be conceived as acting in Time, but must really act in
Time, and in all Time.   Action in Time does not belong to the Deity as a
Person, but quite as much to the Deity as the first principle of all things,
which is what Mr. Mansel means by the Unconditioned.

† On this Mr. Mansel's remark is (pp. 110, 111) that Sir W. Hamilton
did not assert these to be unmeaning abstractions.   I never pretended
that he did ; the gist of my complaint against him is, that he did not perceive them to be unmeaning.   "Hamilton," says Mr. Mansel, "maintains
"that the terms absolute and infinite are perfectly intelligible as abstrac-

"the Infinite," or "the Absolute," but of concrete persons or things possessing infinitely or absolutely certain specific attributes, I cannot think that our author has proved anything ; nor do I think it possible to prove them any otherwise unknowable, than that they can only be known in their relations to us, and not as Noumena, or Things in themselves. This, however, is true of the finite as well as of the infinite, of the imperfect as well as of the completed or absolute. Our author has merely proved the uncognoscibility of a being which is *nothing but* infinite, or *nothing but* absolute: and since nobody supposes that there is such a being, but only beings which are something positive carried to the infinite, or to the absolute, to have established this point cannot be regarded as any great achievement. He has not even refuted M. Cousin ; whose doctrine of an intuitive cognition of the Deity, like every other doctrine relating to intuition, can only be disproved by showing it to be a mistaken interpretation of facts ; which, again, as we shall see hereafter, can only be done by pointing out in what other way the seeming perceptions may have originated, which are erroneously supposed to be intuitive.

"tions, as much so as relative and finite." *Quis dubitavit?* It is not the terms absolute and infinite that are unmeaning ; it is " The Infinite " and " The Absolute." Infinite and Absolute are real attributes, abstracted from concrete objects of thought, if not of experience, which are at least believed to possess those attributes. " The Infinite " and " The Absolute " are illegitimate abstractions of what never were, nor could without self-contradiction be supposed to be, attributes of any concrete. I regret to differ, on this point, from my distinguished reviewer in the Westminster Review, who considers these to be intelligible abstractions, though of a higher reach of abstraction than the preceding (p. 14). The distinction is seized by one of my American critics, Dr. H. B. Smith (p. 134), who regards it as the difference between talking "about the Infinite and Absolute as entities," and considering them "simply as modes and predicates of real existences." That there are persons "in Laputa or the Empire" (as Sir W. Hamilton phrases it) who do talk about them as entities, up to any pitch of wild nonsense, I am quite aware ; and against these Sir W. Hamilton's Essay, as the protest, though the insufficient protest, of a rival Transcendentalist, has its value.

CHAPTER V.

WHAT IS REJECTED AS KNOWLEDGE BY SIR WILLIAM
HAMILTON, BROUGHT BACK UNDER THE NAME OF
BELIEF.

WE have found Sir W. Hamilton maintaining with great
earnestness, and taking as the basis of his philosophy,
an opinion respecting the limitation of human knowledge, which, if he did not mean so much by it as the
language in which he often clothed it seemed to imply,
meant at least this, that the Absolute, the Infinite, the
Unconditioned, are necessarily unknowable by us. I
have discussed this opinion as a serious philosophical
dogma, expressing a definite view of the relation between
the universe and human apprehension, and fitted to guide
us in distinguishing the questions which it is of any
avail to ask, from those which are altogether closed to
our investigations.

But had the doctrine, in the mind of Sir W. Hamilton,
meant ten times more than it did—had he upheld the
relativity of human knowledge in the fullest, instead of
the scantiest meaning of which the words are susceptible
—the question would still have been reduced to naught,
or to a mere verbal controversy, by his admission of a
second kind of intellectual conviction called Belief;
which is anterior to knowledge, is the foundation of it,
and is not subject to its limitations; and through the
medium of which we may have, and are justified in
having, a full assurance of all the things which he has
pronounced unknowable to us; and this not exclusively
by revelation, that is, on the supposed testimony of a
Being whom we have ground for trusting as veracious,
but by our natural faculties.

From some philosophers, this distinction would have the appearance of a mere fetch—one of those transparent evasions which have sometimes been resorted to by the assailants of received opinions, that they might have an opportunity of ruining the rational foundations of a doctrine without exposing themselves to odium by its direct denial: as the writers against Christianity in the eighteenth century, after declaring some doctrine to be contradictory to reason, and exhibiting it in the absurdest possible light, were wont to add that this was not of the smallest consequence, religion being an affair of faith, not of reason. But Sir W. Hamilton evidently meant what he says; he was expressing a serious conviction, and one of the tenets of his philosophy: he really recognised under the name of Belief a substantive source, I was going to say, of knowledge; I may at all events say of trustworthy evidence. This appears in the following passages :—

"The * sphere of our belief is much more extensive "than the sphere of our knowledge, and therefore, when "I deny that the Infinite can by us be *known*, I am far "from denying that by us it is, must, and ought to be, "*believed*. This I have indeed anxiously evinced, both "by reasoning and authority."

"St. Austin † accurately says, 'We know, what rests "upon *reason;* but believe, what rests upon *authority.*' "But reason itself must rest at last upon authority; for "the original data of reason do not rest on reason, but "are necessarily accepted by reason on the authority of "what is beyond itself. These data are, therefore, in "rigid propriety, Beliefs or Trusts. Thus it is that in "the last resort we must perforce philosophically admit, "that belief is the primary condition of reason, and not "reason the ultimate ground of belief. We are com- "pelled to surrender the proud *Intellige ut credas* of "Abelard, to content ourselves with the humble *Crede* "*ut intelligas* of Anselm."

* Letter to Mr Calderwood, in Appendix to Lectures, ii. 530, 531.
† Dissertations on Reid, p. 760.

And in another part of the same Dissertation,* (he is arguing that we do not believe, but know, the external world)—" If asked, indeed, how we know that we know " it ? how we know that what we apprehend in sensible " perception is, as consciousness assures us, an object, " external, extended, and numerically different from the " conscious subject? how we know that this object is " not a mere mode of mind, illusively presented to us as " a mere mode of matter; then indeed we must reply " that we do not in propriety *know* that what we are " compelled to perceive as not-self is not a perception " of self, and that we can only on reflection *believe* such " to be the case, in reliance on the original necessity of " so believing, imposed on us by our nature."

It thus appears that, in Sir W. Hamilton's opinion, Belief is a conviction of higher authority than Knowledge; Belief is ultimate, Knowledge only derivative; Knowledge itself finally rests on Belief; natural beliefs are the sole warrant for all our knowledge. Knowledge, therefore, is an inferior ground of assurance to natural Belief; and as we have beliefs which tell us that we know, and without which we could not be assured of the truth of our knowledge, so we have, and are warranted in having, beliefs beyond our knowledge; beliefs respecting the Unconditioned—respecting that which is in itself unknowable.

I am not now considering what it is that, in our author's opinion, we are bound to believe concerning the unknowable. What here concerns us is, the nullity to which this doctrine reduces the position to which our author seemed to cling so firmly—viz., that our knowledge is relative to ourselves, and that we can have no knowledge of the infinite and absolute. In telling us that it is impossible to the human faculties to know anything about Things in themselves, we naturally suppose he intends to warn us off the ground—to bid us understand that this subject of inquiry is closed to us, and

* Pp. 749, 750.

exhort us to turn our attention elsewhere. It appears that nothing of the kind was intended : we are to understand, on the contrary, that we may have the best grounded and most complete assurance of the things which were declared unknowable—an assurance not only equal or greater in degree, but the same in nature, as we have for the truth of our knowledge : and that the matter in dispute was only whether this assurance or conviction shall be called knowledge, or by another name. If this be all, I must say I think it not of the smallest consequence. If no more than this be intended by the "great axiom" and the elaborate argument against Cousin, a great deal of trouble has been taken to very little purpose ; and the subject would have been better left where Reid left it, who did not trouble himself with nice distinctions between belief and knowledge, but was content to consider us as knowing that which, by the constitution of our nature, we are forced, with entire conviction, to believe. According to Sir W. Hamilton, we believe premises, but know the conclusions from them. The ultimate facts of consciousness * are " given less in "the form of cognitions than of beliefs : " " Conscious- "ness in its last analysis, in other words our primary "experience, is a faith." But if we know the theorems of Euclid, and do not know the definitions and axioms on which they rest, the word knowledge, thus singularly applied, must be taken in a merely technical sense. To say that we believe the premises, but know the conclusion, would be understood by every one as meaning that we had other independent evidence of the conclusion. If we only know it through the premises, the same name ought in reason to be given to our assurance of both.†
In common language, when Belief and Knowledge are distinguished, Knowledge is understood to mean complete

---

* Discussions, p. 86.
† Accordingly Sir W. Hamilton himself, in one of the Dissertations on Reid (p. 763), says that "the principles of our knowledge must be them-"selves knowledge." And there are few who will not approve this use of language, and condemn the other.

conviction, Belief a conviction somewhat short of complete ; or else we are said to believe when the evidence
is probable (as that of testimony), but to know, when it
is intuitive, or demonstrative from intuitive premises :
we believe, for example, that there is a Continent of
America, but know that we are alive, that two and two
make four, and that the sum of any two sides of a triangle
is greater than the third side.   This is a distinction of
practical value : but in Sir W. Hamilton's use of the
term, it is the intuitive convictions that are the Beliefs,
and those which are dependent and contingent upon
them, compose our knowledge.   Whether a particular
portion of our convictions, which are not more certain,
but if anything less certain, than the remainder, and
according to our author rest on the same ultimate basis,
shall in opposition to the common usage of mankind,
receive exclusively the appellation of knowledge, is at
the most a question of terminology, and can only be
made to appear philosophically important by confounding difference of name with difference of fact.   That
anything capable of being said on such a subject should
pass for a fundamental principle of philosophy, and be
one of the chief sources of the reputation of a metaphysical system, is but an example how the mere forms
of logic and metaphysics can blind mankind to the total
absence of their substance.

It must not be supposed, from anything which has
been here said, that I wish to abolish the distinction
between Knowledge and Belief (meaning True Belief)
or maintain that it is necessarily a distinction without a
difference.   Those terms are employed to denote more
than one real difference, and neither of them can conveniently be dispensed with in philosophy.*   What con-

---

* There is much dispute among philosophers as to the difference
between Knowledge and Belief ; and the strife is not likely to terminate,
until they perceive that the real question is, not what the distinction is,
but what it shall be ; what one among several differences already known
and recognised, the words shall be employed to denote. " The word belief,"
says Dr. M'Cosh (p. 36), in this more discerning than the generality, " is
" unfortunately a very vague one, and may stand for a number of very

cerns us in the present chapter is not the rationale of the distinction between knowledge and belief, but whether that distinction is relevant to the question between Sir W. Hamilton and M. Cousin about the Infinite and the Absolute; and whether Sir W. Hamilton is warranted in giving back under the name of Belief, the assurance or conviction respecting these objects which he refuses under the name of knowledge. My position is, that the Infinite and Absolute which Sir W. Hamilton has

"different mental affections. When I am speaking of first or intuitive "principles, I use the term to signify our conviction of the existence of "an object not now present, and thus I distinguish primitive faith from "primitive knowledge, in which the object is present." This distinction agrees well with usage in the cases to which Dr. M'Cosh applies it : we know that which we perceive by the senses, and believe that which we only re- member : we know that we ourselves, and (while we look at them) our house and garden, exist, and believe the existence of the Czar of Russia and the Island of Ceylon. Every definition of Belief, as distinguished from Knowledge, must include these cases, because in them the conviction which receives the name of Belief falls short of the complete assurance implied in the word knowledge : our memory may deceive us ; the Czar or the island may have been swallowed up by an earthquake. But if we attempt to carry out Dr. M'Cosh's distinction through the entire region of thought, the whole of what we call our scientific knowledge, except the primary facts or intuitions on which it is grounded, has to pass into the category of Belief; for the objects with which it is conversant are seldom present.

Mr. Mansel might be supposed to be adopting Dr. M'Cosh's distinction, when he says (p. 126), "We believe that the true distinction between "knowledge and belief may ultimately be referred to the presence or "absence of the corresponding intuition." But his criterion of the dis- tinction, and, according to him, Sir W. Hamilton's also, is the following : we believe that a thing is, but do not know even that it is, unless we can conceive how, or in what manner, it is. "When I say that I believe in "the existence of a spiritual being who can see without eyes, I cannot "conceive the manner in which seeing co-exists with the absence of the "bodily organ of sight" (p. 126). "We cannot conceive the manner in "which the unconditioned and the personal are united in the Divine "Nature ; yet we may believe that, in some manner unknown to us, they "are so united. To conceive the union of two attributes in one object of "thought, I must be able to conceive them as united in some particular "manner: when this cannot be done, I may nevertheless believe that the "union is possible, though I am unable to conceive how it is possible." This may be more briefly expressed by saying that we can believe what is inconceivable, but can know only what is conceivable ; and undoubtedly both these contrasted propositions are maintained by Sir W. Hamilton. But to regard them as a clue to the distinction in his mind between knowledge and belief, would be to misunderstand his opinions : for the convictions which he most emphatically characterised as beliefs, in contra- distinction to knowledge, are what he calls our natural and necessary

been proving to be unknowable, being made up of contradictions, are as incapable of being believed as of being known ; that the only attitude in reference to them, of any intellect which apprehends the meaning of language, is that of disbelief.   On the other hand, there are Infinites and Absolutes which, not being self-contradictory, admit of being believed, namely, concrete realities supposed to be infinite or absolute in respect of certain attributes : but Sir W. Hamilton, as I maintain, has done nothing towards proving that such concrete realities cannot be known, in the way in which we know other things, namely, in their relations to us. When, therefore, he affirms that though the Infinite cannot by us be known, "by us it is, must, and ought to be be-"lieved," I answer, that the Infinite which, as he has so laboriously proved, cannot be known, neither is, must, nor ought to be believed ; not because it cannot be known, but because there exists no such thing for us to

beliefs, "the original data of reason," which, far from being inconceivable, are usually tested by being themselves conceivable while their negations are not. If knowledge were distinguished from belief by our being aware of the manner as well as the fact, we could not believe and know the same fact ; our knowledge could not rest, as he says it does, on a belief that it is itself true.

But indeed, this notion of Sir W. Hamilton that we have two convictions on the same point, one guaranteeing the other—our knowledge of a truth, and a belief in the truth of that knowledge—seems to me a piece of false philosophy, resembling the doctrine he elsewhere rejects, that we have both a feeling and a consciousness of the feeling. We do not know a truth and believe it besides ; the belief *is* the knowledge. Belief, altogether, is a genus which includes knowledge : according to the usage of language we believe whatever we assent to ; but some of our beliefs are knowledge, others are only belief. The first requisite which, by universal admission, a belief must possess, to constitute it knowledge, is that it be true. The second is, that it be well grounded ; for what we believe by accident, or on evidence not sufficient, we are not said to know. The grounds must, moreover, be sufficient for the very highest degree of assurance ; for we do not consider ourselves to know, as long as we think there is any possibility (I mean any appreciable possibility) of our being mistaken. But when a belief is true, is held with the strongest conviction we ever have, and held on grounds sufficient to justify that strongest conviction, most people would think it worthy of the name of knowledge, whether it be grounded on our personal investigations, or on the appropriate testimony, and whether we know only the fact itself, or the manner of the fact. And I am inclined to think that the purposes of philosophy, as well as those of common life, are best answered by making this the line of demarcation.

know; unless, with Hegel, we hold that the Absolute is not subject to the Law of Contradiction, but is at once a real existence and the synthesis of contradictories. And, on the other hand, the Infinite and Absolute which are really capable of being believed, are also, for anything Sir W. Hamilton has shown to the contrary, capable of being, in certain of their aspects, known.

CHAPTER VI.

THE PHILOSOPHY OF THE CONDITIONED.

THE "Philosophy of the Conditioned," in its wider sense, includes all the doctrines that we have been discussing. In its narrower it consists, I think, mainly of a single proposition, which Sir W. Hamilton often reiterates, and insists upon as a fundamental law of human intellect. Though suggested by Kant's Antinomies of Speculative Reason, in the form which it bears in Sir W. Hamilton's writings it belongs, I believe, originally to himself. No doctrine which he has anywhere laid down is more characteristic of his mode of thought, and none is more strongly associated with his fame.

For the better understanding of this theory, it is necessary to premise some explanations respecting another doctrine, which is also his, but not peculiar to him. He protests, frequently and with emphasis, against the notion that whatever is inconceivable must be false. "There is no ground," he says,* "for infer-"ring a certain fact to be impossible, merely from our "inability to conceive its possibility." I regard this opinion as perfectly just. It is one of the psychological truths, highly important, and by no means generally recognised, which frequently meet us in his writings, and which give them, in my eyes, most of their philosophical value. I am obliged to add, that though he often furnishes a powerful statement and vindication of such truths, he seldom or never consistently adheres to them. Too often what he has affirmed in generals is

* Discussions, p. 624.

taken back in details, and arguments of his own are found to rest on philosophical commonplaces which he has himself repudiated and refuted. I am afraid that the present is one of these cases, and that Sir W. Hamilton will sometimes be found contending that a thing cannot possibly be true because we cannot conceive it: but at all events he disclaims any such inference, and broadly lays down, that things not only may be, but are, of which it is impossible for us to conceive even the possibility.

Before showing how this proposition is developed into the "Philosophy of the Conditioned," let us make the ground safe before us, by bestowing a brief consideration upon the proposition itself, its meaning, and the foundations on which it rests.

We cannot conclude anything to be impossible, because its possibility is inconceivable to us; for two reasons. First; what seems to us inconceivable, and so far as we are personally concerned, may really be so, usually owes its inconceivability only to a strong association. When, in a prolonged experience, we have often had a particular sensation or mental impression, and never without a certain other sensation or impression immediately accompanying it, there grows up so firm an adhesion between our ideas of the two, that we are unable to think of the former without thinking the latter in close combination with it. And unless other parts of our experience afford us some analogy to aid in disentangling the two ideas, our incapacity of imagining the one fact without the other grows, or is prone to grow, into a belief that the one cannot exist without the other. This is the law of Inseparable Association, an element of our nature of which few have realised to themselves the full power. It was for the first time largely applied to the explanation of the more complicated mental phenomena by Mr. James Mill; and is, in an especial manner, the key to the phenomenon of inconceivability. As that phenomenon only exists because our powers of conception are determined by our limited experience, Incon-

ceivables are incessantly becoming Conceivables as our
experience becomes enlarged.   There is no need to go
farther for an example than the case of Antipodes.   This
physical fact was, to the early speculators, inconceivable:
not, of course, the fact of persons in that position; this
the mind could easily represent to itself; but the possibility that, being in that position, and not being nailed
on, nor having any glutinous substance attached to their
feet, they could help falling off.   Here was an inseparable, though, as it proved to be, not an indissoluble
association, which while it continued made a real fact
what is called inconceivable ; and because inconceivable,
it was unhesitatingly believed to be impossible.   Inconceivabilities of similar character have, at many periods,
obstructed the reception of new scientific truths: the
Newtonian system had to contend against several of
them ; and we are not warranted in assigning a different
origin and character to those which still subsist, because
the experience that would be capable of removing them
has not occurred.   If anything which is now inconceivable by us were shown to us as a fact, we should soon
find ourselves able to conceive it.   We should even be
in danger of going over to the opposite error, and believing that the negation of it is inconceivable.   There are
many cases in the history of science (I have dilated on
some of them in another work) where something which
had once been inconceivable, and which people had with
great difficulty learnt to conceive, becoming itself fixed
in the bonds of an inseparable association, scientific men
came to think that it alone was conceivable, and that the
conflicting hypothesis which all mankind had believed,
and which a vast majority were probably believing still,
was inconceivable.   In Dr. Whewell's writings on the
Inductive Sciences, this transition of thought is not
only exemplified but defended.   Inconceivability is thus
a purely subjective thing, arising from the mental antecedents of the individual mind, or from those of the
human mind generally at a particular period, and cannot
give us any insight into the possibilities of Nature.

But, secondly, even assuming that inconceivability is not solely the consequence of limited experience, but that some incapacities of conceiving are inherent in the mind, and inseparable from it; this would not entitle us to infer, that what we are thus incapable of conceiving cannot exist. Such an inference would only be warrantable if we could know *à priori* that we must have been created capable of conceiving whatever is capable of existing: that the universe of thought and that of reality, the Microcosm and the Macrocosm (as they once were called) must have been framed in complete correspondence with one another. That this is really the case has been laid down expressly in some systems of philosophy, by implication in more, and is the foundation (among others) of the systems of Schelling and Hegel: but an assumption more destitute of evidence could scarcely be made, nor can one easily imagine any evidence that could prove it, unless it were revealed from above.

What is inconceivable, then, cannot therefore be inferred to be false. But let us vary the terms of the proposition, and express it thus: what is inconceivable, is not therefore incredible. We have now a statement, which may mean either exactly the same as the other, or more. It may mean only that our inability to conceive a thing, does not entitle us to deny its possibility, nor its existence. Or it may mean that a thing's being inconceivable to us is no reason against our believing, and legitimately believing, that it actually is. This is a very different proposition from the preceding. Sir W. Hamilton, as we have said, goes this length. It is now necessary to enter more minutely than at first seemed needful, into the meaning of "inconceivable;" which, like almost all the metaphysical terms we are forced to make use of, is weighed down with ambiguities.

Reid pointed out and discriminated two meanings of the verb "to conceive," * giving rise to two different

* "To conceive, to imagine, to apprehend, when taken in the proper

meanings of inconceivable. But Sir W. Hamilton uses
" to conceive " in three meanings, and has accordingly
three meanings for Inconceivable ; though he does not
give the smallest hint to his readers, nor seems ever to
suspect, that the three are not one and the same.

The first meaning of Inconceivable is, that of which
the mind cannot form to itself any representation ; either
(as in the case of Noumena) because no attributes are
given, out of which a representation could be framed,
or because the attributes given are incompatible with
one another—are such as the mind cannot put together
in a single image. Of this last case numerous instances
present themselves to the most cursory glance. The
fundamental one is that of a simple contradiction. We
cannot represent anything to ourselves as at once being
something, and not being it ; as at once having, and
not having, a given attribute. The following are other
examples. We cannot represent to ourselves time or
space as having an end. We cannot represent to our-

"sense, signify an act of the mind which implies no belief or judgment at
"all. It is an act of the mind by which nothing is affirmed or denied,
"and which, therefore, can neither be true nor false. But there is another
"and a very different meaning of these words, so common and so well
"authorised in language that it cannot be avoided ; and on that account
"we ought to be the more on our guard, that we be not misled by the am-
"biguity. . . .   When we would express our opinion modestly, instead of
"saying, 'This is my opinion,' or 'This is my judgment,' which has the air
"of dogmaticalness, we say, ' I conceive it to be thus—I imagine, or appre-
"hend it to be thus ;' which is understood as a modest declaration of our
"judgment. In like manner, when anything is said which we take to be
"impossible, we say, ' We cannot conceive it :' meaning that we cannot
"believe it. Thus we see that the words *conceive, imagine, apprehend*,
"have two meanings, and are used to express two operations of the mind,
"which ought never to be confounded. Sometimes they express simple
"apprehension, which implies no judgment at all ; sometimes they express
"judgment or opinion. . . .   When they are used to express simple appre-
"hension they are followed by a noun in the accusative case, which
"signifies the object conceived ; but when they are used to express opinion
"or judgment, they are commonly followed by a verb in the infinitive
"mood. 'I conceive an Egyptian pyramid.' This implies no judgment.
"'I conceive the Egyptian pyramids to be the most ancient monuments
"of human art.' This implies judgment. When they are used in the
"last sense, the thing conceived must be a proposition, because judgment
"cannot be expressed but by a proposition."—Reid on the Intellectual
Powers, p. 223 of Sir W. Hamilton's edition, to which edition all my
references will be made.

selves two and two as making five; nor two straight
lines as enclosing a space. We cannot represent to ourselves a round square; nor a body all black, and at the
same time all white.

These things are literally inconceivable to us, our
minds and our experience being what they are. Whether
they would be inconceivable if our minds were the same
but our experience different, is open to discussion. A
distinction may be made, which, I think, will be found
pertinent to the question. That the same thing should
at once be and not be—that identically the same statement should be both true and false—is not only inconceivable to us, but we cannot imagine that it could be
made conceivable. We cannot attach sufficient meaning
to the proposition, to be able to represent to ourselves
the supposition of a different experience on this matter.
We cannot therefore even entertain the question, whether
the incompatibility is in the original structure of our
minds, or is only put there by our experience. The case
is otherwise in all the other examples of inconceivability.
Our incapacity of conceiving the same thing as A and not
A, may be primordial; but our inability to conceive A
without B, is because A, by experience or teaching, has
become inseparably associated with B : and our inability
to conceive A with C, is, because, by experience or
teaching, A has become inseparably associated with some
mental representation which includes the negation of C.
Thus all inconceivabilities may be reduced to inseparable
association, combined with the original inconceivability
of a direct contradiction. All the cases which I have
cited as instances of inconceivability, and which are the
strongest I could have chosen, may be resolved in this
manner. We cannot conceive a round square, not
merely because no such object has ever presented itself
in our experience, for that would not be enough.
Neither, for anything we know, are the two ideas in
themselves incompatible. To conceive a round square,
or to conceive a body all black and yet all white, would
only be to conceive two different sensations as produced

in us simultaneously by the same object; a conception familiar to our experience ; and we should probably be as well able to conceive a round square as a hard square, or a heavy square, if it were not that, in our uniform experience, at the instant when a thing begins to be round it ceases to be square, so that the beginning of the one impression is inseparably associated with the departure or cessation of the other.* Thus our inability to form a conception always arises from our being compelled to form another contradictory to it. We cannot conceive time or space as having an end, because the idea of any portion whatever of time or space is inseparably associated with the idea of a time or space beyond it. We cannot conceive two and two as five, because an inseparable association compels us to conceive it as four ; and it cannot be conceived as both, because four and five, like round and square, are so related in our experience, that each is associated with the cessation, or removal, of the other. We cannot conceive two straight lines as enclosing a space, because enclosing a space means approaching and meeting a second time ; and the mental image of two straight lines which have once met is inseparably associated with the representation of them as diverging. Thus it is not wholly without ground that the notion of a round square, and the assertion that two and two make five, or that two straight lines can enclose a space, are said, in common and even in scientific parlance, to involve a contradiction. The statement is not logically correct, for contra-

* It has been remarked to me by a correspondent, that a round square differs from a hard square or a heavy square in this respect, that the two sensations or sets of sensations supposed to be joined in the first-named combination are affections of the same nerves, and therefore, being different affections, are mutually incompatible by our organic constitution, and could not be made compatible by any change in the arrangements of external nature. This is probably true, and may be the physical reason why when a thing begins to be perceived as round it ceases to be perceived as square ; but it is not the less true that this mere fact suffices, under the laws of association, to account for the inconceivability of the combination. I am willing, however, to admit, as suggested by my correspondent, that "if the imagination employs the organism in its representations," which it probably does, "what is originally unperceivable in consequence of organic laws" may also be "originally unimaginable."

diction is only between a positive representation and its negative. But the impossibility of uniting contradictory conceptions in the same representation, is the real ground of the inconceivability in these cases. And we should probably have no difficulty in putting together the two ideas supposed to be incompatible, if our experience had not first inseparably associated one of them with the contradictory of the other.*

* That the reverse of the most familiar principles of arithmetic and geometry might have been made conceivable, even to our present mental faculties, if those faculties had coexisted with a totally different constitution of external nature, is ingeniously shown in the concluding paper of a recent volume, anonymous, but of known authorship, "Essays, by a Barrister."

"Consider this case. There is a world in which, whenever two pairs of "things are either placed in proximity or are contemplated together, a "fifth thing is immediately created and brought within the contempla-"tion of the mind engaged in putting two and two together. This is "surely neither inconceivable, for we can readily conceive the result by "thinking of common puzzle tricks, nor can it be said to be beyond the "power of Omnipotence. Yet in such a world surely two and two would "make five. That is, the result to the mind of contemplating two two's "would be to count five. This shows that it is not inconceivable that two "and two might make five : but, on the other hand, it is perfectly easy "to see why in this world we are absolutely certain that two and two "make four. There is probably not an instant of our lives in which we "are not experiencing the fact. We see it whenever we count four books, "four tables or chairs, four men in the street, or the four corners of a "paving stone, and we feel more sure of it than of the rising of the sun "to-morrow, because our experience upon the subject is so much wider "and applies to such an infinitely greater number of cases. Nor is it true "that every one who has once been brought to see it, is equally sure of it. "A boy who has just learnt the multiplication table is pretty sure that "twice two are four, but is often extremely doubtful whether seven times "nine are sixty-three. If his teacher told him that twice two made five, "his certainty would be greatly impaired.

"It would also be possible to put a case of a world in which two straight "lines should be universally supposed to include a space. Imagine a man "who had never had any experience of straight lines through the medium "of any sense whatever, suddenly placed upon a railway stretching out "on a perfectly straight line to an indefinite distance in each direction. "He would see the rails, which would be the first straight lines he had "ever seen, apparently meeting, or at least tending to meet at each "horizon ; and he would thus infer, in the absence of all other experience, "that they actually did enclose a space, when produced far enough. "Experience alone could undeceive him. A world in which every object "was round, with the single exception of a straight inaccessible railway, "would be a world in which every one would believe that two straight "lines enclosed a space. In such a world, therefore, the impossibility of "conceiving that two straight lines can enclose a space would not exist."

In the "Geometry of Visibles" which forms part of Reid's "Inquiry

Thus far, of the first kind of Inconceivability ; the first and most proper meaning in which the word is used. But there is another meaning, in which things are often said to be inconceivable which the mind is under no

into the Human Mind," it is contended that if we had the sense of sight, but not that of touch, it would appear to us that "every right line being "produced will at last return into itself," and that "any two right lines "being produced will meet in two points." Ch. vi., Sect. 9 (p. 148). The author adds, that persons thus constituted would firmly believe "that "two or more bodies may exist in the same place." For this they would "have the testimony of sense," and could "no more doubt of it than they "can doubt whether they have any perception at all, since they would "often see two bodies meet and coincide in the same place, and separate "again, without having undergone any change in their sensible qualities "by this penetration." (P. 151.)

Hardly any part of the present volume has been so maltreated, by so great a number of critics, as the illustrations here quoted from an able and highly. instructed contemporary thinker ; which, as they were neither designed by their author nor cited by me as anything more than illustrations, I do not deem it necessary to take up space by defending. When a selection must be made, one is obliged to consider what one can best spare.

[Some of my correspondents, looking upon the illustrations by "A "Barrister" as (what they are not) an essential part of my argument, think me bound either to defend them or to give them up. As they are, in my opinion, perfectly defensible, I am ready, thus challenged, to stand up for them. And I select, among the attacks made on them, that of Dr. M'Cosh (Examination of Mr. J. S. Mill's Philosophy, pp. 209–211), as one of the fairest, and including what is most worthy of notice in the others. Of the first illustration, Dr. M'Cosh says :—

"Were we placed in a world in which two pairs of things were always "followed by a fifth thing, we might be disposed to believe that the pairs "caused the fifth thing, or that there was some prearranged disposition "of things producing them together ; but we could not be made to judge "that $2 + 2 = 5$, or that the fifth thing is not a different thing from the two "and the two. On the other supposition put, of the two pairs always "suggesting a fifth, we should explain their recurrence by some law of "association, but we would not confound the 5 with the $2 + 2$, or think "that the two pairs could make five."

This passage is a correct description of what would happen if the presentation of the fifth thing were posterior, by a perceptible interval, to the juxtaposition of the two pairs, so that we should have time to judge that the two and two make four previously to perceiving the fifth. But the supposition is that the production of the fifth is so instantaneous in the very act of seeing, that we never should see the four things by themselves as four : the fifth thing would be inseparably involved in the act of perception by which we should ascertain the sum of the two pairs. I confess it seems to me that in this case we should have an apparent intuition of two and two making five.

To the second illustration, Dr. M'Cosh 'replies : "I allow that this "person as he looked one way, would see a figure presented to the eye of "two straight lines approaching nearer each other ; and that as he looked incapacity of representing to itself in an image. It is often said, that we are unable to conceive *as possible* that which, in itself, we are perfectly well able to conceive: we are able, it is admitted, to conceive it as an imaginary

"the other way he would see a like figure. But I deny that in combining "the two views he would ever decide that the four lines seen, the two "seen first and the two seen second, make only two straight lines. In "uniting the two perceptions in thought, he would certainly place a bend "or a turn somewhere, possibly at the spot from which he took the two "views. He would continue to do so till he realised that the lines seen "on either side did not in fact approach nearer each other. Or, to state "the whole phenomenon with more scientific accuracy : Intuitively, and "to a person who had not acquired the knowledge of distance by ex- "perience, the two views would appear to be each of two lines approaching "nearer each other ; but without his being at all cognisant of the relation "of the two views, or of one part of the lines being further removed from "him than another. As experience told him that the lines receded from "him on each side, he would contrive some means of combining his obser- "vations, probably in the way above indicated ; but he never could make "two straight lines enclose a space."

Now it seems to me that the supposed percipient *could* not account for his apparent perceptions in the manner indicated ; he *could* not believe that there was a turn or a bend anywhere. "At the spot from which he took the two views" he would have the evidence of his senses that there was no bend. Looking along the interval between the lines, he would again have the evidence of sense that they were not deflected either way, but maintained an uniform direction. Until, therefore, experience of the laws of perspective had corrected his judgment, he would have the apparent evidence of his senses that two straight lines met in two points. This appearance, until shown by further experience to be an illusion, would probably decide his belief : and any doubts that might be raised by a contemplation of straight lines which were nearer to him, would be silenced by the supposition that two straight lines will inclose a space if only they are produced far enough.

Dr. M'Cosh may himself be cited as a witness to the intrinsic possi- bility of conceiving combinations which I should have thought were uni- versally regarded as inconceivable. When distinguishing between the two meanings of inconceivable (in pp. 234, 235 of his book) he says: "We "cannot be made to decide or believe that Cleopatra's Needle should be "in Paris and Egypt at the same time ; yet with some difficulty we can "simultaneously image it in both places." Now when we consider that in order really to image the *same* Needle (and not two Needles exactly similar) in two places at once we must actually imagine the two places, Paris and Alexandria, superposed upon one another and occupying the same portion of space, it seems to me that this conception is quite as impossible to us as the reverse of a geometrical axiom ; and is, indeed, of much the same character.]

The "Geometry of Visibles" has been noticed only by Dr. M'Cosh (pp. 211–213), who rejects it, as founded on the erroneous doctrine (as he considers it) that we cannot perceive by sight the third dimension of space. I regard this, on the contrary, as not only a true doctrine, but one from which Dr. M'Cosh's own opinion does not materially differ : and

object, but unable to conceive it realised.   This extends
the term inconceivable to every combination of facts
which to the mind simply contemplating it, appears incredible.*   It was in this sense that Antipodes were inconceivable.   They could be figured in imagination;
they could even be painted, or modelled in clay.   The
mind could put the parts of the conception together, but
could not realise the combination as one which could
exist in nature.   The cause of the inability was the
powerful tendency, generated by experience, to *expect*
falling off, when a body, not of adhesive quality, was in
contact only with the under side of another body.   The
association was not so powerful as to disable the mind
from conceiving the body as holding on; doubtless because other facts of our experience afforded models on

if it be true, it is impossible to resist Reid's conclusion, that to beings
possessing only the sense of sight, the paradoxes here quoted, and several
others, would be truths of intuition—self-evident truths.
    [Dr. Ward, in the *Dublin Review*, contests this doctrine; and an argu-
ment against it has been sent to me by the intelligent and instructed
correspondent already once referred to. For a reply I might refer them
to the chapter on the Geometry of Visibles, in Reid's work; but I will
point out, in few words, where I think they are in error. They contend
that Reid's Idomenians would not possess the notion which we attach to
the term straight line, but would call by that name what they would really
image to themselves as a circular arc. But Reid's position (and he assigns
good reasons for it) is the reverse of this; that what we, who have the
sense of touch, perceive as a circular arc with ourselves in the centre,
Idomenians could only perceive as a straight line; and that, consequently,
all the appearances which Reid enumerates would be by them apprehended, and, as they would think, perceived, as phenomena of straight
lines.
    Dr. M'Cosh also returns to the charge, but holds a different doctrine
from my other two critics, being of opinion that the Idomenians would
really have the notion of a straight line. For the consequences of this I
refer him back to Reid. He adds, that as touch alone can reveal to us
impenetrability, the Idomenians could argue nothing as to bodies *pene-
trating* one another. But, they could have the conception of the only
penetration Reid contended for, namely, of bodies meeting and coinciding
in the same place, and separating again without alteration. And for this
they would have the evidence of sense. The fact is literally true of the
visual images, which to them would be the whole bodies; and as they
could form no notion of one thing passing behind another, their only
impression would be of penetration.]
    * I do not mean. which is *really* incredible, as Mr. Mansel, in his re-
joinder, supposes I do, and consequently charges me with imputing to Sir
W. Hamilton that in the Law of the Conditioned he maintains that of
two *incredible* alternatives one must be *believed*.

which such a conception could be framed. But though not disabled from conceiving the combination, the mind was disabled from believing it. The difference between belief and conception, and between the conditions of belief and those of simple conception, are psychological questions into which I do not enter. It is sufficient that inability to believe can coexist with ability to conceive, and that a mental association between two facts which is not intense enough to make their separation unimaginable, may yet create, and, if there are no counter associations, always does create, more or less of difficulty in believing that the two can exist apart; a difficulty often amounting to a local or temporary impossibility.

This is the second meaning of Inconceivability ; which by Reid is carefully distinguished from the first, but his editor Sir W. Hamilton employs the word in both senses indiscriminately.* How he came to miss the distinction is tolerably obvious to any one who is familiar with his writings, and especially with his theory of Judgment ; but needs not be pointed out here. It is more remarkable that he gives to the term a third sense, answering to a third signification of the verb " to conceive." To conceive anything, has with him not only its two ordinary meanings—to represent the thing as an image, and to be able to realise it as possible—but an additional one, which

* It is curious that Dr. M'Cosh, with this volume before him, and occupied in criticising it, did not find out until his book was passing through the press, and then only from the sixth edition of my "System of Logic," that I was aware of the difference between these two meanings of "to conceive" (M'Cosh, p. 241, note). He consequently thought it necessary to tell me, what I had myself stated in the text, that Antipodes were inconceivable only in the second sense.

Dr. M'Cosh continually charges me with confounding the two meanings, and arguing from one of them to the other. But he must be well aware that intuitional philosophers in general (I do not say that Dr. M'Cosh) assign as the sufficient, and conclusive proof of inconceivability in the one sense, inconceivability in the other. They argue that a proposition must be true, and ought to be believed—on the ground that we cannot conceive its opposite, meaning that we cannot frame a mental representation of it. It is therefore quite pertinent to show (when it can be done) that this inability to join the ideas together is not inherent in our constitution, but is accounted for by the conditions of our experience ; for to show this, is to destroy the argument principally relied on as a proof that the judgment is a necessary one.

he denotes by various phrases. One of his common expressions for it is, "to construe to the mind in thought." This, he often says, can only be done "through a higher "notion." "We * think, we conceive, we comprehend a "thing only as we think it as within or under some- "thing else." So that a fact, or a supposition, is conceivable or comprehensible by us (conceive and comprehend being with him in this case synonymous) only by being reduced to some more general fact, as a particular case under it. Again,† " to conceive the possibility " of a thing, is defined " conceiving it as the consequent of a "certain reason." The inconceivable, in this third sense, is simply the inexplicable. Accordingly all first truths are, according to Sir W. Hamilton, inconceivable. "The ‡ " primary data of consciousness, as themselves the con- " ditions under which all else is comprehended, are ne- " cessarily themselves incomprehensible. . . . that is . . . " we are unable to conceive through a higher notion how " that is possible, which the deliverance avouches actually " to be." And we shall find him arguing things to be inconceivable, merely on the ground that we have no higher notion under which to class them. This use of the word inconceivable, being a complete perversion of it from its established meanings, I decline to recognise. If all the general truths which we are most certain of are to be called inconceivable, the word no longer serves any purpose. Inconceivable is not to be confounded with unprovable, or unanalysable. A truth which is not inconceivable in either of the received meanings of the term—a truth which is completely apprehended, and without difficulty believed, I cannot consent to call inconceivable merely because we cannot account for it, or deduce it from a higher truth.§

---

* Lectures, iii. 102.   † Ibid. p. 100.
‡ Dissertations on Reid, p. 745.
§ Mr. Mansel refuses to admit (pp. 131 et seqq) that Sir W. Hamilton confounds these different senses of the word Conception, and asserts that he always adheres to the meaning indicated by him in a foot-note to Reid (p. 377), and answering to the first meaning of inconceivable, namely, unimaginable. Of the second meaning Mr. Mansel says (p. 132), "When

These being Sir W. Hamilton's three kinds of inconceivability; is the inconceivability of a proposition in any of these senses, consistent with believing it to be true? The third kind is avowedly compatible not only

"Hamilton speaks of being 'unable to conceive as possible,' he does not "mean, as Mr. Mill supposes, physically possible under the law of gravi-"tation or some other law of matter, but mentally possible as a represen-"tation or image; and thus the supposed second sense is identical with "the first." According to this interpretation, when Sir W. Hamilton says of anything that it cannot be conceived as possible, he does not mean possible in fact, but possible to thought, in other words, that it cannot be conceived as conceivable. I, however, do Sir W. Hamilton the justice of believing, that when he added the words "as possible" to the word conceive, he intended to add something to the idea. Accordingly he uses the phrases "to understand as possible," "to comprehend as possible," as equivalents for "to conceive as possible." I believe that by "possible" he meant, as people usually do, possible in fact. And I have the authority of Mr. Mansel himself for so thinking. Mr. Mansel, in another place (p. 36) expresses what was probably the real meaning of Sir W. Hamilton, and laments that Sir W. Hamilton did not state it distinctly. "To con-"ceive a thing as possible," says Mr. Mansel, "we must conceive the man-"ner in which it is possible: but we may believe in the fact without being "able to conceive the manner." This makes no sense if understood as Mr. Mansel, in his rejoinder, says that it ought to be—"mentally possible "as a notion, not physically possible as a fact." There is no *manner* of being possible as a mere notion: the elements of the notion can be put together in the mind, or they cannot. A *manner* of being possible can only refer to possibility as a fact. When people say that they cannot conceive *how* a thing is possible, they always mean, that but for evidence to the contrary, they should have supposed it impossible. And this I always find to be the case when Sir W. Hamilton uses the phrase. I know not of any *manner* of a possibility that would enable us to conceive the thing "*as* possible" unless it removed some obstacle to believing that the thing *is* possible. Such, for instance, would be the case, if we have found or imagined something which is capable of causing the thing; or some means or mechanism by which it could be brought about (the desideratum in Mr. Mansel's illustration of a being who sees without eyes); or if we have had an actual intuition of the thing as existing: which, when sufficiently familiar, makes it no longer seem to require any ground of possibility beyond the fact itself. In short, the *how* of its existence, which enables us to conceive it as possible, must be a how which affords at least a semblance of explanation of Mr. Mansel's *that*. This is distinctly recognised by Sir W. Hamilton in one of the passages I have quoted, in which "to conceive the possibility" of a thing is defined "con-ceiving it as the consequent of a certain reason." By conceiving a thing as possible, he meant apprehending some fact, or imagining some hypothesis, which would explain its possibility; which would be, in the Leibnitzian sense, its Sufficient Reason. For, an explanation, even hypothetical, of a thing which previously seemed to admit of none, removes a difficulty in believing it. We have a natural tendency to disbelieve anything ⁺which, while it has never been presented in our experience, also contradicts our habitual associations: but the suggestion to our mind of some possible conditions which would be a Sufficient Reason

with belief, but with our strongest and most natural beliefs. An inconceivable of the second kind can not only be believed, but believed with full understanding. In this case we are perfectly able to represent to ourselves mentally what is said to be inconceivable; only, from an association in our mind, it does not look credible : but, this association being the result of experience or of teaching, contrary experience or teaching is able to dissolve it; and even before this has been done—while the thing still feels incredible, the intellect may, on sufficient evidence, accept it as true. An inconceivable of the first kind, inconceivable in the proper sense of the term— that which the mind is actually unable to put together in a representation—may nevertheless be believed, if we attach any meaning to it, but cannot be said to be believed with understanding. We cannot believe it on direct evidence, *i.e.* through its being presented in our experience, for if it were so presented it would immediately cease to be inconceivable. We may believe it because its falsity would be inconsistent with something which we otherwise know to be true. Or we may believe it because it is affirmed by some one wiser than ourselves, who, we suppose, may have had the experience which has not reached us, and to whom it may thus have become conceivable. But the belief is without understanding, for we form no mental picture of what we believe. We do not so much believe the fact, as believe that we should believe it if we could have the needful presentation in our experience; and that some other being has, or may have, had that presentation. Our inability to conceive it, is no argument whatever for its being false, and no hindrance to our believing it, to the above-mentioned extent.

But though facts, which we cannot join together in an

for its existence, takes away its incredibility, and enables us to "conceive "it as possible." This view of Sir W. Hamilton's meaning explains, though it does not justify, his using the term in its third signification; which Mr. Mansel (p. 132) also endeavours to reduce to the first, but which may be better identified with the second : for of First Truths also it is impossible to assign any Sufficient Reason.

image, may be united in the universe, and though we may have sufficient ground for believing that they are so united in point of fact, it is impossible to believe a proposition which conveys to us no meaning at all. If any one says to me, Humpty Dumpty is an Abracadabra, I neither know what is meant by an Abracadabra, nor what is meant by Humpty Dumpty, I may, if I have confidence in my informant, believe that he means something, and that the something which he means is probably true : but I do not believe the very thing which he means, since I am entirely ignorant what it is. Propositions of this kind, the unmeaningness of which lies in the subject or predicate, are not those generally described as inconceivable. The unmeaning propositions spoken of under that name, are usually those which involve contradictions. That the same thing is and is not—that it did and did not rain at the same time and place, that a man is both alive and not alive, are forms of words which carry no signification to my mind. As Sir W. Hamilton truly says,* one half of the statement simply sublates or takes away the meaning which the other half has laid down. The unmeaningness here resides in the copula. The word *is* has no meaning, except as exclusive of *is not*. The case is more hopeless than that of Humpty Dumpty, for no explanation by the speaker of what the words mean can make the assertion intelligible. Whatever may be meant by a man, and whatever may be meant by alive, the statement that a man can be alive and not alive is equally without meaning to me. I cannot make out anything which the speaker intends me to believe. The sentence affirms nothing of which my mind can take hold. Sir W. Hamilton, indeed, maintains the contrary. He says,† " When we conceive the proposition that A is not A, we " clearly comprehend the separate meaning of the terms " *A* and *not A*, and also the import of the assertion of " their identity." We comprehend the separate meaning

---

* Lectures, iii. 99.   † Ibid. p. 113.

G

of the terms, but as to the meaning of the assertion, I think we only comprehend what the same form of words would mean in another case. The very import of the form of words is inconsistent with its meaning anything when applied to terms of this particular kind. Let any one who doubts this, attempt to define what is meant by applying a predicate to a subject, when the predicate and the subject are the negation of one another. To make sense of the assertion, some new meaning must be attached to *is* or *is not*, and if this be done the proposition is no longer the one presented for our assent. Here, therefore, is one kind of inconceivable proposition which nothing whatever can make credible to us. Not being able to attach any meaning to the proposition, we are equally incompetent to assert that it is, or that it is not, possible in itself. But we have not the power of believing it ; and there the matter must rest.

We are now prepared to enter on the peculiar doctrine of Sir W. Hamilton, called the Philosophy of the Conditioned. Not content with maintaining that things which from the natural and fundamental laws of the human mind, are for ever inconceivable to us, may, for aught we know, be true, he goes farther, and says, we know that many such things are true. "Things * there " are which may, nay *must*, be true, of which the under- " standing is wholly unable to construe to itself the pos- " sibility." Of what nature these things are, is declared in many parts of his writings, in the form of a general law. It is thus stated in the review of Cousin: † "The " Conditioned is the mean between the two extremes— " two unconditionates, exclusive of each other, neither " of which can be conceived as possible, but of which, on " the principles of contradiction and excluded middle, " one must be admitted as necessary. . . . The mind is " not represented as conceiving two propositions sub- " versive of each other as equally possible ; but only,

* Discussions, p. 624.   † Ibid. p. 15.

"as unable to understand as possible, either of the
"extremes; one of which, however, on the ground of
"their mutual repugnance, it is compelled to recognise
"as true."

In the Dissertations on Reid * he enunciates, in still
more general terms, as "The Law of the Conditioned:
"That all positive thought lies between two extremes,
"neither of which we can conceive as possible, and yet
"as mutual contradictories, the one or the other we must
"recognise as necessary." And it is (he says) "from
"this impotence of intellect" that "we are unable to
"think aught as absolute. Even absolute relativity
"is unthinkable."

The doctrine is more fully expanded in the Lectures
on Logic,† from which I shall quote at greater length.

"All that we can positively think . . . . lies between
"two opposite poles of thought, which, as exclusive of
"each other, cannot, on the principles of Identity and
"Contradiction, both be true, but of which, on the prin-
"ciple of Excluded Middle, one or the other must. Let
"us take, for example, any of the general objects of
"our knowledge. Let us take body, or rather, since
"body as extended is included under extension, let us
"take extension itself, or space. Now extension alone
"will exhibit to us two pairs of contradictory incon-
"ceivables,‡ that is, in all, four incomprehensibles, but
"of which, though all are equally unthinkable . . . . we
"are compelled, by the law of Excluded Middle, to
"admit some two as true and necessary.

"Extension may be viewed either as a whole or as a
"part; and in each aspect it affords us two incogitable
"contradictions. 1st. Taking it as a whole: space, it
"is evident, must either be limited, that is, have an end,
"and circumference; or unlimited, that is, have no end,

---

* P. 911.   † Lectures, iii. 100, *et seq.*

‡ To save words in the text, I shall simply indicate in foot-notes the
places at which the author passes from one of the three meanings of the
word Inconceivable to another. In this place he is using it in the first
or second meaning, probably in the first.

"no circumference.   These are contradictory supposi-
"tions; both, therefore, cannot, but one must be true.
"Now let us try positively to comprehend, positively to
"conceive,* the possibility of either of these two
"mutually exclusive alternatives.   Can we represent, or
"realise in thought, extension as absolutely limited? in
"other words, can we mentally hedge round the whole of
"space, conceive† it absolutely bounded, that is, so that
"beyond its boundary there is no outlying, no surround-
"ing space?   This is impossible.   Whatever compass of
"space we may enclose by any limitation of thought,
"we shall find that we have no difficulty in transcend-
"ing these limits.   Nay, we shall find that we cannot
"but transcend them ; for we are unable to think any
"extent of space except as within a still ulterior space,
"of which, let us think till the powers of thinking fail,
"we can never reach the circumference.   It is thus im-
"possible for us to think space as a totality, that is, as
"absolutely bounded, but all-containing.   We may,
"therefore, lay down this first extreme as inconceivable.‡
"We cannot think space as limited.

   "Let us now consider its contradictory: can we com-
"prehend the possibility of infinite or unlimited space?
"To suppose this is a direct contradiction in terms ; it is
"to comprehend the incomprehensible.   We think, we
"conceive,§ we comprehend a thing, only as we think it
"as within or under something else ; but to do this of
"the infinite is to think the infinite is finite, which is
"contradictory and absurd.

   "Now here it may be asked, how have we then the
"word *infinite?*   How have we the notion which this
"word expresses?   The answer to this question is con-
"tained in the distinction of positive and negative
"thought.   We have a positive concept of a thing when
"we think it by the qualities of which it is the comple-
"ment.   But as the attribution of qualities is an affir-

---

* First and second senses confused together.
† First sense.   ‡ First sense.   § Third sense.

" mation, as affirmation and negation are relatives, and
" as relatives are known only in and through each other,
" we cannot, therefore, have a consciousness of the
" affirmation of any quality, without having at the same
" time the correlative consciousness of its negation.
" Now, the one consciousness is a positive, the other
" consciousness is a negative notion. But, in point of
" fact, a negative notion is only the negation of a notion ;
" we think only by the attribution of certain qualities,
" and the negation of these qualities and of this attribu-
" tion is simply, in so far, a denial of our thinking at all.
" As affirmation always suggests negation, every positive
" notion must likewise suggest a negative notion : and
" as language is the reflex of thought, the positive and
" negative notions are expressed by positive and negative
" names. Thus it is with the infinite. The finite is the
" only object of real or positive thought ; it is that alone
" which we think by the attribution of determinate
" characters ; the infinite, on the contrary, is conceived
" only by the thinking away of every character by which
" the finite was conceived : in other words, we conceive
" it only as inconceivable.* . . . . .

"It is manifest that we can no more realise the
" thought or conception of infinite, unbounded, or un-
" limited space, than we can realise the conception of
" a finite or absolutely bounded space.† But these two
" inconceivables are reciprocal contradictories : we are
" unable to comprehend ‡ the possibility of either, while,
" however, on the principle of Excluded Middle, one or
" other must be admitted. . . . .

"It is needless to show that the same result is given
" by the experiment made on extension considered as a
" part, as divisible. Here if we attempt to divide ex-
" tension in thought, we shall neither, on the one hand,
" succeed in conceiving the possibility § of an absolute
" minimum of space, that is, a minimum *ex hypothesi*

---

* Third sense, gliding back into the first.
† Here the return to the first sense is completed.
‡ Second sense.   § Second sense.

" extended, but which cannot be conceived as divisible
" into parts,* nor, on the other, of carrying on this
" division to infinity.   But as these are contradictory
" opposites," one or the other of them must be true.

In other passages our author applies the same order
of considerations to Time, saying that we can neither
conceive an absolute commencement, nor an infinite
regress; an absolute termination, nor a duration infinitely
prolonged; though either the one or the other must be
true.   And again, of the Will: we cannot, he says, conceive the Will to be Free, because this would be to conceive an event uncaused, or, in other words, an absolute
commencement: neither can we conceive the Will not
to be Free, because this would be supposing an infinite
regress from effect to cause.   The will, however, must
be either free or not free; and in this case, he thinks we
have independent grounds for deciding one way, namely,
that it is free, because if it were not, we could not be
accountable for our actions, which our consciousness
assures us that we are.

This, then, is the Philosophy of the Conditioned: into
the value of which it now remains to enquire.

In the case of each of the Antinomies which the
author presents, he undertakes to establish two things:
that neither of the rival hypotheses can be conceived by
us as possible, and that we are nevertheless certain that
one or the other of them is true.

To begin with his first position, that we can neither
conceive an end to space, nor space without end.

That we are unable to conceive an end to space I fully
acknowledge.   To account for this there needs no inherent incapacity.   We are disabled from forming this
conception, by known psychological laws.   We have
never perceived any object, or any portion of space,
which had not other space beyond it.   And we have
been perceiving objects and portions of space from the
moment of birth.   How then could the idea of an object,

* First sense.

or of a portion of space, escape becoming inseparably associated with the idea of additional space beyond? Every instant of our lives helps to rivet this association, and we never have had a single experience tending to disjoin it. The association, under the present constitution of our existence, is indissoluble. But we have no ground for believing that it is so from the original structure of our minds. We can suppose that in some other state of existence we might be transported to the end of space, when, being apprised of what had happened by some impression of a kind utterly unknown to us now, we should at the same instant become capable of conceiving the fact, and learn that it was true. After some experience of the new impression, the fact of an end to space would seem as natural to us as the revelations of sight to a person born blind, after he has been long enough couched to have become familiar with them. But as this cannot happen in our present state of existence, the experience which would render the association dissoluble is never obtained; and an end to space remains inconceivable.

One half, then, of our author's first proposition, must be conceded. But the other half? Is it true that we are incapable of conceiving infinite space? I have already shown strong reasons for dissenting from this assertion: and those which our author, in this and other places, assigns in its support, seem to me quite untenable.

He says, "we think, we conceive, we comprehend, a "thing, only as we think it as within or under some-"thing else. But to do this of the infinite is to think "the infinite as finite, which is contradictory and ab-"surd." When we come to Sir W. Hamilton's account of the Laws of Thought, we shall have some remarks to make on the phrase to think one thing "within or under another;" a favourite expression with the Transcendental school, one of whose characteristics is, that they are always using the prepositions in a metaphorical sense. But granting that to think a thing is to think it under something else, we must understand this

statement as it is invariably interpreted by those who
employ it. According to them, we think a thing when
we make any affirmation respecting it, and we think it
under the notion which we affirm of it. Whenever we
judge, we think the subject under the predicate. Consequently when we say "God is good," we think God
under the notion "good." Is this, in our author's
opinion, to think the infinite as finite, and hence "contradictory and absurd"?

If this doctrine hold, it follows that we cannot predicate anything of a subject which we regard as being in
any of its attributes, infinite. We are unable, without
falling into a contradiction, to assert anything not only
of God, but of Time, and of Space. Considered as a
reductio ad absurdum, this is sufficient. But we may
go deeper into the matter, and deny the statement that
to think anything "under" the notion expressed by a
general term is to think it as finite. None of our
general predicates are, in the proper sense of the
term, finite; they are all, at least potentially, infinite.
"Good" is not a name for the things or persons possessing that attribute which exist now, or at any other
given moment, and which are only a finite aggregate.
It is a name for all those which ever did, or ever will,
or even in hypothesis or fiction can, possess the attribute. This is not a limited number. It is the very
nature and constituent character of a *general* notion
that its extension (as Sir W. Hamilton would say) is
without limit.

But he might perhaps say, that though its extension,
consisting of the possible individuals included in it, may
be infinite, its *comprehension*, the set of attributes contained in it (or as I prefer to say, connoted by its name)
is a limited quantity. Undoubtedly it is. But see what
follows. If, because the comprehension of a general
notion is finite, anything infinite cannot without contradiction be thought under it, the consequence is, that a
being possessing in an infinite degree a given attribute,
cannot be thought under that very attribute. Infinite

goodness cannot be thought as goodness, because that would be to think it as finite. Surely there must be some great confusion of ideas in the premises, when this comes out as the conclusion.

Our author goes on to repeat the argument used in his reply to Cousin, that Infinite Space is inconceivable, because all the conception we are able to form of it is negative, and a negative conception is the same as no conception. "The infinite is conceived only by the "thinking away of every character by which the finite "was conceived." To this assertion I oppose my former reply. Instead of thinking away every character of the finite, we think away only the idea of an end, or a boundary. Sir W. Hamilton's proposition is true of "The Infinite," the meaningless abstraction; but it is not true of Infinite Space. In trying to form a conception of that, we do not think away its positive characters. We leave to it the character of Space; all that belongs to it as space; its three dimensions, with all their geometrical properties. We leave to it also a character which belongs to it as Infinite, that of being greater than any finite space. If an object which has these well-marked positive attributes is unthinkable, because it has a negative attribute as well, the number of thinkable objects must be remarkably small. Nearly all our positive conceptions which are at all complex, include negative attributes. I do not mean merely the negatives which are implied in affirmatives, as in saying that snow is white we imply that it is not black; but independent negative attributes superadded to these, and which are so real that they are often the essential characters, or differentiæ, of classes. Our conception of dumb, is of something which *cannot* speak; of the brutes, as of creatures which *have not* reason; of the mineral kingdom, as the part of Nature which *has not* organisation and life; of immortal, as that which *never* dies. Are all these examples of the Inconceivable? So false is it that to think of a thing under a negation is to think it as unthinkable.

In other passages, Sir W. Hamilton argues that we

cannot conceive infinite space, because we should require infinite time to do it in. It would of course require infinite time to carry our thoughts in succession over every part of infinite space. But on how many of our finite conceptions do we think it necessary to perform such an operation? Let us try the doctrine upon a complex whole, short of infinite ; such as the number 695,788. Sir W. Hamilton would not, I suppose, have maintained that this number is inconceivable. How long did he think it would take to go over every separate unit of this whole, so as to obtain a perfect knowledge of that exact sum, as different from all other sums, either greater or less? Would he have said that we could have no conception of the sum until this process had been gone through? We could not, indeed, have an *adequate* conception. Accordingly we never have an adequate conception of any real thing. But we have a *real* conception of an object if we conceive it by any of its attributes that are sufficient to distinguish it from all other things. We have a conception of any large number, when we have conceived it by some one of its modes of composition, such as that indicated by the position of its digits. We seldom get nearer than this to an adequate conception of any large number. But for all intellectual purposes, this limited conception is sufficient : for it not only enables us to avoid confounding the number, in our calculations, with any other numerical whole—even with those so nearly equal to it that no difference between them would be perceptible by sight or touch, unless the units were drawn up in a manner expressly adapted for displaying it—but we can also, by means of this attribute of the number, ascertain and add to our conception as many more of its properties as we please. If, then, we can obtain a real conception of a finite whole without going through all its component parts, why deny us a real conception of an infinite whole because to go through them all is impossible? Not to mention that even in the case of the finite number, though the units composing it are limited, yet, Number being infinite, the possible modes of deriving any given number from other numbers are numerically infinite; and as all these are necessary parts of an adequate conception of any number, to render our conception even of this finite whole perfectly adequate would also require an infinite time. *

But though our conception of infinite space can never be adequate, since we can never exhaust its parts, the conception, as far as it goes, is a real conception. We realise in imagination the various attributes composing it. We realise it as space. We realise it as greater than any given space. We even realise it as endless, in an intelligible manner, that is, we clearly represent to ourselves that however much of space has been already explored, and however much more of it we may imagine ourselves to traverse, we are no nearer to the end of it than we were at first; since, however often we repeat the process of imagining distance extending in any direction from us, that process is always susceptible of being carried further. This conception is both real and perfectly definite. A merely negative notion may correspond to any number of the most heterogeneous positive things, but this notion corresponds to one thing only. We possess it as completely as we possess any of our clearest conceptions, and can avail ourselves of it as well for ulterior mental operations. As regards the Extent of Space, therefore, Sir W. Hamilton has not made out his point: one of the two contradictory hypotheses is not inconceivable.

The same thing may be said, equally decidedly, respecting the Divisibility of Space. According to our author, a minimum of divisibility, and a divisibility without

---

* Mr. Mansel replies (p. 134) that our system of numeration enables us to "exhaust any finite number, by dealing with its items in large masses," but that no such process can "exhaust the infinite." My argument is that we need not exhaust the infinite to be enabled to conceive it; since, in point of fact, we *do* not exhaust the finite numbers which it is admitted that we can and do conceive. Mr. Mansel says we do; which reduces the question to a difference in the meaning of the word exhaust. In the only sense that is of importance to the argument, we do not mentally exhaust any large number, since we do not acquire an adequate idea of it.

limit, are both inconceivable. I venture to think, on the contrary, that both are conceivable. Divisibility of course, does not here mean physical separability of parts, but their mere existence; and the question is, can we conceive a portion of extension so small as not to be composed of parts, and can we, on the other hand, conceive parts consisting of smaller parts, and these of still smaller, without end? As to the latter, smallness without limit is as positive a conception as greatness without limit. We have the idea of a portion of space, and to this we add that of being smaller than any given portion. The other side of the alternative is still more evidently conceivable. It is not denied that there is a portion of extension which to the naked eye appears an indivisible point; it has been called by philsophers the *minimum visibile*. This minimum we can indefinitely magnify by means of optical instruments, making visible the still smaller parts which compose it. In each successive experiment there is still a *minimun visibile*, anything less than which cannot be discerned with that instrument, but can with one of a higher power. Suppose, now, that as we increase the magnifying powers of our instruments, and before we have reached the limit of possible increase, we arrive at a stage at which that which seemed the smallest visible space under a given microscope, does not appear larger under one which, by its mechanical construction, is adapted to magnify more—but still remains apparentlyindivisible. I say, thatif thishappened, we should believe in a minimum of extension; and as we should be able to conceive, that is, to represent to ourselves in an image, anything smaller, any further divisibility would be as inconceivable to us as it would be unbelievable.

There would be no difficulty in applying a similar line of argument to the case of Time, or to any other of the Antinomies, (there is a long list of them, * to some of which I shall have to return for another purpose,) but it would needlessly encumber our pages. In no one case

* See the catalogue at length, in the Appendix to the second volume of the Lectures, pp. 527–529.

mentioned by Sir W. Hamilton do I believe that he could substantiate his assertion, that "the Conditioned," by which he means every object of human knowledge, lies between two "inconditionate" hypotheses, both of them inconceivable.   Let me add, that even granting the inconceivability of the two opposite hypotheses, I cannot see that any distinct meaning is conveyed by the statement that the Conditioned is "the mean" between them, or that "all positive thought," "all that we can positively think," "lies between" these two "extremes," these "two opposite poles of thought."   The extremes are, space in the aggregate considered as having a limit, Space in the aggregate considered as having no limit.   Neither of these, says Sir W. Hamilton, can we think.   But what we can positively think (according to him) is not Space in the aggregate at all; it is some limited Space, and this we think as square, as circular, as triangular, or as elliptical.   Are triangular and elliptical a mean between infinite and finite?   They are, by the very meaning of the words, modes of the finite.   So that it would be more like the truth to say that we think the pretended mean under one of the extremes; and if infinite and finite are "two opposite poles of thought," then in this polar opposition, unlike voltaic polarity, all the matter is accumulated at one pole.   But this counter-statement would be no more tenable than Sir W. Hamilton's; for in reality, the thought which he affirms to be a medium between two extreme statements, has no correlation with those statements at all.   It does not relate to the same object.   The two counter-hypotheses are suppositions respecting Space at large, Space as a collective whole.   The "conditioned" thinking, said to be the mean between them, relates to parts of Space, and classes of such parts: circles and triangles, or planetary and stellar distances.   The alternative of opposite inconceivabilities never presents itself in regard to them; they are all finite, and are conceived and known as such. What the notion of extremes and a mean can signify, when applied to propositions in which different predicates are affirmed of different subjects, passes my comprehension : but it served to give greater apparent profundity to the "Fundamental Doctrine," in the eyes not of disciples (for Sir W. Hamilton was wholly incapable of quackery) but of the teacher himself.

If these arguments are valid, the "Law of the Conditioned" rests on no rational foundation. The proposition that the Conditioned lies between two hypotheses concerning the Unconditioned, neither of which hypotheses we can conceive as possible, must be placed in that numerous class of metaphysical doctrines, which have a magnificent sound, but are empty of the smallest substance.*

* In the first edition, besides denying the inconceivability of the pairs of contradictory hypotheses in Sir W. Hamilton's Antinomies, I also contested the assertion that one or other of them must be true ; arguing, that the law of Excluded Middle, though true of all phenomena, and therefore of Space and Time in their phenomenal character, is not a law of Things. "The law of Excluded Middle is, that whatever predicate we suppose, "either that or its negative must be true of any given subject : and this "I do not admit when the subject is a Noumenon ; inasmuch as every "possible predicate, even negative, except the single one of Non-entity, "involves, as a part of itself, something positive, which part is only known "to us by phenomenal experience, and may have only a phenomenal "existence."   This, being an over-statement, and when reduced to its proper bounds, not necessarily conflicting with anything said by Sir W. Hamilton on the present subject, I abandon.   But I retain a portion of my remarks, illustrative of the abusive application of which the Principle of Excluded Middle is susceptible.   "The universe, for example, must, it "is affirmed, be either infinite or finite ; but what do these words mean ? "That it must be either of infinite or finite magnitude.   Magnitudes "certainly must be either infinite or finite, but before affirming the same "thing of the Noumenon Universe, it has to be established that the "universe as it is in itself is capable of the attribute magnitude.   How do "we know that magnitude is not exclusively a property of our sensations— "of the states of subjective consciousness which objects produce in us ? "Or if this supposition displeases, how do we know that magnitude is "not, as Kant considered it to be, a form of our minds, an attribute with "which the laws of thought invest every conception that we can form, "but to which there may be nothing analogous in the Noumenon, the "Thing in itself ?   The like may be said of Duration, whether infinite or "finite, and of Divisibility, whether stopping at a minimum or prolonged "without limit.   Either the one proposition or the other must of course "be true of duration and of matter as they are perceived by us—as they "present themselves to our faculties ; but duration itself is held by Kant "to have no real existence out of our minds ; and as for matter, not "knowing what it is in itself, we know not whether, as affirmed of matter "in itself, the word divisible has any meaning.   Believing divisibility to "be an acquired notion, made up of the elements of our sensational ex- "perience, I do not admit that the Noumenon Matter must be either "infinitely or finitely divisible."

CHAPTER VII.

THE PHILOSOPHY OF THE CONDITIONED AS APPLIED BY MR. MANSEL TO THE LIMITS OF RELIGIOUS THOUGHT.

MR. MANSEL may be affirmed, by a fair application of the term, to be, in metaphysics, a pupil of Sir W. Hamilton. I do not mean that he agrees with him in all his opinions; for he avowedly dissents from the peculiar Hamiltonian theory of Cause: still less that he has learnt nothing from any other teacher, or from his own independent speculations. On the contrary, he has shown considerable power of original thought, both of a good and of what seems to me not a good quality. But he is the admiring editor of Sir W. Hamilton's Lectures; he invariably speaks of him with a deference which he pays to no other philosopher; he expressly accepts, in language identical with Sir W. Hamilton's own, the doctrines regarded as specially characteristic of the Hamiltonian philosophy, and may with reason be considered as a representative of the same general mode of thought. Mr. Mansel has bestowed especial cultivation upon a province but slightly touched by his master— the application of the Philosophy of the Conditioned to the theological department of thought; the deduction of such of its corollaries and consequences as directly concern religion.

The premises from which Mr. Mansel reasons are those of Sir W. Hamilton. He maintains the necessary relativity of all our knowledge. He holds that the Absolute and the Infinite, or, to use a more significant expression, an Absolute and an Infinite Being, are inconceivable by us; and that when we strive to conceive what

is thus inaccessible to our faculties, we fall into self-contradiction. That we are, nevertheless, warranted in
believing, and bound to believe, the real existence of an
absolute and infinite being, and that this being is God.
God, therefore, is inconceivable and unknowable by us,
and cannot even be thought of without self-contradiction ; that is (for Mr. Mansel is careful thus to qualify
the assertion), thought of *as* Absolute, and *as* Infinite.
Through this inherent impossibility of our conceiving
or knowing God's essential attributes, we are disqualified
from judging what is or is not consistent with them.
If, then, a religion is presented to us, containing any
particular doctrine respecting the Deity, our belief or rejection of the doctrine ought to depend exclusively upon
the evidences which can be produced for the divine origin
of the religion ; and no argument grounded on the incredibility of the doctrine, as involving an intellectual
absurdity, or on its moral badness as unworthy of a good
or wise being, ought to have any weight, since of these
things we are incompetent to judge. This, at least, is
the drift of Mr. Mansel's argument ; but I am bound to
admit that he affirms the conclusion with a certain limitation ; for he acknowledges, that the moral character of
the doctrines of a religion ought to count for something
among the reasons for accepting or rejecting, as of divine
origin, the religion as a whole.   That it ought also to
count for something in the interpretation of the religion
when accepted, he neglects to say ; but we must in fairness suppose that he would admit it.   These concessions,
however, to the moral feelings of mankind, are made at
the expense of Mr. Mansel's logic.   If his theory is
correct, he has no right to make either of them.

There is nothing new in this line of argument as applied to theology.   That we cannot understand God ;
that his ways are not our ways ; that we cannot scruti-
nise or judge his counsels—propositions which, in a reasonable sense of the terms, could not be denied by any
Theist—have often before been tendered as reasons why
we may assert any absurdities and any moral monstrosi-

ties concerning God, and miscall them Goodness and
Wisdom.   The novelty is in presenting this conclusion
as a corollary from the most advanced doctrines of modern
philosophy—from the true theory of the powers and
limitations of the human mind, on religious and on all
other subjects.

My opinion of this doctrine, in whatever way presented, is, that it is simply the most morally pernicious
doctrine now current; and that the question it involves
is, beyond all others which now engage speculative
minds, the decisive one between moral good and evil for
the Christian world.   It is a momentous matter, therefore, to consider whether we are obliged to adopt it.
Without holding Mr. Mansel accountable for the moral
consequences of the doctrine, further than he himself
accepts them, I think it supremely important to examine
whether the doctrine itself is really the verdict of a sound
metaphysic ; and essential to a true estimation of Sir
W. Hamilton's philosophy to enquire, whether the conclusion thus drawn from his principal doctrine, is justly
affiliated on it.   I think it will appear that the conclusion not only does not follow from a true theory of the
human faculties, but is not even correctly drawn from
the premises from which Mr. Mansel infers it.

We must have the premises distinctly before us as
conceived by Mr. Mansel, since we have hitherto seen
them only as taught by Sir W. Hamilton.   Clearness and
explicitness of statement being in the number of Mr.
Mansel's merits, it is easier to perceive the flaws in his
arguments than in those of his master, because he often
leaves us less in doubt what he means by his words.

To have " such a knowledge of the Divine Nature "
as would enable human reason to judge of theology, would
be, according to Mr. Mansel,* " to conceive the Deity as
he is."   This would be to "conceive him as First
Cause, as Absolute, and as Infinite."   The First Cause
Mr. Mansel defines in the usual manner.   About the
meaning of Infinite there is no difficulty.   But when

* Limits of Religious Thought, 4th edition, pp. 29, 30.

H

we come to the Absolute we are on more slippery
ground. Mr. Mansel, however, tells us his meaning
plainly. By the Absolute, he does not mean what Sir
W. Hamilton professes always to mean by it, something
which includes the idea of completed or finished. He
adopts the other meaning, which Sir W. Hamilton men-
tions, but disclaims—the opposite of Relative. "By
"the Absolute is meant that which exists in and by itself,
"having no necessary relation to any other Being."

This explanation by Mr. Mansel of Absolute in the
sense in which it is opposed to Relative, is more definite
in its terms than that which Sir W. Hamilton gives
when attempting the same thing. For Sir W. Hamilton
recognises (as already remarked) this second meaning of
Absolute, and this is the account he gives of it : *
"*Absolutum* means what is freed or loosed ; in which
"sense the Absolute will be what is aloof from relation,
"comparison, limitation, condition, dependence, &c.,
"and thus is tantamount to τὸ ἀπόλυτον of the lower
"Greeks." May it not be surmised that the vagueness
in which the master here leaves the conception, was for
the purpose of avoiding difficulties upon which the pupil,
in his desire of greater precision, has unwarily run ? Mr.
Mansel certainly gains nothing by the more definite
character of his language. The words, " having no
necessary relation to any other Being," admit of two
constructions. The words, in their natural sense, only
mean, *capable of existing out of relation to anything else.*
The argument requires that they should mean, *incapable
of existing in relation with anything else.* Mr. Mansel
cannot intend the latter. He cannot mean that the
Absolute is incapable of entering into relation with any
other being ; for he would not affirm this of God ; on
the contrary, he is continually speaking of God's relations to the world and to us. Moreover, he accepts,
from Dr. Calderwood, an interpretation inconsistent
with this.† This, however, is the meaning necessary
to support his case. For what is his first argument ?

* Discussions, p. 14, note.   † Limits of Religious Thought, p. 200.

That God cannot be known by us as Cause, as Absolute, and as Infinite, because these attributes are, to our conception, incompatible with one another.   And why incompatible?   Because * " a Cause cannot, as such, be " absolute; the Absolute cannot, as such, be a cause. " The cause, as such, exists only in relation to its effect : " the cause is a cause of the effect; the effect is an effect " of the cause.   On the other hand, the conception of the " Absolute involves a possible existence out of all rela- " tion."   But in what manner is a possible existence out of all relation, incompatible with the notion of a cause? Have not causes a possible existence apart from their effects?   Would the sun (for example) not exist if there were no earth or planets for it to illuminate?   Mr. Mansel seems to think that what is capable of existing out of relation, cannot possibly be conceived or known in relation.   But this is not so.   Anything which is capable of existing in relation, is capable of being conceived or known in relation.   If the Absolute Being cannot be conceived as Cause, it must be that he cannot exist as Cause ; he must be incapable of causing.   If he can be in any relation whatever to any finite thing, he is conceivable and knowable in that relation, if no otherwise. Freed from this confusion of ideas, Mr. Mansel's argument resolves itself into this—the same Being cannot be thought by us both as Cause and as Absolute, because a Cause *as such* is not Absolute, and Absolute as such is not a Cause ; which is exactly as if he had said that Newton cannot be thought by us both as an Englishman and as a mathematician, because an Englishman, as such, is not a mathematician, nor a mathematician, as such, an Englishman.†

_____

* Limits of Religious Thought, p. 31.

† Mr. Mansel, in his reply (p. 151) accuses me of mutilating his argument.   I therefore add the remainder of it.   "We attempt to escape from "this apparent contradiction by introducing the idea of succession in "time.   The Absolute exists first by itself, and afterwards becomes a "Cause.   But here we are checked by the third conception, that of the "Infinite.   How can the Infinite become that which it was not from the "first?   If Causation is a possible mode of existence, that which exists

Again, Mr. Mansel argues,* that, "supposing the Absolute to become a cause," since *ex vi termini* it is not necessitated to do so, it must be a voluntary agent, and therefore conscious; for "volition is only possible in a conscious being." But consciousness, again, is only conceivable as a relation; and any relation conflicts with the notion of the Absolute, since relatives are mutually dependent on one another. Here it comes out distinctly as a premise in the reasoning, that to be in a relation at all, even if only a relation to itself, the relation of being "conscious of itself," is inconsistent with being the Absolute.†

Mr. Mansel, therefore, must alter his definition of the Absolute if he would maintain his argument. He must

"without causing is not infinite; that which becomes a cause has passed "beyond its former limits." (Limits of Religious Thought, pp. 31, 32.)

This alleged inconsistency of thought in supposing the Infinite to *become* a cause, because to do so would be to become something which it was not from the first, applies, like nearly all the rest of Mr. Mansel's argumentation, only to the self-contradictory fiction, "The Infinite," which is supposed either infinite without reference to any attributes, or infinite in all possible attributes. Substitute for this the notion of a Being infinite in given attributes, and the incompatibility disappears. Surely the most familiar form of the notion of an infinite being, is that of a Being infinite in power. Power is not only compatible with, but actually means, capability of causing. Can we be told that a Being infinite in its capability of causing, cannot to our conceptions, consistently with its infinity, actually cause anything, but the power, because infinite, must remain dormant through eternity? or, as the opposite alternative, that this Being must be conceived as having exercised from all eternity the whole of its infinite power of causing, because any later exercise of that power would be *passing* into causation? Either hypothesis Mr. Mansel affirms (Limits of Religious Thought, p. 204) to be inconceivable of an Infinite Being. But if an Infinite Being means a Being of infinite wisdom and goodness as well as power, the conception of that infinite power as only partly exercised is so far from being a contradiction, that it is not even a paradox.

* Limits of Religious Thought, p. 32.

† How does Mr. Mansel reconcile this argument with the definition of the Absolute which he himself accepts from Dr. Calderwood (Limits of Religious Thought, p. 200)? "The Absolute is that which is free from "all *necessary* relation, that is, which is free from every relation as a con- "dition of existence; but it may exist in relation, provided that rela- "tion be not a necessary condition of its existence, that is, provided the "relation may be removed without affecting its existence." A better definition of an Absolute Being could scarcely be devised; and that Mr. Mansel should borrow it, and then deny the latter half of it, proves him to be greatly inferior to Dr. Calderwood in the important accomplishment of understanding his own meaning. For before it can be maintained that

either fall back on the happy ambiguity of Sir W. Hamilton's definition, " what is aloof from relation," which does not decide whether the meaning is merely that it can exist out of relation, or that it is incapable of existing in it; or he must take courage, and affirm that an Absolute Being is incapable of all relation. But as he will certainly refuse to predicate this of God, the consequence follows, that God is not an Absolute Being.

The whole of Mr. Mansel's arguments for the inconceivability of the Infinite and of the Absolute is one long *ignoratio elenchi*.   It has been pointed out in a former chapter that the words Absolute and Infinite have no real meaning, unless we understand by them that which is absolute or infinite in some given attribute ; as space is called infinite, meaning that it is infinite in extension ; and as God is termed infinite in the sense of possessing infinite power, and absolute in the sense of absolute goodness, or knowledge.   It has also been shown that Sir W. Hamilton's arguments for the unknowableness of the Unconditioned, do not prove that we cannot know an object which is absolute or infinite in some specific attribute, but only that we cannot know an abstraction called " The Absolute " or " The Infinite," which is supposed to have all attributes at once.   The same remark is applicable to Mr. Mansel,* with only this

to be a conscious being contradicts the notion of the Absolute, because consciousness is a relation, the power just admitted in the Absolute of existing in relation provided it is not bound to any relation, must be either denied or forgotten.

[Mr. Mansel, in his rejoinder, says that he did not mean to admit the second half of Dr. Calderwood's definition ; and he holds to the doctrine " The absolute, as such, must be out of all relation" (not merely capable of existing out of relation) " and consequently cannot be conceived in the relation of plurality." (Philosophy of the Conditioned, p. 117).]

* Mr. Mansel (pp. 153, 154) protests against this passage, as attributing to him the use of the word "Absolute" in the sense attached to it by Sir W. Hamilton, which includes perfection, though he had expressly stated that he used the term in a different sense.   "When Mr. Mill " charges Mr. Mansel with undertaking to prove the impossibility of con- "ceiving a Being *absolutely* just or *absolutely* wise (*i.e.* as he supposes, "*perfectly* just or wise) he actually forgets that he has just been criti- "cising Mr. Mansel's definition of the Absolute, as something having a "possible existence out of relation."   And he asks what I can mean by

difference, that he, with the laudable ambition I have
already noticed of stating everything explicitly, draws
this important distinction himself, and says, of his own
motion, that the Absolute he means is the abstraction.   He says,* that the Absolute and Infinite can be
"nothing less than the sum of all reality," the complex
of all positive predicates, even those which are exclusive
of one another; and expressly identifies it with Hegel's
Absolute Being, which contains in itself "all that is
"actual, even evil included."   "That which is conceived
"as absolute and infinite," says Mr. Mansel,† "must be
"conceived as containing within itself the sum not only
"of all actual, but of all possible modes of being."   One
may well agree with Mr. Mansel that this farrago of

goodness or knowledge "out of all relation." If I have, in this passage,
exchanged Mr. Mansel's definition of the Absolute for Sir W. Hamilton's,
by including in it the notion of "finished, perfected, completed," Mr.
Mansel had set me the example. As long as he kept to his own definition,
I did the same : I only followed him when he himself imported the idea
of perfection from the other meaning of the term, and reasoned from it as
one of the characteristics of the Absolute. Does the reader doubt this?
He shall see. We cannot, says Mr. Mansel, reconcile the idea of the
Absolute with that of a Cause, because "if the condition of causal ac-
"tivity is a higher state than that of quiescence, the Absolute, whether
"acting voluntarily or involuntarily, has passed from a condition of com-
"parative imperfection to one of comparative perfection, and therefore
"was not originally *perfect*. If the state of activity is an inferior state
"to that of quiescence, the Absolute, in becoming a cause, has lost *its*
"*original perfection.*" (Limits of Religious Thought, pp. 34, 35. The
italics are my own.) Again (p. 38) "While it is impossible to represent
"in thought any object except as finite, it is equally impossible to repre-
"sent any finite object, or any aggregate of finite objects, as *exhausting*
"*the universe of being.* Thus the hypothesis which would annihilate the
"Infinite is itself shattered to pieces against the rock of the Absolute."
In spite, therefore, of his own definition, Mr. Mansel thinks it part of the
notion of the Absolute that it is the Perfect, and that it exhausts the universe of being, *i.e.*, is the completed whole of existence.
    It thus appears that if I am chargeable with anything, it is with
having neglected to point out one confusion of ideas the more in Mr.
Mansel, and, this time, a confusion between two ideas which he had expressly discriminated. But even had I really committed the blunder he
imputes to me, it would not have affected the question between us : for he
always (and, as I think, rightly) assumes that the Being whose conceivability by us is the subject of discussion, has to be conceived *both* as absolute and as infinite (the Infinito-Absolute of Sir W. Hamilton) ; and if he
had escaped untouched from my criticism of Sir W. Hamilton in respect
of the Absolute, he would still have been inextricably involved in it as
regards the Infinite.
        * Limits of Religious Thought, p. 30.   † Ibid. p. 31.

contradictory attributes cannot be conceived : but what
shall we say of his equally positive averment that it
must be believed ?   If this be what the Absolute is,
what does he mean by saying that we must believe God
to be the Absolute ?

The remainder of Mr. Mansel's argumentation is
suitable to this commencement. The Absolute, as conceived, that is, as he defines it, cannot be "a whole * com-
" posed of parts," or " a substance consisting of attri-
" butes," or a " conscious subject in antithesis to an
" object. For if there is in the absolute any principle
" of unity, distinct from the mere accumulation of parts
" or attributes, this principle alone is the true absolute.
" If, on the other hand, there is no such principle, then
" there is no absolute at all, but only a plurality of rela-
" tives. The almost unanimous voice of philosophy, in
" pronouncing that the absolute is both one and simple,
" must be accepted as a voice of reason also, so far as
" reason has any voice in the matter. But this absolute
" unity, as indifferent and containing no attributes,
" can neither be distinguished from the multiplicity
" of finite beings by any characteristic feature, nor be
" identified with them in their multiplicity." It will
be noticed that the Absolute, which was just before
defined as having all attributes, is here declared to have
none : but this, Mr. Mansel would say, is merely one
of the contradictions inherent in the attempt to conceive what is inconceivable. "Thus we are landed in
" an inextricable dilemma. The Absolute cannot be
" conceived as conscious, neither can it be conceived as
" unconscious: it cannot be conceived as complex, neither
" can it be conceived as simple : it cannot be conceived
" by difference, neither can it be conceived by the ab-
" sence of difference : it cannot be identified with the
" universe, neither can it be distinguished from it." Is
this chimerical abstraction the Absolute being whom
anybody need be concerned about, either as knowable or
as unknowable ?   Is the inconceivableness of this impos-

* Limits of Religious Thought, p. 33.

sible fiction any argument against the possibility of conceiving God, who is neither supposed to have no attributes nor to have all attributes, but to have good attributes? Is it any hindrance to our being able to conceive a Being absolutely just, for example, or absolutely wise? Yet it is of this that Mr. Mansel undertook to prove the impossibility.

Again, of the Infinite: according to Mr. Mansel,[*] being "that than which a greater is inconceivable," it "consequently can receive no additional attribute or "mode of existence which it had not from all eternity." It must therefore be the same complex of all possible predicates which the Absolute is, and all of them infinite in degree. It "cannot be regarded as consisting of a "limited number of attributes, each unlimited in its "kind. It cannot be conceived, for example, after the "analogy of a line, infinite in length, but not in "breadth; or of a surface, infinite in two dimensions of "space, but bounded in the third; or of an intelligent "being, possessing some one or more modes of conscious-"ness in an infinite degree, but devoid of others." This Infinite, which is infinite in all attributes, and not solely in those which it would be thought decent to predicate of God, cannot, as Mr. Mansel very truly says, be conceived. For[†] "the Infinite, if it is to be conceived "at all, must be conceived as potentially everything and "actually nothing; for if there is anything general which "it cannot become, it is thereby limited; and if there is "anything in particular which it actually is, it is thereby "excluded from being any other thing. But again, "it must also be conceived as actually everything and "potentially nothing; for an unrealised potentiality is "likewise a limitation. If the infinite can be that which "it is not, it is by that very possibility marked out as "incomplete, and capable of a higher perfection. If it "is actually everything, it possesses no characteristic "feature by which it can be distinguished from anything "else, and discerned as an object of consciousness." Here

* Limits of Religious Thought, p. 30.   † Ibid. p. 48.

certainly is an Infinite whose infinity does not seem to
be of much use to it.   But can a writer be serious who
bids us conjure up a conception of something which
possesses infinitely all conflicting attributes, and because
we cannot do this without contradiction, would have us
believe that there is a contradiction in the idea of infinite
goodness, or infinite wisdom? Instead of " the Infinite,"
substitute " an infinitely good Being," and Mr. Mansel's
argument reads thus : If there is anything which an
infinitely good Being cannot become—if he cannot become bad—that is a limitation, and the goodness cannot
be infinite.   If there is anything which an infinitely
good Being actually is (namely good), he is excluded
from being any other thing, as from being wise or
powerful.   I hardly think that Sir W. Hamilton would
patronise this logic, learnt though it be in his school.*

It cannot be necessary to follow up Mr. Mansel's
metaphysical dissertation any farther. It is all, as I have
said, the same *ignoratio elenchi*. I have been able to find
only one short passage in which he attempts to show
that we are unable to represent in thought a particular
attribute carried to the infinite. For the sake of fairness,

* By the time Mr Mansel gets to this place, he grows tired of giving
relevant answers, and thinks that any verbal repartee will suffice. To the
first half of my statement, his answer is this (p. 158): "Is becoming bad
a higher perfection?" I reply, that Mr. Mansel seems to think so ;
inasmuch as he says "If the Infinite can be that which it is not, it is by
"that very possibility marked out as incomplete, and capable of a higher
"perfection." If the infinite is God, and, as such, good, to become bad
would be to become what it is not, and consequently, according to Mr.
Mansel, to attain a higher perfection. To the second half he replies by
identifying the manner in which the Infinite, by being anything in particular, is excluded from being any other thing, with the manner in which
a thing, by being a horse, is excluded from being a dog. Let me remind
him that a horse and a dog are substances, and that we are talking about
attributes. A substance cannot become another substance, but it may
put on any number of additional attributes. Does not the whole of the
discussion turn upon attributes? Does the question, what the Infinite
can or cannot be or become, mean anything but what attributes it can
have or acquire? As a Substance the Infinite is the Infinite, and cannot
become anything else. Does it follow from this that by possessing one
attribute, it is excluded from possessing any other? Or is it possible that
Mr. Mansel means, that the "Infinite, if it is to be conceived at all," must
be conceived as capable of changing its substance, and becoming a finite
dog, thereby excluding itself from being a horse? That would indeed be
a stretch beyond anything I have charged him with.

I cite it in a note.* All the argument that I can discover in it, I conceive that I have already answered,
as stated much better by Sir W. Hamilton.

Mr. Mansel thinks it necessary to declare† that the
contradictions are not in "the nature of the Absolute"
or Infinite "in itself, but only" in "our own conception
of that nature." He did not mean to say that the
Divine Nature is itself contradictory. But he says‡
"We are compelled by the constitution of our minds,
"to believe in the existence of an Absolute and Infinite
"Being." Such being the case, I ask, is the Being whom
we must believe to be infinite and absolute, infinite and
absolute in the meaning which those terms bear in Mr.
Mansel's definition of them? If not, he is bound to tell
us in what other meaning. Believing God to be infinite
and absolute must be believing something, and it must be
possible to say what. If Mr. Mansel means that we
must believe the reality of an Infinite and Absolute
Being in some other sense than that in which he has
proved such a Being to be inconceivable, his point is not
made out, since he undertook to prove the inconceivability of the very Being in whose reality we are required
to believe. But the truth is that the Infinite and Absolute which he says we must believe in, are the very
Infinite and Absolute of his definitions. The Infinite is
that which is opposed to the Finite; the Absolute, that
which is opposed to the Relative. He has therefore

---

* "A thing—an object—an attribute—a person—or any other term sig-
"nifying one out of many possible objects of consciousness, is by that very
"relation necessarily declared to be finite. An infinite thing, or object, or
"attribute, or person, is therefore in the same moment declared to be both
"finite and infinite. . . And on the other hand, if all human attributes are
"conceived under the conditions of difference, and relation, and time, and
"personality, we cannot represent in thought any such attribute magnified
"to infinity; for this again is to conceive it as finite and infinite at the
"same time. We can conceive such attributes, at the utmost, only *indefi-
"nitely*; that is to say, we may withdraw our thoughts, for the moment,
"from the fact of their being limited; but we cannot conceive them as
"*infinite*; that is to say, we cannot positively think of the absence of the
"limit; for, the instant we attempt to do so, the antagonist elements of
"the conception exclude one another, and annihilate the whole."—Limits
of Religious Thought, p. 60.
    † Ibid. p. 39.   ‡ Ibid. p. 45.

either proved nothing, or vastly more than he intended. For the contradictions which he asserts to be involved in the notions, do not follow from an imperfect mode of apprehending the Infinite and Absolute, but lie in the definitions of them ; in the meaning of the phrases themselves. The contradictions are in the very object which we are called upon to believe. If, therefore, Mr. Mansel would escape from the conclusion that an Infinite and Absolute Being is intrinsically impossible, it must be by affirming, with Hegel, that the law of Contradiction does not apply to the Absolute ; that, respecting the Absolute, contradictory propositions may both be true.*

Let us now pass from Mr. Mansel's metaphysical argumentation on an irrelevant issue, to a much more important subject, that of his practical conclusion, namely, that we cannot know the divine attributes in such a manner, as can entitle us to reject any statement respecting the

* Mr. Mansel's summary of his reply on this portion of the case is as follows (pp. 161, 162) : "The reader may now, perhaps, understand the "reason of an assertion which Mr. Mill regards as supremely absurd, "namely, that we must believe in the existence of an absolute and infinite "Being, though unable to conceive the nature of such a Being. To be- "lieve in such a Being is simply to believe that God made the world : to "declare the nature of such a Being inconceivable, is simply to say that "we do not know how the world was made. If we believe that God made "the world, we must believe that there was a time when the world was not, "and when God alone existed, out of relation to any other being. But "the mode of that sole existence we are unable to conceive, nor in what ":manner the first act took place by which the absolute and self-existent "gave existence to the relative and dependent."

I know not how Mr. Mansel discovers that I regard as supremely absurd the notion that we may believe, and may have good grounds for believing things which are inconceivable to us. As he most truly says, there is no one with whose mode of thinking such an opinion would more flagrantly conflict. But I venture to think that one may deem it possible to have a real and positive, though inadequate, conception of an infinite Being, without supposing oneself to know how God made the world. Mr. Mansel resumes (p. 163) "Where is the incongruity of saying, I believe that a "being exists possessing certain attributes, though I am unable in my "present state of knowledge to conceive the manner of that existence ?" Assuredly, nowhere : provided that you do not invest the object of your belief with contradictory attributes ; for my admission of the believability of what is inconceivable, stops at the self-contradictory : consequently I do not admit the believability of such an Absolute and Infinite as Mr. Mansel has been mystifying us with. The sum of what I am maintaining against him is, that the Absolute and Infinite which are believable, and

Deity, on the ground of its being inconsistent with his character.   Let us examine whether this assertion is a legitimate corollary from the relativity of human knowledge, either as it really is, or as it is understood to be by Sir W. Hamilton and by Mr. Mansel.

The fundamental property of our knowledge of God, Mr. Mansel says, is that we do not and cannot know him as he is in himself: certain persons, therefore, whom he calls Rationalists, he condemns as unphilosophical, when they reject any statement as inconsistent with the character of God.   This is a valid answer, as far as words go, to some of the later Transcendentalists—to those who think that we have an intuition of the Divine Nature; though even as to them it would not be difficult to show that the answer is but skin-deep.   But those "Rationalists" who hold, with Mr. Mansel himself, the relativity of human knowledge, are not touched by his reasoning.   We cannot know God as he is in himself (they reply); granted: and what then?   Can we know man as he is in himself, or matter as it is in itself?

the Absolute and Infinite which are inconceivable, are different things : That the Absolute and Infinite of which, as he has shown, the conception annihilates itself by the contradictions it involves, is that which possesses absolutely and infinitely all attributes, and that this is as unbelievable as it is inconceivable : That the Absolute and Infinite which is believable is that which possesses absolutely and infinitely some given attributes, which in their finite degrees are known to us, and is therefore conceivable ; and involves no contradiction, unless we include among the attributes some that contradict one another, in which case it is indeed inconceivable, but also unbelievable.

When Mr. Mansel maintains (pp. 14–18, and 142) that being infinite is, to our conceptive faculty, inconsistent with being a Person, I answer, that it is being "The Infinite" which is so.   When he insists (if he does insist) that the Creator must, in some manner inconceivable to us, *be* this nonentity ; when he identifies the Creator (p. 100) with something which we must believe to be "the sole existence, having no plurality beyond itself," and "simple, having no plurality within itself," thus literally annihilating all plurality in the universe ; when he says (pp. 28, 29) "we believe that" God's "own nature is simple and uniform, admitting of no distinction between various attributes, nor between any attribute and its subject," but yet conceivable by us "only by means of various attributes, distinct from the subject and from each other," *i.e.* conceived by us as he is not ; it appears to me that in thus following the old theologians in the mystical metaphysics which is always at the service of mystical theology he encumbers Theism and Christianity with (to say the least) very unnecessary difficulties.

We do not claim any other knowledge of God than such as we have of man or of matter. Because I do not know my fellow-men, nor any of the powers of nature, as they are in themselves, am I therefore not at liberty to disbelieve anything I hear respecting them as being inconsistent with their character? I know something of Man and Nature, not as they are in themselves, but as they are relatively to us ; and it is as relative to us, and not as he is in himself, that I suppose myself to know anything of God. The attributes which I ascribe to him, as goodness, knowledge, power, are all relative. They are attributes (says the rationalist) which my experience enables me to conceive, and which I consider as proved, not absolutely, by an intuition of God, but phenomenally, by his action on the creation, as known through my senses and my rational faculty. These relative attributes, each of them in an infinite degree, are all I pretend to predicate of God. When I reject a doctrine as inconsistent with God's nature, it is not as being inconsistent with what God is in himself, but with what he is as manifested to us. If my knowledge of him is only phenomenal, the assertions which I reject are phenomenal too. If those assertions are inconsistent with my relative knowledge of him, it is no answer to say that all my knowledge of him is relative. That is no more a reason against disbelieving an alleged fact as unworthy of God, than against disbelieving another alleged fact as unworthy of Turgot, or of Washington, whom also I do not know as Noumena, but only as Phenomena.

There is but one way for Mr. Mansel out of this difficulty, and he adopts it. He must maintain, not merely that an Absolute Being is unknowable in himself, but that the Relative attributes of an Absolute Being are unknowable likewise. He must say that we do not know what Wisdom, Justice, Benevolence, Mercy, are, as they exist in God. Accordingly he does say so. The following are his direct utterances on the subject : as an implied doctrine, it pervades his whole argument.

"It is a fact* which experience forces upon us, and
"which it is useless, were it possible, to disguise, that
"the representation of God after the model of the
"highest human morality which we are capable of
"conceiving, is not sufficient to account for all the
"phenomena exhibited by the course of his natural
"Providence. The infliction of physical suffering.
"the permission of moral evil, the adversity of the
"good, the prosperity of the wicked, the crimes of the
"guilty involving the misery of the innocent, the tardy
"appearance and partial distribution of moral and reli-
"gious knowledge in the world—these are facts which
"no doubt are reconcilable, we know not how, with the
"Infinite Goodness of God, but which certainly are not
"to be explained on the supposition that its sole and
"sufficient type is to be found in the finite goodness of
"man." In other words, it is necessary to suppose that
the infinite goodness ascribed to God is not the goodness which we know and love in our fellow-creatures,
distinguished only as infinite in degree, but is different
in kind, and another quality altogether. When we call
the one finite goodness and the other infinite goodness,
we do not mean what the words assert, but something
else : we intentionally apply the same name to things
which we regard as different.

Accordingly Mr. Mansel combats, as a heresy of his
opponents, the opinion that infinite goodness differs only
in degree from finite goodness. The notion † "that the
"attributes of God differ from those of man in degree
"only, not in kind, and hence that certain mental and
"moral qualities of which we are immediately conscious
"in ourselves, furnish at the same time a true and ade-
"quate image of the infinite perfections of God," (the
word *adequate* must have slipped in by inadvertence,
since otherwise it would be an inexcusable misrepresentation) he identifies with "the vulgar Rationalism which
"regards the reason of man, in its ordinary and normal

---

* Limits of Religious Thought, Preface to the fourth edition, p. 13.
† Ibid. p. 26.

" operation, as the supreme criterion of religious truth."
And in characterising the mode of arguing of this vulgar
Rationalism, he declares its principles to be, that * " all
" the excellences of which we are conscious in the
" creature, must necessarily exist in the same manner,
" though in a higher degree, in the Creator.   God is
" indeed more wise, more just, more merciful, than man ;
" but for that very reason, his wisdom and justice and
" mercy must contain nothing that is incompatible with
" the corresponding attributes in their human character."
It is against this doctrine that Mr. Mansel feels called
on to make an emphatic protest.

Here, then, I take my stand on the acknowledged
principle of logic and of morality, that when we mean
different things we have no right to call them by the
same name, and to apply to them the same predicates,
moral and intellectual.   Language has no meaning
for the words Just, Merciful, Benevolent, save that in
which we predicate them of our fellow-creatures ; and
unless that is what we intend to express by them, we have
no business to employ the words.   If in affirming them
of God we do not mean to affirm these very qualities,
differing only as greater in degree, we are neither philosophically nor morally entitled to affirm them at all.   If
it be said that the qualities are the same, but that we
cannot conceive them as they are when raised to the
infinite, I grant that we cannot adequately conceive them
in one of their elements, their infinity.   But we can
conceive them in their other elements, which are the
very same in the infinite as in the finite development.
Anything carried to the infinite must have all the properties of the same thing as finite, except those which
depend upon the finiteness.   Among the many who
have said that we cannot conceive infinite space, did any
one ever suppose that it is *not* space ? that it does not
possess all the properties by which space is characterised?
Infinite Space cannot be cubical or spherical, because
these are modes of being bounded : but does any one

* Limits of Religious Thought, p. 28.

imagine that in ranging through it we might arrive at some region which was not extended ; of which one part was not outside another ; where, though no body intervened, motion was impossible ; or where the sum of two sides of a triangle was less than the third side ? The parallel assertion may be made respecting infinite goodness. What belongs to it either as Infinite or as Absolute I do not pretend to know ; but I know that infinite goodness must be goodness, and that what is not consistent with goodness, is not consistent with infinite goodness. If in ascribing goodness to God I do not mean what I mean by goodness ; if I do not mean the goodness of which I have some knowledge, but an incomprehensible attribute of an incomprehensible substance, which for aught I know may be a totally different quality from that which I love and venerate—and even must, if Mr. Mansel is to be believed, be in some important particulars opposed to this—what do I mean by calling it goodness ? and what reason have I for venerating it ? If I know nothing about what the attribute is, I cannot tell that it is a proper object of veneration. To say that God's goodness may be different in kind from man's goodness, what is it but saying, with a slight change of phraseology, that God may possibly not be good ? To assert in words what we do not think in meaning, is as suitable a definition as can be given of a moral falsehood. Besides, suppose that certain unknown attributes are ascribed to the Deity in a religion the external evidences of which are so conclusive to my mind, as effectually to convince me that it comes from God. Unless I believe God to possess the same moral attributes which I find, in however inferior a degree, in a good man, what ground of assurance have I of God's veracity ? All trust in a Revelation presupposes a conviction that God's attributes are the same, in all but degree, with the best human attributes.

If, instead of the "glad tidings" that there exists a Being in whom all the excellences which the highest human mind can conceive, exist in a degree inconceivable to us, I am informed that the world is ruled by a being whose attributes are infinite, but what they are we cannot learn, nor what are the principles of his government, except that " the highest human morality which we are capable of conceiving " does not sanction them ; convince me of it, and I will bear my fate as I may.   But when I am told that I must believe this, and at the same time call this being by the names which express and affirm the highest human morality, I say in plain terms that I will not.   Whatever power such a being may have over me, there is one thing which he shall not do : he shall not compel me to worship him.   I will call no being good, who is not what I mean when I apply that epithet to my fellow-creatures ; * and if such a being can sentence me to hell for not so calling him, to hell I will go.

Neither is this to set up my own limited intellect as a criterion of divine or of any other wisdom.   If a person is wiser and better than myself, not in some unknown and unknowable meaning of the terms, but in their known human acceptation, I am ready to believe that what this person thinks may be true, and that what he does may be right, when, but for the opinion I have of him, I should think otherwise.   But this is because I believe that he and I have at bottom the same standard of truth and rule of right, and that he probably understands better than I the facts of the particular case.   If I thought it not improbable that his notion of right might be my notion of wrong, I should not defer to his judgment.   In like manner, one who sincerely believes in an absolutely good ruler of the world, is not warranted in disbelieving any act ascribed to him, merely because the very small part of its circumstances which we can possibly know does not sufficiently justify it. But if what I am told respecting him is of a kind which

---

* Mr. Mansel, in his rejoinder, says that this means that I will call no being good "the phenomena of whose action in any way differ from those of a good man." This is a misconstruction ; he should have said "no "being, the principle or rule of whose action is different from that by " which a good man man endeavours to regulate his actions."

I

no facts that can be supposed added to my knowledge could make me perceive to be right ; if his alleged ways of dealing with the world are such as no imaginable hypothesis respecting things known to him and unknown to me, could make consistent with the goodness and wisdom which I mean when I use the terms, but are in direct contradiction to their signification ; then, if the law of contradiction is a law of human thought, I cannot both believe these things, and believe that God is a good and wise being. If I call any being wise or good, not meaning the only qualities which the words import, I am speaking insincerely ; I am flattering him by epithets which I fancy that he likes to hear, in the hope of winning him over to my own objects.   For it is worthy of remark that the doubt whether words applied to God have their human signification, is only felt when the words relate to his moral attributes ; it is never heard of in regard to his power.   We are never told that God's omnipotence must not be supposed to mean an infinite degree of the power we know in man and nature, and that perhaps it does not mean that he is able to kill us, or consign us to eternal flames.   The Divine Power is always interpreted in a completely human signification, but the Divine Goodness and Justice must be understood to be such only in an unintelligible sense.   Is it unfair to surmise that this is because those who speak in the name of God, have need of the human conception of his power, since an idea which can overawe and enforce obedience must address itself to real feelings ; but are content that his goodness should be conceived only as something inconceivable, because they are so often required to teach doctrines respecting him which conflict irreconcilably with all goodness that we can conceive ? *

* I quote in Mr. Mansel's words nearly the whole of his answer to the preceding remarks (pp. 164–170).

   "Mr. Mill asserts, as many others have asserted before him, that "the relation between the communicable attributes of God and the corre-"sponding attributes of man is one not of identity but of analogy ; that is "to say, that the Divine attributes have the same relation to the Divine

I am anxious to say once more, that Mr. Mansel's conclusions do not go the whole length of his arguments,
and that he disavows the doctrine that God's justice and
goodness are *wholly* different from what human beings

"nature that the human attributes have to human nature. Thus, for
" example, there is a Divine justice and there is a human justice; but God
" is just as the Creator and Governor of the world, having unlimited
" authority over all his creatures, and unlimited jurisdiction over all their
" acts; and man is just in certain special relations, as having authority
" over some persons and some acts only, so far as is required for the needs
" of human society. So, again, there is a Divine mercy and there is a
" human mercy; but God is merciful in such a manner as is fitting com-
" patibly with the righteous government of the universe : and man is
" merciful in a certain limited range, the exercise of the attribute being
" guided by considerations affecting the welfare of society or of indi-
" viduals. Or to take a more general case : Man has in himself a rule of
" right and wrong implying subjection to the authority of a superior (for
" conscience has authority only as reflecting the law of God); while God
" has in himself a rule of right and wrong, implying no higher authority,
" and determined absolutely by his own nature. The case is the same
" when we look at moral attributes not externally in their active mani-
" festations, but internally, in their psychological constitution. If we do
" not attribute to God the same complex mental constitution of reason,
" passion, and will, the same relation to motives and inducements, the
" same deliberation and choice of alternatives, the same temporal succes-
" sion of facts in consciousness, which we ascribe to man,—it will follow
" that those psychological relations between reason, will, and desire,
" which are implied in the conception of human action, cannot represent
" the Divine excellences in themselves, but can only illustrate them by
" analogies from finite things. And if man is liable to error in judging of
" the conduct of his fellow-men, in proportion as he is unable to place
" himself in their position, or to realise to himself their modes of thought
" and principles of action—if the child, for instance, is liable to error in
" judging the actions of the man, or the savage of the civilised man—surely
" there is far more room for error in men's judgment of the ways of God,
" in proportion as the difference between God and man is greater than the
" difference between a man and a child. . . . We will simply ask, whether
" Mr. Mill really supposes the word *good* to lose all community of mean-
" ing when it is applied, as it certainly is, to different persons among our
" fellow creatures with express reference to their different duties and
" different qualifications for performing them ?   The duties of a father
" are not the same as those of a son ; is the word therefore wholly
" equivocal when we speak of one person as a good father, and another as
" a good son? Nay, when we speak generally of a man as good, has not
" the epithet a tacit reference to human nature and human duties ? and
" yet there is no community of meaning when the same epithet is applied
" to other creatures ? Ἡ ἀρετὴ πρὸς τὸ ἔργον τὸ οἰκεῖον,—the goodness of
" any being whatever has relation to the nature and office of that being.
" We may therefore test Mr. Mill's declamation by a parallel case. A
" wise and experienced father addresses a young and inexperienced son :
" 'My son,' he says, 'there may be some of my actions which do not
" seem to you to be wise or good, or such as you would do in my place.
" Remember, however, that your duties are different from mine ; that

understand by the terms.   He would, and does, admit
that the qualities as conceived by us bear *some likeness*
to the justice and goodness which belong to God, since
man was made in God's image.   But such a semi-

"your knowledge of my duties is very imperfect ; and that there may be
"things which you cannot now see to be wise and good, but which you
"may hereafter discover to be so.' 'Father,' says the son, 'your prin-
"ciples of action are not the same as mine ; the highest morality which
"I can conceive at present does not sanction them ; and as for believing
"that you are good in anything of which I do not plainly see the good-
"ness'—we will not repeat Mr. Mill's alternative ; we will only ask
"whether it is not just possible that there may be as much difference
"between man and God as there is between a child and his father ? "
        There is a mode of controversy which I do not remember to have seen
in any enumeration of Fallacies, but which will some day find a place
there, under some such name as the Inversion of Parts.   It consists in
indignantly vindicating as against your adversary the very principle
which he is asserting against yourself.   Would not any reader of the
above passage suppose that it is Mr. Mansel who is contending against
me for the " community of meaning " of the word good, to whatever being
it is applied ; instead of me against him ?   It is I who say that as goodness in a good father is the very same quality with goodness in a good
son, so goodness in a good God must be, in all but degree, the same quality
as goodness in a good man, or we are not entitled to call it goodness.
It is Mr. Mansel who denies this, affirming that there is more than a
difference of degree.   And unless he is to be understood as surrendering
this point by the illustrations he now employs, his defence is no defence
at all ; for it confounds a difference in the outward circumstances in which
a moral quality has to be exercised, with a difference in the quality itself.
In his imaginary dialogue between a son and a father, does the son really
think the father's conduct inconsistent with such goodness as, under the
father's teaching, he has realised in himself, or learnt to recognise in
others ?   Does he not think that it is the same goodness, but acting under
a knowledge of facts, and an appreciation of means, such as he does not
himself · possess ?   Does the son think that the father's conduct is not
justifiable by the same moral law which he prescribes to the son, and
that in order to justify the father it is necessary to suppose him actuated
by another *kind* of morality, not the same, but merely having the same
relation to the father's nature that the other goodness has to the son's
nature ?   If the son has implicit confidence in the father, he will not
answer, in the words put into his mouth by Mr. Mansel, "your principles of action are not the same as mine."   He will say, "your principles of action I well know : they are those which you have taught to
me—those by which, in my best moments, I endeavour, though with
inferior strength, to guide my conduct.   You are incapable of acting on
any others.   Knowing your principles, and not knowing what conduct,
in your different position, the principles require, but being convinced that
you do know, I am certain that you act on those principles."   All the
allowance for human ignorance which can be demanded on similar grounds
in judging of what is ascribed to God, I have amply granted.
        On the latter part of the paragraph in the text, Mr. Mansel makes some
further remarks.   To the statement that " the doubt whether words
("applied to God have their human signification, is only felt when the

concession, which no Christian could avoid making, since without it the whole Christian scheme would be subverted, cannot save him; he is not relieved by it from any difficulties, while it destroys the whole fabric of his argument.   The Divine goodness, which is said to be a different thing from human goodness, but of which the human conception of goodness is some imperfect reflection or resemblance, does it agree with what men call goodness in the *essence* of the quality—in what *constitutes* it goodness?   If it does, the "Rationalists" are right; it is not illicit to reason from the

"words relate to his moral attributes—it is never heard of in regard to "his power," Mr. Mansel makes answer (p. 172), "We meet Mr. Mill's "confident assertion with a direct denial, and take the opportunity of in-"forming him that the conception of infinite Power has suggested the "same difficulties, and has been discussed by philosophers and theologians "in the same manner, as those of infinite Wisdom and infinite Goodness. "Has Mr. Mill never heard of such questions as, Whether Omnipotence can "reverse the past?—Whether God can do that which he does not will to "do?—Whether God's perfect foreknowledge is compatible with his own "perfect liberty?—Whether God could have made a better world than the "existing one?"   In return for the information thus liberally bestowed, I humbly reply, that I have "heard of such questions:" but I see in them (with the exception of the second, which relates to the meaning of Power, not of Infinite power) only inquiries, mostly frivolous, how much *more* power God has than man.   There is no difference in the conception of the power itself, which is in both cases the same, namely, the conformity of the event to the volition.   The divine omnipotence is always supposed to mean an infinite degree of this, and not of anything else.   But infinite goodness, according to Mr. Mansel, means not an infinite degree, but a different kind, not admitting of any common definition with human goodness.

[Mr. Mansel's answer to this is a curious one.   He says that "if power, "as predicated of man, means the conformity of the event to the volition, "man assuredly can do no more than he actually wills to do; for there can "be no conformity except where there is a volition and an event."   We may know that the event would conform to our volition although it has not actually taken place.   Most people, I believe, if they said that they had the power of throwing themselves into a well, would mean that *if* they willed so to throw themselves, the effect would follow.   And if it were asked whether there are any limits to God's power, the question would mean, Is there anything which if willed by him, nevertheless would not take place. What else can be meant when we speak of a living being as having power, I cannot divine.]

The concluding sentence Mr. Mansel censures as attributing discreditable motives to opponents.   Had it not been for this proof, I should have thought it unnecessary to say, that no imputation was intended on the sincerity either of classes or of individuals.   But the effect of men's necessities of position on their opinions as well as on their conduct, is far too widely reaching and influential an element in human affairs, to be *always* passed over in silence for fear of offending personal susceptibilities.

one to the other. If not, the divine attribute, whatever
else it may be, is not goodness, and ought not to be
called by the name. Unless there be some human
conception which agrees with it, no human name can
properly be applied to it; it is simply the unknown
attribute of a thing unknown; it has no existence in
relation to us, we can affirm nothing of it, and owe it
no worship. Such is the inevitable alternative.*

To conclude : Mr. Mansel has not made out any connection between his philosophical premises and his
theological conclusion. The relativity of human knowledge, the uncognoscibility of the Absolute, and the
contradictions which follow the attempt to conceive a
Being with all or without any attributes, are no obstacles

* Mr. Mansel says (p. 175), " The question really at issue is not whether
"the Rationalist argument is licit or illicit, but whether, in its lawful
" use, it is to be regarded as infallible or fallible." If this were all, there
would be nothing for him and the Rationalists to quarrel about ; for who
ever asserted, of any human reasoning, that it is infallible ? Neither, I
believe, would any " Rationalist" dissent from Mr. Mansel's view of the
"lawful use " of the argument, which he declares throughout his Eighth
Lecture to be only admissible (as one argument among others) on the
question of the authenticity of a Revelation. No Rationalists, I should
suppose, believe that what they reject as inconsistent with the Divine
Goodness was really revealed by God. They do not both admit it to be
revealed and believe it to be false. They believe that it is either a mistaken interpretation, or found its way by human means into documents
which they may nevertheless consider as the records of a Revelation. They
concede, therefore, to Mr. Mansel (and unless the hypothesis were admitted
of a God who is not good, they cannot help conceding) that the moral objections to a religious doctrine are only valid against its truth if they are
strong enough to outweigh whatever external evidences there may be of
its having been divinely revealed. But when the question is, *how much*
weight is to be allowed to moral objections, the difference will be radical
between those who think that the Divine Goodness is the same thing with
human goodness carried to the infinite, and Mr. Mansel, who thinks that
it is a different quality, only having some analogy to the human. Indeed
it is hard to see how any one, who holds the latter opinion, can give more
than a nominal weight to any such argument against a religious doctrine.
For, if things may be right according to divine goodness which would be
wrong according to even an infinite degree of the human, and if all that
is known is that there is some analogy between the two, while no one
pretends to have any knowledge how far the analogy reaches, and it may
be presumed to be as distant as the remainder of the Divine Nature is
from the human, it is impossible to assign any determinate weight to an
argument grounded on contradiction of such an analogy. It becomes a
mere dialectical *locus communis :* an argument to be taken up and laid
down as suits convenience, and which different men will hold valid in
different cases, according to their fancies or prepossessions.

to our having the same kind of knowledge of God which we have of other things, namely not as they exist absolutely, but relatively.   The proposition, that we cannot conceive the moral attributes of God in such a manner as to be able to affirm of any doctrine or assertion that it is inconsistent with them, has no foundation in the laws of the human mind: while, if admitted, it would not prove that we should ascribe to God attributes bearing the same name as human ˈqualities, but not to be understood in the same sense; it would prove that we ought not to ascribe any moral attributes to God at all, inasmuch as no moral attributes known or conceivable by us are true of him, and we are condemned to absolute ignorance of him as a moral being.

CHAPTER VIII.

IN the discussion of the Relativity of human knowledge
and the Philosophy of the Conditioned, we have brought
under consideration those of Sir W. Hamilton's metaphysical doctrines which have the greatest share in
giving to his philosophy the colour of individuality
which it possesses, and the most important of those
which can be regarded as belonging specially to himself. On a certain number of minor points, and on one
of primary importance, Causation, we shall again have
to examine opinions of his which are original. But on
most of the subjects which remain to be discussed, at
least in the psychological department (as distinguished
from the logical), Sir W. Hamilton is merely an eminent representative of one of the two great schools of
metaphysical thought; that which derives its popular
appellation from Scotland, and of which the founder
and most celebrated champion was a philosopher whom,
on the whole, Sir W. Hamilton seems to prefer to any
other, Dr. Reid. For the future, therefore, we shall be
concerned less with Sir W. Hamilton's philosophy as
such, than with the general mode of thought to which
it belongs. We shall be engaged in criticising doctrines
common to him with many other thinkers; but in doing
so we shall take his writings as text-books, and deal with
the opinions chiefly in the form in which he presented
them. No other course would be so fair to the opinions
themselves: not only because they have not, within the
last half century, had so able a teacher, and never one

so well acquainted with the teachings of others, but also because he had the great advantage of coming last. All theories, at their commencement, bear the burthen of mistakes and inadvertences not inherent in the theories themselves, but either personal to their authors, or arising from the imperfect state of philosophical thought at the time of their origin. At a later period, the errors which accidentally adhered to the theory are stript off, the most obvious objections to it are perceived, and more or less successfully met, and it is rendered, at least apparently, consistent with such admitted truths as it at first seemed to contradict. One of the unfairest, though commonest tricks of controversy, is that of directing the attack exclusively against the first crude form of a doctrine.* Whoever should judge Locke's philosophy as it is in Locke, Berkeley's philosophy as it is in Berkeley, or Reid's as it is in Reid, would often condemn them on the ground of incidental misapprehensions, which form no essential part of their doctrine, and from which its later adherents and expositors are free. Sir W. Hamilton's is the latest form of the Reidian theory; and by no other of its supporters has that theory been so well guarded, or expressed in such discriminating terms, and with such studious precision. Though there are a few points on which the earlier philosopher seems to me nearer the truth, on the whole it is impossible to pass from Reid to Sir W. Hamilton, or from Sir W. Hamilton back to Reid, and not be struck with the immense progress which their common philosophy has made in the interval between them.

All theories of the human mind profess to be interpretations of Consciousness: the conclusions of all of them are supposed to rest on that ultimate evidence, either immediately or remotely. What Consciousness directly reveals, together with what can be legitimately inferred from its revelations, composes, by universal

---

* This, for example, is the secret of most of the apparent triumphs which are so frequently gained over the population theory of Malthus, and the political economy of Ricardo.

admission, all that we know of the mind, or indeed of
any other thing.   When we know what any philosopher
considers to be revealed in Consciousness, we have the
key to the entire character of his metaphysical system.

There are some peculiarities requiring notice, in Sir
W. Hamilton's mode of conceiving and defining Consciousness.   The words of his definition do not, of
themselves, indicate those peculiarities.   Consciousness,
he says,* is " the recognition by the mind or ego of its
own acts or affections;" and in this, as he truly
observes, " all philosophers are agreed."   But all
philosophers have not, by any means, meant the same
thing by it.   Most of them (including Reid and Stewart)
have meant, as the words naturally mean, Self-consciousness.   They have held, that we can be conscious only of
some state of our own mind.   The mind's " own acts or
affections" are in the mind itself, and not external to
it : accordingly we have, in their opinion, the direct
evidence of consciousness, only for the internal world.
An external world is but an inference, which, according
to most philosophers, is justified, or even, by our
mental constitution, compelled : according to others,
not justified.

Nothing, however, can be farther from Sir W. Hamilton's mind than he declares this opinion to be.   Though
consciousness, according to him, is a recognition of the
mind's own acts and affections, we are nevertheless conscious of things outside the mind.   Some of the mind's
acts are perceptions of outward objects ; and we are, of
course, conscious of those acts : now, to be conscious of
a perception, necessarily implies being conscious of the
thing perceived.   " It is † palpably impossible that we
" can be conscious of an act, without being conscious of
" the object to which that act is relative.   This, how-
" ever, is what Dr. Reid and Mr. Stewart maintain.
" They maintain that I can know *that* I know, without
" knowing *what* I know,—or that I can know the know-
" ledge without knowing what the knowledge is about:

* Lectures, i. 193 and 201.   † Ibid. i. 212.

" for example, that I am conscious of perceiving a book,
" without being conscious of the book perceived,—that
" I am conscious of remembering its contents without
" being conscious of these contents remembered—and so
" forth." "An act * of knowledge existing and being
" what it is only by relation to its object, it is manifest
" that the act can be known only through the object to
" which it is correlative ; and Reid's supposition that an
" operation can be known in consciousness to the ex-
" clusion of its object, is impossible. For example, I
" see the inkstand. How can I be conscious that my
" present modification exists,—that it is a perception
" and not another mental state,—that it is a perception
" of sight, to the exclusion of every other sense,—and
" finally, that it is a perception of the inkstand, and of
" the inkstand only,—unless my own consciousness com-
" prehend within its sphere the object, which at once
" determines the existence of the act, qualifies its kind,
" and distinguishes its individuality ? Annihilate the
" inkstand, you annihilate the perception ; annihilate
" the consciousness of the object, you annihilate the
" consciousness of the operation. It undoubtedly sounds
" strange to say, I am conscious of the inkstand, instead
" of saying, I am conscious of the perception of the ink-
" stand. This I admit, but the admission can avail
" nothing to Dr. Reid, for the apparent incongruity of
" the expression arises only from the prevalence of that
" doctrine of perception in the schools of philosophy,
" which it is his principal merit to have so vigorously
" assailed."

This is Sir W. Hamilton's first difference, on the subject of Consciousness, from his predecessor, Reid. In
being conscious of those of our mental operations which
regard external objects, we are, according to Sir W.
Hamilton, conscious of the objects. Consciousness,
therefore, is not solely of the ego and its modifications,
but also of the non-ego.

This first difference is not the only one. Conscious-

* Lectures, i. 228.

ness, according to Sir W. Hamilton, may be of things external to self, but it can only be of things actually present. In the first place, they must be present in time. We are not conscious of the past. Thus far Sir W. Hamilton agrees with Reid, who holds that memory is of the past, consciousness only of the present. Reid, however, is of opinion that memory is an "immediate knowledge of the past," exactly as consciousness is an immediate knowledge of the present. Sir W. Hamilton contends * that this opinion of Reid is "not only false," but "involves a contradiction in terms." Memory is an act, and an act "exists only in the *now ;*" it can therefore be cognisant only of what now is. In the case of memory, what now is, is not the thing remembered, but a present representation of it in the mind, which representation is the sole object of consciousness. We are aware of the past, not immediately, but mediately, through the representation. "An act of memory, is "merely a present state of mind, which we are con- "scious of, not as absolute, but as relative to, and repre- "senting, another state of mind, and accompanied with "the belief that the state of mind, as now represented, "has actually been. . . . All that is immediately known "in the act of memory, is the present mental modifi- "cation ; that is, the representation and concomitant "belief . . . . So far is memory from being an imme- "diate knowledge of the past, that it is at best only a "mediate knowledge of the past ; while in philosophical "propriety, it is not a knowledge of the past at all, "but a knowledge of the present, and a belief of the "past. . . . We may doubt, we may deny that the "representation and belief are true. We may assert that "they represent what never was, and that all beyond "their present mental existence is a delusion : " but it is impossible for us to doubt or deny that of which we have immediate knowledge.

Again, that of which we are conscious must not only be present in time, it must also, if external to our minds,

* Lectures, i. 218–221.

be present in place. It must be in direct contact with our bodily organs. We do not immediately perceive a distant object. "To say,* for example, that we perceive " by sight the sun or moon, is a false or an elliptical ex-" pression. We perceive nothing but certain modifica-" tions of light, in immediate relation to our organ of " vision; and so far from Dr. Reid being philosophically " correct when he says that 'when ten men look at the " sun or moon, they all see the same individual object,' " the truth is that each of these persons sees a different " object, because each person sees a different complement " of rays, in relation to his individual organ;" to which, in another place, he adds, that each individual sees two different objects, with his right and with his left eye. " It is not by perception, but by a process of reasoning, " that we connect the objects of sense with existences " beyond the sphere of immediate knowledge. It is " enough that perception affords us the knowledge of the " non-ego at the point of sense. To arrogate to it the " power of immediately informing us of external things " which are only the causes of the object we immediately " perceive, is either positively erroneous, or a confusion " of language arising from an inadequate discrimination " of the phenomena." † There can, I think, be no doubt that these remarks on knowledge of the past and per-ception of the distant, are correct, and a great improve-ment upon Reid.

It appears, then, that the true definition of Conscious-ness in Sir W. Hamilton's use of the term, would be Immediate Knowledge. And he expressly says, ‡ " *Con-*

---

* Lectures, ii. 153.

† And elsewhere (foot-note to Reid, p. 302):—"It is self-evident that "if a thing is to be an object *immediately* known, it must be known as it "exists. Now, a body must exist in some definite part of space, in a "certain *place;* it cannot, therefore, be immediately known *as existing,* "except it be known *in its place.* But this supposes the mind to be imme-"diately present to it in space."

I do not guarantee the conclusiveness of this reasoning; but it has been an error of philosophers in all times to flank their good arguments with bad ones.

‡ Discussions, p. 51.

"*sciousness* and *immediate knowledge* are thus terms
"universally convertible : and if there be an immediate
"knowledge of things external, there is consequently
"the Consciousness of an outer world."   Immediate
knowledge, again, he treats as universally convertible
with Intuitive knowledge : * and the terms are really
equivalent. We know intuitively, what we know by its
own evidence—by direct apprehension of the fact, and
not through the medium of a previous knowledge of
something from which we infer it. Regarded in this
light, our author's difference with Reid as to our being
conscious of outward objects, would appear, on his own
showing, to be chiefly a dispute about words : for Reid
also says that we have an immediate and intuitive knowledge of things without, and (if Sir W. Hamilton understands him rightly) that it is immediate and intuitive in
the same meaning and mode, as that claimed for us by
Sir W. Hamilton. Sir W. Hamilton stretches the word
Consciousness so as to include this knowledge, while
Reid, with greater regard for the origin and etymology
of the word, restricts it to the cases in which the mind
is "conscia *sibi*."   Sir W. Hamilton has a right to his
own use of the term ; but care must be taken that it
do not serve as a means of knowingly or unknowingly
begging any question. One of the most disputed questions in psychology is exactly this—Have we, or not,
an immediate intuition of material objects ? and this
question must not be prejudged by affirming that those
objects are in our consciousness. On the contrary, it
is only allowable to say that they are in our consciousness, after it had been already proved that we cognise
them intuitively.

It is a little startling, after so much has been said of
the limitation of Consciousness to immediate knowledge,
to find Sir W. Hamilton, in the Dissertations on Reid,†
maintaining that "consciousness comprehends every
"cognitive act ; in other words, whatever we are not
"conscious of, that we do not know." If consciousness

* Lectures, i. 221, note ; and iv. 73.   † P. 810.

comprehends all our knowledge, but yet is limited to immediate knowledge, it follows that all our knowledge must be immediate, and that we have, therefore, no knowledge of the past or of the absent.   Sir W. Hamilton might have cleared up this difficulty by saying, as he had already done, that our mediate cognitions—those of the past and the absent—though he never hesitates to call them knowledge, are in strict propriety Belief.   We could then have understood his meaning.   But the explanation he actually gives is quite different.   It is, that "all our mediate cognitions are contained in our immediate." This is a manifest attempt to justify himself in calling them, not belief, but knowledge, like our immediate cognitions.   But what is the meaning of " contained " ? If it means that our mediate cognitions are *part* of our immediate, then they are themselves immediate, and we have no mediate cognitions.   Sir W. Hamilton has told us, that in the case of a remembered fact, what we immediately cognise is but a present mental representation of it, "accompanied with the belief that the state of mind, as now represented, has actually been."   Having said this, he also says that the past fact, which does not now exist, is "contained" in the representation and in the belief which do exist.   But if it is contained in them, it must have a present existence too, and is not a past fact. Perhaps, however, by the word "contained," all that is meant is, that it is implied in them ; that it is a necessary or legitimate inference from them.   But if it is only this, it remains absent in time ; and what is absent in time, our author has said, is not a possible object of consciousness.   If, therefore, a past fact is an object of knowledge, we *can* know what we are not conscious of ; consciousness does not comprehend all our cognitions. To state the same thing in another manner ; a remembered fact is either a part of our consciousness, or it is not.   If it is, Sir W. Hamilton is wrong when he says that we are not conscious of the past.   If not, he is wrong, either in saying that we can know the past, or in saying that what we are not conscious of, we do not know.

This inconsistency, which emerges only in the Dissertations, I shall not further dwell upon: it is chiefly important as showing that the most complicated and elaborate version of Sir W. Hamilton's speculations is not always the freest from objection.   The doctrine of his Lectures is, that a part of our knowledge—the knowledge of the past, the future, and the distant—is mediate and representative, but that such mediate knowledge is not Consciousness; consciousness and immediate knowledge being coextensive.

From our author's different deliverances as above quoted, it appears that he gives two definitions of Consciousness.   In the one, it is synonymous with direct, immediate, or intuitive knowledge; and we are conscious not only of ourselves but of outward objects, since, in our author's opinion, we know these intuitively.   According to the other definition, consciousness is the mind's recognition of its own acts and affections.   It is not at once obvious how these two definitions can be reconciled? for Sir W. Hamilton would have been the last person to say that the outward object is identical with the mental act or affection.   He must have meant that consciousness is the mind's recognition of its own acts and affections together with all that is therein implied, or as he would say, contained.   But this involves him in a new inconsistency: for how can he then refuse the name of consciousness to our mediate knowledge— to our knowledge or belief (for instance) of the past? The past reality is certainly implied in the present recollection of which we are conscious: and our author has said that all our mediate knowledge is contained in our immediate, as he has elsewhere said that knowledge of the outward object is contained in our knowledge of the perception. If, then, we are conscious of the outward object, why not of the past sensation or impression?

From the definition of Consciousness as "the recognition by the mind or Ego of its own acts or affections," our author might be supposed to think (as has been actually thought by many philosophers) that conscious-

ness is not the fact itself of knowing or feeling, but a
subsequent operation by which we become aware of that
fact. This however is not his opinion. By "the mind's
recognition of its acts and affections" he does not mean
anything different from the acts and affections themselves. He denies that we have one faculty by which
we know or feel, and another by which we know that
we know, and by which we know that we feel. These
are not, according to him, different facts, but the same
fact seen under another point of view. And he takes
this occasion for making a remark, of wide application
in philosophy, which it would be of signal service to all
students of metaphysics to keep constantly in mind;
that difference of names often does not signify difference
of things, but only difference in the particular aspect
under which a thing is considered. On the real identity
between our various mental states and our consciousness
of them, he seems to be of the opinion which was maintained before him by Brown, and which is stated by Mr.
James Mill, with his usual clearness and force, in the
following passage : *—

"Having a sensation, and having a feeling, are not
" two things. The thing is one, the names only are two.
" I am pricked by a pin. The sensation is one; but I
" may call it sensation, or a feeling, or a pain, as I please.
" Now, when, having the sensation, I say I feel the sen-
" sation, I only use a tautological expression; the sensa-
" tion is not one thing, the feeling another; the sensation
" is the feeling. When instead of the word feeling, I
" use the word conscious, I do exactly the same thing—
" I merely use a tautological expression. To say I feel a
" sensation, is merely to say that I feel a feeling; which
" is an impropriety of speech. And to say I am con-
" scious of a feeling, is merely to say that I feel it. To
" have a feeling is to be conscious; and to be conscious
" is to have a feeling. To be conscious of the prick of the
" pin, is merely to have the sensation. And though I
" have these various modes of naming my sensation, by

* Analysis of the Human Mind, i. 170–172.

K

" saying, I feel the prick of a pin, I feel the pain of a
" prick, I have the sensation of a prick, I have the feel-
" ing of a prick, I am conscious of the feeling ; the thing
" named in all these various ways is one and the same.

" The same explanation will easily be seen to apply to
" ideas.   Though at present I have not the sensation
" called the prick of a pin, I have a distinct idea of it.
" The having an idea, and the not having it, are distin-
" guished by the existence or non-existence of a certain
" feeling. To have an idea, and the feeling of that idea, are
" not two things ; they are one and the same thing.   To
" feel an idea, and to be conscious of that feeling, are not
" two things ; the feeling and the consciousness are but
" two names for the same thing.   In the very word feeling,
" all that is implied in the word Consciousness is involved.

" Those philosophers, therefore, who have spoken of
" Consciousness as a feeling distinct from all other feel-
" ings, committed a mistake, and one, the evil conse-
" quences of which have been most important ; for, by
" combining a chimerical ingredient with the elements
" of thought, they involved their enquiries in confusion
" and mystery from the very commencement.

" It is easy to see what is the nature of the terms
" Conscious and Consciousness, and what is the marking
" function which they are destined to perform.   It was of
" great importance, for the purpose of naming, that we
" should not only have names to distinguish the different
" classes of our feelings, but also a name applicable
" equally to all those classes.   This purpose is answered
" by the concrete term, Conscious, and the abstract of
" it, Consciousness.   Thus, if we are in any way sen-
" tient ; that is, have any of the feelings whatsoever of a
" living creature ; the word Conscious is applicable to
" the feeler, and Consciousness to the feeling ; that is to
" say the words are Generical marks, under which all the
" names of the subordinate classes of the feelings of a
" sentient creature are included.   When I smell a rose,
" I am conscious ; when I have the idea of a fire, I am
" conscious ; when I remember, I am conscious ; when I

"reason, and when I believe, I am conscious; but be-
"lieving and being conscious of belief, are not two
"things, they are the same thing: though this same
"thing I can name at one time without the aid of the
"generical mark, while at another time it suits me to
"employ the generical mark."

Sir W. Hamilton's doctrine is exactly this, except
that he expresses the latter part of it in less perspicuous
phraseology, saying that consciousness is "the fundamental form, the generic condition" of all the modes
of our mental activity;* "in fact, the general condition
of their existence."† But, while holding the same
theory with Brown and Mill, he completes it by the
addition that though our mental states and our consciousness of them are only the same fact, they are the
same fact regarded in different relations. Considered
in themselves, as acts and feelings, or considered in relation to the external object with which they are concerned,
we do not call them consciousness. It is when these
mental modifications are referred to a subject or ego, and
looked at in relation to Self, that consciousness is the
term used; consciousness being "the self-affirmation that
certain modifications are known by me, and that these
modifications are mine."‡ In this self-affirmation,
however, no additional fact is introduced. It "is not to
be viewed as anything different from" the "modifications
themselves." There is but one mental phenomenon,
the act of feeling; but as this implies an acting or feeling Self, we give it a name which connotes its relation to
the self, and that name is Consciousness. Thus, "consciousness and knowledge"§—and I think he would have
added feeling (the mind's "affections") as well as knowledge—"are not distinguished by different words as dif-
"ferent things, but only as the same thing considered in
"different aspects. The verbal distinction is taken for the
"sake of brevity and precision, and its convenience war-
"rants its establishment. . . . Though each term of a

* Discussions, p. 48.   † Lectures, i. 193.
‡ Ibid.   § Ibid. pp. 194, 5.

"relation necessarily supposes the other, nevertheless
"one of these terms may be to us the more interesting,
"and we may consider that term as the principal, and
"view the other only as subordinate and correlative.
"Now, this is the case in the present instance. In an
"act of knowledge, my attention may be principally
"attracted either to the object known, or to myself, as
"the subject knowing; and in the latter case, although
"no new element be added to the act, the condition
"involved in it—*I know that I know*, becomes the
"primary and permanent matter of consideration. And
"when, as in the philosophy of mind, the act of know-
"ledge comes to be specially considered in relation to
"the knowing subject, it is, at last, in the progress of
"the science, found convenient, if not absolutely neces-
"sary, to possess a scientific word in which this point of
"view should be permanently and distinctively em-
"bodied."

If any doubt could have existed, after this passage, of
Sir W. Hamilton's opinion on the question, it would
have been removed by one of the fragments recently
published by his editors, in continuation of the Dissertations on Reid. I extract the words : *—

"Consciousness is not to be regarded as aught dif-
"ferent from the mental modes or movements them-
"selves. It is not to be viewed as an illuminated place
"within which objects coming are presented to, and
"passing beyond are withdrawn from, observation ; nor
"is it to be considered even as an observer—the mental
"modes as phenomena observed. Consciousness is just
"the movements themselves, rising above a certain
"degree of intensity. . . . It is only a comprehensive
"word for those mental movements which rise at once
"above a certain degree of intension." †

* Supplement to Reid, p. 932.
† The qualification here first introduced, of "rising above a certain
degree of intensity," has reference to a doctrine of our author to be fully
considered hereafter, that of latent mental states. It makes no abatement
from the doctrine that consciousness of a feeling *is* the feeling ; for mental
states which are not intense enough to rise into consciousness, are, accord-

We now pass to a question which is of no little importance to the character of Sir W. Hamilton's system of philosophy.   We found, not long ago, that he makes between Knowledge and Belief a broad distinction, on which he lays great stress, and which plays a conspicuous part both in his own speculations and in those of some of his followers.   Let us now look at this distinction in the light thrown upon it by those doctrines of Sir W. Hamilton which are the subject of the present chapter.

Though Sir W. Hamilton allows a mediate, or representative, knowledge of the past and the absent, he has told us that "in philosophical propriety" it ought not to be called knowledge, but belief.   We do not, properly speaking, know a past event, but believe it, by reason

ing to the same theory, not intense enough to be felt; and if felt, the feeling, and the consciousness of the feeling, are one and the same.

It was not without some difficulty, and after considerable study, that I was able to satisfy myself that Sir W. Hamilton held the sound and rational theory with which I have credited him in the text. For he often states and defends his doctrine in a manner which might lead one to think, that in saying that to know, and to know that we know, are but one fact, he does not mean one fact, but two facts which are inseparable. This misapprehension of his meaning is favoured by the repeated use of (what we seldom meet with in his writings) a false illustration; that of the sides and angles of a triangle. "The sides suppose the angles—the angles "suppose the sides,—and, in fact, the sides and angles are in themselves "in reality, one and indivisible." (Lectures, i. 194.) "The sides and angles "of a triangle (or trilateral) as mutually correlative—as together making "up the same simple figure—and as, without destruction of that figure, "actually inseparable from it, and from each other, are *really* one; but "inasmuch as they have peculiar relations, which may, in thought, be "considered severally and for themselves, they are *logically* twofold." (Dissertations on Reid, p. 806.) According to this, the sides are in reality the angles looked at in a particular point of view; and the angles the same thing as the sides, regarded in a particular relation to something else. When this was the illustration selected of the identity between Consciousness and Knowledge, it was natural to suppose that the writer regarded these two as no otherwise one than the sides and angles of a triangle are. But a closer examination has satisfied me that Sir W. Hamilton was only wrong respecting sides and angles, and not respecting Consciousness and Knowledge. On the former subject he has against him not only the reason of the case, but his own authority; for he says, when discoursing on another subject (foot-note to Reid, p. 590): "It is not "more reasonable to identify sense with judgment, because the former "cannot exist without an act of the latter, *than it would be to identify* "*the sides and angles of a mathematical figure, because sides and angles* "*cannot exist apart from each other.*"

of the present recollection which we immediately know.
We do not, properly speaking, perceive or know the
sun, but we perceive and know an image in contact with
our organs, and believe the existence of the sun through
" a process of reasoning," which connects the image
that we directly perceive, with something else as its
cause.   Again, though we cannot know an Infinite or
an Absolute Being, we may and ought to believe in
the reality of such a Being.   But in all these cases the
belief itself, the conviction we feel of the existence of
the sun, and of the reality of the past event, and which
according to Sir W. Hamilton we ought to feel of the
existence of a Being who is the Infinite and the Absolute
—this belief is a fact present in time and in place—a
phenomenon of our own mind; of this we are conscious;
this we immediately know.   Such, it is impossible to
doubt, is Sir W. Hamilton's opinion.

Let us now apply to this the general principle emphatically affirmed by him, and forming the basis of his
argument against Reid and Stewart on the subject of
Consciousness.   "It is palpably impossible that we can
" be conscious of an act, without being conscious of the
" object to which that act is relative.   The knowledge
" of an operation necessarily involves the knowledge of
" its object."   "It is impossible to make consciousness
"conversant about the intellectual operations to the
" exclusion of their objects," and therefore, since we are
conscious of our perceptions, we must be conscious of
the external objects perceived.   Such is Sir W. Hamilton's theory.   But perceptions are not the only mental
operations we are conscious of, which point to an external
object.   This is no less true of beliefs.   We are conscious of belief in a past event, in the reality of a distant
body, and (according to Sir W. Hamilton) in the existence of the Infinite and the Absolute.   Consequently,
on Sir W. Hamilton's principle, we are conscious of the
objects of those beliefs ; conscious of the past event,
conscious of the distant body, conscious of the Infinite
and of the Absolute.   To disclaim this conclusion would

be to bring down upon himself the language in which
he criticised Reid and Stewart; it would be to maintain
"that I can know *that* I [believe] without knowing *what*
"I [believe]—or that I can know the [belief] without
"knowing what the [belief] is about: for example, that
"I am conscious of [remembering a past event] without
"being conscious of [the past event remembered]; that
"I am conscious of [believing in God], without being
"conscious [of the God believed in]." If it be true that
"an act of knowledge" exists, and is what it is, "only
"by relation to its object," this must be equally true
of an act of belief: and it must be as "manifest" of the
one act as of the other, "that it can be known only
through the object to which it is correlative." Therefore past events, distant objects, and the Absolute, inasmuch as they are believed, are as much objects of immediate knowledge as things finite and present; since
they are presupposed and implicitly contained in the
mental fact of belief, exactly as a present object is
implicitly contained in the mental fact of perception.
Either, therefore, Sir W. Hamilton was wrong in his
doctrine that consciousness of our perceptions implies
consciousness of their external object, or if he was right
in this, the distinction between Belief and Knowledge
collapses: all objects of Belief are objects of Knowledge:
Belief and Knowledge are the same thing: and he was
wrong in asserting that the Absolute ought to be believed, or wrong in maintaining against Cousin that it
is incapable of being known.

Another reasoner might escape from this dilemma by
saying that the knowledge of the object of belief, which
is implied in knowledge of the belief itself, is not knowledge of the object as existing, but knowledge of it as
believed—the mere knowledge *what it is* that we believe.
And this is true; but it could not be said by Sir W.
Hamilton; for he rejects the same reasonable explanation in the parallel case. He will not allow it to be
said that when we have what we call a perception, and
refer it to an external object, we are conscious not of the

external object as existing, but of ourselves as inferring
an external existence.   He maintains that the actual
outward existence of the object is a deliverance of consciousness, because "it is impossible that we can be
" conscious of an act without being conscious of the
" object to which that act is relative."   He cannot, then,
reject as applied to the act of Belief, a law which, when
he has occasion for applying it to the acts of Perception
and Knowledge, he affirms to be common to all our
mental operations.   If we can be conscious of an operation without being conscious of its object, the reality of
an external world is not indeed subverted, but there is an
end to Sir W. Hamilton's theory of the mode in which it
is known, and to his particular mode of proving it.

The difficulty in which Sir W. Hamilton is thus
involved seems to have become, though very insuffi-
ciently, perceptible to himself.   Towards the end of his
Lectures on Logic, after saying * that " we may be equally
certain of what we believe as of what we know," and
that, " it has, not without ground, been maintained by
" many philosophers, both in ancient and modern times,
" that the certainty of all knowledge is, in its ultimate
" analysis, resolved into a certainty of belief," he adds,†
" But, on the other hand, the manifestation of this
" belief necessarily involves knowledge ; for we cannot
" believe without some consciousness or knowledge of
" the belief, and consequently without some conscious-
" ness or knowledge of the object of the belief."   The
remark which this tardy reflection suggests to him is
merely this :—" The consideration, however, of the rela-
" tion of Belief and Knowledge does not properly belong
" to Logic, except so far as it is necessary to explain the
" nature of Truth and Error.   It is altogether a meta-
" physical discussion ; and one of the most difficult pro-
" blems of which Metaphysics attempts the solution."
Accordingly, he takes the extremely unphilosophical
liberty of leaving it unsolved.   But when a thinker is
compelled by one part of his philosophy to contradict

* Lectures, iv. 70.   † Ibid. p. 73.

another part, he cannot leave the conflicting assertions standing, and throw the responsibility of his scrape on the arduousness of the subject. A palpable self-contradiction is not one of the difficulties which can be adjourned, as belonging to a higher department of science. Though it may be a hard matter to find the truth, that is no reason for holding to what is self-convicted of error. If Sir W. Hamilton's theory of consciousness is correct, it does not leave the difference between Belief and Knowledge in a state of obscurity, but abolishes that distinction entirely, and along with it a great part of his own philosophy. If his premises are true, we not only cannot believe what we do not know, but we cannot believe that of which we are not conscious; the distinction between our immediate and our mediate or representative cognitions, and the doctrine of things believable but not knowable, must both succumb; or if these can be saved, it must be by abandoning the proposition, which is at the root of so much of his philosophy, that consciousness of an operation is consciousness of the object of the operation.

But when Sir W. Hamilton began to perceive that if his theory is correct nothing can be believed except in so far as it is known, he did not therefore renounce the attempt to distinguish Belief from Knowledge. In the very same Lecture, he says,* "Knowledge and Belief "differ not only in degree but in kind. Knowledge is a "certainty founded upon insight; Belief is a certainty "founded upon feeling. The one is perspicuous and "objective: the other is obscure and subjective. Each, "however, supposes the other: and an assurance is "said to be a knowledge or a belief, according as the "one element or the other preponderates." If Sir W. Hamilton had bestowed any sufficient consideration on the difficulty, he would hardly have consented to pay himself with such mere words. If each of his two certainties supposes the other, it follows that whenever we have a certainty founded upon feeling, we have a parallel

* Lectures, iv. 62.

certainty founded upon insight. We therefore have
always insight when we are certain; and we are never
certain except to the extent to which we have insight.
It is not a case in which we can talk of one or the other
element preponderating. They must be equal and co-
extensive. The whole of what we know we must believe;
and the whole of what we believe we must know: for
we know that we believe it, and the act of belief " can
" only be known through the object to which it is cor-
" relative." Our conviction is not divided, in varying
proportions, between knowledge and belief: the two
must always keep abreast of one another.

All this follows, whatever may be the meaning of
the " in sight " which forms the distinction in kind
between belief and knowledge. But what is this insight ? " The immediate consciousness of an object "
(he goes on to say) " is called an *intuition*, an *insight*." *
So that if knowledge is distinguished from belief by
being grounded on insight, it is distinguished by being
grounded on immediate consciousness. But belief also
supposes immediate consciousness, since " we cannot
" believe without some consciousness or knowledge of
" the belief, and consequently without some conscious-
" ness or knowledge of the object of the belief." Not
merely without some consciousness, but, if our author's
theory is correct, without a consciousness coextensive
with the belief. As far as we believe, so far as we are
conscious of the belief, and so far, therefore, if the
theory be true, we are conscious of the thing believed.

But though Sir W. Hamilton cannot extricate himself
from this entanglement, having, by the premises he laid
down, cut off his own retreat, other thinkers can find a
way through it. For, in truth, what can be more absurd
than the notion that belief of anything implies knowledge of the thing believed ? Were this so, there could
be no such thing as false belief. Every day's experience
shows that belief of the most peremptory kind—assurance
founded on the most intense " feeling," is compatible

* Lectures, iv. 73.

with total ignorance of the thing which is the object of belief; though of course not with ignorance of the belief itself. And this absurdity is a full refutation of the theory which leads to it—that consciousness of an operation involves consciousness of that about which the operation is conversant. The theory does not *seem* so absurd when affirmed of knowledge as of belief, because (the term knowledge being only applied in common parlance to what is regarded as true, while belief may confessedly be false), to say that if we are conscious of our knowledge, we must be conscious of that which we know, is not so manifestly ridiculous, as it is to affirm that if we are conscious of a mistaken belief, we must be conscious of a non-existent fact. Yet the one proposition must be equally true with the other, if consciousness of an act involves consciousness of the object of the act. It is over the ruins of this false theory that we must force our way out of the labyrinth in which Sir W. Hamilton has imprisoned us. It may be true, or it may not, that an external world is an object of immediate knowledge. But assuredly we cannot conclude that we have an immediate knowledge of external things, because we have an immediate knowledge of our cognitions of them; whether those cognitions are to be termed belief, with Reid, or knowledge, with Sir W. Hamilton.*

* Mr. Mansel (p. 129) gets over this criticism on Sir W. Hamilton very easily. "Hamilton," he says, "maintains that we cannot be conscious of a mental operation without being conscious of its object. On this Mr. "Mill retorts, that if, as Hamilton admits, we are conscious of a belief in "the Infinite and the Absolute, we must be conscious of the Infinite and "the Absolute themselves; and such consciousness is knowledge. The "fallacy of this retort is transparent. The immediate object of Belief is "a *proposition* which I hold to be true, not a *thing* apprehended in an act "of conception. I believe in an Infinite God; *i.e.*, I believe *that* God is "infinite. I believe that the attributes which I ascribe to God exist in "him in an infinite degree. Now, to believe this proposition I must, of "course, be conscious of its meaning; but I am not therefore conscious "of the Infinite God as an object of conception; for this would require "further an apprehension of the manner in which these infinite attributes "coexist so as to form one object."

A very simple explanation, if only it be a true one. Sir W. Hamilton had no need to feel embarrassed in applying his doctrine, that the knowledge of an operation involves the knowledge of its object, to the operation called Belief; for the object of Belief is but a proposition, and knowledge of the proposition is the only knowledge required. Strange, that when this explanation stood so obvious, Sir W. Hamilton should have missed it—should not only have felt that there was a difficulty, but remanded it to the abstruser Metaphysics, as part of "one of the most difficult problems of which Metaphysics attempts the solution." Sir W. Hamilton was often confused and inconsistent, but rarely, if ever, on subjects which he had studied, superficial. He would have brushed away Mr. Mansel's distinction with the decisive stroke with which he so often levels a fallacy. The object of Belief is a proposition; but is not the object of Knowledge propositions? Is not all knowledge a series of judgments; and is not a judgment expressed in words, a proposition? It is true that knowledge is of things; but we know things only by their attributes: our knowledge of a thing is made up of our knowledge of a certain number of its attributes, every one of which may be expressed in a proposition. When we are said to know a Thing, the meaning is either that we know it as possessing some attribute, or that we know it and its attributes together as existing. So when we do not know the Thing, but have a belief respecting it, the belief is either that it possesses some attribute, or is a belief of its existence, which is called believing *in* it. When the question is one of attributes, the object of belief is a proposition, but so is the object of knowledge. When the question is one of existence, the object of knowledge is a Thing, but so is the object of belief.

The "Inquirer" (pp. 31–33), unlike Mr. Mansel, thinks that this is "a very intricate point;" that there is a real metaphysical difficulty, and that Sir W. Hamilton was aware of it; that he perceived two facts, both true, which he could not reconcile with one another, and that he died without having had time to find the reconciliation. On this I remark, first, that the difficulty is not in reconciling two facts, but two of Sir W. Hamilton's opinions, and that the only solution would be to give up one of them. Secondly, that, whatever the solution might be, he had nearly the whole of his philosophical life to find it in; for the inconsistent opinions are two of the cardinal doctrines of his philosophy. The "Inquirer" thinks that we ought to look indulgently on inconsistencies, as being mere incidents of growths; as indeed they are in a learner, who, independently of his ignorance of Things, is not yet fully master of his own thoughts: but a teacher is supposed to be full grown. While admitting (p. 7) that I have proved against Sir W. Hamilton "continual inconsistencies and discrepancies," the "Inquirer" maintains that all sound philosophy, while incomplete, must be liable to the objection of inconsistency. I confess I cannot see the necessity that our thoughts should be contradictory because our knowledge is incomplete; that because there is much that we do not know, we should not have sufficiently considered what we do know, to avoid holding in conjunction opinions which conflict with one another. The "Inquirer" probably confounds two different things: the belief in contradictories, and the recognition of positive truths which merely limit one another, but to what extent or at what points we cannot yet determine.

CHAPTER IX.

OF THE INTERPRETATION OF CONSCIOUSNESS.

ACCORDING to all philosophers, the evidence of Consciousness, if only we can obtain it pure, is conclusive. This
is an obvious, but by no means a mere identical proposition. If consciousness be defined as intuitive knowledge,
it is indeed an identical proposition to say, that if we
intuitively know anything, we do know it, and are sure
of it. But the meaning lies in the applied assertion,
that we do know some things immediately, or intuitively.
That we must do so is evident, if we know anything ;
for what we know mediately, depends for its evidence
on our previous knowledge of something else : unless,
therefore, we knew something immediately, we could not
know anything mediately, and consequently could not
know anything at all. That imaginary being, a complete Sceptic, might be supposed to answer, that perhaps
we do not know anything at all. I shall not reply to
this problematical antagonist in the usual manner, by
telling him that if he does not know anything, I do. I
put to him the simplest case conceivable of immediate
knowledge, and ask, if we ever feel anything ? If so,
then, at the moment of feeling, do we know that we
feel ? Or if he will not call this knowledge, will he
deny that when we have a feeling, we have at least some
sort of assurance, or conviction, of having it ? This
assurance or conviction is what other people mean by
knowledge. If he dislikes the word, I am willing in
discussing with him to employ some other. By whatever name this assurance is called, it is the test to which

we bring all our other convictions.   He may say it is
not certain ; but such as it may be, it is our model of
certainty.   We consider all our other assurances and
convictions as more or less certain, according as they
approach the standard of this.   I have a conviction that
there are icebergs in the Arctic seas.   I have not had
the evidence of my senses for it : I never saw an iceberg.
Neither do I intuitively believe it by a law of my mind.
My conviction is mediate, grounded on testimony, and
on inferences from physical laws.   When I say I am
convinced of it, I mean that the evidence is equal to
that of my senses.   I am as certain of the fact as if I
had seen it.   And, on a more complete analysis, when I
say I am convinced of it, what I am convinced of is that
if I were in the Arctic seas I should see it.   We mean
by knowledge, and by certainty, an assurance similar and
equal to that afforded by our senses : if the evidence in
any other case can be brought up to this, we desire no
more.   If a person is not satisfied with this evidence,
it is no concern of anybody but himself, nor, practically,
of himself, since it is admitted that this evidence is
what we must, and may with full confidence, act upon.
Absolute scepticism, if there be such a thing, may be
dismissed from discussion, as raising an irrelevant
issue, for in denying all knowledge it denies none.
The dogmatist may be quite satisfied if the doctrine he
maintains can be attacked by no arguments but those
which apply to the evidence of the senses.   If his
evidence is equal to that, he needs no more ; nay, it is
philosophically maintainable that by the laws of psychology we can conceive no more, and that this is the
certainty which we call perfect.

The verdict, then, of consciousness, or, in other words,
our immediate and intuitive conviction, is admitted, on
all hands, to be a decision without appeal.   The next
question is *to what* does consciousness bear witness ?
And here, at the outset, a distinction manifests itself,
which is laid down by Sir W. Hamilton, and stated, in

a very lucid manner, in the first volume of his Lectures.
I give it in his own words.*

   " A fact of consciousness is that whose existence is
" given and guaranteed by an original and necessary
" belief.   But there is an important distinction to be
" here made, which has not only been overlooked by all
" philosophers, but has led some of the most distin-
" guished into no inconsiderable errors.

   " The facts of consciousness are to be considered in
" two points of view; either as evidencing their own
" ideal or phenomenal existence, or as evidencing the
" objective existence of something else beyond them.
" A belief in the former is not identical with a belief in
" the latter.   The one cannot, the other may possibly,
" be refused.   In the case of a common witness, we
" cannot doubt the fact of his personal reality, nor the
" fact of his testimony as emitted,—but we can always
" doubt the truth of that which his testimony avers.
" So it is with consciousness.   We cannot possibly
" refuse the fact of its evidence as given, but we may
" hesitate to admit that beyond itself of which it assures
" us.   I shall explain by taking an example.   In the
" act of External Perception, consciousness gives as a
" conjunct fact, the existence of Me or Self as perceiving,
" and the existence of something different from Me or
" Self as perceived.   Now the reality of this, as a
" subjective datum—as an ideal phenomenon—it is
" absolutely impossible to doubt without doubting the
" existence of consciousness, for consciousness is itself
" this fact; and to doubt the existence of consciousness
" is absolutely impossible ; for as such a doubt could not
" exist except in and through consciousness, it would,
" consequently, annihilate itself.   We should doubt that
" we doubted.   As contained—as given—in an act of
" consciousness, the contrast of mind knowing and
" matter known cannot be denied.

   " But the whole phenomenon as given in conscious-

* Lectures, i. 271–275.

"ness may be admitted, and yet its inference disputed.
"It may be said, consciousness gives the mental subject
"as perceiving an external object, contradistinguished
"from it as perceived : all this we do not, and cannot,
"deny. But consciousness is only a phenomenon ;—
"the contrast between the subject and object may be
"only apparent, not real ; the object given as an exter-
"nal reality, may only be a mental representation which
"the mind is, by an unknown law, determined uncon-
"sciously to produce, and to mistake for something
"different from itself. All this may be said and be-
"lieved, without self-contradiction,—nay, all this has,
"by the immense majority of modern philosophers, been
"actually said and believed.

  "In like manner, in an act of Memory, consciousness
"connects a present existence with a past. I cannot
"deny the actual phenomenon, because my denial would
"be suicidal, but I can without self-contradiction assert
"that consciousness may be a false witness in regard to
"any former existence ; and I may maintain, if I please,
"that the memory of the past, in consciousness, is
"nothing but a phenomenon, which has no reality
"beyond the present. There are many other facts of
"consciousness which we cannot but admit as ideal
"phenomena, but may discredit as guaranteeing aught
"beyond their phenomenal existence itself. The legality
"of this doubt I do not at present consider, but only its
"possibility ; all that I have now in view being to
"show that we must not confound, as has been done,
"the double import of the facts, and the two degrees of
"evidence for their reality. This mistake has, among
"others, been made by Mr. Stewart. . . .

  "With all the respect to which the opinion of so dis-
"tinguished a philosopher as Mr. Stewart is justly
"entitled, I must be permitted to say, that I cannot
"but regard his assertion that the present existence of
"the phenomena of consciousness and the reality of
"that to which these phenomena bear witness, rest on
"a foundation equally solid—as wholly untenable. The

" second fact, the fact testified to, may be worthy of all
" credit—as I agree with Mr. Stewart in thinking that
" it is; but still it does not rest on a foundation equally
" solid as the fact of the testimony itself. Mr. Stewart
" confesses that of the former no doubt had ever been
" suggested by the boldest sceptic; and the latter, in so
" far as it assures us of our having an immediate know-
" ledge of the external world,—which is the case alleged
" by Mr. Stewart,—has been doubted, nay denied, not
" merely by sceptics, but by modern philosophers almost
" to a man. This historical circumstance, therefore, of
" itself, would create a strong presumption that the two
" facts must stand on very different foundations; and
" this presumption is confirmed when we investigate
" what these foundations themselves are.

  " The one fact,—the fact of the testimony, is an act
" of consciousness itself; it cannot, therefore, be invali-
" dated without self-contradiction. For, as we have
" frequently observed, to doubt of the reality of that of
" which we are conscious is impossible; for as we can
" only doubt through consciousness, to doubt of con-
" sciousness is to doubt of consciousness by conscious-
" ness. If, on the one hand, we affirm the reality of the
" doubt, we thereby explicitly affirm the reality of con-
" sciousness, and contradict our doubt; if, on the other
" hand, we deny the reality of consciousness, we implicitly
" deny the reality of our denial itself. Thus, in the act
" of perception, consciousness gives, as a conjunct fact, an
" ego or mind, and a non-ego or matter, known together,
" and contradistinguished from each other. Now, as a
" present phenomenon, this double fact cannot possibly
" be denied. I cannot, therefore, refuse the fact, that,
" in perception, I am conscious of a phenomenon which
" I am compelled to regard as the attribute of something
" different from my mind or self. This I must perforce
" admit, or run into self-contradiction. But admitting
" this, may I not still, without self-contradiction, main-
" tain that what I am compelled to view as the phe-
" nomenon of something different from me is nevertheless

L

" (unknown to me) only a modification of my mind ?
" In this I admit the fact of the testimony of conscious-
" ness as given, but deny the truth of its report.
" Whether this denial of the truth of consciousness as
" a witness is or is not legitimate, we are not, at this
" moment, to consider : all I have in view at present is,
" as I said, to show that we must distinguish in con-
" sciousness two kinds of facts,—the fact of consciousness
" testifying, and the fact of which consciousness testifies;
" and that we must not, as Mr. Stewart has done, hold
" that we can as little doubt of the fact of the existence
" of the external world, as of the fact that consciousness
" gives in mutual contrast, the phenomenon of self in
" contrast to the phenomenon of not-self."

He adds, that since no doubt has been, or can be,
entertained of the facts given in the act of consciousness
itself, " it is only the authority of these facts as evidence
" of something beyond themselves,—that is, only the
" second class of facts,—which become matter of discus-
" sion ; it is not the reality of consciousness that we
" have to prove, but its veracity."

By the conception and clear exposition of this distinction, Sir W. Hamilton has contributed materially to
make the issues involved in the great question in hand,
more intelligible ; and the passage is a considerable item
for the appreciation both of his philosophy and of his
philosophical powers.   It is one of the proofs that, whatever be the positive value of his achievements in metaphysics, he had a greater capacity for the subject than
many metaphysicians of high reputation, and particularly
than his two distinguished predecessors in the same
school of thought, Reid and Stewart.

There are, however, some points in this long extract
which are open to criticism.   The distinction it draws,
is, in the main, beyond question, just.   Among the facts
which Sir W. Hamilton considers as revelations of consciousness, there is one kind which, as he truly says, no
one does or can doubt, another kind which they can and
do.   The facts which cannot be doubted are those to

THE INTERPRETATION OF CONSCIOUSNESS. 163

which the word consciousness is by most philosophers
confined : the facts of internal consciousness ; "the
mind's own acts and affections." What we feel, we
cannot doubt that we feel. It is impossible to us to feel,
and to think that perhaps we feel not, or to feel not,
and think that perhaps we feel. What admits of being
doubted, is the revelation which consciousness is supposed to make (and which our author considers as itself
consciousness) of an external reality. But according to
him, though we may doubt this external reality, we are
compelled to admit that consciousness testifies to it.
We may disbelieve our consciousness ; but we cannot
doubt what its testimony is. This assertion cannot be
granted in the same unqualified manner as the others.
It is true that I cannot doubt my present impression :
I cannot doubt that when I perceive colour or weight,
I perceive them as in an object. Neither can I doubt
that when I look at two fields, I perceive which of them
is the farthest off. The majority of philosophers, however, would not say that perception of distance by the
eye is testified by consciousness ; because although we
really do so perceive distance, they believe it to be an
acquired perception. It is at least possible to think that
the reference of our sensible impressions to an external
object is, in like manner, acquired ; and if so, though a
fact of our consciousness in its present artificial state, it
would have no claim to the title of a fact of consciousness generally, or to the unlimited credence given to
what is originally consciousness. This point of psychology we shall have to discuss farther on.

Another remark needs to be made. All the world
admits with our author, that it is impossible to doubt a
fact of internal consciousness. To feel, and not to know
that we feel, is an impossibility. But Sir W. Hamilton is
not satisfied to let this truth rest on its own evidence. He
wants a demonstration of it. As if it were not sufficiently
proved by consciousness itself, he attempts to prove it by
a *reductio ad absurdum.* No one, he says, can doubt consciousness, because, doubt being itself consciousness, to

doubt consciousness would be to doubt that we doubt.
He sets so high a value on this argument, that he is
continually recurring to it in his writings ; it actually
amounts to a feature of his philosophy.* Yet it seems
to me no better than a fallacy. It treats doubt as something positive, like certainty, forgetting that doubt is
uncertainty. Doubt is not a state of consciousness, but
the negation of a state of consciousness. Being nothing
positive, but simply the absence of a belief, it seems to
be the one intellectual fact which may be true without
self-affirmation of its truth ; without our either believing
or disbelieving that we doubt. If doubt is anything
other than merely negative, it means an insufficient
assurance ; a disposition to believe, with an inability to
believe confidently. But there are degrees of insuffi-
ciency ; and if we suppose, for argument's sake, that it
is possible to doubt consciousness, it may be possible to
doubt different facts of consciousness in different degrees.
The general uncertainty of consciousness might be the
one fact that appeared least uncertain. The saying of
Socrates, that the only thing he knew was that he knew
nothing, expresses a conceivable and not inconsistent
state of mind. The only thing he felt perfectly sure of
may have been that he was sure of nothing else. Omitting Socrates (who was no sceptic as to the reality of
knowledge, but only as to its having yet been attained)
and endeavouring to conceive the hazy state of mind of a
person who doubts the evidence of his senses, it is quite

---

* It is rather more speciously put in a foot-note on Reid (p. 231) : "To
"doubt that we are conscious of this or that, is impossible. For the
"doubt must at least postulate itself ; but the doubt is only a datum of
"consciousness : therefore in postulating its own reality, it admits the
"truth of consciousness, and consequently annihilates itself." In another
foot-note (p. 442) he says, "In doubting the fact of his consciousness, the
"sceptic must at least affirm the fact of his doubt ; but to affirm a doubt
"is to affirm the consciousness of it ; the doubt would, therefore, be self-
"contradictory—i.e., annihilate itself." And again (Dissertations on
Reid, p. 744) : "As doubt is itself only a manifestation of consciousness,
"it is impossible to doubt that what consciousness manifests, it does
"manifest, without in thus doubting, doubting that we actually doubt ;
"that is, without the doubt contradicting and therefore annihilating
"itself."

possible to suppose him doubting even whether he doubts.   Most people, I should think, must have found themselves in something like this predicament as to particular facts, of which their assurance is all but perfect ; they are not quite certain that they are uncertain.*

But though our author's proof of the position is as untenable as it is superfluous, all agree with him in the position itself, that a real fact of consciousness cannot be doubted or denied.   Let us now, therefore, return to his distinction between the facts "given in the act of consciousness," and those "to the reality of which it only bears evidence."   These last, or, in other words, "the *veracity* of consciousness," Sir W. Hamilton thinks it possible to doubt or deny ; he even says, that such facts, more or fewer in number, have been doubted

---

* In another passage of our author (Lectures, iv. 69), the same argument reappears in different words, and for a different purpose. He is speaking of the Criterion of Truth.   This criterion, he says, "is the neces-"sity determined by the laws which govern our faculties of knowledge, "and the consciousness of this necessity is certainty.   That the necessity "of a cognition, that is, the impossibility of thinking it other than as it is "presented—that this necessity, as founded on the laws of thought, is "the criterion of truth, is shown by the circumstance that where such "necessity is found, all doubt in regard to the correspondence of the "cognitive thought and its object must vanish ; for to doubt whether "what we necessarily think in a certain manner, actually exists as we "conceive it, is nothing less than an endeavour to think the necessary as "the not necessary or the impossible, which is contradictory."

It is very curious to find Sir W. Hamilton maintaining that our necessities of thought are proof of corresponding realities of existence—that things must actually *be* so and so because it is impossible for us to think them as being otherwise ; forgetful of the whole "Philosophy of the Conditioned," and the principle so often asserted by him, that things may, nay, must be true, of which it is impossible for us to conceive even the possibility.   But we are here only concerned with his argument, and in that he forgets that to doubt is not a positive but a negative fact.   It simply means, not to have any knowledge or assured belief on the subject. Now, how can it be asserted that this negative state of mind is "an endeavour to think" anything?   And (even if it were) an endeavour to think a contradiction is not a contradiction.   An endeavour to think what cannot be thought, far from being impossible, is the test by which we ascertain its unthinkability.   The failure of the endeavour in the case supposed, would not prove that what we were endeavouring to think was unreal, but only that it was unthinkable ; which was already assumed in the hypothesis : and our author has carried us round a long circuit, to return to the point from which we set out.

or denied by nearly the whole body of modern philosophers. But this is a statement of the point in issue between Sir W. Hamilton and modern philosophers, the correctness of which, I will venture to affirm that very few if any of them would admit. He represents "nearly the whole body of modern philosophers " as in the peculiar and parodoxical position, of believing that consciousness declares to them and to all mankind the truth of certain facts, and then of disbelieving those facts. That great majority of philosophers of whom Sir W. Hamilton speaks, would, I apprehend, altogether deny this statement. They never dreamed of disputing the veracity of consciousness. They denied what Sir W. Hamilton thinks it impossible to deny ; the fact of its testimony. They thought it did not testify to the facts to which he thinks it testifies. Had they thought as he does respecting the testimony, they would have thought as he does respecting the facts. As it is, many of them maintained that consciousness gives no testimony to anything beyond itself ; that whatever knowledge we possess, or whatever belief we find in ourselves, of anything but the feelings and operations of our own minds, has been acquired subsequently to the first beginnings of our intellectual life, and was not witnessed to by consciousness when it received its first impressions. Others, again, did believe in a testimony of consciousness, but not in the testimony ascribed to it by Sir W. Hamilton. Facts, to which in his opinion it testifies, some of them did not believe at all, others did not believe them to be known intuitively ; nay, many of them both believed the facts, and believed that they were known intuitively, and if they differed from Sir W. Hamilton, differed in the merest shadow of a shade ; yet it is with these last, as we shall see, that he has his greatest quarrel. In his contest, therefore, with (as he says) the majority of philosophers, Sir W. Hamilton addresses his arguments to the wrong point. He thinks it needless to prove that the testimony to which he appeals, is really given by Consciousness, for that he regards as undenied and undeniable : but he is incessantly proving to us that we ought to believe our consciousness, a thing which few, if any, of his opponents denied.* It is true his appeal is always to the same argument, but that he is never tired of reiterating. It is stated the most systematically in the first Dissertation on Reid, that " on the Philosophy of Common Sense." After saying that there are certain primary elements of cognition, manifesting themselves to us as facts of which consciousness assures us, he continues,† " How, it is " asked, do these primary propositions—these cognitions " at first hand—these fundamental facts, feelings, beliefs, " certify us of their own veracity? To this the only " possible answer is, that as elements of our mental con- " stitution—as the essential conditions of our knowledge, " they *must* by us be accepted as true. To suppose their " falsehood, is to suppose that we are created capable of " intelligence, in order to be made the victims of delu- " sion ; that God is a deceiver, and the root of our " nature a lie : " that man is organised ‡ for the attain- " ment, and actuated by the love of truth, only to be- " come the dupe and victim of a perfidious creator." It appears, therefore, that the testimony of consciousness must be believed, because to disbelieve it, would be to impute mendacity and perfidy to the Creator.

But there is a preliminary difficulty to be here resolved, which may be stated without irreverence. If the proof of the trustworthiness of consciousness is the veracity of the Creator, on what does the Creator's veracity itself rest? Is it not on the evidence of consciousness? The divine veracity can only be known in two ways, 1st, by intuition, or 2ndly, through evidence. If it is known by intuition, it is itself a fact of conscious-

---

* The philosophers who have most insisted on the necessity of a test for consciousness, have always found that test in consciousness itself. Hear Mr. Stirling, the latest of them, who in this respect represents them all : " It is the function of consciousness, though itself infallible, inviolable, and veracious as nothing else is or can be, to test and try and question consciousness to the uttermost " (p. 58).

     † Dissertations on Reid, p. 743.   ‡ Ibid. p. 745.

ness, and to have ground for believing it, we must assume that consciousness is trustworthy. Those who say that we have a direct intuition of God, are only saying in other words that consciousness testifies to him. If we hold, on the contrary, with our author, that God is not known by intuition, but proved by evidence, that evidence must rest, in the last resort, on consciousness. All proofs of religion, natural or revealed, must be derived either from the testimony of the senses, or from internal feelings of the mind, or from reasonings of which one or other of these sources supplied the premises. Religion, thus itself resting on the evidence of consciousness, cannot be invoked to prove that consciousness ought to be believed. We must already trust our consciousness, before we can have any evidence of the truth of religion.

I know not whether it is from an obscure sense of this objection to his argument, that Sir W. Hamilton adopts what, in every other point of view, is a very extraordinary limitation of it. After representing the veracity of the Creator as staked on the truth of the testimony of Consciousness, he is content to claim this argument as not amounting to proof, but only to a *primâ facie* presumption. "Such * a supposition" as that of a perfidious creator, "if gratuitous, is manifestly illegitimate." "The data of our original consciousness must, it is evident, *in the first instance*" (the italics are the author's), "be presumed true. It is only if proved false," which it can only be by showing them to be inconsistent with one another, "that their authority can, "*in consequence of that proof*, be, in the second instance, "disallowed." "Neganti incumbit probatio. Nature "is not gratuitously to be assumed to work, not only "in vain, but in counteraction of herself; our faculty of "knowledge is not, without a ground, to be supposed "an instrument of illusion." It is making a very humble claim for the veracity of the Creator, that it should be held valid merely as a presumption, in the

* Dissertations on Reid, pp. 743–745.

absence of contrary evidence ; that the Divine Being,
like a prisoner at the bar, should be presumed innocent
until proved guilty.   Far, however, from intending this
remark in any invidious sense against Sir W. Hamilton,
I regard it as one of his titles to honour, that he has not
been afraid, as many men would have been, to subject a
proposition surrounded by reverence to the same logical
treatment as any other statement, and has not felt himself obliged, as a philosopher, to consider it from the
first as final.   My complaint could only be, that his logic
is not sufficiently consistent; and that the divine veracity
is entitled either to more or to less weight than he accords
to it.   He is bound by the laws of correct reasoning
to prove his premise without the aid of the conclusion
which he means to draw from it.   If he can do this—
if the divine veracity is certified by stronger evidence
than the testimony of consciousness, it may be appealed
to, not merely as a presumption, but as a proof.   If not,
it is entitled to no place in the discussion, even as a
presumption.   There is no intermediate position for it,
good enough for the one purpose, but not good enough
for the other.   It would be a new view of the fallacy
of *petitio principii* to contend that a conclusion is no
proof of the premises from which it is deduced, but
is *primâ facie* evidence of them.

Our author, however, cannot be convicted of *petitio
principii*.   Though he has not stated, I think he has
enabled us to see, in what manner he avoided it.   True,
he has deduced the trustworthiness of consciousness
from the veracity of the Deity ; and the veracity of the
Deity can only be known from the evidence of consciousness.   But he may fall back upon the distinction
between facts given in consciousness itself, and facts " to
the reality of which it only bears evidence."   It is for
the trustworthiness of these last, that he assigns as pre-
sumptive evidence (which the absence of counter-evidence
raises into proof) the divine veracity.   That veracity itself,
he may say, is proved by consciousness, but to prove it
requires only the other class of facts of consciousness,

those given in the act of consciousness itself.   There
are thus two steps in the argument.   "The phenomena
of consciousness considered merely in themselves," with
reference to which "scepticism is confessedly impossible," * suffice (we must suppose him to think) for
proving the divine veracity; and that veracity, being
proved, is in its turn a reason for trusting the testimony
which consciousness pronounces to facts without and
beyond itself.

Unless, therefore, Sir W. Hamilton was guilty of a
paralogism, by adducing religion in proof of what is necessary to the proof of religion, his opinion must have
been that our knowledge of God rests upon the affirmation which Consciousness makes of itself, and not of
anything beyond itself; that the divine existence and
attributes may be proved without assuming that consciousness testifies to anything but our own feelings
and mental operations.   If this be so, we have Sir W.
Hamilton's authority for affirming, that even the most
extreme form of philosophical scepticism, the Nihilism
(as our author calls it) of Hume, which denies the objective existence of both Matter and Mind, does not
touch the evidences of Natural Religion.   And it really
does not touch any evidences but such as religion can
well spare.   But what a mass of religious prejudice has
been directed against this philosophical doctrine, on the
strength of what we have now Sir W. Hamilton's authority for treating as a mere misapprehension.†

But something more is necessary to render the divine
veracity available in support of the testimony of consciousness, against those, if such there be, who admit
the fact of the testimony, but hesitate to admit its

* Dissertations on Reid, p. 745.
† Accordingly Sir W. Hamilton says elsewhere (Appendix to Lectures,
i. 394) : "Religious disbelief and philosophical scepticism are not merely
not the same, but have no natural connection." I regret that this statement is followed by a declaration that the former, "must ever be a matter"
not merely "of regret," but of "reprobation."   This imputation of moral
blame to an opinion sincerely entertained and honestly arrived at, is a
blot which one would willingly not have found in a thinker of so much
ability, and in general of so high a moral tone.

truth. The divine veracity can only be implicated in
the truth of anything, by proving that the Divine Being
intended it to be believed. As it is not pretended that
he has made any revelation in the matter, his intention
can only be inferred from the result: and our author
draws the inference from his having made it an original
and indestructible part of our nature that our consciousness should declare to us certain facts. Now this is
what the philosophers who disbelieve the facts, would
not, any of them, admit. Many indeed have admitted
that we have a *natural tendency* to believe something
which they considered to be an illusion : but it cannot
be affirmed that God intended us to do whatever we have
a natural tendency to. On every theory of the divine
government, it is carried on, intellectually as well as
morally, not by the mere indulgence of our natural tendencies, but by the regulation and control of them. One
philosopher, Hume, has said that the tendency in question seems to be an " instinct," and has called a psychological doctrine, which he regarded as groundless, an
" universal and primary opinion of all men." But he
never dreamed of saying that we are compelled by our
nature to believe it ; on the contrary, he says that this
illusive opinion " is soon destroyed by the slightest
philosophy." Of all eminent thinkers, the one who
comes nearest to our author's description of those who
reject the testimony of consciousness, is Kant. That
philosopher did maintain that there is an illusion inherent in our constitution ; that we cannot help conceiving as belonging to Things themselves, attributes
with which they are only clothed by the laws of our
sensitive and intellectual faculties. But he drew a
marked distinction between an illusion and a delusion.
He did not believe in a mystification practised on us by
the Supreme Being, nor would he have admitted that
God intended us permanently to mistake the conditions
of our mental conceptions for properties of the things
themselves. If God has provided us with the means
of correcting an error, it is probable that he does not

intend us to be misled by it : and in matters speculative as well as practical, it surely is more religious to
see the purposes of God in the dictates of our deliberate
reason, than in those of a "blind and powerful instinct
of nature."

As regards almost all, however, if not all philosophers,
it may truly be said, that the questions which have
divided them have never turned on the veracity of consciousness. Consciousness, in the sense usually attached
to it by philosophers,—consciousness of the mind's own
feelings and operations, cannot, as our author truly
says, be disbelieved. The inward fact, the feeling in
our own minds, was never doubted, since to do so
would be to doubt that we feel what we feel. What
our author calls the *testimony* of consciousness to something beyond itself, may be, and is, denied ; but what
is denied, has almost always been that consciousness
gives the testimony ; not that, if given, it must be
believed.

At first sight it might seem as if there could not possibly be any doubt whether our consciousness does or
does not affirm any given thing. Nor can there, if consciousness means, as it usually does, self-consciousness.
If consciousness tells me that I have a certain thought
or sensation, I assuredly have that thought or sensation.
But if consciousness, as with Sir W. Hamilton, means a
power which can tell me things that are not phenomena
of my own mind, there is immediately the broadest
divergence of opinion as to what are the things to which
consciousness testifies. There is nothing which people
do not think and say that they know by consciousness,
provided they do not remember any time when they did
not know or believe it, and are not aware in what manner
they came by the belief. For Consciousness, in this
extended sense, is, as I have so often observed, but
another word for Intuitive Knowledge : and whatever
other things we may know in that manner, we certainly
do not know by intuition what knowledge is intuitive.
It is a subject on which both the vulgar and the ablest

thinkers are constantly making mistakes. No one is
better aware of this than Sir W. Hamilton. I transcribe
a few of the many passages in which he has acknowledged it.   " Errors " * may arise by attributing to " in-
" telligence as necessary and original data, what are
" only contingent generalisations from experience, and
" consequently, make no part of its complement of native
" truths." †   And again : ‡ " Many philosophers have
" attempted to establish on the principles of common
" sense propositions which are not original data of con-
" sciousness ; while the original data of consciousness,
" from which their propositions were derived, and to
" which they owed their whole necessity and truth—these
" data the same philosophers were (strange to say) not
" disposed to admit."   It fares still worse with the
philosophers chargeable with this error, when Sir W.
Hamilton comes into personal controversy with them.
M. Cousin's mode of proceeding, for example, he characterises thus : § " Assertion is substituted for proof ; facts
" of consciousness are alleged, which consciousness never
" knew ; and paradoxes that baffle argument, are pro-
" mulgated as intuitive truths, above the necessity of
" confirmation."   M. Cousin's particular misinterpreta-
tion of consciousness was, as we saw, that of supposing
that each of its acts testifies to three things, of which
three Sir W. Hamilton thinks that it testifies only to
one.   Besides the finite element, consisting of a Self and
a Not-self, M. Cousin believes that there are directly
revealed in Consciousness an infinite (God) and a relation between this Infinite and the Finite.   But it is not
only M. Cousin who, in our author's opinion, mistakes
the testimony of consciousness.   He brings the same
charge against a thinker with whom he agrees much

---

* Lectures, iv. 137.

† There are writers of reputation in the present day, who maintain in
unqualified terms, that we know by intuition the impossibility of miracles.
" La négation du miracle," says M. Nefftzer (*Revue Germanique* for September 1863, p. 183), " n'est pas subordonnée à l'expérience ; elle est une
" nécessité logique et un fait de certitude interne ; elle doit être le premier
" article du *credo* de tout historien et de tout penseur."

‡ Dissertations on Reid, p. 749.   § Discussions, p. 25.

oftener than with M. Cousin; against Reid. That
philosopher, as we have seen, is of opinion, contrary to
Sir W. Hamilton, that we have an immediate knowledge
of things past. This is to be conscious of them in Sir
W. Hamilton's sense of the word, though not in Reid's.
Finally, Sir W. Hamilton imputes a similar error, no
longer to any particular metaphysician, but to the world
at large. He says that we do not see the sun, but only
a luminous image, in immediate contiguity to the eye,
and that no two persons see the same sun, but every
person a different one. Now it is assuredly the universal
belief of mankind that all of them see the same sun, and
that this is the very sun which rises and sets, and which
is 95 (or according to more recent researches 92) millions
of miles distant from the earth. Nor can any of the
appeals of Reid and Sir W. Hamilton from the sophistries
of metaphysicians to Common Sense and the universal
sentiment of mankind, be more emphatic than that to
which Sir W. Hamilton here lays himself open from
Reid and from the non-metaphysical world.*

We see, therefore, that it is not enough to say that
something is testified by Consciousness, and refer all

* Reid himself places the "natural belief" which Sir W. Hamilton rejects,
on exactly the level of those which he most strenuously maintains, saying
(Works, Hamilton's edition, p. 284) in a passage which our author himself
quotes, "The vulgar are firmly persuaded that the very identical objects
"which they perceive continue to exist when they do not perceive them :
"and are no less firmly persuaded that when ten men look at the sun
"or the moon, they all see the same individual object." And Reid avows
that he agrees with the vulgar in both opinions. But Sir W. Hamilton,
while he upholds the former of these as one to deny which would be to
declare our nature a lie, thinks that nothing can be more absurd than
the latter of them. "Nothing," he says (Lectures, ii. 129) "can be con-
"ceived more ridiculous than the opinion of philosophers in regard to
"this. For example, it has been curiously held (and Reid is no exception)
"that in looking at the sun, moon, or any other object of sight, we are,
"on the one doctrine, actually conscious of these distant objects, or on the
"other, that these distant objects are those really represented in the mind.
"Nothing can be more absurd : we perceive, through no sense, aught ex-
"ternal but what is in immediate relation and in immediate contact with
"its organ. . . . Through the eye we perceive nothing but the rays of
"light in relation to, and in contact with, the retina."
The basis of the whole Ideal System, which it is thought to be the great
merit of Reid to have exploded, was a natural prejudice, supposed to be
intuitively evident, namely, that that which knows, must be of a similar

dissentients to consciousness to prove it.   Substitute for Consciousness the equivalent phrase (in our author's acceptation at least) Intuitive Knowledge, and it is seen that this is not a thing which can be proved by mere introspection of ourselves.   Introspection can show us a present belief or conviction, attended with a greater or a less difficulty in accommodating the thoughts to a different view of the subject : but that this belief, or conviction, or knowledge, if we call it so, is intuitive, no mere introspection can ever show ; unless we are at liberty to assume that every mental process which is now as unhesitating and as rapid as intuition, was intuitive at its outset.   Reid, in his commencements at least, often expressed himself as if he believed this to be the case : Sir W. Hamilton, wiser than Reid, knew better.   With him (at least in his better moments) the question, what is and is not revealed by Consciousness, is a question for philosophers.   "The first * problem of philosophy" is " to seek out, purify, and establish, by intellectual analysis " and criticism, the elementary feelings or beliefs, in " which are given the elementary truths of which all are " in possession : " this problem, he admits, is " of no easy

nature to that which is known by it.   " This principle," says our author (foot-note to Reid, p. 300), " has, perhaps, exerted a more extensive influ-" ence on speculation than any other. . . . It would be easy to show that "the belief, explicit or implicit, that what knows and what is immediately "known must be of an analogous nature, lies at the root of almost every "theory of cognition, from the very earliest to the very latest speculations. ". . . And yet it has not been proved, and is incapable of proof, nay, is " contradicted by the evidence of consciousness itself."

But though Sir W. Hamilton manifests himself thus thoroughly aware how wide the differences of opinion may be and are respecting our intuitive perceptions, I by no means intend to deny that he on certain occasions affirms the contrary.   In the fourth volume of the Lectures (p. 95), he says, " I have here limited the possibility of error to Probable Reasoning, "for in Intuition and Demonstration, there is but little possibility of im-" portant error."   After a certain amount of reading of Sir W. Hamilton, one is used to these contradictions.   What he here asserts to be so nearly impossible, that no account needs to be taken of it in a classification of Error, he is continually fighting against in detail, and imputing to nearly all philosophers.   And when he says (Lectures, i. 266) that the "revela-tion" of consciousness is " naturally clear," and only mistaken by philoso-phers because they resort to it solely for confirmation of their own opinions, he merely transports into psychology the dogmatism of theologians.

    * Dissertations on Reid, p. 752.

accomplishment;" and the "argument from common
sense" is thus "manifestly dependent on philosophy as
"an art, as an acquired dexterity, and cannot, notwith-
"standing the errors which they have so frequently
"committed, be taken out of the hands of the philoso-
"phers. Common sense is like Common Law. Each may
"be laid down as the general rule of decision; but in
"the one case it must be left to the jurist, in the other
"to the philosopher, to ascertain what are the contents
"of the rule; and though in both instances the common
"man may be cited as a witness for the custom or the
"fact, in neither can he be allowed to officiate as advo-
"cate or as judge."

So far, good. But now, it being conceded that the
question, what do we know intuitively, or, in Sir W.
Hamilton's phraseology, what does our· consciousness
testify, is not, as might be supposed, a matter of simple
self-examination, but of science, it has still to be determined in what manner science should set about it. And
here emerges the distinction between two different methods of studying the problems of metaphysics, forming
the radical difference between the two great schools into
which metaphysicians are fundamentally divided. One
of these I shall call, for distinction, the introspective
method; the other, the psychological.

The elaborate and acute criticism on the philosophy
of Locke, which is perhaps the most striking portion of
M. Cousin's Lectures on the History of Philosophy, sets
out with a remark which sums up the characteristics of
the two great schools of mental philosophy, by a summary
description of their methods. M. Cousin observes, that
Locke went wrong from the beginning, by placing before
himself, as the question to be first resolved, the *origin* of
our ideas. This was commencing at the wrong end. The
proper course would have been to begin by determining
what the ideas now are; to ascertain what it is that
consciousness actually tells us, postponing till afterwards
the attempt to frame a theory concerning the origin of
any of the mental phenomena.

I accept the question as M. Cousin states it, and I contend, that no attempt to determine what are the direct revelations of consciousness, can be successful, or entitled to any regard, unless preceded by what M. Cousin says ought only to follow it, an inquiry into the origin of our acquired ideas. For we have it not in our power to ascertain, by any direct process, what Consciousness told us at the time when its revelations were in their pristine purity. It only offers itself to our inspection as it exists now, when those original revelations are overlaid and buried under a mountainous heap of acquired notions and perceptions.

It seems to M. Cousin that if we examine, with care and minuteness, our present states of consciousness, distinguishing and defining every ingredient which we find to enter into them—every element that we seem to recognise as real, and cannot, by merely concentrating our attention upon it, analyse into anything simpler—we reach the ultimate and primary truths, which are the sources of all our knowledge, and which cannot be denied or doubted without denying or doubting the evidence of consciousness itself, that is, the only evidence which there is for anything. I maintain this to be a misapprehension of the conditions imposed on inquirers by the difficulties of psychological investigation. To begin the inquiry at the point where M. Cousin takes it up, is in fact to beg the question. For he must be aware, if not of the fact, at least of the belief of his opponents, that the laws of the mind—the laws of association according to one class of thinkers, the Categories of the Understanding according to another —are capable of creating, out of those data of consciousness which are uncontested, purely mental conceptions, which become so identified in thought with all our states of consciousness, that we seem, and cannot but seem, to receive them by direct intuition ; and, for example, the belief in Matter, in the opinion of some of these thinkers, is, or at least may be, thus produced. Idealists, and Sceptics, contend that the belief in Matter

M

is not an original fact of consciousness, as our sensations are, and is therefore wanting in the requisite which, in M. Cousin's and Sir W. Hamilton's opinion, gives to our subjective convictions objective authority.   Now, be these persons right or wrong, they cannot be refuted in the mode in which M. Cousin and Sir W. Hamilton attempt to do so—by appealing to Consciousness itself. For we have no means of interrogating consciousness in the only circumstances in which it is possible for it to give a trustworthy answer.   Could we try the experiment of the first consciousness in any infant—its first reception of the impressions which we call external; whatever was present in that first consciousness would be the genuine testimony of Consciousness, and would be as much entitled to credit, indeed there would be as little possibility of discrediting it, as our sensations themselves.   But we have no means of now ascertaining, by direct evidence, whether we were conscious of outward and extended objects when we first opened our eyes to the light.   That a belief or knowledge of such objects is in our consciousness now, whenever we use our eyes or our muscles, is no reason for concluding that it was there from the beginning, until we have settled the question whether it could possibly have been brought in since.   If any mode can be pointed out in which within the compass of possibility it might have been brought in, the hypothesis must be examined and disproved before we are entitled to conclude that the conviction is an original deliverance of consciousness.   The proof that any of the alleged Universal Beliefs, or Principles of Common Sense, are affirmations of consciousness, supposes two things; that the beliefs exist, and that there are no means by which they could have been acquired.   The first is in most cases undisputed, but the second is a subject of inquiry which often taxes the utmost resources of psychology.   Locke was therefore right in believing that " the origin of our ideas" is the main stress of the problem of mental science, and the subject which must be first considered in forming the theory of the Mind. Being unable to examine the actual contents of our consciousness until our earliest, which are necessarily our most firmly knit associations, those which are most intimately interwoven with the original data of consciousness, are fully formed, we cannot study the original elements of mind in the facts of our present consciousness. Those original elements can only come to light as residual phenomena, by a previous study of the modes of generation of the mental facts which are confessedly not original; a study sufficiently thorough to enable us to apply its results to the convictions, beliefs, or supposed intuitions which seem to be original, and to determine whether some of them may not have been generated in the same modes, so early as to have become inseparable from our consciousness before the time to which memory goes back. This mode of ascertaining the original elements of mind I call, for want of a better word, the psychological, as distinguished from the simply introspective mode. It is the known and approved method of physical science, adapted to the necessities of psychology.*

It might be supposed from incidental expressions of Sir W. Hamilton that he was alive to the need of a methodical scientific investigation, to determine what portion of our "natural beliefs" are really original, and

---

* The "Inquirer" thinks he refutes the preceding paragraph when he says (pp. 52, 53) that Consciousness may not have given its full revelation in the infant, and that it would be "contrary to all analogy" to suppose "that consciousness alone, of all our natural properties, needs no development, no education." If this supposed improvement of consciousness by exercise be admitted, it goes even harder with the Introspective Method than I had maintained. I pointed out an experiment not realisable, but conceivable, which by ascertaining the contents of consciousness antecedently to any acquired experience, would authenticate as the original data of consciousness whatever that experiment revealed. But if consciousness does not tell its tale at once, but requires time and practice to tell it, and does not get it completed until there has been time for impressions originating in experience to be formed, then there is no period at which the Introspective Method, applied to the case, would yield a conclusive result: the natural and acquired testimonies of consciousness are inseparably blended at every stage, and to separate them by mere self-observation, and show that any particular item belongs to the one and not to the other, involves a double impossibility, instead of the single one I contended for.

what are inferences, or acquired impressions, mistakenly deemed intuitive.* To the declarations already quoted to this effect, the following may be added. Speaking of Descartes' plan, of commencing philosophy by a reconsideration of all our fundamental opinions, he says, " There are among our prejudices, or pretended cogni- " tions, a great many hasty conclusions, the investiga- " tion of which requires much profound thought, skill, " and acquired knowledge. . . . To commence philo- " sophy by such a review, it is necessary for a man to " be a philosopher before he can attempt to become " one." And he elsewhere † bestows high praise upon Aristotle for not falling " into the error of many modern " philosophers, in confounding the natural and necessary " with the habitual and acquired connections of thought," nor attempting " to evolve the conditions under which " we think from the tendencies generated by thinking ; " a praise which cannot be bestowed on our author him- self. But, notwithstanding the ample concession which he appeared to make when he admitted that the problem was one of extreme difficulty, essentially scientific, and ought to be reserved for philosophers, I regret to say that he as completely sets at naught the only possible method of solving it, as M. Cousin himself. He even expresses his contempt for that method. Speaking of Extension, he says,‡ " It is truly an idle problem to " attempt imagining the steps by which we may be sup- " posed to have acquired the notion of Extension, when " in fact, we are unable to imagine to ourselves the possi- " bility of that notion not being always in our posses- " sion." That things which we " are unable to imagine " to ourselves the possibility of," may be, and many of them must be, true, was a doctrine which we thought we had learnt from the author of the Philosophy of the Conditioned. That we cannot imagine a time at which we had no knowledge of Extension, is no evidence that there has not been such a time. There are mental laws,

* Lectures, iv. 92.   † Dissertations on Reid, p. 894.
‡ Ibid. p. 882.

recognised by Sir W. Hamilton himself, which would inevitably cause such a state of things to become inconceivable to us, even if it once existed. There are artificial inconceivabilities equal in strength to any natural. Indeed it is questionable if there are any natural inconceivabilities, or if anything is inconceivable to us for any other reason than because Nature does not afford the combinations in experience which are necessary to make it conceivable.

I do not think that there can be found, in all Sir W. Hamilton's writings, a single instance in which, before registering a belief as a part of our consciousness from the beginning, he thinks it necessary to ascertain that it cannot have grown up subsequently. He demands, indeed,* " that no fact be assumed as a fact of consciousness but " what is ultimate and simple." But to pronounce it ultimate, the only condition he requires is that we be not able to " reduce it to a generalisation from experience." This condition is realised by its possessing the "character " of necessity." " It must be impossible not to think it. " In fact, by its necessity alone can we recognise it as an " original datum of intelligence, and distinguish it from " any mere result of generalisation and custom." In this Sir W. Hamilton is at one with the whole of his own section of the philosophical world ; with Reid, with Stewart, with Cousin, with Whewell, and we may add, with Kant.† The test by which they all decide a belief

* Lectures, i. 268–270.

† In the first edition I added, "and even with Mr. Herbert Spencer :" but that powerful thinker, in his paper in the *Fortnightly Review*, disclaims the doctrine. As I now understand Mr. Spencer, he maintains that the impossibility of getting rid of a belief is a proof of its truth, and also of its being a primary, or ultimate, truth, but not of its being intuitive, since even our primary forms of thought are, in Mr. Spencer's opinion, products of experience, either our own, or inherited by us from ancestors by the laws of the development of organisation. I had confounded the two ideas, of a primary truth and an intuitive truth, which had never, as far as I know, been distinguished by any one except Mr. Spencer; and had, therefore, identified his theory with the ordinary doctrine of the intuitive philosophy ; which I now see to be a misconception, though I think both theories open to refutation by the same arguments, and the difference between them not material to the test of truth, though highly important to psychology.

I perceive also that I was mistaken, when, in an early chapter of this to be part of our primitive consciousness—an original intuition of the mind—is the necessity of thinking it. Their proof that we must always, from the beginning, have had the belief, is the impossibility of getting rid of it now.   This argument, applied to any of the disputed questions of philosophy, is doubly illegitimate : neither the major nor the minor premise is admissible. For, in the first place, the very fact that the questions are disputed, disproves the alleged impossibility.   Those against whose dissent it is needful to defend the belief which is affirmed to be necessary, are unmistakable examples that it is not necessary.   It may be a necessary

work (chap. ii.) I classed Mr. Spencer among the philosophers who hold, in its widest sense, the doctrine of the Relativity of human knowledge : for the external things which, he contends, we cannot help believing to be connected with all our sensations, are not, according to him, entirely un-cognisable by us.   On the contrary, he believes (p. 548) that "the more or "less coherent relations among" one's "states of consciousness, are gene-"rated by experience of the more or less constant relations in something "beyond his consciousness :" *i.e.*, that for every proposition which we can truly assert about the similitudes, successions, and coexistences of our states of consciousness, there is a corresponding similitude, succession, or coexistence really obtaining among Noumena beyond our consciousness, and even that we can have "experience" of the same.   This prodigious amount of knowledge respecting the "Unknowable" is only consistent with the doctrine of Relativity if we understand that doctrine in the very limited sense in which Sir W. Hamilton holds it.   This abates nothing from the value of the psychological analyses due to Mr. Spencer, whose services to philosophy as an applier and defender of the "experience hypothesis" are beyond all price.

Mr. Spencer, in the same paper, adheres to his doctrine that the test of truth in the last resort is the inconceivability of its negation, and maintains that doctrine with his usual argumentative power.   In one part of his argument, he seems to put a sense upon it which would leave little, if any, difference between his opinion and my own.   He seems to say (p. 539) that the proposition, Things equal to the same thing are equal to one another, is known to be true by the inconceivability of its negation, in the same manner in which it might be said that two unequal lines placed side by side are known to be unequal by the inconceivability of their being equal, *i.e.*, "I find it impossible, while contemplating the lines, to get rid of the consciousness" of their inequality.   If the inconceivableness of the negative only means that I cannot resist the evidence of my senses for the affirmative, I have no objection to admit this as the test of any truth, even a geometrical axiom.   I believe that my knowledge of the axiom is of exactly the same kind as my knowledge of the inequality of the two lines : I know it because I see it ; and as I cannot have this positive intuition together with its negative, this may be called, if any one pleases, the inconceivability of the negative.   But I do not therefore rest the belief that things equal to the same thing are equal to one another on an *à priori* incapacity of my mind to conceive them unequal.   I believe that

belief to those who think it so; they may personally be
quite incapable of not holding it.   But even if this in-
capability extended to all mankind, it might be merely
the effect of a strong association ; like the impossibility
of believing Antipodes ; and it cannot be shown that even
where the impossibility is, for the time, real, it might
not, as in that case, be overcome.   The history of science
teems with inconceivabilities which have been conquered,
and supposed necessary truths which have first ceased to
be thought necessary, then to be thought true, and have
finally come to be deemed impossible.*   These philosophers, therefore, and among them Sir W. Hamilton,

I am only unable to conceive them unequal because I have always seen
them to be equal, and am renewing that experience at almost every instant
of my life.
   Mr. Spencer asks (p. 549), If an axiom of mathematics is said to be
known "only by induction from personal experiences," on what warrant
"are personal experiences asserted ?   The testimony of experience is given
"only through memory," and "the trustworthiness of memory" is open
to more doubt than the "immediate consciousness" of the mathematical
truth.   Instead, however, of immediate consciousness, let us call it immediate observation, which is a mode of consciousness, and the "personal
experiences" which it yields become the most certain evidence which it
is possible to have : not depending upon memory, but upon direct perception, which can be repeated at any moment ; corroborated, however, by a
vast mass of memories, both of our own and of other people, which by
their number, ubiquity, and variety operate as a complete insurance against
the possible error of memory in any single instance.
   * Mr. Mahaffy, after distinguishing, as I have done, between the two
kinds of so-called inconceivables, the Unimaginable and the simply
Incredible, says (pp. viii. ix.), "There seems to be a definite distinction
"between them, not of degree, but of kind.   We may safely defy Mr. Mill
"to point out a case where an unimaginable (inconceivable) was proved
"true, or even possible.   And the reason is plain.   The latter depends
"upon the form of the thinking or intuiting faculty ; the former, merely
"upon empirical association."   In Mr. Mahaffy's philosophical system
the distinction passes for one of kind, but he must surely see that it
admits of being construed as a difference only of degree.   If an empirical
association between two ideas, not so strong as to be altogether irresistible,
makes it difficult to imagine in our own minds the corresponding facts as
disjoined, it is but rational to believe that a stronger empirical association,
produced by still more incessant repetition, will convert that difficulty
into a conditional impossibility ; an inability only to be overcome by contrary experience, which experience the conditions of our terrestrial existence may not permit.   And if, as I have before observed, "a mental
"association between two facts, which is not intense enough to make
"their separation unimaginable, may yet create, and if there are no
"counter-associations, always does create, more or less of difficulty in
"believing that the two can exist apart ; a difficulty often amounting to
"a local or temporary impossibility ;" an association which is so intense

mistake altogether the true conditions of psychological investigation, when, instead of proving a belief to be an original fact of consciousness by showing that it cannot, by any known means, have been acquired, they conclude that it was not acquired, for the reason, often false, and never sufficiently substantiated, that our consciousness cannot get rid of it now.

Since, then, Sir W. Hamilton not only neglects, but repudiates, the only scientific mode of ascertaining our original beliefs, what does he mean by treating the question as one of science, and in what manner does he apply science to it? Theoretically, he claims for science an exclusive jurisdiction over the whole domain, but practically he gives it nothing to do except to settle

as to make the separation unimaginable, may surely create an impossibility of belief, not local or temporary, but as durable as the experience which gave rise to the association.

Mr. Spencer, who is almost willing to rest the claims of inconceivability as a test of truth on its expressing "the net result of our experience up to the present time," has given an excellent exposition of this point. He sees clearly that the difference between the two kinds of inconceivable is only one of degree—the degree of strength of the cohesion between the two ideas. The proposition "the ice was hot" he justly classes as not unimaginable, but merely unbelievable ; the unbelievableness, however, arising from a difficulty, though not amounting to an impossibility, of combining the two ideas in a representation. "The elements of the pro- "position cannot be put together in thought without great resistance. "Between those other states of consciousness which the word ice connotes, "and the state of consciousness named cold, there is an extremely strong "cohesion—a cohesion measured by the resistance to be overcome in "thinking the ice as hot." (Spencer, p. 543.) The merely unbelievable is thus distinguished from Mr. Mahaffy's unimaginable, not by a generic difference, but by a minor degree of unimaginability. And the seeming incredibility is strictly proportioned to the degree of difficulty in com- bining the two thoughts in one representation.

With regard to Mr. Mahaffy's assertion, that nothing unimaginable has ever been "proved true, or even possible ;" the point would have been more effectually maintained if he could have said "nothing which *seemed* unimaginable ;" for whatever has been "proved true" or even "possible" has thereby become imaginable. People had much difficulty, and most people have some difficulty still, in representing to themselves sunrise as a motion not of the sun but of the earth ; but no one has called this notion of sunrise either inconceivable or unimaginable after knowing it to be the true notion. Let us first, then, state the question correctly : Has anything which *seemed* unimaginable been proved true, or possible ? It is hardly practicable to give such an answer to this question as will silence the retort, that what was called unimaginable was really no more than incredible ; for since unimaginableness, as I have said, exists in

the relations of the supposed intuitive beliefs among themselves.   It is the province of science, he thinks, to resolve some of these beliefs into others.   He prescribes, as a rule of judgment, what he calls " the Law of Parsimony."   No greater number of ultimate beliefs are to be postulated than is strictly indispensable.   Where one such belief can be looked upon as a particular case of another—the belief in Matter, for instance, of the cognition of a Non-ego—the more special of the two necessities of thought merges in the more general one.   This identification of two necessities of thought, and subsumption of one of them under the other, he is not wrong in regarding as a function of science. He affords an example of it, when, in a manner which we shall hereafter characterise, he denies to Causation the character, which philosophers of his school

numerous degrees, graduating from a slight difficulty to at least a temporary impossibility, there is no definite line of demarcation between the absolutely unimaginable (if there be such a thing) and the totally incredible, nor even between what is unimaginable by a given person, and what is merely incredible to him.   Most of the questions which lie on that border land are still disputed.   For example : is a creation *a nihilo*, or Matter capable of thinking, unimaginable, or only incredible ?   Both the one and the other are habitually ranked among the most unimaginable of all things.   Yet the one is firmly believed by all Materialists, and the other by all Christians.   Every Materialist, therefore, and every Christian, may be called as a witness that things which are unimaginable are not only possible but true.   To take another instance—an event without a cause.   Is that unimaginable, or only incredible ?   All who regard the category of Cause and Effect as a necessity of thought, including Sir W. Hamilton, and Mr. Mahaffy himself, maintain it to be unimaginable. Yet most of these believe it to be both possible and true in the case of human freewill.   Not only therefore what to one man seems unimaginable, another believes to be true, but the same man believes to be true what to himself seems unimaginable : witness the whole Philosophy of the Conditioned.

Dr. M'Cosh thinks that antipodes were unbelievable, not in consequence of an association, but because (p. 240) " the alleged fact seemed contrary " to a law of nature established by observation.   A gathered experience " seemed to show that there was an absolute up and down, and that heavy " bodies tended downwards."   Of course it was the apparent experience that generated the association.   But if there had been no more in the matter than an intellectual conviction, the conviction would have given way as soon as any one made the remark that the experience was confined to a region in which the direction of *down* coincided with direction towards the earth.   It is because our intellectual convictions generate temporarily inseparable associations, that they give way so slowly before evidence.

have commonly assigned to it, of an ultimate belief,
and attempts to identify it with another and more
general law of thought. This limited function is the
only one which, it seems to me, is reserved for science
in Sir W. Hamilton's mode of studying the primary
facts of consciousness. In the mode he practises of
ascertaining them to be facts of consciousness, there is
nothing for science to do. For, to call them so because
in his opinion he himself, and those who agree with him,
cannot get rid of the belief in them, does not seem
exactly a scientific process.* It is, however, characteristic
of what I have called the introspective, in contradistinction to the psychological, method of metaphysical
inquiry. The difference between these methods will
now be exemplified by showing them at work on a
particular question, the most fundamental one in philosophy, the distinction between the Ego and the Non-ego.

We shall first examine what Sir W. Hamilton has
done by his method, and shall afterwards attempt to
exemplify the use which can be made of the other.

* The "Inquirer" (p. 54) thinks that Sir W. Hamilton demanded, as
evidence that a supposed fact of consciousness is not acquired, but original, not only that it should not be reducible to a generalisation from
experience, but that it should lie "at the root of all experience ;" which
the "Inquirer" understands to mean "that no experience is possible unless
this belief, this mode of thought, is already present with us." If Sir W.
Hamilton meant this, he took no pains to show that he meant it. The
authority quoted is a passing expression (Lectures, i. 270) : "Whenever
"in an analysis of the intellectual phenomenon, we arrive at an element
"which we cannot reduce to a generalisation from experience, *but which*
"*lies at the root of all experience,* and which we cannot, therefore, resolve
"into any higher principle, this we properly call a fact of consciousness."
The idea of the words in italics is no further developed ; it is omitted from
the definition in the next page, "A fact of consciousness is thus, that
"whose existence is given and guaranteed by an original and necessary
"belief" (unless the idea is supposed to be implied in the word "original") ;
and Sir W. Hamilton never, as far as I am aware, recurs to it in his
attempts to prove the originality of a belief. This is the more remarkable,
because Kant makes a continual and obtrusive use of this criterion ; we
are always hearing from him that this or that mental element cannot be
the product of experience, because its pre-existence is required to render
experience possible ; which goes far to show that Sir W. Hamilton's
abstinence was intentional, and grounded on a sense of the extreme
difficulty of proving, in any of the disputed cases, what Kant so confidently
affirms. It is not unusual with Sir W. Hamilton to adopt, from other
philosophers, single expressions of which the full meaning forms no part
of his own mode of thought.

CHAPTER X.

SIR WILLIAM HAMILTON'S VIEW OF THE DIFFERENT THEORIES
RESPECTING THE BELIEF IN AN EXTERNAL WORLD.

SIR W. HAMILTON brings a very serious charge against
the great majority of philosophers. He accuses them of
playing fast and loose with the testimony of consciousness; rejecting it when it is inconvenient, but appealing
to it as conclusive when they have need of it to establish
any of their opinions. "No* philosopher has ever
"openly thrown off allegiance to the authority of con-
"sciousness." No one denies "that † as all philosophy
"is evolved from consciousness, so on the truth of con-
"sciousness, the possibility of all philosophy is depen-
"dent." But if any testimony of consciousness be supposed false, "the ‡ truth of no other fact of consciousness
"can be maintained. The legal brocard, *Falsus in uno,*
"*falsus in omnibus,* is a rule not more applicable to other
"witnesses than to consciousness. Thus every system
"of philosophy which implies the negation of any fact
"of consciousness is not only necessarily unable, without
"self-contradiction, to establish its own truth by any
"appeal to consciousness; it is also unable, without self-
"contradiction, to appeal to consciousness against the
"falsehood of any other system. If the absolute and
"universal veracity of consciousness be once surrendered,
"every system is equally true, or rather all are equally
"false; philosophy is impossible, for it has now no in-
"strument by which truth can be discovered, no standard
"by which it can be tried; the root of our nature is a
"lie. But though it is thus manifestly the common
"interest of every scheme of philosophy to preserve

---

* Lectures, i. 377.　　† Ibid p. 285.　　‡ Ibid. p. 283.

"intact the integrity of consciousness, almost every
"scheme of philosophy is only another mode in which
"this integrity has been violated.   If, therefore, I am
"able to prove the fact of this various violation, and to
"show that the facts of consciousness have never, or
"hardly ever, been fairly evolved, it will follow, as I
"said, that no reproach can be justly addressed to con-
"sciousness as an ill-informed, or vacillating, or perfi-
"dious witness, but to those only who were too proud
"or too negligent to accept its testimony, to employ its
"materials, and obey its laws."   That nearly all philosophers have merited this imputation, our author endeavours to show by a classified enumeration of the various
theories which they have maintained respecting the perception of material objects.   No instance can be better
suited for trying the dispute.   The question of an external world is the great battle-ground of metaphysics,
not so much from its importance in itself, as because
while it relates to the most familiar of all our mental
acts, it forcibly illustrates the characteristic differences
between the two metaphysical methods.

"We are immediately conscious in perception," says
Sir W. Hamilton,* "of an ego and a non-ego, known
"together, and known in contrast to each other.   This
"is the fact of the Duality of Consciousness.   It is clear
"and manifest.   When I concentrate my attention in the
"simplest act of perception, I return from my observa-
"tion with the most irresistible conviction of two facts,
"or rather two branches of the same fact; that I am,
"and that something different from me exists.   In this
"act I am conscious of myself as the perceiving subject,
"and of an external reality as the object perceived; and
"I am conscious of both existences in the same indi-
"visible moment of intuition.   The knowledge of the
"subject does not precede, nor follow, the knowledge of
"the object ; neither determines, neither is determined
"by the other.   Such is the fact of perception revealed
"in consciousness, and as it determines mankind in

* Lectures, i. 288–295.

" general in their almost equal assurance of the reality of
" an external world, as of the existence of our own minds.

" We may, therefore, lay it down as an undisputed
" truth, that consciousness gives, as an ultimate fact, a
" primitive quality ; a knowledge of the ego in relation
" and contrast to the non-ego ; and a knowledge of the
" non-ego in relation and contrast to the ego.   The ego
" and non-ego are thus given in an original synthesis, as
" conjoined in the unity of knowledge, and in an original
" antithesis, as opposed in the contrariety of existence.
" In other words, we are conscious of them in an indi-
" visible act of knowledge together and at once, but we
" are conscious of them, as, in themselves, different and
" exclusive of each other.

" Again, consciousness not only gives us a duality, but
" it gives its elements in equal counterpoise and inde-
" pendence.   The ego and non-ego—mind and matter—
" are not only given together, but in absolute co-equality.
" The one does not precede, the other does not follow ;
" and in their mutual relation, each is equally dependent,
" equally independent.   Such is the fact as given in and
" by consciousness."   Or rather (he should have said)
such is the answer we receive, when we examine and
interrogate our *present* consciousness.   To assert more
than this, merely on this evidence, is to beg the question instead of solving it.

" Philosophers have not, however, been content to
" accept the fact in its integrity, but have been pleased
" to accept it only under such qualifications as it suited
" their systems to devise.   In truth, there are just as
" many different philosophical systems originating in this
" fact, as it admits of various possible modifications.   An
" enumeration of these modifications, accordingly, affords
" an enumeration of philosophical theories.

" In the first place, there is the grand division of
" philosophers into those who do, and those who do not,
" accept the fact in its integrity.   Of modern philosophers,
" almost all are comprehended under the latter category,
" while of the former, if we do not remount to the

" schoolmen and the ancients, I am only aware of a single
" philosopher before Reid, who did not reject, at least in
" part, the fact as consciousness affords it.

" As it is always expedient to possess a precise name
" for a precise distinction, I would be inclined to de-
" nominate those who implicitly acquiesce in the primi-
" tive duality as given in consciousness, the Natural
" Realists, or Natural Dualists, and their doctrine,
" Natural Realism or Natural Dualism." This is, of
course, the author's own doctrine.

" In the second place, the philosophers who do not
" accept the fact, and the whole fact, may be divided and
" subdivided into various classes by various principles of
" distribution.

" The first subdivision will be taken from the total, or
" partial, rejection of the import of the fact. I have
" previously shown that to deny any fact of conscious-
" ness as an actual phenomenon is utterly impossible."
(But it is very far from impossible to believe that something which we now confound with consciousness, may
have been altogether foreign to consciousness when this
was unmingled with acquired impressions.) " But
" though necessarily admitted as a present phenomenon,
" the import of this phenomenon—all beyond our actual
" consciousness of its existence—may be denied. We
" are able, without self-contradiction, to suppose, and
" consequently to assert, that all to which the pheno-
" menon of which we are conscious refers, is a decep-
" tion ;" (say rather, an unwarranted inference ;) that
" for example, the past, to which an act of memory
" refers, is only an illusion involved in our consciousness
" of the present—that the unknown subject to which
" every phenomenon of which we are conscious involves
" a reference, has no reality beyond this reference itself,
" —in short, that all our knowledge of mind or matter
" is only a consciousness of various bundles of baseless
" appearances. This doctrine, as refusing a substantial
" reality to the phenomenal existence of which we are
" conscious, is called Nihilism; and consequently, philo-

" sophers, as they affirm or deny the authority of con-
" sciousness in guaranteeing a substratum or substance
" to the manifestation of the ego and non-ego, are
" divided into Realists or Substantialists, and into
" Nihilists or Non-Substantialists.   Of positive or
" dogmatic Nihilism there is no example in modern
" philosophy. . . . But as a sceptical conclusion from
" the premises of previous philosophers, we have an
" illustrious example of Nihilism in Hume ; and the
" celebrated Fichte admits that the speculative prin-
" ciples of his own idealism would, unless corrected by
" his practical, terminate in this result."

The Realists, or Substantialists, those who do believe
in a substratum, but reject the testimony of consciousness
to an *immediate* cognisance of an Ego and a Non-ego,
our author divides into two classes, according as they
admit the real existence of two substrata, or only of one.
These last, whom he denominates Unitarians or Monists,
either acknowledge the ego alone, or the non-ego alone,
or regard the two as identical.   Those who admit the
ego alone, looking upon the non-ego as a product
evolved from it (*i.e.* as something purely mental) are
the Idealists.   Those who admit the non-ego alone, and
regard the ego as evolved from it (*i.e.* as purely material)
are the Materialists.   The third class acknowledge the
equipoise of the two, but deny their antithesis, maintaining " that mind and matter are only phenomenal
" modifications of the same common substance.   This is
" the doctrine of Absolute Identity, a doctrine of which
" the most illustrious representatives among recent
" philosophers are Schelling, Hegel, and Cousin." *

There remain those who admit the coequal reality of
the Ego and the Non-ego, of mind and matter, and also
their distinctness from one another, but deny that they
are known immediately.   These are Dualists, " but are †
" distinguished from the Natural Dualists of whom we
" formerly spoke, in this—that the latter establish the
" existence of the two worlds of mind and matter on the

* Lectures, i. 296–297.   † Ibid. 295–296.

"immediate knowledge we possess of both series of
"phenomena—a knowledge of which consciousness
"assures us; whereas the former, surrendering the
"veracity of consciousness to our immediate knowledge
"of material phenomena, and consequently, our imme-
"diate knowledge of the existence of matter, still en-
"deavour, by various hypotheses and reasonings, to
"maintain the existence of an unknown external world.
"As we denominate those who maintain a Dualism as
"involved in the fact of consciousness, Natural Dualists;
"so we may style those dualists who deny the evidence
"of consciousness to our immediate knowledge of aught
"beyond the sphere of mind, Hypothetical Dualists, or
"Cosmothetic Idealists.

"To the class of Cosmothetic Idealists, the great
"majority of modern philosophers are to be referred.
"Denying an immediate or intuitive knowledge of the
"external reality, whose existence they maintain, they,
"of course, hold a doctrine of mediate or representative
"perception; and, according to the various modifications
"of that doctrine, they are again subdivided into those
"who view, in the immediate object of perception, a
"representative entity present to the mind, but not a
"mere mental modification, and into those who hold
"that the immediate object is only a representative
"modification of the mind itself.   It is not always easy
"to determine to which of these classes some philoso-
"phers belong.   To the former, or class holding the
"cruder hypothesis of representation, certainly belong
"the followers of Democritus and Epicurus, those Aris-
"totelians who held the vulgar doctrine of species
"(Aristotle himself was probably a natural dualist), and
"in recent times, among many others, Malebranche,
"Berkeley, Clarke, Newton, Abraham Tucker, &c.   To
"these is also, but problematically, to be referred, Locke.
"To the second, or class holding the finer hypothesis
"of representation, belong, without any doubt, many
"of the Platonists, Leibnitz, Arnauld, Crousaz, Con-
"dillac, Kant, &c., and to this class is also probably to

"be referred Descartes."   In our own country the best known and typical specimen of this mode of thinking, is Brown; and it is upon him that our author discharges most of the shafts which this class of thinkers, as being the least distant from him of all his opponents, copiously receive from him." *

With regard to the various opinions thus enumerated, I shall first make a remark of general application, and shall then advert particularly to the objects of Sir W. Hamilton's more especial animadversion, the Cosmothetic Idealists.

Concerning all these classes of thinkers, except the Natural Realists, Sir W. Hamilton's statement is, that they deny some part of the testimony of consciousness, and by so doing invalidate the appeals which they nevertheless make to consciousness, as a voucher for

---

* In one of the Dissertations on Reid (Dissertation C.) Sir W. Hamilton gives a much more elaborate, and more minutely discriminated enumeration and classification of the opinions which have been or might be held respecting our knowledge of mind and of matter. But the one which I have quoted from the Lectures is more easily followed, and sufficient for all the purposes for which I have occasion to advert to it. I shall only cite from the latter exposition a single passage (p. 817) which exhibits in a strong light the sentiments of our author towards philosophers of the school of Brown.

"Natural Realism and Absolute Idealism are the only systems worthy "of a philosopher; for, as they alone have any foundation in conscious-"ness, so they alone have any consistency in themselves. . . . Both build "upon the same fundamental fact, that the extended object immediately "perceived is identical with the extended object actually existing;—for "the truth of this fact, both can appeal to the common sense of mankind; "and to the common sense of mankind Berkeley did appeal not less con-"fidently, and perhaps more logically than Reid. . . . The scheme of "Hypothetical Realism or Cosmothetic Idealism, which supposes that "behind the non-existent world perceived, lurks a correspondent but un-"known world existing, is not only repugnant to our natural beliefs, but "in manifold contradiction with itself. The scheme of Natural Realism "may be ultimately difficult—for, like all other truths, it ends in the "inconceivable, but Hypothetical Realism—in its origin—in its develop-"ment—in its result, although the favourite scheme of philosophers, is "philosophically absurd."

Sir W. Hamilton may in general be depended on for giving a perfectly fair statement of the opinion of adversaries; but in this case his almost passionate contempt for the later forms of Cosmothetic Idealism has misled him. No Cosmothetic Idealist would accept as a fair statement of his opinion, the monstrous proposition that a "non-existent world" is "perceived."

N

their own doctrines.   If he had said that they all run
counter, in some particular, to the general sentiment of
mankind—that they all deny some common opinion,
some natural belief (meaning by natural, not one
which rests on a necessity of our nature, but merely
one which, in common with innumerable varieties of
false opinion, mankind having a strong tendency to
adopt) ; had he said only this, no one could have contested its truth ; but it would not have been a *reductio
ad absurdum* of his opponents.   For all philosophers,
Sir W. Hamilton as much as the rest, deny some
common opinions, which others might call natural
beliefs, but which those who deny them consider, and
have a right to consider, as natural prejudices; held,
nevertheless, by the generality of mankind in the persuasion of their being self-evident, or, in other words,
intuitive, and deliverances of consciousness.   Some of
the points on which Sir W. Hamilton is at issue with
natural beliefs, relate to the very subject in hand—the
perception of external things.   We have found him
maintaining that we do not see the sun ; but an image
of it, and that no two persons see the same sun ; in contradiction to as clear a case as could be given of natural
belief.   And we shall find him affirming, in opposition
to an equally strong natural belief, that we immediately
perceive extension only in our own organs, and not in
the objects we see or touch.   Beliefs, therefore, which
seem among the most natural that can be entertained,
are sometimes, in his opinion, delusive ; and he has told
us that to discriminate which these are, is not within
the competence of everybody, but only of philosophers.
He would say, of course, that the beliefs which he rejects
were not in our consciousness originally.   And nearly
all his opponents say the same thing of those which *they*
reject.   Those, indeed, who, like Kant, believe that
there are elements present, even at the first moment of
internal consciousness, which do not exist in the object,
but are derived from the mind's own laws, are fairly
open to Sir W. Hamilton's criticism.   It is not my

business to justify, in point of consistency, any more than of conclusiveness, the reasoning, by which Kant, after getting rid of the outward reality of all the attributes of Body, persuades himself that he demonstrates the externality of Body itself.*   But, as regards all existing schools of thought not descended from Kant, Sir W. Hamilton's accusation is without ground.

There is something more to be said respecting the mixed multitude of metaphysicians whom our author groups together under the title of Cosmothetic Idealists, and whose mode of thought he judges more harshly than that of any other school.   He represents them as holding the doctrine that we perceive external objects, not by an immediate, but by a mediate or representative perception.   And he recognises three divisions of them,† according to three different forms in which this hypothesis may be entertained.   The supposed representative object may be regarded, first, as not a state of mind, but something else ; either external to the mind, like the *species sensibiles* of some of the ancients, and the " motions of the brain " of some of the early moderns ; or in the mind, like the Ideas of Berkeley.   Secondly, it may be regarded as a state of mind, but a state different from the mind's act in perceiving or being conscious of it : of this kind, perhaps, are the Ideas of Locke. Or, thirdly, as a state of mind, identical with the act by which we are said to perceive it.   This last is the form in which, as Sir W. Hamilton truly says,‡ the doctrine was held by Brown.

Now, the first two of these three opinions may fairly be called what our author calls them—theories of mediate or representative perception.   The object which, in

---

* In the *Lehrsatz* of the 21st Supplement to the Kritik der Reinen Vernunft ; the Lemma at p. 184 of Mr. Heywood's Translation. See also, in Heywood, the note at p. xxxix. of the Second Preface ; being Supplement II. in Rosenkranz and Schubert's edition of the collected works, vol. ii. p. 684. This reasoning of Kant, to my mind, strangely sophistical, nevertheless does not place the externality of Bodies out of the mind. It is "externality in Space," and Space, in his philosophy, does not exist out of the mind.

† Discussions, p. 57.   ‡ Ibid. p. 58.

these theories, the mind is supposed directly to perceive, is a *tertium quid*, which by the one theory is, and by the other is not, a state or modification of mind, but in both is distinct equally from the act of perception, and from the external object : and the mind is cognisant of the external object vicariously, through this third thing, of which alone it has immediate cognisance—of which alone, therefore, it is, in Sir W. Hamilton's sense of the word, conscious. Against both these theories Reid, Stewart, and our author, are completely triumphant, and I am in no way interested in pressing for a rehearing of the cause.

But the third opinion, which is Brown's, cannot with any justness of thought or propriety of language be called a theory of mediate or representative perception. Had Sir W. Hamilton taken half the pains to under-stand Brown which he took to understand far inferior thinkers, he never would have described Brown's doc-trine in terms so inappropriate.

Representative knowledge is always understood by our author to be knowledge of a thing by means of an image of it ; by means of something which is *like* the thing itself. "Representative knowledge," he says, " is " only deserving of the name of knowledge in so far as " it is comformable with the intuitions which it repre-" sents." * The representation must stand in a rela-tion to what it represents, like that of a picture to its original : as the representation in memory of a past impression of sense, does to that past impression ; as a representation in imagination does to a supposed pos-sible presentation of sense ; and as the Ideas of the earlier Cosmothetic Idealists were supposed to do to the out-ward objects of which they were the image or impress. But the Mental Modifications of Brown and those who think with him, are not supposed to bear any resem-blance to the objects which excite them. These ob-jects are supposed to be unknown to us, except as the causes of the mental modifications. The only relation

* Dissertations on Reid, p. 811.

between the two is that of cause and effect. Brown being free from the vulgar error that a cause must be like its effect, and admitting no knowledge of the cause (beyond its bare existence) except the effect itself, naturally found nothing in it which it was possible to compare with the effect, or in virtue of which any resemblance could be affirmed to exist between the two. In another place, * Sir W. Hamilton makes an ostensible distinction between the fact of *resembling* and that of *truly representing* the objects; but defines the last expression to mean, affording us " such a know- " ledge of their nature as we should have were an im- " mediate intuition of the reality in itself competent to " man." No one who is at all acquainted with Brown's opinions will pretend him to have maintained that we have anything of this sort. He did not believe that the mental modification afforded us any knowledge whatever of the nature of the external object. There is no need to quote passages in proof of this; it is a fact patent to whoever reads his Lectures. It is the more strange that Sir W. Hamilton should have failed to recognise this opinion of Brown, because it is exactly the opinion which he himself holds respecting our knowledge of objects in respect of their Secondary Qualities. These, he says, are "in their own nature occult and inconceivable," and are known only in their effects on us, that is, by the mental modifications which they produce.†

Further, Brown's is not only not a theory of *representative* perception, but it is not even a theory of *mediate* perception. He assumes no *tertium quid*, no object of thought intermediate between the mind and the outward object. He recognises only the perceptive act; which with him means, and is always declared to mean, the mind itself perceiving. It will hardly be pretended that the mind itself is the " representative object" interposed by him between itself and the outward thing

* Dissertations on Reid, p. 842.
† Dissertations on Reid, p. 846 : and the fuller explanation at pp. 854 and 857.

which is acting upon it; and if it is not, there certainly
is no other.   But if Brown's theory is not a theory of
mediate perception, it loses all that essentially distinguishes it from Sir W. Hamilton's own doctrine.   For
Brown also thinks that we have, on the occasion of
certain sensations, an instantaneous and irresistible conviction of an outward object.   And if this conviction is
immediate and necessitated by the constitution of our
nature, in what does it differ from our author's direct
consciousness?   Consciousness, immediate knowledge,
and intuitive knowledge, are, Sir W. Hamilton tells us,
convertible expressions; and if it be granted that whenever our senses are affected by a material object, we
immediately and intuitively recognise that object as
existing and distinct from us, it requires a great deal of
ingenuity to make out any substantial difference between
this immediate intuition of an external world, and Sir
W. Hamilton's direct perception of it.

The distinction which our author makes, resolves
itself, as explained by him, into the difference of which
he has said so much, but of which he seemed to have so
confused an idea, between Belief and Knowledge.   In
Brown's opinion, and I will add, in Reid's, the mental
modification which we experience from the presence of
an object, raises in us an irresistible *belief* that the
object exists.   No, says Sir W. Hamilton: it is not a
belief, but a *knowledge :* we have indeed a belief, and our
knowledge is certified by the belief; but this belief of
ours regarding the object is a belief that we *know* it.
"In perception, * consciousness gives, as an ultimate
"fact, *a belief of the knowledge of the existence of some-*
"*thing different from self.*   As ultimate, this belief cannot
"be reduced to a higher principle; neither can it be
"truly analysed into a double element.   We only believe
"that this something *exists* because we believe that we
"*know* (are conscious of) this something as existing;
"the belief of the existence is necessarily involved in the
"belief of the knowledge of the existence.   Both are

* Discussions, p. 89.

"original, or neither.   Does consciousness deceive us in
"the latter, it necessarily deludes us in the former; and
"if the former, *though* a fact of consciousness, is false,
"the latter, *because* a fact of consciousness, is not true.
"The beliefs contained in the two propositions,
     "1°. I believe that a material world exists;
     "2°. I believe that I immediately know a material
          "world existing (in other words, I believe that
          "the external reality itself is the object of which
          "I am conscious in perception),
"though distinguished by philosophers, are thus vir-
"tually identical.   The belief of an external world was
"too powerful, not to compel an acquiescence in its truth.
"But the philosophers yielded to nature, only in so far
"as to coincide in the dominant result.   They falsely
"discriminated the belief in the existence, from the belief
"in the knowledge.   With a few exceptions, they held
"fast by the truth of the first; but they concurred, with
"singular unanimity, in abjuring the second."
     Accordingly, Brown is rebuked because, while reject-
ing our natural belief that we *know* the external object,
he yet accepts our natural belief that it *exists* as a sufficient warrant for its existence.   But what real distinction
is there between Brown's intuitive belief of the existence
of the object, and Sir W. Hamilton's intuitive knowledge
of it? Just three pages previous,* Sir W. Hamilton had
said, "Our knowledge rests ultimately on certain facts of
"consciousness, which as primitive, and consequently
"incomprehensible, are given less in the form of cogni-
"tions than of beliefs."   The consciousness of an external world is, on his own showing, primitive and
incomprehensible; it therefore is less a cognition than
a belief.   But if we do not so much know as believe an
external world, what is meant by saying that we believe
that we know it? Either we do not know, but only
believe it, and if so, Brown and the other philosophers
assailed were right; or knowledge and belief, in the case
of ultimate facts, are identical, and then, believing that

* Discussions, p. 86.

we know is only believing that we believe, which according to our author's and to all rational principles, is but another word for simple believing.

It would not be fair, however, to hold our author to his own confused use of the terms Belief and Knowledge. He never succeeds in making anything like an intelligible distinction between these two notions considered generally, but in particular cases we may be able to find something which he is attempting to express by them. In the present case his meaning seems to be, that Brown's Belief in an external object, though instantaneous and irresistible, was supposed to be *suggested* to the mind by its own sensation ; which suggestion Brown regarded as a case of a more general law, whereby every fact suggests the intuitive belief of a cause or antecedent with which it is invariably connected : while Sir W. Hamilton's Knowledge of the object is supposed to arise along with the sensation, and to be co-ordinate with it.   And this is what Sir W. Hamilton means by calling Brown's a mediate, his own an immediate cognition of the object : the real difference being that on Sir W. Hamilton's theory, the cognition of the ego or of its modification, and that of the non-ego, are simultaneous, while on Brown's the one immediately precedes the other.   Our author expresses this meaning, though much less clearly, when he declares * Brown's theory to be "that in perception, the external reality is not the " immediate object of consciousness, but that the ego is " only determined in some unknown manner to represent " the non-ego, which representation, though only a modi- " fication of mind or self, we are compelled by an illusion " of our nature to mistake for a modification of matter, " or non-self."   This being our author's conception of the doctrine which he has to refute, let us see in what manner he proceeds to refute it.

"You will remark," he says,† "that Brown (and " Brown only speaks the language of all the philosophers " who do not allow the mind a consciousness of aught

* Lectures, ii. 86.   † Ibid. ii. 106.

" beyond its own states,) misstates the phenomenon
" when he asserts that, in perception, there is a reference
" from the internal to the external, from the known to
" the unknown.   That this is not the fact, our observa-
" tion of the phenomenon will at once convince you.
" In an act of perception, I am conscious of something
" as self and of something as not self : this is the simple
" fact.   The philosophers, on the contrary, who will not
" accept this fact, misstate it.   They say that we are
" conscious of nothing but a certain modification of
" mind ; but this modification involves a reference to,—
" in other words, a representation of,—something external
" as its object.   Now this is untrue.   We are conscious
" of no reference, of no representation : we believe that
" the object of which we are conscious is the object which
" exists."   To this argument (of the worth of which
something has been said already) I shall return presently.
But he subjoins a second.

" Nor could there possibly be such reference or repre-
" sentation ; for reference or representation supposes a
" knowledge already possessed of the object referred to
" or represented ; but perception is the faculty by which
" our first knowledge is acquired, and therefore cannot
" suppose a previous knowledge as its condition."   And
further on :* " Mark the vice of the procedure.   We can
" only, 1°, assert the existence of an external world in-
" asmuch as we know it to exist ; and we can only, 2°,
" assert that one thing is representative of another, inas-
" much as the thing represented is known, independently
" of the representation.   But how does the hypothesis
" of a representative perception proceed ?   It actually
" converts the fact into an hypothesis : actually converts
" the hypothesis into a fact.   On this theory, we do not
" know the existence of an external world, except on the
" supposition that that which we do know truly repre-
" sents it as existing.   The hypothetical realist cannot,
" therefore, establish the fact of the external world,
" except upon the fact of its representation.   This is

* Lectures, ii. 138, 139.

" manifest.   We have, therefore, next to ask him, how
" he knows the fact that the external world is actually
" represented.   A representation supposes something
" represented, and the representation of the external
" world supposes the existence of that world.   Now the
" hypothetical realist, when asked how he proves the
" reality of the outer world, which, *ex hypothesi*, he does
" not know, can only say that he infers its existence from
" the fact of its representation.   But the fact of the re-
" presentation of an external world supposes the exis-
" tence of that world ; therefore he is again at the
" point from which he started.   He has been arguing
" in a circle."

Let me first remark that this reasoning assumes the
whole point in dispute ; it presupposes that the supposition which it is brought to disprove is impossible.   The
theory of the third form of Cosmothetic Idealism is, that
though we are conscious only of the sensations which
an object gives us, we are determined by a necessity of
our nature, which some call an instinct, others an intuition, others a fundamental law of belief, to ascribe these
sensations to something external, as their substratum, or
as their cause.   There is surely nothing *à priori* impossible in this supposition.   The supposed instinct or intuition seems to be of the same family with many other
Laws of Thought, or Natural Beliefs, which our author
not only admits without scruple, but enjoins obedience to,
under the usual sanction, that otherwise our intelligence
must be a lie.   In the present case, however, he, without
the smallest warrant, excludes this from the list of possible hypotheses.   He says that we cannot infer a reality
from a mental representation, unless we already know
the reality independently of the mental representation.
Now he could hardly help being aware that this is the
very matter in dispute.   Those who hold the opinion he
argues against, do not admit the premise upon which he
argues.   They say that we may be, and are, necessitated
to infer a cause, of which we know nothing whatever
except its effect.   And why not?   Sir W. Hamilton

thinks us entitled to infer a substance from attributes, though he allows that we know nothing of the substance except its attributes.

But this is not the worst, and there are few specimens of our author in which his deficiencies as a philosopher stand out in a stronger light. As Burke in politics, so Sir W. Hamilton in metaphysics, was too often a polemic rather than a connected thinker: the generalisations of both, often extremely valuable, seem less the matured convictions of a scientific mind, than weapons snatched up for the service of a particular' quarrel. If Sir W. Hamilton can only seize upon something which will strike a hard blow at an opponent, he seldom troubles himself how much of his own edifice may be knocked down by the shock. Had he examined the argument he here uses, sufficiently to determine whether he could stand by it as a deliberate opinion, he would have perceived that it committed him to the doctrine that there is no such thing as representative knowledge. But it is one of Sir W. Hamilton's most positive tenets that there *is* representative knowledge, and that Memory, among other things, is an example of it. Let us turn back to his discussion of that subject, and see what he, at that time, considered representative knowledge to be.

"Every act,* and consequently every act of know-
"ledge, exists only as it now exists; and as it exists
"only in the Now, it can be cognisant only of a now-
"existent object. But the object known in memory is,
"*ex hypothesi,* past; consequently, we are reduced to
"the dilemma, either of refusing a past object to be
"known in memory at all, or of admitting it to be only
"mediately known, in and through a present object.
"That the latter alternative is the true one, it will
"require a very few explanatory words to convince you.
"What are the contents of an act of memory? An act
"of memory is merely *a present state of mind which we*
"*are conscious of not as absolute, but as relative to, and*
"*representing, another state of mind, and accompanied*

* Lectures, i. 219, 220.

" *with the belief that the state of mind, as now represented,*
" *has actually been.* I remember an event I saw—the
" landing of George IV. at Leith. This remembrance is
" only *a consciousness of certain imaginations, involving*
" *the conviction that these imaginations now represent*
" *ideally what I formerly really experienced.* All that is
" immediately known in the act of memory, is the present
" mental modification, that is, the representation and
" concomitant belief. Beyond this mental modification
" we know nothing; and this mental modification is not
" only known to consciousness, but only exists in and
" by consciousness. *Of any past object, real or ideal, the*
" *mind knows and can know nothing,* for, *ex hypothesi,* no
" such object now exists; or if it be said to know such
" an object, it can only be said to know it mediately, *as*
" *represented in the present mental modification.* Properly
" speaking, however, we know only the actual and pre-
" sent, and all real knowledge is an immediate know-
" ledge. What is said to be mediately known, is, in
" truth not known to be, but only believed to be: for
" its existence is *only an inference resting on the belief,*
" *that the mental modification truly represents what is*
" *in itself beyond the sphere of knowledge.*"

Had Sir W. Hamilton totally forgotten all this, when
a few lectures afterwards, having then in front of him
a set of antagonists who needed the theory here laid
down, he repudiated it—denying altogether the possibility of the mental state so truly and clearly expressed
in this passage, and affirming that we cannot possibly
recognise a mental modification to be representative of
something else, unless we have a present knowledge of
that something else, otherwise obtained? With merely
the alteration of putting instead of a past state of mind,
a present external object, the Cosmothetic Idealists
might borrow his language down to the minutest detail.
They, too, believe that the mental modification is a present state of mind, which we are conscious of, not as
absolute, but as relative to, and representing, "an ex-
" ternal object, and accompanied with the belief that

"the object as now represented, actually" is : that we know something (viz. matter) only "as represented in "the present mental modification," and that "its exis- "tence is only an inference, resting on the belief that " the mental modification truly represents what is in "itself beyond the sphere of knowledge."   They do not, strictly speaking, require quite so much as this : for the word " represents," especially with " truly " joined to it, suggests the idea of a resemblance, such as does, in reality, exist between the picture of a fact in memory and the present impression to which it corresponds; but the Cosmothetic Idealists only maintain that the mental modification arises from *something*, and that the reality of this unknown something is testified by a natural belief.   That they apply to one case the same theory which our author applies to another, does not, of course, prove them to be right ; but it proves the suicidal character (to use one of his favourite expressions) of our author's argument, when he scouts the supposition of an instinctive inference from a known effect to an un- known cause, as an hypothesis which can in no possible case be legitimate ; forgetful that its legitimacy is re- quired by his own psychology, one of the leading doc- trines of which is entirely grounded on it.

It is not only in treating of Memory, that Sir W. Hamilton requires a process of thought precisely similar to that which, when employed by opponents, he declares to be radically illegitimate.   I have already mentioned that in his opinion our perceptions of sight are not per- ceptions of the outward object, but of its image, a " modi- "fication of light in immediate relation to our organ of " vision " and that no two persons see the same sun ; pro- positions in direct conflict with the " natural beliefs " to which he so often refers, and to which Reid, not without reason, appeals in this instance ; for assuredly people in general are as firmly convinced that what they see is the real sun, as that what they touch is the real table.   Let us hear Sir W. Hamilton once more on the subject.   " It is *

* Lectures, ii. 153, 154.

" not by perception, but by a process of reasoning, that
" we connect the objects of sense with existences beyond
" the sphere of immediate knowledge. It is enough that
" perception affords us the knowledge of the non-ego
" at the point of sense. To arrogate to it the power of
" immediately informing us of external things, *which are*
" *only the causes of the object we immediately perceive, is*
" either positively erroneous, or a confusion of language
" arising from an inadequate discrimination of the pheno-
" menon."   Here is a case in which we know something
to be a representation, though, in our author's opinion,
that which it represents not only is not, at the present
time, known to us, but never was, and never will be so.
The Cosmothetic Idealists desire only the same liberty
which Sir W. Hamilton here exercises, of concluding from
a phenomenon directly known, to something unknown
which is the cause of the phenomenon.   They postulate
the possibility that what our author holds to be true of
the non-ego at a distance, may be true of the non-ego at
the point of sense, namely, that it is not known immediately, but as a necessary inference from what is known.
To shut the door upon this supposition as inherently
inadmissible, and make an exactly similar one ourselves
as often as our system requires it, does not befit a philosopher, or a critic of philosophers.*

* Some of the inconsistencies here pointed out in Sir W. Hamilton's
speculations respecting Perception have been noticed, and ably discussed
by Mr. Bailey, in the fourth letter of the Second Series of his Letters on
the Philosophy of the Human Mind.
    In treating of Modified Logic (Lectures, iv. 67, 68), Sir W. Hamilton
justifies, after his own manner, the assumption made alike by himself and
by the Cosmothetic Idealists ; and the grounds of justification are as available to them as to him. " Real truth is the correspondence of our thoughts
" with the existences which constitute their objects. But here a difficulty
" arises : how can we know that there is, that there can be such a corre-
" spondence ?   All that we know of the objects is through the presenta-
" tions of our faculties ; but whether these present the objects as they are
" in themselves, we can never ascertain, for to do this it would be requisite
" to go out of ourselves,—out of our faculties,—to obtain a knowledge of
" the objects by other faculties, and thus to compare our old presentations
" with our new."   The very difficulty which we have seen him throwing
in the teeth of the Cosmothetic Idealists. " But all this, even were the
" supposition possible, would be incompetent to afford us the certainty
" required.   For were it possible to leave our old, and to obtain a new, set

In the controversy with Brown, which forms the second paper in the "Discussions," and much of which is reproduced verbatim in our author's Lectures, the argument which I have now examined does not appear. In the room of it, we have the following argument.* If Brown is right, " the mind either *knows* the reality of what it "represents, or it does not." The first supposition is dismissed for the absurdities it involves, and because it is inconsistent with Brown's doctrine. But if the mind does not know the reality of what it represents, the " alternative remains, that the mind is *blindly* determined " to *represent*, and *truly* to represent, the reality which it " does not know." And if so, the mind "either blindly " determines itself " or " is blindly determined " by a supernatural power. The latter supposition he rejects because it involves a standing miracle; the former as " utterly irrational, inasmuch as it would explain an

---

"of faculties, by which to test the old, still the veracity of these new "faculties would be equally obnoxious to doubt as the veracity of the old. "For what guarantee could we obtain for the credibility in the one case, "which we do not already possess in the other? The new faculties could "only assert their own truth ; but this is done by the old ; and it is impos- "sible to imagine any presentations of the non-ego by any finite intelli- "gence to which a doubt might not be raised, whether these presentations "were not merely subjective modifications of the conscious ego itself." It is a very laudable practice in philosophising to state the difficulties strongly. But when the difficulty is one which in any case has to be surmounted, we should allow others to surmount it in the same mode which we adopt for ourselves. This mode, in the present case, is our author's usual one : "All that could be said in answer to such a doubt is that if "such were true, our whole nature is a lie :" in other words, our nature prompts us to believe that the modification of the conscious ego points to, and results from, a non-ego with corresponding properties. The Cosmothetic Idealists do but say the same thing : and they have as good a right to say it as our author.

In saying that the Cosmothetic Idealists can make out as good a case for their opinion as Sir W. Hamilton for his, I do not say that their case is good against Berkeley, who held that the non-ego we are compelled to postulate as the cause of our sensations is not matter, but a mind. Minds, Berkeley would say, we know to exist, in ourselves by consciousness, in other beings by evidence. Matter we do not know to exist, for all the indications of it are otherwise explicable : we ought not, therefore, to assume its existence until it is shown that our sensations cannot be caused by a Mind. Sir W. Hamilton escapes from this argument by his doctrine, that Matter with its Primary and Secundo-primary qualities is directly and immediately perceived.

* Discussions, p. 67.

" effect, by a cause wholly inadequate to its production.
" On this alternative, knowledge is supposed to be the
" effect of ignorance,—intelligence of stupidity—life of
" death." All this artillery is directed against the simple
supposition that by a law of our nature, a modification
of our own minds may assure us of the existence of an
unknown cause. The author's persistent ignorance of
Brown's opinion is surprising. Brown knows nothing
of the mental modification as *truly representing* the unknown reality ; he claims no knowledge as arising out of
ignorance, no intelligence growing out of stupidity. He
claims only an instinctive belief implanted by nature ;
and the menacing alternative, that the mind must either
determine itself to this belief, or be determined to it by
a special interference of Providence, could be applied
with exactly as much justice to the earth's motion. But
though Sir W. Hamilton's weapon falls harmless upon
Brown, it recoils with terrible effect upon his own
theories of representative cognition. A remembrance,
for example, does represent, and truly represent, the
past fact remembered : and we do, through that representation, mediately know the past fact, which in any
other sense of the word, according to our author, we do
not know. Although therefore the conclusion " that the
mind is blindly determined to represent, and truly to
represent, the reality which it does not know," is not
obligatory upon Brown, it is upon Sir W. Hamilton.
On his own showing he has to choose between the
absurdity that the mind " blindly determines itself,"
and the perpetual miracle of its being determined by
divine interference. This is one of the weakest exhibi-
tions of Sir W. Hamilton that I have met with in his
writings. For the difficulty by which he thought to
overwhelm Brown, and which does not touch Brown,
but falls back upon himself, is no difficulty at all, but
the merest moonshine. The transcendent absurdity, as
he considers it, that the mind should be blindly determined to represent, and truly to represent, the reality
which " it does not know," instead of an absurdity, is

the exact expression of a fact.   It is a literal description
of what takes place in an act of memory.   As often as
we recollect a past event, and on the faith of that recollection, believe or know that the event really happened,
the mind, by its constitution, is "blindly determined to
represent, and truly to represent" a fact which, except as
witnessed by that representation, "it does not know."*

It may generally, I think, be observed of Sir W.
Hamilton, that his most *recherché* arguments are his
weakest ; they certainly are so in the present case.   It
would have been wiser in him to have been contented
with his first and simpler argument, that Brown's
doctrine conflicts with consciousness, inasmuch as "we
are conscious of no reference, of no representation :"
or, to speak more clearly, we are not aware that the
existence of an eternal reality is suggested to us by

* Our belief in the veracity of Memory is evidently ultimate : no reason
can be given for it which does not presuppose the belief, and assume it to
be well grounded.   This point is forcibly urged in the Philosophical Introduction to Dr. Ward's able work, "On Nature and Grace :" a book the
readers of which are likely to be limited by its being addressed specially
to Catholics, but showing a capacity in the writer which might otherwise
have made him one of the most effective champions of the Intuitive school.
Though I do not believe morality to be intuitive in Dr. Ward's sense, I
think his book of great practical worth, by the strenuous manner in which
it maintains morality to have another foundation than the arbitrary decree
of God, and shows, by great weight of evidence, that this is the orthodox
doctrine of the Roman Catholic Church.

Dr. Ward, returning to this subject in the *Dublin Review* (p. 309), says
that in declaring our belief in the veracity of Memory to be ultimate, I am
admitting "an exception" to the doctrine of what he calls the Phenomenist school, and " an exception which no phenomenist had made before."
The necessity of making this exception, he deems a powerful argument
against the doctrine itself.   "If ever there were a paradoxical position"
mine, according to him, "is one on the surface.   It is most intelligible to
"say that there are no trustworthy institutions ; and it is most intelligible
"to say that there are many such ; but on the surface it is the *ne plus
"ultra* of paradox, to say that there is *just one* such, and no more."

First, on what account is it more improbable that there should be "just
one" source of intuitive knowledge besides present consciousness, making
two in all, than that there should be three, four, or any other number?
To me it seems that there is no antecedent presumption in the case, but a
mere question of evidence.   Dr. Ward, with good reason, challenges me
to explain "where the distinction lies between acts of memory and other
alleged intuitions" which I do not admit as such.   The distinction is,
that as all the explanations of mental phenomena presuppose Memory,
Memory itself cannot admit of being explained.   Whenever this is shown
to be true of any other part of our knowledge, I shall admit that part to

O

our sensations.   We seem to become aware of both at once.

The fact is as alleged, but it proves nothing, being consistent with Brown's doctrine.   Whether the belief in a non-ego arose in our first act of perception, simultaneously with the sensation, or not until suggested by the sensation, we have, as I before remarked, no means

be intuitive.   Dr. Ward thinks that there are various other intuitions "more favourably circumstanced for the establishment of their trust-"worthiness" than Memory itself, and he gives as an example our conviction of the wickedness of certain acts.   My reason for rejecting this as a case of intuition is, that the conviction can be explained without presupposing, as part of the explanation, the very fact itself; which the belief in Memory cannot.

Dr. Ward has been too hasty in saying that no phenomenist ever before made this "exception."   I doubt if he could point out any phenomenist who has not made it, either expressly or by implication.   All who have attempted the explanation of the human mind by sensation have postulated the knowledge of past sensations as well as of present; some of them have expressly said so.   Take Hume, for instance, the most extreme of Phenomenists; he always excepts Memory from the sources of knowledge of which he attempts to find an explanation.   In his "Sceptical Doubts," he says "It may be a subject worthy curiosity, to inquire what is the "nature of that evidence which assures us of any real existence and matter "of fact, beyond the present testimony of our senses, *or the records of our* "*memory.*"   And again, "all reasonings concerning matter of fact seem "to be founded in the relation of Cause and Effect.   By means of that "relation alone can we go beyond the evidence of our *memory* and senses." And in his "Sceptical Solution of these Doubts," where he is attempting to explain Belief by the laws of Association, he asserts that belief "where it reaches beyond the *memory* and senses" is amenable to his theory. It would be easy to quote equally decisive passages from other Phenomenists.   How, indeed, could any one make Experience the source of all our knowledge without postulating the belief in Memory as the fundamental fact?   What is Experience but Memory?

For myself, I do admit other sources of knowledge than sensation and the memory of sensation, though not than consciousness and the memory of consciousness.   I have distinctly declared that the elementary *relations* of our sensations to one another, viz. their resemblances, and their successions and coexistences, are subjects of direct apprehension.   And I have avowedly left the question undecided whether our perception of ourselves— of our own personality—is not a case of the same kind.   It is curious that while Dr. Ward thinks I am bound to explain why I acknowledge only one case of intuition, Dr. M'Cosh charges me with postulating as great a number of first principles as are demanded by either the Scotch or the German metaphysicians, and has devoted a whole chapter of his book to an enumeration of them; including several which, as he might have known, I regard as truths indeed, but not as ultimate principles.   I do not know what extreme of supposed psychological analysis Dr. M'Cosh thought it incumbent on me to profess.   In my estimation, the doctrine of "all or none" is no more a necessity in philosophy than in politics.

of directly ascertaining.   As far as depends on direct evidence, the subject is inscrutable.   But this we may know, that even if the suggestion theory were true, the belief suggested would by the laws of association become so intimately blended with the sensation suggesting it, that long before we were able to reflect on our mental operations, we should have become entirely incapable of thinking of the two things as other than simultaneous. An appeal to consciousness avails nothing, when, even though the doctrine opposed were true, the appeal might equally, and with the same plausibility, be made.   The facts are alike consistent with both opinions, and, for aught that appears, Brown's is as likely to be true as Sir W. Hamilton's.   The difference between them, as already observed, is extremely small, and I will add, supremely unimportant.   If the reality of matter is certified to us by an irresistible belief, it matters little whether we reach the belief by the two steps, or by only one.

The really important difference of opinion on the subject of Perception between Brown and Sir W. Hamilton, is far other than this. It is, that Sir W. Hamilton belives us to have a direct intuition not solely of the reality of matter, but also of its primary qualities, Extension, Solidity, Figure, &c., which, according to him, we know as in the material object, and not as modifications of ourselves : while Brown believes that matter is suggested to us only as an unknown something, all whose attributes, as known or conceived by us, are resolvable into affections of our senses.   In Brown's opinion we are cognisant of a non-ego in the perceptive act, only in the indefinite form of something external ; all else we are able to know of it is only that it produces certain affections in us : which is also our author's opinion as regards the Secondary Qualities.   The difference therefore, between Brown and Sir W. Hamilton, is not of the kind which Sir W. Hamilton considers it to be, but consists mainly in this, that Brown really held what Sir W. Hamilton held only verbally, the doctrine of the

Relativity of our knowledge.   I shall attempt, further
on, to show that on the point on which they really
differed, Brown was right and Sir W. Hamilton totally
wrong. *

The considerations which have now been adduced
are subversive of a great mass of triumphant animadversion by our author on the ignorance and carelessness
of Brown and some milder criticism on Reid.   Sir W.
Hamilton thinks it astonishing that neither of these
philosophers should have recognised Natural Realism,
and the third form of Cosmothetic Idealism, as two
different modes of thought.   Reid, whom he makes a
great point of claiming as a Natural Realist, was, he
says, quite unaware of the possibility of the other opinion,
and did not guard against it by his language, leaving it,
therefore, open to dispute whether, instead of being a
Natural Realist, he was not, like Brown, a Cosmothetic
Idealist of the third class; while Brown, on the other
hand, never conceived Natural Realism, nor thought it
possible that Reid held any other than his own opinion,
as he invariably affirms him to have done.   I apprehend
that both philosophers are entirely clear of the blame
thus imputed to them.   Reid never imagined Brown's
doctrine, nor Brown Reid's, as anything different from
his own, because in truth they were not different.   If

---

* There is also a difference between Brown and Sir W. Hamilton in the
particular category of intuitive knowledge to which they referred the
cognition of the existence of matter.   Brown deemed it a case of the belief
in causation, which again he regarded as a case of our intuitive belief in the
constancy of the order of nature.   "I do not," he says (Lecture xxiv.
vol. ii. p. 11), "conceive that it is by any peculiar intuition we are led to
"believe in the existence of things without.   I consider this belief as the
"effect of that more general intuition, by which we consider a new con-
"sequent, in any series of accustomed events, as the sign of a new ante-
"cedent, and of that equally general principle of association, by which
"feelings that have frequently co-existed, flow together and constitute after-
"wards one complex whole."   That is, he thought that when an infant
finds the motions of his muscles, which have been accustomed to take place
unimpeded, suddenly stopped by what he will afterwards learn to call the
resistance of an external object, the infant intuitively (though perhaps not
instantaneously) believes that this unexpected phenomenon, the stoppage
of a series of sensations, is conjoined with, or as we now say, caused by
the presence of some new antecedent : which, not being the infant himself,
nor a state of his sensations, we may call an outward object.

the distinction between a Natural Realist and a Cosmothetic Idealist of the third class, be that the latter
believes the existence of the external object to be inferred from, or suggested by, our sensations, while the
former holds it to be neither the one nor the other, but
to be apprehended in consciousness simultaneously and
co-ordinately with the sensations, Reid was as much a
Cosmothetic Idealist as Brown. The question does not
concern philosophy, but the history of philosophy, which
is Sir W. Hamilton's strongest point, and was not at all
a strong point with either Brown or Reid; but the
matter of fact is worth the few pages necessary for
clearing it up, because Sir W. Hamilton's vast and
accurate learning goes near to obtaining for his statements, on any such matter, implicit confidence, and it
is therefore important to show that even where he is
strongest, he is sometimes wrong.

In the severe criticism on Brown from which I have
quoted, and which, though in some respects unjust, in
others I cannot deny to be well merited, some of the
strongest expressions have reference to the gross misunderstanding of Reid, of which Brown is alleged to have
been guilty in not perceiving him to have been a Natural
Realist. " We proceed," says our author,* " to consider
" the greatest of all Brown's errors, in itself and in its
" consequences, his misconception of the cardinal position
" of Reid's philosophy, in supposing that philosopher as
" a *hypothetical* realist, to hold with himself the third
" form of the *representative* hypothesis, and not, as a
" *natural* realist, the doctrine of an *intuitive* Perception."
" Brown's † transmutation of Reid from a *natural* to a
" *hypothetical* realist, as a misconception of the grand
" and distinctive tenet of a school by one even of its
" disciples, is without a parallel in the whole history
" of philosophy; and this portentous error is prolific;
" *chimæra chimæram parit*. Were the evidence of the
" mistake less unambiguous, we should be disposed
" rather to question our own perspicacity than to tax so

* Discussions, p. 58.   † Ibid. p 56.

" subtle an intellect with so gross a blunder." And he did, in time, feel some misgiving as to his " own perspicacity." When, in preparing an edition of Reid, he was obliged to look more closely into that author's statements, we find a remarkable lowering of the high tone of these sentences ; and he felt obliged, in revising the paper for the Discussions, to write "This is too strong," after a passage in which he had said that * " Brown's "interpretation of the fundamental tenet of Reid's philo-"sophy is not a simple misconception, but an absolute "reversal of its real and even *unambiguous* import." Well would it have been for Brown's reputation if all Sir W. Hamilton's attempts to bring home blunders to him had been as little successful as this.

In the work in which Reid first brought his opinions before the world, the " Inquiry into the Human Mind," his language is so unequivocally that of a Cosmothetic Idealist, that it admits of no mistake. It is almost more unambiguous than that of Brown himself. The external object is always said to be perceived through the medium of " natural signs :" these signs being our sensations, interpreted by a natural instinct. Our sensations, he says,† belong to that " class of natural signs "which . . though we never before had any notion or "conception of the thing signified, do suggest it, or "conjure it up, as it were, by a natural kind of magic, "and at once give us a conception and create a belief of "it." " I take,‡ it for granted that the notion of hard-"ness, and the belief of it, is first got by means of that "particular sensation which, as far back as we can "remember, does invariably suggest it, and that, if we "had never had such a feeling, we should never have "had our notion of hardness." Again,§ " when a coloured "body is presented, there is a certain apparition to the "eye, or to the mind, which we have called *the appearance* "*of colour*. Mr. Locke calls it *an idea*, and, indeed, it

---

* Discussions, p. 60.
† Inquiry into the Human Mind, Works (Hamilton's ed.), p. 122.
‡ Ibid.   § Ibid. p. 137.

" may be called so with the greatest propriety. This
" idea can have no existence but when it is perceived.
" It is a kind of thought, and can only be the act of a
" percipient, or thinking being. By the constitution of
" our nature, we are led to conceive this idea as a sign
" of something external, and are impatient till we learn
" its meaning."

I must be excused if I am studious to prove, by an
accumulation of citations, that these are not passing
expressions of Reid, but the deliberate doctrine of his
treatise. " I think it appears from what hath been said,
" that there are natural suggestions; particularly, that
" sensation suggests the notion of present existence, and
" the belief that what we perceive or feel does now
" exist. . . And, in like manner, certain sensations of
" touch, by the constitution of our nature, suggest to us
" extension, solidity, and motion." *   " By an original
" principle of our constitution, a certain sensation of
" touch both suggests to the mind the conception of
" hardness, and creates the belief of it: or, in other
" words, this sensation is a natural sign of hardness." †
" The word *gold* has no similitude to the substance
" signified by it; nor is it in its own nature more fit to
" signify this than any other substance; yet, by habit
" and custom, it suggests this and no other. In like
" manner, a sensation of touch suggests hardness al-
" though it hath neither similitude to hardness, nor, as
" far as we can perceive, any necessary connection with
" it. The difference betwixt these two signs lies only
" in this—that, in the first, the suggestion is the effect
" of habit and custom; in the second, it is not the
" effect of habit, but of the original constitution of our
" minds." ‡   " Extension, therefore, seems to be a quality
" *suggested* to us" (the italics are Reid's) " by the very
" same sensations which suggest the other qualities
" above mentioned. When I grasp a ball in my hand,
" I perceive it at once hard, figured, and extended.

* Inquiry into the Human Mind, Works, p. 111.
† Ibid. p. 121.   ‡ Ibid. p. 121.

"The feeling is very simple, and hath not the least
"resemblance to any quality of body.   Yet it suggests
" to us three primary qualities perfectly distinct from one
" another, as well as from the sensation which indicates
"them.   When I move my hand along the table, the
" feeling is so simple that I find it difficult to distinguish
"it into things of different natures, yet it immediately
" suggests hardness, smoothness, extension, and motion
" —things of very different natures, and all of them as
" distinctly understood as the feeling which suggests
"them." *   " The feelings of touch, which suggest
" primary qualities, have no names, nor are they ever
" reflected upon.   They pass through the mind instan-
" taneously, and serve only to introduce the notion and
" belief of external things, which by our constitution,
" are connected with them.   They are natural signs,
" and the mind immediately passes to the thing signified,
" without making the least reflection upon the sign,
" or observing that there was any such thing." †
This passage, with many others of like import, Sir
W. Hamilton might usefully have meditated on, before
he laid so much stress on the testimony of consciousness that the apprehension is *not* through the medium
of a sign.

"Let a man press his hand against the table—he feels
"it hard.   But what is the meaning of this?   The
" meaning undoubtedly is, that he hath a certain feeling
" of touch from which he concludes, without any rea-
" soning or comparing ideas, that there is something
" external really existing, whose parts stick so firmly
" together, that they cannot be displaced without con-
" siderable force.   There is here a feeling, and a con-
" clusion drawn from it, or some way suggested by
" it. . . . . The hardness of the table is the conclusion,
" the feeling is the medium by which we are led to that
" conclusion."‡   "How a sensation should instantly make
" us conceive and believe the existence of an external

* Inquiry into the Human Mind, Works, p. 123.
  † Ibid. p. 124.   ‡ Ibid. p. 125.

" thing altogether unlike to it, I do not pretend to know ;
" and when I say that the one suggests the other, I
" mean not to explain the manner of their connection,
" but to express a fact, which every one may be conscious
" of namely, that by a law of our nature, such a con-
" ception and belief constantly and immediately follow
" the sensation." *   There are three ways in which the
" mind passes from the appearance of a natural sign to
" the conception and belief of the thing signified—by
" original principles of our constitution, by custom, and
" by reasoning.   Our original perceptions are got in the
" first of these ways. . . .   In the first of these ways,
" Nature, by means of the sensations of touch, informs
" us of the hardness and softness of bodies ; of their
" extension, figure, and motion ; and of that space in
" which they move and are placed." †   " In the testi-
" mony of Nature given by the senses, as well as in
" human testimony given by language, things are signi-
" fied to us by signs : and in one as well as the other,
" the mind, either by original principles or by custom,
" passes from the sign to the conception and belief of
" the things signified. . . .   The signs in original per-
" ceptions are sensations, of which Nature hath given
" us a great variety, suited to the variety of the things
" signified by them.   Nature hath established a real con-
" nection between the signs and the things signified,
" and Nature hath also taught us the interpretation of
" the signs—so that, previous to experience, the sign
" suggests the thing signified and creates the belief of
" it." ‡   " It is by one particular principle of our con-
" stitution that certain features express anger ; and by
" another particular principle that certain features ex-
" press benevolence.   It is, in like manner, by one parti-
" cular principle of our constitution that a certain sensa-
" tion signifies hardness in the body which I handle ;
" and it is by another particular principle that a certain
" sensation signifies motion in that body." §

* Inquiry into the Human Mind, Works, p. 131.
† Ibid. p. 188.   ‡ Ibid. pp, 194, 195.   § Ibid. p. 195.

I doubt if it would be possible to extract from Brown himself an equal number of passages expressing as clearly and positively, and in terms as irreconcilable with any other opinion, the doctrine which our author terms the third form of Cosmothetic Idealism; in the exact shape, too, in which Brown held it, unencumbered by the gratuitous addition which Sir W. Hamilton fastens on him, that the sign must "truly represent" the thing signified,—a notion which Reid takes good care that he shall not be supposed to entertain, since he repeatedly declares that there is no resemblance between them. That Reid, at least when he wrote the Inquiry, was a Cosmothetic Idealist; that up to that time it had never occurred to him that the convictions of the existence and qualities of external objects could be regarded as anything but suggestions by, and conclusions from, our sensations—is too obvious to be questioned by any one who has the text fresh in his recollection. Accordingly Sir W. Hamilton acknowledges as much in his edition of Reid, both in the footnotes and in the appended Dissertations. After restating his own doctrine, that our natural beliefs assure us of outward objects, only by assuring us that we are immediately conscious of them, he adds,* " Reid himself seems " to have become obscurely aware of this condition : and " though he never retracted his doctrine concerning the " mere *suggestion* of extension, we find in his Essays on " the Intellectual Powers assertions in regard to the " immediate perception of external things, which would " tend to show that his later views were more in unison " with the necessary convictions of mankind." And in another place † he says of the doctrine maintained by Reid " in his earlier work," that it is one which " if he " did not formally retract in his later writings, he did " not continue to profess." It is hard that Brown should be charged with blundering to a degree which is " portentous " and "without a parallel in the whole history of philosophy," for attributing to Reid an opinion which

* Foot-note to Reid, p. 129.   † Dissertations on Reid, p. 821.

Sir W. Hamilton confesses that Reid maintained in one of his only two important writings, and did not retract in the other.   But Sir W. Hamilton is still more wrong than he confesses.   He is in a mistake when he says that Reid, though he did not retract the opinion, did not continue to profess it.   For some reason, not apparent, he did cease to employ the word Suggestion.   But he continued to use terms equivalent to it.   "Every dif-
" ferent perception is conjoined with a sensation that is
" proper to it.   *The one is the sign,* the other the thing
" signified." *   " I touch the table gently with my hand,
" and I feel it to be smooth, hard, and cold.   These are
" qualities of the table perceived by touch : but I *perceive*
" *them by means* of a sensation which indicates them." †
" Observing that the agreeable sensation is raised when
" the rose is near, and ceases when it is removed, I am
" led by my nature to *conclude* some quality to be in the
" rose, which is the cause of this sensation.   This quality
" in the rose is the object perceived ; and that act of my
" mind by which I have the conviction and belief of this
" quality, is what in this case I call perception." ‡   Of this passage even Sir W. Hamilton honestly says in a foot-note, that it " appears to be an explicit disavowal of the doctrine of an intuitive or immediate perception." Again : " When a primary quality is perceived, *the sensa-*
" *tion immediately leads our thought to the quality signified*
" *by it,* and is itself forgot. . .   The sensations belonging
" to primary qualities . . . carry the thought to the ex-
" ternal object, and immediately disappear and are forgot.
" *Nature intended them only as signs;* and when they have
" served that purpose they vanish." §   " Nature has con-
" nected our perception of external objects with certain
" sensations.   *If the sensation is produced, the correspond-*
" *ing perception follows,* even when there is no object, and
" in that case is apt to deceive us." ‖   " In perception,
" whether original or acquired, there is something which
" may be called *the sign,* and something which is signified

* Essays on the Intellectual Powers, Works, p. 312.
† Ibid. p. 311.   ‡ Ibid. p. 310.   § Ibid. p. 315.   ‖ Ibid. p. 320.

" to us, or *brought to our knowledge by that sign.*   In
" original perception, *the signs are the various sensations*
" which are produced by the impressions made upon our
" organs.   *The things signified are the objects perceived*
" in consequence of those sensations, by the original
" constitution of our nature.   Thus, when I grasp an
" ivory ball in my hand, I have a certain sensation of
" touch.   Although this sensation be in the mind, and
" have no similitude to anything material ; yet, by the
" laws of my constitution, *it is immediately followed* by
" the conception and belief, that there is in my hand a hard
" smooth body of a spherical figure, and about an inch
" and a half in diameter.   This belief is grounded neither
" upon reasoning nor upon experience ; it is the imme-
" diate effect of my constitution, and this I call original
" perception."

All these are as unequivocal, and the last passage as
full and precise a statement of Cosmothetic Idealism, as
any in the Inquiry.   In the Dissertations appended to
Reid,† Sir W. Hamilton, who never fails in candour,
acknowledges in the fullest manner the inferences which
may be drawn from passages like these, but thinks that
they are balanced by others which " seem to harmonise
" exclusively with the conditions of natural presenta-
" tionism," ‡ and on the whole is decidedly § of opinion
" that, as the great end—the governing principle of Reid's
" doctrine, was to reconcile philosophy with the neces-
" sary convictions of mankind, he intended a doctrine
" of natural, consequently a doctrine of presentative,
" realism ; and that he would have at once surrendered
" as erroneous, every statement which was found at
" variance with such a doctrine."   But it is clear that
the doctrine of perception through natural signs did not,
in Reid's opinion, contradict " the necessary convictions
of mankind ; " being brought into harmony with them
by his doctrine, that the signs, after they have served

---

* Essays on the Intellectual Powers, p. 332.
† Dissertations on Reid, pp. 819–824 and 882–885.
‡ Ibid. p. 882.   § Ibid. p. 820.

their purpose, are "forgot," which, as he conclusively shows in many places, it was both natural and inevitable that they should be.   The passages which Sir W. Hamilton cites as inconsistent with any doctrine but Natural Realism, are those in which Reid affirms that we perceive objects *immediately*, and that the external things which really exist are the very ones which we perceive.   But Reid evidently did not think these expressions inconsistent with the doctrine that the notion and belief of external objects are irresistibly suggested through natural signs.   Having this notion and belief irresistibly suggested, is what he means by perceiving the external object.   He says so in more than one of the passages I have just quoted : and neither in his chapter on Perception, or anywhere else, does he speak of perception as implying anything more.   In that chapter he says,* " If we attend to that act of our mind " which we call the perception of an external object of " sense, we shall find in it these three things : First, " some conception or notion of the object perceived ; " Secondly, a strong and irresistible conviction and belief " of its present existence ; and, Thirdly, that this con- " viction and belief are immediate, and not the effect of " reasoning."   We see in this as in a hundred other places, what Reid meant when he said that our perception of outward objects is immediate.   He did not mean that it is not a conviction suggested by something else, but only that the conviction is not the effect of reasoning. " This conviction † is not only irresistible, but it is " immediate ; that is, it is not by a train of reasoning " and argumentation that we come to be convinced of " the existence of what we perceive."   As Nature has given us the signs, so it is by an original law of our nature that we are enabled to interpret them.   When Reid means anything but this in contending for an immediate perception of objects, he merely means to deny that it takes place through an image in the brain

---

* Essays on the Intellectual Powers, Essay ii. chap. v. p. 258.
† Same Essay, p. 259.

or in the mind, as maintained by Cosmothetic Idealists
of the first or the second class.

The only plausible argument produced by Sir W.
Hamilton in proof of Reid's Natural Realism, and
against his having held, as Brown thought, Brown's
own opinion, is, that when in the speculations of Arnauld
he had before him exactly the same opinion, he failed to
recognise it.*   But on a careful examination of Reid's
criticism on Arnauld, it will be seen, that as long as
Reid had to do with Arnauld's direct statement of his
opinion, he found nothing in it different from his own ;
but was puzzled, and thought that Arnauld attempted
to unite inconsistent opinions, because, after throwing
over the "ideal theory," and saying that the only real
ideas are our perceptions, he maintained that it is still
true, in a sense, that we do not perceive things directly,
but through our ideas.   What! asks Reid, do we perceive
things through our perceptions?   But if we merely put
the word sensations instead of perceptions, the doctrine
is exactly that of Reid in the Inquiry—that we perceive
things through our sensations.   Most probably Arnauld
meant this, but was not so understood by Reid.   If he
meant anything else, his opinion was not the same as
Reid's, and we need no explanation of Reid's not recognising it.

One of the collateral indications that Reid's opinion
agreed with Brown's, and not with Sir W. Hamilton's,
is that in treating this question he seldom or never
uses the word Knowledge, but only Belief.   On Sir W.
Hamilton's doctrine, the distinction between these two
terms, however vaguely and mistily conceived by him,
is indispensable.   The total absence of any recognition
of it in Reid, shows that of the two opinions, if there
was one which he had never conceived the possibility of,
it was not Brown's, as Sir W. Hamilton supposes, but
Sir W. Hamilton's.   In our author's mind this indica-

---

* Same Essay, chap. xiii.   For Sir W. Hamilton's remarks, see
Lectures, ii. 50-53; Discussions, pp. 75-77; and Dissertations on Reid,
p. 823.

tion ought to have decided the question : for in the case of another philosopher he, on precisely the same evidence, brings in a verdict of Cosmothetic Idealism. Krug's system, he says,* as first promulgated, "was, "like Kant's, a mere Cosmothetic Idealism ; for while "he allowed a *knowledge* of the internal world, he only "allowed a *belief* of the external."

It is true, Reid did not believe in what our author terms "representative perception," if by this be meant perception through an image in the mind, supposed, like the picture of a fact in memory, to be *like* its original. But neither (as I have repeatedly observed) did Brown. What Brown held was exactly the doctrine of Reid in the passages that I have extracted. He thought that certain sensations, irresistibly, and by a law of our nature, suggest, without any process of reasoning, and without the intervention of any *tertium quid*, the notion of something external, and an invincible belief in its real existence. If representative perception be this, both Reid and Brown believed in it ; if anything else, Brown believed in it no more than Reid. Not only was Reid a Cosmothetic Idealist of Brown's exact type, but in stating his own doctrine, he has furnished, as far as I am aware, the clearest and best statement extant of their common opinion. They differed, indeed, as to our having, in this or in any other manner, an intuitive perception of any of the *attributes* of objects ; Reid, like Sir W. Hamilton, affirming, while Brown denied, that we have a direct intuition of the Primary Qualities of bodies. But Brown did not deny, nor would Sir W. Hamilton accuse him of denying, the wide difference between his opinion and Reid's on this latter point.

Before closing this chapter, I will notice the curious fact, that after insisting with so much emphasis upon the recognition of an Ego and a Non-ego as an element in all consciousness, Sir W. Hamilton is obliged to admit that the distinction is in certain cases a mistake, and that our consciousness sometimes recognises a Non-ego

* Dissertations on Reid, p. 797.

where there is only an Ego. It is a doctrine of his, repeated in many parts of his works, that in our *internal* consciousness there is no non-ego. Even the remembrance of a past fact, or the mental image of an absent object, is not a thing separable or distinguishable from the mind's act in remembering, but is another name for that act itself. Now it is certain, that in thinking of an absent or an imaginary object, we naturally imagine ourselves to be thinking of an objective something, distinguishable from the thinking act. Sir W. Hamilton, being obliged to acknowledge this, resolves the difficulty in the very manner for which he so often rebukes other thinkers—by representing this apparent testimony of consciousness as a kind of illusion. "The object," he says,[*] "is in this case given as really identical with the "conscious ego, but still consciousness distinguishes it, "as an accident from the ego, as the subject of that "accident: it projects, as it were, this subjective phe-"nomenon from itself,—views it at a distance,—in a "word, objectifies it." But if, in one-half of the domain of consciousness—the internal half—it is in the power of consciousness to "project" out of itself what is merely one of its own acts, and regard it as external and a non-ego, why are those accused of declaring consciousness a lie, who think that this may possibly be the case with the other half of its domain also, and that the non-ego altogether may be but a mode in which the mind represents to itself the possible modifications of the ego? How the truth stands in respect to this matter I will endeavour, in the following chapter, to investigate. For the present, I content myself with asking, why the same liberty in the interpretation of Consciousness, which Sir W. Hamilton's own doctrine cannot dispense with, should be held to be an insurmountable objection to the counter doctrine?

* Lectures, ii. 432.

CHAPTER XI.

THE PSYCHOLOGICAL THEORY OF THE BELIEF IN AN
EXTERNAL WORLD.

WE have seen Sir W. Hamilton at work on the question
of the reality of Matter, by the introspective method,
and, as it seems, with little result.   Let us now approach
the same subject by the psychological.   I proceed,
therefore, to state the case of those who hold that the
belief in an external world is not intuitive, but an
acquired product.

This theory postulates the following psychological
truths, all of which are proved by experience, and are
not contested, though their force is seldom adequately
felt, by Sir W. Hamilton and the other thinkers of the
introspective school.

It postulates, first, that the human mind is capable of
Expectation.   In other words, that after having had
actual sensations, we are capable of forming the conception of Possible sensations ; sensations which we are not
feeling at the present moment, but which we might feel,
and should feel if certain conditions were present, the
nature of which conditions we have, in many cases,
learnt by experience.

It postulates, secondly, the laws of the Association of
Ideas.   So far as we are here concerned, these laws are
the following: 1st. Similar phenomena tend to be thought
of together.   2nd. Phenomena which have either been
experienced or conceived in close contiguity to one
another, tend to be thought of together.   The contiguity is of two kinds ; simultaneity, and immediate
succession.   Facts which have been experienced or

P

thought of simultaneously, recall the thought of one another. Of facts which have been experienced or thought of in immediate succession, the antecedent, or the thought of it, recalls the thought of the consequent, but not conversely. 3rd. Associations produced by contiguity become more certain and rapid by repetition. When two phenomena have been very often experienced in conjunction, and have not, in any single instance, occurred separately either in experience or in thought, there is produced between them what has been called Inseparable, or less correctly, Indissoluble Association : by which is not meant that the association must inevitably last to the end of life—that no subsequent experience or process of thought can possibly avail to dissolve it ; but only that as long as no such experience or process of thought has taken place, the association is irresistible ; it is impossible for us to think the one thing disjoined from the other. 4th. When an association has acquired this character of inseparability—when the bond between the two ideas has been thus firmly riveted, not only does the idea called up by association become, in our consciousness, inseparable from the idea which suggested it, but the facts or phenomena answering to those ideas come at last to seem inseparable in existence : things which we are unable to conceive apart, appear incapable of existing apart ; and the belief we have in their co-existence, though really a product of experience, seems intuitive. Innumerable examples might be given of this law. One of the most familiar, as well as the most striking, is that of our acquired perceptions of sight. Even those who, with Mr. Bailey, consider the perception of distance by the eye as not acquired, but intuitive, admit that there are many perceptions of sight which, though instantaneous and unhesitating, are not intuitive. What we see is a very minute fragment of what we think we see. We see artificially that one thing is hard, another soft. We see artificially that one thing is hot, another cold. We see artificially that what we see is a book, or a stone, each of these being not merely an inference, but a heap of inferences, from the signs which we see, to things not visible. We see, and cannot help seeing, what we have learnt to infer, even when we know that the inference is erroneous, and that the apparent perception is deceptive. We cannot help seeing the moon larger when near the horizon, though we know that she is of precisely her usual size. We cannot help seeing a mountain as nearer to us and of less height, when we see it through a more than ordinarily transparent atmosphere.

Setting out from these premises, the Psychological Theory maintains, that there are associations naturally and even necessarily generated by the order of our sensations and of our reminiscences of sensation, which, supposing no intuition of an external world to have existed in consciousness, would inevitably generate the belief, and would cause it to be regarded as an intuition.

What is it we mean, or what is it which leads us to say, that the objects we perceive are external to us, and not a part of our own thoughts? We mean, that there is concerned in our perceptions something which exists when we are not thinking of it; which existed before we had ever thought of it, and would exist if we were annihilated; and further, that there exists things which we never saw, touched, or otherwise perceived, and things which never have been perceived by man. This idea of something which is distinguished from our fleeting impressions by what, in Kantian language, is called Perdurability; something which is fixed and the same, while our impressions vary; something which exists whether we are aware of it or not, and which is always square (or of some other given figure) whether it appears to us square or round—constitutes altogether our idea of external substance. Whoever can assign an origin to this complex conception, has accounted for what we mean by the belief in matter. Now all this, according to the Psychological Theory, is but the form impressed by the known laws of association, upon the conception or notion, obtained by experience, of Contingent Sensations ; by which are meant, sensations that are not in our present consciousness, and individually never were in our consciousness at all, but which in virtue of the laws to which we have learnt by experience that our sensations are subject, we know that we should have felt under given supposable circumstances, and under these same circumstances, might still feel.

I see a piece of white paper on a table. I go into another room. If the phenomenon always followed me, or if, when it did not follow me, I believed it to disappear *è rerum naturâ,* I should not believe it to be an external object. I should consider it as a phantom—a mere affection of my senses : I should not believe that there had been any Body there. But, though I have ceased to see it, I am persuaded that the paper is still there. I no longer have the sensations which it gave me ; but I believe that when I again place myself in the circumstances in which I had those sensations, that is, when I go again into the room, I shall again have them ; and further, that there has been no intervening moment at which this would not have been the case. Owing to this property of my mind, my conception of the world at any given instant consists, in only a small proportion, of present sensations. Of these I may at the time have none at all, and they are in any case a most insignificant portion of the whole which I apprehend. The conception I form of the world existing at any moment, comprises, along with the sensations I am feeling, a countless variety of possibilities of sensation : namely, the whole of those which past observation tells me that I could, under any supposable circumstances, experience at this moment, together with an indefinite and illimitable multitude of others which though I do not know that I could, yet it is possible that I might, experience in circumstances not known to me. These various possibilities are the important thing to me in the world. My present sensations are generally of little importance, and are moreover fugitive : the possibilities, on the contrary, are permanent, which is the character that mainly distinguishes our idea of Substance or Matter from our notion of sensation.   These possibilities, which are conditional certainties, need a special name to distinguish them from mere vague possibilities, which experience gives no warrant for reckoning upon.   Now, as soon as a distinguishing name is given, though it be only to the same thing regarded in a different aspect, one of the most familiar experiences of our mental nature teaches us, that the different name comes to be considered as the name of a different thing.

There is another important peculiarity of these certified or guaranteed possibilities of sensation; namely, that they have reference, not to single sensations, but to sensations joined together in groups.   When we think of anything as a material substance, or body, we either have had, or we think that on some given supposition we should have, not some *one* sensation, but a great and even an indefinite number and variety of sensations, generally belonging to different senses, but so linked together, that the presence of one announces the possible presence at the very same instant of any or all of the rest.   In our mind, therefore, not only is this particular Possibility of sensation invested with the quality of permanence when we are not actually feeling any of the sensations at all; but when we are feeling some of them, the remaining sensations of the group are conceived by us in the form of Present Possibilities, which might be realised at the very moment.   And as this happens in turn to all of them, the group as a whole presents itself to the mind as permanent, in contrast not solely with the temporariness of my bodily presence, but also with the temporary character of each of the sensations composing the group; in other words, as a kind of permanent substratum, under a set of passing experiences or manifestations: which is another leading character of our idea of substance or matter, as distinguished from sensation.

Let us now take into consideration another of the general characters of our experience, namely, that in

addition to fixed groups, we also recognise a fixed Order
in our sensations ; an Order of succession, which, when
ascertained by observation, gives rise to the ideas of
Cause and Effect, according to what I hold to be the true
theory of that relation, and is on any theory the source
of all our knowledge what causes produce what effects.
Now, of what nature is this fixed order among our sensations? It is a constancy of antecedence and sequence. But
the constant antecedence and sequence do not generally
exist between one actual sensation and another. Very
few such sequences are presented to us by experience.
In almost all the constant sequences which occur in
Nature, the antecedence and consequence do not obtain
between sensations, but between the groups we have
been speaking about, of which a very small portion is
actual sensation, the greater part being permanent possibilities of sensation, evidenced to us by a small and
variable number of sensations actually present. Hence,
our ideas of causation, power, activity, do not become
connected in thought with our sensations as *actual* at
all, save in the few physiological cases where these figure
by themselves as the antecedents in some uniform
sequence. Those ideas become connected, not with
sensations, but with groups of possibilities of sensation.
The sensations conceived do not, to our habitual thoughts,
present themselves as sensations actually experienced,
inasmuch as not only any one or any number of them
may be supposed absent, but none of them need be
present. We find that the modifications which are
taking place more or less regularly in our possibilities of
sensation, are mostly quite independent of our consciousness, and of our presence or absence. Whether we are
asleep or awake the fire goes out, and puts an end to
one particular possibility of warmth and light. Whether
we are present or absent the corn ripens, and brings a
new possibility of food. Hence we speedily learn to
think of Nature as made up solely of these groups of
possibilities, and the active force in Nature as manifested
in the modification of some of these by others. The

sensations, though the original foundation of the whole,
come to be looked upon as a sort of accident depending
on us, and the possibilities as much more real than the
actual sensations, nay, as the very realities of which
these are only the representations, appearances, or effects.
When this state of mind has been arrived at, then, and
from that time forward, we are never conscious of a
present sensation without instantaneously referring it
to some one of the groups of possibilities into which a
sensation of that particular description enters; and if
we do not yet know to what group to refer it, we at
least feel an irresistible conviction that it must belong
to some group or other; *i.e.* that its presence proves
the existence, here and now, of a great number and
variety of possibilities of sensation, without which it
would not have been.   The whole set of sensations as
possible, form a permanent background to any one or
more of them that are, at a given moment, actual; and
the possibilities are conceived as standing to the actual
sensations in the relation of a cause to its effects, or of
canvas to the figures painted on it, or of a root to the
trunk, leaves, and flowers, or of a substratum to that
which is spread over it, or, in transcendental language,
of Matter to Form.

When this point has been reached, the Permanent
Possibilities in question have assumed such unlikeness
of aspect, and such difference of apparent relation to us,
from any sensations, that it would be contrary to all we
know of the constitution of human nature that they
should not be conceived as, and believed to be, at least
as different from sensations as sensations are from one
another.   Their groundwork in sensation is forgotten,
and they are supposed to be something intrinsically distinct from it.   We can withdraw ourselves from any of
our (external) sensations, or we can be withdrawn from
them by some other agency.   But though the sensations
cease, the possibilities remain in existence; they are
independent of our will, our presence, and everything
which belongs to us.   We find, too, that they belong as

much to other human or sentient beings as to ourselves.
We find other people grounding their expectations and
conduct upon the same permanent possibilities on which
we ground ours.   But we do not find them experiencing
the same actual sensations.   Other people do not have
our sensations exactly when and as we have them : but
they have our possibilities of sensation ; whatever indicates a present possibility of sensations to ourselves, indicates a present possibility of similar sensations to them,
except so far as their organs of sensation may vary
from the type of ours.   This puts the final seal to our
conception of the groups of possibilities as the fundamental reality in Nature.   The permanent possibilities
are common to us and to our fellow-creatures ; the actual
sensations are not.   That which other people become
aware of when, and on the same grounds, as I do, seems
more real to me than that which they do not know of
unless I tell them.   The world of Possible Sensations
succeeding one another according to laws, is as much
in other beings as it is in me ; it has therefore an existence outside me ; it is an External World.

If this explanation of the origin and growth of the
idea of Matter, or External Nature, contains nothing at
variance with natural laws, it is at least an admissible
supposition, that the element of Non-ego which Sir W.
Hamilton regards as an original datum of consciousness,
and which we certainly do find in what we now call our
consciousness, may not be one of its primitive elements—
may not have existed at all in its first manifestations.
But if this supposition be admissible, it ought, on Sir
W. Hamilton's principles, to be received as true.   The
first of the laws laid down by him for the interpretation
of Consciousness, the law (as he terms it) of Parsimony,
forbids to suppose an original principle of our nature in
order to account for phenomena which admit of possible
explanation from known causes.   If the supposed ingredient of consciousness be one which might grow up
(though we cannot prove that it did grow up) through
later experience ; and if, when it had so grown up, it

would, by known laws of our nature, appear as completely intuitive as our sensations themselves ; we are bound, according to Sir W. Hamilton's and all sound philosophy, to assign to it that origin. Where there is a known cause adequate to account for a phenomenon, there is no justification for ascribing it to an unknown one. And what evidence does Consciousness furnish of the intuitiveness of an impression, except instantaneousness, apparent simplicity, and unconsciousness on our part of how the impression came into our minds ? These features can only prove the impression to be intuitive, on the hypothesis that there are no means of accounting for them otherwise. If they not only might, but naturally would, exist, even on the supposition that it is not intuitive, we must accept the conclusion to which we are led by the Psychological Method, and which the Introspective Method furnishes absolutely nothing to contradict.

Matter, then, may be defined, a Permanent Possibility of Sensation. If I am asked, whether I believe in matter, I ask whether the questioner accepts this definition of it. If he does, I believe in matter : and so do all Berkeleians. In any other sense than this, I do not. But I affirm with confidence, that this conception of Matter includes the whole meaning attached to it by the common world, apart from philosophical, and sometimes from theological, theories. The reliance of mankind on the real existence of visible and tangible objects, means reliance on the reality and permanence of Possibilities of visual and tactual sensations, when no such sensations are actually experienced. We are warranted in believing that this is the meaning of Matter in the minds of many of its most esteemed metaphysical champions, though they themselves would not admit as much : for example, of Reid, Stewart, and Brown. For these three philosophers alleged that all mankind, including Berkeley and Hume, really believed in Matter, inasmuch as unless they did, they would not have turned aside to save themselves from running against a post.

Now all which this manœuvre really proved is, that they believed in Permanent Possibilities of Sensation.   We have therefore the unintentional sanction of these three eminent defenders of the existence of matter, for affirming, that to believe in Permanent Possibilities of Sensation is believing in Matter.   It is hardly necessary, after such authorities, to mention Dr. Johnson, or any one else who resorts to the *argumentum baculinum* of knocking a stick against the ground.   Sir W. Hamilton, a far subtler thinker than any of these, never reasons in this manner. He never supposes that a disbeliever in what he means by Matter, ought in consistency to act in any different mode from those who believe in it.   He knew that the belief on which all the practical consequences depend, is the belief in Permanent Possibilities of Sensation, and that if nobody believed in a material universe in any other sense, life would go on exactly as it now does.   He, however, did believe in more than this, but, I think, only because it had never occurred to him that mere Possibilities of Sensation could, to our artificialised consciousness, present the character of objectivity which, as we have now shown, they not only can, but unless the known laws of the human mind were suspended, must necessarily, present.

Perhaps it may be objected, that the very possibility of framing such a notion of Matter as Sir W. Hamilton's —the capacity in the human mind of imagining an external world which is anything more than what the Psychological Theory makes it—amounts to a disproof of the theory.   If (it may be said) we had no revelation in consciousness, of a world which is not in some way or other identified with sensation, we should be unable to have the notion of such a world.   If the only ideas we had of external objects were ideas of our sensations, supplemented by an acquired notion of permanent possibilities of sensation, we must (it is thought) be incapable of conceiving, and therefore still more incapable of fancying that we perceive, things which are not sensations at all.   It being evident however that some philosophers believe this, and it being maintainable that the mass of mankind do so, the existence of a perdurable basis of sensations, distinct from sensations themselves, is proved, it might be said, by the possibility of believing it.

Let me first restate what I apprehend the belief to be. We believe that we perceive a something closely related to all our sensations, but different from those which we are feeling at any particular minute ; and distinguished from sensations altogether, by being permanent and always the same, while these are fugitive, variable, and alternately displace one another. But these attributes of the object of perception are properties belonging to all the possibilities of sensation which experience guarantees. The belief in such permanent possibilities seems to me to include all that is essential or characteristic in the belief in substance. I believe that Calcutta exists, though I do not perceive it, and that it would still exist if every percipient inhabitant were suddenly to leave the place, or be struck dead. But when I analyse the belief, all I find in it is, that were these events to take place, the Permanent Possibility of Sensation which I call Calcutta would still remain; that if I were suddenly transported to the banks of the Hoogly, I should still have the sensations which, if now present, would lead me to affirm that Calcutta exists here and now. We may infer, therefore, that both philosophers and the world at large, when they think of matter, conceive it really as a Permanent Possibility of Sensation. But the majority of philosophers fancy that it is something more ; and the world at large, though they have really, as I conceive, nothing in their minds but a Permanent Possibility of Sensation, would, if asked the question, undoubtedly agree with the philosophers : and though this is sufficiently explained by the tendency of the human mind to infer difference of things from difference of names, I acknowledge the obligation of showing how it can be possible to believe in an existence transcending all possibilities of sensation, unless on the hypothesis that such an existence actually is, and that we actually perceive it.

The explanation, however, is not difficult. It is an admitted fact, that we are capable of all conceptions which can be formed by generalising from the observed laws of our sensations. Whatever relation we find to exist between any one of our sensations and something different from *it*, that same relation we have no difficulty in conceiving to exist between the sum of all our sensations and something different from *them*. The differences which our consciousness recognises between one sensation and another, give us the general notion of difference, and inseparably associate with every sensation we have, the feeling of its being different from other things : and when once this association has been formed, we can no longer conceive anything, without being able, and even being compelled, to form also the conception of something different from it. This familiarity with the idea of something different from *each* thing we know, makes it natural and easy to form the notion of something different from *all* things that we know, collectively as well as individually. It is true we can form no conception of what such a thing can be ; our notion of it is merely negative ; but the idea of a substance, apart from its relation to the impressions which we conceive it as making on our senses, *is* a merely negative one. There is thus no psychological obstacle to our forming the notion of a something which is neither a sensation nor a possibility of sensation, even if our consciousness does not testify to it ; and nothing is more likely than that the Permanent Possibilities of sensation, to which our consciousness does testify, should be confounded in our minds with this imaginary conception. All experience attests the strength of the tendency to mistake mental abstractions, even negative ones, for substantive realities ; and the Permanent Possibilities of sensation which experience guarantees, are so extremely unlike in many of their properties to actual sensations, that since we are capable of imagining something which transcends sensation, there is a great natural probability that we should suppose these to be it.

But this natural probability is converted into certainty, when we take into consideration that universal law of our experience which is termed the law of Causation, and which makes us mentally connect with the beginning of everything, some antecedent condition, or Cause. The case of Causation is one of the most marked of all the cases in which we extend to the sum total of our consciousness, a notion derived from its parts. It is a striking example of our power to conceive, and our tendency to believe, that a relation which subsists between every individual item of our experience and some other item, subsists also between our experience as a whole, and something not within the sphere of experience. By this extension to the sum of all our experiences, of the internal relations obtaining between its several parts, we are led to consider sensation itself—the aggregate whole of our sensations—as deriving its origin from antecedent existences transcending sensation. That we should do this, is a consequence of the particular character of the uniform sequences, which experience discloses to us among our sensations. As already remarked, the constant antecedent of a sensation is seldom another sensation, or set of sensations, actually felt. It is much oftener the existence of a group of possibilities, not necessarily including any actual sensations, except such as are required to show that the possibilities are really present. Nor are actual sensations indispensable even for this purpose; for the presence of the object (which is nothing more than the immediate presence of the possibilities) may be made known to us by the very sensation which we refer to it as its effect. Thus, the real antecedent of an effect—the only antecedent which, being invariable and unconditional, we consider to be the cause—may be, not any sensation really felt, but solely the presence, at that or the immediately preceding moment, of a group of possibilities of sensation. Hence it is not with sensations as actually experienced, but

with their Permanent Possibilities, that the idea of
Cause comes to be identified : and we, by one and the
same process, acquire the habit of regarding Sensation
in general, like all our individual sensations, as an Effect,
and also that of conceiving as the causes of most of our
individual sensations, not other sensations, but general
possibilities of sensation.   If all these considerations put
together do not completely explain and account for our
conceiving these Possibilities as a class of independent
and substantive entities, I know not what psychological
analysis can be conclusive.

It may perhaps be said, that the preceding theory
gives, indeed, some account of the idea of Permanent
Existence which forms part of our conception of matter,
but gives no explanation of our believing these permanent objects to be external, or out of ourselves.   I
apprehend, on the contrary, that the very idea of anything out of ourselves is derived solely from the knowledge experience gives us of the Permanent Possibilities.
Our sensations we carry with us wherever we go, and
they never exist where we are not ; but when we change
our place we do not carry away with us the Permanent
Possibilities of Sensation : they remain until we return, or
arise and cease under conditions with which our presence
has in general nothing to do.   And more than all—
they are, and will be after we have ceased to feel, Permanent Possibilities of sensation to other beings than
ourselves.   Thus our actual sensations and the permanent possibilities of sensation, stand out in obtrusive
contrast to one another : and when the idea of Cause has
been acquired, and extended by generalisation from the
parts of our experience to its aggregate whole, nothing
can be more natural than that the Permanent Possibilities should be classed by us as existences generically
distinct from our sensations, but of which our sensations
are the effect.*

---

* My able American critic, Dr. H. B. Smith, contends through several
pages (152–157) that these facts afford no proofs that objects *are* external
to us.   I never pretended that they do.   I am accounting for our conceiving,

The same theory which accounts for our ascribing to
an aggregate of possibilities of sensation, a permanent
existence which our sensations themselves do not possess,
and consequently a greater reality than belongs to our
sensations, also explains our attributing greater objectivity to the Primary Qualities of bodies than to the
Secondary.   For the sensations which correspond to
what are called the Primary Qualities (as soon at least
as we come to apprehend them by two senses, the eye as
well as the touch) are always present when any part of
the group is so.   But colours, tastes, smells, and the
like, being, in comparison, fugacious, are not, in the
same degree, conceived as being always there, even when
nobody is present to perceive them.   The sensations
answering to the Secondary Qualities are only occasional,
those to the Primary, constant.   The Secondary, moreover, vary with different persons, and with the temporary
sensibility of our organs ; the Primary, when perceived
at all, are, as far as we know, the same to all persons
and at all times.

or representing to ourselves, the Permanent Possibilities as real objects
external to us.   I do not believe that the real externality to us of anything,
except other minds, is capable of proof.   But the Permanent Possibilities
are external to us in the only sense we need care about ; they are not
constructed by the mind itself, but merely recognised by it ; in Kantian
language, they are *given* to us, and to other beings in common with us.
"Men cannot act, cannot live," says Professor Fraser (p. 26), "without
"assuming an external world, in some conception of the term external.
"It is the business of the philosopher to explain what that conception
" ought to be.   For ourselves we can conceive only—(1) An externality to
"our present and transient experience in *our own* possible experience past
" and future, and (2) An externality to our own conscious experience, in
" the contemporaneous, as well as in the past or future experience of *other*
"*minds*."   The view I take of externality, in the sense in which I acknowledge it as real, could not be more accurately expressed than in Professor
Fraser's words.   Dr. Smith's criticisms continually go wide of the mark
because he has somehow imagined that I am defending, instead of attack-
ing the belief in Matter as an entity *per se*.   As when he says (pp. 157–
158) that my reasoning assumes, contrary to my own opinion, " an
"*à priori* necessity and validity of the law of cause and effect, or in-
"variable antecedence and consequence."   This might fairly have been
said if I were defending the belief in the supposed hidden cause of our
sensations : but I am only accounting for it ; and to do so I assume only
the tendency, but not the legitimacy of the tendency, to extend all the
laws of our own experience to a sphere beyond our experience.

CHAPTER XII.

THE PSYCHOLOGICAL THEORY OF THE BELIEF IN MATTER, HOW FAR APPLICABLE TO MIND.

IF the deductions in the preceding chapter are correctly drawn from known and admitted laws of the human mind, the doctrine which forms the basis of Sir W. Hamilton's system of psychology, that Mind and Matter, an ego and a non-ego, are original data of consciousness, is deprived of its foundation. Although these two elements, an Ego and a Non-ego, are in (what we call) our consciousness now, and are, or seem to be, inseparable from it, there is no reason for believing that the latter of them, the non-ego, was in consciousness from the beginning; since, even if it was not, we can perceive a way in which it not only might, but must have grown up. We can see that, supposing it absent in the first instance, it would inevitably be present now, not as a deliverance of consciousness in Sir W. Hamilton's sense, for to call it so is to beg the question; but as an instantaneous and irresistible suggestion and inference, which has become by long repetition undistinguishable from a direct intuition. I now propose to carry the inquiry a step farther, and to examine whether the Ego, as a deliverance of consciousness, stands on firmer ground than the Non-ego; whether, at the first moment of our experience, we already have in our consciousness the conception of Self as a permanent existence; or whether it is formed subsequently, and admits of a similar analysis to that which we have found that the notion of Not-self is susceptible of.

It is evident, in the first place, that our knowledge of

mind, like that of matter, is entirely relative ; Sir W.
Hamilton indeed affirms this of mind, in an even more
unqualified manner than he believes it of matter, making
no distinction between Primary and Secondary Qualities.
" In so far * as mind is the common name for the states
" of knowing, willing, feeling, desiring, &c., of which I
" am conscious, it is only the name for a certain series of
" connected phenomena or qualities, and consequently
" expresses only what is known.   But in so far as it
" denotes that subject or substance in which the phe-
" nomena of knowing, willing, &c., inhere—something
" behind or under these phenomena—it expresses what,
" in itself, or in its absolute existence, is unknown."   We
have no conception of Mind itself, as distinguished from
its conscious manifestations.   We neither know nor can
imagine it, except as represented by the succession of
manifold feelings which metaphysicians call by the name
of States or Modifications of Mind.   It is nevertheless
true that our notion of Mind, as well as of Matter, is
the notion of a permanent something, contrasted with
the perpetual flux of the sensations and other feelings or
mental states which we refer to it ; a something which
we figure as remaining the same, while the particular
feelings through which it reveals its existence, change.
This attribute of Permanence, supposing that there were
nothing else to be considered, would admit of the same
explanation when predicated of Mind, as of Matter.   The
belief I entertain that my mind exists when it is not
feeling, nor thinking, nor conscious of its own existence,
resolves itself into the belief of a Permanent Possibility
of these states.   If I think of myself as in dreamless
sleep, or in the sleep of death, and believe that I, or in
other words my mind, is or will be existing through
these states, though not in conscious feeling, the most
scrupulous examination of my belief will not detect in
it any fact actually believed, except that my capability
of feeling is not, in that interval, permanently destroyed,
and is suspended only because it does not meet with the

* Lectures, i. 138.

combination of conditions which would call it into action : the moment it did meet with that combination it would revive, and remains, therefore, a Permanent Possibility. Thus far, there seems no hindrance to our regarding Mind as nothing but the series of our sensations (to which must now be added our internal feelings), as they actually occur, with the addition of infinite possibilities of feeling requiring for their actual realisation conditions which may or may not take place, but which as possibilities are always in existence, and many of them present.

In order to the further understanding of the bearings of this theory of the Ego, it is advisable to consider it in its relation to three questions, which may very naturally be asked with reference to it, and which often have been asked, and sometimes answered very erroneously. If the theory is correct, and my mind is but a series of feelings, or, as it has been called, a thread of consciousness, however supplemented by believed Possibilities of consciousness which are not, though they might be, realised ; if this is all that Mind, or Myself, amounts to, what evidence have I (it is asked) of the existence of my fellow-creatures ? What evidence of a hyperphysical world, or, in one word, of God ? and, lastly, what evidence of immortality?

Dr. Reid unhesitatingly answers, None. If the doctrine is true, I am alone in the universe.

I hold this to be one of Reid's most palpable mistakes. Whatever evidence to each of the three points there is on the ordinary theory, exactly that same evidence is there on this.

In the first place, as to my fellow-creatures. Reid seems to have imagined that if I myself am only a series of feelings, the proposition that I have any fellow-creatures, or that there are any Selves except mine, is but words without a meaning. But this is a misapprehension. All that I am compelled to admit if I receive this theory, is that other people's Selves also are but series of feelings, like my own. Though my Mind, as I am capable of conceiving it, be nothing but the succession of my feelings, and though Mind itself may be merely a possibility of feelings, there is nothing in that doctrine to prevent my conceiving, and believing, that there are other successions of feelings besides those of which I am conscious, and that these are as real as my own. The belief is completely consistent with the metaphysical theory. Let us now see whether the theory takes away the grounds of it.

What are those grounds? By what evidence do I know, or by what considerations am I led to believe, that there exist other sentient creatures; that the walking and speaking figures which I see and hear, have sensations and thoughts, or in other words, possess Minds? The most strenuous Intuitionist does not include this among the things that I know by direct intuition. I conclude it from certain things, which my experience of my own states of feeling proves to me to be marks of it. These marks are of two kinds, antecedent and subsequent; the previous conditions requisite for feeling, and the effects or consequences of it. I conclude that other human beings have feelings like me, because, first, they have bodies like me, which I know, in my own case, to be the antecedent condition of feelings; and because, secondly, they exhibit the acts, and other outward signs, which in my own case I know by experience to be caused by feelings. I am conscious in myself of a series of facts connected by an uniform sequence, of which the beginning is modifications of my body, the middle is feelings, the end is outward demeanour. In the case of other human beings I have the evidence of my senses for the first and last links of the series, but not for the intermediate link. I find, however, that the sequence between the first and last is as regular and constant in those other cases as it is in mine. In my own case I know that the first link produces the last through the intermediate link, and could not produce it without. Experience, therefore, obliges me to conclude that there must be an intermediate link;

which must either be the same in others as in myself, or
a different one : I must either believe them to be alive,
or to be automatons : and by believing them to be alive,
that is, by supposing the link to be of the same nature
as in the case of which I have experience, and which is
in all other respects similar, I bring other human beings,
as phenomena, under the same generalisations which I
know by experience to be the true theory of my own
existence.   And in doing so I conform to the legitimate
rules of experimental enquiry.   The process is exactly
parallel to that by which Newton proved that the force
which keeps the planets in their orbits is identical with
that by which an apple falls to the ground.   It was not
incumbent on Newton to prove the impossibility of its
being any other force ; he was thought to have made
out his point when he had simply shown that no other
force need be supposed.   We know the existence of other
beings by generalisation from the knowledge of our
own : the generalisation merely postulates that what
experience shows to be a mark of the existence of something within the sphere of our consciousness, may be concluded to be a mark of the same thing beyond that sphere.

This logical process loses none of its legitimacy on
the supposition that neither Mind nor Matter is anything but a permanent possibility of feeling.   Whatever sensation I have, I at once refer it to one of the
permanent groups of possibilities of sensation which I
call material objects.   But among these groups I find
there is one (my own body) which is not only composed,
like the rest, of a mixed multitude of sensations and possibilities of sensation, but is also connected, in a peculiar
manner, with all my sensations.   Not only is this special
group always present as an antecedent condition of every
sensation I have, but the other groups are only enabled
to convert their respective possibilities of sensation into
actual sensations, by means of some previous change in
that particular one.   I look about me, and though
there is only one group (or body) which is connected
with all my sensations in this peculiar manner, I

observe that there is a great multitude of other bodies, closely resembling in their sensible properties (in the sensations composing them as groups) this particular one, but whose modifications do not call up, as those of my own body do, a world of sensations in my consciousness.   Since they do not do so in my consciousness, I infer that they do it out of my consciousness, and that to each of them belongs a world of consciousness of its own, to which it stands in the same relation in which what I call my own body stands to mine.   And having made this generalisation, I find that all other facts within my reach accord with it.   Each of these bodies exhibits to my senses a set of phenomena (composed of acts and other manifestations) such as I know, in my own case, to be effects of consciousness, and such as might be looked for if each of the bodies has really in connection with it a world of consciousness.   All this is as good and genuine an inductive process on the theory we are discussing, as it is on the common theory.   Any objection to it in the one case would be an equal objection in the other.   I have stated the postulate required by the one theory : the common theory is in need of the same.   If I could not, from my personal knowledge of one succession of feelings, infer the existence of other successions of feelings, when manifested by the same outward signs, I could just as little, from my personal knowledge of a single spiritual substance, infer by generalisation, when I find the same outward indications, the existence of other spiritual substances.

As the theory leaves the evidence of the existence of my fellow-creatures exactly as it was before, so does it also with that of the existence of God.   Supposing me to believe that the Divine Mind is simply the series of the Divine thoughts and feelings prolonged through eternity, that would be, at any rate, believing God's existence to be as real as my own.   And as for evidence, the argument of Paley's Natural Theology, or, for that matter, of his Evidences of Christianity, would stand exactly where it does.   The Design argument is drawn

from the analogy of human experience.   From the relation which human works bear to human thoughts and
feelings, it infers a corresponding relation between works,
more or less similar but superhuman, and superhuman
thoughts and feelings.   If it proves these, nobody but
a metaphysician needs care whether or not it proves a
mysterious substratum for them.   Again, the arguments
for Revelation undertake to prove by testimony, that
within the sphere of human experience works were done
requiring a greater than human power, and words said
requiring a greater than human wisdom.   These positions, and the evidences of them, neither lose nor gain
anything by our supposing that the wisdom only means
wise thoughts and volitions, and that the power means
thoughts and volitions followed by imposing phenomena.

As to immortality, it is precisely as easy to conceive
that a succession of feelings, a thread of consciousness,
may be prolonged to eternity, as that a spiritual substance for ever continues to exist: and any evidence
which would prove the one, will prove the other.   Metaphysical theologians may lose the *à priori* argument by
which they have sometimes flattered themselves with
having proved that a spiritual substance, by the essential constitution of its nature, *cannot* perish.   But they
had better drop this argument in any case.   To do them
justice, they seldom insist on it now.

The notion that metaphysical Scepticism, even at the
utmost length to which it ever has been, or is capable of
being, carried, has for its logical consequence atheism,
is grounded on an entire misapprehension of the Sceptical argument, and has no *locus standi* except for persons
who think that whatever accustoms people to a rigid
scrutiny of evidence is unfavourable to religious belief.
This is the opinion, doubtless, of those who do not
believe in any religion, and seemingly of a great number
who do : but it is not the opinion of Sir W. Hamilton,
who says * that "religious disbelief and philosophical
" scepticism are not merely not the same, but have no

* Lectures, i. 394.

" natural connection ; " and who, as we have seen, makes use of the veracity of the Deity as his principal argument for trusting the testimony of consciousness to the substantiality of Matter and of Mind, which would have been a gross *petitio principii* if he had thought that our assurance of the divine attributes required that the objective existence of Matter and Mind should be first recognised.

The theory, therefore, which resolves Mind into a series of feelings, with a background of possibilities of feeling, can effectually withstand the most invidious of the arguments directed against it.   But, groundless as are the extrinsic objections, the theory has intrinsic difficulties which we have not yet set forth, and which it seems to be beyond the power of metaphysical analysis to remove.   Besides present feelings, and possibilities of present feeling, there is another class of phenomena to be included in an enumeration of the elements making up our conception of Mind.   The thread of consciousness which composes the mind's phenomenal life, consists not only of present sensations, but likewise, in part, of memories and expectations.   Now what are these ?   In themselves, they are present feelings, states of present consciousness, and in that respect not distinguished from sensations.   They all, moreover, resemble some given sensations or feelings, of which we have previously had experience.   But they are attended with the peculiarity, that each of them involves a belief in more than its own present existence.   A sensation involves only this : but a remembrance of sensation, even if not referred to any particular date, involves the suggestion and belief that a sensation, of which it is a copy or representation, actually existed in the past : and an expectation involves the belief, more or less positive, that a sensation or other feeling to which it directly refers, will exist in the future. Nor can the phenomena involved in these two states of consciousness be adequately expressed, without saying that the belief they include is, that I myself formerly had, or that I myself, and no other, shall hereafter have,

the sensations remembered or expected. The fact believed is, that the sensations did actually form, or will
hereafter form, part of the self-same series of states, or
thread of consciousness, of which the remembrance or expectation of those sensations is the part now present. If,
therefore, we speak of the Mind as a series of feelings,
we are obliged to complete the statement by calling it a
series of feelings which is aware of itself as past and
future ; and we are reduced to the alternative of believing that the Mind, or Ego, is something different from
any series of feelings, or possibilities of them, or of accepting the paradox, that something which *ex hypothesi* is
but a series of feelings, can be aware of itself as a series.

The truth is, that we are here face to face with that
final inexplicability, at which, as Sir W. Hamilton
observes, we inevitably arrive when we reach ultimate
facts ; and in general, one mode of stating it only
appears more incomprehensible than another, because
the whole of human language is accommodated to the
one, and is so incongruous with the other, that it cannot
be expressed in any terms which do not deny its truth.
The real stumbling block is perhaps not in any theory
of the fact, but in the fact itself. The true incomprehensibility perhaps is, that something which has ceased,
or is not yet in existence, can still be, in a manner,
present : that a series of feelings, the infinitely greater
part of which is past or future, can be gathered up, as
it were, into a single present conception, accompanied
by a belief of reality. I think, by far the wisest thing
we can do, is to accept the inexplicable fact, without
any theory of how it takes place : and when we are
obliged to speak of it in terms which assume a theory,
to use them with a reservation as to their meaning.

I have stated the difficulties attending the attempt to
frame a theory of Mind, or the Ego, similar to what I
have called the Psychological Theory of Matter, or the
Non-ego. No such difficulties attend the theory in its
application to Matter ; and I leave it, as set forth, to pass
for whatever it is worth as an antagonist doctrine to that

of Sir W. Hamilton and the Scottish School, respecting the non-ego as a deliverance of consciousness.*

* Mr. Mansel, in his "Prolegomena Logica," shows a perception of the difference here pointed out between the character of the Psychological explanation of the belief in Matter, and that of the belief in Mind ; and he resolves the question by drawing a distinction between the two Noumena, not often drawn by philosophers posterior to Berkeley. He considers the Ego to be a direct presentation of consciousness, while with regard to the Non-ego he is not far from adopting the Berkeleian theory. The whole of his remarks on the subject are well worth reading. See "Prolegomena Logica," pp. 123–135.

APPENDIX TO THE TWO PRECEDING CHAPTERS.

THIS attempt to bring out into distinctness the mode in which the notions of Matter and Mind, considered as Substances, may have been generated in us by the mere order of our sensations, has naturally received from those whose metaphysical opinions were already made up, a much greater amount of opposition than of assent. I think I have observed, however, that the repugnance shown to it by writers has been in tolerably correct proportion to the evidence they give of deficiency in that indispensable aptitude of a metaphysician, facility in placing himself at the point of view of a theory different from his own : and that those who have ever (if the expression may be pardoned) thought themselves into the Berkeleian or any other Idealistic scheme of philosophy, however little favourable towards other parts of the present volume, have either let this part of it alone, or expressed more or less approbation of it. Those who are completely satisfied with the popular every-day notion of Matter, or whose metaphysics have been adopted from any of the Realistic thinkers who undertake to legitimate that common notion, are usually content with going round the counter-theory on the outside, and seldom place themselves sufficiently at the centre of it to perceive what a person ought to think or do, who occupies that position. They no longer, indeed, commit so gross a blunder as that which, not very long ago, even Reid, Stewart, and Brown rushed blindly into—that of charging a Berkeleian with inconsistency if he did not walk iuto the water or into the fire. Acquaintance with the German metaphysicians, and (it is but just to add) the teachings of Sir W. Hamilton, have had that much of beneficial result. But if such thinkers as these three could pass judgment on Berkeley's doctrine while showing by such conclusive proof that they had never understood its very alphabet—that, however much consideration they may have given to the mere arguments of Berkeley, they had not begun to realise his doctrine in their own minds —to look at the sensible universe as he saw it, and see what consequences would follow ; it is not wonderful that those who have got on a few steps further than this, have still much to do, before they are able to accommodate their conceptive faculties to the conditions of what I have called the Psycho-

logical Theory, and follow that theory correctly into the rami-
fication of its applications.

In principle, I must admit that my opponents, as a body,
have referred the Psychological Theory to the right test.   They
have aimed at showing that its attempt to account for the belief
in Matter (I say Matter only, because I do not profess to have
adequately accounted for the belief in Mind) implies or requires
that the belief should already exist, as a condition of its own
production.   The objection, if true, is conclusive; but they are
not very particular about the proof of its truth.   They, one and
all, think their case made out if I employ, in any part of the
exposition, the language of common life—a language constructed on the basis of the notions into the origin of which I
am inquiring.   If I say, that after we have seen a piece of paper
on a table, our belief that it is still there during our absence
means a belief that if we went again into the room we should
see it, they cry out, Here is belief in Matter already assumed;
the idea of going into a room implies belief in matter.   If, as
a proof that modifications may take place in our possibilities of
sensation while the sensations are not in actual consciousness,
I say that whether we are asleep or awake the fire goes out, I
am told that I am assuming a knowledge of ourselves as a substance, and of the difference between being asleep and awake.
They forget that to go into a room, to be asleep or awake, are
expressions which have a meaning in the Psychological Theory
as well as in theirs; that every assertion that can be made
about the external world, which means anything on the Realistic
theory, has a parallel meaning on the Psychological.   Going into
a room, on the Psychological theory, is a mere series of sensations felt, and possibilities of sensation inferred,* but distinguishable from every other combination of sensations and
possibilities, and which, with others like to itself, forms as
vast and variegated a picture of the universe as can be had on
the other theory; indeed, as I maintain, the very same picture.
The Psychological theory requires that we should have a conception of this series of actual and contingent sensations, as
distinct from any other; but it does not require that we should
have referred these sensations to a substance ulterior to all
sensation or possibility of sensation.   To suppose so, is to
commit the same kind of misapprehension, though in a less
extreme degree, which Reid, Stewart, and Brown committed.

When, in attempting an intelligible discussion of an abstruse

* This particular series includes volitions in addition to sensations; but
the difference is of no consequence; and the theory would stand if we
suppose ourselves carried into the room instead of walking into it.

metaphysical question, I have occasion to speak of any combination of physical facts, I must speak of it by the only names
there are for it. I must employ language, every word of which
expresses, not things as we perceive them, or as we may have
conceived them originally, but things as we conceive them now.
I was addressing readers, all of whom had the acquired notion
of Matter, and nearly all of them the belief in it : and it was
my business to show, to these believers in Matter, a possible
mode in which the notion and belief of it might have been
acquired, even if Matter, in the metaphysical meaning of the
term, did not exist. In endeavouring to point out to them by
what facts the notion might have been generated, it was competent to me to state those facts in the language which was not
only the most intelligible, but, to the minds I was addressing,
the truest. The real paralogism would have been, if I had said
anything implying, not the existence of Matter, but that the
belief in it or the notion of it was part of the facts by which I
was maintaining that this belief and notion may have been
generated. But in no single instance have any adversaries
whom I am aware of, been able to show this : and if they fairly
placed themselves at the point of view of the Psychological
explanation, they would see that I could not, in any circumstances whatever, have been reduced to this necessity : because
there is, as I have said, for every statement which can be made
concerning material phenomena in terms of the Realistic
theory, an equivalent meaning in terms of Sensation and Possibilities of Sensation alone, and a meaning which would justify
all the same processes of thought. In fact, almost all philosophers who have narrowly examined the subject, have decided
that Substance need only be postulated as a support for phenomena, or as a bond of connection to hold a group or series of
otherwise unconnected phenomena together : let us only, then,
think away the support, and suppose the phenomena to remain,
and to be held together in the same groups and series by some
other agency, or without any agency but an eternal law, and
every consequence follows without Substance, for the sake of
which Substance was assumed. The Hindoos thought that
the earth required to be supported by an elephant ; but
the earth turned out quite capable of supporting itself, and
"hanging self-balanced " on its own " centre." Descartes thought
that a material medium filling the whole space between the
earth and the sun, was required to enable them to act on
one another ; but it has been found sufficient to suppose an
immaterial law of attraction, and the medium and its vortices
dropped off as superfluities.

To dispel some of the haze which seems still to hang about the data assumed by the Psychological theory of the belief in Matter, it will be well that, as I have stated what laws and capacities, in one word what conditions, that theory postulates in the mind itself, I should also state what conditions it postulates in Nature; in that which, to use the Kantian phraseology, is given to the mind, as distinguished from the mind's own constitution.

First, then, it postulates Sensations; and a certain Order among sensations. And the Order postulated is of more kinds than one.

In the first place, there is the mere fact of succession. Sensations exist before and after one another. This is as much a primordial fact as sensation itself; it is a feature always present in sensation, and we have the strongest ground that can ever be had for regarding it as ultimate, because every genesis we assign to any other fact of perception or thought, includes it as a condition. I shall be told, that this is postulating the reality of Time: and it is so, if by Time be understood an indefinite succession of successions, unequal in rapidity. But an entity called Time, and regarded as not a succession of successions, but as something *in* which the successions take place, I do not and need not postulate.* Neither do I decide whether this inseparable attribute of our sensations is annexed to them by the laws of mind, or given in the sensations themselves; nor whether, at this great height of abstraction, the distinction does not disappear. Let me say also, that I have never pretended to account by association for the idea of Time. It is the seeming infinity of Time, as of Space, which, after Mr. James Mill, I have tendered that explanation of: and that of this it is the true and sufficient one, is to me obvious.

Sensations are not only successive, they are also simultaneous: it often happens that several of them are felt, apparently at the same instant. This attribute of sensations is not so evidently primordial as their succession. There are philosophers who

---

* This objective conception of Time, as *holding* the successions instead of *being* them, is probably suggested by our being able to measure time, and number its parts. But what we call measuring Time is only comparing successions, and measuring the length or rapidity of one series of successions by that of another. Rapidity of succession, indeed, is a phrase which derives all its meaning from such a comparison. I say that the words of a person to whom I am listening succeed one another more rapidly than the tickings of a clock, because, after I have heard a word and a ticking simultaneously, a second word occurs before a second ticking. The only ultimate facts or primitive elements in Time are Before and After; which (the knowledge of opposites being one) involve the notion of Neither before nor after, *i.e.*, simultaneous.

think that the sensations deemed simultaneous are very rapidly successive, their distinction from other cases of succession being that they may succeed one another in any order. I do not agree in this opinion; but, even supposing it correct, we should equally have to postulate the distinction. We should have to assume that plurality of sensations exists in two modes, one consciously successive, the other felt as simultaneous, and that the mind is able to distinguish between the one sort and the other.

Besides this twofold order inherent in sensations, of being either successive or simultaneous, there is an order within that order : they are successive or simultaneous in constant combinations. The same antecedent sensation is followed by the same consequent sensation ; the same sensation is accompanied by the same set of simultaneous sensations. I use these expressions for shortness, for the uniformity of order is not quite so simple as this. The consequent sensation is not always *actually* felt after the antecedent, nor are all the synchronous sensations actually felt whenever one of them is felt. But the one which is felt gives us assurance, grounded on experience, that each of the others, if not felt, is feelable, *i.e.*, will be felt if the other facts be present which are the known antecedent conditions of such a sensation as it is. For example, I have the sensations of colour and of a visible disc, which are parts of our present conception of a cast-iron ball. I infer that there are, now or presently to be had by me, simultaneously with those visual sensations, another feeling, called the sensation of hardness. But I do not have this last sensation inevitably and at once. Why ? Because (as I also know by experience) no sensation of hardness is ever felt unless preceded by a condition, the same in all cases, but itself sensational, the sensations of muscular exertion and pressure. The visual sensation is synchronous, not necessarily with the actual sensation of hardness, but with a present possibility of that sensation. When we feel the one, we are not always feeling the other, but we know that it is to be felt on the ordinary terms: we know that so soon as the muscular sensations take place which are the observed preliminary to *every* sensation of hardness, that particular sensation of hardness will certainly be had, simultaneously with the visual sensation. This is what is meant by saying that a Body is a group of simultaneous possibilities of sensation, not of simultaneous sensations. It rarely happens that the sensations which enter into the group can all be experienced at once; because many of them are never had without a long series of antecedent sensations, including volitions, which may be incompatible with the sensations and volitions necessary for having others. The sensations which we receive when we study the internal structure of a closed body, are not to be obtained without having previously the complex series of sensations and volitions concerned in the operation of opening it. The sensations we receive from the complicated process by which food nourishes us must be long waited for after our first sight of the food, and many of them are not even then to be had without our being led up to them through a long series of muscular and other sensations. But the very first sensations we have, that are sufficient to identify the group, guarantee to us the possibility or potentiality of all the others. The potentiality becomes actuality on the occurrence of certain known conditions *sine quâ non* of each, which are conditions not of having that particular sensation at a given moment, but of having any sensation of that kind; conditions which, when analysed, are themselves also merely sensational. Any one who had thrown his mind, by an act of imagination, into the Psychological theory, would see at a glance all these applications and developments of it, even if he did not follow them out into detail. But men will not, and mostly cannot, throw their minds into any theory with which they are not familiar; and the bearings and consequences of the Psychological theory will have to be developed and minutely expounded innumerable times, before it will be seen as it is, and have whatever chance it deserves of being accepted as true.

I have postulated first, Sensation; secondly, succession and simultaneousness of sensations; thirdly, an uniform order in their succession and simultaneousness, such that they are united in groups, the component sensations of which are in such a relation to one another, that when we experience one, we are authorised to expect all the rest, conditionally on certain antecedent sensations called organic, belonging to the *kind* of each. This is all we need postulate with regard to the groups, considered in themselves, or considered in relation to the perceiving Subject. Let us examine whether it is necessary to postulate anything additional respecting the groups considered in relation to one another.

In Dr. M'Cosh's opinion, the Psychological theory overlooks this part of the subject.* In quoting the analysis of our conception of Matter into Resistance, Extension, and Figure, together with miscellaneous powers of exciting other sensations, he observes, "There is a palpable omission here, for it omits

---

* M'Cosh, p. 118. The same observation applies to another of my critics, the writer in *Blackwood's Magazine*, who says (p. 28) "The qualities by which they [Things] act upon each other, cannot be resolved into any receptivity or subjectivity of mine."

" those powers by which one body operates upon another; thus " the sun has a power to make wax white, and fire to make lead " fluid." If Dr. M'Cosh had entered even a very little way into the mode of thought which he is combating, he must have seen that after mentioning the attribute of exciting sensations, it could not be necessary to add that of making something else excite sensations. If Body altogether is only conceived as a power of exciting sensations, the action of one body upon another is simply the modification by one such power of the sensations excited by another ; or to use a different expression, the joint action of two powers of exciting sensations. It is easy for any one competent to such enquiries who will make the attempt, to understand how one group of Possibilities of Sensation can be conceived as destroying or modifying another such group.

Let there be granted a synchronous group, connected by the contingent simultaneousness already described, which renders each of the component sensations a mark of the possibility of having all the others; while each, independently of the others, has conditions *sine qua non* of its own, also sensational, but of the kind which, in common language, we call organic, and refer to an internal sense. Let us suppose that these organic conditions, instead of existing for one or more sensations of the group and not for the rest, do not at present exist for any of them. The whole of the possibilities of sensation which form the group, and which mutually testify to each other's presence, are now dormant : but they are ready to start into actuality at any moment, when the conditions *sine qua non* which belong to them separately are realised : and whenever any of them thus starts up, it informs us (so far as our experience happens to have reached) what others are ready to do so in the same manner. This dormancy of all the possibilities, while, as real possibilities guaranteeing one another, they continue to exist, constitutes, on the Psychological theory, the fact which is at the bottom of the assertion that the body is in existence when we are not perceiving it. This fact is all that we need postulate to account for our conceiving the groups of Possibilities of Sensation as permanent and independent of us; for our projecting them into objectivity ; and for our conceiving them as perhaps capable of being Possibilities of Sensation to other beings in like manner as to ourselves, as soon as we have conceived the idea of other sentient beings than ourselves. And since we do actually recognise other sentient beings as existing, and receive impressions from them which entirely accord with this hypothesis, we accept the hypothesis as a truth, and believe that the Permanent Possibilities of Sensation really are common to ourselves and other beings.

Having thus arrived at the conception of an absent group of Possibilities, there is surely no more difficulty in conceiving the annihilation or alteration of the Possibilities while absent, than of the sensations themselves when present. The log which I saw on the fire an hour ago, has been consumed and has disappeared when I look again; the Possibilities of Sensation which I called by that name, are possibilities no longer. The ice which I placed in front of the fire at the same time, is now water; such Possibilities of Sensation as form part of the groups called ice and not of the groups called water, have ceased and given place to others. All this is intelligible without supposing the wood, the ice, or the water, to be anything underneath or beyond Permanent Possibilities of Sensation. Why, then, when I ascribe the disappearance of the wood, and the conversion of the ice into water, to the presence of the fire, must I suppose the fire to be something underneath a Possibility of Sensation? My experience informs me that those other Possibilities of Sensation do not vanish or change in the manner mentioned, unless another Possibility of Sensation known by the name of fire, has existed immediately before, and continued to exist simultaneously with the change. Changes in the Permanent Possibilities I find to have always for their antecedent conditions, other Permanent Possibilities, and to be connected with them by an order or law, as uniform as that which connects the elements of each group with one another; indeed by a still stricter order, for the laws of succession, those of Cause and Effect, are laws of more rigid precision than those of simultaneousness. But the facts, between which the observed uniformities of succession exist, are facts of sense; that is, either actual sensations, or possibilities of sensation inferred from the actual. Thus the whole variety of the facts of nature as we know it, is given in the mere existence of our sensations, and in the laws or order of their occurrence.*

I have now given an exposition of the Psychological Theory, and of the mode in which it accounts for what is supposed to be our natural conviction of the existence of Matter, from the

* Mr. O'Hanlon, in his little pamphlet (pp. 12 and 14) puts his difficulty on this subject in the following terms: "Your permanent possi-"bilities of sensation are, so long as they are not felt, nothing actual. Yet "you speak of change taking place in them, and that independently of "our consciousness and of our presence or absence. . . . If the fire, apart "from any consciousness, be some positive condition or conditions of "warmth and light, if the corn be some positive condition or conditions of "food, my thesis is made out, and your Pure Idealism falls to the ground.

R

objective point of view, as I had previously done from the subjective ; and I think it will be found that the exposition does not presuppose anything which I have not expressly postulated, and that I have not postulated any of the facts or notions which I undertake to explain. It may be said that I postulate an Ego—the sentient Subject of the sensations. I have stated what subjective, as well as what objective data I postulate. Expectation being one of these, in so far as reference to an Ego is implied in Expectation I do postulate an Ego. But I am entitled to do so, for up to this stage it is not Self, but Body, that I have been endeavouring to trace to its origin as an acquired notion.*

I now pass to this very subject, the Ego, and to the objections which have been made against the manner in which it is treated in the preceding chapter.

" If, on the other hand, the fire be nothing positive apart from any con-
"sciousness, then, since it is nothing at all when so apart, you can have
"no right to speak of modifications taking place in it whether we are
"asleep or awake, present or absent."

I give great credit to my young antagonist, not only for the neatness of his dilemma, but for having gone so directly to the point at which is the real stress of the dispute. But I think he will perceive, from what I have said in the text, in what manner one may have a right to speak of modifications as taking place in a possibility. And I think he will be able to see that the condition of a phenomenon needs not necessarily be anything positive, in his sense of the word, or objective ; it may be anything, positive or negative, actuality or possibility, without which the phenomenon would not have occurred, and which may therefore be justly inferred from its occurrence.

* Mr. O'Hanlon says (p. 14) : " Conceding the entire truth of the posi-
"tion, that there are associations naturally and even necessarily generated
"by the order of our sensations, and of our reminiscences of sensation,
"which, supposing no intuition of an external world to have existed in
"consciousness, would inevitably generate the belief, and would cause it
"to be regarded as an intuition ;—conceding, I say, for argument's sake,
"the entire truth of this position, it may still be true that though we have
"no intuition of the external world, the inference that such a world exists
"is a legitimate one." Undoubtedly it may. Malebranche, for instance, according to whose system Matter is not perceived, nor in any way cognised, nor capable of being cognised by our minds, all the things that we see or feel existing only as ideas in the Divine Mind, nevertheless fully believed in the reality of this superfluous wheel in the mechanism of the universe, which merely revolves while the machinery does its work independently of it—because he thought that God himself had asserted its existence in the Scriptures : and whoever agrees with Malebranche in his premises is likely to agree with him in his conclusion. But with most people, whether philosophers or common men, the evidence on which Matter is believed to exist independently of our minds, is either that we perceive it by our senses, or that the notion and belief of it come to us by an original law of our nature. If it be shown that there is no ground for either of these opinions—that all we are conscious of may be accounted

Having shown that in order to account for the belief in Matter, or, in other words, in a non-ego supposed to be presented in or along with sensation, it is not necessary to suppose anything but sensations and possibilities of sensation connected in groups ; it was natural and necessary to enquire whether the Ego, supposed to be presented in or along with all consciousness whatever, is also an acquired notion, inexplicable in the same manner. I therefore stated this phenomenal theory of the Ego; freed it from the prejudice which attaches to it on the score of consequences to which it does not lead, the non-existence, first, of our fellow-creatures, and secondly, of God ;* but showed that it has

for without supposing that we perceive Matter by our senses, and that the notion and belief in Matter may have come to us by the laws of our constitution without being a revelation of any objective reality, the main evidences of Matter are at an end ; and though I am perfectly willing to listen to any other evidence, Malebranche's argument is, I must confess, quite as conclusive as any that I expect to find.

* Some of my critics have impugned the arguments of the preceding chapter on this particular point. They have said (Mr. O'Hanlon is the one who has said it with the greatest compactness and force) that persons, equally with inanimate things, may be conceived as mere states of my own consciousness; that the same processes of thought which, according to the Psychological theory, can generate the belief in Matter even if it does not exist, must be equally competent to engender the belief of the existence of other Minds: and that the principles of the theory require us, under the law of Parsimony, to conclude that if the belief may have been, it has been, thus generated : consequently the theory takes away all evidence of the existence of other minds, or of other threads of consciousness than our own.

It would undoubtedly do so, if the only evidence of the existence of other threads of consciousness was a natural belief, as a natural belief is the only evidence which rational persons now acknowledge of the existence of Matter. But there is other evidence, which does not exist in the case of Matter, and which is as conclusive as the other is inconclusive. The nature of this has been stated, with sufficient fulness of development, in the preceding chapter, and Mr. O'Hanlon has rightly understood it to be a simple extension of "the principles of inductive evidence, which experience "shows hold good of my states of consciousness, to a sphere without my "consciousness." But he objects (p. 7): "The doing so postulates two "things : (a) That there is a sphere beyond my consciousness, the very "thing to be proved. (b) That the laws which obtain in my conscious-"ness, also obtain in the sphere beyond it."

To this I reply, that it does not postulate these two things, but, to the extent required by the present question, proves them. There is nothing in the nature of the inductive principle that confines it within the limits of my own consciousness, when it exceptionally happens that an inference surpassing the limits of my consciousness can conform to inductive conditions.

I am aware, by experience, of a group of Permanent Possibilities of Sensation which I call my body, and which my experience shows to be an universal condition of every part of my thread of consciousness. I am also aware of a great number of other groups, resembling the one that I

intrinsic difficulties, which no one has been able to remove;
since certain of the attributes comprised in our notion of the
Ego, and which are at the very foundation of it, namely
Memory and Expectation, have no equivalent in Matter, and
cannot be reduced to any elements similar to those into which
Matter is resolved by the Psychological theory.   Having stated
these facts, as inexplicable by the Psychological theory, I left
them to stand as facts, without any theory whatever : not
adopting the Permanent Possibility hypothesis as a sufficient

call my body, but which have no connection, such as that has, with the
remainder of my thread of consciousness. This disposes me to draw an
inductive inference, that those other groups are connected with other
threads of consciousness, as mine is with my own. If the evidence stopped
here, the inference would be but an hypothesis ; reaching only to the
inferior degree of inductive evidence called Analogy. The evidence, however, does not stop here : for,—having made the supposition that real
feelings, though not experienced by myself, lie behind those phenomena
of my own consciousness which, from their resemblance to my body, I
call other human bodies,—I find that my subsequent consciousness presents those very sensations, of speech heard, of movements and other
outward demeanour seen, and so forth, which, being the effects or consequents of actual feelings in my own case, I should expect to follow upon
those other hypothetical feelings if they really exist : and thus the hypothesis is verified. It is thus proved inductively that there is a sphere
beyond my consciousness : i.e., that there are other consciousnesses beyond
it ; for there exists no parallel evidence in regard to Matter. And it is
proved inductively, that so far as respects those other consciousnesses
linked to as many groups of Permanent Possibilities of Sensation similar
to my own body, the laws which obtain in my consciousness also obtain
in the sphere beyond it ; that those other threads of consciousness are
beings similar to myself.
    The legitimacy of this process is open to no objections, either real or
imaginary, but such as may equally be made against inductive inferences
within the sphere of our own actual or possible consciousness. Facts of
which I never *have* had consciousness are as much unknown facts, as
much apart from my actual experience, as facts of which I cannot have
consciousness. When I conclude, from facts that I immediately perceive,
to the existence of other facts such as *might* come into my actual consciousness (which the feelings of other people never can) but which never
did come into it, and of which I have no evidence but an induction from
experience ; how do I know that I am concluding rightly—that the inference is warranted, from an actual consciousness to a contingent possibility of consciousness which has never become actual? Surely because
this conclusion from experience is verified by further experience ; because
those other experiences which I ought to have if my inference was correct,
really present themselves. This verification, which is the source of all
my reliance on induction, justifies the same reliance wherever it is found.
The alien threads of consciousness of which I presume the existence from
the analogy of my own body, manifest the truth of the presumption by
visual and tactual effects within my own consciousness, resembling those
which follow from sensations, thoughts, or emotions felt by myself. The
reality beyond the sphere of my consciousness rests on the twofold

theory of Self in spite of the objections to it, as some of my critics have imagined, and have wasted no small amount of argument and sarcasm in exposing the untenability of such a position: neither, on the other hand, did I, as others have supposed, accept the common theory of Mind, as a so-called Substance.   Since the state in which I profess to leave the question has been so ill understood, it is incumbent on me to explain myself more fully.

Since the fact which alone necessitates the belief in an Ego,

evidence, of its antecedents, and its consequents.   It is an inference upwards from the manifestations, and downwards from the antecedent conditions; and whichever of these inferences is first drawn, the other is its verification.

I venture to hope that these considerations may remove Mr. O'Hanlon's difficulty.   But whatever the difficulty may be, it is not peculiar to the Psychological theory, but has equally to be encountered on every other. For no one supposes that other people's feelings or states of consciousness are a matter of direct intuition to us, or of Natural Belief.   We do not directly perceive other minds: their reality is not known to us immediately, but by means of evidence.   And there is no evidence by which it can be proved to me that there is a conscious being within each of the human bodies that I see, without a process of induction involving the very same assumptions which are required by the Psychological Theory.

I will delay the reader a few moments more while I reply to a minor difficulty of Mr. O'Hanlon.   He urges, that the Psychological theory inserts an alien consciousness between two consciousnesses of my own, as the effect of one of them and the cause of the other.   " A boy cuts his "finger and screams.   The knife, the blood, and the boy's body are only "(in Mr. Mill's view) actual and possible groups of my sensations, and "the scream is an actual sensation.   I infer, continuing to accept Mr. "Mill's theory, that between the scream and the other sensations, namely "between two sets of states of my own consciousness, a foreign conscious- "ness had the feeling I call pain, and also that the sensations of cutting "its finger, the same sensations, belong as much to it as to me, combined "with certain additions, and in a very peculiar manner.   Yet if I was not "by, the boy, the knife, the blood, the scream would only exist poten- "tially" (pp. 8, 9).   Whatever seeming absurdity, and real confusion, exist here, are only attributable to the fact, that Mr. O'Hanlon, notwithstanding his acuteness, has not yet sufficiently thought himself into the theory he denies.   On the same evidence on which I recognise foreign threads of consciousness, I believe that the Permanent Possibilities of Sensation are common to them and to me; but not the actual sensations. The evidence proves to me, that although the knife, the blood, and the boy's body would, if I were absent, be mere potentialities of sensation relatively to me, the similar potentialities which I infer to exist in him have been realised as actual sensations; and it is as conditions of the sensations in him, and not of sensations in me, that they form a part of the series of causes and effects which take place out of my consciousness. The chain of causation is the following: 1. A modification in a set of Permanent Possibilities of Sensation common to the boy and me.   2. A sensation of pain in the boy, not felt by me.   3. The scream, which is a sensation in me.

the one fact which the Psychological theory cannot explain, is the fact of Memory (for Expectation I hold to be, both psychologically and logically, a consequence of Memory), I see no reason to think that there is any cognisance of an Ego until Memory commences. There seems no ground for believing, with Sir W. Hamilton and Mr. Mansel, that the Ego is an original presentation of consciousness ; that the mere impression on our senses involves, or carries with it, any consciousness of a Self, any more than I believe it to do of a Not-self. Our very notion of a Self takes its commencement (there is every reason to suppose) from the representation of a sensation in memory, when awakened by the only thing there is to awaken it before any associations have been formed, namely, the occurrence of a subsequent sensation similar to the former one. The fact of recognising a sensation, of being reminded of it, and, as we say, remembering that it has been felt before, is the simplest and most elementary fact of memory : and the inexplicable tie, or law, the organic union (as Professor Masson calls it) which connects the present consciousness with the past one, of which it reminds me, is as near as I think we can get to a positive conception of Self. That there is something real in this tie, real as the sensations themselves, and not a mere product of the laws of thought without any fact corresponding to it, I hold to be indubitable. The precise nature of the process by which we cognise it, is open to much dispute. Whether we are directly conscious of it in the act of remembrance, as we are of succession in the fact of having successive sensations, or whether, according to the opinion of Kant, we are not conscious of a Self at all, but are compelled to assume it as a necessary condition of Memory,* I do not undertake to decide. But this original element, which has no community of nature with any of the things answering to our names, and to which we cannot give any name but its own peculiar one without implying some false or ungrounded theory, is the Ego, or Self. As such, I ascribe a reality to the Ego—to my own Mind—different from that real existence as a Permanent Possibility, which is the only reality I acknowledge in Matter : and by fair

---

* Mr. Mahaffy thinks that the question may be decided in favour of Kant on the evidence of consciousness itself. "Are you," he asks (p. lvi.) "conscious of being presented with yourself as a substance? or are you "only conscious that in every act of thought you must presuppose a per- "manent self, and always refer it to self, while still that self you cannot "grasp, and it remains a hidden basis upon which you erect the structure "of your thoughts? Which of these opinions will most men adopt? "After all, Kant's view is the simpler and the more consistent with the "ordinary language."

experiential inference from that one Ego, I ascribe the same reality to other Egoes, or Minds.

Having thus, as I hope, more clearly defined my position in regard to the reality of the Ego, considered as a question of Ontology, I return to my first starting point, the Relativity of human knowledge, and affirm (being here in entire accordance with Sir W. Hamilton) that whatever be the nature of the real existence we are compelled to acknowledge in Mind, the Mind is only known to itself phenomenally, as the series of its feelings or consciousnesses. We are forced to apprehend every part of the series as linked with the other parts by something in common, which is not the feelings themselves, any more than the succession of the feelings is the feelings themselves : and as that which is the same in the first as in the second, in the second as in the third, in the third as in the fourth, and so on, must be the same in the first and in the fiftieth, this common element is a permanent element. But beyond this, we can affirm nothing of it except the states of consciousness themselves. The feelings or consciousnesses which belong or have belonged to it, and its possibilities of having more, are the only facts there are to be asserted of Self—the only positive attributes, except permanence, which we can ascribe to it. In consequence of this, I occasionally use the words " mind " and "thread of consciousness" interchangeably, and treat Mind as existing, and Mind as known to itself, as convertible: but this is only for brevity, and the explanations which I have now given must always be taken as implied.*

---

* Dr. M'Cosh has renewed his attack upon the doctrine of Permanent Possibilities. But I cannot find in his later remarks, so far as they are to the purpose, much more than a repetition of his earlier. On some minor points he does present some novelties. He is severe upon me for hesitating to decide whether the attribute of succession as between our sensations is given in the sensations themselves, or annexed to them by a law of the mind. The first supposition he characterises as a mere verbal generalisation like those which I have laid to the charge of Condillac ; forgetting the opinion held by some acute metaphysicians, and which is no mere verbal generalisation, that to have sensations in succession is only the same thing as having more sensations than one. The other supposition, that the attribute of succession is annexed to our sensations by a law of the mind, he says is giving to the mind the " power of generating " in the course of its exercise a totally new idea," an opinion, he says, utterly inconsistent with my " empirical theory ;" he does not say with what theory. In any scheme of human knowledge that I am able to form, the resemblances and the successions and coexistences of our sensations are real facts, and objects of direct apprehension. Whether we are said to apprehend them by our senses or by our minds (which is the real meaning of the alternative I have left open) affects no theory of mine, and is to me a matter of indifference.

The most curious part of Dr. M'Cosh's reply is that he thinks, according to my " theory " there is no difference between sensations and thoughts. According to him, if I am right, the facts of external nature being only possibilities of sensation, ought to succeed one another according to " mental laws, say the laws of association." The reader will scarcely believe that I am not misrepresenting Dr. M‘Cosh ; but I refer him to the article, pp. 345 and 346.

Dr. M‘Cosh still maintains that the action of bodies on one another cannot be accountèd for on the hypothesis of Immateriality, takes credit for having, on this point, detected me in an oversight, and seems to consider the answer I was "obliged" to give him as an afterthought of my own. This only proves that Dr. M‘Cosh has forgotten, if he ever knew, the very elements of the Berkeleian controversy. Whoever knows anything of that, has got far beyond the stage of thought at which Dr. M‘Cosh remains. Berkeley would indeed have been easily answered if his doctrine could give no account of the greater part of all the phenomena of physical nature.

CHAPTER XIII.

THE PSYCHOLOGICAL THEORY OF THE PRIMARY QUALITIES
OF MATTER.

FOR the reasons which have been set forth, I conceive
Sir W. Hamilton to be wrong in his statement that a
Self and a Not-self are immediately apprehended in our
primitive consciousness. We have, in all probability, no
notion of Not-self, until after considerable experience of
the recurrence of sensations according to fixed laws, and
in groups.* Nor is it credible that the first sensation
which we experience awakens in us any notion of an
Ego or Self. To refer it to an Ego is to consider it as
part of a series of states of consciousness, some portion
of which is already past. The identification of a present
state with a remembered state cognised as past, is what,
to my thinking, constitutes the cognition that it is I who
feel it. " I " means he who saw, touched, or felt something yesterday or the day before. No single sensation
can suggest personal identity: this requires a series of
sensations, thought of as forming a line of succession,
and summed up in thought into a Unity.

But (however this may be) throughout the whole of our
sensitive life except its first beginnings, we unquestion-
ably refer our sensations to a *me* and a not-me. As soon as
I have formed, on the one hand, the notion of Permanent

* In the first edition I said : " But without the notion of not-self, we
" cannot have that of self, which is contrasted with it." In saying this I
overlooked the fact, that my own sensations and other feelings, as distinguished from what I call Myself, are a sufficient Not-self to make the
Self apprehensible. The contrast necessary to all cognition is sufficiently
provided for by the antithesis between the Ego and particular modifications of the Ego.

Possibilities of Sensation, and on the other, of that continued series of feelings which I call my life, both these
notions are, by an irresistible association, recalled by
every sensation I have. They represent two things, with
both of which the sensation of the moment, be it what
it may, stands in relation, and I cannot be conscious of
the sensation without being conscious of it as related
to these two things. They have accordingly received
relative names, expressive of the double relation in
question. The thread of consciousness which I apprehend the sensation as a part of, is the *subject* of the sensation. The group of Permanent Possibilities of Sensation
to which I refer it, and which is partially realised and
actualised in it, is the *object* of the sensation. The
sensation itself ought to have a correlative name ; or
rather, ought to have two such names, one denoting the
sensation as opposed to its Subject, the other denoting
it as opposed to its Object. But it is a remarkable fact,
that this necessity has not been felt, and that the need
of a correlative name to every relative one has been considered to be satisfied by the terms Object and Subject
themselves ; the object and the subject not being attended to in the relation which they respectively bear
to the sensation, but being regarded as directly corre-
lated with one another. It is true that they are related
to one another, but only through the sensation : their
relation to each other consists in the peculiar and different relation in which they severally stand to the
sensation. We have no conception of either Subject or
Object, either Mind or Matter, except as something to
which we refer our sensations, and whatever other feelings we are conscious of. The very existence of them
both, so far as cognisable by us, consists only in the
relation they respectively bear to our states of feeling.
Their relation to each other is only the relation between
those two relations. The immediate correlatives are
not the pair, Object, Subject, but the two pairs, Object,
Sensation objectively considered ; Subject, Sensation
subjectively considered. The reason why this is over-

looked, might easily be shown, and would furnish a good illustration of that important part of the Laws of Association which may be termed the Laws of Obliviscence.

I have next to speak of a psychological fact, also a consequence of the Laws of Association, and without a full appreciation of which the idea of Matter can only be understood in its original groundwork, but not in the superstructure which the laws of our actual experience have raised upon it.   There are certain of our sensations which we are accustomed principally to consider subjectively, and others which we are principally accustomed to consider objectively.   In the case of the first, the relation in which we most frequently, most habitually, and therefore most easily consider them, is their relation to the series of feelings of which they form a part, and which, consolidated by thought into a single conception, is termed the Subject.   In the case of the second, the relation in which we by preference contemplate them is their relation to some group, or some kind of group, of Permanent Possibilities of Sensation, the present existence of which is certified to us by the sensation we are at the moment feeling—and which is termed the Object. The difference between these two classes of our sensations, answers to the distinction made by the majority of philosophers between the Primary and the Secondary Qualities of Matter.

We can, of course, think of all or any of our sensations in relation to their Objects, that is, to the permanent groups of possibilities of sensation to which we mentally refer them.   This is the main distinction between our sensations, and what we regard as our purely mental feelings.   These we do not refer to any groups of Permanent Possibilities; and in regard to them the distinction of Subject and Object is merely nominal. These feelings have no Objects, except by metaphor. There is nothing but the feeling and its Subject.   Metaphysicians are obliged to call the feeling itself the object.   Our sensations, on the contrary, have all of them objects; they all are capable of being classed under some group of Permanent Possibilities, and being referred to the presence of that particular set of possibilities as the antecedent condition or cause of their own existence. There are, however, some of our sensations, in our consciousness of which the reference to their Object does not play so conspicuous and predominant a part as in others. This is particularly the case with sensations which are highly interesting to us on their own account, and on which we willingly dwell, or which by their intensity compel us to concentrate our attention on them. These are, of course, our pleasures and pains. In the case of these, our attention is naturally given in a greater degree to the sensations themselves, and only in a less degree to that whose existence they are marks of. And of the two conceptions to which they stand in relation, the one to which we have most tendency to refer them is the Subject; because our pleasures and pains are of no more importance as marks than any of our other sensations, but are of very much more importance than any others as parts of the thread of consciousness which constitutes our sentient life. Many indeed of our internal bodily pains we should hardly refer to an Object at all, were it not for the knowledge, late and slowly acquired, that they are always connected with a local organic disturbance, of which we have no present consciousness, and which is therefore a mere Possibility of Sensation. Those of our sensations, on the contrary, which are almost indifferent in themselves, our attention does not dwell on; our consciousness of them is too momentary to be distinct, and we pass on from them to the Permanent Possibilities of Sensation which they are the signs of, and which alone are important to us. We hardly notice the relation between these sensations and the subjective chain of consciousness of which they form so extremely insignificant a part: the sensation is hardly anything to us but the link which draws into our consciousness a group of Permanent Possibilities; this group is the only thing distinctly present to our thoughts. The unimpressive organic sensation merges in the mere mental suggestion, and we seem to cognise directly that which we think of only by association, and know only by inference. Sensation is in a manner blotted out, and Perception seems to be installed in its place. This truth is expressed, though not with sufficient distinctness, in a favourite doctrine of Sir W. Hamilton, that in the operations of our senses Sensation is greatest when Perception is least, and least when it is greatest; or, as he, by a very inaccurate use of mathematical language, expresses it, Sensation and Perception are in the inverse ratio of one another.

With regard to those sensations which, without being absolutely indifferent, are not, in any absorbing degree, painful or pleasurable, we habitually think of them only as connected with, or proceeding from, Objects. And I am disposed to believe, contrary to the opinion of many philosophers, that any of our senses, or at all events any combination of more than one sense, would have been sufficient to give us some idea of Matter. If we had only the senses of smell, taste, and hearing, but had the sensations according to fixed laws of coexistence so that whenever we had any one of them it marked to us a present possibility of having all the others, I am inclined to think that we should have formed the notion of groups of possibilities of sensation, and should have referred every particular sensation to one of these groups, which, in relation to all the sensations so referred to it, would have become an Object, and would have been invested in our thoughts with the permanency and externality which belong to matter. But though we might, in this supposed case, have had an idea of Matter, that idea would necessarily have been of a very different complexion from what we now have. For, as we are actually constituted, our sensations of smell, taste, and hearing, and as I believe (with the great majority of philosophers) those of sight also, are not grouped together directly, but through the connection which they all have, by laws of coexistence or of causation, with the sensations which are referable to the sense of touch and to the muscles ; those which answer to the terms Resistance, Extension, and Figure. These, therefore, become the leading and conspicuous elements in all the groups : where these are, the group is : every other member of the group presents itself to our thoughts, less as what it is in itself, than as a mark of these. As the entire group stands in the relation of Object to any one of the component sensations which is realised at a given moment, so do these special parts of the group become, in a manner, Object, in relation not only to actual sensations, but to all the remaining Possibilities of Sensation which the group includes. The Permanent Possibilities of sensations of touch and of the muscles, form a group within the group—a sort of inner nucleus, conceived as more fundamental than the rest, on which all the other possibilities of sensation included in the group seem to depend ; these being regarded, in one point of view, as effects, of which that nucleus is the cause, in another as attributes, of which it is the substratum or substance. In this manner our conception of Matter comes ultimately to consist of Resistance, Extension, and Figure, together with miscellaneous powers of exciting other sensations. These three attributes become its essential constituents, and where these are not found, we hesitate to apply the name.

Of these properties, which are consequently termed the Primary Qualities of Matter, the most fundamental is Resistance : as is proved by numerous scientific controversies. When the question arises whether something which affects our senses in a peculiar way, as for instance whether Heat, or Light, or Electricity, is or is not Matter, what seems always to be meant is, does it offer any, however trifling, resistance to motion? If it were shown that it did, this would at once terminate all doubt. That Resistance is only another name for a sensation of our muscular frame, combined with one of touch, has been pointed out by many philosophers, and can scarcely any longer be questioned. When we contract the muscles of our arm, either by an exertion of will, or by an involuntary discharge of our spontaneous nervous activity, the contraction is accompanied by a state of sensation, which is different according as the locomotion consequent on the muscular contraction continues freely, or meets with an impediment. In the former case, the sensation is that of motion through empty space. After having had (let us suppose) this experience several times repeated, we suddenly have a different experience : the series of sensations accompanying the motion of our arm is brought, without intention or expectation on our part, to an abrupt close. This interruption would not, of itself, necessarily suggest the belief in an external obstacle. The hindrance might be in our organs; it might arise from paralysis, or simple loss of power through fatigue. But in either of these cases, the muscles would not have been contracted, and we should not have had the sensation which accompanies their contraction. We may have had the will to exert our muscular force, but the exertion has not taken place.* If it does take place, and is accompanied by the usual muscular sensation, but the distinctive feeling which I have called the sensation of motion in empty space does not follow, we have what is called the feeling of Resistance, or in other words, of muscular action impeded ; and that feeling is the fundamental element in the notion of Matter which results from our common experience. But simultaneously with this feeling of Resistance, we have also feelings of touch ; sensations of

* Sir W. Hamilton thinks (Dissertations on Reid, pp. 854, 855) that we are conscious of resistance through a "mental effort or nisus to move," distinct both from the original will to move, and from the muscular sensation : "for we are," he says, "conscious of it, though, by a narcosis or "stupor of the sensitive nerves we lose all feeling of the movement of the "limb ; though by a paralysis of the motive nerves no movement of the limb "follows the mental effort to move ; though by an abnormal stimulus of the "muscular fibres, a contraction in them is caused even in opposition to our "will." If all this is true—though by what experiments it has been substantiated we are not told—it does not by any means show that there is a mental *nisus* not physical, but merely removes the seat of the *nisus* from the nerves to the brain.

which the organs are not the nerves diffused through our muscles, but those which form a network under the skin ; the sensations which are produced by passive contact with bodies, without muscular action. As these skin sensations of simple contact invariably accompany the muscular sensation of resistance—for we must touch the object before we can feel it resisting our pressure— there is early formed an inseparable association between them. Whenever we feel resistance we have first felt contact. Whenever we feel contact, we know that were we to exercise muscular action, we should feel more or less resistance. In this manner is formed the first fundamental group of Permanent Possibilities of Sensation ; and as we in time recognise that all our other sensations are connected in point of fact with Permanent Possibilities of resistance—that in coexistence with them we should always, by sufficient search, encounter something which would give us the feeling of contact combined with the muscular sensation of resistance ; our idea of Matter, as a Resisting Cause of miscellaneous sensations, is now constituted.

Let us observe, in passing, the elementary example here afforded of the Law of Inseparable Association, and the efficacy of that law to construct what, after it has been constructed, is undistinguishable, by any direct interrogation of consciousness, from an intuition. The sensation produced by the simple contact of an object with the skin, without any pressure—or even with pressure, but without any muscular reaction against it—is no more likely than a sensation of warmth or cold would be, to be spontaneously referred to any cause external to ourselves. But when the constant coexistence, in experience, of this sensation of contact with that of Resistance to our muscular effort whenever such effort is made, has erected the former sensation into a mark or sign of a Permanent Possibility of the latter ; from that time forward, no sooner do we have the skin sensation which we call a sensation of contact, than we cognise, or, as we call it, perceive, something external, corresponding to the idea we now form of Matter as a *resisting* object.   Our sensations of touch have become *representative* of the sensations of resistance with which they habitually coexist: just as philosophers have shown that the sensations of different shades of colour given by our sense of sight, and the muscular sensations accompanying the various movements of the eye, become representative of those sensations of touch and of the muscles of locomotion, which are the only real meaning of what we term the distance of a body from us.*

The next of the primary qualities of Body is Extension ; which has long been considered as one of the principal stumbling blocks of the Psychological Theory. Reid and Stewart were willing to let the whole question of the intuitive character of our knowledge of Matter, depend on the inability of psychologists to assign any origin to the idea of Extension, or analyse it into any combination of sensations and reminiscences of sensation.   Sir W. Hamilton follows their example in laying great stress on this point.

The answer of the opposite school I will present in its latest and most improved form, as given by Professor Bain, in the First Part of his great work on the Mind.†

* Sir. W. Hamilton draws a distinction between two kinds of resistance, or rather, between two senses of the word : the one, that which I have mentioned, and which is a sensation of our muscular frame ; the other, the property of Matter which the old writers called Impenetrability, being that by which, however capable of being compressed into a smaller space, it refuses to part with all its extension, and be extruded from space altogether.   But these two kinds of resistance are merely two modes of regarding and naming the same state of consciousness ; for if the body could be pressed entirely out of space, the only way in which we should discover that it had vanished would be by the sudden cessation of all sensations of resistance.   It is always the muscular sensation which constitutes the presence, and its negation the absence, of body, in any given portion of space.

† "The Senses and the Intellect," pp. 113–117.   My first extract is from the original edition ; for in the one recently published (and enriched by many valuable improvements) the exposition I now quote is given more summarily, and in a manner otherwise less suited for my purpose.

[Dr. M'Cosh, without any warrant, speaks (p. 121) of Mr. Bain as having "elaborated into a minute system the general statements scattered throughout Mr. Mill's Logic ;" and in another passage (pp. 123, 124)

Mr. Bain recognises two principal kinds or modes of descriminative sensibility in the muscular sense : the one corresponding to the degree of intensity of the muscular effort—the amount of energy put forth ; the other corresponding to the duration—the longer or shorter continuance of the same effort.   The first makes us acquainted with degrees of resistance ; which we estimate by the intensity of the muscular energy required to overcome it.   To the second we owe, in Mr. Bain's opinion, our idea of Extension.

" When a muscle begins to contract, or a limb to bend,
" we have a distinct sense of how far the contraction
" and the bending are carried ; there is something in the
" special sensibility that makes one mode of feeling for
" half-contraction, another mode for three-fourths, and
" another for total contraction.   Our feeling of moving
" organs, or of contracting muscles, has been already
" affirmed to be different from our feeling of dead ten-
" sion—something more intense, keen, and exciting ;
" and I am now led to assert, from my best observations

refers to him and to Mr. Herbert Spencer (Mr. Herbert Spencer !) as merely following out an investigation indicated by me.   Coleridge re- minded one of his critics, that there are such things in the world as springs, and that the water a man draws does not necessarily come from a hole made in another man's cistern.   Mr. Bain did not stand in need of any predecessor except our common precursors, and has taught much more to me, on these subjects, than there is any reasonable probability that I can have taught to him.   Dr. M'Cosh falls into a corresponding mistake concerning myself, when he ascribes (pp. 7, 8) my regarding it " as impossible for the mind to rise to first or final causes, or to know the " nature of things," to "the influence" of M. Comte.   The larger half of my "System of Logic," including all its fundamental doctrines, was written before I had ever seen the "Cours de Philosophie Positive." That work was indebted to M. Comte for many valuable thoughts, but a short list would exhaust the chapters, and even the pages, which contain them.   As for the general doctrine which Dr. M'Cosh's words so imper- fectly express — that our knowledge is only of the coexistences and sequences, or the similitudes, of phenomena ; I was familiar with it before I was out of boyhood from the teachings of my father, who had learnt it where M. Comte learnt it—from the methods of physical science, and the writings of their philosophical predecessors.   Ever since the days of Hume, that doctrine has been the general property of the philosophic world.   From the time of Brown it has entered even into popular philosophy.   I have given a brief history of it in "Auguste Comte and Positivism."]

"and by inference from acknowledged facts, that the
" extent of range of a movement, the degree of shorten-
" ing of a muscle, is a matter of discriminative sensi-
" bility. I believe it to be much less pronounced, less
" exact, than the sense of resistance above described,
" but to be not the less real and demonstrable.

" If we suppose a weight raised, by the flexing of the
" arm, first four inches, and then eight inches, it is
" obvious that the mere amount of exertion or expended
" power will be greater, and the sensibility increased in
" proportion. In this view, the sense of range would
" simply be the sense of a greater or less continuance of
" the same effort, that effort being expended in move-
" ment. We can have no difficulty in believing that
" there should be a discriminating sensibility in this
" case; it seems very natural that we should be diffe-
" rently affected by an action continued four or five times
" longer than another. If this be admitted, as true to
" observation, and as inevitably arising from the exist-
" ence of any discrimination whatsoever of degrees of
" expended power, everything is granted that is con-
" tended for at present. It is not meant to affirm that
" at each degree of shortening of a muscle, or each inter-
" mediate attitude of a limb, there is an impression made
" on the centres that can be distinguished from the im-
" pression of every other position or degree of shorten-
" ing ; it is enough to require that the range or amount
" of movement gone over should be a matter of distinct
" perception, through the sensibility to the amount of
" force expended *in time*, the degree of effort being the
" same. The sensibility now in question differs from
" the former (from sensibility to the intensity of effort)
" chiefly in making the degree turn upon *duration*, and
" not upon the amount expended each instant; and it
" seems to me impossible to deny that force increased
" or diminished simply as regards continuance, is as
" much a subject of discriminative sensibility as force
" increased or diminished in the intensity of the sus-
" tained effort. . . .

"If the sense of degrees of range be thus admitted as
"a genuine muscular determination, its functions in out-
"ward perception are very important. The attributes of
"extension and space fall under its scope. In the first
"place, it gives the feeling of *linear extension*, inasmuch
"as this is measured by the sweep of a limb, or other
"organ moved by muscles. The difference between six
"inches and eighteen inches is expressed to us by the
"different degrees of contraction of some one group of
"muscles; those, for example, that flex the arm, or, in
"walking, those that flex or extend the lower limb.
"The inward impression corresponding to the outward
"fact of six inches in length, is an impression arising
"from the continued shortening of a muscle, a true
"muscular sensibility. It is the impression of a mus-
"cular effort having a certain continuance; a greater
"length produces a greater continuance (or a more rapid
"movement) and in consequence an increased feeling
"of expended power.

"The discrimination of length in any one direction
"includes *extension* in any direction. Whether it be
"length, breadth, or height, the perception has pre-
"cisely the same character. Hence superficial and solid
"dimensions, the size or magnitude of a solid object,
"come to be felt in a similar manner. . . .

"It will be obvious that what is called *situation* or
"Locality must come under the same head, as these are
"measured by distance taken along with direction;
"direction being itself estimated by distance, both in
"common observation and in mathematical theory. In
"like manner, *form* or *shape* is ascertained through the
"same primitive sensibility to extension or range.

"By the muscular sensibility thus associated with
"prolonged contraction we can therefore compare dif-
"ferent degrees of the attribute of space, in other words,
"difference of length, surface, situation, and form. When
"comparing two different lengths we can feel which is
"the greater, just as in comparing two different weights
"or resistances. We can also, as in the case of weight,

" acquire some absolute standard of comparison, through
" the permanency of impressions sufficiently often re-
" peated. We can engrain the feeling of contraction of
" the muscles of the lower limb due to a pace of thirty
" inches, and can say that some one given pace is less
" or more than this amount. According to the delicacy
" of the muscular tissue we can, by shorter or longer
" practice, acquire distinct impressions for every standard
" dimension, and can decide at once whether a given
" length is four inches or four and a half, nine or ten,
" twenty or twenty-one. This sensibility to size, en-
" abling us to dispense with the use of measures of
" length, is an acquirement suited to many mechanical
" operations. In drawing, painting, and engraving, and
" in the plastic arts, the engrained discrimination of the
" most delicate differences is an indispensable qualifi-
" cation.

" The third attribute of muscular discrimination is
" the *velocity* or speed of the movement. It is difficult
" to separate this from the foregoing. In the feeling of
" range, velocity answers the same purpose as continu-
" ance ; both imply an enhancement of effort, or of ex-
" pended power, different in its nature from the increase
" of dead effort in one fixed situation. We must learn
" to feel that a slow motion for a long time is the same as
" a quicker motion with less duration ; which we can
" easily do by seeing that they both produce the same
" effect in exhausting the full range of a limb. If we
" experiment upon the different ways of accomplishing
" a total sweep of the arm, we shall find that the slow
" movements long continued are equal to quick motions
" of short continuance, and we are thus able by either
" course to acquire to ourselves a measure of range and
" lineal extension. . . .

" We would thus trace the perception of the mathe-
" matical and mechanical properties of matter to the
" muscular sensibility alone. We admit that this per-
" ception is by no means very accurate if we exclude the
" special senses, but we are bound to show at the outset

" that these senses are not essential to the perception, as
" we shall afterwards show that it is to the muscular
" apparatus associated with the senses that their more
" exalted sensibility must be also ascribed.   The space
" moved through by the foot in pacing may be appre-
" ciated solely through the muscles of the limb, as well
" as by the movements of the touching hand or the
" seeing eye.   Whence we may accede to the assertion
" sometimes made, that the properties of space might be
" conceived, or felt, in the absence of an external world,
" or of any other matter than that composing the body
" of the percipient being ; for the body's own movements
" in empty space would suffice to make the very same
" impressions on the mind as the movements excited by
" outward objects.   A perception of length, or height, or
" speed, is the mental impression, or state of conscious-
" ness, accompanying some mode of muscular movement,
" and this movement may be generated from within as
" well as from without ; in both cases the state of con-
" sciousness is exactly the same."

A theory of Extension somewhat similar, though less
clearly unfolded, was advanced by Brown, and as it
stands in his statement, fell under the criticism of Sir
W. Hamilton ; who gives it, as he thinks, a short and
crushing refutation, as follows :— *

" As far as I can find his meaning in his cloud of words,
" he argues thus :—The notion of Time or succession
" being supposed, that of *longitudinal* extension is given
" in the succession of feelings which accompanies the
" gradual contraction of a muscle ; the notion of this
" succession constitutes, *ipso facto*, the notion of a certain
" length ; and the notion of this length (he quietly takes
" for granted) is the notion of longitudinal extension
" sought.   The paralogism here is transparent.   Length
" is an ambiguous term ; and it is length in space,
" extensive length, and not length in time, protensive
" length, whose notion it is the problem to evolve.   To
" convert, therefore, the notion of a certain kind of

* Dissertations on Reid, p. 869.

" length (and that certain kind being also confessedly
" only length in time) into the notion of a length in
" space, is at best an idle begging of the question—Is
" it not ?   Then I would ask, whether the series of feel-
" ings of which we are aware in the gradual contraction
" of a muscle, involves the consciousness of being a suc-
" cession in length, (1) in time alone ? or (2) in space
" alone ? or (3) in time and space together?   These
" three cases will be allowed to be exhaustive.   If the
" first be affirmed ; if the succession appear in conscious-
" ness a succession in time exclusively, then nothing has
" been accomplished ; for the notion of extension or
" space is in no way contained in the notion of duration
" or time.   Again, if the second or third is affirmed ; if
" the series appear to consciousness a succession in
" length, either in space alone, or in space and time
" together, then is the notion it behoved to generate
" employed to generate itself."

The dilemma looks formidable, but one of its horns
is blunt; for the very assertion of Brown, and of all
who hold the Psychological theory, is that the notion of
length in space, not being in our consciousness originally,
is constructed by the mind's laws out of the notion of
length in time. Their argument is not, as Sir W.
Hamilton fancied, a fallacious confusion between two
different meanings of the word length ; they maintain
the one to be a product of the other. Sir W. Hamilton
did not fully understand the argument. He saw that a
succession of feelings, such as that which Brown spoke
of, could not possibly give us the idea of *simultaneous*
existence. But he was mistaken in supposing that
Brown's argument implied this absurdity. The notion
of simultaneity must be supposed to have been already
acquired : as it necessarily would be at the very earliest
period, from the familiar fact that we often have
sensations simultaneously. What Brown had to show
was, that the idea of the particular mode of simultaneous existence called Extension, might arise, not
certainly out of a mere succession of muscular sensa-

tions, but out of that added to the knowledge already possessed that sensations of touch may be simultaneous. Suppose two small bodies, A and B, sufficiently near together to admit of their being touched simultaneously, one with the right hand, the other with the left.   Here are two tactual sensations which are simultaneous, just as a sensation of colour and one of odour might be ; and this makes us cognise the two objects of touch as both existing at once.   The question then is, what have we in our minds when we represent to ourselves the relation between these two objects already known to be simultaneous, in the form of Extension, or intervening Space —a relation which we do not suppose to exist between the colour and the odour.   Now those who agree with Brown, say that whatever the notion of Extension may be, we *acquire* it by passing our hand or some other organ of touch in a longitudinal direction from A to B : that this process, as far as we are conscious of it, consists of a series of varied muscular sensations, differing according to the amount of muscular effort, and, the effort being given, differing in length of time.   When we say that there is a space between A and B, we mean that some amount of these muscular sensations must intervene ; and when we say that the space is greater or less, we mean that the series of sensations (amount of muscular effort being given) is longer or shorter.   If another object, C, is farther off in the same line, we judge its distance to be greater, because to reach it the series of muscular sensations must be further prolonged, or else there must be the increase of effort which corresponds to augmented velocity.   Now this, which is not denied to be the mode in which we become aware of extension, by any other sense than sight, is considered by the psychologists in question to *be* extension.   The idea of Extended Body they consider to be that of a variety of resisting points, existing simultaneously, but which can be perceived by the same tactile organ only successively, at the end of a series of muscular sensations which constitutes their distance ; and are said to be at different distances from one another because the series of intervening muscular sensations is longer in some cases than in others.*

The theory may be recapitulated as follows. The sensation of muscular motion unimpeded constitutes our notion of empty space, and the sensation of muscular motion impeded constitutes that of filled space. Space in Room—room for movement; which its German name, *Raum*, distinctly confirms. We have a sensation which accompanies the free movement of our organs, say for instance of our arm. This sensation is variously modified by the direction, and by the amount of the movement. We have different states of muscular sensation corresponding to the movements of the arm upward, downward, to right, to left, or in any radius whatever of a sphere of which the joint, that the arm revolves round, forms the centre. We have also different states of muscular sensation according as the arm is moved *more;* whether this consists in its being moved with greater velocity, or with the same velocity during a longer time: and the equivalence of these two is speedily learnt, by finding that a greater effort conducts the hand in a shorter time from

---

* It is not pretended that all this was clearly seen by Brown. It is impossible to defend the theory as Brown stated it. He seems to have thought that the essence of extension consisted in divisibility into parts. "A succession of feelings" (he says) "when remembered by the mind "which looks back upon them, was found to involve, necessarily, the "notion of *divisibility into separate parts*, and therefore of *length, which* "*is only another name for continued divisibility.*" (Lecture xxiv. vol. ii. p. 3 of the 19th edition, 1851.) He thought that he had explained all that needed explanation in the idea of space, when he had shown how the notion of continued divisibility got into it. This appears when he says, " It would not be easy for any one to define matter more simply, than as "that which has parts, and that which resists our efforts to grasp it; "and in our analysis of the feelings of infancy, we have been able to dis- " cover how both these notions may have arisen in the mind." But if divisibility into parts constitutes all our notion of extension, every sensation we have must be identified with extension, for they are all divisible into parts (parts in succession, which Brown thinks sufficient) when they are prolonged beyond the shortest instant of duration which our consciousness recognises. It is probable that Brown did not mean this, but thought that all he had to account for in the conception of space was its divisibility, because he tacitly assumed that all the rest of the notion was already given in the fact of muscular movement. And this, properly understood, is maintainable; but Brown cannot here be acquitted of a charge to which he is often liable, that of leaving an important philosophical question only half thought out.

the same point to the same point ; from the tactual
impression A to the tactual impression B. These different kinds and qualities of muscular sensation, experienced in getting from one point to another (that is,
obtaining in succession two sensations of touch and
resistance, the objects of which are regarded as simultaneous) are all we mean by saying that the points are
separated by spaces, that they are at different distances,
and in different directions. An intervening series of
muscular sensations before the one object can be reached
from the other, is the only peculiarity which (according
to this theory) distinguishes simultaneity in space from
the simultaneity which may exist between a taste and a
colour, or a taste and a smell : and we have no reason
for believing that Space or Extension in itself, is anything different from that which we recognise it by.   It
appears to me that this doctrine is sound, and that the
muscular sensations in question are the sources of all the
notion of Extension which we should ever obtain from
the tactual and muscular senses without the assistance
of the eye.

But the participation of the eye in generating our
actual notion of Extension, very much alters its character, and is, I think, the main cause of the difficulty
felt in believing that Extension derives its meaning to
us from a phenomenon which is not synchronous but
successive. The fact is, that the conception we now
have of Extension or Space is an eye picture, and
comprehends a great number of parts of Extension at
once, or in a succession so rapid that our consciousness
confounds it with simultaneity.   How then (it is naturally asked) can this vast collection of consciousnesses
which are sensibly simultaneous, be generated by the
mind out of its consciousness of a succession—the succession of muscular feelings ?   An experiment may be
conceived, which would throw great light on this subject, but which unfortunately is more easily imagined
than obtained. There have been persons born blind who
were mathematicians, and I believe even naturalists ; and

it is not impossible that one day a person born blind may be a metaphysician. The first who is so, will be able to enlighten us on this point. For he will be an *experimentum crucis* on the mode in which extension is conceived and known, independently of the eye. Not having the assistance of that organ, a person blind from birth must necessarily perceive the parts of extension— the parts of a line, of a surface, or of a solid—in conscious succession. He perceives them by passing his hand along them, if small, or by walking over them if great. The parts of extension which it is possible for him to perceive simultaneously, are only very small parts, almost the minima of extension. Hence, if the Psychological theory of the idea of extension is true, the blind metaphysician would feel very little of the difficulty which seeing metaphysicians feel, in admitting that the idea of Space is, at bottom, one of time—and that the notion of extension or distance, is that of a motion of the muscles continued for a longer or a shorter duration. If this analysis of extension appeared as paradoxical to the metaphysician born blind, as it does to Sir W. Hamilton, this would be a strong argument against the Psychological theory. But if, on the contrary, it did not at all startle him, that theory would be very strikingly corroborated.

We have no experiment directly in point. But we have one which is the very next thing to it. We have not the perceptions and feelings of a metaphysician blind from birth, told and interpreted by himself. But we have those of an ordinary person blind from birth, told and interpreted for him by a metaphysician. And the English reader is indebted for them to Sir W. Hamilton. Platner, "a man no less celebrated as an acute philosopher than "as a learned physician and an elegant scholar," endeavoured to ascertain by observation what notion of extension was possessed by a person born blind, and made known the result in words which Sir W. Hamilton has rendered into his clear English.* "In regard to the

* Lectures, ii. 174.

"visionless representation of space or extension, the
"attentive observation of a person born blind, which I
"formerly instituted in the year 1785, and again, in
"relation to the point in question, have continued for
"three whole weeks—this observation, I say, has con-
"vinced me, that the sense of touch, by itself, is alto-
"gether incompetent to afford us the representation of
"extension and space, and is not even cognisant of local
"exteriority ; in a word, that a man deprived of sight
"has absolutely no perception of an outer world, beyond
"the existence of something effective, different from his
"own feeling of passivity, and in general only of the
"numerical diversity—shall I say of impressions, or of
"things ? In fact, to those born blind, *time serves instead
"of space.*   Vicinity and distance means in their mouths
"nothing more than the shorter or longer time, the
"smaller or greater number of feelings which they find
"necessary to attain from some one feeling to another.
"That a person blind from birth employs the language
"of vision—that may occasion considerable error; and did,
"indeed at the commencement of my observations, lead
"me wrong ; but, in point of fact, he knows nothing
"of things as existing out of each other ; and (this in
"particular I have very clearly remarked) if objects, and
"the parts of his body touched by them, did not make
"different *kinds* of impression on his nerves of sensation,
"he would take everything external for one and the
"same.   In his own body, he absolutely did not dis-
"criminate head and foot at all by their distance, but
"merely by the difference of the feelings (and his per-
"ception of such differences was incredibly fine) which
"he experienced from the one and from the other, and
"moreover through time.   In like manner, in external
"bodies, he distinguished their figure, merely by the
"varieties of impressed feelings ; inasmuch, for example,
"as the cube, by its angles, affected his feeling differ-
"ently from the sphere."

The highly instructive representation here given by
Platner, of this person's state of mind, is exactly that

which we have just read in Mr. Bain, and which that philosopher holds to be the primitive conception of extension by all of us, before the wonderful power of sight and its associations in abridging the mental processes, has come into play. The conclusion which, as we have seen, Platner draws from the case, is that we obtain the idea of extension solely from sight; and even Sir W. Hamilton is staggered in his belief of the contrary. But Platner, though unintentionally, puts a false colour on the matter when he says that his patient had no perception of extension. He used the terms expressive of it with such propriety and discrimination, that Platner, by his own account, did not at first suspect him of not meaning by those terms all that is meant by persons who can see. He therefore meant something; he had impressions which the words expressed to his mind; he had conceptions of extension, after his own manner. But his idea of degrees of extension was but the idea of a greater or smaller number of sensations experienced in succession "to attain from some one feeling to another;" that is, it was exactly what, according to Brown's and Mr. Bain's theory, it ought to have been. And, the sense of touch and of the muscles not being aided by sight, the sensations continued to be conceived by him only as successive; his mental representation of them remained a conception of a series, not of a coexistent group. Though he must have had experience of simultaneity, for no being who has a plurality of senses can be without it, he does not seem to have thoroughly realised the conception of the parts of space as simultaneous. Since what was thus wanting to him, is the principal feature of the conception as it is in us, he seemed to Platner to have no notion of extension. But Platner, fortunately, being a man who could both observe, and express his observations precisely, has been able to convey to our minds the conception which his patient really had of extension; and we find that it was the same as our own, with the exception of the element which, if the Psychological theory be true, was certain to be added to it by the sense of sight. For, when this sense is awakened, and its sensations of colour have become *representative* of the tactual and muscular sensations with which they are coexistent, the fact that we can receive a vast number of sensations of colour at the same instant (or what appears such to our consciousness) puts us in the same position as if we had been able to receive that number of tactual and muscular sensations in a single instant. The ideas of all the successive tactual and muscular feelings which accompany the passage of the hand over the whole of the coloured surface, are made to flash on the mind at once : and impressions which were successive in sensation become coexistent in thought. From that time we do with perfect facility, and are even compelled to do, what Platner's patient never completely succeeded in doing, namely, to think all the parts of extension as coexisting, and to believe that we perceive them as such. And if the laws of inseparable association, which are already admitted as the basis of other acquired perceptions of sight, are considered in their application to this case, it is certain that this apparent perception of successive elements as simultaneous would be generated and would supply all that there is in our idea of extension, more than there was in that of Platner's patient.*

---

* Mr. Mahaffy thinks (pp. xx., xxi.) that Platner omitted to ascertain whether his patient was capable of recognising simultaneity ; and is of opinion that he could not do so, or that if he could, it must have been owing to his education among people possessed of sight. " The question "remains : can we postulate a sense of such simultaneity originally, be- "fore any space or extension is given ? I am disposed to agree with " Brown, that, although we can afterwards analyse them, all simultaneous "feelings form originally one mental state ; which of course excludes "simultaneity until the analysis obtained by the aid of space and exten- "sion give us the elements separately. Hence, until at least one body " was given as extended, we should not obtain the notion." Brown may very possibly be right, but it does not follow that the analysis necessary to our distinguishing different sensations in one mass of simultaneous feeling, can only take place by means of space and extension. If the simultaneous sensations differ in kind, as a sound, for instance, and a smell, all that is necessary to our being able to distinguish them when together is that we should at some other time have experienced them separate. We should then know the compound, and also the elements : and since these are not chemically fused into a product bearing no resem-

I shall quote, in continuation, part of the exposition by Mr. Bain, of the machinery by which our consciousness of Extension becomes an appendage of our sensations of Sight. It is a striking example of the commanding influence of that sense; which, though it has no greater variety of original impressions than our other special senses, yet owing to the two properties of being able to receive a great number of its impressions at once, and to receive them from all distances, takes the lead altogether from the sense of touch : and is not only the organ by which we read countless possibilities of tactual and muscular sensations which can never, to us, become realities, but substitutes itself for our touch and our muscles even where we can use them—causes their actual use as avenues to knowledge to become, in many cases, obsolete,—the sensations themselves to be little heeded and very indistinctly remembered,—and communicates its own prerogative of simultaneousness to impressions and conceptions originating in other senses, which it could never have given, but only suggests, through visible marks associated with them by experience.

"The distinctive impressibility of the eye," says Mr. Bain,* " is for Colour. This is the effect specific to it

blance to its factors, but retain when combined their identity with what they are in their separate state, our knowledge of them separately would enable us to recognise them in the compound ; in other words, to feel two sensations as simultaneous.

Dr. M'Cosh says (p. 143) that the experience of other observers (and particularly Mr. Kinghan, Principal of the Institution for the Blind at Belfast) as well as experiments by Dr. M'Cosh himself on young children born blind, do not confirm Platner's statement, but prove that those born blind have "a very clear notion of figure and distance, got directly from the sense of touch." This is just what might have been expected, for I am far from agreeing with Platner that the notions of figure and distance come originally from sight. The sense of sight is not necessary to give the perception of simultaneity : but, giving a prodigious number of simultaneous sensations in one glance, it greatly quickens all processes dependent on observation of the fact of simultaneousness. A person born blind can acquire, by a more gradual process, all that there is in our notion of Space except the visible Picture : but he will be much longer before he realises it completely, and in the case of Platner's patient that point does not seem to have been reached.

* The Senses and the Intellect, pp. 370–374. I now quote from the second edition (1864). The corresponding passage in the first edition begins at p. 363.

" as a sense.   But the feeling of Colour by itself, im-
" plies no knowledge of any outward object, as a cause
" or a thing wherein the colour inheres.   It is simply a
" mental effect or influence, a feeling or conscious state,
" which we should be able to distinguish from other con-
" scious states, as for example, a smell or a sound.   We
" should also be able to mark the difference between it
" and others of the same kind, more or less vivid, more
" or less enduring, more or less voluminous.   So we
" should distinguish the qualitative differences between
" one colour and another.   Pleasure or pain, with dis-
" crimination of intensity and of duration, would attach
" to the mere sensation of colour.   Knowledge or belief
" in an external or material coloured body, there would
" be none.

" But when we add the active or muscular sensibility
" of the eye, we obtain new products.   The sweep of the
" eye over the coloured field gives a feeling of a definite
" amount of *action*, an exercise of internal power, which
" is something totally different from the passive feeling
" of light.   This action has many various modes, all of
" the same quality, but all distinctively felt and recog-
" nised by us.   Thus the movements may be in any
" direction—horizontal, vertical, or slanting; and every
" one of these movements is felt as different from every
" other.   In addition to these, we have the movements
" of adjustment of the eye, brought on by differences in
" the remoteness of objects.   We have distinctive feelings
" belonging to these different adjustments, just as we
" have towards the different movements across the field
" of view.   If the eyes are adjusted, first to clear vision
" for an object six inches from the eye, and afterwards
" change their adjustment to suit an object six feet dis-
" tant, we are distinctly conscious of the change, and of
" the degree or amount of it; we know that the change is
" greater than in extending the adjustment to a three-feet
" object, while it is less than we should have to go
" through for a twenty-feet object.   Thus in the altera-
" tions of the eyes for near and far, we have a distinctive

" consciousness of amount or degree, no less than in the
" movements for right and left, up and down. Feelings
" with the character of activity are thus incorporated
" with the sensibility to colour; the luminous impression
" is associated with exertion on our part, and is no
" longer a purely passive state. We find that the light
" changes as our activity changes, we recognise in it a
" certain connection with our movements; an association
" springs up between the passive feeling and the active
" energy of the visible [" visual "] organ, or rather of the
" body generally; for the changes of view are owing to
" movements of the head and trunk, as well as to the
" sweep of the eye within its own orbit. . . . .
     " When, along with a forward movement, we behold
" a steadily varying change of appearance in the objects
" before us, we associate the change with the locomotive
" effort, and after many repetitions, we firmly connect
" the one with the other. We then know what is im-
" plied in a certain feeling in the eye, a certain adjust-
" ment of the lenses and a certain inclination of the
" axes, of all of which we are conscious; we know that
" these things are connected with the further experience
" of a definite locomotive energy needing to be expended,
" in order to alter this consciousness to some other con-
" sciousness. Apart from this association, the eye-feel-
" ing might be recognised as differing from other eye-
" feelings, but there could be no other perception in the
" case. Experience connects these differences of ocular
" adjustment with the various exertions of the body at
" large, and the one can then imply and reveal the
" others. The feeling that we have when the eyes are
" parallel and vision distinct, is associated with a great
" and prolonged effort of walking, in other words, with
" a long distance. An inclination of the eyes of two
" degrees, is associated with two paces to bring us up to
" the nearest limit of vision, or with a stretch of some
" other kind, measured in the last resort by pacing, or
" by passing the hand along the object. The change
" from an inclination of 30° to an inclination of 10°, is

T

"associated with a given sweep of the arm, carrying the "hand forward over eight inches and a half."

These slight changes in the action of the muscles that move the eye, habitually effected in a time too short for computation, are the means by which our visual impressions from the whole of that portion of the universe which is visible from the position where we stand, may be concentrated within an interval of time so small that we are scarcely conscious of any interval; and they are, in my apprehension, the generating cause of all that we have in our notion of extension over and above what Platner's patient had in his. He had to conceive two or any number of bodies (or resisting objects) with a long train of sensations of muscular contraction filling up the interval between them: while we, on the contrary, think of them as rushing upon our sight, many of them at the same instant, all of them at what is scarcely distinguishable from the same instant; and this visual imagery effaces from our minds any distinct consciousness of the series of muscular sensations of which it has become representative. The simultaneous visual sensations are to us *symbols* of tactual and muscular ones which were slowly successive. "This symbolic relation being far briefer, is habitually "thought of in place of that it symbolises: and by the "continued use of such symbols, and the union of them "into more complex ones, are generated our ideas of "visible extension—ideas which, like those of the "algebraist working out an equation, are wholly unlike "the ideas symbolised; and which yet, like his, occupy "the mind to the entire exclusion of the ideas sym- "bolised." This last extract is from Mr. Herbert Spencer,* whose Principles of Psychology, in spite of some doctrines which he holds in common with the intuitive school, are on the whole one of the finest examples we possess of the Psychological Method in its full power. His treatment of this subject, and Mr. Bain's, are at once corroborative and supplementary of

* Principles of Psychology, p. 224.

one another: and to them I must refer the reader who desires an ampler elucidation of the general question. The remainder of this chapter will be devoted to the examination of some peculiarities in Sir W. Hamilton's treatment of it.

Sir W. Hamilton relies mainly upon one argument to prove that Vision, without the aid of Touch, gives an immediate knowledge of Extension: which argument had been anticipated in a passage which he quotes from D'Alembert.* The following is his own statement of it. "It can† easily be shown that the perception of " colour involves the perception of extension. It is " admitted that we have by sight a perception of colours, " consequently a perception of the difference of colours. " But a perception of the distinction of colours neces- " sarily involves the perception of a discriminating line ; " for if one colour be laid beside or upon another, we " only distinguish them as different by perceiving that " they limit each other, which limitation necessarily " affords a breadthless line,—a line of demarcation. " One colour laid upon another, in fact, gives a line " returning upon itself, that is, a figure. But a line and " a figure are modifications of extension. The percep- " tion of extension, therefore, is necessarily given in the " perception of colours."

And farther on : ‡—" All parties are, of course, at one " in regard to the fact that we see colour. Those who " hold that we see extension, admit that we see it only " as coloured ; and those who deny us any vision of " extension, make colour the exclusive object of sight. " In regard to this first position, all are, therefore, agreed, " Nor are they less harmonious in reference to the " second ;—that the power of conceiving colour involves " the power of perceiving the differences of colours. By " sight we, therefore, perceive colour, and discriminate " one colour, that is, one coloured body,—one sensation " of colour, from another. This is admitted. A third

* Lectures ii. 172.   † Ibid. p. 165.
‡ Ibid. p. 167.

"position will also be denied by none, that the colours
"discriminated in vision, are, or may be, placed side by
"side in immediate juxtaposition: or, one may limit
"another by being superinduced partially over it.   A
"fourth position is equally indisputable; that the con-
"trasted colours, thus bounding each other, will form by
"their meeting a visible line, and that, if the superin-
"duced colour be surrounded by the other, this line will
"return upon itself, and thus constitute the outline of
"a visible figure.   These four positions command a
"peremptory assent; they are all self-evident.   But
"their admission at once explodes the paradox under
"discussion"—(that extension cannot be cognised by
sight alone).   "And thus: A line is extension in one
"dimension,—length; a figure is extension in two,—
"length and breadth.   Therefore, the vision of a line is
"a vision of extension in length; the vision of a figure,
"the vision of extension in length and breadth."

I must acknowledge that I cannot make the answer
to this argument as thorough and conclusive as I could
wish; for we have not the power of making an experiment, the completing converse of Platner's.   There is
no example of a person born with the sense of sight, but
without those of touch and the muscles; and nothing
less than this would enable us to define precisely the extent and limits of the conceptions which sight is capable
of giving, independently of association with impressions
of another sense.   There are, however, considerations
well adapted to moderate the extreme confidence which
Sir W. Hamilton places in this argument.   First, it
must be observed that when the eye, at present, takes
cognisance of a visible figure, it does not cognise it by
means of colour alone, but by all those motions and
modifications of the muscles connected with the eye,
which have so great a share in giving us our acquired
perceptions of sight.   To determine what can be cognised by sight alone, we must suppose an eye incapable
of these changes; which can neither have the curvature
of its lenses modified nor the direction of its axis changed

by any mode of muscular action; which cannot, therefore, travel along the boundary line that separates two colours, but must remain fixed with a steady gaze on a definite spot. If we once allow the eye to follow the direction of a line or the periphery of a figure, we have no longer merely sight, but important muscular sensations superadded. Now there is nothing more certain than that an eye with its axis immovably fixed in one direction, gives a full and clear vision of but a small portion of space, that to which the axis directly points, and only a faint and indistinct one of the other points surrounding it. When we are able to see any considerable portion of a surface so as to form a distinct idea of it, we do so by passing the eye over and about it, changing slightly the direction of the axis many times in a second. When the eye is pointed directly to one spot, the faint perceptions we have of others are barely sufficient to serve as indications for directing the axis of the eye to each of them in turn, when withdrawn from the first. Physiologists have explained this by the fact, that the centre of the retina is furnished with a prodigiously greater number of nervous papillæ, much finer and more delicate individually, and crowded closer together, than any other part. Whatever be its explanation, the fact itself is indubitable ; and seems to warrant the conclusion that if the axis of the eye were immovable, and we were without the muscular sensations which accompany and guide its movement, the impression we should have of a boundary between two colours would be so vague and indistinct as to be merely rudimentary.

A rudimentary conception must be allowed, for it is evident that even without moving the eye we are capable of having two sensations of colour at once, and that the boundary which separates the colours must give some specific affection of sight, otherwise we should have no discriminative impressions capable of afterwards becoming, by association, representative of the cognitions of lines and figures which we owe to the tactual and the muscular sense. But to confer on these discriminative im-

pressions the name which denotes our matured and perfected cognition of Extension, or even to assume that they
have in their nature anything in common with it, seems
to be going beyond the evidence. Berkeley acknowledged a very considerable amount of perception by the
eye alone, of something which it was possible to call by
the name of extension ; and that which is so perceived
has, since his time, been known to philosophers as
Visible Extension, in contradistinction to Tangible.
But Berkeley maintained that Visible Extension, not
only is not the same thing as Tangible Extension, but
has not the smallest likeness to it, and that a person
born with only one of the two senses, and afterwards
acquiring the other, would, until there had been time to
learn their mutual relation by experience, never suspect
that there was any connection between them. In point
of fact, those who are born blind and afterwards acquire
sight, know by the information of others that the eye
pictures and the tactual sensations come from the same
objects : yet even with that help it is always a work of
time and difficulty to connect the one with the other.
Sir W. Hamilton appears to think that extension as
revealed by the eye, is identical with the extension which
we know by touch, except that it is only in two dimensions. " It is not," he says,* " all kind of extension
" and form that is attributed to sight. It is not figured
" extension in all the three dimensions, but only extension
" as involved in plane figures ; that is, only length and
" breadth." But to have the notion of extension even in
length and breadth as we have it, is to have it in such a
manner that we might know certain muscular facts
without having tried : as, for instance, that if we placed
our finger on the spot corresponding to one end of a line,
or boundary of a surface, we should have to go through
a muscular motion before we could place it on the other.
Is there the smallest reason to suppose that on the
evidence of sight alone, we could arrive at this conclusion in anticipation of the sense of touch ? I cannot

* Lectures, ii. 160.

admit that we could have what is meant by a perception of superficial space, unless we conceived it as something which the hand could be moved across ; and, whatever may be the retinal impression conveyed by the line which bounds two colours, I see no ground for thinking that by the eye alone we could acquire the conception of what we now mean when we say that one of the colours is outside the other.*　On this point I may again quote

* The following case, however, which I quote from Dr. M'Cosh (pp. 163–165), if correctly reported, would require a considerable modification of the preceding doctrine. " The best reported case " of a person born blind, but who acquired eyesight by means of a surgical operation, " is that of Dr. Franz of Leipsig (Phil. Trans. of Roy. Soc. 1841). The " youth had been born blind, and was seventeen years of age when the " experiment was wrought which gave him the use of one eye. When the " eye was sufficiently restored to bear the light, a sheet of paper on which " two strong black lines had been drawn, the one horizontal, the other " vertical, was placed before him at the distance of about three feet. He " was now allowed to open the eye, and after attentive examination he " called the lines by their right denominations," that is, according to Dr. M'Cosh, horizontal and vertical. " ' The outline in black of a square, " six inches in diameter, within which a circle had been drawn, and within " the latter a triangle, was, after careful examination, recognised and " correctly described by him.' ' At the distance of three feet, and on a " level with the eye, a solid cube and a sphere, each of four inches dia- " meter, was placed before him.' After attentively examining these " bodies, he said he saw a quadrangular and a circular figure, and after " some consideration he pronounced the one a square and the other a disc. " His eye being then closed, the cube was taken away and a disc of equal " size substituted and placed next to the sphere. On again opening his " eye he observed no difference in these objects, but regarded them both " as discs. The solid cube was now placed in a somewhat oblique posi- " tion before the eye, and close beside it a figure cut out of pasteboard, " representing a plane outline prospect of the cube when in this position. " Both objects he took to be something like flat quadrates." [qy. quadri- laterals ?] " A pyramid placed before him with one of its sides towards " his eye he saw as a plain " [plane ?] " triangle. This object was now " turned a little, so as to present two of its sides to view, but rather more " of one side than of the other : after considering and examining it for a " long time, he said that this was a very extraordinary figure ; it was " neither a triangle, nor a quadrangle, nor a circle ; he had no idea of it, " and could not describe it ; in fact, said he, I must give it up. On the " conclusion of these experiments, I asked him to describe the sensations " the objects had produced, whereupon he said, that immediately on " opening his eye he had discovered a difference in the two objects, the " cube and the sphere, placed before him, and perceived that they were " not drawings ; but that he had not been able to form from them the " idea of a square and a disc, until he perceived a sensation of what he saw " in the points of his fingers, as if he really touched the object." (A very significant fact, both psychologically and physiologically.) " When I " gave the three bodies (the sphere, cube, and pyramid) into his hand, he

Mr. Bain.* " I do not see how one sensation can be
" felt as out of another, without already supposing that we
" have a feeling of space.   If I see two distinct objects
" before me, as two candle flames, I apprehend them as
" different objects, and as distant from one another by an
" interval of space ; but this apprehension presupposes
" an independent experience and knowledge of lineal
" extension.   There is no evidence to show that, at the

" was much surprised he had not recognised them as such by sight, as he
" was well acquainted with mathematical figures by his touch."
     The case as stated looks like an experimental proof, that not only some-
thing which admits of being called extension, but an extension which is
promptly identified with that already known by touch, though in two
dimensions only, may be perceived by sight at the very first use of the
eyes, before the muscular action necessary for directing the eye has been
learnt by practice.   There is one suspicious circumstance in the recital
—the youth's instantaneous perception that the cube and the sphere were
not drawings ; for how could one who had never before had any sensation
of sight, distinguish without help a drawing from its object ?   Cheselden's
patient was for a long time deceived by pictures, and asked which was the
lying sense, feeling or seeing.   We ought, moreover, to have been expressly told whether, previous to the operation, the blindness was absolutely complete ; which in many of the cases cited by Mr. Samuel Bailey
it was not, and, according to Cheselden, in cases of congenital cataract it
seldom is so.   If no material circumstance is omitted in the report of
Dr. Franz's case, the doctrine in the text will require a certain amount of
correction.   What is there called a rudimentary conception of figure by
the eye, must be more than rudimentary ; it must be, in its way, considerably developed ; and it must be such that " after attentive examination " it could be recognised as corresponding with the circles and
quadrangles already known by touch.   On this last point the report does
not agree with other recorded cases.   In a recent case, for example, recorded by Mr. Nunneley (I quote at second hand from Professor Fraser
in the *North British Review*) the boy could indeed, after couching, " at
once perceive a difference in the shapes of objects," could see that the
cube and the sphere " were not of the same visible figure," but could not
tell which was which : " it was not till they had been many times placed
" in his hands, that he learnt to distinguish by sight the one which he
" had just had in his hands from the other placed beside it.   He gradually
" became more correct in his judgments, but it was only after several days
" that he could tell by the eye alone which was the sphere and which the
" cube ; when asked, he always, before answering, wished to take both in
" his hands.   Even when this was allowed, when immediately afterwards
" the objects were placed before the eyes, he was not certain of the
" figure."
     If Dr. Franz's case is fairly reported, his patient was probably of more
than ordinary natural quickness of observation, and identified the figures
not by resemblance proper, but by analogy, or resemblance of relations.

---

* The Senses and the Intellect, 2nd ed. p. 376 ; 1st ed. p. 368.

" first sight of these objects, and before any association
" is formed between visible appearances and other move-
" ments, I should be able to apprehend in the double
" appearance a difference of place. I feel a distinctness
" of impression, undoubtedly, partly optical and partly
" muscular, but in order that this distinctness may mean
" to me a difference of position in space, it must reveal
" the additional fact, that a certain movement of my arm

Though beholding for the first time a visual square and circle, he was no
doubt aware through the persons who surrounded him, that the objects
shown to his sight were objects which could be touched—which he already
knew by touch. During the "careful examination" and "consideration"
which preceded his recognition of them, he was probably employed in
asking himself to what, in his experience of tangible objects, these visible
objects bore the greatest affinity. Now, he was "well acquainted with
mathematical figures by touch," and had therefore acquired a complete
idea of a closed figure, and of the boundary which encloses it—the outline
separating object from not-object. A relation similar to that between a
tangible figure and its boundary, exists between the visual periphery and
the mass of colour it encloses. This mere analogy might be sufficient to
direct his choice, when a visual object had at any rate to be identified with
a tangible. The grand difficulty was in discovering that any visual object
was the same with any tangible : but, this difficulty once surmounted by
the information of others, a small circumstance might give him a hint for
pairing the one class of objects with the other. In his familiarity, by
touch and the muscles, with (let us say) a triangular outline, he had become
aware of sudden and sharp bends in it, and knew that there were three
of these in the tangible periphery. There was the same number of peculiar points in the visual outline, which might not spontaneously have
reminded him of the bends he knew by touch, but, if a choice had to be
made, were more analogous to them than anything in a circular outline.
Being required therefore to give to this object the name of something
tangible, he was naturally led to calling it a triangle. It is by no means
evident that if left entirely to himself, he would have found out, except by
gradual experience, that the phenomenon analogous to extension, which
he perceived by sight, was the extension which he already knew by touch.
I may add, that since we have from sight distinctive sensations answering
to the various figures, it is no more than natural that these sensations,
however unlike the tactual sensations which they represent, should have
relations among themselves, resembling the mutual relations of those.
The same explanation may probably serve for the lad's ability to distinguish by sight a vertical line from a horizontal. He was probably told
that one of them was horizontal and the other vertical, and was only
asked which was which ; and without further information we cannot tell
what small circumstance may have determined him to guess the one
rather than the other. To sum up my view of Dr. Franz's case, it does
not prove that we perceive extension by sight, but only that we have
discriminative sensations of sight corresponding to all the diversities of
superficial extension : but, if rightly reported, it greatly widens the range
of those discriminative sensations, and almost shows that by sight alone
we might rise to the height of Reid's Geometry of Visibles.

" would carry my hand from the one flame to the other ;
" or that some other movement of mine would change by
" definite amount the appearance I now see. If no
" information is conveyed respecting the possibility of
" movements of the body generally, no idea of space is
" given, for we never consider that we have a notion
" of space, unless we distinctly recognise this possi-
" bility. But how a vision to the eye can reveal
" beforehand what would be the experience of the
" hand or the other moving members, I am unable to
" understand." *

* To this passage, Mr. Bain has appended, in his second edition (p. 377),
the following instructive note :—

" In following a wide ranging movement, or in expatiating over a large
" prospect, we must move the eyes or the head ; and probably every one
" would allow that, in such a case, feelings of movement make a part of
" our sensation and our subsequent idea. The notion of a mountain
" evidently contains feelings of visual movement. But when we look at a
" circle, say one-tenth of an inch in diameter, the eye can take in the
" whole of it without movement, and we might suppose that the sensa-
" tion is, in that case, purely optical, there being no apparent necessity
" for introducing the muscular consciousness. A characteristic optical
" impression is produced ; we should be able to discriminate between the
" small circle and a square, or an oval, or between it and a somewhat larger
" or somewhat smaller circle, from the mere optical difference of the effect
" on the retina. Why then may we not say, that, through the luminous
" tracing alone, we have the feeling of visible form ?

" By making an extreme supposition of this nature, it is possible to
" remove the case from a direct experimental test. We may still, how-
" ever, see very strong grounds for maintaining the presence of a muscu-
" lar element even in this instance. In the first place, our notions of
" form are manifestly obtained by working on the large scale, or by the
" survey of objects of such magnitude as to demand the sweep of the eye,
" in order to comprehend them. We lay the foundations of our knowledge
" of visible outline in circumstances where the eye must be active, and
" must mix its own activity with the retinal feelings. The idea of a
" circle is first gained by moving the eye round some circular object of
" considerable size. Having done this, we transfer the fact of motion to
" smaller circles, although they would not of themselves demand an ex-
" tensive ocular sweep. So that when we look at a little round body, we
" are already preoccupied with the double nature of visible form, and are
" not in a position to say how we should regard it, if that were our first
" experience of a circle.

" But, in the second place, the essential import of visible form is some-
" thing not attainable without the experience of moving the eye. If we
" looked at a little round spot, we should know an optical difference be-
" tween it and a triangular spot, and we should recognise it as identical
" with another round spot ; but that is merely retinal knowledge, or
" optical discrimination. That would not be to recognise form, because
" by form we never mean so little as a mere change of colour. We mean

Sir W. Hamilton does not limit the perception of Extension to sight and touch, either separately or combined with one another. "The opinions," he says,[*] "so generally prevalent, that through touch, or touch "and muscular feeling, or touch and sight, or touch, "muscularfeeling, and sight,—that through these senses, "exclusively, we are percipient of extension, &c., I do "not admit. On the contrary, I hold that all sensations "whatsoever, of which we are conscious as one out of "another, *eo ipso* afford us the condition of immediately "and necessarily apprehending extension; for in the con- "sciousness itself of such reciprocal outness is actually "involved a perception of difference of place in space, "and, consequently, of the extended." It may safely be admitted that whenever we are conscious of two sensa- tions as "one out of another," in the sense of locality, we have a perception of space ; for the two expressions are equivalent. But to have a consciousness of difference between two sensations which are felt simultaneously, is not to feel them as "one out of another" in this sense; and the very question to be decided is, whether any of our senses, apart from feelings of muscular motion, gives us the notion of "one out of another" in the sense necessary to support the idea of Extension.

Sir W. Hamilton thinks that whenever two different nervous filaments are simultaneously affected at their extremities, the sensations received through them are felt as one out of the other. It is extremely probable that the affection of two distinct nervous filaments is the condition of the discriminative sensibility which furnishes us with sensations capable of becoming representative of objects one out of the other. But that is a different thing from giving us the perception directly. Un-

"by a round form something that would take a given sweep of the eye to "comprehend it; and unless we identify the small spot with the circles "previously seen, we do not perceive it to be a circle. It may remain in "our mind as a purely optical meaning ; but we can never cross the chasm "that separates an optical meaning from an effect combining light and "movement, in any other way than by bringing in an experience of move- "ment."

* Dissertations on Reid, p. 861.

doubtedly we recognise difference of place in the objects
which affect our senses, whenever we are aware that those
objects affect different parts of our organism.   But when
we are aware of this, we already have the notion of Place.
We must be aware of the different parts of our body as
one out of another, before we can use this knowledge as
a means of cognising a similar fact in regard to other
material objects.   This Sir W. Hamilton admits ; and
what, therefore, he is bound to prove is, that the very
first time we received an impression of touch, or of any
other sense, affecting more than one nervous filament, we
were conscious of being affected in a plurality of places.
This he does not even attempt to do ; and direct proof is
palpably unattainable.   As a matter of indirect evidence,
we may oppose to this theory Mr. Bain's, according to
which, apart from association, we should not have any
impression of this kind, and should in general be conscious only of a greater mass or "volume" of sensation
when we were affected in two places, than when only in
one ; like the more massive sensation of heat which we
feel when our bodies are immersed in a warm bath, compared with that which we feel when heat of the same, or
even of greater intensity, is applied only to our hands or
feet.   Mr. Bain's doctrine, being as consistent with the
admitted facts of the case as Sir W. Hamilton's, has a
good claim, on his own law of Parsimony, to be preferred to it.   But, besides, there are recorded facts which
agree with Mr. Bain's theory, and are quite irreconcilable
with Sir W. Hamilton's ; and to find such we need not
travel beyond Sir W. Hamilton's own pages.

One of them is the very case we have already had before
us, that recorded by Platner.   The facts of this case are
quite inconsistent with the opinion, that we have a direct
perception of extension when an object touches us in
more than one place, including the extremities of more
than one nervous filament.   Platner expressly says that
his patient, when an object touched a considerable part
of the surface of his body, but without exciting more
than one *kind* of sensation, was conscious of no local

difference—no " outness " of one part of the sensation in relation to another part—but only (we may presume) of a greater *quantity* of sensation; as Mr. Bain would call it, a greater volume. As Platner expresses it, " if objects " and the parts of his body touched by them, did not " make different kinds of impression on his nerves of " sensation, he would take everything external for one " and the same. In his own body, he absolutely did not " discriminate head and foot at all by their distance, but " merely by the difference of the feelings." Such an experiment, reported by a competent observer, is of itself almost enough to overthrow Sir W. Hamilton's theory.

In like manner, the patient in Cheselden's celebrated case, after his second eye was couched, described himself as seeing objects twice as large with both eyes as with one only; that is, he had a double quantity, or double volume of sensation, which suggested to his mind the idea of a double size.*

Another case, for the knowledge of which I am also indebted to Sir W. Hamilton, who knew it through an abstract given by M. Maine de Biran of the original report by M. Rey Régis, a medical observer, in his " Histoire Naturelle de l'Ame "—is as incompatible with Sir W. Hamilton's theory as Platner's case. It is the case

---

* I may here observe that Sir W. Hamilton (and the same mistake has been made by Mr. Bailey) considers Cheselden's case as evidence that the "perception of externality," as distinguished from that of distance from the eye, is given by sight as well as by touch, because the young man said that objects at first seemed "to touch his eyes, as what he felt did his skin." (Foot-note to Reid, p. 177.) He seems to think that, on the other theory, the boy should have been metaphysician enough to recognise in the perception "a mere affection of the organ," or at least should have perceived the objects "as if in his eyes." But he was not accustomed to conceive tangible objects as if in his fingers. He conceived them as touching his fingers : and he simply transferred the experience of touch to the newly-acquired sense. All his notions of perception were associated with direct contact ; and as he did not perceive any of the objects of sight to be at a distance from the organ by which he perceived them, he concluded that they must be in contact with it.

Mr. Nunneley's case, on this point, agrees with Cheselden's. "The boy "said everything touched his eyes, and walked carefully about with his "hands held up before him, to prevent things hurting his eyes by touch-"ing them."

of a patient who lost the power of movement in one-half of his body, apparently from temporary paralysis of the motory nerves, while the functions of the sensory nerves seemed unimpaired. This patient, it was found, had lost the power of localising his sensations. "Experi- "ments,* various and repeated, were made to ascertain "with accuracy, whether the loss of motive faculty had "occasioned any alteration in the capacity of feeling; and "it was found that the patient, though as acutely alive "as ever to the sense of pain, felt, when this was secretly "inflicted, as by compression of his hand under the "bedclothes, a sensation of suffering or uneasiness, by "which, when the pressure became strong, he was com- "pelled lustily to cry out; but a sensation merely "general, he being altogether unable to localise the "feeling, or to say whence the pain proceeded. . . . The "patient, as he gradually recovered the use of his limbs, "gradually also recovered the power of localising his "sensations." It would be premature to establish a scientific inference upon a single experiment: but if confirmed by repetition, this is an *experimentum crucis*. So far as one experiment can avail, it proves, that sensation without motion does not give the perception of difference of place in our bodily organs (not to speak of outward objects), and that this perception is even now entirely an inference, dependent on the muscular feelings.†

It gives a very favourable idea of Sir W. Hamilton's sincerity and devotion to truth, that he should have drawn from their obscurity, and made generally known, two cases which make such havoc with his own opinions

---

* Dissertations on Reid, pp. 874, 875.

† Dr. M'Cosh says (p. 151): "This case is valueless, as evidently the functions of the nervous apparatus were deranged." I am far from pre- tending that this single experiment is conclusive; but I can as little admit that it ought to count for nothing. The functions of the motor nerves were deranged; but no derangement appears to have been re- marked in those of the nerves of sensation; unless, by a *petitio principii*, the incapacity of localising the sensations is considered to prove it. We cannot indeed prove that those nerves were not also in a morbid state: but pathological cases, which are admitted to be the nearest equivalents

as this and Platner's; for though he did not believe the
cases to be really inconsistent with his theory, he can
hardly have been entirely unaware that they could be
used against it.

The only other point in Sir W. Hamilton's doctrines
respecting the Primary Qualities which it is of importance to notice, is one, I believe, peculiar to himself, and
certainly not common to him with any of his eminent
predecessors in the same school of thought. It is the
doctrine, that those qualities are not perceived—are not
directly and immediately cognised—in things external
to our bodies, but only in our bodies themselves. · "A
" Perception," he says,* " of the Primary Qualities does
" not, originally, and in itself, reveal to us the existence,
" and qualitative existence, of aught beyond the organism,
" apprehended by us as extended, figured, divided, &c.
" The primary qualities of things external to our organism
" we do not perceive, *i.e.* immediately know. For these
" we only learn to *infer*, from the affections which we
" come to find that they determine in our organs;—affec-
" tions which, yielding us a perception of organic ex-
" tension, we at length discover, by observation and
" induction, to imply a corresponding extension in the
" extra-organic agents."   Neither, according to him, do
we perceive, or immediately know, ' extension in its true
and absolute magnitude;" our perceptions giving different impressions of magnitude from the same object,
when placed in contact with different parts of our body.
" As perceived extension is only the recognition of one
" organic affection in its outness from another; as a
" minimum of extension is thus, to perception, the

in physiology to experiments in inorganic science, would lose all their
scientific value if it could be assumed without evidence that the disease
extended to other functions than those in which it was observed.   Even
if a physical derangement were proved, one not unimportant point would
have been ascertained by the experiment—that a morbid affection may
take away the power of localising sensations, without taking away the
sensations. Localisation, therefore, does not depend on the same conditions with the sensations themselves, still less is it inseparably involved
in them.
    * Dissertations on Reid, pp. 881, 882.

"smallest extent of organism in which sensations can
"be discriminated as plural ; and as in one part of the
"organism this smallest extent is perhaps some million,
"certainly some myriad, times smaller than in others ;
"it follows that, to perception, the same real exten-
"sion will appear, in this place of the body, some
"million or myriad times greater than in that.   Nor
"does this difference subsist only as between sense
"and sense; for in the same sense, and even in that
"sense which has very commonly been held exclu-
"sively to afford a knowledge of absolute extension, I
"mean Touch proper, the minimum, at one part of
"the body, is some fifty times greater than it is at
"another."

Thus, according to Sir W. Hamilton, all our cognitions of extension and figure in anything except our own
body, and of the real amount of extension even in that,
are not perceptions, or states of direct consciousness, but
"inferences," and even inferences "by observation and
induction" from our experience.   Now, we know how
contemptuous he is of Brown, and other "Cosmothetic
Idealists," for maintaining that the existence of extension or extended objects otherwise than as an affection
of our own minds, is not a direct perception but an
inference.   We know how he reproaches this opinion
with being subversive of our Natural Beliefs ; how often
he repeats that the testimony of consciousness must be
accepted entire, or not accepted at all ; how earnestly
and in how many places he maintains "that we have
"not merely a notion, a conception, an imagination, a
"subjective representation of Extension, for example,
"called up or suggested in some incomprehensible man-
"ner to the mind, on the occasion of an extended object
"being presented to the sense ; but that in the percep-
"tion of such an object we have, *as by nature we believe*
"*we have*, an immediate knowledge or consciousness of
"that external object *as extended*.   In a word, that in
"sensitive perception, the extension as known, and the
"extension as existing, are convertible ; known because

"existing, and existing, since known." * All this, it appears, is only true of the extension of our own bodies. The extension of any other body is not known immediately or by perception, but as an inference from the former. I ask any one, whether this opinion does not contradict our "natural beliefs" as much as any opinion of the Cosmothetic Idealists can do ; whether to the natural, or non-metaphysical man, it is not as great a paradox to affirm that we do not perceive extension in anything external to our bodies, as that we do not perceive extension in anything external to our minds ; and whether, if the natural man can be brought to assent to the former, he will find any additional strangeness or apparent absurdity in the latter. This is only one of the many instances in which the philosopher who so vehemently accuses other thinkers of affirming the absolute authority of Consciousness when it is on their own side, and rejecting it when it is not, lays himself open to a similar charge. The truth is, it is a charge from which no psychologist, not Reid himself, is exempt. No person of competent understanding has ever applied himself to the study of the human mind, and not discovered that some of the common opinions of mankind respecting their mental consciousness are false, and that some notions, apparently intuitive, are really acquired. Every psychologist draws the line where he thinks it can be drawn most truly. Of course it is possible that Sir W. Hamilton has drawn it in the right place, and Brown in the wrong. Sir W. Hamilton would say that the common opinions which he contests are not Natural Beliefs, though mistaken for such. And Brown thinks exactly the same of those which are repugnant to his own doctrine. Neither of them can justify himself but by pointing out a mode in which the apparent perceptions, supposed to be original, may have been acquired ; and neither can charge the other with anything worse than having made a mistake in this extremely delicate

* Dissertations on Reid, p. 842.

U

process of psychological analysis. Neither of them has a right to give to a mistake in such a matter, the name of a rejection of the testimony of consciousness, and attempt to bring down the other by an argument which is of no possible value except *ad invidiam*, and which in its invidious sense is applicable to them both, and to all psychologists deserving the name.

NOTE TO THE PRECEDING CHAPTER.

A host of critics, headed by Dr. M'Cosh, Mr. Mahaffy, and the writer in *Blackwood*, have directed their shafts against this chapter; but Professor Fraser, himself a host, is on my side. The essential point in the controversy being the analysis of Extension, I shall confine my notice to the arguments bearing upon that point.

The principal objection is the same which was made to the two preceding chapters: that the explanation given of Extension presupposes Extension: that the notion itself is surreptitiously introduced, to account for its own origin. The case of the objectors is most compactly stated by Mr. Mahaffy, in the following extract : *—

"The briefest way of criticising the long passage" [quoted from Mr. Bain] "will be to enumerate its fallacies in general heads. (*a*) A know-"ledge of our organism as extended must not be begged, when we are "going to explain extension ; hence, such expressions as the 'range of a "limb' or 'sweep of a limb,' must either be carefully confined to the "mere succession of feelings in moving it, or they beg the question : and "indeed, as suggesting extension in the very statement, they should be "avoided when we are describing the phenomena from which extension is "to be derived. (*β*) Any mention or postulating of *direction* cannot be "for a moment allowed ; for what possible meaning can direction have ex-"cept in space? In particular, lineal (by which I suppose Mr. Bain "principally means rectilinear) direction would be only given with great "difficulty by the moving of limbs, and we should be brought back to "the old Greek notion of circular motion being the most natural. This "difficulty, as well as a host of others, are urged with great acuteness "by Mr. Abbott. (*Sight and Touch*, chap. v.) More especially he states, "from E. H. Weber, that touch cannot give us the idea of a right line at "all, and consequently not the slightest idea of direction. (*γ*) No such "notion as velocity or rapidity can be admitted, far less such a notion as "the comparison of quicker and slower motions. In fact, the idea of motion "requires as its logical antecedent both space and time, and is not iden-"tical with pure succession. Suppose we had nothing but the series of "our thoughts to analyse, we could never get beyond the idea of a series, "nor could we ever by any chance get the notion of acceleration or retar-"dation in it. For what is quicker or slower? Nothing but more space "traversed in less time and *vice versâ*. Motion cannot be apprehended "without something fixed, which is only given us by relations of space, as "Kant has well shown. The *motion* of our thoughts, then, is in the first

---

* Mahaffy, pp. xviii.-xx.

"place, only an analogical expression; and secondly, could never have
"been felt without something in space whereby not only to measure the
"increased or diminished velocity of our thinking, but even to learn
"that there is any velocity at all in the matter. The evidence of dreaming
"seems to corroborate this view. Why is it that the intuitions of velocity
"afforded us by space being removed, the current of thoughts is found
"by itself completely incompetent to suggest or estimate speed at all ?
"(δ) What we necessarily use to *measure* extension must not for that reason
"have originally *suggested* it. And yet all that the association school
"ever attempt to prove is only this : that all the measures of extension
"can be traced to series of muscular feelings in time. The knowledge of
"extension is one thing, and primitive ; the measure of extension is
"another, and empirical ; and we should not accept Mr. Bain's confusion
"of them together (perhaps identification of them), without some further
"proof than his bare statement.

"Upon all these assumptions, however, the theory of Mr. Bain is based,
"and the intelligent reader will find them scattered over the very surface
"of the argument. I would call particular attention to the passage . . .
"'We must learn to feel that a slow motion for a long time is the same
"as a quicker motion with less duration, which we can easily do by seeing
"that they both produce the same effect in exhausting the full range of
"the limb.' Surely it is clear that without space we could never get the
"idea of motion, which involves space as much as time—in fact, a series
"in time only changes, it does not move ; and even granting we had the
"idea, we could never discriminate whether that motion was quicker or
"slower, except the notion of something permanent in space, and motion
"in space, were given. The same *petitio principii* is made by Mr. Mill."

This orderly and succinct mode of setting forth the objection is a great
convenience for answering it. I shall take Mr. Mahaffy's points in his
own order.

(α) The phraseology employed to express the data common to both
parties must, at least in the commencement, be that which common language affords ; since no other would enable the reader to understand, without a laborious process, on a subject already so difficult, what are the facts
meant. But the phraseology, of course, must not be so used as to assume
anything which either the theory itself, or the theory opposed to it, does
not admit. As Mr. Mahaffy observes, "such expressions as the range of
a limb, or the sweep of a limb," must "be carefully confined to the
mere succession of feelings in moving it." And if the reader turns back
to the first of the quoted passages, he will find that Mr. Bain has been
most industrious in directing attention to the feelings involved in the
motion of a limb, as the point to be attended to, in contradistinction to
the motion itself, and in showing that his expressions are to be understood of the former, and not of the latter.

(β) Direction, Mr. Mahaffy maintains, must not be mentioned or referred to in the analysis of extension, because direction means space, and
space must not be called in to account for itself. It would have been
nearer the truth if, instead of saying that direction means space, he had
said that space means direction. Space is the aggregate of directions, as
Time is of successions. To postulate direction, therefore, is to postulate,
not space, but the element which the notion of space is made of. Mr.
Bain, however, does not postulate direction. He postulates the distinctive sensations which, from the first, accompany the motions of a limb in
what we, with our acquired perceptions, call variety of directions. There
are such distinctive sensations, otherwise we should not even now know,

when our eyes are shut, in what direction our arm is moving. According to Mr. Bain, the difference in the sensations depends on the difference in the muscles exerted. "All directions that call forth the play of the same "muscles, are similar directions as respects the body : different muscles "mean different directions."* These sensations, shading, as they do, gradually into one another, without abruptness or break, are well fitted to give rise to the feeling of continuity, which unites all our different notions of different directions into one notion of space.†

(γ) Velocity or rapidity, comparison of quicker and slower motions. must not, Mr. Mahaffy says, be postulated, because quicker or slower have no meaning but with reference to the greater, or smaller space traversed in a given time. It is true that the two motions derive their name from space ; but are the motions themselves therefore undistinguishable ? A saw and a hatchet are so called on account of the different kind of work they do ; but can we not also distinguish the two objects when we see them ? Again I say, what is postulated is not the space traversed, but the greater or less energy of the muscular sensation. It only remains to be explained how we learn that a more energetic sensation lasting a shorter time, is equivalent to a less energy continued for a longer time. Mr. Bain thinks we learn this by their both producing the same effect in "exhausting the full range of the limb ;" by which he means, attaining the extreme limit of the sensation which accompanies protension—the point beyond which no further addition to it can be made. Where is the *petitio principii* here ? I think that the solution is an admissible one— that we may fairly be supposed to take the entire series of the sensations

---

* The Senses and the Intellect, p. 203 (second edition).

† With regard to Mr. Abbot's difficulties, the following is a specimen of them : "Let us suppose a blind man trying to get the notion "of distance from the motion of his hand. He finds a certain sweep of "the hand brings it into contact with a desk ; the distance of which, "therefore, is represented by that effort. But it requires a greater effort "to reach the eyes or the nose ; and distance being=locomotive effort, it is "demonstrated that the nose extends beyond the desk. The top of the "head must be conceived as more remote, and the back farthest of all." Mr. Abbot seems to suppose that a blind man's permanent impression of the distance of objects from him, will be derived from his very first experiment ; and denies him the common privilege belonging to all experience, of correcting and completing itself. If the nose is really nearer to his hand than the desk, will he not soon find a way of reaching the nearer object with less locomotive effort than the more distant ? If it be said, that this can only be done by bending his arm, and that flexure of the arm is attended with more sense of effort than protension of it, the answer is that even if this were true, the effort is of a different kind ; and the blind man would speedily distinguish between the two, and would learn that objects reached by his bended arm are nearer to his body, by all the other tests of proximity, than those which can only be reached with the arm extended. Dr. M'Cosh (p. 135) falls into a fallacy of the same kind.

Mr. Abbot's book, a repetition of the attack made by Mr. Bailey on Berkeley's Theory of Vision, has sufficient ability to require an answer by itself, had not this been effectually done by Professor Fraser in an elaborate and able paper in the *North British Review* for August, 1864, which I trust will eventually be reprinted in a more permanent form.

which accompany the stretching out of the limb, as a unit of measurement, divisible into an ascending scale of degrees, which may be passed through in a shorter or a longer time, but the sum of which is always equal to itself. I have myself pointed out another road by which we might arrive at the same equivalence. We have two simultaneous sensations of touch with our two hands. We then move the right hand until it joins the left, and touches the same object. It need not be supposed that we yet know them as our hands, or the object as a body, or know of our right hand as moving through space. But the two simultaneous sensations of touch, either of which we may prolong or repeat at pleasure, have given us the notion of a permanent element in touch, and of two such permanent elements as coexisting. We have now had the two sensations of touch with a single hand, but separated by a series of the sensations accompanying muscular movement : and we find that to get from one of the tactual sensations to the other requires a shorter time, in proportion to the energy of the intervening muscular sensations. In this mental process time is postulated, but not space : and it is contended that the shorter time, or its equivalent, the greater energy, required to get from one object of touch to another already recognised as simultaneous, is the measure, in the last resort, of their distance in space. The eye then comes in, and with its greater powers of simultaneous sensation, it gathers up, by its acquired perceptions, a host of such measurements in one apparent intuition.

(δ) "What we necessarily use to measure extension" need not, as Mr. Mahaffy justly observes, have originally suggested it : but if all the facts of consciousness involved in what we call extension can be accounted for on the supposition that the measure is the thing itself, no other evidence needs be required.* The apparent testimony of consciousness to a difference between them, is perfectly explicable by the totally altered aspect which, as I have shown in the text, our cognisance of Extension puts on when the sense of sight has assumed the lead of it. When a larger collection of carefully observed facts respecting persons blind from birth, shall have been subjected to an acuter and more discriminating analysis, the additional insight which we may hope to obtain into the psychology of such persons, will probably dissipate the remains of obscurity which still hang over some of the details of the subject.

Dr. M'Cosh and the writer in *Blackwood* are constructive thinkers as well as critics, and endeavour to prove, in a direct manner, that the notion of extension is not acquired through our muscular sensations. The evidence on which they chiefly insist is that antecedently to experience, we localise our sensations at different points of our body : according to Dr. M'Cosh, at the extremities of the nerve-fibres ; every sensation being, by nature,† felt at the point where the nerve terminates. The writer in *Blackwood* † says, "We do not commence our sentient life with

---

* The writer in *Blackwood* thinks it absurd that the measure should "measure itself" (p. 32)—that muscular sensation, as a measure of distance, should be employed in measuring muscular sensation. But are not quantities usually measured by quantities of the same kind ? A foot rule measures length by its own length. A bushel measures solid contents by its own contents. The tickings of a clock measure other successions by their own succession. A weight measures other weights by itself.

† Pp. 26, 27.

"sensations felt nowhere—we certainly have no memory of pains that
"were not felt somewhere—in that arena, in fact, which we come to call
"our body." The absence of remembrance of what took place soon after
birth being, as I have so often observed, no proof that it did not happen,
the proof offered is, "that no ingenuity whatever will get our pains into
"our bodies, or give us knowledge of these bodies, unless we commence
"with the admission that certain pains and pleasures of a physical order
"are, as soon as they attain to any distinctness, felt in different parts of
"a certain arena, thus localising each other. . . . Many writers describe
"this localisation as an acquired perception. Now, no one doubts for a
"moment that the accurate localisation of our sensations is acquired by
"experience; but that experience, we maintain, would not be possible
"were there not some vague localisation given us at once, by simulta-
"neous sensations felt in different parts of our system. How else do we
"get our first idea of space or position?" To this last question I have
already endeavoured to give an answer.* With regard to the localisation, so far as it regards our external sensations, I see no difficulty in
believing that it takes place altogether by the process to which, as the
writer admits, we are indebted for our power of "accurate localisation."
I am bit by an animal, or my skin is irritated at some point, and I am at
first unable, as occasionally happens even now, to fix the exact place of
the sensation. I move my hand along the surface until I find the place
where the friction of the hand relieves the irritation, or where its contact
increases the smart. I am now expressing these facts in the ordinary
language of mankind, but I have sufficiently explained the sense which
that language bears in my own doctrine. The view I have taken of the
manner in which we obtain our cognition of place, does not rest on any
previous localisation, even vague, of our sensations. Nor does the localising of a sensation, say in one of our limbs, amount to anything but
attributing to the sensation an uniform and close conjunction, either synchronous or by immediate succession, with the group of sensations of
various kinds which constitute my perception of the limb. In general
we probably first discover that the sensation is connected with the limb,
by perceiving that the exciting cause of the sensation is connected with it.
Mr. Bain states the matter as follows:† "I can associate one pain with
"the sight of my finger, another pain with the sight of my toe,
"and a third with the position of my arm that determines the crown of
"my head. An infant at the outset knows not where to look for the
"cause of an irritation when anything touches it; by and by the child
"observes a coincidence between a feeling and a pressure operating on
"some one part; whence a feeling in the hand is associated with the
"sight of the hand, and so for other members.—When the feeling is more

---

* If distance and direction are explicable in the way I have pointed
out, place and position follow by obvious consequence. If once it be
admitted that impressions of touch can be cognised as at once simultaneous and separated by a series of muscular feelings, i.e. at once distant
and simultaneous, and that this amounts to cognising them as in space;
the position of these impressions among one another, which constitutes
their place, will easily result from the different quantities of muscular
sensation required for passing from one to the other, combined with the
distinctive qualities of the muscular sensations dependent on what we call
difference in the direction of the motion.

† The Senses and the Intellect, pp. 397, 398 (2nd ed.)

"internal, as in the interior of the trunk, we have greater difficulty in "tracing the precise seat, often we are quite at a loss on the point. In "this case we have to trust to some indications that come to the surface, "or to the effect of superficial pressure on the deep parts. By getting a "blow on the ribs we come to connect feelings in the chest with the place "in our map of the body: we can thus make experiments on the deep-"seated organs and learn the meaning of their indications. But the more "inaccessible the parts, the more uncertainty is there in assigning the "locality of their sensations." There are some difficulties, not yet completely resolved, respecting the localisation of our internal pains, for the solution of which we need more careful and intelligent observation of infants. But I think enough is known to show that the localisation of our sensations is not the starting point of our knowledge of place and position, but follows it. It is true that (as Dr. M'Cosh observes*) "if a child is wounded in the arm, it will not hold out its foot." But, before it has given evidence of having "any acquired perceptions," will it hold out its arm either? On the theory that the localisation is an acquired perception, it should do neither the one nor the other.†

Dr. M'Cosh has another argument to prove that we have an original power of localising our sensations, and, strange to say, it is the very one which is usually thought to be the strongest proof that the power is acquired: viz., the persistence of the association which makes us refer sensations to a limb, after the limb has been cut off. "Müller," says Dr. M'Cosh,‡ "has collected a number of such cases," of which one will be a sufficient sample: "a student named Schmidts, from Aix, had his arm "amputated above the elbow thirteen years ago; he has never ceased to "have sensations as if in the fingers." It is a singular oversight in Dr. M'Cosh to adduce these facts as proof that we localise the sensation at the extremities of the nerves. He forgets that after the arm was cut off, the extremity of the nerve was in the stump, and that it is there, and not in the fingers, that, if his theory were true, the sensation ought to have been felt. The reference of it to the limb which was gone could only be a case of irresistible association. It does not directly negative the existence of an instinctive localisation; but it proves that, if there be any such, an acquired association can overpower it. So in respect to the following fact, also quoted from Müller:§ "When, in the restoration of a nose, a "flap of skin is turned down from the forehead and made to unite with "the stump of the nose, the new nose thus formed has, as long as the "isthmus of skin by which it maintains its original connections remains "undivided, the same sensations as if it were still on the forehead; in "other words, when the nose is touched, the patient feels the impression "in the forehead." But the nerve that conveys the impression no longer

---

* M'Cosh, p. 150.

† Dr. M'Cosh says (same page) "It is hard to believe that the "instantaneous voluntary drawing back of a limb when wounded, and "the shrinking of the frame when boiling liquid is poured down the "throat, can proceed from an application of an observed law as to the "seat of sensations." The obvious solution of this difficulty is, that both the drawing back and the shrinking, when they take place in an extremely young infant, are purely automatic; a reflex action, produced, without the intervention of the will, by the irritation of the motor nerves: a solution quite conformable to physiology.

‡ P. 148.   § P. 149.

terminates in the forehead; it terminates in the new nose; and according to Dr. M'Cosh's theory the sensation should be felt there, exactly as it is after the "isthmus of skin" has been divided, the old nervous connection cut off, and a new one gradually formed. Dr. M'Cosh's facts well nigh destroy his own theory; but they are such as, on the association theory, would certainly happen. The last, especially, is of great value to that theory, because it is one of the strongest instances which show that there is a distinctive "Quale" (as one of Dr. M'Cosh's German authorities calls it) belonging to the sensation conveyed by each one of the nerves, which hinders it from being confounded with the sensation conveyed by any other nerve, and enables it to form associations special to itself with the part of the body it serves, which, as we see, persist even after it has been taken away to serve another part.

Dr. M'Cosh, in his reply, denies that his facts conflict with his theory, for his theory is, that we intuitively localise our sensations, not where the nerves really terminate, but where they "normally" terminate; that is, not where the termination is, but where it ought to be. In other words, we, naturally and intuitively, feel our sensations in a place which, in the case of an amputated limb, is not only outside our body, but may be at a distance of one or two feet from it : and this seat of sensation in the space outside our bodies follows us wherever we go. This is what Dr. M'Cosh would rather believe, than that the reference of the feeling to such a place is an illusion produced by association. In support of his opinion he refers to a case mentioned by Professor Valentin (along with three others of a similar character) in which a girl whose left hand was congenitally imperfect, said she had the internal sensation of a palm of the hand and five fingers (which she did not possess) as perfectly in her left hand as in her right. But what does this prove, except that she had the same sensations in the nerves of her left hand as in those of her right, which of course, therefore, carried the same association. Dr. M'Cosh should show a case in which sensations were referred to non-existent fingers when there were no real fingers to suggest the notion.

According to Dr. M'Cosh, the reference of sensations to a lost limb contradicts not his but the association theory : since the lapse of years after the loss of the limb would be sufficient to destroy the old association. And this, in the great majority of cases, it probably does. But it is a frequent experience that a sensation exactly like one we have formerly felt, and like nothing else, revives even after many years a long forgotten remembrance. Again, Dr. M'Cosh says that in the case of the new nose, the affection, according to the association theory, "should have been felt in "the forehead, not till the isthmus was cut, but till the old association was "gone ; and this," according to me, "might not have been for twenty "years." This overlooks an important feature in the case. When not only the old nervous connection has been cut off, but a new one formed, between the new nose and the nervous trunk which connected the old nose with the brain, the sensations become identical with those which were referred to the old nose when it existed ; and the reference of them to the nose is thus supported by as old and strong an asssociation as the previous reference of them to the forehead ; with the difference that while every day helps to dissolve the one association, every day strengthens and rivets the other.

The only further case referred to by Dr. M'Cosh, is one mentioned by Schopenhauer * on the authority of Frorieps ; that of "Eva Lauk, an Estho-

* Die Welt als Wille und Vorstellung, ed. 1844, vol. ii. p. 40.

" nian girl, fourteen years old, born without arms or legs, but who, according
" to her mother, had developed herself intellectually quite as rapidly as her
" brothers and sisters, and without the use of limbs had reached a correct
" judgment concerning the magnitude and distance of visible objects, quite
" as quickly as they." This, unfortunately, is all the information which
Schopenhauer gives on this interesting case. In Dr. M'Cosh's judgment, it
entirely disproves the opinion " that a sweep of the arm or leg, considered
merely as a group of sensations without extension," could give the idea of
extension. He means, probably, that it proves that the idea can be acquired
without any use of arms or legs. But we do not know of what nature the
girl's idea of extension was. What we are told is, that she had notions
of magnitude and distance, which she applied to objects with the same
correctness as other people. But her notion of distance may have been
only such as could be formed by the time expended in being carried to
the spot ; and her notion of magnitude may have been acquired when
objects were in contact with her body—perhaps still by means of muscular
feelings of pressure and motion. Above all, it must be remembered that
the girl was surrounded by people possessing legs and arms, and had
their aid in associating the discriminating sensations of sight with the
facts, of touch and of the muscles, to which they correspond. Such assistance is a great help even to children who have the ordinary complement
of legs and arms ; they all must acquire the association much more
quickly through the help given them by the acts and words of other
people. It may be confidently assumed that Eva Lauk had this help,
probably in more than usual measure, and did not find out wholly by
herself that a greater mass of visual sensation indicated a greater mass
of tactual sensation answering to it.

I believe I have noticed every plausible objection to Mr. Bain's and my
own analysis of Extension, which has a sufficiently individual character
to require an answer by itself. The subject is in need of further study
before all its obscure corners will be completely lighted up ; but this it
can hardly fail to receive, now that highly competent thinkers are engaged
in extending our knowledge of the Mind by the application of the Psychological Method, grounded on the Laws of Association.

CHAPTER XIV.

HOW SIR WILLIAM HAMILTON AND MR. MANSEL DISPOSE OF THE LAW OF INSEPARABLE ASSOCIATION.

IT has been obvious in the preceding discussions, and is known to all who have studied the best masters of what I have called the Psychological, in opposition to the merely Introspective method of metaphysical enquiry, that the principal instrument employed by them for unlocking the deeper mysteries of mental science, is the Law of Inseparable Association. This law, which it would seem specially incumbent on the Intuitive school of metaphysicians to take into serious consideration, because it is the basis of the rival theory which they have to encounter at every point, and which it is necessary for them to refute first, as the condition of establishing their own, is not so much rejected as ignored by them. Reid and Stewart, who had met with it only in Hartley, thought it needless to take the trouble of understanding it. The best informed German and French philosophers are barely aware, if even aware, of its existence.* And in this country and age, in which it has been employed by thinkers of the highest order as the most potent of all instruments of psychological analysis, the opposite school usually dismiss it with a few sentences, so smoothly gliding over the surface of the subject, as to prove that

---

* As lately as the year 1864 has been published the first work (I believe) in the French language, which recognises the Association Psychology in its modern developments: an able and instructive "Etude sur l'Association des Idées," by M. P. M. Mervoyer. Since then, the excellent introductory discourses prefixed by M. Cazelles to his translations from the English psychologists, and the remarkable work of M. Taine, "De l'Intelligence," have, it is to be hoped, permanently naturalised the Association Psychology among French thinkers and students.

they have never, even for an instant, brought the powers of their minds into real and effective contact with it.

Sir W. Hamilton has written a rather elaborate Dissertation on the Laws of Association; and the more elementary of them had engaged a considerable share of his attention.* But he nowhere shows that he had the smallest suspicion of this, the least familiar and most imperfectly understood of these laws.   I find in all his writings only two or three passages in which he touches,

---

* In this Dissertation, which originally broke off abruptly, but the conclusion of which has recently been supplied from the author's papers, he attempts to simplify the theory of Association; reducing Association by Resemblance, not indeed to Association by Contiguity, but to that combined with an elementary law, for the first time expressly laid down by Sir W. Hamilton, though implied in all Association and in all Memory: viz., that a present sensation or thought suggests the remembrance of what he calls *the same* sensation or thought (meaning one exactly similar) experienced at a former time.   This leaves Resemblance of simple sensations as a distinct principle of association, the foundation of all the rest, while it resolves resemblance of complex phenomena into that simple principle combined with the law of Contiguity.

By virtue of this speculation, Sir W. Hamilton thinks it possible to reduce Association to a single law: "Those thoughts suggest each other, "which had previously constituted parts of the same entire or total act of "cognition." (Lectures, ii. 238, and the corresponding passages of the Dissertation.)   This appears to me, I confess, far from a happy effort of generalisation; for there is no possibility of bringing under it the elementary case of suggestion, which our author has the merit of being the first to put into scientific language.   The sweet taste of to-day, and the similar sweet taste of a week ago which it reminds me of, have not "previously constituted parts of the same act of cognition;" unless we take literally the expression by which they are spoken of as the *same* taste, though they are no more the same taste than two men are the same man if they happen to be exactly alike.   It is a further objection, that the attempted simplification, even if otherwise correct, would merely unite two clear notions into one obscure one; for the notion of feelings ' which suggest one another because they resemble, or because they have been experienced together, is universally intelligible, while that of forming parts of the same act of cognition involves all the metaphysical difficulties which surround the ideas of Unity, Totality, and Parts.

After thus, as he fancies, reducing all the phenomena of Association to a single law, Sir W. Hamilton asks, how is this law itself explained? and justly observes that it may be an ultimate law, and that ultimate laws are necessarily unexplainable.   But he nevertheless quotes, with some approbation, an attempt by a German writer, H. Schmid, to explain it by an *à priori* theory of the human mind, which may be recommended to notice as a choice specimen of a school of German metaphysicians who have remained several centuries behind the progress of philosophical inquiry, having never yet felt the influence of the Baconian reform.   See Lectures, ii. 240–243.

even cursorily, on this mode of explaining mental phenomena. The first and longest of these occurs in the treatment, not of any of the greater problems of mental philosophy, but of a very minor question; whether, in the perception of outward objects, our cognition of wholes precedes that of their component parts, or the contrary. More fully; "whether, in Perception, do we "first obtain a general knowledge of the complex wholes "presented to us by sense, and then, by analysis and "limited attention, obtain a special knowledge of their "several parts; or do we not first obtain a particular "knowledge of the smallest parts to which sense is "competent, and then, by synthesis, collect them into "greater and greater wholes?" * Sir W. Hamilton declares for the first theory, and quotes as supporters of the second, Stewart and James Mill; to the latter of whom, more than to any other thinker, mankind are indebted for recalling the attention of philosophers to the law of Inseparable Association, and pointing out the important applications of which it is susceptible. Through the conflict with Mr. Mill on the very subordinate question which he is discussing, Sir W. Hamilton is led to quote a part of that philosopher's exposition of Inseparable Association; and it is a sign how little he was aware of the importance of the subject, that a theory of so wide a scope and such large consequences should receive the only recognition he ever gives it in a bye corner of his work, incidentally to one of the smallest questions therein discussed. I shall extract the very passages which he quotes from Mr. Mill, because, in a small space, they state and illustrate very happily the two most characteristic properties of our closest associations: that the suggestions they produce are, for the time, irresistible; and that the suggested ideas (at least when the association is of the synchronous kind as distinguished from the successive) become so blended together, that the compound result appears, to our consciousness, simple.

* Lectures ii. 144.

"Where two or more ideas," says Mr. Mill,* "have
"been often repeated together, and the association has
"become very strong, they sometimes spring up in such
"close combination, as not to be distinguishable. Some
"cases of sensation are analogous. For example, when
"a wheel, on the seven parts of which the seven pris-
"matic colours are respectively painted, is made to re-
"volve rapidly, it appears not of seven colours, but of
"one uniform colour, white. By the rapidity of the
"succession, the several sensations cease to be distin-
"guishable; they run, as it were, together, and a new
"sensation, compounded of all the seven, but apparently
"a single one, is the result. Ideas, also, which have
"been so often conjoined, that whenever one exists in
"the mind, the others immediately exist along with it,
"seem to run one into another, to coalesce, as it were,
"and out of many to form one idea; which idea, how-
"ever in reality complex, appears to be no less simple
"than any one of those of which it is compounded. . . .
    "It is to this great law of association that we trace
:"the formation of our ideas of what we call external
"objects; that is, the ideas of a certain number of sensa-
"tions received together so frequently that they coalesce,
"as it were, and are spoken of under the idea of unity.
"Hence what we call the idea of a tree, the idea of a
"stone, the idea of a horse, the idea of a man.
    "In using the names, tree, horse, man, the names of
"what I call objects, I am referring, and can be referring,
"only to my own sensations; in fact, therefore, only
"naming a certain number of sensations, regarded as
"in a particular state of combination; that is, of con-
"comitance. Particular sensations of sight, of touch, of
"the muscles, are the sensations, to the ideas of which,
"colour, extension, roughness, hardness, smoothness,
"taste, smell, so coalescing as to appear one idea, I
"give the name idea of a tree.
    "To this case of high association, this blending to-
"gether of many ideas, in so close a combination that

* Analysis of the Human Mind, i. 68-75.

"they appear not many ideas, but one idea, we owe, as
"I shall afterwards more fully explain, the power of
"classification, and all the advantages of language.
"It is obviously, therefore, of the greatest moment,
"that this important phenomenon should be well
"understood.

"Some ideas are by frequency and strength of asso-
"ciation so closely combined that they cannot be sepa-
"rated. If one exists, the other exists along with it, in
"spite of whatever effort we may make to disjoin them.

"For example; it is not in our power to think of
"colour, without thinking of extension; or of solidity,
"without figure. We have seen colour constantly in
"combination with extension, spread, as it were, upon a
"surface. We have never seen it except in this con-
"nection. Colour and extension have been invariably
"conjoined. The idea of colour, therefore, uniformly
"comes into mind, bringing that of extension along
"with it; and so close is the association, that it is not
"in our power to dissolve it. We cannot, if we will,
"think of colour, but in combination with extension.
"The one idea calls up the other, and retains it, so
"long as the other is retained.

"This great law of our nature is illustrated in a man-
"ner equally striking by the connection between the ideas
"of solidity and figure. We never have the sensations
"from which the idea of solidity is derived, but in con-
"junction with the sensations whence the idea of figure
"is derived. If we handle anything solid it is always
"either round, square, or of some other form. The ideas
"correspond with the sensations. If the idea of solidity
"rises, that of figure rises along with it. The idea of
"figure which rises is, of course, more obscure than that
"of extension; because, figures being innumerable, the
"general idea is exceedingly complex, and hence, of
"necessity, obscure. But such as it is, the idea of figure
"is always present when that of solidity is present; nor
"can we, by any effort, think of the one without think-
"ing of the other at the same time."

Other illustrations follow, concluding with these words: " The following of one idea after another, or after a sen- " sation, so certainly that we cannot prevent the com- " bination, nor avoid having the *consequent* feeling as " often as we have the *antecedent,* is a law of association, " the operation of which we shall afterwards find to be " extensive, and bearing a principal part in some of the " most important phenomena of the human mind." And the promise of this sentence is amply redeemed in the sequel of the treatise.

The only remark which this highly philosophical exposition suggests to Sir W. Hamilton, is a disparaging reflection on Mr. Mill's philosophy in general. He says that Mr. Mill, in his "ingenious" treatise, " has "pushed the principle of Association to an extreme which "refutes its own exaggeration,—analysing not only our "belief in the relation of effect and cause into that " principle, but even the primary logical laws," so that it is no wonder he should "account for our knowledge of " complex wholes in perception, by the same universal "principle."   Having, on the strength of this previous verdict of exaggeration, dispensed with inquiring how much the law of Inseparable Association can really accomplish, he makes no use of its most obvious applications, even while transcribing them into his own pages. One of the psychological facts stated in the passage quoted, the impossibility, to us, of separating the idea of extension and that of colour, is a truth strongly insisted on by Sir W. Hamilton himself.   In the very next Lecture but one to that from which I have been quoting, he strenuously maintains that we can neither conceive colour without extension, nor extension without colour.   Even the born blind, he thinks, have the sensation of darkness, that is, of black colour, and mentally clothe all extended objects with it.*   Except the last position, which has no evidence and no probability,† the

* Lectures, ii. 168–172.
† According to the doctrine of all advanced psychologists, to which Sir W. Hamilton gives an express adhesion, it is impossible to have a conscious.

doctrine is undoubtedly true, and the fact is so obviously
a case of the law of association, that even Stewart, little
partial as he was to that mode of explaining mental
phenomena, does not dream of attributing it to anything
else. "In consequence," says Stewart, "of our always
"perceiving extension at the same time at which the
"sensation of colour is excited in the mind, we find it
"impossible to think of that sensation without conceiving
"extension along with it." He gives this as one of the
instances "of very intimate associations formed between
"two ideas which have no necessary connection with one
"another." A mental analysis by way of association
which was sufficiently obvious to recommend itself to
Stewart, will scarcely be charged with "pushing the
principle to an extreme." In fact, if an association can
ever become inseparable by dint of repetition, how
could the association between colour and extension fail
of being so? The two facts never exist but in immediate conjunction, and the experience of that conjunction
is repeated at every moment of life which is not spent
in darkness. Yet after transcribing this explanation
both from Stewart and from Mill, Sir W. Hamilton
remains as insensible to it as if it had never been given ;
and without a word of refutation, composedly registers
the inseparableness of the two ideas as an ultimate mental fact proving them both to be original perceptions of
the same organ, the eye. Sir W. Hamilton's authority
can have little weight against the doctrine which accounts for the more complex parts of our mental constitution by the laws of association, when it is so evident
that he rejected that doctrine not because he had ex-

---

ness of darkness without having had a consciousness of light. Besides,
it is a notorious optical fact that a completely black object occupying the
whole sphere of vision is invisible : it reflects no light. Blackness, therefore
(the complete blackness of absolute darkness), is not a sensation, but the
total absence of sensation ; it is, in fact, nothing at all ; and to say that a
person born blind cannot imagine extension without clothing it with
nothing at all, is to assert something not very intelligible. In the case
of a person who has *become* blind, it might have a meaning ; for blackness
to him, like darkness to us, does not stand for mere inability to see, but
for the usual effort to see, not followed by the usual consequence.

amined it and found it wanting, but without examining it; having taken for granted that it did not deserve examination.*

How imperfect was his acquaintance with the secondary laws, the *axiomata media* of association, is plainly seen in his argument against Stewart and Mill on the comparatively insignificant question with which he started. The thesis he is asserting is, that "in place of "ascending upwards, from the minimum of perception "to its maxima, we descend from masses to details."

"If the opposite doctrine" (says Sir W. Hamilton) † "were correct, what would it involve? It would involve

---

* In one of the unfinished dissertations left among his papers, and intended for his edition of Reid (in which it now stands as note E) Sir W. Hamilton did attempt to disprove the doctrine that our incapacity to conceive colour without extension is an effect of association. His arguments (pp. 919, 920), are first, that of D'Alembert (discussed in a former chapter), that when two colours meet we must be conscious of the line which separates them; and the junction, therefore, of two colours cannot be conceived apart from extension. But suppose that we are only perceiving a single colour, which occupies the whole field of vision : our invariably seeing this as extended cannot be explained by something which only happens when we see two colours; unless the impression received from the two adheres to the one by association. Sir W. Hamilton, therefore, is reduced to say that the field of vision "has a right and a left, an upper and an under side, and may be divided into halves, quarters, &c., indefinitely," an argument which begs the question, since it assumes that the homogeneously coloured field is already perceived as composed of parts, that is, as extended.

Sir W. Hamilton's other argument is that "we cannot be conscious of "a colour without being conscious of that colour in contrast to, and "therefore out of, another colour,—without, therefore, being conscious of "the extended." This seems an assumption without grounds. If a single colour occupies the whole field of vision, it can surely be recognised as colour. The contrast, which is essential to consciousness, needs not be between one colour and another : it may be between colour and the absence of sensation, or between colour and a sensation of some other sense. I am supposing the sensation of colour to be intermittent; or if it were constant, I admit that it would cease to be felt at all.

The converse incapacity to conceive extension without colour, Sir W. Hamilton deals with very summarily (p. 917), by saying that there is no object of vision, either actual or conceivable, which is not coloured. This is the very explanation given by the Association theory. All objects of vision are coloured, counting black as a colour, which when it stands in contrast with positive colours, we may legitimately do ; by the laws of Association, therefore, what is always seen as coloured is always conceived as coloured. In combating, as he thinks, the Association theory, Sir W. Hamilton is obliged to have recourse to it.

† Lectures, ii. 149, 150.

"as a primary inference, that, as we know the whole
"through the parts, we should know the parts better
"than the whole. Thus, for example, it is supposed
"that we know the face of a friend, through the
"multitude of perceptions which we have of the different
"points of which it is made up; in other words, that
"we should know the whole countenance less vividly
"than we know the forehead and eyes, the nose and
"mouth, &c., and that we should know each of these
"more feebly than we know the various ultimate points,
"in fact, unconscious minima of perception, which go
"to constitute them. According to the doctrine in
"question, we perceive only one of these ultimate points
"at the same instant, the others by memory incessantly
"renewed. Now let us take the face out of perception
"into memory altogether. Let us close our eyes, and
"let us represent in imagination the countenance of our
"friend. This we can do with the utmost vivacity; or
"if we see a picture of it, we can determine with a con-
"sciousness of the most perfect accuracy, that the portrait
"is like or unlike. It cannot, therefore, be denied that
"we have the fullest knowledge of the face as a whole,
"that we are familiar with its expression, with the
"general results of its parts. On the hypothesis, then,
"of Stewart and Mill, how accurate should be our know-
"ledge of these parts themselves. But make the ex-
"periment. You will find, that unless you have analysed,
"—unless you have descended from a conspectus of the
"whole face to a detailed examination of its parts,—with
"the most vivid impression of the constituted whole,
"you are almost totally ignorant of the constituted parts.
"You may probably be unable to say what is the colour
"of the eyes, and if you attempt to delineate the mouth
"or nose, you will inevitably fail. Or look at the por-
"trait. You may find it unlike, but unless, as I said,
"you have analysed the countenance, unless you have
"looked at it with the analytic scrutiny of a painter's
"eye, you will assuredly be unable to say in what respect
"the artist has failed,—you will be unable to specify

"what constituent he has altered, though you are fully
"conscious of the fact and effect of the alteration. What
"we have shown from this example may equally be done
"from any other—a house, a tree, a landscape, a concert
"of music, &c." *

I have already made mention of a very important part
of the Laws of Association, which may be termed the
Laws of Obliviscence. If Sir W. Hamilton had sufficiently attended to those laws, he never could have
maintained, that if we knew the parts before the whole,
we must continue to know the parts better than the
whole. It is one of the principal Laws of Obliviscence,
that when a number of ideas suggest one another by
association with such certainty and rapidity as to coalesce
together in a group, all those members of the group
which remain long without being specially attended to,
have a tendency to drop out of consciousness. Our consciousness of them becomes more and more faint and
evanescent, until no effort of attention can recall it into
distinctness, or at last recall it at all. Any one who
observes his own mental operations will find this fact
exemplified in every day of his life. Now the law of
attention is admitted to be, that we attend only to that
which, either on its own or on some other account,
interests us. In consequence, what interests us only
momentarily we only attend to momentarily; and do not
go on attending to it, when that, for the sake of which
alone it interested us, has been attained. Sir W. Hamilton would have found these several laws clearly set forth,
and abundantly exemplified, in the work of Mr. Mill
which he had before him. It is there shown how large
a proportion of all our states of feeling pass off without
having been attended to, and in many cases so habitually

---

* Those who are acquainted with Mr. Bailey's attempt to disprove
Berkeley's Theory of Vision, will be reminded by this passage of an
exactly similar argument employed by that able thinker and writer, to
prove the intuitive character of what philosophers almost unanimously
consider as the acquired perceptions of sight. I have given the same
answer to Mr. Bailey on another occasion, which I give to Sir W.
Hamilton here.

that we become finally incapable of attending to them. This subject was also extremely well understood by Reid, who, little as he had reflected on the principle of Association, was much better acquainted with the laws of Obliviscence than his more recent followers, and has excellently illustrated and exemplified some of them.* Among those which he has illustrated the most success-fully, one is, that the very great number of our states of feeling which, being themselves neither painful nor pleasurable, are important to us only as signs of some-thing else, and which by repetition have come to do their work as signs with a rapidity which to our feelings is instantaneous, cease altogether to be attended to; and through that inattention our consciousness of them either ceases altogether, or becomes so fleeting and indistinct as to leave no reliable trace in the memory. This happens, even when the impressions which serve the purpose of signs are not mere ideas, or reminiscences, of sensation, but actual sensations. After reading a chapter of a book, when we lay down the volume do we remember to have been individually conscious of the printed letters and syllables which have passed before us? Could we recall, by any effort of mind, the visible aspect presented by them, unless some unusual circum-stance has fixed our attention upon it during the perusal? Yet each of these letters and syllables must have been present to us as a sensation for at least a passing moment, or the sense could not have been conveyed to us. But the sense being the only thing in which we are interested —or, in exceptional cases, the sense and a few of the words or sentences—we retain no impression of the separate letters and syllables. This instance is the more instructive, inasmuch as, the whole process taking place within our means of observation, we know that our knowledge begins with the parts, and not with the whole. We know that we perceived and distinguished

* See his Inquiry into the Human Mind, chap. v. sections 2 and 8; chap. vi. sects. 2, 3, 4, 7, 8, 19; Intellectual Powers, Essay ii. chaps. 16 and 17.

letters and syllables before we learnt to understand
words and sentences ; and the perceptions could not, at
that time, have passed unattended to ; on the contrary,
the effort of attention of which those letters and syllables
must have been the object, was probably, while it lasted,
equal in intensity to any which we have been called
upon to exercise in after life.   Were Sir W. Hamilton's
argument valid, one of two things would follow.   Either
we have even now, when we read in a book, a more vivid
consciousness of the letters and syllables than of the
words and sentences (and by parity of reason a more
vivid consciousness of the words and sentences than of
the general purport of the discourse) : or else, we could
read sentences off hand at first, and only by subsequent
analysis discovered the letters and syllables.   If ever
there was a *reductio ad absurdum*, this is one.

The facts on which Sir W. Hamilton's argument
rests, are obviously accounted for by the laws which he
ignores.   In our perceptions of objects, it is generally
the wholes, and the wholes alone, that interest us.   In
his example, that of a friend's countenance, it is (special
motives apart) only the friend himself that we are
interested about; we care about the features only as
signs that it is our friend whom we see, and not another
person.   Unless therefore the face commands our attention by its beauty or strangeness, or unless we stamp
the features on our memory by acts of attention directed
upon them separately, they pass before us and do their
work as signs, with so little consciousness that no distinct
trace may be left in the memory.   We forget the details
even of objects which we see every day, if we have no
motive for attending to the parts as distinguished from
the wholes, and have cultivated no habit of doing so.
That this is consistent with having known the parts
earlier than the wholes, is proved not only by the case of
reading, but by that of playing on a musical instrument,
and a hundred other familiar instances ; by everything,
in fact, which we learn to do.   When the wholes alone
are interesting to us, we soon forget our knowledge of

the component parts, unless we purposely keep it alive by conscious comparison and analysis.

This is not the only fallacy in Sir W. Hamilton's argument. Considered as a reply to Mr. Mill's explanation of the origin of our ideas of objects, it entirely misses the mark. If the argument and examples had proved their point, which it has been seen that they do not, they would have proved that we perceive and know, to some extent or other, the object as a whole, before knowing its *integrant* parts. But it is not of integrant parts that Mr. Mill was speaking; and he might have admitted all that Sir W. Hamilton contends for, without surrendering his own opinion. The question does not relate to parts in extension. It does not concern Mr. Mill's theory whether we know, or do not know, a man as such, before we distinguish, in thought or in perception, his head from his feet. What Mr. Mill said was, that our idea of an object, whether it be of the man, or of his head, or of his feet, is compounded by association from our ideas of the colour, the shape, the resistance, &c., which belong to those objects. These are what philosophers have called the metaphysical parts, not the integrant part, of the total impression. Now I have never heard of any philosopher who maintained that *these* parts were not known until after the objects which they characterise; that we perceive the body first, and its colour, shape, form, &c., only afterwards. Our senses, which on all theories are at least the avenues through which our knowledge of bodies comes to us, are not adapted by nature to let in the perception of the whole object at once. They only open to let pass single attributes at a time. And this is as much Sir W. Hamilton's opinion as any one's else, except where he is sustaining an argument which makes him blind to it.

As is often the case with our author, the conclusion he is maintaining is worth more than his argument to prove it, and though not the whole truth, has truth in it. That we perceive the whole before the parts will not tand examination as a general law, but is very often true

as a particular fact: our first impression is often that of
a confused mass, of which all the parts seem blended,
and our subsequent progress consists in elaborating this
into distinctness. It was well to point out this fact: but
if our author had paid more attention to its limits, he
might have been able to give us a complete theory of
it, instead of leaving it, as he has done, an empirical
observation, which waits for some one to raise it into a
scientific law.

The same want of comprehension of the power of an
inseparable association, which was shown by Sir W.
Hamilton in the case of Colour and Extension, is exhibited in the only other case in which he adduces any
argument to prove that an idea was not produced by
association. The case is that of causality, and the argument is the ordinary one of metaphysicians of his school.
"The *necessity** of so thinking cannot be derived from a
" *custom* of so thinking. The force of custom, influential
" as it may be, is still always limited to the customary;
" and the customary never reaches, never even approaches
" to the necessary." If this were so, not only could an
inseparable association generate no necessity of belief, but
there could be no such thing as inseparable association;
no entirely irresistible conjunction between two mental
states. The paviour, however, who cannot use his
rammer without the accustomed cry, the orator who had
so often while speaking twirled a string in his hand
that he became unable to speak when he accidentally
dropped it, are, it seems to me, examples of a
" customary " which did approach to, and even reach,
the " necessary." " Association may explain a strong
" and special, but it can never explain a universal and
" absolutely irresistible belief." Not when the conjunction of facts which engenders the association, is
itself universal and irresistible? " What † I cannot but
" think, must be *à priori*, or original to thought: it
" cannot be engendered by experience upon custom." As

---

* Discussions, Appendix i. on Causality, p. 615.
† Lectures, ii. 191.

if experience, that is to say, association, were not perpetually engendering both inabilities to think, and inabilities not to think. " We can * think away each " and every part of the knowledge we have derived "from experience." Associations derived from experience are doubtless separable by a sufficient amount of contrary experience ; but, in the cases we are considering, no contrary experience is to be had.   On the theory that the belief in causality results from association, "when † asso- " ciation is recent, the causal judgment should be weak, " and rise only gradually to full force, as custom becomes " inveterate."   And how do we know that it does not ? The whole process of acquiring our belief in causation takes place at an age of which we have no remembrance, and which precludes the possibility of testing the matter by experiment : and all theories agree that our first type of causation is our own power of moving our limbs ; which is as complete as it can be, and has formed as strong associations as it is capable of forming, long before the child can observe or communicate its mental operations.

It is strange that almost all the opponents of the Association psychology should found their main or sole argument in refutation of it upon the feeling of neces- sity ; for if there be any one feeling in our nature which the laws of association are obviously equal to producing, one would say it is that.   Necessary, according to Kant's definition, and there is none better, is that of which the negation is impossible.   If we find it impossible, by any trial, to separate two ideas, we have all the feeling of necessity which the mind is capable of.   Those, therefore, who deny that association can generate a necessity of thought, must be willing to affirm that two ideas are never so knit together by association as to be practically inseparable.   But to affirm this is to contradict the most familiar experience of life.   Many persons who have been frightened in childhood can never be alone in the dark without irrepressible terrors.   Many a person is

* Lectures, iv. 74.   † Discussions, *ut supra*.

unable to revisit a particular place, or to think of a particular event, without recalling acute feelings of grief or reminiscences of suffering.   If the facts which created these strong associations in individual minds, had been common to all mankind from their earliest infancy, and had, when the associations were fully formed, been forgotten, we should have had a necessity of Thought—one of the necessities which are supposed to prove an objective law, and an *à priori* mental connection between ideas.*   Now, in all the supposed natural beliefs and necessary conceptions which the principle of Inseparable Association is employed to explain, the generating causes of the association did begin nearly at the beginning of life, and are common either to all, or to a very large portion of mankind.†

* Dr. Ward (p. 291) takes exception to these instances, as exemplifying not a necessity of thought but a necessity of feeling—which has never been affirmed to prove an objective law, or an *à priori* connection between ideas. I answer that what I sought to prove by the instances, was that two ideas may be "so knit together by association as to be practically inseparable."   And I added, not that a necessity of feeling proves a necessity of thought, but that under certain conditions it would generate one. If the person in whose mind a given spot is associated with terrors, had entirely forgotten the fact by which it came to be so; and if the rest of mankind, or even only a great number of them, felt the same terror on coming to the same place, and were equally unable to account for it; there would certainly grow up a conviction that the place had a natural quality of terribleness, which would probably fix itself in the belief that the place was under a curse, or was the abode of some invisible object of terror.   Feelings common to many persons, which are at once irresistible and unaccountable, almost always pass into equivalent judgments and beliefs.   Indeed, this is the precise way in which the fact of our sensations is translated into belief in an external world; and we should, in the case supposed, seem to have the same evidence of the terrific quality, which we have of any of the qualities of objects.

† I find it necessary here to correct a misunderstanding to which I never should have suspected myself to be liable.   Dr. M'Cosh employs nearly the whole of his ninth chapter (Judgment or Comparison) in protesting against the doctrine, that an inseparable association necessarily produces belief; and concludes with a solemn appeal to the young to raise themselves above the influence of mere association, and learn "that it is "our duty to found our beliefs on a previous judgment" and "to base our "beliefs on an inspection of realities and actualities."   (Pp. 214, 215.)   In all of which, aimed as it is at myself, Dr. M'Cosh is preaching not only to a person already converted, but to an actual missionary of the same doctrine.   I have certainly called attention to the important psychological truth, not unrecognised by Dr. M'Cosh, that a strong mental association between two facts, even short of inseparability, has a great tendency to

The beggarly account now exhibited, is, I believe, all
that Sir W. Hamilton has anywhere written against the
Association psychology. But it is not all that has been
said against that psychology from Sir W. Hamilton's
point of view. In this as in various other cases, to
supply what Sir W. Hamilton has omitted, recourse
may advantageously be had to Mr. Mansel.

Mr. Mansel, though in some sense a pupil of Sir W.
Hamilton, is a pupil who may be usefully consulted even
after his master. Besides that he now and then sees
things which his master did not see, he very often fights
a better battle against adversaries. Moreover, as I before
remarked, he has a decided taste for clear statements and
definite issues ; and this is no small advantage when the
object is, not victory, but to understand the subject.

Mr. Mansel joins a distinct issue with the Association
psychology, and brings the question to the proper test.
" It has been already observed," he says, in his Prolegomena Logica,* " that whatever truths we are com-
" pelled to admit as everywhere and at all times neces-
" sary, must have their origin, not without, in the laws
" of the sensible world, but within, in the constitution
" of the mind itself. Sundry attempts have, indeed,
" been made to derive them from sensible experience and
" constant association of ideas ; but this explanation is
" refuted by a criterion decisive of the fate of all hypo-
" theses : it does not account for the phenomena. It
" does not account for the fact that *other associations, as*
" *frequent and as uniform, are incapable of producing a*

make us believe in a connection between the facts themselves ; but I thought
that if there ever had been a writer who was assiduous in warning people
against this tendency (to which, in my Logic, I have given a conspicuous
place in the enumeration of Fallacies) and exhorting them to ground their
beliefs exclusively on the evidence, that writer was myself. Dr. M'Cosh's
work is unimpeachable in point of candour and fairness ; but this instance
shows how little he is to be relied on for correctly apprehending the
maxims and tendencies of a philosophy different from his own.

Dr. M'Cosh, in his reply, interprets the phraseology of this Note as if I
had accused him of "preaching" in some disparaging sense. I was merely
alluding to the almost proverbial expression, "prêcher un converti,"
which I thought that Dr. M'Cosh would have understood.

* Beginning of chap. iv. p. 90.

BY SIR WILLIAM HAMILTON AND MR. MANSEL. 331

" higher conviction than that of a relative and physical
" necessity only."

This is coming to the point, and evinces a correct apprehension of the conditions of scientific proof. If other
associations, as close and as habitual as those existing
in the cases in question, do not produce a similar feeling
of necessity of thought, the sufficiency of the alleged cause
is disproved, and the theory must fall. Mr. Mansel is
within the true conditions of the Psychological Method.

But what are these cases of uniform and intimate
association, which do not give rise to a feeling of mental
necessity? The following is Mr. Mansel's first example
of them : * " I may imagine the sun rising and setting
" as now for a hundred years, and afterwards remaining
" continually fixed in the meridian. Yet my experiences
" of the alternations of day and night have been at least
" as invariable as of the geometrical properties of bodies.
" I can imagine the same stone sinking ninety-nine times
" in the water, and floating the hundredth, but my expe-
" rience invariably repeats the former phenomenon only."

The alternation of day and night is invariable in our
experience; but is the phenomenon day so closely linked
in our experience with the phenomenon night, that we
never perceive the one, without, at the same or the immediately succeeding moment, perceiving the other? That
is a condition present in the inseparable associations
which generate necessities of thought. Uniformities of
sequence in which the phenomena succeed one another
only at a certain interval, do not give rise to inseparable
associations.† There are also mental conditions, as well

---

* Prolegomena Logica, pp. 96, 97.

† Mr. Mahaffy has misunderstood (p. xxiv.) the meaning of this statement, which is certainly too incautiously expressed. The phenomena
which must have been simultaneous or immediately successive to create
an inseparable association, need not have been actual perceptions : an
association, and even an inseparable association, may be created between
two ideas, if they have been habitually present together, or in immediate
succession, merely in thought. This truth is so universally recognised by
writers on Association, that it did not seem to require statement. But
the succession which generates an inseparable association, must, either in
fact or in thought, be an immediate succession ; or rather, one without any
conscious or perceptible interval.

as physical, which are required to create such an association.   Let us take Mr. Mansel's other instance, a stone
sinking in the water.   We have never seen it float, yet
we have no difficulty in conceiving it floating.   But, in
the first place, we have not been seeing stones sinking
in water from the first dawn of consciousness, and in
nearly every subsequent moment of our lives, as we have
been seeing two and two making four, intersecting
straight lines diverging instead of enclosing a space,
causes followed by effects and effects preceded by causes.
But there is a still more radical distinction than this.
No frequency of conjunction between two phenomena
will create an inseparable association, if counter-associations are being created all the while.   If we sometimes
saw stones floating as well as sinking, however often we
might have seen them sink, nobody supposes that we
should have formed an inseparable association between
them and sinking.   We have not seen a stone float, but
we are in the constant habit of seeing either stones or
other things which have the same tendency to sink, remaining in a position which they would otherwise quit,
being maintained in it by an unseen force.   The sinking
of a stone is but a case of gravitation, and we are abundantly accustomed to see the force of gravity counteracted.
Every fact of that nature which we ever saw or heard of,
is *pro tanto* an obstacle to the formation of the inseparable
association which would make a violation of the law of
gravity inconceivable to us.   Resemblance is a principle
of association, as well as contiguity: and however contradictory a supposition may be to our experience *in hác
materiá*, if our experience *in aliá materiá* furnishes us
with types even distantly resembling what the supposed
phenomenon would be if realised, the associations thus
formed will generally prevent the specific association
from becoming so intense and irresistible, as to disable
our imaginative faculty from embodying the supposition
in a form moulded on one or other of those types.*

* In an able manuscript critique on " the Experience Hypothesis " which
has been communicated to me, the familiar truth that fire burns is given

Again, says Mr. Mansel,* "experience has uniformly "presented to me a horse's body in conjunction with a "horse's head, and a man's head with a man's body; "just as experience has uniformly presented to me space "inclosed within a pair of curved lines and not within "a pair of straight lines:" yet I have no difficulty in imagining a centaur, but cannot imagine a space inclosed by two straight lines. "Why do I, in the "former case, consider the results of my experience as "contingent only and transgressible, confined to the

as an example of an uniform sequence which does not generate a necessity of thought. No one (the writer observes) will say that we have a more frequent perception of the fact that parallel lines do not inclose a space, than we have of the fact that fire burns: yet we can without difficulty imagine human beings remaining unburnt in a fiery furnace ; nay, we may even believe it, if we admit the supposition either of magic or of a miracle. No doubt : but this is fully explained by the counter-associations. Though we have never seen a human being in the fire unburnt, being in the fire is not inseparably associated with destruction, for we have seen abundance of other objects, immersed in intense fire, yet resisting its action. The conception of a man in the same position, is within the limits of the power characteristic of imagination, of varying (only slightly in this instance) our mental combinations of the elements given by experience. The writer asks, why then cannot imagination produce all combinations? The only ones it cannot produce are precisely those which are prevented by associations really irresistible, associations that, have never been counteracted by counter-associations, and by the operation of which, elements with which certain combinations in imagination would be incompatible, are forced into our mental representations.

The same writer says, we believe by a necessity of thought that a tangent touches a circle at one point only, yet this necessary belief, far from being the result of uniform experience, is contradicted by uniform experience, since the tangents and circles of experience touch one another at more than one point—coalesce in an appreciable portion of their extent. I answer, that the circle in our imagination is copied from those only, among the circles of our experience, in which sense can detect no variation from the definition of a circle, i.e. whose radii are not perceptibly unequal. Now, if the radii are, to our perception, equal, a line which is to our perception straight, will touch the circle in what is to our perception a single point. And there are many such circles, not perhaps in nature, but certainly in the products of mechanical art. The belief therefore does not conflict, but accords, with an uniform experience. And even on the contrary supposition—even if there were no circles in experience but such as are appreciably different from the geometrical ideal, our senses would no less inform us that in the degree in which a visible circle and straight line approximate to the definitions, the extent of their contact with one another approximates to a point : which, by the principles of Induction, makes the ultimate truth as much a truth of experience, as if it were directly cognised by the senses.

* Prolegomena Logica, pp. 99, 100.

"actual phenomena of a limited field, and possessing
"no value beyond it; while in the latter I am compelled
"to regard them as necessary and universal? Why can
"I give in imagination to a quadruped body what expe-
"rience assures me is possessed by bipeds only? And
"why can I not, in like manner, invest straight lines
"with an attribute which experience has uniformly
"presented in curves?"

I answer:—Because our experience furnishes us with
a thousand models on which to frame the conception of
a centaur, and with none on which to frame that of two
straight lines enclosing a space. Nature, as known in
our experience, is uniform in its laws, but extremely
varied in its combinations. The combination of a horse's
body with a human head has nothing, *primâ facie*, to
make any wide distinction between it and any of the
numberless varieties which we find in animated nature.
To a common, even if not to a scientific mind, it is within
the limits of the variations in our experience. Every
similar variation which we have seen or heard of, is a
help towards conceiving this particular one; and tends
to form an association, not of fixity but of variability,
which frustrates the formation of an inseparable association between a human head and a human body exclusively.
We know of so many different heads, united to so many
different bodies, that we have little difficulty in imagining
any head in combination with any body. Nay, the
mere mobility of objects in space is a fact so universal in
our experience, that we easily conceive any object whatever occupying the place of any other; we imagine
without difficulty a horse with his head removed, and a
human head put in its place. But what model does our
experience afford on which to frame, or what elements
from which to construct, the conception of two straight
lines enclosing a space? There are no counter associations in that case, and consequently the primary association, being founded on an experience beginning from
birth, and never for many minutes intermitted in our
waking hours, easily becomes inseparable. Had but

experience afforded a case of persistent illusion, in which
two straight lines after intersecting had appeared again
to approach, the counter association formed might have
been sufficient to render such a supposition imaginable,
and defeat the supposed necessity of thought.   In the
case of parallel lines, the laws of perspective do present
such an illusion : they do, to the eye, appear to meet in
both directions, and consequently to inclose a space: and
by supposing that we had no access to the evidence
which proves that they do not really meet, an ingenious
thinker, whom I formerly quoted, was able to give the
idea of a constitution of nature in which all mankind
might have believed that two straight lines could inclose
a space.   That we are unable to believe or imagine it in
our present circumstances, needs no other explanation
than the laws of association afford : for the case unites
all the elements of the closest, intensest, and most inseparable association, with the greatest freedom from conflicting counter-associations which can be found within
the conditions of human life.*

In all the instances of phenomena invariably conjoined
which fail to create necessities of thought, I am satisfied
it would be found that the case is wanting in some of
the conditions required by the Association psychology,
as essential to the formation of an association really

* Mr. Mahaffy says that I need not have gone beyond our present world
for illusions which, according to my doctrine, ought to have made it possible to conceive something that is contradictory to a mathematical axiom :
and proceeds to mention illusions the illusory character of which is at once
seen, from the immediate accessibility of the evidence which disproves
them ; double vision, and the apparent crookedness of a stick in the water
(p. xxvii.).   As a protection against future irrelevances of this kind, I have
inserted in the text the word "persistent" before "illusion."   Mr. Mahaffy
argues as if the illusions in our experience never got corrected by contrary
experience, but would permanently deceive us unless overridden by an
à priori conviction.   "Every child," he says, "who looks down a long
"street, sees two parallel right lines converging, and we very rarely pro-
"ceed to verify or question the result. . . . Most assuredly no child has
"verified for himself that the very long parallel lines which he has met,
"and sees to be equidistant, as far as he can easily judge, and which he
"sees do not change their direction suddenly—that these parallel lines do
"not meet."   Does a child, then, never walk down a street ? or does Mr
Mahaffy think it necessary to the child's enlightenment that he should
walk down every street ?

inseparable. It is the more to be wondered at that Mr.
Mansel should not have perceived the easy answer which
could be given to his argument, since he himself comes
very near to giving the same explanation of many impos-
sibilities of thought, which is given by the Association
theory. "We can only," he says,* "conceive in thought
what we have experienced in presentation;" and no
other reason is necessary for our being unable to conceive
a thing, than that we have never experienced it. He
even holds that the stock example of a necessity of
thought, the belief in the uniformity of the course of
nature, can be accounted for by experience, without any
objective necessity at all. "We cannot conceive," he
says,† "a course of nature without uniform succession,
"as we cannot conceive a being who sees without eyes
"or hears without ears; because we cannot, under exist-
"ing circumstances, experience the necessary intuition.
"But such things may nevertheless exist; and under
"other circumstances, they might become objects of
"possible conception, the laws of the process of concep-
"tion remaining unaltered." I am aware that when
Mr. Mansel uses the words Presentation and Intuition
he does not mean exclusively presentation by the senses.
Nevertheless, if he had only written the preceding passage, no one would have suspected that he could have
required any other cause for our inability to conceive a
bilineal figure, than the impossibility of our perceiving
one. It is sufficient, in his opinion,‡ to constitute any
propositions necessary, that "while our constitution *and*
"*circumstances* remain as they are, we cannot but think
"them." It is superabundantly manifest that many
propositions which all admit to be grounded only on
experience, are necessary under this definition. Mr.
Mansel even asserts a more complete dependence of our
possibilities of thought upon our opportunities of experience than there appears to me to be ground for: since
he affirms that "we can only conceive in thought what

* Prolegomena Logica, p. 112.
† Ibid. p. 149.   ‡ Ibid. p. 150.

we have experienced in presentation," while in reality it is sufficient that we should have experienced in presentation things bearing some similarity to it.

NOTE TO THE PRECEDING CHAPTER.

Dr. Ward, one of the ablest living defenders of the intuitional metaphysics, has, in the *Dublin Review* for October 1871, made a vigorous attack upon the doctrines of this chapter. His arguments in part coincide (though with a difference in the illustrations) with those already noticed, of Mr. Mansel: several of them, however, are distinct: and as I believe that in answering them, I am answering the best that is likely to be said by any future champion, I will take up Dr. Ward's points one by one.

Dr. Ward thus expresses the test of necessary truth : " If in any case I " know by my very conception of some ens, that a certain attribute, not " included in that conception, is truly predicable of that ens, such predica- " tion is a self-evidently necessary proposition. Take, for instance, the " axiom that all trilateral figures are triangular. If, by my very concep- " tion of a trilateral figure, I know its triangularity . . . then I know " infallibly that a trilateral non-triangular figure is an intrinsically repug- " nant chimera ; that in no possible region of existence could such a figure " be found ; that not even an Omnipotent Being could form one." Consequently "the triangularity of all trilateral figures is cognisable as " a self-evidently necessary truth ;" not grounded on, nor deriving its evidence from, experience.

It is not denied, nor deniable, that there are properties of things which we know to be true (as Dr. Ward expresses it) by our "very conception " of the thing. But this is no argument against our knowing them solely by experience, for (as is truly and aptly said by Professor Bain in his Logic) these are cases in which in the very process of forming the conception, we have experience of the fact. It is not likely that Dr. Ward has returned to the notion (so long abandoned and even forgotten by intuitionists) of ideas literally innate, and thinks that we bring with us into the world the conception of a trilateral figure ready made. He doubtless believes that it is at least suggested by observation of objects. Now, the fact of three sides and that of three angles are so intimately linked together in external nature, that it is impossible for the conception of a three-sided figure to get into the mind without carrying with it the conception of three angles. Therefore, when we have once got the conception of a trilateral, we have no need of further experience to prove triangularity. The conception itself, which represents all our previous experience, suffices. And if the Association theory be true, it must follow from it, that whenever any property of external things is in the relation to the things which is required for the formation of an inseparable association, that property will get into the conception, and be believed without further proof. Dr. Ward will say that triangularity is not included in the conception of a trilateral. But this is only true in the sense that triangularity is not in the connotation of the name. Many attributes not included in the definition are included in the conception. Dr. Ward cannot but see that on the experience hypothesis, this not only may, but must be the case.*

---

* The belief, however, when grounded on the conception without a fresh

Y

Dr. Ward goes on to deny that uniformity of experience can produce the belief that the truth thus uniformly experienced is necessary. If it could, he says, the fact itself of the uniformity of nature—the fact that phenomena succeed each other according to uniform laws—resting on a broader basis of experience than any particular law of nature, has all the conditions for being regarded as a necessary truth, and must produce " a " practical necessity of fancying that in every possible region of existence " phenomena succeed each other by uniform laws ; " * now, we are under no such necessity, as I myself have strenuously maintained. But my answer to Mr. Mansel's instances is applicable to this of Dr. Ward's. Is it seriously that he compares our experience of the uniformity of nature, in point of obviousness and familiarity, with our experience of the straightness of straight lines ? The uniformity is, in the first stages of our experience, an actual paradox ; first appearances are against it ; they seem to show that some events do indeed succeed each other with an approach, though only an approach, to uniformity, but that a far greater number have no fixed order whatever. How can it be maintained that we have, at that early period of our observations, such experience of this universal truth, as to incorporate it in our conception of every object in nature, and create an irresistible association of uniformity of sequence with all possible events ? As we gradually learn the correct *interpretation* of our experience, and become aware that uniformity of sequence *is* an universal truth, a powerful, though even then, not an irresistible association, does grow up ; accordingly the law that whatever begins to exist has a cause, is classed by most of the intuitional philosophers as a necessary truth, though (strange to say) a necessary truth with an exception.

But Dr. Ward † contends (Dr. M'Cosh had already said the same thing) ‡ that there is a fallacy of ambiguity in the phrase "necessity of thought." He charges me with using the phrase " in two senses funda- " mentally different. A necessity of thought may, no doubt, be most " intelligibly understood to mean a law of nature whereby under certain " circumstances I *necessarily think* this, that, and the other judgment. " But it may also be understood to mean a law of nature whereby I *think* " *as necessary* this, that, and the other judgment." He agrees with me " that from a necessity of thought in the *former* sense, no legitimate " argument whatever can be deduced for a necessity of objective truth. " Supposing I felt unusually cold a few moments ago, it is a necessity " of thought that I should now *remember* the circumstance. Yet that " past experience was no necessary truth. It is a necessity of thought

---

appeal to experience—when got at, as Dr. Ward expresses it, not by observation of external nature, but of our own mind—is only justified exactly so far as we are entitled to assume that the conception in our mind represents the facts of outward experience. Only if space itself is everywhere what we conceive it to be, can our conclusions from the conception be everywhere objectively true. The truths of geometry are valid wherever the constitution of space agrees with what it is within our means of observation. That space cannot anywhere be differently constituted, or that almighty power could not make a different constitution of it, we know not. This may serve as an answer to some other remarks of Dr. Ward (pp. 301 to 303), to which it would tax the reader's patience too much to give a fuller reply.

    * P. 290.

    † P. 292.   ‡ Examination of Mr. J. S. Mill's Philosophy (pp. 43, 44).

"again that I expect the sun to rise to-morrow: and many similar "instances could be adduced. The only necessity of thought which proves "the self-evident necessity of objective truth, is the necessity of thinking "that such truth is self-evidently necessary."

Not denying the validity of this distinction, I maintain that it does not affect the argument; because the one necessity is always proved by the other. The evidence always given, and the only evidence which I believe can be given, that we must think anything as necessary, is that we necessarily think it. This, under various names, a Fundamental Law of Belief, the Inconceivability of the Opposite, and so on, is the staple of the Intuitionist argument. Surely, if I disprove the necessity of thinking the thing at all, I disprove that it must be thought as necessary. What other proof can be given of the necessity of a truth, I confess myself ignorant. The consensus of mankind will not do, since that is disproved by being disputed; and Dr. Ward's argument, that a truth must be independent of experience if it can be deduced from the conception, has been met by showing that it is deduced from the conception only after experience has put it there.

Dr. Ward says* that "mere constant and uniform experience cannot "possibly account for the mind's conviction of self-evident necessity." Nor do I pretend that it does. The experience must not only be constant and uniform, but the juxtaposition of the facts in experience must be immediate and close, as well as early, familiar, and so free from even the semblance of an exception that no counter association can possibly arise. Dr. Ward gives two contrasted examples: "I have never even once "experienced the equality of 2 + 9 to 3 + 8, and yet am convinced that "not even Omnipotence could overthrow that equality. I have most "habitually experienced the warmth-giving property of fire, and yet see "no reason for doubting that Omnipotence can at any time suspend or "remove that property. That which I have *never* experienced I regard "as *necessary;* that which I have habitually and unexceptionably expe- "rienced I regard as *contingent.*"

To the first example I answer, that if the equality of 2 + 9 and 3 + 8 does not come to us in the first instance by direct experience (though fully ratified by it), neither does it come by direct intuition. It is gained by a succession of steps, each resting on actual trial. True, it may be but a mental trial; as by merely fancying myself "holding two pebbles in one "hand and nine in the other, and then transferring one pebble from the "larger to the smaller group." But the mere imagination of this transfer would not, and ought not to carry conviction to me, if I had not previously observed that change of place makes no difference in the number of objects. All reasoning from conceptions is open to, and finally rests upon, an appeal to the sensations. With respect to the warmth-giving property of fire, the instance is not happily chosen; for warmth is so much the *differentia* of fire, the principal connotation of the word, that what was believed not to warm would certainly not be called fire. But (disregarding this) Dr. Ward's illustration may be met in the same manner in which I have met the similar illustrations of Mr. Mansel. Fire, it is true, will always, under certain needful conditions, give warmth; but the sight of fire is very often unattended with any sensation of warmth. It is not concomitance of the outward facts that creates the association, but concomitance of the sensible impressions. The visible presence of fire and the sensation of

* Pp. 298, 299.

warmth are not in that invariable conjunction and immediate juxtaposition, which might disable us from conceiving the one without the other, and might therefore lead us to suppose their conjunction to be a necessary truth.

Dr. Ward's criticisms on the view I take of the Law of Causation belong not to the present work, but to my System of Logic. One more of his objections, however, may be noticed here. He says,* that while I account for the "power of ascertaining axioms by mere mental experience" from "one of the characteristic properties of geometrical forms," viz., that they can be painted in the imagination with a distinctness equal to reality, I entirely leave out of account arithmetical and algebraic axioms, though these, equally with geometrical, can be arrived at by merely mental experimentation. I do not leave them out of account, but have assigned, in my Logic, another and equally conclusive reason why they can be studied in our conceptions alone, namely, that arithmetical and algebraic truths being true not of any particular kind of things, but of all things whatever, any mental conceptions whatever will adequately represent them.

---

* P. 302.

CHAPTER XV.

SIR WILLIAM HAMILTON'S DOCTRINE OF UNCONSCIOUS MENTAL MODIFICATIONS.

THE laws of Obliviscence noticed in the preceding chapter, are closely connected with a question raised by Sir W. Hamilton, and discussed at some length in his Lectures: Whether there are unconscious states of mind: or, as he expresses it in the eighteenth Lecture, "Whether the mind exerts energies, and is the subject "of modifications, of neither of which it is conscious." Our author pronounces decidedly for the affirmative, in opposition to most English philosophers, by whom, he says, "the supposition of an unconscious action or passion "of the mind, has been treated as something either "unintelligible or absurd;" and in opposition, no less, to at least one expression of opinion by our author himself.* This is one of the numerous inconsistencies in Sir W. Hamilton's professed opinions, which a close examination and comparison of his speculations brings to light, and which show how far he was in reality from being the systematic thinker which, on a first impression of his writings, he seems to be. In one point of view, these self-contradictions are fully as much an honour as a discredit to him; since they frequently arise from his having acutely seized some important psychological truth, greatly in advance of his general mode of thought, and not having brought the

---

* "Every act of mind is an act of consciousness" (Lectures, ii. 277). Another statement to the same effect which I erroneously quoted in former editions (Lectures, ii. 73) does not belong to Sir W. Hamilton.

remainder of his philosophy up to it. Instead of having
reasoned out a consistent scheme of thought, of which
every part fits in with the other parts, he seems to have
explored the deeper regions of the mind only at the
points which had some direct connection with the conclusions he had adopted on a few special questions of
philosophy : and from his different explorations he
occasionally, as in the present case, brought back
different results. But, in the place where he treats
directly of this particular question, he decides unequivocally for the existence of latent mental modifications.
The subject is in itself not unimportant, and his
treatment of it will serve as an example by which to
estimate his powers of thought in the province of pure
psychology.

Sir W. Hamilton recognises three different kinds, or,
as he calls them, degrees, of mental latency. Two of
these will be seen, on examination, to be entirely
irrelevant.

The first kind of latency, is that which belongs to all
the parts of our knowledge which we are not thinking
of at the very moment. "I know a science of lan-
"guage, not merely while I make a temporary use of it,
"but inasmuch as I can apply it when and how I will.
"Thus the infinitely greater part of our spiritual treasures
"lies always beyond the sphere of consciousness, hid in
"the obscure recesses of the mind." *   But this stored-
up knowledge, I submit, is not an "unconscious action
or passion of the mind." It is not a mental state, but a
capability of being put into a mental state. When I am
not thinking of a thing, it is not present to my mind at all.
It may become present when something happens to recall
it ; but it is not latently present now ; no more than any
physical thing which I may have hoarded up. I may
have a stock of food with which to nourish myself hereafter ; but my body is not in a state of latent nourish-
ment by the food which is in store. I have the power

* Lectures, i. 339.

to walk across the room, though I am sitting in my chair; but we should hardly call this power a latent act of walking.   What required to be shown was, not that I may possess knowledge without recalling it, but that it can be recalled to my mind, I remaining unconscious of it all the time.*

"The† second degree of latency exists when the mind "contains systems of knowledge, or certain habits of

---

* Sir W. Hamilton deliberately rejects this obvious distinction, and in his Lecture on memory (Lect. xxx.) maintains that all the knowledge we possess, whether we are thinking of it or not, is at all times present to us, though unconsciously.   "This is certainly," (he says) "an hypothesis, " because whatever is out of consciousness can only be assumed ; but it "is an hypothesis which we are not only warranted, but necessitated by "the phenomena, to establish." (Lectures, ii. 209.)   This confident assertion is supported only by a passage from an author of whom the reader has already heard something, H. Schmid (*Versuch einer Metaphysik*) ; by whom, however, the conclusion is not elicited from "the phenomena," but drawn, *à priori*, from the assertion that the act of knowledge is " an energy "of the self-acting powers of a subject one and indivisible ; consequently "a part of the ego must be detached or annihilated if a cognition once "existent be again extinguished."   This palpable begging of the whole point in dispute (which Schmid makes no scruple of propping up by half-a-dozen other arbitrary assumptions) of course makes it necessary to explain how anything can be forgotten ; which Schmid resolves by declaring that nothing ever is ; it merely passes into latency.   Of all this, not a shadow of evidence is exhibited ; anything being set down as fact, which can be educed from the idea of the Ego evolved by Schmid out of the depths of his moral consciousness.   His style of philosophising may be judged from the following specimen : "Every mental activity belongs to "the one vital activity of mind in general ; it is, therefore, indivisibly "bound up with it, and can be neither torn from, nor abolished in it." Therefore he has only to call every impression in memory a "mental activity" to prove that when we have once had it, we can never more get rid of it.   If he had but happened to call it a mental *act*, it would have been all over with his argument ; for there may surely be passing acts of one permanent activity.   Schmid further argues, from the same premises, that feelings, volitions, and desires are retained in the mind without the medium of memory, that is, we retain the states themselves, not the notions or remembrances of them : from which it follows, that I am at this moment desiring and willing to rise from my bed yesterday morning, and every previous morning since I began to have a will.   Schmid has an easy answer to all attempts at explaining mental phenomena by physiological hypothesis, viz., that "Mind, howbeit conditioned by bodily relations, still ever preserves its self-activity and independence."   As if to determine whether it does so or not, was not the very point in dispute between him and the physiological hypothesis.   These reasonings are quite worthy of Schmid ; but it is extremely unworthy of Sir W. Hamilton to accept and endorse them.

† Lectures, i. 339-346.

" action, which it is wholly unconscious of possessing in
" its ordinary state, but which are revealed to conscious-
" ness in certain extraordinary exaltations of its powers.
" The evidence on this point shows that the mind fre-
" quently contains the whole systems of knowledge, which,
" though in our normal state they have faded into abso-
" lute oblivion, may, in certain abnormal states, as mad-
" ness, febrile delirium, somnambulism, catalepsy, &c.,
" flash out into luminous consciousness, and even throw
" into the shade of unconsciousness those other systems
" by which they had, for a long period, been eclipsed
" and even extinguished." He then cites from various
authors some of the curious recorded cases, " in which
" the extinct memory of whole languages was suddenly
" restored, and, what is even still more remarkable, in
" which the faculty was exhibited of actually repeating,
" in known or unknown tongues, passages which were
" never within the grasp of conscious memory in the
" normal state." These, however, are not cases of latent
states of mind, but of a very different thing—of latent
memory. It is not the mental impressions that are
latent, but the power of reproducing them. Every one
admits, without any apparatus of proof, that we may
have powers and susceptibilities of which we are not
conscious; but these are capabilities of being affected,
not actual affections. I have the susceptibility of being
poisoned by prussic acid, but this susceptibility is not
a present phenomenon, constantly taking place in
my body without my perceiving it. The capability of
being poisoned is not a present modification of my
body; nor is the capability I perhaps have of recollect-
ing, should I become delirious, something which I have
forgotten while sane, a present modification of my
mind. These are future contingent states, not present
actual ones. The real question is, can I undergo a
present actual mental modification without being aware
of it?

We come, therefore, to the third case, which is the
only one really in point, and inquire, whether there are,

in our ordinary mental life, "mental* modifications, *i.e.*
"mental activities and passivities, of which we are un-
"conscious, but which manifest their existence by effects
"of which we are conscious?" Sir W. Hamilton decides
that there are : and even "that what we are conscious of
"is constructed out of what we are not conscious of;"
that "the sphere of our conscious modifications is only
"a small circle in the centre of a far wider sphere of
"action and passion, of which we are only conscious
"through its effects."

His first example is taken from the perception of external objects. The facts which he adduces are these.
1st. Every *minimum visibile* is composed of still smaller
parts, which are not separately capable of being objects
of vision ; "they are, severally and apart, to conscious-
"ness as zero." Yet every one of these parts "must by
"itself have produced in us a certain modification, real
"though unperceived," since the effect of the whole can
only be the sum of the separate effects of the parts.
2nd. "When we look at a distant forest, we perceive a
"certain expanse of green. Of this as an affection of
"our organism, we are clearly and distinctly conscious.
"Now, the expanse of which we are conscious is evidently
"made up of parts of which we are not conscious. No leaf,
"perhaps no tree, may be separately visible. But the
"greenness of the forest is made up of the greenness of
"the leaves ; that is, the total impression of which we are
"conscious, is made up of an infinitude of small impres-
"sions of which we are not conscious." 3rd. Our sense of
hearing tells the same tale. There is a *minimum audibile;*
the faintest sound capable of being heard. This sound,
however, must be made up of parts, each of which must
affect us in some manner, otherwise the whole which
they compose could not affect us. When we hear the
distant murmur of the sea, "this murmur is a sum
"made up of parts, and the sum would be as zero if the
"parts did not count as something . . . . If the noise
"of each wave made no impression on our sense, the

* Lectures, i. 347-349.

"noise of the sea, as the result of these impressions,
"could not be realised. But the noise of each several
"wave, at the distance we suppose, is inaudible; we
"must, however, admit that they produce a certain
"modification beyond consciousness, on the percipient
"subject; for this is necessarily involved in the reality
"of their result." *

It is a curious question how Sir W. Hamilton failed
to perceive that an unauthorised assumption has slipped
into his argument. Because the *minimum visibile* consists of parts (as we know through the microscope), and
because the *minimum visibile* produces an impression on
our sense of sight, he jumps to the conclusion that each
one of the parts does so too. But it is a supposition
consistent with what we know of nature, that a certain
quantity of the cause may be a necessary condition to the
production of *any* of the effect. The *minimum visibile*
would on that supposition *be* this certain quantity; and
the two halves into which we can conceive it divided,
though each contributing its half to the formation of
that which produces vision, would not each separately
produce half of the vision, the concurrence of both being
necessary to produce any vision whatever. And so of the
distant murmur of the sea: the agency which produces
it is made up of the rolling of many different waves,
each of which, if sufficiently near, would affect us with
a perceptible sound; but at the distance at which they
are, it may require the rolling of many waves to excite
an amount of vibration in the air sufficient, when en-
feebled by extension, to produce any effect whatever on
our auditory nerves, and through them, on our mind.
The supposition that each wave affects the mind separately because their aggregate affects it, is therefore, to
say the least, an unproved hypothesis.

The counter-hypothesis, that in order to the production
of any quantity whatever of the effect, there is needed
a certain minimum quantity of the cause, it is the more
extraordinary that Sir W. Hamilton should have over-

* Lectures, i. 349-351.

looked, since he has not only himself adopted a similar supposition in some other cases,* but it is a necessary part of his theory in this very case.   He will not admit as possible, that less than a certain quantity of the external agent, produces no mental modification; but he himself supposes that less than a certain quantity of mental modification produces no consciousness.   Yet if his *à priori* argument is valid for the one sequence, it is valid for the other.   If the effect of a whole must be the sum of similar effects produced by all its parts, and if every state of consciousness is the effect of a modification of mind which is made up of an infinitude of small parts, the state of consciousness also must be made up of an infinitude of small states of consciousness, produced by these infinitely small mental modifications respectively.   We are not at liberty to adopt the one theory for the first link in the double succession, and the other theory for the other link.   Having shown no reason why either theory should be preferred, our author would have acted more philosophically in not deciding between them.   But to accommodate half the fact to one theory and half to the other, without assigning any reason for the difference, is to exceed all rational license of scientific hypothesis.

After these examples from Perception, our author passes to cases of Association: and as he here states some important mental phenomena well and clearly, I shall quote him at some length.†

"It sometimes happens, that we find one thought "rising immediately after another in consciousness, but "whose consecution we can reduce to no law of associa-"tion.   Now in these cases we can generally discover "by an attentive observation, that these two thoughts,

---

* "In the internal perception of a series of mental operations, a certain "time, a certain duration, is necessary for the smallest section of conti-"nuous energy to which consciousness is competent.   Some minimum of "time must be admitted as the condition of consciousness."   (Lectures, i. 369.)   And again (Lectures, ii. 102): "It cannot certainly be said, that "the minimum of sensation infers the maximum of perception; for per-"ception always supposes a certain quantum of sensation."

† Lectures, i. 352, 353.

" though not themselves associated, are each associated
" with certain other thoughts ; so that the whole conse-
" cution would have been regular, had these intermediate
" thoughts come into consciousness, between the two
" which are not immediately associated. Suppose, for
" instance, that A, B, C, are three thoughts,—that A
" and C cannot immediately suggest each other, but
" that each is associated with B, so that A will naturally
" suggest B, and B naturally suggest C. Now it may
" happen, that we are conscious of A, and immediately
" thereafter of C. How is the anomaly to be explained ?
" It can only be explained on the principle of latent
" modifications. A suggests C, not immediately, but
" through B ; but as B, like the half of the *minimum*
" *visibile* or *minimum audibile*, does not rise into con-
" sciousness, we are apt to consider it as non-existent.
" You are probably aware of the following fact in
" mechanics. If a number of billiard balls be placed in a
" straight row and touching each other, and if a ball
" be made to strike in the line of the row, the ball at
" one end of the series, what will happen ? The motion
" of the impinging ball is not divided among the whole
" row : this, which we might *à priori* have expected, does
" not happen, but the impetus is transmitted through
" the intermediate balls which remain each in its place to
" the ball at the opposite end of the series, and this ball
" alone is impelled on. Something like this seems often
" to occur in the train of thought. One idea immediately
" suggests another into consciousness—the suggestion
" passing through one or more ideas which do not them-
" selves rise into consciousness. The awakening and
" awakened ideas here correspond to the ball striking
" and the ball struck off; while the intermediate ideas
" of which we are unconscious, but which carry on the
" suggestion, resemble the intermediate balls which re-
" main moveless, but communicate the impulse. An
" instance of this occurs to me with which I was recently
" struck. Thinking of Ben Lomond, this thought was
" immediately followed by the thought of the Prussian

" system of education.   Now conceivable connection be-
" tween these two ideas in themselves, there was none.
" A little reflection, however, explained the anomaly.
" On my last visit to the mountain, I had met upon its
" summit a German gentleman, and though I had no
" consciousness of the intermediate and unawakened
" links between Ben Lomond and the Prussian schools,
" they were undoubtedly these,—the German,—Ger-
" many, Prussia,—and, these media being admitted, the
" connection between the extremes was manifest."

Though our author says that the facts here described
can only be explained on the supposition that the intervening ideas never came into consciousness at all, he
is aware that another explanation is conceivable, namely
that they were momentarily in consciousness, but were
forgotten, agreeably to the law of Obliviscence already
spoken of: which, in fact, is the explanation given by
Stewart.   The same two explanations may be given of
his final example, drawn from a class of phenomena also
governed by laws of association " our acquired dexterities
and habits." *   When we learn any manual operation,
suppose that of playing on the pianoforte, the operation
is at first a series of conscious volitions, followed by
movements of the fingers : but when, by sufficient repetition, a certain facility has been acquired, the motions
take place without our being able to recognise afterwards
that we have been conscious of the volitions which preceded them.   In this case, we may either hold with Sir
W. Hamilton, that the volitions (to which must be added
the feelings of muscular contraction, and of the contact
of our fingers with the keys) are not, in the practised
performer, present to consciousness at all ; or, with
Stewart, that he is conscious of them, but for so brief
an interval, that he has no remembrance of them afterwards.   The motions, in this case, are said by Hartley
to have become secondarily automatic, which our author
supposes to be a third opinion, but the difference, if

* Lectures, iii. 355.

difference it was, between this and Stewart's theory, is not material to the present inquiry.

Let us now consider the reasons given by Sir W. Hamilton for preferring his explanation to Stewart's. The first and principal of them is, that to suppose a state of consciousness which is not remembered,* "violates "the whole analogy of consciousness." "Consciousness "supposes memory; and we are only conscious as we "are able to connect and contrast one instance of our "intellectual existence with another." "Of conscious-"ness, however faint, there must be some memory, "however short. But this is at variance with the "phenomenon, for the ideas of A and C may precede "and follow each other without any perceptible interval, "and without any the feeblest memory of B."

Here again I am obliged, not without wonder, to point out the inconclusive character of the argument. When Sir W. Hamilton says that consciousness implies memory, he means, as his words show, that we are only conscious by means of change; by discriminating the present state from a state immediately preceding. Granting this, as with proper explanations I do, all it proves is, that any conscious state of mind must be re-membered long enough to be compared with the mental state immediately following it. The state of mind, therefore, which he supposes to have been latent, must, if it passed into consciousness, have been remembered until one other mental modification had supervened : which there is assuredly not a particle of evidence that it was not : for our having totally forgotten it a minute after, is no evidence, but a common consequence of the laws of Obliviscence. It is perhaps true that all consciousness must be followed by a memory, but I see no reason why an evanescent state of consciousness must be followed, if by any, by a more than evanescent memory. "It is "a law of mind," our author says further on,† "that the "intensity of the present consciousness determines the

---

* Lectures, i. 354, 355.   † Lectures, i. 368, 369.

"vivacity of the future memory. Vivid consciousness, "long memory; faint consciousness, short memory." Well, then: in the case supposed, the intensity of consciousness is at a minimum, therefore on his own showing the duration of memory should be so too. If the consciousness itself is too fleeting to fix the attention, so, à *fortiori*, must the remembrance of it. In reality, the remembrance is often evanescent when the consciousness is by no means so, but is so distinct and prolonged as to be in no danger whatever of being supposed latent. Take the case of a player on the pianoforte while still a learner, and before the succession of volitions has attained the rapidity which practice ultimately gives it. In this stage of progress there is, beyond all doubt, a conscious volition, anterior to the playing of each particular note. Yet has the player, when the piece is finished, the smallest remembrance of each of these volitions, as a separate fact? In like manner, have we, when we have finished reading a volume, the smallest memory of our successive volitions to turn the pages? On the contrary, we only know that we must have turned them, because, without doing so, we could not have read to the end. Yet these volitions were not latent: every time we turned over a leaf, we must have formed a conscious purpose of turning; but, the purpose having been instantly fulfilled, the attention was arrested in the process for too short a time to leave a more than momentary remembrance of it. The sensations of sight, touch, and the muscles, felt in turning the leaves, were as vivid at the moment as any of our ordinary sensible impressions which are only important to us as means to an end. But because they had no pleasurable or painful interest in themselves ; because the interest they had as means passed away in the same instant by the attainment of the end ; and because there was nothing to associate the act of reading with these particular sensations, rather than with other similar sensations formerly experienced; their trace in the memory was only momentary, unless something unusual and remarkable connected with the particular leaves turned over, detained them in remembrance.

If sensations which are evidently in consciousness may leave so brief a memory that they are not felt to leave any memory whatever, what wonder that the same should happen when the sensations are of so fugitive a character, that it can be debated whether they were in consciousness at all? However true it may be that there must be some memory wherever there is consciousness, what·argument is this against a theory which supposes a low degree of consciousness, attended by just the degree of memory which properly belongs to it?

Imagine an argument in physics, corresponding to this in metaphysics. Some of my readers are probably acquainted with the important experiments of M. Pasteur, which appear to have finally exploded the ancient hypothesis of Equivocal Generation, by showing that even the smallest microscopic animalcules are not produced in a medium from which their still more microscopic germs have been effectually excluded. What should we think of any one who deemed it a refutation of M. Pasteur, that the germs are not discernible by the naked eye? who maintained that invisible animalcules must proceed, if from germs at all, from visible germs? This reasoning would be an exact parallel to that of Sir W. Hamilton.

The only other argument of our author against Stewart's doctrine, is confined to the phenomenon of acquired habits, in which case, he says,* the supposition of real but forgotten consciousness "would constrain our assent to the most monstrous conclusions:" since, in reading aloud, if the matter be uninteresting, we may be carrying on a train of thought (even of "serious meditation") on a totally different subject, and this, too, "without distraction or fatigue:" which, he says, would be impossible, if we were separately conscious of, or (as he rather gratuitously alters the idea), separately attentive to, "each least movement in either process." Sir W.

* Lectures, i. 360.

Hamilton here loses sight of a part of his own philosophy, which deserves his forgetfulness the less as it is a very valuable part.   In one of the most important psychological discussions in his Lectures,* he forcibly maintains that we are capable of carrying on several distinct series of states of consciousness at once ; and goes so far as to contend not only that our consciousness, but what is more than consciousness, our "*concentrated* consciousness, or attention," is capable of being divided among as many as six simultaneous impressions.†   Returning to the same subject in another place, he quotes from a modern French philosopher, Cardaillac (in a work entitled *Etudes Elémentaires de Philosophie*), an excellent and conclusive passage, showing the great multitude of states more or less conscious, which often coexist in the mind, and help to determine the subsequent trains of thought or feeling; and illustrating the causes that determine which of these shall in any particular case predominate over the rest.‡   Our consciousness, therefore, according to Sir W. Hamilton, ought not to have much difficulty in finding room for the two simultaneous series of states which he quarrels with Stewart's hypothesis for requiring : and we are not bound, under the penalty of "monstrous conclusions," to consider one of these series as latent.   Sir W. Hamilton indeed says § truly, that "the greater the number of objects to "which our consciousness is simultaneously extended, the "smaller is the intensity with which it is able to con-

---

* Lectures, i. 238–254.   † Ibid. p. 254.
   ‡ Lectures, ii. 250–258.   From this long exposition I shall only extract a single passage (p. 258), but I recommend the whole of it to the attentive consideration of readers.
   "Thus, if we appreciate correctly the phenomena of Reproduction or "Reminiscence, we shall recognise, as an incontestable fact, that our "thoughts suggest each other not one by one successively, as the order to "which language is restricted might lead us to infer; but that the com-"plement of circumstances under which we at every moment exist, "awaken simultaneously a great number of thoughts; these it calls into "the presence of the mind, either to place them at our disposal, if we find 'it requisite to employ them, or to make them co-operate in our deli-"berations, by giving them, according to our nature and our habits, an "influence, more or less active, on our judgments and consequent acts."
   § Lectures, i. 237.

" sider each ; " but the intensity of consciousness necessary for reading aloud with correctness in a language familiar to us, not being very considerable, a great part of our power of attention is disposable for "the train of serious meditation" which is supposed to be passing through our minds at the same time.   For all this, I would not advise any person (unless one with the peculiar gift ascribed to Julius Cæsar) to stake anything on the substantial value of a train of thought carried on by him while reading aloud a book on another subject.   Such thoughts, I imagine, are always the better for being revised when the mind has nothing else to do than to consider them.

It is strange, but characteristic, that Sir W. Hamilton cannot be depended on for remembering, in one part of his speculations, the best things which he has said in another; not even the truths into which he has thrown so much of the powers of his mind, as to have made them, in an especial manner, his own.

Notwithstanding the failure of Sir W. Hamilton to adduce a single valid reason for preferring his hypothesis to that of Stewart, it does not follow that he is not, at least in certain cases, in the right.   The difference between the two opinions being beyond the reach of experiment, and both being equally consistent with the facts which present themselves spontaneously, it is not easy to obtain sure grounds for deciding between them.   The essential part of the phenomenon is, that we have, or once had, many sensations, and that many ideas do, or once did, enter into our trains of thought, which sensations and ideas we afterwards, in the words of James Mill, are "under an acquired incapacity of attending to : " * and that when our incapacity of attending to them has become complete, it is, to our subsequent consciousness, exactly as if we did not have them at all : we are incapable, by any self-examination, of being aware of them.   We know that these lost sensations and ideas, for lost they appear to be, leave traces of having existed ;

* Analysis of the Human Mind, i. 33.

they continue to be operative in introducing other ideas by association. Either, therefore, they have been consciously present long enough to call up associations, but not long enough to be remembered a few moments later; or they have been, as Sir W. Hamilton supposes, unconsciously present ; or they have not been present at all, but something instead of them, capable of producing the same effects. I am myself inclined to agree with Sir W. Hamilton, and to admit his unconscious mental modifications, in the only shape in which I can attach any very distinct meaning to them, namely, unconscious modifications of the nerves. There are much stronger facts in support of this hypothesis than those to which Sir W. Hamilton appeals—facts which it is far more difficult to reconcile with the doctrine that the sensations are felt, but felt too momentarily to leave a recognisable impression in memory. In the case, for instance, of a soldier who receives a wound in battle, but in the excitement of the moment is not aware of the fact, it is difficult not to believe that if the wound had been accompanied by the usual sensation, so vivid a feeling would have forced itself to be attended to and remembered. The supposition which seems most probable is, that the nerves of the particular part were affected as they would have been by the same cause in any other circumstances, but that, the nervous centres being intensely occupied with other impressions, the affection of the local nerves did not reach them, and no sensation was excited. In like manner, if we admit (what physiology is rendering more and more probable) that our mental feelings, as well as our sensations, have for their physical antecedent particular states of the nerves ; it may well be believed that the apparently suppressed links in a chain of association, those which Sir W. Hamilton considers as latent, really are so ; that they are not, even momentarily, felt; the chain of causation being continued only physically, by one organic state of the nerves succeeding another so rapidly that the state of mental consciousness appropriate to each is not produced. We have only to suppose, either that a nervous modification of too short duration does not produce any sensation or mental feeling at all, or that the rapid succession of different nervous modifications makes the feelings produced by them interfere with each other, and become confounded in one mass. The former of these suppositions is extremely probable, while of the truth of the latter we have positive proof. An example of it is the experiment which Sir W. Hamilton quoted from Mr. Mill, and which had been noticed before either of them by Hartley. It is known that the seven prismatic colours, combined in certain proportions, produce the white light of the solar ray. Now, if the seven colours are painted on spaces bearing the same proportion to one another as in the solar spectrum, and the coloured surface so produced is passed rapidly before the eyes, as by the turning of a wheel, the whole is seen as white. The physiological explanation of this phenomenon may be deduced from another common experiment. If a lighted torch, or a bar heated to luminousness, is waved rapidly before the eye, the appearance produced is that of a ribbon of light ; which is universally understood to prove that the visual sensation persists for a certain short time after its cause has ceased. Now, if this happens with a single colour, it will happen with a series of colours : and if the wheel on which the prismatic colours have been painted is turned with the same rapidity with which the torch was waved, each of the seven sensations of colour will last long enough to be contemporaneous with all the others, and they will naturally produce by their combination the same colour as if they had, from the beginning, been excited simultaneously. If anything similar to this obtains in our consciousness generally (and that it obtains in many cases of consciousness there can be no doubt) it will follow that whenever the organic modifications of our nervous fibres succeed one another at an interval shorter than the duration of the sensations or other feelings corresponding to them, those sensations or feelings will, so to speak, overlap one another, and becoming simultaneous instead of successive, will blend into a state of feeling, probably as unlike the elements out of which it is engendered, as the colour white is unlike the prismatic colours.   And this may be the source of many of those states of internal or mental feeling which we cannot distinctly refer to a prototype in experience, our experience only supplying the elements from which, by this kind of mental chemistry, they are composed.   The elementary feelings may then be said to be latently present, or to be present but not in consciousness.   The truth, however, is, that the feelings themselves are not present, consciously or latently, but that the nervous modifications which are their usual antecedents have been present, while the consequents have been frustrated, and another consequent has been produced instead.*

* These considerations may serve as an answer to Dr. M'Cosh, when he maintains, with many other of the intuitive philosophers, that association cannot generate a mental state specifically distinct from the elements out of which it it composed ; which amounts to a denial of the possibility of mental chemistry.   I had thought that such an experiment as that of the wheel with the seven colours, in which seven sensations, following one another very rapidly, become, or at least generate, one sensation, and that one totally different from any of the seven, sufficiently proved the possibility of what Dr. M'Cosh denies ; but he writes as if he had never heard of that experiment.   "I can discover," he says (p. 185), "no evidence "that two sensations succeeding one another will ever be anything else "than two sensations."   The analogous facts in the case of ideas cannot be appealed to, for they are the very matter disputed ; but there is abundance of similar instances in sensation.   Dropping succession of colours, let Dr. M'Cosh look at an ordinary wheel revolving with the rapidity which is often seen in machinery, and he will have a sensation which is not one of rotatory motion at all, but a dizzy spectrum apparently stationary, with the exception of a slight degree of tremulous movement.   Dr. M'Cosh, in his reply, says he was perfectly aware of the experiments of the luminous ring and the wheel with the seven colours.   He does not seem to have known of the other fact which I mentioned, that a wheel may be in such rapid rotation as to seem stationary ; for he offers instead of it "a wheel in rapid motion appearing stationary when made visible by instantaneous electric light," of which he gives the true explanation, that, seeing the wheel only for the instant, we do not really see it move.   The wheel in my example is rotating in broad daylight.   But these examples of mental chemistry, being taken from sensation, are (says Dr. M'Cosh) merely organic.   He requires me to produce examples from purely mental affections.   And how do we know that our mental affections are not also organic, having for their immediate antecedents states of the nerves and brain ?   This is not only possible, but the progress of science has rendered it almost certain, even to those who are far from being Materialists in the ordinary sense of the term.

There are, however, abundant proofs that association can generate new mental affections. Let us take, as one of the obvious examples, the love of money. Does any one think that money has intrinsically, by its own nature, any more value to us than the first shining pebbles we pick up, except for the things it will purchase? Yet its association with these things not only makes it desired for itself, but creates in many minds a passionate love of it, far surpassing the desire they feel for any of the uses to which it can be put. Not only the love of money, but the love of acquisition, of possession, of accumulation, is a feeling created by association. What is desired for itself is the use and enjoyment of individual objects : the possession of a store of them is at first desired as a means to that ; but after it has been long pursued as a means, it becomes itself an end—the object of the passion of appropriation, or property, a passion *sui generis*, and (as life has hitherto been carried on) one of the principal moving powers in human affairs. These, Dr. M'Cosh may say, are feelings, and what I want is intellectual states ; I desiderate examples of "the power of association to generate new ideas, and to produce belief." As an example, then, of new ideas, take the idea of infinity. Infinity is not a fact of intuition, nor of consciousness. We do not perceive space (for example) to be infinite. But every object we see or touch, and every portion of space that we cognise, is cognised along with something beyond it. We hence become incapable of conceiving any object or space without something beyond ; that is, we conceive space as infinite. And along with this new idea a belief is generated ; for it has been, and is, the general belief of mankind, without any other evidence of it, that space is actually infinite. As a further example of a belief generated by association, take the acquired perceptions of sight. On the lowest estimate of these which is made by any psychologist, we spontaneously believe that we see much which we only infer : the ideas of the inferred facts are so blended by the power of association with the sensations which suggest them, that the ideas are confounded with sensations, and believed to be direct perceptions of sight.

CHAPTER XVI.

SIR WILLIAM HAMILTON'S THEORY OF CAUSATION.

SIR W. HAMILTON commences his treatment of the question of Causation, by warning the reader against "some philosophers who, instead of accommodating their solutions to the problem, have accommodated the problem to their solutions." It might almost have been supposed that this expression had been invented to be applied to Sir W. Hamilton himself. He has defined the problem in a manner in which it had been defined by no one else, for no visible reason but to adapt it to a solution which no one else had thought of.[*]

"When we are aware," he says,[†] "of something "which begins to exist, we are, by the necessity of our "intelligence, constrained to believe that it has a Cause. "But what does this expression, that it has a cause, "signify? If we analyse our thought, we shall find "that it simply means, that as we cannot conceive any "new existence to commence, therefore all that now is "seen to arise under a new appearance, had previously "an existence under a prior form. We are utterly "unable to realise in thought, the possibility of the "complement of existence being either increased or "diminished. We are unable, on the one hand, to con- "ceive nothing becoming something, or, on the other, "something becoming nothing. When God is said to "create out of nothing, we construe this to thought by "supposing that he evolves existence out of himself; we

---

[*] When I say no one else, I ought perhaps to except Krug, from whom in another place (Lectures, iv. 135) our author quotes a sentence, containing at least the germ of his own theory.

[†] Lectures, ii. 377, 378.

" view the Creator as the cause of the universe. 'Ex
" nihilo nihil, in nihilum nil posse reverti,' expresses, in
" its purest form, the whole intellectual phenomenon of
" causality.

" There is thus conceived an absolute tautology be-
" tween the effect and its causes. We think the causes
" to contain all that is contained in the effect, the effect
" to contain nothing which was not contained in the
" causes. Take as example: A neutral salt is an effect
" of the conjunction of an acid and an alkali. Here we
" do not, and here we cannot, conceive that, in effect,
" any new existence has been added, nor can we con-
" ceive that any has been taken away. Put another
" example: Gunpowder is the effect of a mixture of
" sulphur, charcoal, and nitre, and those three substances
" are again the effect,—result, of simpler constituents,
" either known or conceived to exist. Now, in all this
" series of compositions we cannot conceive that aught
" begins to exist. The gunpowder, the last compound,
" we are compelled to think, contains precisely the same
" quantum of existence that its ultimate elements con-
" tained prior to the combination. Well, we explode
" the powder. Can we conceive that existence has been
" diminished by the annihilation of a single element
" previously in being, or increased by the addition of a
" single element which was not heretofore in nature?
" 'Omnia mutantur; nihil interit,' is what we think—
" what we must think. This then is the mental phe-
" nomenon of causality,—that we necessarily deny in
" thought that the object which appears to begin to be,
" really so begins; and that we necessarily identify its
" present with its past existence."

This being Sir W. Hamilton's idea of what Causality
means, he thinks it unnecessary to suppose, with most
of the philosophers of the intuitive school, a special
principle of our nature to account for our believing that
every phenomenon must have a cause. The belief is
accounted for, "not * from a power, but from an impo-

* Lectures, ii. 397.

tence of mind," namely, from the Law of the Conditioned; or in other words, from the incapacity of the human mind to conceive the Absolute. We are unable to conceive and construe to ourselves an absolute commencement. Whatever we think, we cannot help thinking as existing; and whatever we think as existing, we are compelled to think as having existed through all past, and as destined to exist through all future, time. It does not at all follow that this is really the fact, for there are many things inconceivable to us, which not only may, but must, be true. Accordingly it may be true that there is an absolute commencement; it may not be true that every phenomenon has a cause. Human volitions in particular may come into existence uncaused; and, in Sir W. Hamilton's opinion, they do so. But to us a beginning and an end of existence are both inconceivable. "We are * unable to construe in thought, "that there can be an atom absolutely added to, or an "atom absolutely taken away from, existence in general. "Make the experiment. Form to yourselves a notion of "the universe; now, can you conceive that the quantity "of existence, of which the universe is the sum, is either "amplified or diminished? You can conceive the "creation of the world as lightly as you can conceive "the creation of an atom. But what is creation? It is "not the springing of nothing into something. Far "from it: it is conceived, and is by us conceivable, "merely as the evolution of a new form of existence, by "the fiat of the Deity. Let us suppose the very crisis "of creation. *Can we realise it to ourselves, in thought,* "*that the moment after the universe came into mani-* "*fested being, there was a larger complement of existence* "*in the universe and its Author together, than there was* "*the moment before, in the Deity himself alone?* This "we cannot imagine. What I have now said of our con- "ceptions of creation, holds true of our conceptions of "annihilation. We can conceive no real annihilation— "no absolute sinking of something into nothing. But,

* Lectures, ii. 405, 406.

"as creation is cogitable by us only as an exertion of
"divine power, so annihilation is only to be conceived
"by us as a withdrawal of the divine support.   All that
"there is now actually of existence in the universe, we
"conceive as having virtually existed, prior to creation,
"in the Creator; and in imagining the universe to be
"annihilated by its Author, we can only imagine this
"as the retraction of an outward energy into power."

Had this extraordinary view of Causation proceeded
from a thinker of less ability and authority than Sir
W. Hamilton, I think there are few readers who, on
reading the sentence which I have marked by italics,
would not have set down the entire speculation as a
mauvaise plaisanterie.

But since any opinion, however strange, of Sir W.
Hamilton, must be believed to be serious, and no serious
opinion of such a man ought to be dismissed unexamined,
I shall proceed to inquire, whether the problem of which
he propounds this solution, *is* the problem of Causation,
and whether the solution is a true one.   To take the
last question first; is it a fact that we cannot conceive a
beginning of existence?   Is it true that whenever we
conceive a thing as existing, we are incapable of conceiving a time when it did not exist, or a time when it
will exist no longer?

If, by incapacity to conceive an absolute commencement, were only meant that we cannot imagine a time
when nothing existed; and if our incapacity of conceiving annihilation, only means that we cannot represent to
ourselves an universe devoid of existence; I do not deny
it.   Whatever else we may suppose removed, there always
remains the conception of empty space: and Sir W.
Hamilton is probably right in his opinion, that we cannot
imagine even empty space without clothing it mentally
with some sort of colour or figure.   Whoever admits the
possibility of Inseparable Association, can scarcely avoid
thinking that these are cases of it; and that we are unable to imagine any object but as occupying space, or to
imagine it removed without leaving that space either

vacant or filled by something else. But we can conceive both a beginning and an end to all physical existence. As a mere hypothesis, the notion that matter cannot be annihilated arose early; but as a settled belief, it is the tardy result of scientific inquiry. All that is necessary for imagining matter annihilated is presented in our daily experience. We see apparent annihilation whenever water dries up, or fuel is consumed without a visible residuum. The fact could not offer itself to our immediate perceptions in a more palpable shape, if the annihilation were real. Having an exact type on which to frame the conception of matter annihilated, the vulgar of all countries easily and perfectly conceive it. Those to whom, if to anybody, it is inconceivable, are philosophers and men of science, who, having formed their familiar conception of the universe on the opposite theory, have acquired an inseparable association of their own, which they cannot overcome. To them the vapour which has succeeded to the water dried up by the sun, the gases which replace the fuel transformed by combustion, have become irrevocably a part of their conception of the entire phenomenon. But the ignorant, who never heard of these things, are not in the least incommoded by the want of them; and if they were not told the contrary, would live and die without suspecting that the water, and the wood or coal, were not destroyed.

All this is not denied by Sir W. Hamilton; but his answer to it is, that if the universe were to perish it would still remain capable of existing, which, it seems, amounts to the same thing. We conceive it as having " virtually existed before it was created," and as virtually existing after it is destroyed. We cannot conceive that there was, at the moment after creation, " a larger " complement of existence in the universe and its Author " together, than there was the moment before in the " Deity himself alone." Creation is to us merely the conversion of power into outward existence; annihilation only " the retraction of an outward energy into power." So that potential existence is exactly the same thing as actual existence ; the difference is formal only. Not only is power a real entity, but the power to create an universe *is* the universe : all created things are but a part of its substance, and can be reabsorbed into it. And this is presented to us, not as a recondite ontological theory, forced upon philosophers as an escape from an otherwise insuperable difficulty, but as a statement of what we all think, and cannot but think, from the very constitution of our thinking faculty. Is this the fact? Does any one, except Sir W. Hamilton, think that in computing the sum total of existence, worlds which God might have created but did not, count for exactly as much as they would if he had really created them? There is a corollary from this doctrine which also deserves attention. If the sum of potential and actual existence is always the same, then with every increase of actual existence, there must be a diminution of power : for if there was once the power without the universe, and is now the same quantity of power and also the universe, what our author nautically terms the " complement of existence " has been increased : which is contrary to the theory. By every exercise, therefore, of creative power, God is less powerful : he has less power now, by a whole universe, than before his power of creating the universe had been transmuted into act ; and were he to " retract " the actual existence into potential, he would be more powerful than he now is, by that exact amount. Is this what all mankind think, and are under an original necessity of thinking? Is this the mode in which, by the " law of the Conditioned," every one of us is absolutely necessitated to construe the idea of Creation? Sir W. Hamilton says it is.

By a desperate attempt to put an intelligible meaning into the theory, somebody may interpret it to mean that before the universe existed in fact, it existed as a thought in the Divine Mind ; and that the idea of an universe, complete in all its details, is equivalent in the " complement of existence " to an actual universe. This is not, perhaps, incapable of being maintained; but it affords no escape from the difficulty. For, this idea in the Divine Mind—is the Divine Mind now denuded of it? Has the Deity *forgotten* the universe, from the time when the divine conception was reduced into act? If not, there are now *both* the universe and the idea of the universe; that is, a double "complement of existence" instead of a single.*

But were it ever so true that we are incapable of conceiving a commencement of anything, and are necessitated to believe that whatever now exists must have existed in the same or another shape through all past time:—that Sir W. Hamilton should imagine *this* to be the law of Cause and Effect, must be accounted one of the most singular hallucinations to be found in the writings of any eminent thinker. According to Sir W. Hamilton, when we say that everything must have a cause, we mean that nothing begins to exist, but everything has always existed. I ask any one, either philosopher or common man, whether he does not mean the exact reverse; whether it is not because things do begin to exist, that a cause must be supposed for their existence. The very words in which the axiom of Causation is commonly stated, and which our author, in the first words of his exposition, adopts, are, that everything which *beings to exist* must have a cause. Is it possible that this axiom can be grounded on the fact that we

* The curious notion that potential existence is tantamount to actual reappears in the Appendix to the Discussions (p. 620). "The creation *a* "*Nihilo* means only, that the universe, when created, was not merely put "into form, an original chaos, or complement of brute matter, having "preceded a plastic energy of intelligence; but that the universe was "called into actuality from potential existence by the Divine fiat. The "Divine fiat therefore was the proximate cause of the creation; and the "Deity, containing the cause, contained, potentially, the effect."

It is so frequent in our author's writings to find doctrines of a very decided character laid down in one page, and implicitly or even directly denied in another, that so strange a doctrine as the one in question could not be expected to escape that fate. Accordingly, in p. 703 of the same volume, "the Potential" is defined to be, "what is not at this, but may be at another time." If so, the universe, when it only existed potentially, *was not:* and did not count as part of the "complement" of present existence.

never suppose anything to begin to exist? Does not he who takes away a beginning of existence, take away all causation, and all need of a cause? Sir W. Hamilton entirely mistakes what it is which causation is called in to explain. The Matter composing the universe, whatever philosophical theory we hold concerning it, we know by experience to be constant in quantity; never beginning or ending, only changing its forms. But its forms have a beginning and ending: and it is its forms, or rather its changes of form—the end of one form and beginning of another—which alone we seek a cause for, and believe to have a cause. It is *events*, that is to say, *changes*, not substances, that are subject to the law of Causation. The question for the psychologist is not why we believe that a substance, but why we believe that a change in the form of a substance, must have a cause. Sir W. Hamilton, in a tardy defence of his theory against objections,* is forced, in a sort of way, to admit this, and virtually to acknowledge that all which we really consider as caused, we consider as beginning to exist. Nothing is caused but events: and it will hardly be said that we conceive an event as having never had a beginning, but been in existence as an event just as much before it happened as when it did happen. An event then being the only thing which suggests the belief or the idea of having or requiring a cause, Sir W. Hamilton may be charged with the scientific blunder which he imputes, far less justly, to Brown: he "professes to explain the phenomenon of causality, "but previously to explanation evacuates the pheno-"menon of all that desiderates explanation."†

Sir W. Hamilton was familiar with the teaching of the Aristotelian schools concerning the four Causes—or rather the four meanings of the word Cause, for synonymy and homonymy were, in their classifications, very often confounded: 1, Materia. 2, Forma. 3, Efficiens. 4, Finis: Efficiens being the only one of these which

---

* Appendix on Causation, Lectures, ii. 538.
† Lectures, ii. 384.

answers either to the common or to the modern philosophical notion of Cause.   Sir W. Hamilton confounds
Materia with Efficiens ; or rather ignores Efficiens altogether, and imagines that when the rest of the world
are speaking of Efficiens, they mean Materia.   It is the
very thing which they pre-eminently do not mean.   Sir
W. Hamilton may choose to call nothing Existence except the permanent element in phenomena; but it is the
changeable element, and no other, which is referred to
a cause, or which could ever have given the notion of
causation.

Sir W. Hamilton says * that the total cause—that the
" concurring or co-efficient causes, in fact, constitute the
" effect."   And again,† "an effect" is "nothing more than
" the sum or complement of all the partial causes, the
" concurrence of which constitutes its existence."   " An
" effect‡ is nothing but the actual union of its constituent
" entities ; "   " causes always continue actually to exist
" in their effects."   Because the original matter continues
to exist in the matter transformed, the Efficiens which
transformed it continues to exist in the fact of the change!
Of course he takes as his example a case in which the
material is the prominent thing, that of a salt, compounded
of an acid and an alkali.   " Considering § the salt as an
" effect, what are the concurrent causes,—the co-effi-
" cients,—which constitute it what it is?   There are,
" first, the acid, with its affinity to the alkali; secondly,
" the alkali, with its affinity to the acid; and thirdly,
" the translating force (perhaps the human hand) which
" made their affinities available, by bringing the two
" bodies within the sphere of mutual attraction.   Each
" of these three concurrents must be considered as a
" partial cause ; for abstract any one, and the effect is
" not produced."   Strange that even this first degree of
analysis should not have opened his eyes to the fact,
that the moment he admits into *causa efficiens* anything
more than *materia*, his theory is at an end.   For he

---

* Lectures, i. 59.   † Ibid. p. 97.
‡ Ibid. ii. p. 540.   § Ibid. i. p. 59.

will indeed find in the salt, two of his three "co-effi-
cients," the acid and the alkali, with their affinity; but
where will he find in it "the translating force, perhaps
the human hand?" This essential "concause" does not
embarrass him at all; it costs him nothing to make away
with it altogether. "This last," he says,* "as a tran-
"sitory condition and not always the same, we shall
"throw out of account." If we throw out of account
all that is transitory, we have no difficulty in proving
that all that is left is permanent. But the transitory
conditions are as much a part of the cause as the permanent conditions. Our author has just before said that
he takes the term causes "as synonymous for all without
"which the effect would not be;" and if the effect is
"the sum or complement" of all the causes, the transitory as well as the permanent elements must be found
in it. To exclude all the transitory part of the cause, is
to exclude the whole cause, except the materials. Suppose the effect to be St. Paul's: in assigning its causes,
the will of the government, the mind of the architect, and
the labour of the builders, are all cast out, for they are
all transitory, and only the stones and mortar remain.†

It will have been remarked, that in propounding this

* Lectures, i. 97.
† On the same shoal is stranded an argument appended to the same
discussion, which our author seems to think of considerable value in
the establishment of a First Cause. The progress from cause to effect, he
says, (Lectures, i. 59, 60,) is from the simpler to the more complex. "The
"lower we descend in the series of causes, the more complex will be the
"product; the higher we ascend, it will be the more simple." To prove
this, he appeals to his example, the composition of a salt. Now, the salt
is indeed more complex than either of its chemical ingredients, the acid
and the alkali; but need it be, or is it, more complex than the remaining
"co-efficient," the human hand, or whatever power, natural or artificial,
brings the acid and alkali together? The event which causes, may be in any
degree whatever a more complex fact, than the event which is caused by it.
Professor Bain (Logic, ii. 36) considers Sir W. Hamilton's theory of
Causation to be an anticipation of the scientific doctrine of the Conservation of Force. There is, doubtless, some analogy between them, but they
seem to me radically different. Force is the principle of Change, and is,
therefore, really the leading ingredient in causation: but the conservation
in Sir W. Hamilton's theory is conservation of the element which has
nothing to do with change. It is only equivalent to the old-established
fact of the unchangeableness in the quantity of Matter, in other words, of
Resistance.

theory of the belief in Causation, Sir W. Hamilton gives up Causation as a necessary law of the universe ; maintaining that a fact is not to be supposed impossible to Nature because we are impotent to conceive it, and indeed regarding the free acts of an intelligent being as an exception to the universality of the law of Cause and Effect. But while in one place he pays this homage to his own principles, in another he entirely takes leave of them, and glides back into the beaten path of the school of thought which, erecting human capacities of conception into the measure of the universe, maintains that causes must be, because we are incapable of conceiving phenomena without them. After describing the process of ascending from cause to cause, quite gratuitously, as a progress towards unity, Sir W. Hamilton says,* " Philo-" sophy thus, as the knowledge of effects in their causes, " necessarily tends, not towards a plurality of ultimate " or first causes, but towards one alone. This first cause, " the Creator, it can indeed never reach, as an object of " immediate knowledge; but, as the convergence towards " unity in the ascending series is manifest in so far as " that series is within our view " (here he confounds convergence from many to few with convergence towards one) "*and as it is even impossible for the mind to suppose* " *the convergence not continuous and complete*, it follows, " unless all analogy be rejected—unless our intelligence " be declared a lie, that we must, philosophically, believe " in that ultimate or primary unity which, in our present " existence, we are not destined in itself to apprehend."

A deliverance more radically at variance with the author's own canons, could scarcely have been made. For, first, one of the principal of them is, that our inability to conceive a thing as possible, is no argument whatever against its being true. In the second place, the alleged impossibility of conceiving any of the phenomena of the universe to be uncaused, applies equally, on his own showing, to the First Cause itself. For, though he here talks only of one inconceivability, we are, if his

* Lectures, i. 60.

2 A

theory be correct, under the pressure of two counter-inconceivabilities—being equally unable to conceive an uncaused beginning, or an infinite regress from effect to cause: it is equally inconceivable to us that there should, as that there should not, be a first Cause. In this difficulty, by what right does he (I mean merely as a philosopher, and on his own principles) select one of the rival inconceivabilities as the real interpreter of Nature, in preference to the other? And, having selected it, why apply it up to a certain point, and there stop? Why must all the phenomena of experience be referred to a single Cause, because we cannot conceive anything uncaused, and that single cause be proclaimed uncaused, notwithstanding the same impossibility? An argument by Sir W. Hamilton would not be complete unless it wound up with his tiresome final appeal, "unless our intelligence be declared a lie." It is time to understand, once for all, what this means. Does it mean that if our intelligence cannot conceive one thing apart from another, the one thing cannot exist without the other? If yes, what becomes of the Philosophy of the Conditioned? If no, what becomes of the present argument? *

* It has been suggested to me by a correspondent to whom I have more than once adverted, as an explanation of Sir W. Hamilton's conflicting language respecting conceivability as a test of truth, that he probably distinguished between what may be termed unilateral and bilateral inconceivableness. I state the distinction in the words of my able correspondent. "Bilateral inconceivableness is no test of truth, for the obvious reason "that it applies equally to two contradictory propositions. But Hamilton "thought unilateral inconceivableness—an inconceivableness limited to "one side of a question only—a proof of a positive deliverance of con-"sciousness on the other side. Hamilton therefore frequently employs "the principle that what is unilaterally inconceivable must be false, while "he invariably denies that bilateral inconceivableness is any test of "falsehood."

Sir W. Hamilton may have had some such distinction in his mind, though if he had, it would not have been going out of his way to have stated it, instead of constantly enunciating the doctrine that things inconceivable to us may be true, in language which recognises no difference between the two cases. But the distinction, if he made it, is of no service to him. If it is possible for anything to be true which is inconceivable to us, the inconceivability of a supposition cannot be a deliverance of consciousness against it. On the contrary, the fact that both sides of an alternative which has no third side may be inconceivable, is a *reductio ad absurdum* of the opinion that inconceivability is an evidence of falsehood.

Sir W. Hamilton makes a far better figure when arguing against other theories of Causation, than when maintaining his own. He is usually acute in finding the weak points in other people's philosophies; and he brings this talent into play, effectively enough, on the present subject. He is not, indeed, at all successful in combating the doctrine (substantially that of Hume and Brown) that it is experience which proves the fact of causation, and association which generates the idea: for against this he only has to say, that experience and association cannot account for necessity. Now, as to real necessity, we do not know that it exists in the case. Sir W. Hamilton himself is of opinion that it does not, and that there are phenomena (the volitions of rational intelligences) which do not depend on causes. And as for the *feeling* of necessity, or what is termed a necessity of thought, it is (as I have already observed), of all mental phenomena positively the one which an inseparable association is the most evidently competent to generate. I cannot, therefore, attribute any value to Sir W. Hamilton's discussion of this point; but in his refutation of some of the theories of causation which have originated in his own hemisphere of the intellectual world, he is very felicitous. Take, for example, the doctrine of Wolf and the Leibnitzians (though not of Leibnitz), which " attempts to establish the principle " of Causality upon the principle of Contradiction." " Listen," says our author,* " to the pretended demon- " stration :—Whatever is produced without a cause, is " produced by nothing ; in other words, has nothing for " its cause. But nothing can no more be a cause than " it can be something. The same intuition which makes " us aware that nothing is not something, shows us that " everything must have a real cause of its existence.— " To this, it is sufficient to say, that the existence " of causes being the point in question, the existence " of causes must not be taken for granted, in the very " reasoning which attempts to prove their reality. In

* Lectures, ii. 396, 397.

" excluding causes, we exclude all causes; and conse-
" quently we exclude Nothing, considered as a cause; it
" is not, therefore, allowable, contrary to that exclusion,
" to suppose Nothing as a cause, and then from the
" absurdity of that supposition to infer the absurdity of
" the exclusion itself. If everything must have a cause, it
" follows that, upon the exclusion of other causes, we must
" accept of Nothing as a cause. But it is the very point
" at issue, whether everything must have a cause or not;
" and therefore it violates the first principles of reasoning
" to take this quæsitum itself as granted. This opinion,"
adds our author, " is now universally abandoned."

But there is another theory of Causation which is not
abandoned, but has formed for some time past the strong-
hold of the Intuitive school. This is, that we acquire
both our notion of Causation, and our belief in it, from
an internal consciousness of power exerted by ourselves,
in our voluntary actions: that is, in the motions of our
bodies, for our will has no other direct action on the outward world. This relation of the act of will to the
bodily movement, it is maintained, is "not a simple
" relation of succession. The will is not for us a pure
" act without efficiency; it is a productive energy; so
" that in volition there is given to us the notion of
" cause; and this notion we subsequently transport—
" project out from our internal activities, into the changes
" of the external world."

To this doctrine Sir W. Hamilton gives the following
conclusive answer.[*] "This reasoning, in so far as re-
" gards the mere empirical fact of our consciousness of
" causality, in the relation of our will as moving and of
" our limbs as moved, is refuted by the consideration,
" that between the overt fact of corporeal movement of
" which we are cognisant, and the internal act of mental
" determination of which we are also cognisant, there
" intervenes a numerous series of intermediate agencies
" of which we have no knowledge; and consequently,
" that we can have no consciousness of any causal con-

---

* Lectures, ii. 391, 392.

" nection between the extreme links of this chain,—the
" volition to move and the limb moving, as this hypo-
" thesis asserts.   No one is immediately conscious, for
" example, of moving his arm through his volition.
" Previously to this ultimate movement, muscles, nerves,
" a multitude of solid and fluid parts must be set in
" motion by the will, but of this motion we know, from
" consciousness, actually nothing.   A person struck with
" paralysis is conscious of no inability in his limb to
" fulfil the determination of his will ; and it is only after
" having willed, and finding that his limbs do not obey
" his volition, that he learns by this experience, that the
" external movement does not follow the internal act.
" But as the paralytic learns after the volition that his
" limbs do not obey his mind ; so it is only after the
" volition that the man in health learns that his limbs
" do obey the mandates of his will." *

With this reasoning, borrowed as our author admits
from Hume, I entirely agree ; and I wonder that it did
not prove to Sir W. Hamilton how little the objection
to a doctrine, that it is opposed to our natural beliefs,
deserves the exaggerated value he sets upon it ; for if
there is a natural belief belonging to us, I should sup-

---

* The same argument is restated in the Dissertations on Reid (pp. 866,
867) with some additional development.   " Volition to move a limb, and
" the actual moving of it, are the first and last in a series of more than
" two successive events, and cannot, therefore, stand to each other, imme-
" diately, in the relation of cause and effect.   They may, however, stand
" to each other in the relation of cause and effect, mediately.   But then,
" if they can be known in consciousness as thus mediately related, it is a
" necessary condition of such knowledge, that the intervening series of
" causes and effects, through which the final movement of the limb is sup-
" posed to be mediately dependent on the primary volition to move, should
" be known to consciousness immediately under that relation.   But this
" intermediate, this connecting series is confessedly unknown to conscious-
" ness at all, far less as a series of causes and effects.   It follows there-
" fore à fortiori, that the dependency of the last on the first of these events,
" as of an effect upon its cause, must be to consciousness unknown.   In
" other words : having no consciousness that the volition to move is the
" efficacious force (power) by which even the event immediately conse-
" quent on it (say the transmission of the nervous influence from brain to
" muscle) is produced, such event being, in fact, itself to consciousness
" occult ; multo minus can we have a consciousness of that volition being
" the efficacious force by which the ultimate movement of the limb is
" mediately determined."

pose it to be, that we are directly conscious of ability to move our limbs. It is, nevertheless, our author's opinion that the belief is groundless, and that we learn even a fact so closely connected with us, in the way in which any bystander learns it; by outward observation.*

Mr. Mansel, who agrees with Sir W. Hamilton in so many of his opinions, separates from him here, and adopts a modified form of the Volitional Theory. He acknowledges the validity of Hume's and Sir W. Hamilton's argument, and does not derive the idea of Power or Causation from mind acting upon body—from my will producing my bodily motions—but from myself producing my will. "In† every act of volition, I am " fully conscious that it is in my power to form the reso- "lution or to abstain ; and this constitutes the presenta- "tive consciousness of free will and of power." And the sole notion we have of causation in the outward uni- verse, as anything more than invariable antecedence and consequence, is that ‡ of a relation between two objects, " similar to that which exists between ourselves and our "volitions." Thus interpreted, continues Mr. Mansel,§ it is an interesting illustration of the universal ten- "dency of men to identify, as far as may be, other agents "with themselves, even when the identification tends to "the destruction of all clear thinking:—furnishing a psy- "chological explanation of a form of speech which has "prevailed and will continue to prevail among all people "in all times, but not properly to be called a *neces- "sary truth*, nor capable of any scientific application ; "inasmuch as, in any such application, it may be true or "false, without our being able to determine which, as "the object of which it treats never comes within the "reach of our faculties. What is meant by *power* in a

* Sir W. Hamilton adds, as a further objection to the theory, that it does not account for that, in our notion of causation, which is the sole ground for rejecting the Experience theory of it : its "quality of necessity and universality." And this is true: the philosophers who combat the Experience theory of causation by the Volitional one, deprive themselves of a very bad, but still the best argument on their side of the question.

† Prolegomena Logica, p. 139.

‡ Ibid. p. 140.   § Ibid. pp. 142, 143.

" fire to melt wax ?   How and when is it exerted, and in
" what manner does it come under our cognisance ?   Sup-
" posing such power to be suspended by an act of Omni-
" potence, the Supreme Being at the same time producing
" the succession of phenomena by the immediate inter-
" position of his own will,—could we in any way detect
" the change ?   Or suppose the course of nature to be
" governed by a pre-established harmony, which ordained
" that at a certain moment fire and wax should be in the
" neighbourhood of each other, that, at the same moment,
" fire by itself should burn, and wax by its own laws
" should melt, neither affecting the other,—would not
" all the perceptible phenomena be precisely the same as
" at present ?   These suppositions may be extravagant,
" though they are supported by some of the most emi-
" nent names in philosophy ; but the mere possibility of
" making them shows that the rival hypothesis is not a
" necessary truth ; the various principles being opposed,
" only like the vortices of Descartes and the gravitation
" of Newton, as more or less plausible methods of account-
" ing for the same physical phenomena."   Mr. Mansel
recognises the possibility that in some other portion of
the universe, phenomena may succeed one another at
random, without laws of causation, or by laws which are
continually changing.   We cannot, he says, conceive this
state of things, but we can suppose it ; and this very inability to conceive a phenomenon as taking place without
a cause—in other words, this subjective necessity of the
law of cause and effect—results, in his opinion, merely
from the conditions of our experience.   If we were asked,
why a physical change must have a cause, " we * should
" probably reply—Because matter cannot change of
" itself.   But why cannot we think of matter as changing
" itself? Because *power*, and the *origination of change*, or
" self-determination, have never been given to us, save
" in one form, that of the actions of the conscious self.
" What I am to conceive as taking place, I must con-
" ceive as taking place in the only manner of taking

* Prol. Log. p. 148.

"place in which it has ever been presented to me."
(Here Mr. Mansel exaggerates one of the consequences
of the law of Inseparable Association, through his having
reached the consequence only empirically, and not analysed it by means of the law.) "This reduces the law
" of Causality, in one sense indeed to an empirical prin-
" ciple, but to an empirical principle of a very peculiar
" character; one namely, in which it is psychologically
" impossible that experience should testify in more than
" one way. Such principles, however empirical in their
" origin, are co-extensive in their application with the
" whole domain of thought."

And further on,* " To call the principle of Causality
" as thus explained a Law of Thought, would be incor-
" rect. We cannot think the contrary, not because the
" laws of thought forbid us, but because the material for
" thought is wanting. Thought is subject to two diffe-
" rent modes of restriction: firstly, from its own laws,
" by which it is restricted as to its form; and secondly,
" from the laws of intuition, by which it is restricted as
" to its matter. The restriction, in the present instance,
" is of the latter kind. We cannot conceive a course of
" nature without uniform succession, as we cannot con-
" ceive a being who sees without eyes or hears without
" ears; because we cannot, under existing circumstances,
" experience the necessary intuition. But such things
" may, notwithstanding, exist; and under other circum-
" stances, they might become objects of possible concep-
" tion, the laws of the process of conception remaining
" unaltered."

In this exposition, which, I do not hesitate to say,
contains more sound philosophy than is to be found on
the same subject in all Sir W. Hamilton's writings, I
must, nevertheless, take exception to the main doctrine
—that the type on which we frame our notion of Power
or Causation in general, is the power, not of our volitions
over matter, but of our Self over our volitions. In common with one half of the psychological world, I am

* Prol. Log. p. 149.

wholly ignorant of my possessing any such power. I can indeed influence my own volitions, but only as other people can influence my volitions, by the employment of appropriate means. Direct power over my volitions I am conscious of none. However possible it may be that I possess this power without knowing it, a fact of consciousness contestable and contested cannot well be the source and prototype of an idea common to all mankind. I agree, however, with Mr. Mansel in the opinion which he shares with Comte, James Mill, and many others who see nothing in causation but invariable antecedence; that we naturally, and unavoidably, form our first conception of all the agencies in the universe from the analogy of human volitions. The obvious reason is, that nearly everything which is interesting to us, comes, in our earliest infancy, either from our own voluntary motions, or (a consideration too much neglected) from the voluntary motions of others; and, among the few sequences of phenomena which at that time fall within the scope of our perceptions, scarcely any others afford us the spectacle of an apparently absolute commencement; of one thing setting others in motion without being in motion itself—or originating changes in other things, while not itself undergoing any visible change. But as I do not believe, any more than Sir W. Hamilton or Mr. Mansel, that the state of mind called volition carries with it a prophetic anticipation, which can inform us prior to experience that volition will be followed by an effect; I conceive that, no more in this than in any other case of causation, have we evidence of anything more than what experience informs us of: and it informs us of nothing except immediate, invariable, and unconditional sequence.

It is allowed on all hands that part, at least, of our idea of power, is the expectation we feel, that when the cause exists, we shall perceive the effect; but Hume himself admits that in the common notion of power there is an additional element, an animal *nisus*, as he calls it, which would be more properly termed a conception of

effort.   That this idea of effort enters into our notion of
Power, is to my mind one of the strongest proofs that
this notion is not derived from the relation of ourselves
to our volitions, but from that of our volitions to our
actions.   The idea of Effort is essentially a notion derived
from the action of our muscles, or from that combined
with affections of our brain and nerves.   Every one of
our muscular movements has to contend against resistance, either that of an outward object, or the mere friction and weight of the moving organ ; every voluntary
motion is consequently attended by the muscular sensation of resistance, and if sufficiently prolonged, by the
additional muscular sensation of fatigue.   Effort, considered as an accompaniment of action upon the outward
world, means nothing, to us, but those muscular sensations.   Since we experience them whenever we voluntarily move an object, we by a mere act of natural
generalisation, the unconscious result of association, on
beholding the same object moved by the wind or by any
other agent, conceive the wind as overcoming the same
obstacle, and figure it to ourselves as putting forth the
same effort.   Children and savages sincerely mistake it
for a conscious effort.   We outgrow that belief; but
it is not conformable to the mode of action of the human
intellect that it should pass *uno saltu*, from a complete
assimilation of the two phenomena, to conceiving them
as totally different.   The "natural tendency of men" so
justly characterised by Mr. Mansel, "to identify, as far as
may be, other agents with themselves," does not admit
itself baffled and give up the attempt after the first
failure.   The consequents being the same, when the
mind is no longer able to suppose an exact parity in the
antecedents, it still thinks that there must be something
in common between them : and when obliged to admit
that there is volition in one case, and a mere unconscious
object, in the other, it interposes between the antecedent
and the consequent an abstract entity, to express what
is supposed common to the animate and the inanimate
agency—through which they both work, and in the ab-

sence of which nothing would be effected. This purely subjective notion, the product of generalisation and abstraction acting on the real feeling of muscular or nervous effort, is Power. And this, I conceive, is the psychological rationale of Comte's great historical generalisation, that the metaphysical conception (as he terms it) of the universe succeeds by a natural law to the Fetish conception, and becomes the agent by which the Fetish theory is transformed into Polytheism, this into Monotheism, this into Monotheism, and Monotheism itself is frittered away into energies and attributes of Nature, and other subordinate abstractions.

Thus much respecting Causation as a conception of the mind. The law of Cause and Effect in its objective aspect, as the fundamental principle in the order of the universe, the basis of most of our knowledge, and the guide of all our action, has been so fully treated in its numerous bearings in my System of Logic, that it is needless for me to speak further of it here.

CHAPTER XVII.

THE DOCTRINE OF CONCEPTS, OR GENERAL NOTIONS.

WE now arrive at the questions which form the transition from Psychology to Logic—from the analysis and laws of the mental operations, to the theory of the ascertainment of objective truth : the natural link between the two being the theory of the particular mental operations whereby truth is ascertained or authenticated. According to the common classification, from which Sir W. Hamilton does not deviate, these operations are three : Conception, or the formation of General Notions ; Judgment ; and Reasoning. We begin with the first.

On this subject two questions present themselves: first, whether there are such things as General Notions, and secondly, what they are. If there are General Notions, they must be the notions which are expressed by general terms ; and concerning general terms, all who have the most elementary knowledge of the history of metaphysics are aware that there are, or once were, three different opinions.

The first is that of the Realists, who maintained that General Names are the names of General Things. Besides individual things, they recognised another kind of Things, not individual, which they technically called Second Substances, or Universals *a parte rei*. Over and above all individual men and women, there was an entity called Man—Man in general, which inhered in the individual men and women, and communicated to them its essence. These Universal Substances they considered to be a much more dignified kind of beings than individual substances, and the only ones the cognisance of which deserved the names of Science and Knowledge. Individual existences were fleeting and perishable, but the beings called Genera and Species were immortal and unchangeable.

This, the most prevalent philosophical doctrine of the middle ages, is now universally abandoned, but remains a fact of great significance in the history of philosophy; being one of the most striking examples of the tendency of the human mind to infer difference of things from difference of names,—to suppose that every different class of names implied a corresponding class of real entities to be denoted by them. Having two such different names as "man" and "Socrates," these inquirers thought it quite out of the question that man should only be a name for Socrates, and others like him, regarded in a particular light. Man, being a name common to many, must be the name of a substance common to many, and in mystic union with the individual substances, Socrates and the rest.

In the latter middle ages there grew up a rival school of metaphysicians, termed Nominalists, who repudiating Universal Substances, held that there is nothing general except names. A name, they said, is general, if it is applied in the same acceptation to a plurality of things : but every one of the things is individual. The dispute between these two sects of philosophers was very bitter, and assumed the character of a religious quarrel : authority, too, interfered in it, and as usual on the wrong side. The Realist theory was represented as the orthodox doctrine, and belief in it was imposed as a religious duty. It could not, however, permanently resist philosophical criticism, and it perished. But it did not leave Nominalism in possession of the field. A third doctrine arose, which endeavoured to steer between the two. According to this, which is known by the name of Conceptualism, generality is not an attribute solely of names, but also of thoughts. External objects indeed are all individual, but to every general name corresponds a General Notion, or Conception, called by

Locke and others an Abstract Idea.   General Names
are the names of these Abstract Ideas.

Realism being no longer extant, nor likely to be
revived, the contest at present is between Nominalism
and Conceptualism; each of which counts illustrious
names among its modern adherents.   Sir W. Hamilton
professes allegiance to both, affirming* "that the opposing parties are really at one."   But his general mode of
thought, and habitual phraseology, are purely Conceptualist.   This in already apparent in the passage I shall
first quote, which contains his statement of the fact to
be explained.   It is preceded by a remark on Abstraction
which is perfectly just, and throws great light on the
processes of human thought.   Abstraction, he says,† is
simply the concentration of our attention on a particular object, or a particular quality of an object, and
diversion of it from everything else.   There may be
abstraction, therefore, without generalisation.   "The
"notion of the figure of the desk before me is an
"abstract idea,—an idea that makes part of the total
"notion of that body, and on which I have concen-
"trated my attention, in order to consider it exclusively.
"This idea is abstract, but it is at the same time indi-
"vidual; it represents the figure of this particular desk,
"and not the figure of any other body."

There are, therefore, "individual abstract notions;"
but there are also "Abstract General Notions."   These
are formed "when,‡ comparing a number of objects, we
"seize on their resemblances, when we concentrate our
"attention on these points of similarity, thus abstracting
"the mind from a consideration of their differences; and
"when we give a name to our notion of that circum-
"stance in which they all agree.   The general notion is
"thus one which makes us know a quality, property,
"power, notion, relation; in short, any point of view
"under which we recognise a plurality of objects as a
"unity.   It makes us aware of a quality, a point of

* Lectures, ii. 286 ; and foot-note on Reid, p. 412.
† Ibid. ii. 287.   ‡ Ibid. pp. 287–290.

" view, common to many things. It is a notion of re-
" semblance; hence the reason why general names or
" terms, the signs of general notions, have been called
" *terms of resemblance (termini similitudinis).* In this
" process of generalisation, we do not stop short at a
" first generalisation. By a first generalisation we have
" obtained a number of classes of resembling individuals.
" But these classes we can compare together, observe
" their similarities, abstract from their differences, and
" bestow on their common circumstance a common name.
" On these second classes we can again perform the same
" operation, and thus ascending the scale of general no-
" tions, throwing out of view always a greater number
" of differences, and seizing always on fewer similarities
" in the formation of our classes, we arrive at length at
" the limit of our ascent in the notion of *being* or *exis-
" tence.* Thus placed on the summit of the scale of
" classes, we descend by a process the reverse of that by
" which we have ascended; we divide and subdivide the
" classes, by introducing always more and more cha-
" racters, and laying always fewer differences aside; the
" notions become more and more composite, until we at
" length arrive at the individual.

" I may here notice that there is a twofold quantity to
" be considered in notions. It is evident that, in pro-
" portion as the class is high, it will, in the first place,
" contain under it a greater number of classes, and in
" the second, will include the smallest complement of
" attributes. Thus *being* or *existence* contains under it
" every class; and yet when we say that a thing exists,
" we say the very least of it that is possible. On the
" other hand, an individual, though it contain nothing
" but itself, involves the largest amount of predication.
" For example, when I say—this is Richard, I not only
" affirm of the subject every class from existence down
" to man, but likewise a number of circumstances proper
" to Richard as an individual. Now, the former of these
" quantities, the external, is called the Extension of a
" notion; the latter, the internal quantity, is called its

" Comprehension or Intension. . . . . The internal and ex-
" ternal quantities are in the inverse ratio of each other.
" The greater the extension, the less the comprehension ;
" the greater the comprehension, the less the extension."

As a popular account of Classification, for learners, to
be followed by a more scientific exposition, this fully
answers its purpose ; but it is expressed in the common
language of Conceptualists, and we should naturally conclude from it that the author was a Conceptualist. He
however asserts the doctrine of the Nominalists, that
there are no general notions, and that the notion suggested by a general name is always singular or individual, to be " not only true but self-evident." * And he
quotes as " irrefragable " the argument of Berkeley,
directed against the very possibility of Abstract Ideas.
The passage from Berkeley is in the Introduction to his
" Principles of Human Knowledge," and is as follows :—

" It is agreed, on all hands, that the qualities or modes
" of things, do never really exist each of them apart by
" itself, and separated from all others, but are mixed, as
" it were, and blended together, several in the same
" object. But, we are told, the mind, being able to con-
" sider each quality singly, or abstracted from those other
" qualities with which it is united, does by that means
" frame to itself abstract ideas. For example, there is
" perceived by sight an object extended, coloured, and
" moved ; this mixed or compound idea the mind resolv-
" ing into its simple constituent parts, and viewing each
" by itself, exclusive of the rest, does frame the abstract
" ideas of extension, colour, and motion. Not that it is
" possible for colour or motion to exist without exten-
" sion ; but only that the mind can frame to itself by
" *abstraction* the idea of colour exclusive of extension,
" and of motion exclusive of both colour and extension.

" Again, the mind having observed that in the par-
" ticular extensions perceived by sense, there is some-
" thing common and alike in all, and some other things

* Lectures, ii. 298.

" peculiar, as this or that figure or magnitude, which
" distinguish them one from another ; it considers apart
" or singles out by itself that which is common, making
" thereof a most abstract idea of extension, which is
" neither line, surface, nor solid, nor has any figure or
" magnitude, but is an idea entirely prescinded from all
" these. So, likewise, the mind, by leaving out of the
" particular colours perceived by sense, that which dis-
" tinguishes them one from another, and retaining that
" only which is common to all, makes an idea of colour
" in abstract, which is neither red, nor blue, nor white,
" nor any other determinate colour. And, in like man-
" ner, by considering motion abstractedly not only from
" the body moved, but likewise from the figure it de-
" scribes, and all particular directions and velocities, the
" abstract idea of motion is framed ; which equally cor-
" responds to all particular motions whatever that may
" be perceived by sense.

   " Whether others have this wonderful faculty of ab-
" stracting their ideas, they best can tell ; for myself I
" find, indeed, I have a faculty of imagining, or repre-
" senting to myself the ideas of those particular things
" I have perceived, and of variously compounding and
" dividing them. I can imagine a man with two heads,
" or the upper part of a man joined to the body of a
" horse. I can consider the hand, the eye, the nose,
" each by itself abstracted or separated from the rest of
" the body. But then whatever hand or eye I imagine,
" it must have some particular shape and colour. Like-
" wise the idea of man that I frame to myself, must be
" either of a white, or a black, or a tawny, a straight, or
" a crooked, a tall, or a low, or a middle-sized man. I
" cannot by any effort of thought conceive the abstract
" idea above described. And it is equally impossible
" for me to form the abstract idea of motion distinct
" from the body moving, and which is neither swift nor
" slow, curvilinear nor rectilinear ; and the like may be
" said of all other abstract general ideas whatsoever. To
" be plain, I am myself able to abstract in one sense, as

2 B

"when I consider some particular parts or qualities
"separated from others, with which though they are
"united in some object, yet it is possible they may
"really exist without them. But I deny that I can
"abstract one from another, or conceive separately, those
"qualities which it is impossible should exist so sepa-
"rated; or that I can frame a general notion by ab-
"stracting from particulars in the manner aforesaid.
"Which two last are the proper acceptations of *abstrac-*
"*tion.* And there are grounds to think most men will
"acknowledge themselves to be in my case." It is
evident, indeed, that the existence of Abstract Ideas—
the conception of the class-qualities by themselves, and
not as embodied in an individual—is effectually precluded by the law of Inseparable Association.

In what manner, Sir W. Hamilton manages to combine two theories, which in words are, and in substance
have always been believed to be, directly contradictory
of one another, we learn only from his Lectures on
Logic. The hearers of those on Metaphysics, unless the
Professor supplied oral elucidations which do not appear
in the text, must have been considerably puzzled by
finding the task of reconciling the two doctrines thrown
entirely on themselves. In the Lectures on Logic, however, an attempt is made to perform it for them. It is
there stated,* that the General Notion, which Sir W.
Hamilton terms a Concept, and which is the notion we
form of some "point of similarity" between individual
objects, "is not cognisable in itself, that is, it affords no
"absolute or irrespective object of knowledge, but can
"only be realised in consciousness by applying it as a
"term of relation, to one or more of the objects, which
"agree in the point or points of resemblance which it
"expresses. . . . The moment we attempt to represent
"to ourselves any of these concepts, any of these ab-
"stract generalities, as absolute objects, by themselves,
"and out of relation to any concrete or individual
"realities, their relative nature at once reappears; for

* Lectures, iii. 128, 129.

" we find it altogether impossible to represent any of the
" qualities expressed by a concept, except as attached to
" some individual and determinate object, and their whole
" generality consists in this, that though we must realise
" them in thought under some singular of the class, we
" may do it under any.   Thus, for example, we cannot
" actually represent the bundle of attributes contained
" in the concept *man* as an absolute object by itself, and
" apart from all that reduces it from a general cognition
" to an individual representation.   We cannot figure in
" imagination any object adequate to the general notion
" or term *man;* for the man to be here imagined must
" be neither tall nor short, neither fat nor lean, neither
" black nor white, neither man nor woman, neither young
" nor old, but all and yet none of these at once.   The
" relativity of our concepts is thus shown in the contra-
" diction and absurdity of the opposite hypothesis."

This is sound doctrine, but it is pure Nominalism ;
as the passage first quoted from our author was pure
Conceptualism.   It is very necessary that I should
quote the additional elucidations given in the succeeding
Lecture.*   A Concept or (General) Notion, he there
says, is in this distinguished from a " Presentation of
" Perception, or Representation of Phantasy," that " our
" knowledge through either of the latter is a direct, im-
" mediate, irrespective, determinate, individual, and ade-
" quate cognition ; that is, a singular or individual object
" is known in itself, by itself, through all its attributes,
" and without reference to aught but itself.   A concept,
" on the contrary, is an indirect, mediate, indeterminate,
" and partial cognition of any one of a number of objects,
" but not an actual representation either of them all, or
" of the whole attributes of any one object. . . . . . .

"Formed by comparison," concepts "express only a
" relation.   They cannot, therefore, be held up as an
" absolute object to consciousness—they cannot be repre-
" sented as universals, in imagination.   They can only
" be thought of in relation to some one of the individual

* Lectures, iii. 131–137.

" objects they classify, and when viewed in relation to it
" they can be represented in imagination ; but then, as
" actually represented, they no longer constitute general
" attributions, they fall back into mere special determi-
" nations of the individual object in which they are
" represented.   Thus it is, that the generality or uni-
" versality of concepts is potential, not actual.   They
" are only generals inasmuch as they may be applied to
" any of the various objects they contain ; but while they
" cannot be actually elicited into consciousness, except in
" application to some one or other of these, so they
" cannot be so applied without losing, *pro tanto*, their
" universality.   Take, for example, the concept *horse*.
" In so far as by *horse* we merely think of the word, that
" is, of the combination formed by the letters *h, o, r, s, e,*
" —this is not a concept at all, as it is a mere representa-
" tion of certain individual objects.   This I only state
" and eliminate, in order that no possible ambiguity
" should be allowed to lurk.   By *horse*, then, meaning
" not merely a representation of the word, but a concept
" relative to certain objects classed under it,—the con-
" cept *horse*, I say, cannot, if it remain a concept, that is,
" a universal attribution, be represented in imagination ;
" but, except it be represented in imagination, it cannot
" be applied to any object, and except it be so applied, it
" cannot be realised in thought at all.   You may try to
" escape the horns of the dilemma, but you cannot.   You
" cannot realise in thought an absolute or irrespective
" concept, corresponding in universality to the applica-
" tion of the word ; for the supposition of this involves
" numerous contradictions.   An existent horse is not a
" relation, but an extended object possessed of a deter-
" minate figure, colour, size, &c. ; *horse,* in general, cannot,
" therefore, be represented, except by an image of some-
" thing extended and of a determinate figure, colour,
" size, &c.   Here now emerges the contradiction.   If,
" on the one hand, you do not represent something ex
" tended, and of a determinate figure, colour, and size,
" you have no representation of any horse.   There is,

"therefore, in this alternative, nothing which can be
"called the actual concept or image of a horse at all. If,
"on the other hand, you do represent something ex-
"tended, and of a determinate figure, colour, and size,
"then you have, indeed, the image of an individual
"horse, but not a universal concept coadequate with *horse*
"in general. For how is it possible to have an actual
"representation of a figure, which is not a determinate
"figure? but if of a determinate figure, it must be that
"of some one of the many different figures under which
"horses appear; but then if it be only of one of these,
"it cannot be the general concept of the others, which
"it does not represent. In like manner, how is it
"possible to have the actual representation of a thing
"coloured, which is not the representation of a de-
"terminate colour, that is, either white, or black, or
"grey, or brown, &c.? but if it be any one of these,
"it can only represent a horse of this or that particular
"colour, and cannot be the general concept of horses of
"every colour. The same result is given by the other
"attributes; and what I originally stated is thus mani-
"fest—that concepts have only a potential, not an actual,
"universality, that is, they are only universal, inasmuch
"as they may be applied to any of a certain class of
"objects, but as actually applied, they are no longer
"general attributions, but only special attributes."

But if, as our author says, concepts are "incapable of
being realised in thought at all," except as representations of individual objects, how are they, even potentially universal? Being mere mental creations, they *are*
nothing except what they can be thought as being;
and they cannot be thought as being universal, but
only as being part of the thought of an individual
object, though the individual object needs not always
be the same. This is not a potential universality,
though it is an universal potentiality. If, then, the
Nominalists are thus completely right, how can it be
that the Conceptualists are not wrong?

Our author thinks that the apparent difference between

them is a mere case of verbal ambiguity; arising from "the employment of the same terms to express the "representations of Imagination, and the notions or "concepts of the Understanding." "A relation," he "says,* cannot be represented in imagination. The "two terms,—the two relative objects, can be severally "imaged in the sensible phantasy, but not the relation "itself. This is the object of the Comparative Faculty, "or of Intelligence Proper. To objects so different as "the images of sense and the unpicturable notions of "intelligence, different names ought to be given." "In "Germany,† the question of nominalism and concep-"tualism has not been agitated, and why? Simply "because the German language supplies terms by which "concepts (or notions of thought proper) have been con-"tradistinguished from the presentations and representa-"tions of the subsidiary faculties." ‡ We are therefore to understand that although Imagination cannot figure to itself anything general or universal, Thought Proper, or the Comparative Faculty, or the Understanding, can. But I do not believe that Berkeley, whose argument our author declares "irrefragable," or any other of the great Nominalist thinkers whom he enumerates, would have accepted this distinction. They would, I apprehend, have denied that the attributes included in the so-called General Notion can be thought separately, any more than they can be imaged separately. But why do I talk of Berkeley? Sir W. Hamilton has himself nega-tived the distinction in the very passage just quoted, when he says, "the concept *horse* cannot, if it remain a "concept, that is, a universal attribution, be represented "in imagination; but, *except it be represented in imagi-*"*nation,* it cannot be applied to any object, and except "it be so applied, *it cannot be realised in thought.*" The simple question is, Can the attributes of horse as a class be objects of thought, except as part of a representation

---

of some individual horse? If the Concept cannot exist
in the mind except enveloped in the miscellaneous attributes of an individual (which is the truth, and fully
recognised as such in the passages quoted from Sir W.
Hamilton) then it can no more be thought separately by
the intellect than depicted separately in the imagination.

This notion of a Concept as something which can be
thought, but "cannot in itself be depicted to sense or
"imagination," * is supported, as we saw, by calling it
a relation. "As the result of a comparison," a concept
"necessarily † expresses a relation:" and a "relation
cannot be represented in imagination." If a concept
is a relation, what relation is it, and between what?
"As the result of a comparison," it must be a relation
of resemblance among the things compared. I might
observe that a concept, which is defined by our author
himself "a bundle of attributes," does not signify the
mere fact of resemblance between objects; it signifies our
mental representation of that in which they resemble;
of the "common circumstance" which Sir W. Hamilton
spoke of in his exposition of Classification. The attributes are not the relation, they are the *fundamentum
relationis*. This objection, however, I can afford to waive.
However inappropriate the expression, let us admit that
a concept is a relation. But if a relation cannot be
represented in imagination, our author has just said that
"the two terms, the two relative objects," can. The
relation, according to him, though it cannot be imagined,
can be thought. But can a relation be thought without
thinking the related objects between which it exists?
Assuredly, no: and this impossibility can the less be
denied by Sir W. Hamilton, as it is the basis on which he
founds his theory of Consciousness—of the direct appre-

* Mansel, Prolegomena Logica, p. 15. What a mere play upon words
the distinction is, is shown by Mr. Mansel's saying, a few pages later,
(p. 29), "In every complete act of conception, the attributes forming the
concept are contemplated as co-existing in a possible object of intuition."
So that they *are* "depicted to imagination;" only they are not depicted
separately.
† Lectures, iii. 128.

hension of the Ego and the Non-ego. Consequently, when we think a relation, we must think it as existing between some particular objects which we think along with it : and a Concept, even if it be the apprehending of a relation, can only be thought as individual, not as general.

The true theory of Concepts needs not, I think, be sought farther off than in our author's own account of their origin. "In the formation," he says,* "of a con-"cept or notion, the process may be analysed into four "momenta. In the first place, we must have a plurality "of objects presented or represented by the subsidiary "faculties. These faculties must furnish the rude ma-"terial for elaboration. In the second place, the objects "thus applied are, by an act of the Understanding, com-"pared together, and their several qualities judged to "be similar or dissimilar. In the third place, an act of "volition, called Attention, concentrates consciousness "on the qualities thus recognised as similar ; and that "concentration, by attention, on them, involves an "abstraction of consciousness from those which have "been recognised and thrown aside as dissimilar ; for "the power of consciousness is limited, and it is clear or "vivid precisely in proportion to the simplicity or one-"ness of the object. Attention and Abstraction are the "two poles of the same act of thought : they are like the "opposite scales in a balance, the one must go up as the "other goes down. In the fourth place, the qualities, "which by comparison are judged similar, and by at-"tention are constituted into an exclusive object of "thought,—these are already, by this process, identified "in consciousness ; for they are only judged similar, "inasmuch as they produce in us indiscernible effects. "Their synthesis in consciousness may, however, for "precision's sake, be stated as a fourth step in the pro-"cess. But it must be remembered, that at least the "three latter steps are not in reality, distinct and inde-"pendent acts, but are only so distinguished and stated,

* Lectures, iii., 132, 133.

" in order to enable us to comprehend and speak about
" the indivisible operation in the different aspects in
" which we may consider it." Let me remark, in passing, the fresh recognition in the last sentence, of an
important principle, already several times adverted to,
in the theory of Naming.

The formation, therefore, of a Concept, does not consist in separating the attributes which are said to compose it, from all other attributes of the same object,
and enabling us to conceive those attributes, disjoined
from any others. We neither conceive them, nor think
them, nor cognise them in any way, as a thing apart, but
solely as forming, in combination with numerous other
attributes, the idea of an individual object. But, though
thinking them only as part of a larger agglomeration,
we have the power of fixing our attention on them, to
the neglect of the other attributes with which we think
them combined. While the concentration of attention
actually lasts, if it is sufficiently intense, we may be temporarily unconscious of any of the other attributes, and
may really, for a brief interval, have nothing present to
our mind but the attributes constituent of the concept.
In general, however, the attention is not so completely
exclusive as this ; it leaves room in consciousness for
other elements of the concrete idea : though of these the
consciousness is faint, in proportion to the energy of the
concentrative effort ; and the moment the attention re-
laxes, if the same concrete idea continues to be contemplated, its other constituents come out into consciousness. General concepts, therefore, we have, properly
speaking, none ; we have only complex ideas of objects
in the concrete : but we are able to attend exclusively
to certain parts of the concrete idea : and by that exclusive attention, we enable those parts to determine exclusively the course of our thoughts as subsequently
called up by association ; and are in a condition to
carry on a train of meditation or reasoning relating to
those parts only, exactly as if we were able to conceive
them separately from the rest.

What principally enables us to do this is the employment of signs, and particularly the most efficient and familiar kind of signs, viz. Names. This is a point which Sir W. Hamilton puts well and strongly, and there are many reasons for stating it in his own language.[*]

"The concept thus formed by an abstraction of the "resembling from the non-resembling qualities of "objects, would again fall back into the confusion "and infinitude from which it has been called out, "were it not rendered permanent for consciousness, "by being fixed and ratified in a verbal sign. Con- "sidered in general, thought and language are recipro- "cally dependent; each bears all the imperfections "and perfections of the other; but without language "there could be no knowledge realised of the essential "properties of things, and of the connection of their "accidental states."

The rationale of this is, that when we wish to be able to think of objects in respect of certain of their attributes—to recall no objects but such as are invested with those attributes, and to recall them with our attention directed to those attributes exclusively—we effect this by giving to that combination of attributes, or to the class of objects which possess them, a specific Name. We create an artificial association between those attributes and a certain combination of articulate sounds, which guarantees to us that when we hear the sound, or see the written characters corresponding to it, there will be raised in the mind an idea of some object possessing those attributes, in which idea those attributes alone will be suggested vividly to the mind, our consciousness of the remainder of the concrete idea being faint. As the name has been directly associated only with those attributes, it is as likely, in itself, to recall them in any one concrete combination as in any other. What combination it shall recall in the particular case, depends on recency of experience, accidents of memory, or the in-

_____
[*] Lectures, iii. 137.

fluence of other thoughts which have been passing, or
are even then passing, through the mind; accordingly, the
combination is far from being always the same, and seldom gets itself strongly associated with the name which
suggests it ; while the association of the name with the
attributes that form its conventional signification, is
constantly becoming stronger.   The association of that
particular set of attributes with a given word, is what
keeps them together in the mind by a stronger tie than
that with which they are associated with the remainder
of the concrete image.   To express the meaning in Sir
W. Hamilton's phraseology, this association gives them
an unity * in our consciousness.   It is only when this
has been accomplished, that we possess what Sir W.
Hamilton terms a Concept ; and this is the whole of the
mental phenomenon involved in the matter.   We have
a concrete representation, certain of the component elements of which are distinguished by a mark, designating
them for special attention ; and this attention, in cases
of exceptional intensity, excludes all consciousness of
the others.

Sir W. Hamilton thinks, however, that we can form,
though scarcely preserve, concepts without the aid of
signs.   "Language," † he says, "is the attribution of
"signs to our cognition of things.   But as a cognition
"must have been already there, before it could receive a
"sign ; consequently, that knowledge which is denoted
"by the formation and application of a word, must have

---

* One of the best and profoundest passages in all Sir W. Hamilton's
writings, is that in which he points out (though only incidentally) what
are the conditions of our ascribing Unity to any aggregate.   "Though it
"is only by experience we come to attribute an external unity to aught
"continuously extended, that is, consider it as a system or constituted
"whole ; still, in so far as we do so consider it, *we think the parts as held*
"*together by a certain force*, and the whole, therefore, as endowed with a
"power of resisting their distraction.   It is, indeed, only by finding that
"a material continuity resists distraction, that we view it as more than a
"fortuitous aggregation of many bodies, that is, as a single body.   The
"material universe, for example, though not *de facto* continuously ex-
"tended, we consider as one system in so far, but only in so far, as we
'find all bodies tending together by reciprocal attraction."   Dissertations on Reid, pp. 852, 853.

† Lectures, iii. 138–140.

" preceded the symbol which denotes it." A sign, however, he continues, in one of his happiest specimens of
illustration, " is necessary to give stability to our intel-
" lectual progress,—to establish each step in our advance
" as a new starting point for our advance to another be-
" yond. A country may be overrun by an armed host,
" but it is only conquered by the establishment of for-
" tresses. Words are the fortresses of thought. They
" enable us to realise our dominion over what we have
" already overrun in thought; to make every intellectual
" conquest the basis of operations for others still beyond.
" Or another illustration : You have all heard of the pro-
" cess of tunnelling—of tunnelling through a sand-bank.
" In this operation it is impossible to succeed, unless
" every foot, nay almost every inch in our progress, be
" secured by an arch of masonry, before we attempt the
" excavation of another. Now, language is to the mind
" precisely what the arch is to the tunnel. The power of
" thinking and the power of excavation are not depen-
" dent on the word in the one case, on the mason-work
" in the other ; but without these subsidiaries, neither
" process could be carried on beyond its rudimentary
" commencement. Though, therefore, we allow that
" every movement forward in language must be deter-
" mined by an antecedent movement forward in thought ;
" still, unless thought be accompanied at each point of
" its evolution, by a corresponding evolution of language,
" its further development is arrested. . . . . Admitting
" even that the mind is capable of certain elementary
" concepts without the fixation and signature of lan-
" guage, still these are but sparks which would twinkle
" only to expire, and it requires words to give them pro-
" minence, and by enabling us to collect and elaborate
" them into new concepts, to raise out of what would
" otherwise be only scattered and transitory scintilla-
" tions, a vivid and enduring light."

Mr. Mansell, who agrees with Sir W. Hamilton in the
essentials of his doctrine of Concepts, goes beyond him
on this point, being of opinion that without signs we

could not form concepts at all. The objection, that we must have had the concept before we could have given it a name, he meets by the suggestion that names when first used are names only of individual objects, but being extended from one object to another under the law of Association by Resemblance, they become specially associated with the points of Resemblance, and thus generate the Concept. In Mr. Mansel's opinion,[*] no one, " without the aid of symbols," can advance " beyond the " individual objects of sense or imagination. In the pre- " sence of several individuals of the same species, the " eye may observe points of similarity between them ; " and in this no symbol is needed ; but every feature " thus observed is the distinct attribute of a distinct indi- " vidual, and however similar, cannot be regarded as " identical. For example : I see lying on the table be- " fore me a number of shillings of the same coinage. " Examined severally, the image and superscription of " each is undistinguishable from that of its fellow ; but " in viewing them side by side, *space* is a necessary con- " dition of my perception, and the difference of locality " is sufficient to make them distinct, though similar in- " dividuals. The same is the case with any representa- " tive image, whether in a mirror, in a painting, or in " the imagination, waking or dreaming. It can only be " depicted as occupying a certain place ; and thus as an " individual, and the representative of an individual. It " is true that I cannot say that it represents this particu- " lar coin rather than that ; and consequently it may be " considered as the representative of all, successively but " not simultaneously. To find a representative which " shall embrace all at once, I must divest it of the con- " dition of occupying space ; and this, experience assures " us, can only be done by means of *symbols*, verbal or " other, by which the concept is fixed in the understand- " ing. Such, for example, is a verbal description of the " coin in question, which contains a collection of attributes " freed from the condition of locality, and hence from all

* Prolegomena Logica, pp. 15–17.

"resemblance to an object of sense.   If we substitute
" Time for Space, the same remarks will be equally ap-
" plicable to the objects of our internal consciousness.
" Every appetite and desire, every affection and volition, as
" *presented*, is an individual state of consciousness, distin-
" guished from every other by its relation to a different
" period of time.   States in other respects exactly similar
" may succeed one another at regular intervals ; but the
" hunger which I feel to-day is an individual feeling as
" numerically distinct from that which I felt yesterday
" or that which I shall feel to-morrow, as a shilling lying
" in my pocket is from a similar shilling lying at the
" bank.   Whereas my *notion* of hunger, or fear, or voli-
" tion, is a general concept, having no relation to one
" period of time rather than to another, and, as such,
" requires, like other concepts, a representative sign.
" Language, taking the word in its widest sense, is thus
" indispensable, not merely to the communication, but to
" the formation of Thought."

This is a step in advance of Sir W. Hamilton's doctrine, but is open to the same criticism, namely, that
after showing all Concepts to be concrete and individual,
it endeavours to make out by an indirect process, a
sort of abstract existence for them.   According to Mr.
Mansel, signs are necessary to concepts, because signs
alone can give this abstract existence.   Signs are wanted,
to emancipate our mental apprehension from the conditions of space and time which are in all our concrete
representations.   The other miscellaneous attributes
which have to be cast out, do not, he seems to think,
embarrass the formation of the Concept ; but it is ham-
pered by the conditions of space and time, and only by
means of a sign can we get rid of these.   But *do* we
get rid of them by employing signs ?   To take Mr.
Mansel's own instance : When we establish our concept
of a shilling by a verbal description of the coin, does
the description enable us to conceive a shilling as not
occupying any space ?   When we think of a shilling,
either by name or anonymously, is not the circumstance

of occupying space called up as an inevitable part of the mental representation ? Not, indeed, the circumstance of occupying a *given part* of space ; but if that is what Mr. Mansel means, it would follow that we need signs to enable us to form a mental representation even of an individual object, provided it be movable : for the same object does not always occupy the same part of space. The truth is, that the condition of space cannot be excluded ; it is an essential part of the concept of Body, and of every kind of bodies. But any given space, or any given time, is not a part of the concept, any more than any of the slight peculiarities in which one shilling differs from another are part of the concept of a shilling. Some space and time, and some individual peculiarities, are always thought along with the concept, and make up the whole, of which it can only be thought as a part: but these are not directly recalled by the class-name, and the attributes composing the concept are. Mr. Mansel, therefore, has not, I conceive, hit the mark : but in the passages which follow, there is real power of metaphysical discrimination.

" Observe * what actually takes place in the formation
" of language and thought among ourselves. To the
" child learning to speak, words are not the signs of
" thoughts, but of intuitions : † the words *man* and *horse*
" do not represent a collection of attributes, but are only
" the name of the individual now before him. It is not
" until the name has been successively appropriated to
" various individuals, that reflection begins to inquire
" into the common features of the class. Language,
" therefore, as taught to the infant, is chronologically
" prior to thought and posterior to sensation. In inquir-
" ing how far the same process can account for the
" invention of language, which now takes place in the
" learning it, the real question at issue is simply this.
" Is the act of giving names to *individual objects of sense,*

* Prolegomena Logica, pp. 19, 20, and 29–31.
† By intuitions Mr. Mansel means the Anschauungen of Kant, or what Mr. Mansel himself otherwise calls Presentations of Sense, to which he adds Representations of Imagination.

" a thing so completely beyond the power of a man
" created in the full maturity of his faculties, that we
" must suppose a Divine Instructor performing precisely
" the same office as is now performed for the infant by
" his mother or his nurse ; teaching him, that is, to
" associate *this sound* with *this sight ?* . . . . All con-
" cepts are formed by means of signs which have
" previously been representative of individual objects
" only. . . . Similarities are noticed earlier than dif-
" ferences : and our first abstractions may be said to be
" performed for us, as we learn to give the same name
" to individuals presented to us under slight, and at first
" unnoticed, circumstances of distinction. The same
" name is thus applied to different objects, long before
" we learn to analyse the growing powers of speech and
" thought, to ask what we mean by each several instance
" of its application, to correct and fix the signification
" of words used at first vaguely and obscurely. To
" point out each successive stage of the process by which
" signs of intuition become gradually signs of thought,
" is as impossible as to point out the several moments
" at which the growing child receives each successive
" increase of his stature."

These remarks of Mr. Mansel remove, as it seems to
me, the only real argument for the supposition that Concepts, or what are called General Notions, are formed
without the aid of signs. But the counter-doctrine
must be received with an important reservation. Signs
are necessary, but the signs need not be artificial ; there
are such things as natural signs. The only reality there
is in the Concept is, that we are somehow enabled and
led, not once or accidentally, but in the common course
of our thoughts, to attend specially, and more or less
exclusively, to certain parts of the presentation of sense
or representation of imagination which we are conscious
of. Now, what is there to make us do this ? There must
be something which, as often as it recurs either to our
senses or to our thoughts, *directs* our attention to those
particular elements in the perception or in the idea : and

whatever performs this office is virtually a sign; but it needs not be a word; the process certainly takes place, to a limited extent, in the inferior animals; and even with human beings who have but a small vocabulary, many processes of thought take place habitually by other symbols than words. It is a doctrine of one of the most fertile thinkers of modern times, Auguste Comte, that besides the logic of signs, there is a logic of images, and a logic of feelings. In many of the familiar processes of thought, and especially in uncultured minds, a visual image serves instead of a word. Our visual sensations—perhaps only because they are almost always present along with the impressions of our other senses—have a facility of becoming associated with them. Hence, the characteristic visual appearance of an object easily gathers round it, by association, the ideas of all other peculiarities which have, in frequent experience, coexisted with that appearance: and, summoning up these with a strength and certainty far surpassing that of the merely casual associations which it may also raise, it concentrates the attention on them. This is an image serving for a sign—the logic of images. The same function may be fulfilled by a feeling. Any strong and highly interesting feeling, connected with one attribute of a group, spontaneously classifies all objects according as they possess or do not possess that attribute. We may be tolerably certain that the things capable of satisfying hunger form a perfectly distinct class in the mind of any of the more intelligent animals; quite as much so as if they were able to use or understand the word food. We here see in a strong light the important truth, that hardly anything universal can be affirmed in psychology except the laws of association. As almost all general propositions which can be laid down respecting Mind, are consequences of these laws, so do these ultimate laws, in varying cases, generate different derivative laws; and are continually raising up exceptions to the empirical generalisations yielded by direct psychical observation, which, so far as true, being mere cases of the wider laws, are always limited by them.

We have now attained a theory of Classification, of Class Notions, and of Class Names, which is clear, free from difficulties, and, in its essential elements, understood and assented to by Sir W. Hamilton. With the exception of a few minor matters, I find no fault in his theory. It is where his theory ends and his practice begins, that I am obliged to diverge from him. His theory is a complete condemnation of his practice. His theory is that of Nominalism; but he affirms, in opposition to every Conceptualist, that Nominalism and Conceptualism are the same, and on this justification expounds all the operations of the intellect in the language, and on the assumptions, of Conceptualism. If a Concept does not exist as a separate or independent object of thought, but is always a mere part of a concrete image, and has nothing that discriminates it from the other parts except a special share of attention, guaranteed to it by special association with a name; what is meant by the paramount place assigned to Concepts in all the intellectual processes? Can it be right to found the whole of Logic, the entire theory of Judgment and Reasoning, upon a thing which has merely a fictitious or constructive existence? Is it correct to say that we think by means of Concepts? Would it not convey both a clearer and a truer meaning, to say that we think by means of ideas of concrete phenomena, such as are presented in experience or represented in imagination, and by means of names, which being in a peculiar manner associated with certain elements of the concrete images, arrest our attention on those elements? Sir W. Hamilton has told us that a concept cannot, as such, be "realised in thought," or "elicited into consciousness." Can it be, that we think and reason by means of that which cannot be thought, of which we cannot become conscious? Of course Sir W. Hamilton did not mean, nor do I, that we cannot think or be conscious of the attributes which are said to compose the concept; but we can only be conscious of them as forming a representation jointly with other attributes which do not enter into the concept. And the difference between the parts of the same representation which are inside and those which are outside what is called the concept, is not that the former are attended to and the latter not, for neither of these is always true. It is, that foreseeing that we shall frequently or occasionally desire to attend only to the former, we have made for ourselves, or have received from our predecessors, a contrivance for being reminded of them, which also serves for fixing our exclusive attention upon them when called to mind. To say, therefore, that we think by means of concepts, is only a circuitous and obscure way of saying that we think by means of general or class names.* To give an intelligible idea of the fact, we always need to translate it out of the former language into the latter. It is possible, no doubt, so to define the terms that both expressions shall mean the same thing. But the less appropriate language has the immense disadvantage, that it cannot be used without tacitly assuming that these mere parts of our complex concrete perceptions and ideas have a separate mental existence, which is admitted not to belong to them. No one, more fully than Sir W. Hamilton, recognises the true theory; but the acknowledgment only serves him

---

* It is for want of apprehending this view of the matter that Sir W. Hamilton (Lectures, iii. 31, 32) brings a charge of self-contradiction against Archbishop Whately, because, having in the commencement and throughout his treatise on Logic, represented Reasoning as the object-matter of that science, he, in certain passages, says that Logic is entirely conversant with the use of language. This is a contradiction only from Sir W. Hamilton's point of view. If Archbishop Whately's had been the same— if he had thought as Sir W. Hamilton did respecting Concepts, considered as the object-matter of reasoning—he would have been justly liable to the imputation cast upon him. But the Archbishop's two statements are perfectly consistent, if we suppose his opinion to have been, that the formation of Concepts, and the subsequent process of combining them in arguments, are themselves processes of language. This doctrine (which is in fact Mr. Mansel's) Sir W. Hamilton deems too absurd to be imputed to the Archbishop (Discussions, p. 138). Yet he fancies himself a Nominalist, and does understand and assent to all the arguments of Nominalism. Unfortunately an intelligent assent to one of two conflicting doctrines is in his case no guarantee against holding, for all practical purposes of thought, the other.

as an excuse for delivering himself up unreservedly to all the logical consequences of the false theory. To read the account which he and Mr. Mansel, in common with the great majority of modern logicians, give of our intellectual processes—which they always make to consist essentially of some operation practised upon concepts—no one would ever imagine that concepts were not complete, rounded off, distinct and separate possessions of the mind, habitually dealt with by it quite apart from anything else ; and this, in the general opinion of Conceptualists, they are : but according to Sir W. Hamilton and Mr. Mansel, they are secretly, all the while, incapable of being thought except as parts of something else which has always to be dealt with along with them, but which these philosophers, in their expositions, suppress as completely, as if they had forgotten that its necessary presence is part of their theory. For these and other reasons, I think that the words Concept, General Notion, and other phrases of like import, convenient as they are for the lighter and every-day uses of philosophical discussion, should be abstained from where precision is required. Above all, I hold that nothing but confusion ever results from introducing the term Concept into Logic, and that instead of the Concept of a class, we should always speak of the signification of a class name.*

The signification of a class name has two aspects, corresponding to the distinction to which Sir W. Hamilton attaches so much importance, between the Extension and

---

* Dr. M'Cosh says (p. 276), "I think it desirable to have a phrase to "denote, not the 'signification of a class name,' but the thing signified by "the class name : and the fittest I can think of is Concept." But the "thing signified" by the class name is the class ; the various objects called by the name : and class is a sufficient name for these, nor has the word Concept, to my knowledge, ever been predicated of them, but only of Sir W. Hamilton's "bundles of attributes." Dr. M'Cosh's use of the word Concept, for the thing conceived, not the conception, is, I believe, peculiar to himself.

I must add, that the chapter of Dr. M'Cosh from which I am now quoting, that headed, "The Logical Notion," contains much sound philosophy, and little with which I disagree except the persistent impression which the author keeps up throughout the chapter that I do disagree with him.

the Comprehension of a concept; which is merely a bad expression for the distinction between the two modes of signification of a concrete general name. Most names are still, what according to Mr. Mansel they all were originally, names of objects; and do not cease to be so by becoming class names; but, though names of objects, they become expressive of certain attributes of those objects, and when predicated of an object, they affirm of it those attributes. The name is said, in the language of logicians, to *de*note the objects and *con*note the attributes. *White* denotes chalk and other white substances, and connotes the particular colour which is common to them. *Bird* denotes eagles, sparrows, crows, geese, and so forth, and connotes life, the possession of wings, and the other properties by which we are guided in applying the name. The various objects denoted by the class name are what is meant by the Extension of the concept, while the attributes connoted are its Comprehension. It must be remarked, however, that the Extension is not anything intrinsic to the concept; it is the sum of all the objects, in our concrete images of which, the concept is included: but the Comprehension is the very concept itself, for the concept means nothing but our mental representation of the sum of the attributes composing it.

And here it is important to take notice of a psychological truth, which forms an additional reason for preferring the expression that we think by general names, to that of thinking by concepts. Since the concept only exists as a part of a concrete mental state; if we say that we think by means of it, and not by the whole which is a part of it, it ought at least to be *the* part by which we think. Since that is the only distinction between it and the remainder of the presentation or representation in which it is imbedded, at least that distinction should be real: all which enters into the concept ought to be operative in thought. So far is this from being true, that in our processes of thought, seldom more than a part, sometimes a very small part, of what is comprehended in the concept, is attended to, or comes into play. This is forcibly stated, though in Conceptualist phraseology, by Mr. Mansel. "We can," he says,[*] "and in the majority of cases do, employ concepts as "instruments of thought, without submitting them to "the test of even possible individualisation. . . . I can- "not *conceive* a triangle which is neither equilateral, nor "isosceles, nor scalene; but I can judge and reason about "a triangle without at the moment trying to conceive it "at all. This is one of the consequences of the repre- "sentation of concepts by language. *The sign is substi- "tuted for the notion signified;* a step which consider- "ably facilitates the performance of complex operations "of thought; but in the same proportion endangers the "logical accuracy of each successive step, as we do not, "in each, stop to verify our signs. Words, as thus em- "ployed, resemble algebraical symbols, which, during "the process of a long calculation, we combine in various "relations to each other, without at the moment think- "ing of the original signification assigned to each." The attempt to stand at once on two incompatible theories, leads to strange freaks of expression. Mr. Mansel describes us as thinking by means of concepts which we are incapable of forming, and do not even attempt to form, but use the signs instead. Yet he will not consent to call this thinking by the signs, but insists that it is the concepts which are even in this case the "instruments of thought." It is surely a very twisted logical position which, when he is so entirely right in what he has to say, compels him to use so strangely contorted a mode of saying it.

The same important psychological fact is excellently illustrated by Sir W. Hamilton in one of the very best chapters of his works, the Tenth Lecture on Logic, in which it is stated as follows:[†] "As a notion or "concept is the fictitious whole or unity made up of a "plurality of attributes,—a whole, too, often of a very "complex multiplicity; and as this multiplicity is only "mentally held together, inasmuch as the concept is

---

* Prolegomena Logica, pp. 31, 32.   † Lectures, iii. 171.

" fixed and ratified in a sign or word ; it frequently hap-
" pens that, in its employment, the word does not sug-
" gest the whole amount of thought for which it is the
" adequate expression, but, on the contrary, we frequently
" give and take the sign, either with an obscure or indis-
" tinct consciousness of its meaning, or even without an
" actual consciousness of its signification at all." The
word does not always serve the purpose of fixing our
attention on the whole of the attributes which it connotes; some of them may be only recalled to mind faintly,
others possibly not at all: a phenomenon easily to be
accounted for by the laws of Obliviscence. But the part
of the attributes signified which the word does recall,
may be all that is necessary for us to think of, at the
time and for the purpose in hand ; it may be a sufficient
part to set going all the associations by means of which
we proceed through that thought to ulterior thoughts.
Indeed, it is because part of the attributes have generally sufficed for that purpose, that the habit is acquired
of not attending to the remainder. When the attributes
not attended to are really of no importance for the end
in view, and if attended to would not have altered the
results of the mental process, there is no harm done :
much of our valid thinking is carried on in this manner,
and it is to this that our thinking processes owe, in a
great measure, their proverbial rapidity. This kind of
thinking was called by Leibnitz, Symbolical. A passage
of one of the early writings of that eminent thinker, in
which it is brought to notice with his accustomed clearness, is translated by Sir W. Hamilton, from whom I
re-quote it.*

" For the most part, especially in an analysis of any
" length, we do not view at once (non simul intuemur)
" the whole characters or attributes of the thing, but in
" place of these we employ signs, the explication of which
" into what they signify we are wont, at the moment of
" actual thought, to omit, knowing or believing that we
" have this explication always in our power. Thus, when

* Lectures, iii. 181.

" I think a chiliagon (or polygon of a thousand sides) I
" do not always consider the various attributes of the
" side, of the equality, and of the number or thousand,
" but use these words (whose meaning is obscurely and
" imperfectly presented to the mind) in lieu of the notions
" which I have of them, because I remember, that I
" possess the signification of these words, though their
" application and explication I do not at present deem
" to be necessary:—this mode of thinking, I am used
" to call *blind* or *symbolical:* we employ it in Algebra
" and in Arithmetic, but in fact universally. And cer-
" tainly when the notion is very complex, we cannot
" think at once all the ingredient notions: but where
" this is possible,—at least, inasmuch as it is possible,—
" I call the cognition *intuitive.* Of the primary elements
" of our notions, there is given no other knowledge than
" the intuitive: as of our composite notions there is, for
" the most part, possible only a symbolical." *

Yet the elements which are thus habitually left out,
and of which in the case of a composite notion, if Leibnitz is right, some *must* be left out, are really parts of
the signification of the name, and if the word Concept
has any meaning, are parts of the concept.   Leibnitz

---

* It will be remarked that Leibnitz here employs the word Intuitive in
a sense entirely different from that which British metaphysicians, and Sir
W. Hamilton himself, attach to the word. In Leibnitz's sense, we cognise
a thing intuitively in as far as we are conscious of the attributes of the
thing itself; symbolically in as far as we merely think of its name, as
standing for an aggregate of attributes, without having all, or perhaps any,
of those attributes present to our mind. I cannot help being surprised
that Sir W. Hamilton should have regarded this distinction of Leibnitz as
coinciding with that of Kant and the modern German thinkers between
Begriff and Anschauung, in other words, Concept and Presentation. Sir
W. Hamilton considers Begriff to be a name for " the symbolical notions
of the understanding," in contrast with Anschauung, which means "the
intuitive presentations of Sense and representations of Imagination."
(Lectures, iii. 183.) He is right as to Anschauung, but as for "symbolical
notions of the understanding," our thinking is called by Leibnitz symbolical
exactly in so far as it takes place without any "notions," any concept or
Begriff at all, by virtue of the mere knowledge that there is a Begriff which
the word represents, and which we could recall if we wanted it. When
thinking is completely symbolical, the meaning of the word is eliminated
from thought, and only the word remains: as in Leibnitz's own illustration
from algebra.

accordingly knew better than to say, as Mr. Mansel says and Sir W. Hamilton implies, that even in these cases we think by means of the concept. According to him we sometimes think entirely without the concept, generally only by a part of it, which may be the wrong part, or an insufficient part, but which may be, and in all sound thinking is, sufficient. On this point, therefore, a false apprehension of the facts of thought is conveyed by the doctrine which speaks of Concepts as its instrument. Leibnitz would perhaps have said, that the name is the instrument in one of the two kinds of thinking, and the concept in the other. The more reasonable doctrine surely is, that the name is the instrument in both; the difference being, that in one case it does the whole, and in the other only a part, perhaps the minimum, of the work for which it is intended and fitted, that of reminding us of the portions of our concrete mental representations which we expect that we shall have need of attending to.

In summary; if the doctrine, that we think by concepts, means that a concept is the only thing present to the mind along with the individual object which (to use Sir W. Hamilton's language) we think under the concept, this is not true: since there is always present a concrete idea or image, of which the attributes comprehended in the concept are only, and cannot be conceived as anything but, a part. Again, if it be meant that the concept, though only a part of what is present to the mind, is the part which is operative in the act of thought, neither is this true: for what is operative is, in a great majority of cases, much less than the entire concept, being that portion only which we have retained the habit of distinctly attending to. In neither of these senses, therefore, do we think by means of the concept: and all that is true is, that when we refer any object or set of objects to a class, some at least of the attributes included in the concept are present to the mind; being recalled to consciousness and fixed in attention, through their association with the class-name.

Before leaving this part of the subject, it seems necessary to remark, that Sir W. Hamilton is by no means
consistent in the extension which he gives to the signification of the word Concept.   In most cases in which he
uses it, he makes it synonymous with General Notion,
and allows concepts of classes only, not of individuals.*
It is thus that he expressly defines the term.   "A Con-
"cept," he says,† "is the cognition or idea of the gene-
"ral character or characters, point or points, in which
"a plurality of objects coincide."   "Concept," he says
again ‡ "is convertible with *general notion*, or more cor-
"rectly, *notion* simply."   He speaks of the extending of
the term to our direct knowledge of individuals, as an
"abusive employment" of it.§   He also says,‖ "No-
"tions and Concepts are sometimes designated by the
"style of *general notions,—general conceptions*.   This
"is superfluous, for in propriety of speech, notions and
"concepts are, in their very nature, general."   In certain places, however, he speaks of concepts of individuals.   "If I think ¶ of Socrates as son of Sophroniscus,
"as Athenian, as philosopher, as pugnosed, these are
"only so many characters, limitations, or determinations
"which I predicate of Socrates, which distinguish him
"from all other men, and together make up my *notion*
"or *concept* of him."   And again,** "When the Exten-
"sion of a concept becomes a minimum, that is, when it
"contains no other notions under it, it is called an indi-
"vidual."   And further on,†† "It is evident that the
"more distinctive characters the concept contains, the
"more minutely it will distinguish and determine, and
"that if it contain a plenum of distinctive characters, it
"must contain the distinctive, the determining cha-
"racters of some individual object.   How do the two
"quantities now stand?   In regard to the comprehen-
"sion or depth, it is evident that it is here at its maxi-
"mum, the concept being a complement of the whole

---

* Lectures, iii. 119, 121, 127, 128, 130, *cum multis aliis.*
        † Ibid. p. 122.   ‡ Discussions, p. 283.
§ Lectures, iii. 121.   ‖ Ibid. p. 212   ¶ Ibid. p. 78.
        ** Ibid. p. 146.   †† Ibid. p. 148.

" attributes of an individual object, which, by these attri-
" butes, it thinks and discriminates from every other.
" On the contrary, the extension or breadth of the con-
" cept is here at its minimum; for, as the extension is
" great in proportion to the number of objects to which
" the concept can be applied, and as the object here is
" only an individual one, it is evident that it could not
" be less without ceasing to exist at all." But, in the
sequel of the same exposition, he again seems to surrender this use of the word Concept as an improper one,
saying,* "If a concept be an individual, that is, only
" a bundle of individual qualities, it is . . . . not a proper
" abstract concept at all, but only a concrete represen-
" tation of Imagination." And indeed, no other doctrine
is consistent with the proposition elsewhere laid down
by our author (though founded, as I think, on an error),
that "the words Conception, Concept, Notion, should
" be limited to the thought of what cannot be repre-
" sented in imagination, as the thought suggested by
" a general term." †

Mr. Mansel, on the contrary, justifies the phrase, concept of an individual, maintaining that "the subjects of
all logical judgments are concepts." ‡ "The man," he
says,§ " as an individual existing at some past time, can-
" not become immediately an object of thought, and
" hence is not, properly speaking, the subject of any
" logical proposition. If I say, Cæsar was the conqueror
" of Pompey, the immediate object of my thought is not
" Cæsar as an individual existing two thousand years
" ago, but a concept now present in my mind, compris-
" ing certain attributes which I believe to have coex-
" isted in a certain man. I may *historically* know that
" these attributes existed in one individual only; and
" hence my concept, virtually universal, is actually singu-
" lar, from the accident of its being predicable of that
" individual only. But there is no *logical* objection to
" the theory that the whole history of mankind may be

* Lectures, iii. p. 152.   † Foot-note to Reid, p. 360.
‡ Prolegomena Logica, p. 63.   § Ibid. p. 62.

"repeated at recurring intervals, and that the name and
"actions of Cæsar may be successively found in various
"individuals at corresponding periods of every cycle."

If this be so, one of two things follows. Either, if
I met with a person who exactly corresponded to the
concept I have formed of Cæsar, I must suppose that
this person actually is Cæsar, and lived in the century
preceding the birth of Christ; or else, I cannot think of
Cæsar as Cæsar, but only as *a* Cæsar; and all those which
are mistakenly called proper names are general names,
the names of virtual classes, signifying a set of attributes
which carry the name with them, wherever they are found.
Either theory seems to be sufficiently refuted by stating
it. Surely the true doctrine is that of Sir W. Hamilton,
that what is called my concept of Cæsar is the presentation in imagination of the individual Cæsar as such. Mr.
Mansel might have learnt better from Reid, who says:
"Most words (indeed all general words) are the signs of
"ideas: but proper names are not: they signify indivi-
"dual things, and not ideas." * And again, soon after:†
"The same proper name is never applied to several indi-
"viduals on account of their similitude, because the
"very intention of a proper name is to distinguish one
"individual from all others; and hence it is a maxim in
"grammar that proper names have no plural number.
"A proper name signifies nothing but the individual
"whose name it is; and when we apply it to the indivi-
"dual, we neither affirm nor deny anything concerning
"him." The whole of Reid's doctrine respecting names
and general notions is not only far more clear, but nearer
to the true doctrine of the connotation of names, than Sir
W. Hamilton's or Mr. Mansel's.‡

* Essays on the Intellectual Powers, Works, p. 404. By ideas Reid
here means (as he fully explains) attributes.
† Ibid. p. 412.
‡ Accordingly, when Sir W. Hamilton (foot-note to p. 691) contends, in
opposition to Reid, that there are definitions which are not nominal but
notional, since they have for their object "the more accurate determination
of the contents of a notion," there is no real difference of meaning between
them: the contents of a notion being simply the connotation of a name.
   Sir W. Hamilton enters, at some length, into the explanation of what

is meant by the clearness, and the distinctness, of Concepts. A concept, according to him, is clear, if we can distinguish it as a whole from other concepts; distinct, if we can discriminate the characters or attributes of which it is the sum (Lectures, iii. 158). The last statement is intelligible, but what does the first mean? If we do not know of what characters the concept is composed, seeing that it has no existence but in those characters, how can we know it so as to distinguish it from other concepts? Our author certainly had not a clear conception of what makes a conception clear; and the proof is, that he adopts as part of his text a quotation from Esser's Logic, in which Esser makes the clearness of a concept to depend on our being able to distinguish, not the concept itself, but the objects included under it; on our being able, in short, to apply the class-name correctly. According to Esser, "a concept is said to be clear, when "the degree of consciousness by which it is accompanied is sufficient to "discriminate" not itself from other concepts, but "what we think in and "through it, from what we think in and through other notions:" and "notions absolutely clear" are "notions whose *objects*" (not as Sir W. Hamilton says, *themselves*) cannot "possibly be confounded with aught else, whether known or unknown." (Lectures, iii. 160, 161.) So that, according to Esser, the clearness of a concept has reference to its Extension, the distinctness to its Comprehension. This is not the only instance in which our author helps out his own expositions by passages from other authors, written from a point of view more or less different from his own.

CHAPTER XVIII.

OF JUDGMENT.

THOUGH, as has appeared in the last chapter, the proposition that we think by concepts is, if not positively untrue, at least an unprecise and misleading expression of the truth, it is not, however, to be concluded that Sir W. Hamilton's view of Logic, being wholly grounded on that proposition, must be destitute of value. Many writers have given good and valuable expositions of the principles and rules of Logic, from the Conceptualist point of view. The doctrines which they have laid down respecting Conception, Judgment, and Reasoning, have been capable of being rendered into equivalent statements respecting Terms, Propositions, and Arguments; these, indeed, were what the writers really had in their thoughts, and there was little amiss except a mode of expression which attempted to be more philosophical than it knew how to be. To say nothing of less illustrious examples, this is true of all the properly logical part of Locke's Essay. His admirable Third Book requires hardly any other alteration to bring it up to the scientific level of the present time, than to be corrected by blotting out everywhere the words Abstract Idea, and replacing them by "the connotation of the class name."

We shall, accordingly, proceed to examine the explanation of Judgment, and of Reasoning, which Sir W. Hamilton has built on the foundation of the doctrine of Concepts.

"To judge," he says,* "is to recognise the relation

* Lectures, iii. 225, 226.

" of congruence or of confliction in which two concepts,
" two individual things, or a concept and an individual,
" compared together, stand to each other. This recog-
" nition, considered as an internal consciousness, is called
" a Judgment; considered as expressed in language, it
" is called a Proposition or Predication."

To be certain of understanding this, we must inquire
what is meant by a relation of congruence or of confliction between concepts. To consult Sir W. Hamilton's
definitions of words is, as we have seen, not a sure way
of ascertaining the sense in which he practically uses
them; but it is one of the ways, and we are bound to
employ it in the first instance. A few pages before, he
has given a sort of definition of these terms.* "Con-
" cepts, in relation to each other, are said to be either
" *Congruent* or *Agreeing*, inasmuch as they may be con-
" nected in thought; or *Conflictive*, inasmuch as they
" cannot. The confliction constitutes the *Opposition* of
" notions." This Opposition is twofold. " 1°. *Imme-*
" *diate* or *Contradictory* Opposition, called likewise
" *Repugnance*; and 2°. *Mediate* or *Contrary* Opposi-
" tion. The former emerges when one concept abolishes
" directly, or by simple negation, what another estab-
" lishes; the latter, when one concept does this not
" directly, or by simple negation, but through the
" affirmation of something else."

Congruent Concepts, therefore, does not mean concepts which coincide, either wholly or in any of their
parts, but such as are mutually compatible; capable of
being predicated of the same individual; of being combined in the same presentation of sense or representation
of imagination. This is more clearly expressed in a
passage from Krug, which our author adopts as part of
his own exposition.† "Identity is not to be confounded
" with Agreement or Congruence, nor Diversity with
" Confliction. All identical concepts are, indeed, con-
" gruent, but all congruent notions are not identical.
" Thus *learning* and *virtue*, *beauty* and *riches*, *magnani-*

* Lectures, iii. 213, 214.   † Ibid. p. 214.

" *mity* and *stature*, are congruent notions, inasmuch as,
" in thinking a thing, they can easily be combined in
" the notion we form of it, although themselves very
" different from each other.   In like manner all con-
" flicting notions are diverse or different notions, for
" unless different, they could not be mutually conflic-
" tive ; but, on the other hand, all different concepts
" are not conflictive ; but those only whose difference is
" so great that each involves the negation of the other ;
" as for example, *virtue* and *vice*, *beauty* and *deformity*,
" *wealth* and *poverty*."   Thus interpreted, our author's
doctrine is, that to judge, is to recognise whether two
concepts, two things, or a concept and a thing, are
capable of coexisting as parts of the same mental representation.   This I will call Sir W. Hamilton's first
theory of Judgment; I will venture to add, his best.

But he soon after proceeds to say,* " When two or
" more thoughts are given in consciousness, there is in
" general an endeavour on our part to discover in them,
" and to develop, a relation of congruence or of conflic-
" tion ; that is, we endeavour to find out whether these
" thoughts will or will not coincide—may or may not
" be blended into one.   If they coincide, we judge, we
" enounce, their congruence or compatibility : if they do
" not coincide, we judge, we enounce, their confliction
" or incompatibility.   Thus, if we compare the thoughts,
" *water, iron*, and *rusting*, find them congruent, and
" connect them into a single thought, thus—*water rusts
" iron*—in that case we form a judgment.

" But if two notions be judged congruent, in other
" words, be conceived as one, this their unity can only
" be realised in consciousness, inasmuch as one of these
" notions is viewed as an attribute or determination of
" the other.   For, on the one hand, it is impossible
" for us to think as one two attributes, that is, two
" things viewed as determining, and yet neither deter-
" mining or qualifying the other ; nor, on the other
" hand, two subjects, that is, two things thought as

* Lectures, iii. 226, 227.

"determined, and yet neither of them determined or
" qualified by the other."

In this regress from *ignotum* to *ignotius*, the next thing
to be ascertained is, what relation between one thought
and another is signified by the verb "to determine."
Such explanation as our author deemed it necessary
to give, may be found a few pages further back. He
there stated,* that by determining a notion, he means
adding on more characters, by each of which " we limit
" or determine more and more the abstract vagueness or
" extension of the notion ; until at last, if every attribute
" be annexed, the sum of attributes contained in the
" notion becomes convertible with the sum of attributes
" of which some concrete individual or reality is the com-
" plement."   Substituting, then, the definition for what
it defines, we find our author's opinion to be, that two
notions can only be congruent, that is, capable of being
blended into one, if we conceive one of them as adding
on additional attributes to the other.   This is not yet
very clear.   We must have recourse to his illustration.
" For example,† we cannot think the two attributes *elec-*
" *trical* and *polar* as a single notion, unless we convert
" the one of these attributes into a subject, to be deter-
" mined or qualified by the other."   Do we ever think
the two attributes electrical and polar as a single notion?
We think them as distinct parts of the same notion, that
is, as attributes which are constantly combined.   "But
" if we do,—if we say, *what is electrical is polar,* we at
" once reduce the duality to unity ; *we judge that*
" *polar is one of the constituent characters of the notion*
" *electrical, or that what is electrical is contained under*
" *the class of things, marked out by the common character*
" *of polarity.*"   The last italics are mine, intended to
mark the place where an intelligible meaning first
" emerges.   " We may,‡ therefore, articulately define a
" judgment or proposition to be the product of that act
" in which we pronounce that of two notions, thought

* Lectures, iii. 194.   † Ibid. p. 227.
‡ Ibid. p. 229.

2 D

"as subject and as predicate, *the one does or does not*
"*constitute a part of the other*, either in the quantity of
"Extension, or in the quantity of Comprehension."

This is Sir W. Hamilton's second theory of Judgment,
enunciated at a distance of exactly three pages from the
first, without the smallest suspicion on his part that they
are not one and the same. Yet they differ by the whole
interval which separates *a part of* from *along with*. According to the first theory, concepts are recognised as
congruent whenever they are not mutually repugnant;
when they are capable of being objectively realised along
with one another; when the attributes comprehended in
both of them can be simultaneously possessed by the
same object. According to the second theory, they are
only congruent when the one concept is actually a part
of the other. The only circumstance in which the two
theories resemble is, that both of them are unfolded out
of the vague expression "capable of being connected in
thought." They are, in fact, two different and conflicting
interpretations of that expression. How irreconcilable
they are, is apparent when we descend to particulars.
Krug's examples, learning and virtue, beauty and riches,
&c., are congruent in the first sense, since they are attributes which can be thought as existing together in the
same subject. But is the concept learning a part of the
concept virtue, the concept beauty a part of the concept
riches, or *vice versâ?* Sir W. Hamilton would scarcely
affirm that they are in a relation of part and whole in
Comprehension; and such relation as they have in Extension is not a relation between the concepts, but between the aggregates of real things of which they are
predicable. One of those aggregates might be part of
the other, though it is not; but one of the concepts can
never be part of the other. No one can ever find the
notion beauty in the notion riches, nor conversely.

Our author having thus gently slid back into the common Conceptualist theory of judgment, that it consists in
recognising the identity or non-identity of two notions,
adheres to it thenceforward with as much consistency

as we need ever expect to find in him. We may consider as his final theory of Judgment, on which his subsequent logical speculations are built, that a judgment is a recognition in thought, a proposition a statement in words, that one notion is or is not a part of another. He makes use of the word notion (doubtless) to include the case in which either of the terms of the proposition is singular. The two notions, one of which is recognised as being or not being a part of the other, may be either Concepts, that is, General Notions, or one of them may be a mental representation of an individual object.

The first objection which, I think, must occur to any one, on the contemplation of this definition, is that it omits the main and characteristic element of a judgment and of a proposition. Do we never judge or assert anything but our mere notions of things? Do we not make judgments and assert propositions respecting actual things? A Concept is a mere creation of the mind: it is the mental representation formed within us of a phenomenon; or rather, it is a part of that mental representation, marked off by a sign, for a particular purpose. But when we judge or assert, there is introduced a new element, that of objective reality, and a new mental fact, Belief. Our judgments, and the assertions which express them, do not enunciate our mere mode of mentally conceiving things, but our conviction or persuasion that the facts as conceived actually exist: and a theory of Judgments and Propositions which does not take account of this, cannot be the true theory. In the words of Reid,[*] "I give the name of Judgment to every determination "of the mind concerning *what is true* or *what is false*. "This, I think, is what logicians, from the days of "Aristotle, have called judgment." And this is the very element which Sir W. Hamilton's definition omits from it.

I am aware that Sir W. Hamilton would have an apparent answer to this. He would, I suppose, reply, that the belief of actual reality, implied in assent to a proposi-

---

[*] Essays on the Intellectual Powers, Works, p. 415.

tion, is not left out of account, but brought to account
in another place.   The belief, he would say, is not
inherent in the judgment, but in the notions which are
the subject and predicate of the judgment; these being
either mental representations of real objects, which if
represented in the mind at all, must be represented as
real, or Concepts formed by a comparison of real objects,
which therefore exist in the mind as concepts of realities.
Accordingly, when we judge and make assertions respecting objects known to be imaginary, the judgments are
accompanied with no belief in any real existence except
that of the mental images; what our author calls the
" presentations of phantasy."   When, indeed, a judgment is formed or an assertion is made respecting
something imaginary which is supposed to be real, as for
instance concerning a ghost, there is a belief in the real
existence in more than the mental image; but this belief
is not anything superadded to the comparison of concepts; it already existed in the concepts; a ghost was
thought as something having a real existence.

This, at least, is what might be said in behalf of Sir
W. Hamilton, though he has not himself said it.   But
though it escapes from the objection against omitting the
element Belief from the definition of Judgment, it does
so by an entire inversion of the logical process of definition.   The element of Belief, or Reality, may indeed be
in the concepts; but it never could have got into the
concepts if it had not first been in the judgments by
which the concepts were constructed.   If the belief of
reality had been absent from those judgments originally,
it never could have come round to them through the
concepts.   Belief is an essential element in a judgment;
it may be either present or absent in a concept.   Our
author, and those who agree with him, postpone this part
of the subject until they are treating of the distinction
between True and False Propositions.   They then say,
that if the relation which is judged to exist between the
notions, exists between the corresponding realities, the
proposition is true, and if not, false.   But if the opera-

tion of forming a judgment or a proposition includes anything at all, it includes judging that the judgment or the proposition is true. The recognition of it as true is not only an essential part, but the essential element of it as a judgment; leave that out, and there remains a mere play of thought, in which no judgment is passed. It is impossible to separate the idea of Judgment from the idea of the truth of a judgment; for every judgment consists in judging something to be true. The element Belief, instead of being an accident which can be passed in silence, and admitted only by implication, constitutes the very difference between a judgment and any other intellectual fact, and it is contrary to all the laws of Definition to define Judgment by anything else. The very meaning of a judgment, or a proposition, is something which is capable of being believed or disbelieved; which can be true or false; to which it is possible to say yes or no. And though it cannot be believed until it has been conceived, or (in plain terms) understood, the real object of belief is not the concept, or any relation of the concept, but the fact conceived. That fact need not be an outward fact; it may be a fact of internal or mental experience. But even then the fact is one thing, the concept of it is another, and the judgment is concerning the fact, not the concept. The fact may be purely subjective, as that I dreamed something last night; but the judgment is not the cognition of a relation between the presentation *I* and the concept *having dreamed*, but the cognition of the real memory of a real event.

This first, and insuperable objection, the force of which will be seen more and more the further we proceed, is applicable to the Conceptualist doctrine of Judgment, howsoever expressed, and to Sir W. Hamilton's as one of the modes of expressing that doctrine. There are other objections special to Sir W. Hamilton's form of it.

In what I have called Sir W. Hamilton's first theory of judgment, we found him saying that the comparison, ending in a recognition of congruence or confliction, may be between " individual things " as well as between

concepts. But in his second theory, one at least of the
terms of comparison must be a concept. For a judgment, according to this theory, is "the product of that act
"in which we pronounce that of two notions, thought
"as subject and predicate, the one does or does not con-
"stitute a part of the other." Now a concept, that is,
a bundle of attributes, may be a part of another concept,
and may be a part of our mental image of an individual
object; but one notion of an individual object cannot
be a part of another notion of an individual object.
One object may be an integrant part of another, but
it cannot be a part in Comprehension or in Extension,
as these words are understood of a Concept. St. Paul's
is an integrant part of London, but neither an attribute
of it, nor an object of which it is predicable.

Since, therefore, a judgment, in Sir W. Hamilton's
second theory, is the recognition of the relation of part
and whole, either between two concepts, or between a
concept and an individual presentation; the theory supposes that the mind furnishes itself with concepts, or
general notions, before it begins to judge. Now this is
not only evidently false, but the contrary is asserted, in
the most decisive terms, by Sir W. Hamilton himself.
He affirms, and it is denied by nobody, that every Concept is built up by a succession of judgments. We
conceive an object mentally as having such and such an
attribute, because we have first judged that it has that
attribute in reality. Let us see what our author says on
this point in his Lectures on Metaphysics. He says that
there is a judgment involved in every mental act.

"The fourth * condition of consciousness, which may
"be assumed as very generally acknowledged, is that
"it involves judgment. A judgment is the mental act
"by which one thing is affirmed or denied of another.
"It may to some seem strange that consciousness, the
"simple and primary act of intelligence, should be a
"judgment, which philosophers in general" (including
Sir W. Hamilton in his second theory) "have viewed as

* Lectures, i. 204.

" a compound and derivative operation. This is, how-
" ever, altogether a mistake. A judgment is, as I shall
" hereafter show you, a simple act of mind, for every
" act of mind implies a judgment. Do we perceive or
" imagine without affirming, in the act, the external
" or internal existence of the object? Now these
" fundamental affirmations are the affirmations,—in
" other words, the judgments,—of consciousness."

And in a subsequent part of his Course : " You will *
" recollect that, when treating of Consciousness in general,
" I stated to you that consciousness necessarily involves
" a judgment; and as every act of mind is an act of
" consciousness, every act of mind, consequently, involves
" a judgment. A consciousness is necessarily the con-
" sciousness of a determinate something, and we cannot
" be conscious of anything without virtually affirming
" its existence, that is, judging it to be. Consciousness
" is thus primarily a judgment or affirmation of existence.
" Again, consciousness is not merely the affirmation of
" naked existence, but the affirmation of a certain quali-
" fied or determinate existence. We are conscious that
" we exist, only in and through our consciousness that
" we exist in this or that particular state—that we are
" so and so affected,—so and so active : and we are only
" conscious of this or that particular state of existence,
" inasmuch as we discriminate it as different from some
" other state of existence, of which we have been previously
" conscious and are now reminiscent; but such a dis-
" crimination supposes, in consciousness, the affirmation
" of the existence of one state of a specific character, and
" the negation of another. On this ground it was that
" I maintained, that consciousness necessarily involves,
" besides recollection, or rather a certain continuity of
" representation, also judgment and comparison; and
" consequently, that, *so far from comparison or judgment*
" *being a process always subsequent to the acquisition of*
" *knowledge through perception and self-consciousness,*
" *it is involved as a condition of the acquisitive process.*"

* Lectures, ii. 277, 278.

But if judgment is a comparison of two concepts, or of a concept and an individual object, and a recognition that one of them is a part of (or even merely congruent with) the other, it *must* be a process "always subsequent to the acquisition of knowledge," or, in other words, to the formation of Concepts. The theory of Judgment in the third volume of the Lectures, belongs to a different mode of thinking altogether from the theory of Consciousness in the first and second ; and when Sir W. Hamilton was occupied with either of them, he must have temporarily forgotten the other.

But in the third volume itself the same inconsistency is obtruded on us still more openly. We are there told in plain words,* "Both concepts and reasonings may be "reduced to judgments : for the act of judging, that is, "the act of affirming or denying one thing of another "in thought, is that in which the Understanding or "Faculty of comparison is essentially expressed. A "concept is a judgment : for, on the one hand, *it is* "*nothing but the result of a foregone judgment or series* "*of judgments fixed and recorded in a word,* a sign, and it "is only amplified by the annexation of a new attribute, "through a continuance of the same process. On the "other hand, as *a concept is thus the synthesis or com-* "*plexion, and the record, I may add, of one or more prior* "*acts of judgment,* it can, it is evident, be analysed into "these again ; every concept is, in fact, a judgment or "a fasciculus of judgments,—these judgments only not "explicitly developed in thought, and not formally "expressed in terms."

That the same philosopher should have written these words, and a little more than a hundred pages after should have defined a judgment as the result of a comparison of concepts, either between themselves, or with individual objects, is, I think, the very crown of the self-contradictions which we have found to be sown so thickly in Sir W. Hamilton's speculations. Coming from a thinker of such ability, it almost makes one despair

* Lectures, iii. 117.

of one's own intellect and that of mankind, and feel as if the attainment of truth on any of the more complicated subjects of thought were impossible.

It is necessary to renounce one of these theories or the other. Either a concept is not the "synthesis and record of one or more prior acts of judgment," or a judgment is not, at least in all cases, the recognition of a relation of which one or both of the terms are Concepts. The least that could be required of Sir W. Hamilton would be so to modify his doctrine as to admit two kinds of judgment: the one kind, that by which concepts are formed, the other that which succeeds their formation. When concepts have been formed, and we subsequently proceed to analyse them, then, he might say, we form judgments which recognise one concept as a whole, of which another is a part. But the judgments by which we constructed the concepts, and every subsequent judgment by which, to use his own words, we amplify them by the addition of a new attribute, have nothing to do with comparison of concepts: it is the Anschauungen, the intuitions, the presentations of experience, which we in this case compare and judge.*

Take, for instance, Sir W. Hamilton's own example of a judgment, "Water rusts iron:" and let us suppose this truth to be new to us. Is it not like a mockery to say with our author, that we know this truth by com-

---

* This mode of escape from contradiction is the one which has, in substance, been resorted to by Mr. Mansel. He distinguishes what he terms Psychological from what he denominates Logical judgments. Psychological judgments merely assert that some object of consciousness, either external or internal, is present : they "may be generally stated in the proposition, This is here." These are the only judgments which are implied in, and necessary to, the formation of Concepts : and these judgments, as they assert a matter of present consciousness, are necessarily true. "But the psychological judgment must not be confounded with the "logical. The former is the judgment of a relation between the conscious "subject and the immediate object of consciousness : the latter is the "judgment of a relation which two objects of thought bear to each "other. . . . The logical judgment necessarily contains two concepts, and "hence must be regarded as logically and chronologically posterior to the "conception, which requires one only." (Prolegomena Logica, pp. 53–56).
But the operation by which a concept is built up, supposes much more than a cognition of the present existence of a fact or facts of conscious-

paring " the *thoughts*, water, iron, and rusting?" Ought
he not to have said the *facts*, water, iron, and rusting?
and even then, is comparing the proper name for the
mental operation? We do not examine whether three
thoughts agree, but whether three outward facts coexist.
If we lived till doomsday we should never find the proposition that water rusts iron in our concepts, if we had
not first found it in the outward phenomena. The
proposition expresses a sequence, and what we call a
causation, not between our concepts, but between the
two sensible presentations of moistened iron and rust.
When we have already judged this sequence to exist outside us, that is, independently of our intellectual combinations, we know it, and once known, it may find its way
into our concepts. But we cannot elicit out of a concept any judgment which we have not first put into it;
which we have not consciously assented to, in the act of
forming the concept. Whenever, therefore, we form a new
judgment—judge a truth new to us—the judgment is not
a recognition of a relation between concepts, but of a
succession, a coexistence, or a similitude, between facts.

This is the smallest sacrifice on the part of Sir W.
Hamilton's theory of judgment which would satisfy
his theory of Consciousness. But when thus reconciled
with a part of his system with which it now conflicts, it
would not be the better founded. It might still be
chased from point to point, unable to make a stand anywhere. For let us next suppose, that the judgment is
not new; that the truth, Water rusts iron, is known to
us of old. When we again think of it, and think it

ness, and a judgment in the form, "This is here." It supposes the whole
process of comparing facts of consciousness, and recognising, or in other
words, judging, in what points they resemble. It implies that the mind,
in its "psychological" judgments, does to the Intuitions or Presentations
everything which it is supposed to do to the Concepts in the "logical"
ones. Consequently the distinction between Mr. Mansel's two kinds of
judgments is in their matter only, not in the mental operation, and is
therefore, as he would say, extra-logical; to which I will add, insignificant.
It will be shown in the text that there is no psychological difference
between the two, and that the discrimination of one class of judgments as
conversant with Presentations and another with Concepts, and the attribution to the latter class of the name of logical, are founded on a false theory.

as a truth, and assent to it, should we even then give a correct account of what passes in our mind, by calling this act of judgment a comparison of our thoughts—our concepts—our notions—of water, rust, and iron? We do not compare our artificial mental constructions, but consult our direct remembrance of facts. We call to mind that we have seen or learned from credible testimony, that when iron is long in contact with water, it rusts. The question is not one of notions, but of beliefs; belief of past and expectation of future presentations of sense. Of course it is psychologically true that when I believe, I have a notion of that which I believe; but the ultimate appeal is not to the notion, but to the presentation or intuition. If I am in any doubt, what is the question I ask myself? Is it—Do I think of, or figure to myself, water as rusting iron? or is it—Did I ever perceive, and have other people perceived, that water rusts iron? There are persons, no doubt, whose criterion of judgment is the relation between their own concepts, but these are not the persons whose judgments the world has usually found worth adopting. If the question between Copernicus and Ptolemy had depended on whether we *conceive* the earth moving and the sun at rest, or the sun moving and the earth at rest, I am afraid the victory would have been with Ptolemy.

But, again, even if judging were entirely a notional operation, consisting of the recognition of some relation between concepts, it remains to be proved that the relation is that of Whole and Part. Could it, even then, be said, that every judgment in which I predicate one thing of another, on the faith of previous judgments recorded, as our author says, in the concepts, consists in recognising that one of the concepts includes the other as a part of itself? When I judge that Socrates is mortal, or that all men are mortal, does the judgment consist in being conscious that my concept mortal is part of my representation of Socrates, or of my concept man?

This doctrine ignores the famous distinction, admitted, I suppose, in some shape or other, by all philosophers,

but most familiar to modern metaphysics in the form in
which it is stated by Kant—the distinction between
Analytical and Synthetical judgments. Analytical judgments are supposed to unfold the contents of a concept;
affirming explicitly of a class, attributes which were
already part of the corresponding concept, and may be
brought out into distinct consciousness by mere analysis
of it. Synthetical judgments, on the contrary, affirm of
a class, attributes which are not in the concept, and
which we therefore do not and cannot judge to be a part
of the concept, but only to be conjoined in fact with
the attributes composing the concept. This distinction,
though obtruded upon our author by many of the writers
with whom he was familiar, has so little in common with
his mode of thought, that he only slightly refers to it,
in a very few passages of his works: in one of these,
however,* he speaks of it as of something very important, expresses his preference for the terms Explicative
and Ampliative as names for it, and discusses, not the
distinction itself, but its history; apparently unconscious
that his own theory entirely does away with it. According to that, all judgments are analytical, or, as he prefers to say, explicative. Even giving up so much of his
theory as contradicts his own doctrine on the formation
of concepts, the part remaining would compel him to
maintain that all judgments which are not new are
analytical, and that synthetical judgments are limited to
truths, or supposed truths, which we learn for the first
time.

This discrepancy between our author and almost all
philosophers, even of his own general way of thinking
(including, among the rest, Mr. Mansel), arises from the
fact, that he understands by concept something different
from what they have usually understood by it. The
concept of a class, in Sir W. Hamilton's acceptation of
the term, includes all the attributes which we have
judged, and still judge, to be common to the whole class.
It means, in short, our entire knowledge of the class.

* Dissertations on Reid, pp. 787, 788.

But, with philosophers in general, the concept of the class as such,—my concept of man, for example, as distinguished from my mental representation of an individual man,—includes, not all the attributes which I ascribe to man, but such of them only as the classification is grounded on, and as are implied in the meaning of the name. Man is a living being, or Man is rational, they would call analytical judgments, because the attributes of life and rationality are of the number of those which are already given in the concept Man: but Man is mortal, they would account synthetical, because, familiar as the fact is, it is not already affirmed in the very name Man, but has to be superadded in the predicate.

It is quite lawful for a philosopher (though seldom prudent) to alter the meaning of a word, provided he gives fair notice of his intention; but he is bound, if he does so, to remain consistent with himself in the new meaning, and not to transfer to it propositions which are only true in the old. This condition Sir W. Hamilton does not observe. It often happens that different opinions of his belong to different and inconsistent systems of thought apparently through his retaining from former writers some doctrine, the grounds of which he has, by another doctrine, subverted. His whole theory of Concepts being infected by an inconsequence of this description, the retention of all the Conceptualist conclusions along with Nominalist premises, it is no wonder if further oversights of the same kind meet us in every part of the details. The following is one of the most palpable. As we just mentioned, the concept of a class in our author's sense, includes all the attributes of the class, so far as the thinker is acquainted with them; the whole of the thinker's knowledge of the class. This is Sir W. Hamilton's own doctrine; but along with it he retains a doctrine belonging to the other meaning of Concept, which I have contrasted with his. "The* "exposition of the Comprehension of a notion is called

* Lectures iii. 143.

" its Definition :" and again * " Definition is the analysis
" of a complex concept into its component parts or
" attributes." But a thing is not analysed into its component parts if any of the parts are left out. The two
opinions taken together lead, therefore, to the remarkable consequence, that the definition of a class ought to
include the whole of what is known of the class. Those
who mean by the concept not all known attributes of
the class, but such only as are included in the connotation of the name, may be permitted to say of a Definition that it is the analysis of the concept : but to Sir W.
Hamilton this was not permissible. To crown the inconsistency, he still presents † the stock example, Man
is a rational animal, as a good definition, and a typical
specimen of what a Definition is ; as if the notions
animal and rational exhausted the whole of the concept
Man, according to his meaning of Concept—the entire
sum of the attributes common to the class. It would
hardly be believed, prior to a minute examination of his
writings, how much vagueness of thought, leading to
the unsuspecting admission of opposite doctrines in the
same breath, lurks under the specious appearance of
philosophical precision which distinguishes him.‡

To return, from Sir W. Hamilton's self-contradictions,
to the merits of the question itself ; the word Judgment,
by universal consent, is coextensive with the word Proposition : a Judgment must be so defined that a Proposition shall be the expression of it in words. Now, if
a Judgment expresses a relation between Concepts (which

---

* Lectures, iii. 151.   † Ibid., pp. 143, 144.

‡ In his non-recognition of the difference between Analytical and
Synthetical judgments, it is already implied that he never recognises the
Connotation of Names ; which in itself is enough to vitiate his whole
logical system, and is a great point of inferiority in him to the best
Conceptualist thinkers, who do recognise it, though in a misleading
phraseology. To the same cause may be ascribed the extremely vulgar
character of the explanation of some of the leading metaphysical terms,
in his eighth Lecture. For example, the distinction between essential and
accidental qualities he defines thus—that the essential qualities of a thing
are those "which it cannot lose without ceasing to be." This, which is a
retrogression from Conceptualism to Realism, does but prove that he

for the purpose of the present discussion I have conceded) the corresponding Proposition represents that
same relation by means of names : the names, therefore,
must be signs of the concepts, and the concepts must be
the meaning of the names. To make this tenable, the
Concept must be so construed as to consist of those
attributes only which are connoted by the name. Cor-
poreity, life, rationality, and any other attributes of man
which are part of the meaning of the word, insomuch
that where those attributes were not, we should with-
hold the name of man—these are part of the concept. But mortality, and all the other human attributes
which are the subject of treatises either on the human
body or on human nature, are not in the concept, because we do not affirm them of any individual by merely
calling him a man ; they are so much additional knowledge. The concept Man is not the sum of all the
attributes of a man, but only of the essential attributes
—of those which constitute him a man; in other words,
those on which the class Man is grounded, and which
are connoted by the name—what used to be called the
essence of Man, that without which Man cannot be, or
in other words, would not be what he is called. Without mortality, or without thirty-two teeth, he would
still be called a man : we should not say, This is not a
man ; we should say, This man is not mortal, or has
fewer than thirty-two teeth.

Instead, therefore, of saying with Sir W. Hamilton,
that the attributes composing the concept of the predicate are part of those which compose the concept of the

simply transcribed his definition from the Realistic Schoolmen. In a
later part of his Lectures (iv. 11) he, *more suo*, forgets this definition, and
replaces it by one of his own ; but in this second definition he betrays
that he never saw the genuine meaning which lay under the distinction,
so badly expressed by the schoolmen in the language of a false system.
Sir W. Hamilton, in distinguishing Essential from Unessential properties,
means only the difference between attributes of the whole genus, and
those confined to some of its species. Sir W. Hamilton's knowledge of
the scholastic writings was extraordinary ; but many students of them who
had not a tithe of that knowledge, have brought back and appropriated
much more of the important materials for thought which those writings
abundantly contain.

subject, we ought to say, they are either a part, or are
invariably conjoined with them, not in our conception,
but in fact. Propositions in which the concept of the
predicate is part of the concept of the subject, or, to express ourselves more philosophically, in which the attributes connoted by the predicate are part of those connoted by the subject, are a kind of Identical Propositions : they convey no information, but at most remind
us of what, if we understood the word which is the
subject of the proposition, we knew as soon as the
word was pronounced. Propositions of this kind are
either definitions, or parts of definitions. These judgments are analytical : they analyse the connotation of
the subject-name, and predicate separately the different
attributes which the name asserts collectively.   All
other affirmative judgments are synthetical, and affirm
that some attribute or set of attributes is, not a part of
those connoted by the subject-name, but an invariable
accompaniment of them.[*]

There remains something to be said on another very
prominent feature in Sir W. Hamilton's theory of Judgment. Having said, that in every judgment we compare "two notions, thought as subject and predicate,"

<hr />

[*] This is perfectly understood by Mr. Mansel, who says (Prolegomena
Logica, p. 58), "When I assert that A is B, I do not mean that the
"attributes constituting the concept A are identical with those constituting
"the concept B, for this is only true in identical judgments ; but that the
"object in which the one set of attributes is found, is the same as that in
"which the other is found. To assert that all philosophers are liable to
"error is not to assert that the signification of the term *philosopher* is
"identical with that of *liable to error;* but that the attributes compre-
"hended in these two distinct terms are in some manner united in the
"same subject." What Mr. Mansel here enunciates distinctly, was contained, though less distinctly, in Sir W. Hamilton's first theory of judgment, especially as he illustrated it from Krug. In adhering to that first
theory, as well as in limiting the concept to the attributes connoted by the
name—for that limitation clearly results from his definition of a Concept
(p. 60), in combination with other passages—Mr. Mansel, as it appears to
me, is much nearer the truth than Sir W. Hamilton ; and would perhaps
be nearer still, if he were not entangled in the meshes of the Hamiltonian
phraseology.
    An example how that phraseology controls him, in his strange assertion
(pp. 184, 185) that every concept "must contain a plurality of attributes "
as a condition of its conceivability ; for a simple idea, like a *summum genus,*

and pronounce that "the one does or does not constitute a part of the other," he adds, "either in the
quantity of Extension, or in the quantity of Comprehension."* He develops this distinction as follows : †—

"If the subject or determined notion be viewed as the
"containing whole, we have an Intensive or Compre-
"hensive proposition; if the Predicate or determining
"notion be viewed as the containing whole, we have an
"Extensive proposition. . . . The relation of subject
"and predicate is contained within that of whole and
"part, for we can always view either the determining
"or the determined notion as the whole which contains
"the other. The whole, however, which the subject
"constitutes, and the whole which the predicate consti-
"tutes, are different, being severally determined by the
"opposite quantities of comprehension and of extension;
"and as subject and predicate necessarily stand to each
"other in the relation of these inverse quantities, it is
"manifestly a matter of indifference, in so far as the
"meaning is concerned, whether we view the subject as
"the whole of comprehension which contains the predi-

is by itself inconceivable." Inconceivable it truly is, but not in any sense
in which conceivability is required of a concept : only in the sense of not
being conceivable separately. "Simple ideas are never conceived as such,
but only as forming parts of a complex object;" in other words, they are
inconceivable in the sense in which, according to Sir W. Hamilton's
doctrine and Mr. Mansel's own, all concepts are inconceivable.

From a similar entanglement, although his account of Definition and
Division is decidedly better than Sir W. Hamilton's, he follows that philosopher in treating the latter logical operation as a division of the Concept :
as if the concept were divided by dividing the things which it is predicable
of (pp. 191–194).

Dr. M'Cosh thinks (p. 294) that there are judgments (other than those
in which the predicates are proper names) which do not affirm or deny
attributes, viz. those in which we compare what he terms "mere Abstracts."
"We cannot call such attributive; thus, there would be no propriety in
"saying that 4 is an attribute of 2+2." But is not *making* 4, an attribute
of 2+2? Further on (p. 333) he says, that the predicate in this class of
propositions "has no quantity or extension, for it is not a class notion.
"When we say that 3×3=9, neither subject nor predicate has an in-
"definite number of objects embraced in it." The objects embraced in 9
are nine apples, nine marbles, nine hours, nine miles, and all the other
aggregations of which nine can be predicated. Every numeral is the
name of a class, and a most comprehensive class, consisting of things of
all imaginable qualities. And the same observation applies to 3 × 3.

* Lectures, iii. 229.   † Ibid. pp. 231–233.

2 E

" cate or the predicate, as the whole of extension which
" contains the subject. In point of fact, in single pro-
" positions it is rarely apparent which of the two wholes
" is meant; for the copula *is, est,* &c., equally denotes
" the one form of the relation or the other. Thus, in the
" proposition *man is two-legged,*—the copula here is con-
" vertible with *comprehends or contains in it,* for the pro-
" position means *man contains in it two-legged,* that is,
" the subject *man* as an intensive whole or complex
" notion, comprehends as a part the predicate *two-legged.*
" Again, in the proposition, *man is a biped,* the copula
" corresponds to *contained under,* for this proposition is
" tantamount to *man is contained under biped,*—that is,
" the predicate *biped,* as an extensive whole or class,
" contains under it as a part the subject *man.* But in
" point of fact, neither of the two propositions unam-
" biguously shows whether it is to be viewed as of an
" intensive or of an extensive purport; nor in a single
" proposition is this of any moment. All that can be
" said is that the one form of expression is better accom-
" modated to express the one kind of proposition, the
" other better accommodated to express the other. It is
" only when propositions are connected into syllogisms,
" that it becomes evident whether the subject or the
" predicate be the whole in or under which the other
" is contained; and it is only as thus constituting two
" different—two contrasted, forms of reasoning—forms
" the most general, as under each of these every other
" is included,—that the distinction becomes necessary
" in regard to concepts and propositions."

I shall not insist on such of the objections to this
passage as have been sufficiently stated; the impropriety,
for instance, of saying that the notion Man *contains* the
predicate two-legged, when that attribute is evidently
not part of the signification of the word; or that the
meaning of a proposition is, that an attribute is part
of a notion: which the first time it is observed, it cannot
possibly be, and at no time is this the thing asserted by
a proposition, unless by those which are avowedly defini-

tions. All these considerations I at present forego : and I will even give our author's theory its necessary correction, by restoring to Propositions the alternative meaning which belongs to them, namely, that a certain attribute is *either* part of a given set of attributes, or invariably coexists with them. Having thus dissociated the doctrine in the quotation from all errors which are incidental and not essential to it, we may state it as follows :—Every proposition is capable of being understood in two meanings, which involve one another, inasmuch as if either of them is true the other is so, but which are nevertheless different ; of which only one may be, and commonly is, in the mind ; and the words used do not always show which. Thus, All men are bipeds, may either mean, that the objects called men are all of them numbered among the objects called bipeds, which is interpreting the proposition in Extension ; or that the attribute of having two feet is one of, or coexists with, the attributes which compose the notion Man : which is interpreting the proposition in Comprehension.

I maintain, that these two supposed meanings of the proposition are not two matters of fact or of thought, reciprocally inferrible from one another, but one and the same fact, written in different ways ; that the supposed meaning in Extension is not a meaning at all, until interpreted by the meaning in Comprehension ; that all concepts and general names which enter into Propositions, require to be construed in Comprehension, and that their Comprehension is the whole of their meaning.

That the meaning in Extension follows if the meaning in Comprehension is granted, is a point which both sides are agreed in. If the attribute signified by biped is either one of, or always conjoined with, the attributes signified by man, we are entitled to assert that the class Man is included in, is a part of, the class Biped. But my position is, that this second assertion is not a conclusion from, but a mere repetition of, the first. For what is the second assertion, if we leave out of it all reference to the attributes ? It can then only mean, that we have

ascertained the fact independently of the attributes—that
is, that we have examined the aggregate whole "all men,"
and the still greater aggregate whole "all bipeds," and
that all the former were found among the latter. Now,
do we assert this? or would it be true? Assuredly no
one of us ever represented or contemplated, even with
his mind's eye, either of these wholes : still less did we
ever compare them as realities, and ascertain that the
fact is as stated. Neither could this be done, by anything
short of infinite power : for all men and all bipeds, except a comparatively few, have either ceased to exist, or
have not yet come into existence. What, then, do we
mean by making an assertion concerning all men? The
phrase does not mean, all and each of a certain great number of objects, known or represented individually. It
means, all and each of an unascertained and indefinite
number, mostly not known or represented at all, but
which if they came within our opportunities of knowledge, might be recognised by the possession of a certain
set of attributes, namely, those forming the connotation
of the word. "All men," and "the class man," are
expressions which point to nothing but attributes ; they
cannot be interpreted except in comprehension. To say,
all men are bipeds, is merely to say, given the attributes
of man, that of being a biped will be found along with
them ; which is the meaning in Comprehension. If the
proposition has nothing to do with the concept Man
except as to its comprehension, still less has it with the
concept Biped. When I say, All men are bipeds, what
has my assertion to do with the class biped as to its
Extension? Have I any concern with the remainder of
the class, after Man is subtracted from it? Am I necessarily aware even whether there is any remainder at all?
I am thinking of no such matter, but only of the attribute two-footed, and am intending to predicate that. I am
thinking of it as an attribute of man, but of what else
it may happen to be an attribute does not concern me.
Thus, all propositions into which general names enter,
and consequently all reasonings, are in Comprehension

only. Propositions and Reasonings may be written in
Extension, but they are always understood in Comprehension. The only exception is in the case of propositions which have no meaning in Comprehension, and
have nothing to do with Concepts—those of which both
the subject and the predicate are proper names; such
as, Tully is Cicero, or, St. Peter is not St. Paul. These
words connote nothing, and the only meaning they
have is the individual whom they *de*note. But where a
meaning in Comprehension, or, in other words, in Connotation, is possible, that is always the one intended.
And Sir W. Hamilton's distinction (though he lays
great stress on it) between Reasoning in Comprehension
and Reasoning in Extension, will be found (as we shall
see hereafter) to be a mere superfetation on Logic.

It is worth while to add, that even could it be admitted
that general propositions have a meaning in Extension
capable of being conceived as different from their meaning in Comprehension, Sir W. Hamilton would still be
wrong in deeming that the recognition of this meaning
depends on, or can possibly result from, a comparison of
the Concepts. The Extension of a concept, as I have
before remarked, is not, like the Comprehension, intrinsic
and essential to the concept; it is an external and wholly
accidental relation of the concept, and no contemplation
or analysis of the concept itself will tell us anything
about it. It is an abstract name for the aggregate of
objects possessing the attributes included in the concept:
and whether that aggregate is greater or smaller does
not depend on any properties of the concept, but on the
boundless productive powers of Nature.

CHAPTER XIX.

OF REASONING.

IN common with the majority of modern writers on Logic, whose language is generally that of the Conceptualist school, Sir W. Hamilton considers Reasoning, as he considers Judgment, to consist in a comparison of Notions : either of Concepts with one another, or of Concepts with the mental representations of individual objects. Only, in simple Judgment, two notions are compared immediately ; in Reasoning, mediately. Reasoning is the comparison of two notions by means of a third. As thus : * "Reasoning is an act of mediate Comparison "or Judgment; for to reason is to recognise that two "notions stand to each other in the relation of a whole "and its parts, through a recognition that those notions "severally stand in the same relation to a third." The foundation, therefore, of all Reasoning is "the self-evi- "dent † principle that a part of the part is a part of the "whole." "Without ‡ reasoning we should have been "limited to a knowledge of what is given by immediate "intuition ; we should have been unable to draw any "inference from this knowledge, and have been shut "out from the discovery of that countless multitude of "truths, which, though of high, of paramount impor- "tance, are not self-evident." This recognition that we discover a "countless multitude of truths," composing a vast proportion of all our real knowledge, by mere reasoning, will be found to jar considerably with our author's theory of the reasoning process, and with his whole view of the nature and functions of Logic, the science of

---

* Lectures, iii. 274.   † Ibid. p. 271.   ‡ Ibid. p. 277.

Reasoning: but this inconsistency is common to him with nearly all the writers on Logic, because, like him, they teach a theory of the science too small and narrow to contain their own facts.

Notwithstanding the great number of philosophers who have considered the definition cited above to be a correct account of Reasoning, the objections to it are so manifest, that until after much meditation on the subject, one can scarcely prevail on oneself to utter them : so impossible does it seem that difficulties so obvious should always be passed over unnoticed, unless they admitted of an easy answer. Reasoning, we are told, is a mode of ascertaining that one notion is a part of another; and the use of reasoning is to enable us to discover truths which are not self-evident. But how is it possible that a truth, which consists in one notion being part of another, should not be self-evident? The notions, by supposition, are both of them in our mind. To perceive what parts they are composed of, nothing surely can be necessary but to fix our attention on them. We cannot surely concentrate our consciousness on two ideas in our own mind, without knowing with certainty whether one of them as a whole includes the other as a part. If we have the notion biped and the notion man, and know what they are, we must know whether the notion of a biped is part of the notion we form to ourselves of a man. In this case the simply Introspective method is in its place. We cannot need to go beyond our consciousness of the notions themselves.

Moreover, if it were really the case that we can compare two notions and fail to discover whether one of them is a part of the other, it is impossible to understand how we could be enabled to accomplish this by comparing each of them with a third. A, B, and C, are three concepts, of which we are supposed to know that A is a part of B, and B of C, but until we put these two propositions together we do not know that A is a part of C. We have perceived B in C intuitively, by direct comparison: but what is B? By supposition it is, and is

perceived to be, A and something more. We have therefore, by direct intuition, perceived that A and something
more is a part of C, without perceiving that A is a part
of C. Surely there is here a great psychological difficulty to be got over, to which logicians of the Conceptualist school have been surprisingly blind.

Endeavouring, not to understand what they say, for
they never face the question, but to imagine what they
might say, to relieve this apparent absurdity, two things
occur to the mind. It may be said, that when a notion is
in our consciousness, but we do not know whether something is or is not a part of it, the reason is that we have
forgotten some of its parts. We possess the notion, but
are only conscious of part of it, and it does its work in
our trains of thought only symbolically. Or, again, it
may be said that all the parts of the notion are in our
consciousness, but are in our consciousness indistinctly.
The meaning of having a distinct notion, according to Sir
W. Hamilton, is that we can discriminate the characters
or attributes of which it is composed. The admitted
fact, therefore, that we can have indistinct notions, may
be adduced as proof that we can possess a notion, and
not be able to say positively what is included in it.
These are the best, or rather the only presentable arguments I am able to invent, in support of the paradox involved in the Conceptualist theory of Reasoning.

It is a great deal easier to refute these arguments
than it was to discover them. The refutation, like the
original difficulty, is two deep. To begin; a notion,
part of which has been forgotten, is to that extent a lost
notion, and is as if we had never had it. The parts
which we can no longer discern in it are not in it, and
cannot therefore be proved to be in it, by reasoning, any
more than by intuition. We may be able to discover by
reasoning that they ought to be there, and may, in consequence, put them there; but that is not recognising
them to be there already. As a notion in part forgotten
is a partially lost notion, so an indistinct notion is a
notion not yet formed, but in process of formation. We

have an indistinct notion of a class when we perceive
in a general way that certain objects differ from others,
but do not as yet perceive in what; or perceive some
of the points of difference, but have not yet perceived,
or have not yet generalised, the others. In this case
our notion is not yet a completed notion, and the parts
which we cannot discern in it, are undiscernible because
they are not yet there. As in the former case, the
result of reasoning may be to put them there; but it
certainly does not affect this by proving them to be
there already.

But even if these explanations had solved the mystery
of our being conscious of a whole and unable to be
directly conscious of its part, they would yet fail to make
intelligible how, not having this knowledge directly, we
are able to acquire it through a third notion. By hypothesis we have forgotten that A is a part of C, until we
again become aware of it through the relation of each
of them to B. We therefore had not forgotten that A
is a part of B, nor that B is a part of C. When we
conceived B, we conceived A as a part of it; when we
conceived C, we conceived B as a part of it. In the
mere fact, therefore, of conceiving C, we were conscious
of B in it, and consciousness of A is a necessary part
of that consciousness of B, and yet our consciousness
of C did not enable us to find in it our consciousness
of A, though it was really there, and though they both
were distinctly present. If any one can believe this,
no contradiction and no impossibility in any theory of
Consciousness need stagger him. Let us now substitute for the hypothesis of forgetfulness, the hypothesis
of indistinctness. We had a notion of C, which was
so indistinct that we could not discriminate A from the
other parts of the notion. But it was not too indistinct to enable us to discriminate B, otherwise the
reasoning would break down as well as the intuition.
The notion of B, again, indistinct as it may have been
in other respects, must have been such that we could
with assurance discriminate A as contained in it. Here

then returns the same absurdity : A is distinctly present in B, which is distinctly present in C, therefore A, if there be any force in reasoning, is distinctly present in C ; yet A cannot be discriminated or perceived in the consciousness in which it is distinctly present : so that, before our reasoning commenced, we were at once distinctly conscious of A, and entirely unconscious of it. There is no such thing as a reduction to absurdity if this is not one.

The reason why a judgment which is not intuitively evident, can be arrived at through the medium of premises, is that judgments which are not intuitively evident do not consist in recognising that one notion is part of another. When that is the case, the conclusion is as well known to us *ab initio* as the premises ; which is really the case in analytical judgments. When reasoning really leads to the "countless multitudes of truths" not self-evident, which our author speaks of—that is, when the judgments are synthetical—we learn, not that A is part of C, because A is part of B and B of C, but that A is conjoined with C, because A is conjoined with B, and B with C. The principle of the reasoning is not, a part of the part is a part of the whole, but, a mark of the mark is a mark of the thing marked, *Nota notæ est nota rei ipsius*. It means, that two things which constantly coexist with the same third thing, constantly coexist with one another ; the things meant not being our concepts, but the facts of experience on which our concepts ought to be grounded.

This theory of reasoning is free from the objections which are fatal to the Conceptualist theory. We cannot discover that A is a part of C through its being a part of B, since if it really is so, the one truth must be as much a matter of direct consciousness as the other. But we can discover that A is conjoined with C through its being conjoined with B ; since our knowledge that it is conjoined with B, may have been obtained by a series of observations in which C was not perceptible. C, we must remember, stands for an attribute, that is, not an actual presentation of sense, but a power of producing such presentations : and that a power may have been present without being apparent, is in the common course of things, implying nothing more than that the conditions necessary to determine it into act were not all present. This power or potentiality, C, may in like manner have been ascertained to be conjoined with B, by another set of observations, in which it was A's turn to be dormant, or perhaps to be active, but not attended to. By combining the two sets of observations, we are enabled to discover what was not contained in either of them, namely, a constancy of conjunction between C and A, such that one of them comes to be a mark of the other : though, in neither of the two sets of observations, nor in any others, may C and A have been actually observed together ; or, if observed, not with the frequency, or under the experimental conditions, which would warrant us in generalising the fact. This is the process by which we do, in reality, acquire the greater part of our knowledge ; all of it (as our author says) which is not " given by immediate intuition." But no part of this process is at all like the operation of recognising parts and a whole ; or of recognising any relation whatever between Concepts ; which have nothing to do with the matter, more than is implied in the fact, that we cannot reason about things without conceiving them, or representing them to the mind.

The theory which supposes Judgment and Reasoning to be the comparison of concepts, is obliged to make the term concept stand for, not the thinker's or reasoner's own notion of a thing, but a sort of normal notion, which is understood as being owned by everybody, though everybody does not always use it ; and it is this tacit substitution of a concept floating in the air for the very concept I have in my own mind, which makes it possible to fancy that we can, by reasoning, find out something to be in a concept, which we are not able to discover in it by consciousness, because, in truth, *that* concept is not in our consciousness. But a concept of a thing, which is not that whereby I conceive it, is to

me as much an external fact, as a presentation of the
senses can be : it is another person's concept, not mine.
It may be the conventional concept of the world at
large—that which it has been tacitly agreed to associate
with the class ; in other words, it may be the connotation of the class-name ; and if so, it may very possibly
contain elements which I cannot directly recognise in it,
but may have to learn from external evidence : but this
is because I do not know the signification of the word,
the attributes which determine its application—and
what I have to do is to learn them : when I have done
this, I shall have no difficulty in directly recognising as
a part of them, anything which really is so.   But with
regard to all attributes not included in the signification
of the name, not only I do not find them in the concept,
but they do not even become part of it after I have
learnt them by experience ; unless we understand by
the concept, not, with philosophers in general, only
the essence of the class, but with Sir W. Hamilton, all
its known attributes.   Even in Sir W. Hamilton's sense,
they are not found in the concept, but added to it ; and
not until we have already assented to them as objective
facts—subsequently, therefore, to the reasoning by
which they were ascertained.

Take such a case as this.   Here are two properties
of circles.   One is, that a circle is bounded by a line,
every point of which is equally distant from a certain
point within the circle.   This attribute is connoted by
the name, and is, on both theories, a part of the concept.   Another property of the circle is, that the length
of its circumference is to that of its diameter in the
approximate ratio of 3·14159 to 1.   This attribute was
discovered, and is now known, as a result of reasoning.
Now, is there any sense, consistent with the meaning
of the terms, in which it can be said that this recondite
property formed part of the concept circle, before it had
been discovered by mathematicians ?   Even in Sir W.
Hamilton's meaning of concept, it is in nobody's but a
mathematician's concept even now : and if we concede

that mathematicians are to determine the normal concept of a circle for mankind at large, mathematicians themselves did not find the ratio of the diameter to the circumference in the concept, but put it there; and could not have done so until the long train of difficult reasoning which culminated in the discovery was complete.

It is impossible, therefore, rationally to hold both the opinions professed simultaneously by Sir W. Hamilton —that Reasoning is the comparison of two notions through the medium of a third, and that Reasoning is a source from which we derive new truths. And the truth of the latter proposition being indisputable, it is the former which must give way. The theory of Reasoning which attempts to unite them both, has the same defect which we have shown to vitiate the corresponding theory of Judgment: it makes the process consist in eliciting something out of a concept which never was in the concept, and if it ever finds its way there, does so after the process, and as a consequence of its having taken place.

CHAPTER XX.

ON SIR WILLIAM HAMILTON'S CONCEPTION OF LOGIC AS
A SCIENCE. IS LOGIC THE SCIENCE OF THE LAWS,
OR FORMS, OF THOUGHT?

HAVING discussed the nature of the three psychological
processes which, together, constitute the operations of
the Intellect, and having considered Sir W. Hamilton's
theory of each, we are in a condition to examine the
general view which he takes of the Science or Art, whose
purpose it is to direct our intellectual operations into
their proper course, and to protect them against error.

Sir W. Hamilton defines Logic "the Science of the
Laws of Thought as Thought."* He proceeds to
justify each of the component parts of this definition.
And first, is Logic a Science?

Archbishop Whately says that it is both a Science
and an Art. He says this is an intelligible sense. He
means that Logic both determines what is, and prescribes what should be. It investigates the nature of the
process which takes place in Reasoning, and lays down
rules to enable that process to be conducted as it ought.
For this distinction, Sir W. Hamilton is very severe on
Archbishop Whately. In the Archbishop's sense of
the words, he says, it never has been, and never could
have been, disputed that Logic is both a Science and an
Art. But † "the discrimination of art and science is
"wrong. Dr. Whately considers science to be any know-
"ledge viewed absolutely, and not in relation to practice,
"—a signification in which every art would, in its doc-

* Lectures, iii. 4.
† Ibid. p. 11 ; see also Discussions, pp. 133, 134.

"trinal part, be a science; and he defines art to be
"the application of knowledge to practice, in which
"sense Ethics, Politics, and all practical sciences, would
"be arts. The distinction of arts and sciences is thus
"wrong. But . . . were the distinction correct it
"would be of no value, for it would distinguish
"nothing, since art and science would mark out no
"real difference between the various branches of know-
"ledge, but only different points of view under which
"the same branch might be contemplated by us,—each
"being in different relations at once a science and an
"art. In fact, Dr. Whately confuses the distinction
"of science theoretical and science practical with the
"distinction of science and art."

But if the difference between science and art is not
the same as that between knowledge theoretical and
practical, we are entitled to ask, what is it? If Archbishop Whately has placed the distinction where it is
not, does his rather peremptory critic and censor tell us
where it is? He declines the problem. " I am well
"aware that it would be no easy matter to give a gene-
"ral definition of science as contradistinguished from
"art, and of art as contradistinguished from science;
"but if the words themselves cannot validly be discri-
"minated, it would be absurd to attempt to discriminate
"anything by them." In the only other part of his
Lectures where the distinction between Art and Science
is touched on,* he says that the "apparently vague
"and capricious manner in which the terms art and
"science are applied," is not "the result of some acci-
"dental and forgotten usage," but is founded on a
"rational principle which we are able to trace." But
when the reader is expecting a statement of this rational
principle, Sir W. Hamilton puts him off with a merely
historical explanation. Without stating what the usage
actually is, he derives it from a distinction drawn by
Aristotle between "a habit productive," and "a habit
practical," which he admits to be "not perhaps beyond

* Lectures, i. 115–119.

the reach of criticism : " which he does not undertake to
" vindicate," and which he confesses to have been lost
sight of by the moderns ever since they ceased to think
" mechanical " arts " beneath their notice," all these
being called arts without any reference to Aristotle's
supposed criterion.* So that Sir W. Hamilton cannot
claim even accordance with usage for the distinction
which he seems, but does not distinctly profess, to
patronise. Yet the principal fault he finds with Archbishop Whately's distinction, is that it does not agree
with usage. According to it, he says, † " ethics, politics,
" religion, and all other practical sciences would be
" arts : " and he speaks of the " incongruity we feel in
" talking of the art of Ethics, the art of Religion, &c.,
" though these are eminently practical sciences." ‡

Religion may be here placed out of the question, for
if there be incongruity with common feelings in calling

---

* I give the Aristotelian distinction in Sir W. Hamilton's words : " In
" the Aristotelic philosophy the terms πρᾶξις and πρακτικός, that is, *practice*
" and *practical*,—were employed both in a generic or looser, and in a
" special or stricter signification. In its generic meaning, πρᾶξις, *practice*,
" was opposed to theory or speculation, and it comprehended under it,
" practice in its special meaning, and another co-ordinate term to which
" practice, in this its stricter signification, was opposed. This term was
" ποίησις, which we may inadequately translate by *production*. The dis-
" tinction of πρακτικός and ποιητικός consisted in this : the former denoted
" that action which terminated in action,—the latter, that action which
" resulted in some permanent product. For example, dancing and music
" are practical, as leaving no work after their performance : whereas
" painting and statuary are productive, as leaving some product over and
" above their energy. Now Aristotle, in formally defining art, defines
" it as a habit productive, and not as a habit practical, ἕξις ποιητικὴ μετὰ
" λόγου ; and though he has not always himself adhered strictly to this limi-
" tation, his definition was adopted by his followers, and the term in its
" application to the practical sciences (the term practical being here used in
" its genuine meaning), came to be exclusively confined to those whose end
" did not result in mere action or energy. Accordingly as Ethics, Politics,
" &c., proposed happiness as their end, and as happiness was an energy,
" or at least the concomitant of energy, these sciences terminated in action,
" and were consequently practical, not productive. On the other hand,
" Logic, Rhetoric, &c., did not terminate in a mere—an evanescent action,
" but in a permanent—an enduring product. For the end of Logic was
" the production of a reasoning, the end of Rhetoric the production of an
" oration, and so forth." (Lectures, i. pp. 117, 118.) The English language expresses the same distinction by the two verbs, *to do* and *to
make*.

† Discussions, p. 134.   ‡ Lectures, i. 116.

Religion an art, there is quite as much in calling it a science, and especially a practical science, as if the theoretical doctrines of religion were no part of religion. If religion is either a science or an art, it must be both, and it is commonly understood to consist pre-eminently in things different from either, namely a state of the feelings, and a disposition of the will. As for Ethics and Politics, the one and the other are, like Logic, both sciences and arts. Ethics, so far as it consists of the theory of the moral sentiments, and the investigation of those conditions of human well-being, disclosed by experience, which the practical part of Ethics has for its object to secure, is, in all senses of the word, a science. The rules or precepts of morals are an art. If there is any reluctance felt to speak of an art of morals, it is not because people prefer calling morals a science, but because most people are unwilling to look upon it as scientific at all, but prefer to regard it as a matter of instinct, or of religious belief, or as depending solely on the state of the will and the affections. In the case of Politics there is not, even to the vulgarest apprehension, any incongruity in the use of the word art: on the contrary, "the art of government" is the vernacular expression, and "science of government" a sort of speculative refinement. Philosophic writers on politics have generally preferred to call their subject a science, in order to indicate that it is a fit subject for speculative thinkers, the word art being apt to suggest to modern ears (it did not to the ancients) something which is the proper business only of practitioners. In reality Politics includes both a science and an art. The Science of Politics treats of the laws of political phenomena; it is the science of human nature under social conditions. The Art of Politics consists (or would consist if it existed) of rules, founded on the science, for the right guidance and government of the affairs of society.

But, says Sir W. Hamilton, if the difference between Science and Art were merely that between affirmations and precepts, the distinctions would be of no value, since it would "mark out no real difference between the "various branches of knowledge, but only different "points of view under which the same branch might "be contemplated by us,—each being in different rela- "tions at once a science and an art." Was it from Sir W. Hamilton we should have expected to hear that a distinction is of no value, because it does not mark a difference between two things, but a difference in the points of view in which we may regard the same thing? How often has he told us, of many of the most impor- tant distinctions in philosophy, that they are precisely of this character! The remark, moreover, in the par- ticular case, is so extremely superficial, that, coming from an author of whom it was by no means the habit to look only at the surface of things, it is one of the strongest of the many proofs which appear in his works, how little thought he had bestowed upon the sciences or arts, beyond his own speciality. The reason why systems of precepts require to be distinguished from systems of truths, is, that an entirely different classifica- tion is required for the purposes of theoretical know- ledge, and for those of its practical application. Take the art of navigation, for example: where is the single science corresponding to this art, or which could with any propriety be included under the same name with it? Navigation is an art dependent on nearly the whole circle of the physical sciences: on astronomy, for the marks by which it determines the ship's place on the ocean; on optics, for the construction and use of its instruments; on abstract mechanics, to understand and regulate the ship's movements; on pneumatics, for the laws of winds; or hydrostatics, for the tides and currents, and the waves as influenced by winds; on meteorology, for the weather; on electricity, for thunderstorms; on magnetism, for the use of the compass; on physical geography, and so on nearly to the end of the list. Not only has each one of all these sciences furnished its contingent towards the rules composing the one art of navigation, but many single rules could only have been framed by the

union of considerations drawn from several different
sciences. For the purposes of the art, the rules by
themselves are sufficient, wherever it has been found
practicable to make them sufficiently precise. But
if the learner, not content with knowing and prac-
tising the rules, wishes to understand their reasons,
and so possess science as well as art, he finds no one
science corresponding in its object-matter with the
art; he must extract from many sciences those truths
of each which have been turned to practical account
for the furtherance of navigation. All this is obvious
to any one (not to say a person of Sir W. Hamilton's sagacity), who has sufficiently reflected on the
sciences and arts, to be aware of the relation between
them. Archbishop Whately's distinction, therefore, in
no way merits the contemptuous treatment which it
receives in the Lectures, and still more in the Discussions. It is eminently practical, it conforms to
the natural and logical order of thought, and accords
better with the ends and even with the custom of
language, than any other mode in which Arts can
be distinguished from Sciences. Sir W. Hamilton,
though he condemns it, has not ventured to set up
any competing distinction in its place, but (as we have
seen) almost intimates that no satisfactory one can be
found.

Next after the question whether Logic is a science,
comes the consideration of its object-matter as a science,
namely, " the Laws of Thought as Thought." "The
" consideration of this head," says our author,* " divides
" itself into three questions—1. What is Thought ?
" 2. What is Thought as Thought ? 3. What are the
" Laws of Thought as Thought ? " These three questions are successively discussed.

To the question, "What is Thought ?" Sir W. Hamilton answers—It is not the direct perception of an object,
nor its representation in memory or imagination, nor its
mere suggestion by association, but is a product of in-

* Lectures, iii. 12.

telligence. Intelligence acts only by comparison. "All
" thought * is a comparison, a recognition of similarity or
" difference, a conjunction or disjunction, in other words
" a synthesis or analysis of its objects. In Conception,
" that is, in the formation of Concepts (or general notions)
" it compares, disjoins or conjoins, attributes; in an act
" of Judgment, it compares, disjoins or conjoins, con-
" cepts; in Reasoning, it compares, disjoins or conjoins,
" judgments. In each step of this process there is one
" essential element; to think, to compare, to conjoin or
" disjoin, it is necessary to recognise one thing *through*
" or *under* another, and therefore, in defining Thought
" proper, we may either define it as an act of Comparison,
" or as a recognition of one notion as *in* or *under* another.
" It is in performing this act of thinking a thing under
" a general notion, that we are said to understand or
" comprehend it. For example : An object is presented,
" say a book : this object determines an impression, and
" I am even conscious of the impression, but without
" recognising to myself what the thing is ; in that case,
" there is only a perception, and not properly a thought.
" But suppose I do recognise it for what it is, in other
" words, compare it with and *reduce it under* a certain
" concept, class, or complement of attributes, which I call
" *book;* in that case, there is more than a perception,—
" there is a thought."

Further on, he again † defines an act of thought as
" the recognition of a thing as coming *under* a concept ;
" in other words, the marking an object by an attribute
" or attributes previously known as common to sundry
" objects, and to which we have accordingly given a
" general name."   And subsequently,‡ as " the comprehension of a thing under a general notion or attribute ; "
and again,§ " the cognition of any mental object by
" another in which it is considered as included ; in other
" words, thought is *the knowledge of things under con-*
" *ceptions.*"   And again,|| " Thought is the Knowledge

" of a thing *through* a concept or general notion, or of
" one notion *through* another."

From these different expressions we may infer, that
the author confines the name Thought to cases where
there is a judgment; and, it would seem, a judgment
affirming more than mere existence. We think an object, or make anything an object of thought, when we
are able to predicate something of it; to affirm that it
is something in particular; that it is a certain sort of
thing; that it belongs to a class—has something which
is (or may be) common to it with a number of other
things; that it has, in short, a certain attribute, or attributes. This is intelligible, and unobjectionable: but
our author's technical expressions, instead of facilitating
the understanding of it, tend, on the contrary, very
much to confuse it. Like the transcendental metaphysicians generally, Sir W. Hamilton, when he attempts to
state the nature of a mental phenomenon with peculiar
precision, does it by a peculiarly unprecise employment
of the common prepositions. What light is thrown upon
the simple process of referring objects to a class, by
calling it the recognition of one thing through, or in,
or under, another? What distinct signification is conveyed by the phrases, "thinking a thing under a general
notion," "reducing it under a concept," "knowing things
under, or through, conceptions"? To find the meaning
of the explanation we have to resort to the thing explained. The only passage in which the author speaks
distinctly, is that in which he paraphrases these expressions by the following: "the marking an object by an
" attribute or attributes previously known as common to
" sundry objects, and to which we have accordingly given
" a general name." To think of an object, then, is to
mark it by an attribute or set of attributes, which has
received a name, or (what is much more essential) which
gives a name to the object. It gives to the object the
concrete name, to which its own abstract name, if it
has an abstract name, corresponds: but it is not indispensable that the attribute should have received a name,

provided it gives one to the object possessing it.   An
animal is called a bull, in sign of its possessing certain
attributes, but there does not exist an abstract word
bullness. Having, then, in Sir W. Hamilton's language,
thought the object, by marking it with a name derived
from an attribute, it is perhaps an allowable, though an
obscure, expression, to say that we know the thing
through the attribute, or through the notion of the
attribute : but what is meant by saying that we know
it, or think it *under* the attribute? We know it and
think it, simply as possessing the attribute. The other
phrase, while seeming to mean more, means less. Again,
when we are asserted to " know one notion through
another ; " when, for example, we think, or judge, that
men, meaning all men, are mortal; is this to know the
notion Man through the notion Mortal? The knowledge we really have, is that the objects Men have the
attribute mortality; in other words, that the outward
facts by which we distinguish men, exist along with
subjection to the outward fact, death.   If there is a
recommendation I would inculcate on every one who
commences the study of metaphysics, it is, to be always
sure what he means by his particles.   A large portion
of all that perplexes and confuses metaphysical thought,
comes from a vague use of those small words.

   After this definition of Thought, our author proceeds
to explain what he means by Thought as Thought. He
means,* " that Logic is conversant with the form of
thought, to the exclusion of the matter." We have here
arrived at one of the cardinal points in Sir W. Hamilton's
philosophy of Logic.   However he may vary on other
doctrines, to this he is constant, that the province of
Logic is the form, not the matter, of thought.   It is a
pity that the only terms he can find to denote the distinction, are a pair of the obscurest and most confusing
expressions in the whole range of metaphysics.   Still
more unfortunate it is, that, thinking it necessary to employ such terms, he has never, in unambiguous language,

* Lectures, iii. 15.

explained their meaning. When Archbishop Whately, in somewhat similar phraseology, tells us that Logic has to do with the form of the reasoning process, but not with its matter, we know what he means. It is, that Logic is not concerned with the actual truth either of the conclusion or of the premises, but considers only whether the one follows from the other; whether the conclusion must be true if the premises are true. Sir W. Hamilton is not content to mean only this. He means much more; but if we wish to know what, the only information he here gives us is a quotation from a German philosopher, Esser. "We are able, by abstraction, "to distinguish from each other,—1°. The object "thought of; and 2°. The kind and manner of think-"ing it. Let us, employing the old established tech-"nical expressions, call the first of these the *matter*, the "second the *form*, of the thought. For example, when "I think that the book before me is a folio, the matter "of the thought is book and folio, the form of it is a "judgment." Thus far Esser. The Form, therefore, of Thought, with which alone Logic is conversant, is not the object thought of, but "the kind and manner of thinking it." It is not necessary to show that this explanation is insufficient. But to find any other, we must have recourse, not to Sir W. Hamilton, but to Mr. Mansel. One of the chapters of Mr. Mansel's "Prolegomena Logica" is entitled "On the Matter and Form of Thought." It commences as follows:*—

"The distinction between Matter and Form in com-"mon language relatively to works of Art, will serve to "illustrate the character of the corresponding distinction "in Thought. The term Matter is usually applied to "whatever is given to the artist, and consequently, as "given, does not come within the province of the art "itself to supply. The Form is that which is given in "and through the proper operation of the art. In "Sculpture, for example, the Matter is the marble in its "rough state as given to the sculptor; the Form is that

* Prolegomena Logica, pp. 226, 227.

" which the sculptor in the exercise of his art communi-
" cates to it." Let me here ask, had the block of marble
no form at all when it came out of the quarry? "The
" distinction between Matter and Form in any mental
" operation is analogous to this. The former includes
" all that is given *to*, the latter all that is given *by*, the
" operation. In the division of notions, for example,
" whether performed by an act of pure thinking or
" not, the generic notion is that given to be divided ;
" the addition of the difference in the act of division
" constitutes the species. And accordingly, Genus
" is frequently designated by logicians the *material*,
" Difference the *formal*, part of the Species." (An
illustration which, whatever else it may do, does not
illustrate.) "So likewise in any operation of pure
" thinking, the Matter will include all that is given
" to and out of the thought ; the Form is what is con-
" veyed in and by the thinking act itself."

This is a fair account of the meaning of Matter and
Form in the Kantian philosophy, and the philosophies
which descend genealogically from the Kantian. But
this meaning must always be taken with, and interpreted by, the characteristic doctrine of the Kantian
metaphysics, that the mind does not perceive, but itself
creates, all the most general attributes which, by a
natural illusion, we ascribe to outward things ; which
attributes, consequently, are called, by that philosophy,
Forms. Extension and Duration, for example, it calls
forms of our sensitive faculty ; Substance, Causality,
Quantity, forms of our Understanding, which is our
faculty of thought. These, however, are not what Sir
W. Hamilton and Mr. Mansel mean, when they say that
Logic is the science of the forms of thought. They do
not mean that it is the science of Substance, Causality,
and Quantity. The truth is, that as soon as the word
Form is stretched beyond its proper signification of
bodily figure, it becomes entirely vague : every thinker
uses it in a sense of his own. The only bond connecting its various meanings, is the negative one of oppo-

sition to Matter. Whenever anything is called Form,
there is something which, relatively to it, is regarded
as Matter: and whenever anything is called Matter,
there is something capable of being superinduced upon
it, which when superinduced will be styled its Form.
How completely the notion of Form accompanies that
of Matter as its relative opposite, we have an illustrious
example in Aristotle, when he defines the soul as the Form
of the Body; so, at least, Sir W. Hamilton, very freely,
translates ἐντελέχεια.* It would be quite warranted by
the practice of metaphysicians, to call any compound
the form of its component elements; water, for instance,
the form of hydrogen and oxygen. And since there is
nothing that may not be regarded as matter relatively to
something which can be constructed out of it, and which
is form relatively to it, but matter relatively to some
other thing, we have form within form, like a nest of
boxes. Kant actually calls the conclusion of a syllogism
the form of it, the premises being its matter: so that
in every train of reasoning, the successive conclusions
pass over one by one from Form to Matter. Without
going this length, Sir W. Hamilton,† after Krug, considers the propositions and terms as the matter of the
syllogism, and the mode in which they are connected as
its form. Yet propositions and terms (*i.e.* concepts)
are classed by him as Forms of Thought. Thus it
is impossible to draw any line between the Matter of
Thought and its Form, or to convey any distinct conception of the province of a science by saying that it is
conversant with the one and not with the other. We
may, however, in a general way, understand Sir W.
Hamilton to mean, that Logic is not concerned with

---

* See Reid, p. 202, and Sir W. Hamilton's foot-note. A still odder
example is given by Reid in his Essays on the Active Powers (Works,
pp. 649, 650). "In the scholastic ages, an action good in itself was said to
"be *materially* good, and an action done with a right intention was called
"*formally* good. This last way of expressing the distinction is still familiar
"among theologians."

† Lectures, iii. 287, 288. So also Mr. Mansel, Prolegomena Logica,
p. 235.

the actual contents of our knowledge—with the particular objects, or truths, which we know—but only with
our mode of knowing them : with what the mind does
when it knows, or thinks, irrespectively of the particular
things which it thinks about : with the theory of the act
or fact of thinking, so far as that fact is the same in all
our thought, or can be reduced to universal principles.

But the fact of thinking is a psychological phenomenon ; and Logic is a different thing from Psychology.
It is for the purpose of marking this difference that Sir
W. Hamilton adds a third point to his definition of
Logic, calling it the science not simply of Thought as
Thought, but of the Laws of Thought as Thought. For
Psychology also treats of thought, considered merely as
thought ; and professes to give an account of Thought
as a mental operation. In what, then, consists the
difference between the two? I cannot venture to state
it in any but our author's own words.*

"The phenomena of the formal, or subjective phases
" of thought, are of two kinds. They are either such as
" are contingent, that is, such as may or may not appear;
" or they are such as are necessary, that is, such as
" cannot but appear.   These two classes of phenomena
" are, however, only manifested in conjunction; they
" are not discriminated in the actual operations of
" thought; and it requires a speculative analysis to
" separate them into their several classes.   In so far as
" these phenomena are considered merely as pheno-
" mena, that is, in so far as philosophy is merely obser-
" vant of them as manifestations in general, they belong
" to the science of Empirical or Historical Psychology.
" But when philosophy, by a reflective abstraction,
" analyses the necessary from the contingent forms of
" thought, there results a science, which is distin-
" guished from all others by taking for its object-matter
" the former of these classes ; and this science is Logic.
" Logic, therefore, is at last fully and finally defined as
" the science of the necessary forms of thought."

* Lectures, iii. 24.

If language has any meaning, this passage must be understood to say, that the "laws" or "forms" which are the province of Logic, are certain "phenomena" of thought, distinguished from its other phenomena by being necessarily present in it,—"such as cannot but appear,"—while the remaining phenomena "may or may not appear." If this be meant, we are landed in a strange conclusion. There is a science, Psychology, which is the science of all mental phenomena, and among others, of the phenomena of Thought, and yet another science, Logic, is required to teach us its *necessary* phenomena. There is a portion of the properties of Thought which are expressly excluded from the science which treats of Thought, to be reserved as the matter of another science, and these are precisely its Necessary qualities. Those which are merely contingent, "such as may or may not appear"—the properties which are not common to all thought, or do not belong to it at all times—these, it seems to be said, Psychology knows something about: but the Necessary properties, "such as cannot but appear"—the properties which all thoughts possess, which thought must possess, without the possession of which it would not be thought—these Psychology knows not of, and it is the office of a different science to investigate them. We may next expect to be told, that the science of dynamics knows nothing of the laws of motion, the composition of forces, the theory of continuous and accelerating force, the doctrines of Momentum and Vis Viva, &c.; it only knows of wind power and water power, steam power and animal power, and the accidents by flood and field which accompany them and disturb their operation.

This, however, supposes that our author means what he expressly says. It assumes that by the "Laws of Thought," and the "Necessary Forms of Thought," he means the modes in which, and the conditions subject to which, by the constitution of our nature, we cannot but think. But when we turn over a few pages, to the place where he is preparing to treat of those laws or necessary forms one by one, it appears that this is an entire mistake. Laws now no longer mean necessities of nature; they are laws in a totally different sense; they mean precepts: and the "necessary forms of thought" are not attributes which it must, but only which it ought to possess. "When * I speak of laws, and of their absolute "necessity in relation to thought, you must not suppose "that these laws and that necessity are the same in "the world of mind as in the world of matter. For "free intelligences, a law is an ideal necessity given in "the form of a precept, which we ought to follow, but "which we may also violate if we please; whereas, for "the existences which constitute the universe of nature, "a law is only another name for those causes which ope- "rate blindly and universally in producing certain inevi- "table results. By *law of thought,* or by *logical necessity,* "we do not, therefore, mean a physical law, such as the "law of gravitation, but a general precept which we are "able certainly to violate, but which if we do not obey, "our whole process of thinking is suicidal, or absolutely "null. These laws are, consequently, the primary con- "ditions of the possibility of valid thought; and ... the "whole of Pure Logic is only an articulate development "of the various modes in which they are applied." †

So that, after all, the real theory of Thought—the laws, in the scientific sense of the term, of Thought as Thought—do not belong to Logic, but to Psychology: and it is only the *validity* of thought which Logic takes

---

* Lectures, iii. 78.

† It might have been supposed that the double meaning of the word law, though in the last century it could blind even a Montesquieu, had been sufficiently written about since that time, to be understood by minds of far less calibre than Sir W. Hamilton's: yet in this passage he does not recognise it, but seems rather to think that the difference between a law in the scientific, and a law in the legislative or ethical sense, does not turn on an ambiguity of the word, but on the difference between "the world of mind" and "the world of matter:" a "free intelligence" knowing only precepts, which it has power to disobey, and not being ruled, like the physical world, by laws from which it cannot escape. Yet Sir W. Hamilton is the same philosopher who is for ever telling us of necessities of thought which are absolutely irresistible to us—from which we can by no mental effort emancipate ourselves; and upon this alleged fact the larger half of his philosophy is grounded. When we find all this forgotten, we almost

cognisance of.   It is not with Thought as Thought, but
only as Valid thought, that Logic is concerned.   There
is nothing to prevent us from thinking contrary to the
laws of Logic : only, if we do, we shall not think rightly,
or well, or conformably to the ends of thinking, but
falsely, or inconsistently, or confusedly.   This doctrine
is at complete variance with the saying of our author in
his controversy with Whately, that Logic is, and never
could have been doubted to be, in Whately's sense of
the terms, both a Science and an Art.   For the present
definition reduces it to the narrowest conception of an
Art—that of a mere system of rules.   It leaves Science
to Psychology, and represents Logic as merely offering
to thinkers a collection of precepts, which they are
enjoined to observe, not in order that they may think,
but that they may think correctly, or validly.

It appears to me, however, that our author, though
inconsistent with himself, is much nearer the mark in
this mode of regarding Logic than in the previous one.
I conceive it to be true that Logic is not the theory of
Thought as Thought, but of valid Thought; not of
thinking, but of correct thinking.   It is not a Science
distinct from, and co-ordinate with, Psychology.   So far
as it is a science at all, it is a part, or branch, of Psychology ; differing from it, on the one hand as a part
differs from the whole, and on the other, as an Art
differs from a Science.   Its theoretic grounds are wholly
borrowed from Psychology, and include as much of that

fancy that we have opened a volume of some other writer by mistake.
Treating of the same question in another place, our author remembers his
own philosophy much better.   In the Lecture in which he divides mental
science into the "Phenomenology of Mind" and its "Nomology," the
former a classification and analysis of our mental faculties, the latter an
investigation of their "laws" (Lectures, i. 121, et seqq.), the word Laws
always stands for "necessary and universal facts," "the Laws by which our
faculties are governed," not precepts by which they ought to be governed :
and of these necessary and universal facts it is expressly said that the Laws
of thought, with which Logic is concerned, are a part.   They are classed
with "the Laws of Memory," "the Laws of Association," "the laws which
govern our capacities of enjoyment," all of which are correctly described
as necessary facts, and not as precepts.   The whole of this is thrown to the
winds when the time comes for taking up Logic as a separate science.

science as is required to justify the rules of the art. Logic has no need to know more of the Science of Thinking, than the difference between good thinking and bad. A consequence of this is, that the Necessary Laws of Thought, those which our author in his first doctrine reserved especially to Logic, are precisely those with which Logic has least to do, and which belong the most exclusively to Psychology. What is common to all thought, whether good or bad, and inseparable from it, is irrelevant to Logic, unless by the light it may indirectly throw on something besides itself. The properties of Thought which concern Logic, are some of its contingent properties; those, namely, on the presence of which depends good thinking, as distinguished from bad.

I therefore accept our author's second view of the province of Logic, which makes it a collection of precepts or rules for thinking, grounded on a scientific investigation of the requisites of valid thought. It is this doctrine which governs his treatment of the details of Logic, and it is by this that we must interpret the assertion that Logic has for its only subject the Form of Thought. By the Form of Thought we must understand Thinking itself; the whole work of the Intellect. The Matter of Thought is the sensations, perceptions, or other presentations (intuitions, as Mr. Mansel calls them), in which the intellect has no share; which are supplied to it, independently of any action of its own. What the mind adds to these, or puts into them, is Forms of Thought. Logic, therefore, is concerned only with Forms, since, being rules for thinking, it can have no authority but over that which depends on thought. Logic and Thinking are coextensive; it is the art of Thinking, of all Thinking, and of nothing but Thinking. And since every distinguishable variety of thinking act is called a Form of Thought, the Forms of Thought compose the whole province of Logic; though it would be hardly possible to invent a worse phrase for expressing so simple a fact.

But what *are* the Forms of Thought? Kant, as already observed, gives to that expression a very wide extent. He holds that every fundamental attribute which we ascribe to external objects is a Form of Thought, being created, not simply discerned, by our thinking faculty. Neither Sir W. Hamilton nor Mr. Mansel goes this length; and at all events they do not consider the theory of the various attributes of bodies to be a part of Logic. It was incumbent on them, therefore, to state clearly what are the Forms of Thought with which Logic is concerned, and for which it supplies precepts. This question is never put, in an express form, by Sir W. Hamilton: but the answer which he rather leaves to be picked up than directly presents, may be gathered from his classification of our intellectual operations. These he reduces to three, Conception, Judgment, and Reasoning. He must have recognised, therefore, that number of general Forms of Thought. The Forms of Thought are Conception, Judgment, and Reasoning: Logic is the Science of the Laws (meaning the rules) of these three operations. If, however, we rigorously hold our author to this short list, we shall perpetually mistake his meaning: for (as already observed) the mode in which the word Form is used, allows of form within form to an unlimited extent. Every concept, judgment, or reasoning, after having received its form from the mind, may again be contemplated as the Matter of some further mental act; and the product of that further act (according to Kant), or the relation of the product to the matter (according to Sir W. Hamilton and Mr. Mansel), is again a Form of Thought; as we find, to our confusion, when we proceed further, and the more profusely, the further we proceed. We have, first, however, to consider a proposition of Sir W. Hamilton, which qualifies his definition of the province of Logic. He says: *

"Logic considers Thought, not as the operation of

* Lectures, iii. 73.

" thinking, but as its product ; it does not treat of Con-
" ception, Judgment, and Reasoning, but of Concepts,
" Judgments, and Reasonings."

Let me begin by saying that I give my entire adhesion to this distinction, and propose to reform the definition of Logic accordingly.   It does not, as we now see,
relate to the Laws of Thought as Thought, but to those
of the Products of Thought.   Instead of the Laws of
Conception, Judgment, and Reasoning, we must speak
of the Laws of Concepts, Judgments, and Reasonings.
This would be mere nonsense in the scientific sense of
the word law : for a product, as such, can have no laws
but those of the operation which produces it.   But understanding by laws, as it seems we are intended to do,
Precepts, Logic becomes the science of the precepts for
the formation of concepts, judgments, and reasonings : or
rather (a science of precepts being an improper expression) the science of the conditions on which right concepts, judgments, and reasonings depend.   Thus, Logic
is the Art of Thinking, which means of correct thinking,
and the Science of the Conditions of correct thinking.
This seems to me a sufficiently accurate definition of it.
But, in attempting a deeper metaphysical analysis of the
distinction he has just drawn, our author raises fresh
difficulties.   He says : *

" The form of thought may be viewed on two sides,
" or in two relations.   It holds, as has been said, a rela-
" tion both to its subject and to its object, and it may
" accordingly be viewed either in the one of these rela-
" tions or in the other.   In so far as the form of thought
" is considered in reference to the thinking mind,—to
" the mind by which it is exerted,—it is considered as
" an act, or operation, or energy ; and in this relation it
" belongs to Phenomenal Psychology.   Whereas, in so
" far as this form is considered in reference to what
" thought is about, it is considered as the product of
" such an act, and in this relation it belongs to Logic.

* Lectures, iii. 73, 74.

" Thus Phenomenal Psychology treats of thought proper
"as conception, judgment, reasoning: Logic, or the
"Nomology of the Understanding, treats of thought
"proper as a concept, as a judgment, as a reasoning."

Just when the puzzled reader fancied that he had at
last arrived at something clear, comes an explanation
which throws all back into darkness. The learner who
had been wandering in the mazes of "Thought as
Thought," laws which are not laws, and "Forms of
Thought" in which Form stands for something which he
never before heard of in connection with that word, at last
descried what seemed to be firm ground : he was told
that Conception, Judgment, and Reasoning are acts of
the mind, that Concepts, Judgments, and Reasonings
are products of those acts, and that Psychology is conversant with the former and Logic with the latter. And
now it turns out that the products *are* the acts. The
two series of things are one and the same series. They
are both of them only "Thought proper." The product is another word for the act itself, considered in one
of its aspects—"in reference to what thought is about."
It is curious that this should occur only a few pages after
Whately has been rebuked for reducing a distinction to
inutility, by making it coincide with a difference not
between things, but between the aspects in which the
same thing is regarded.

Sir W. Hamilton therefore is of opinion that the
thinking act, though verbally, is not psychologically
different from the thought itself. He does not hold,
with Berkeley, that an Idea is a concrete object distinct
from the mind, and contained in it, like furniture in a
house ; nor with Locke (if that was Locke's opinion),
that it is a modification of the mind, but a modification
distinct from the mind's act in cognising it ; but with
Brown, that a sensation is only myself feeling, and a
thought only myself thinking. Concepts, Judgments,
and Reasonings, are only acts of conceiving, judging, and
reasoning ; acts of thought, considered not in their relation to the thinking mind, but to their object, to "what

2 G

thought is about." * But what *is* thought about? Not
about Concepts, for all our thoughts are not about the
thinking act. It must be about the objective presentation, the Anschauung, or Intuition, which the Concept
represents, or from which it has been abstracted. According, therefore, to the doctrine here distinctly laid
down by Sir W. Hamilton, there are but two things
present in any of our intellectual operations; on one
hand, the mind itself thinking (that is, conceiving,
judging, or reasoning), and, on the other, a mental
presentation or representation of the phenomenal
Reality which it conceives, or concerning which it
judges or reasons. I can understand that the thinking
act, or in other words, the mind in a thinking state,
may be contemplated in its relation to the Reality
thought of, and may receive a name which connotes
that Reality; but how does this entitle us to call it a
product of thought? How can the act of thought, or
the mind thinking, be looked upon, even hypothetically,
as a product of thinking? How can Concepts, Judgments, and Reasonings be regarded as products of
thought, if they are the thought itself? Can they be
both the act and something resulting from the act?
Are they results and products of themselves?

I conceive that there is a way out of this difficulty:
a sense in which the two assertions can be reconciled,
though it has not been pointed out by Sir W. Hamilton,

---

* Sir W. Hamilton holds a corresponding theory in regard to the
identity of an imagination with the imagining act. "A representation
"considered as an object is logically, not really, different from a represen-
"tation considered as an act. Here object and act are merely the same in-
"divisible mode of mind viewed in two different relations. Considered by
"reference to a mediate object represented, it is a representative object:
"considered by reference to the mind representing and contemplating the
"representation, it is a representative act. A representative object being
"viewed as posterior in the order of nature, but not of time, to the repre-
"sentative object, is viewed as a *product ;* and the representative act being
"viewed as prior in the order of nature, though not of time, to the repre-
"sentative object, is viewed as a producing process." (Dissertations on
Reid, p. 809.) Sir W. Hamilton has not explained how, in the order of
nature, or in any other order, a thing can be prior, or posterior, or prior
and posterior, to itself.

and is hardly compatible with some of his opinions.
There is a difference between what can properly be
called Acts of the mind, and the other mental phenomena which may be termed its passive States.   And I
know but one way of conceiving the distinction, in
which it can possibly be upheld, namely, by considering
as Acts only those mental phenomena which are results
of Volition.   Now, the first formation of a Concept, and
generally (though not always) any fresh operation of
judgment or reasoning, requires a mental effort, a concentration of consciousness upon certain definite objects,
which concentration depends on the will, and is called
Attention.   When this takes place, the mind is properly
said to be active.   But after frequent repetition of this
act of will, the associations to which it has given rise are
sufficiently riveted to do their work spontaneously; the
effort of attention, after becoming less and less, is finally
null, and the operation, originally voluntary, becomes,
in Hartley's language, secondarily automatic.   When
this transition has been completed, what remains of the
mental phenomenon has lost the character of an Act,
and become numbered among passive States.   It is now
either a mere mental representation of an object, differing
from those copied directly from sense, only in having certain of its parts artificially made intense and prominent;
or it is a *fasciculus* of representations of imagination,
held together by the tie of an association artificially
produced.   When the mental phenomenon has assumed
this passive character, it comes to be termed a Concept,
or, more familiarly and vaguely, an Idea, and to be felt
as if it were, not the mind modified, but something in the
mind: and in this ultimate phasis of its existence we may
properly consider it, not as an act, but as the product
of a previous act ; since it now takes place without any
conscious activity, and becomes a subject on which
fresh activity may be exercised, by an act of voluntary
attention concentrating consciousness on it, or on some
particular part of it.   This explanation, which I leave
for the consideration of philosophers, would not have

suited Sir W. Hamilton, since it would have required
him to limit the extent which he habitually gave to the
expression "mental act." Every phenomenon of mind,
down to the mere reception of a sensation, he regards
as an act: therein differing from Kant, and annihilating
the need and use of the word, the sole function of
which is to distinguish what the mind originates, from
what something else originates in the mind.

To return to the definition of Logic, as the science of
the Forms of Thought, considered in relation, not to the
thinking act itself, but, so far as they are distinguishable
from it, to the products of thought. The products of
thought are Concepts, Judgments, and Reasonings, and
the Forms of Thought are Conception, Judgment, and
Reasoning. Logic is the science of those Forms, so far as
concerns the rules for the right formation of the products:
or, as our author elsewhere phrases it, the science of
the "formal conditions" of valid thinking. These modes
of expression have a rare power of darkening the subject, but I am endeavouring to give them an intelligible
interpretation, by means of that which they profess to
explain. If, then, all thinking consists in adding, to
given matter, a Form derived from the mind itself, what
shall we say of the division, on which so much stress
is laid, of Thinking itself into two kinds, Formal and
Material Thinking, the first of which alone belongs to
Logic, or at all events to pure Logic? Mr. Mansel has
written a volume for the express purpose of showing that
Logic is only concerned with Formal Thinking; and Sir
W. Hamilton's division of Logic into Pure and Modified,
agrees with Mr. Mansel's distinction. Yet, according
to the definition we have just considered, all thinking
whatever is Formal Thinking: since all thinking is either
conceiving, judging, or reasoning, and these are the
Forms of Thought. If Logic investigates the conditions requisite for the right formation of concepts, of
judgments, and of reasonings, it investigates all the conditions of right thought, for there are no other kinds of
thought than these; and if it does all this, what is left

for the so-called Material Thinking which Logic is said not to be concerned with?

The answer to this question affords an additional specimen of the incurable confusion, in which the processes of thought are involved by the unhappy misapplication to them of the metaphorical word Form. Though Concepts, Judgments, and Reasonings, are said to be the forms of thought, and the only forms which thought takes, or rather gives; the metaphysicians who deal in Forms are in the habit of using phrases which signify that Concepts, Judgments, and Reasonings, though themselves Forms, have also, in themselves, a formal part and a material. Different concepts, judgments, and reasonings, have different matter, according to what it is that the conception, the judgment, or the reasoning, is about: and as whatever part of anything is not its Matter, is always styled its Form, whatever is common to all Concepts, or whatever belongs to them irrespectively of all differences in their matter, is said to be their Form; and so of Judgments and of Reasonings. Thus, the difference between an affirmative and a negative judgment is a difference of form, because a judgment may be either affirmative or negative whatever be the matter to which it relates. The difference between a categorical and an hypothetical syllogism is a difference of form, because it neither depends on, nor is it at all affected by, any differences in the matter. Logic, according to Mr. Mansel—pure Logic, according to Sir W. Hamilton—is conversant only with the Forms of Concepts, Judgments, and Reasonings, not with their Matter. Not only is it concerned exclusively with the Forms of thought, but exclusively with the Forms of those Forms. And here I fairly renounce any further attempt to deduce Sir W. Hamilton's or Mr. Mansel's conception of Logic from their definitions of it. I collect it from the general evidence of their treatises, and I proceed to show why I consider it to be wrong.

Logic, Sir W. Hamilton has told us, lays down the laws or precepts indispensable to Valid Thought; the

conditions to which thought is bound to conform, under
the penalty of being invalid, ineffectual, not accomplishing its end. And what is, peculiarly and emphatically, the end of Thinking? Surely it is the attainment
of Truth. Surely, if not the sole, at all events the first
and most essential constituent of valid thought, is that
its results should be true. Concepts, Judgments, and
Reasonings, should agree with the reality of things,
meaning by things the Phenomena or sensible presentations, to which those mental products have reference.
A concept, to be rightly framed, must be a concept of
something real, and must agree with the real fact which
it endeavours to represent, that is, the collection of attributes composing the concept must really exist in the
objects marked by the class-name, and in no others.   A
judgment, to be rightly framed, must be a true judgment, that is, the objects judged of must really possess
the attributes predicated of them.   A reasoning, to be
rightly framed, must conduct to a true conclusion, since
the only purpose of reasoning is to make known to us
truths which we cannot learn by direct intuition.   Even
those who take the most limited view of Logic, allow
that the conclusion must be true conditionally—provided
that the premises are true.   The most important, then,
and at bottom the only important quality of a thought
being its truth, the laws or precepts provided for the
guidance of thought must surely have for their principal
purpose that the products of thinking shall be true.
Yet with this, according to Mr. Mansel, Logic has no
concern ; and Sir W. Hamilton reserves it for a sort of
appendix to the science, under the title of Modified
Logic.   Questions of truth and falsity, according to
both writers, regard only Material Thinking, while
Formal Thinking is the province of Logic.   The only
precepts for thinking with which Logic concerns itself,
are those which have some other purpose than the conformity of our thoughts to the fact.   Yet every possible
precept for thought, if it be an honest one, must have
this for at least its ultimate object.   What, then, is ex-

cluded from Logic, and what is left in it, by the doctrine
that it is only concerned with Formal Thinking? What
is excluded is the whole of the evidences of the validity
of thought. What is included is part of the evidences
of its invalidity.

In no case can thinking be valid unless the concepts,
judgments, and conclusions resulting from it are conformable to fact. And in no case can we satisfy ourselves that they are so, by looking merely at the relations
of one part of the train of thought to another. We must
ascend to the original sources, the presentations of
experience, and examine the train of thought in its relation to these. But we can sometimes discover, without
ascending to the sources, that the process of thought is
not valid; having been so conducted that it cannot possibly avail for obtaining concepts, judgments, or conclusions in accordance with fact. This, for example, is
the case, if we have allowed ourselves to travel from premises to a conclusion through an ambiguous term. The
process then gives no ground at all for believing the
conclusion to be true: it is perhaps true, but we have
no more reason to believe so than we had before. Or
again, the concept, the judgment, or the reasoning may
involve a contradiction, and so cannot possibly correspond to any real state of facts. It is with this part of
the subject only, in the opinion of these philosophers,
that Logic concerns itself. According to Mr. Mansel,*
Logic "accepts, as logically valid, all such concepts,
"judgments and reasonings, as do not, directly or in-
"directly, imply contradictions; pronouncing them thus
"far to be legitimate as thoughts, that they do not in
"ultimate analysis destroy themselves. . . . leaving to
"this or that branch of material science to determine
"how far the same products of thought are guaranteed
"by the testimony of this or that special experience."
Mr. Mansel has not here conceived his own view of the
subject with his usual precision. He narrows the field
of Logic more than he intends. That to which he con-

* Prolegomena Logica, p. 265.

fines the name of Logic, accepts as valid all concepts and judgments that do not imply contradictions, but by no means all reasonings. It rejects these not only when self-contradictory, but when simply inconclusive. It condemns a reasoning not only if it draws a conclusion inconsistent with the premises, but if it draws one which the premises do not warrant: not only if the conclusion must, but if it may, be false though the premises be true. For the notion of true and false *will* force its way even into Formal Logic, whatever pains Sir W. Hamilton and Mr. Mansel give themselves to make the notions of consistent and inconsistent, or of thinkable and unthinkable, do duty instead of it. The ideas of truth and falsity cannot be eliminated from reasoning. We may abstract from actual truth, but the validity of reasoning is always a question of conditional truth—whether one proposition must be true if others are true, or whether one proposition can be true if others are true. When Judgments or Reasonings are in question, "the conditions of the thinkable" are simply the conditions of the believable.

What Mr. Mansel and Sir W. Hamilton really mean, is to segregate from the remainder of the theory of the investigation of truth, as much of it as does not require any reference to the original sufficiency of the groundwork of facts, or the correctness of their interpretation, and call this exclusively Logic, or Pure Logic. They assume that concepts have been formed and judgments made somehow; and if there is nothing within the four corners of the concept or the judgment which proves it absurd, that is, no self-contradiction, they do not question it further. Whether it is grounded on fact or on mere supposition, and if on fact, whether the fact is represented correctly, they do not ask; but think only of the conditions necessary for preventing errors from getting into the process of thought, which were not in the notions or the premises from whence it started. The theory of these conditions (of which the doctrine of the Syllogism is the principal part) Mr. Mansel calls Logic,

and Sir W. Hamilton Pure Logic. The expression
" Formal Logic," which is sometimes applied to it, is
perhaps as distinctive and as little misleading as any
other, and is that which, for want of a better, I am content to use. That this part of Logic should be distinguished and named, and made an object of consideration
separately from the rest, is perfectly natural. What I
protest against, is the doctrine of Sir W. Hamilton, Mr.
Mansel, and many other thinkers, that this part is the
whole ; that there is no other Logic, or Pure Logic, at
all ; that whatever is more than this, belongs not to a
general science and art of Thinking, but (in the words
of Mr. Mansel) to this or that material science.

This doctrine assumes, that with the exception of the
rules of Formal, that is, of Syllogistic Logic, no other
rules can be framed which are applicable to thought
generally, abstractedly from particular matter : That a
general theory is possible respecting the relations which
the parts of a process of thought should bear to one
another, but not respecting the proper relations of all
thought to its matter : That the problem which Bacon
set before himself, and led the way towards resolving, is
an impossible one : That there is not, and cannot be, any
general Theory of Evidence : That when we have taken
care that our notions and propositions concerning Things
shall be consistent with themselves and with one another,
and have drawn no inferences from them but such the
falsity of which would be inconsistent with assertions
already made, we have done all that a philosophy of
Thought can do—and the agreement and disagreement
of our beliefs with the laws of the thing itself, is in each
case a special question, belonging to the science of that
thing in particular : That the study of nature, the search
for objective truth, does not admit of any rules, nor its
attainment, of any general test. For if there are such
rules, if there is such a test, and the consideration of it
does not belong to Logic, to what science or study does
it belong ? There is no other science, which, irrespectively of particular matter, professes to direct the intel-

lect in the application of its powers to any matter on which knowledge is possible. These philosophers must therefore think that there can be no such rules, or that if there are, they can only be of the vaguest possible description. Sir W. Hamilton says as much. " If we * abstract " from the specialities of particular objects and sciences, " and consider only the rules which ought to govern " our procedure in reference to the object-matter of the " sciences in general,—and this is all that a universal " Logic can propose,—these rules are few in number, and " their applications simple and evident. A material or " Objective Logic, except in special subordination to the " circumstances of particular sciences, is therefore of very " narrow limits, and all that it can tell us is soon told." It is very true that all Sir W. Hamilton can tell us of it is soon told. Nothing can be more meagre, trite, and indefinite than the little which he finds to say respecting what he calls Modified Logic. And no wonder, when we consider the following extraordinary deliverance, which I quote from the conclusion of his Thirtieth Lecture on Logic. Speaking of Physical Science generally, Sir W. Hamilton thus expresses himself : †—

" In this department of Knowledge there is chiefly " demanded a patient habit of attention to details, in " order to detect phenomena; and, these discovered, their " generalisation is usually so easy that there is little " exercise afforded to the higher energies of Judgment " and Reasoning. It was Bacon's boast that Induc- " tion, as applied to nature, would equalise all talents, " level the aristocracy of genius, accomplish marvels by " co-operation and method, and leave little to be done by " the force of individual intellects. This boast has been " fulfilled; Science has, by the Inductive Process, been " brought down to minds, who previously would have " been incompetent for its cultivation, and physical " knowledge now usefully occupies many who would " otherwise have been without any rational pursuit."

---

* Lectures, iv. 232. (Appendix I.)   † Ibid. p. 138.

Sir W. Hamilton had good reason for confining his own logical speculations to a minor and subordinate department of the Science and Art of Thinking, when he was so destitute as this passage proves, of the preliminary knowledge required for making any proficiency in the other and higher branch.   Every one who has obtained any knowledge of the physical sciences from really scientific study, knows that the questions of evidence presented, and the powers of abstraction required, in the speculations on which their greater generalisations depend, are such as to task the very highest capacities of the human intellect : and a thinker, however able, who is too little acquainted with the processes actually followed in the investigation of objective truth, to be aware of this fact, is entitled to no authority when he denies the possibility of a Philosophy of Evidence and of the Investigation of Nature; inasmuch as his own acquirements do not furnish him with the means of judging whether it is possible or not.*

If any general theory of the sufficiency of Evidence and the legitimacy of Generalisation be possible, this must be Logic κατ' ἐξοχήν, and anything else called by the name can only be ancillary to it.   For the Logic called Formal only aims at removing one of the obstacles to the attainment of truth, by preventing such mistakes as render our thoughts inconsistent with themselves or with one another : and it is of no importance whether

* Accordingly all that Sir W. Hamilton has to say concerning the requisites of a legitimate Induction, is that there must be no instances to the contrary, and that the number of observed instances must be "competent." (Lectures, iv. 168, 169.)   If this were all that "a Material or Objective Logic" could "tell us," Sir W. Hamilton's treatment of it would be quite justified.   The point of view of a complete induction, namely one in which the nature of the instances is such, that no other result than the one arrived at is consistent with the universal Law of Causation, had never risen above Sir W. Hamilton's horizon.   The same low reach of thought, not for want of power, but of the necessary knowledge, shows itself in every part of the little he says concerning the investigation of Nature. For example, he implicitly follows the mistake of Kant in affirming an intrinsic difference between the inferences of Induction and those of Analogy.   Induction, he says (Lectures, iv. 165, 166), infers that "if a "number of objects of the same class possess in common a certain attribute, ". . . this attribute is possessed by all the objects of that class;" while

we think consistently or not, if we think wrongly. It
is only as a means to material truth, that the formal,
or to speak more clearly, the conditional, validity of an
operation of thought is of any value; and even that
value is only negative : we have not made the smallest
positive advance towards right thinking, by merely keeping ourselves consistent in what is, perhaps, systematic
error. This by no means implies that Formal Logic,
even in its narrowest sense, is not of very great, though
purely negative, value. On the contrary, I subscribe
heartily to all that is said of its importance by Sir W.
Hamilton and Mr. Mansel. It is good to have our path
clearly marked out, and a parapet put up at all the dangerous points, whether the path leads us to the place we
desire to reach, or to another place altogether. But to
call this alone Logic, or this alone Pure Logic, as if all
the rest of the Philosophy of Thought and Evidence
were merely an adaptation of this to something else, is
to ignore the end to which all rules laid down for our
thinking operations are meant to be subservient. The
purpose of them all, is to enable us to decide whether anything, and what, is proved true. Formal Logic conduces
indirectly to this end, by enabling us to perceive, either
that the process which has been performed is one which
could not possibly prove anything, or that it is one
which will prove something to be true, unless the premises happen to be false. This indirect aid is of the
greatest importance; but it is important because the end,

Analogy infers that "if . . . two or more things agree in several internal
"and essential characters . . . they agree, likewise, in all other essential
"characters, that is, they are constituents of the same class." A little
more familiarity with the subject would have shown him that the two kinds
of argument are homogeneous, and differ only in degree of evidence. The
type of them both is, the inference that things which agree with one
another in certain respects, agree in certain other respects. Any argument
from known points of agreement to unknown, is an inference of analogy :
and induction is no more. Induction concludes that if a number of As
have the attribute B, all things which agree with them in being As agree
with them also in having the attribute B. The only peculiarity of Induction, as compared with other cases of analogy, is, that the known points of
agreement from which further agreement is inferred, have been summed
up in a single word and made the foundation of a class. For further explanations, see my System of Logic, Book iii. chap. xx.

the ascertainment of truth, is important ; and it is important only as complementary to a still more fundamental part of the operation, in which Formal Logic affords no help.

I do not deny the scientific convenience of considering this limited portion of Logic apart from the rest—the doctrine of the Syllogism, for instance, apart from the theory of Induction ; and of teaching it in an earlier stage of intellectual education. It can be taught earlier, since it does not, like the inductive logic, presuppose a practical acquaintance with the processes of scientific investigation ; and the greatest service to be derived from it, that of keeping the mind clear, can be best rendered before a habit of confused thinking has been acquired. Not only, however, is it indispensable that the larger Logic, which embraces all the general conditions of the ascertainment of truth, should be studied in addition to the smaller Logic, which only concerns itself with the conditions of consistency ; but the smaller Logic ought to be, at least finally, studied as part of the greater—as a portion of the means to the same end ; and its relation to the other parts—to the other means— should be distinctly displayed. If thought be anything more than a sportive exercise of the mind, its purpose is to enable us to know what can be known respecting the facts of the universe : its judgments and conclusions express, or are intended to express, some of those facts : and the connection which Formal Logic, by its analysis of the reasoning process, points out between one proposition and another, exists only because there is a connection between one objective truth and another, which makes it possible for us to know objective truths which have never been observed, in virtue of others which have. This possibility is an eternal mystery and stumbling-block to Formal Logic. The bare idea that any new truth can be brought out of a Concept—that analysis can ever find in it anything which synthesis has not first put in—is absurd on the face of it : yet this is all the explanation that Formal Logic, as viewed by Sir

W. Hamilton, is able to give of the phenomenon; and Mr. Mansel expressly limits the province of Logic to analytic judgments—to such as are merely identical. But what the Logic of mere consistency cannot do, the Logic of the ascertainment of truth, the Philosophy of Evidence in its larger acceptation, can.   It can explain the function of the Ratiocinative process as an instrument of the human intellect in the discovery of truth, and can place it in its true correlation with the other instruments.   It is therefore alone competent to furnish a philosophical theory of Reasoning.   Such partial account as can be given of the process by looking at it solely by itself, however useful and even necessary to accurate thought, does not dispense with, but points out in a more emphatic manner the need of, the more comprehensive Logic of which it should form a part, and which alone can give a meaning or a reason of existence to the Logic styled Formal, or to the reasoning process itself.

CHAPTER XXI.

THE FUNDAMENTAL LAWS OF THOUGHT ACCORDING TO SIR WILLIAM HAMILTON.

HAVING marked out, as the sole province of Logic, the
"Laws of Thought," Sir W. Hamilton naturally proceeds to specify what these are. The "Fundamental
Laws of Thought," of which all other laws that can be
laid down for thought are but particular applications,
are, according to our author, three in number: the Law
of Identity; the Law of Contradiction; and the Law
of Excluded Middle. In his Lectures he recognised a
fourth, "the Law of Reason and Consequent," which
seems to be compounded of the Law of Causation, and
the Leibnitzian "Principle of Sufficient Reason." But
as, in his later speculations, he no longer considered this
as an ultimate law, it needs not be further spoken of.

These three laws he otherwise denominates "The
Conditions of the Thinkable:" * from which it might
have been supposed that he regarded them as Laws of
Thought in the scientific sense of the word law; conditions to which thought *cannot but* conform, and apart
from which it is impossible. One would have said, *à
priori*, that he could not mean anything but this: since
otherwise the expression "Conditions of the Thinkable"
is perverted from its meaning. Nevertheless, this is not
what he means, at least in this place. It is on this
very occasion that he disclaims, as applicable to laws of
thought, the scientific meaning of the term, and declares

---

* Lectures, iii. 79. In the Appendix to the Lectures (iv. 244, 245) he
calls them the Laws of the Thinkable; and the laws of Conception,
Judgment, and Reasoning he distinguishes from them under the name of
"the laws of Thinking in a strict sense."

them to be (like the laws made by Parliament) general
precepts; not necessities of the thinking act, but in-
structions for right thinking.   Yet it would not have
been claiming too much for these three laws, to have
regarded them as laws in the more peremptory sense;
as actual necessities of thought.   Our author could
hardly have meant that we are able to disbelieve that a
thing is itself, or to believe that a thing is, and at the
same time that it is not.   He not only, like other people,
constantly assumes this to be an impossibility, but makes
that impossibility the ground of some of his leading
philosophical doctrines; as when he says that it is impossible for us to doubt the actual facts of consciousness
" because the doubt implies a contradiction." *   It is
true that a person may, in one sense, believe contradictory propositions, that is, he may believe the affirmative at some times and the negative at others, alternately
forgetting the two beliefs.   It is also true that he may
yield a passive assent to two forms of words, which, had
he been fully conscious of their meaning, he would have
known to be, either wholly or in part, an affirmation and
a denial of the same fact.   But when once he is made
to see that there is a contradiction, it is totally impossible
for him to believe it.

Now, to compel people to see a contradiction where
a contradiction is, constitutes the entire office of Logic in
the limited sense in which Sir W. Hamilton conceives
it : and he is quite right in regarding the whole of Logic,
in that narrow sense, as resting on the three laws speci-
fied by him.   To call them the fundamental laws of
Thought is a misnomer; but they are the laws of Consistency.   All inconsistency is a violation of some one
of these laws; an unconscious violation, for knowingly
to violate them is impossible.

Something remains to be said respecting the three
Laws considered singly, as well as respecting our author's
mode of regarding them.

The Law or Principle of Identity (*Principium Identi-*

* Foot-note to Reid, p. 113, and in many other places.

tatis) is no other than the time-honoured axiom, "Whatever is, is," or, in another phraseology, "A thing is the same as itself:" the proposition which Locke, in his chapter on Maxims, treated. with so much disrespect. Sir W. Hamilton, probably finding it difficult to establish the "principle of all logical affirmation" on such a basis as this, presents the axiom * in a modified shape, as an assertion of the identity between a whole and its parts; or rather between a whole Concept, and its parts in Comprehension—the attributes which compose it; for Logic, as conceived by him, has nothing to do with any wholes but Concepts, abstracting altogether (as he asserts) from the reality of the things conceived.†

Although our author still so far defers to the old version of the Principle of Identity, as to say that it is "expressed in the formula A *is* A, or $A = A$," I must admit that while paying this tribute of respect to our ancient friend, he has taken a very substantial and useful liberty with him, and has made him mean much more than he ever meant before. The only fault that can be found (but that is a serious one) is, that if we accept this view of the maxim, we shall require many "principles of logical affirmation" instead of one. For if we are to make a separate principle for every mode in which we have occasion to re-affirm the same thing in different words, we need a large number of them. If we require a special principle to entitle us, when we have affirmed a set of attributes jointly, to affirm over again

---

* Lectures, iii. 79, 80.

† We here see our author by implication admitting that a Concept has no parts except its parts in Comprehension; what he elsewhere calls its parts in Extension being in no sense parts of the Concept, but parts of something else, namely, of the aggregate of concrete objects to which the Concept corresponds. Had Sir W. Hamilton adhered to this rational doctrine, he must have given up his Judgments in Extension: instead of which he not only retains them, but considers them as also founded on the Principle of Identity: though he has expressly limited that principle in a manner inconsistent with founding any judgments on it save Judgments in Comprehension. This contradiction was worth pointing out, but is not worth insisting on, since it may be rectified by extending the scope of the First Law to the identity of *any* whole with its parts, instead of limiting it to the identity of a Concept with its parts in Comprehension only.

2 H

the same attributes severally, we require also a long list of such principles as these : When one thing is before another, the other is after.   When one thing is after another, the other is before.   When one thing is along with another, the other is along with the first.   When one thing is like, or unlike, another, the other is like (or unlike) the first: in short, as many fundamental principles as there are kinds of relation.   For we have need of all these changes of expression in our processes of thought and reasoning.   What is at the bottom of them all is, that Logic (to borrow a phrase from our author) postulates to be allowed to assert the same meaning in any words which will, consistently with their signification, express it.   The use and meaning of a Fundamental Law of Thought is, that it asserts in general terms the right to do something, which the mind needs to do in cases as they arise.   It is in this sense that the Dictum de Omni et Nullo is called the fundamental law of the Syllogism.   But, for this purpose, it is necessary that the Law or Postulate should be stated in so comprehensive and universal a manner as to cover every case in which the act authorised by it requires to be done.   Looked at in this light, the Principle of Identity ought to have been expressed thus : Whatever is true in one form of words, is true in every other form of words which conveys the same meaning. Thus worded, it fulfils the requirements of a First Principle of Thought ; for it is the widest possible expression of an act of thought which is always legitimate, and continually has to be done.*

Understood in this sense, the Principle of Identity absorbs into itself a Postulate of Logic on which Sir W. Hamilton lays great stress, and which he did good service in making prominent, though we shall hereafter find that he sometimes misapplies it.   He expresses it

---

* This principle provides for the whole of what Kant terms Conclusions of Understanding, and Dr. M'Cosh (p. 290) Implied or Transposed Judgments.   They are not conclusions, nor fresh acts of judgment, but the original judgment, expressed in other words.

as follows : * " The only Postulate of Logic which re-
" quires an articulate enouncement is the demand, that
" before dealing with a judgment or reasoning expressed
" in language, the import of its terms should be fully
" understood ; in other words, Logic postulates to be
" allowed to state explicitly in language, all that is
" implicitly contained in the thought." There cannot
be a more just demand : but let us carefully note the
terms in which our author enunciates it, that he may
be held to them afterwards. Everything may be stated
explicitly in language, which is " implicitly contained
in the thought," that is (according to his own interpretation) in the " import of the terms " used. In other
words, we have a right to express explicitly, what has
already been asserted in terms which really mean, though
they do not explicitly declare it. Observe, what has
been already asserted ; not what can be *inferred* from
something that has been asserted. One proposition may
imply another, but unless the implication is in the very
meaning of the terms, it avails nothing. It may be impossible that the one proposition should be true without
the other being true also, and yet Logic cannot " postulate " to be allowed to affirm this last ; she must be required to prove it. Interpreted in this, its true sense,
Sir W. Hamilton's postulate is legitimate, but is only
a particular case of the Principle of Identity in its
most generalised shape. It is a case of postulating
to be allowed to express a given meaning in another
form of words.

As already mentioned, Sir W. Hamilton represents
the Principle of Identity to be " the principle of all
logical affirmation." This I can by no means admit,
whether the Principle in question is taken in Sir W.
Hamilton's narrower, or in my own wider sense. The
reaffirmation in new language of what has already been
asserted—or (descending to particulars and adopting
our author's phraseology) the thinking of a Concept
through an attribute which is a part of itself—can, as

* Lectures, iii. 114.

I formerly observed, be admitted as a correct account of
the nature of affirmation, only in the case of Analytical
Judgments.   In a Synthetical Judgment, the attribute
predicated is thought not as part of, but as existing in a
common subject along with, the group of attributes composing the Concept : and of this operation of thought it
is plain that no principle of Identity can give any account,
since there is a new element introduced, which is not
identical with any part of what pre-existed in thought.
This is clearly seen by Mr. Mansel, who expressly limits
the dominion of the Law of Identity to analytical judgments ; * and, with perfect consistency, regards these as
the only judgments with which Logic, as such, is concerned.   If, then, the Law of Identity is to be upheld
as the principle "of all logical affirmation," we must
understand that logical affirmation does not mean all
affirmation, but only affirmations which communicate
no fact, and merely assert that what is called by a
name, is what the name declares it to be.

   If our author had stated the Law of Identity to be the
principle not of "logical affirmation," but of affirmative
Reasoning, he would have said something far more plausible, and which had been maintained by many of his
predecessors.   The truth is, however, that as far as that
law is a principle of reasoning at all, it is as much a
principle of negative, as of affirmative reasoning.   In
proving a negative, as much as in proving an affirmative,
we require the liberty of exchanging a proposition for
any other that is equipollent with it, and of predicating separately of any subject, all attributes which have
been predicated of it jointly.   These liberties the mind
rightfully claims in all its intellectual operations.   The
principle of Identity is not the peculiar groundwork
of any special kind of thinking, but an indispensable
postulate in all thinking.

   The second of the "Fundamental Laws" is the Law or
Principle of Contradiction (*Principium Contradictionis*);
that two assertions, one of which denies what the other

* Prolegomena Logica, pp. 196, 197.

affirms, cannot be thought together. Most people would
have said, cannot be believed together; but our author
resolutely refuses to recognise belief as any element in
the scientific analysis of a proposition. "This law," he
says, "is the principle of all logical negation and distinction," * and "is logically expressed in the formula,
What is contradictory is unthinkable." † To this he
subjoins, as an equivalent mathematical formula, "A =
not A = o, or A — A = o : " a misapplication and perversion of algebraical symbols, not to be omitted among
other evidences how little familiar he was with mathematical modes of thought.

Concerning the name of this law, Sir W. Hamilton
observes ‡ that "as it enjoins the absence of contradiction
"as the indispensable condition of thought, it ought to
"be called, not the Law of Contradiction, but the Law
"of Non-Contradiction, or of *non-repugnantia*." It seems
that no extent and accuracy of knowledge concerning
the opinions of predecessors, can preserve a thinker from
giving an erroneous interpretation of their meaning by
antedating a confusion of ideas which exists in his own
mind.   The Law of Contradiction does not "enjoin the
absence of contradiction;" it is not an injunction at all.
If those who wrote before Sir W. Hamilton of the Law
or Principle of Contradiction, had meant by those terms
what he did, namely, a rule or precept, it would have
been, no doubt, absurd in them to have given the name
Law of Contradiction, to a Precept of Non-Contradiction.
But I venture to assert that when they spoke of the Law
of Contradiction (which most of them, I believe, never
did, but called it the Principle) they were no more
dreaming of enjoining anything, than when they spoke
of the Law or Principle of Identity they intended to
enjoin identity.   They used those terms in their proper
scientific, and not, as Sir W. Hamilton does, in their
moral or legislative sense.   By the Law of Identity they
meant one of the properties of identity, namely, that a
proposition which is identical must be true.   And by the

* Lectures, iii. 82.   † Ibid. p. 81.   ‡ Ibid. p. 82.

Law of Contradiction they meant one of the properties of contradiction, namely, that what is contradictory cannot be true. We should express their meaning
better if instead of the word Law, we used the expressions, Doctrine of Identity, and Doctrine of Contradiction.
This is what they had in their minds, and even expressed
by their words; for the word Principle, with them, meant
a particular kind of Doctrine, namely, one which is the
groundwork, and justifying authority, of a whole class
of operations of the mind. If the word Law is to be
retained, *Principium Contradictionis* would be better
translated, not Law of Contradiction, but Law of Contradictory Propositions; were it not for the consideration, that the principle of Excluded Middle is also a
law of contradictory propositions.

The Law of Contradiction, according to Sir W. Hamilton, is the "principle of all logical negation." * I do not
see how it can be the principle of any negation except the
denial that a thing is the contradictory of itself. That
a sight is not a taste is a negation, and it must be a very
narrow use of the term which refuses it the title of a
logical negation. But there is no contradiction between
a sight and a taste. That blue is not green, involves no
logical contradiction. We could believe that a green
thing may be blue, as easily as we believe that a round
thing may be blue, if experience did not teach us the
incompatibility of the former attributes, and the compatibility of the latter. The negative judgment, that a
man is not a horse, may indeed be said to be grounded on
the Principle of Contradiction, inasmuch as the opposite
assertion, that a man is a horse, is in certain of its parts
contradictory, though in others only false. The word
man may be understood as signifying (in precise logical
language, connoting) among the other properties, that of
having exactly two legs—the word horse, that of having
four; and in respect of this particular part of the meaning of the terms, the subject and the predicate are contradictory, the one affirming and the other denying the

* Lectures, iii. 82.

extra number of legs. But suppose the subject and predicate of the judgment to be names of classes constituted by positive attributes without negative, as mathematician and moralist, or merchant and philosopher. An affirmation uniting them may then be false, but cannot possibly be self-contradictory. The Law of Contradiction cannot be the ground on which it is asserted that a mathematician is not a moralist, for the two Concepts are only different, not contradictory, nor even repugnant.

Others have said, that the Law or Doctrine of Contradiction is the principle of Negative Reasoning. But the obvious truth is, that it is the principle of all Reasoning, so far as reasoning can be regarded apart from objective truth or falsehood. For, abstractedly from that consideration, the only meaning of validity in reasoning is that it neither involves a contradiction, nor infers anything the denial of which would not contradict the premises. Valid reasoning, from the point of view of merely Formal Logic, is a negative conception ; it means, reasoning which is not self-destructive ; which cannot be discovered to be worthless from its own data. It would be absurd to suppose that the validity of the reasoning process itself, either affirmative or negative, could be proved from the Doctrine of Contradiction ; for though a given syllogism may be proved valid by showing that the falsity of the conclusion, combined with the truth of one premise, would contradict the truth of the other, this can only be done by another syllogism, so that the validity of Reasoning would be taken for granted in the attempt to prove it. The Law of Contradiction is a principle of reasoning in the same sense, and in the same sense only, as the Law of Identity is. It is the generalisation of a mental act which is of continual occurrence, and which cannot be dispensed with in reasoning. As we require the liberty of substituting for a given assertion, the same assertion in different words, so we require the liberty of substituting, for any assertion, the denial of its contradictory. The affirmation of the one and the denial of the other are logical equivalents, which it is allowable and indispensable to make use of as mutually convertible.

The third "Fundamental Law" is the law or principle of Excluded Middle (*principium Exclusi Medii vel Tertii*), of which the purport is, that, of two directly contradictory propositions, one or the other must be true. I am now expressing the axiom in my own language, for the tortuous phraseology * by which our author escapes from recognising the ideas of truth and falsity, having already been sufficiently exemplified, may here be disregarded. This axiom is the other half of the doctrine of Contradictory Propositions. By the law of Contradiction, contradictory propositions cannot both be true; by the law of Excluded Middle, they cannot both be false. Or, to state the meaning in other language, by the law of Contradiction a proposition cannot be both true and false; by the law of Excluded Middle it must be either true or false—there is no third possibility.

Sir W. Hamilton says that this law is "the principle of disjunctive judgments." †   By disjunctive judgments, logicians have always meant, judgments in this form : Either this is true or that is true.   The law of Excluded Middle cannot be the principle of any disjunctive judgment but those in which the subject of both the members is the same, and one of the predicates a simple negation of the other : as, A is either B or not B.   That indeed rests on the principle of Excluded Middle, or rather, is the very formula of that principle. It is here to be remarked that Sir W. Hamilton, after Krug, but by a very unaccountable departure from the common usage of logicians, confines the name of Disjunctive Judgments to those in which all the alternative propositions have the same subject : " D is either B, or C, or A." ‡   This is not only an arbitrary change in the meaning of words, but renders the classification of propositions incomplete, leaving two kinds of disjunctive propositions (Either B, C, or D, is A, and Either A is E

* Lectures, iii. 83.   † Ibid. p. 84.   ‡ Ibid. p. 239.

or C is D) unrecognised and without a name.   But even
in our author's restricted sense of the word Disjunctive,
I cannot see how the Law of Excluded Middle can be
said to be the principle of *all* disjunctive judgments.
The judgment that A is either B or not B, is warranted
and its truth certified by the Law of Excluded Middle:
but the judgment that A is either B or C, both B and
C being positive, requires some other voucher than the
law that one or other of two contradictories must be true.
Thus, " X is either a man or a brute," is not a judgment
grounded on the principle of Excluded Middle, since
brute is not a bare negation of man, but includes the
positive attribute of being an animal, which X may
possibly not be.

It might be said, with more plausibility, that the Law
of Excluded Middle is the principle of Disjunctive Reasoning.   Thus, in the last example, " X is either a man
or a brute" may be a conclusion from two premises, that
X is an animal, and that every animal is either a man
or a brute: the latter of which is a disjunctive judgment grounded on the Law of Excluded Middle.   But
it is not the fact that all disjunctive conclusions are
inferred from premises of this nature.   Having been
told that A has lost a son, I conclude that either B, C,
or D (A having no other sons) is dead: what kind of
reasoning is this?   Disjunctive, surely: it has a disjunctive premise, and leads to a disjunctive conclusion.
But the disjunctive premise (Every son of A is either B,
C, or D) does not rest on the Law of Excluded Middle,
or on any necessity of thought; it rests on my knowledge of the individual fact.

The third Law, however, like the two others, is one
of the principles of all reasonings, being the generalisation of a process which is liable to be required in all of
them.   As the Doctrine of Contradiction authorises us
to substitute for the assertion of either of two contradictory propositions, the denial of the other, so the doctrine of Excluded Middle empowers us to substitute for
the denial of either of two contradictory propositions,

the assertion of the other.   Thus all the three principles which our author terms the Fundamental Laws of Thought, are universal postulates of Reasoning ; and as such, are entitled to the conspicuous position which our author assigns to them in Logic : though it is evident that they ought not to be placed at the very beginning of the subject, but at the earliest, in its Second Part, the theory of Judgments, or Propositions : since they essentially involve the ideas of Truth and Falsity, which are attributes only of judgments, not of names, or Concepts.

It is another question altogether, what we ought to think of these three principles, considered not as general expressions of legitimate intellectual processes, but as themselves speculative truths.   Sir W. Hamilton considers them to be such in a very universal sense indeed, since he thinks we are bound to regard them as true beyond the sphere of either real or imaginable phenomenal experience—to be true of Things in Themselves —of Noumena.   " Whatever," he says,* " violates the " laws, whether of Identity, of Contradiction, or of Ex- " cluded Middle, we feel to be absolutely impossible, " not only in thought, but in existence.   Thus we cannot " attribute even to Omnipotence the power of making " a thing different from itself, of making a thing at " once to be and not to be, of making a thing neither to " be nor not to be.   These three laws thus determine to " us the sphere of possibility and of impossibility : and " this not merely in thought but in reality, not only " logically but metaphysically."   And in another place :† " if the true character of objective validity be univer- " sality, the laws of Logic are really of that character, " for those laws constrain us, by their own authority, to " regard them as the universal laws not only of human " thought, but of universal reason."   A few pages before, our author took pains to impress upon us that we were not to regard these laws as necessities of thought, but as general precepts " which we are able to violate : " but

* Lectures, iii. 98.   † Ibid. iv. 65.

they now appear to be necessities of thought and something more.

I readily admit that these three general propositions
are universally true of all phenomena.   I also admit
that if there are any inherent necessities of thought,
these are such.   I express myself in this qualified manner, because whoever is aware how artificial, modifiable,
the creatures of circumstances, and alterable by circumstances, most of the supposed necessities of thought are
(though real necessities to a given person at a given
time), will hesitate to affirm of any such necessities that
they are an original part of our mental constitution.
Whether the three so-called Fundamental Laws are laws
of our thoughts by the native structure of the mind, or
merely because we perceive them to be universally true
of observed phenomena, I will not positively decide:
but they are laws of our thoughts now, and invincibly
so.   They may or may not be capable of alteration by
experience, but the conditions of our existence deny to
us the experience which would be required to alter them.
Any assertion, therefore, which conflicts with one of these
laws—any proposition, for instance, which asserts a contradiction, though it were on a subject wholly removed
from the sphere of our experience, is to us unbelievable.
The belief in such a proposition is, in the present constitution of nature, impossible as a mental fact.*

---

* "When remembering a certain thing as in a certain place, the place
"and the thing are mentally represented together; while to think of the
"non-existence of the thing in that place, implies a consciousness in which
"the place is represented but not the thing. Similarly, if instead of
"thinking of an object as colourless, we think of it as having colour, the
"change consists in the addition to the concept of an element that was
"before absent from it—the object cannot be thought of first as red and
"then as not red, without one component of the thought being totally
"expelled from the mind by another. The law of the Excluded Middle,
"then, is simply a generalisation of the universal experience that some
"mental states are directly destructive of other states. It formulates a
"certain absolutely constant law, that the appearance of any positive
"mode of consciousness cannot occur without excluding a correlative
"negative mode: and that the negative mode cannot occur without ex-
"cluding the correlative positive mode: the antithesis of positive and
"negative being, indeed, merely an expression of this experience. Hence
"it follows that if consciousness is not in one of the two modes it must
"be in the other."—Mr. Herbert Spencer, in *Fortnightly Review* for July
15, 1865.

But Sir W. Hamilton goes beyond this : he thinks
that the obstacle to belief does not lie solely in an
incapacity of our believing faculty, but in objective incapacities of existence ; that the "Fundamental Laws
of Thought" are laws of existence too, and may be
known to be true not only of Phenomena but also of
Noumena.   Of this, however, as of all else relating to
Noumena, the verdict of philosophy, I apprehend, must
be that we are entirely ignorant. The distinction itself
is but an idle one ; for since Noumena, if they exist, are
wholly unknowable by us, except phenomenally, through
their effects on us ; and since all attributes which exist
for us, even in our fancy, are but phenomena, there is
nothing for us either to affirm or deny of a Noumenon
except phenomenal attributes : existence itself, as we
conceive it, being merely the power of producing phenomena.   Now in respect to phenomenal attributes, no
one denies the three "Fundamental Laws" to be universally true.   Since then they are laws of all Phenomena, and since Existence has to us no meaning but
one which has relation to Phenomena, we are quite safe
in looking upon them as laws of Existence.   This is
sufficient for those who hold the doctrine of the Relativity of human knowledge.   But Sir W. Hamilton, as
has been seen, does not hold that doctrine, though he
holds a verbal truism which he chooses to call by the
same name.   His opinion is that we do know something
more than phenomena : that we know the Primary
Qualities of bodies as existing in the Noumena, in the
things themselves, and not as mere powers of affecting
us.   Sir W. Hamilton, therefore, needs another kind
of argument to establish the doctrine that the Laws of
Identity, Contradiction, and Excluded Middle, are laws
of all existence : and here we leave it : *

"To deny the universal application of the three laws
" is, in fact, to subvert the reality of thought; and as this
" subversion is itself an act of thought, it in fact annihi-
" lates itself.   When, for example, I say that A is, and

* Lectures, iii. 90, 100.

" then say that A is not, by the second assertion I sub-
" late or take away what, by the first assertion, I posited
" or laid down; thought, in the one case, undoing by
" negation what, in the other, it had by affirmation
" done." This proves only that a contradiction is unthinkable, not that it is impossible in point of fact.
But what follows goes more directly to the mark.   " But
" when it is asserted that A existing and A non-existing
" are at once true, what does it imply? It implies that
" negation and affirmation correspond to nothing out of
" the mind,—that there is no agreement, no disagree-
" ment between thought and its objects; and this is
" tantamount to saying that truth and falsehood are
" merely empty sounds. For if we only think by affirma-
" tion and negation, and if these are only as they are
" exclusive of each other, it follows that unless existence
" and non-existence be opposed objectively in the same
" manner as affirmation and negation are opposed sub-
" jectively, all our thought is a mere illusion. Thus
" it is that those who would assert the possibility of
" contradictions being at once true, in fact annihilate
" the possibility of truth itself, and the whole significance
" of thought."
Of this favourite style of argument with our author
we have already had many specimens, and have said so
much about them, that we can afford to be brief in the
present instance. Assuming it to be true that "to deny
the universal application of the three laws" as laws
of existence "is to subvert the reality of thought:" is
anything added to the force of this consideration by
saying that "this subversion is itself an act of thought"?
If the reality of thought *can* be subverted, is there any
peculiar enormity in doing it by means of thought itself?
In what other way can we imagine it to be done? And
if it were true that thought is an invalid process, what
better proof of this could be given than that we could,
by thinking, arrive at the conclusion that our thoughts
are not to be trusted? Sir W. Hamilton always seems
to suppose that the imaginary sceptic, who doubts the

validity of thought altogether, is obliged to claim a greater validity for his subversive thoughts than he allows to the thoughts they subvert. But it is enough for him to claim the same validity, so that all opinions are thrown into equal uncertainty.* Sir W. Hamilton, of all men, ought to know this, for when he is himself on the sceptical side of any question, as when speaking of the Absolute, or anything else which he deems inaccessible to the human faculties, this is the very line of argument he employs. He proves the invalidity, as regards those subjects, of the thinking process, by showing that it lands us in contradictions.†

But it is entirely inadmissible that to suppose that a law of thought need not necessarily be a law of existence, invalidates the thinking process. If, indeed, there were any law necessitating us to think a relation between *phenomena* which does not in fact exist between the phenomena, then certainly the thinking process would

---

* The principal extant interpreter of the ancient Scepticism, Sextus Empiricus, expressly defines as its essence and scope, τὸ παντὶ λόγῳ λόγον ἴσον ἀντικεῖσθαι. (Pyrrh. Hypot.) It is, indeed, impossible to conceive Scepticism otherwise. Anything more would not be Scepticism, but Negative Dogmatism.

† "If I," says our author (Appendix to Lectures, i. 402), "have done "anything meritorious in philosophy, it is in the attempt to explain the "phenomena of these contradictions, in showing that they arise only "when intelligence transcends the limits to which its legitimate exercise "is restricted." "In generating its antinomies, Kant's Reason transcended "its limits, violated its laws. . . . Reason is only self-contradictory when "driven beyond its legitimate bounds." (Appendix to Lectures, ii. 543.) "It is only when transcending that sphere, when founding on its illegiti- "mate as on its legitimate exercise, that it affords a contradictory "result. . . . The dogmatic assertion of necessity—of Fatalism, and the "dogmatic assertion of Liberty, are the counter and equally inconceivable "conclusions from reliance on the illegitimate and one-sided." (Appendix to Lectures, i. 403.) To the same effect Mr. Mansel, throughout his "Limits of Religious Thought."

In one of the Appendices to the Lectures on Metaphysics (ii. 527, 528), Sir W. Hamilton makes out a long list of contradictions or antinomies (of which we shall have something to say hereafter) involved, as he thinks, in the attempt to conceive the Infinite, and which he considers as evidence that the notion is beyond the reach of the human faculties. Yet he will not allow that the fact of leading to contradictions, which he habitually urges as an argument against the validity of some thought, would be admissible as an argument against Thought in general, if it could be brought home to it. At least he will not allow it in this place: for in his theory of the veracity of Consciousness he does (Lectures, i. 277).

be proved invalid, because we should be compelled by it to think true something which would really be false. But if the mind is incapable of thinking anything respecting Noumena except the Phenomena which it considers as proceeding from them, and to which it can appeal to test its thoughts; and if we are under no necessity of thinking these otherwise than in conformity to what they really are; we may refuse to believe that our generalisations from the Phenomenal attributes of Noumena can be applied to Noumena in any other aspect, without in the least invalidating the operation of thought in regard to anything to which thought is applicable. We may say to Sir W. Hamilton what he says himself in another case : * "I only say that thought is "limited; but, within its limits, I do not deny, I do not "subvert, its truth." As he elsewhere observes, translating from Esser,† truth consists "solely in the correspondence of our thoughts with their objects." If the only real object of thought, even when we are nominally speaking of Noumena, are Phenomena, our thoughts are true when they are made to correspond with Phenomena : and, the possibility of this being denied by no one, the thinking process is valid whether our laws of thought are laws of absolute existence or not.

* Lectures, iii. 100.   † Ibid. p. 107 ; see also iv. 61.

CHAPTER XXII.

OF SIR WILLIAM HAMILTON'S SUPPOSED IMPROVEMENTS IN
FORMAL LOGIC.

OF all Sir W. Hamilton's philosophical achievements,
there is none, except perhaps his "Philosophy of the
Conditioned," on account of which so much merit has
been claimed for him, as the additions and corrections
which he is supposed to have contributed to the doctrine of the Syllogism. These may be summed up in
two principal theories, with their numerous corollaries
and applications; the recognition of two kinds of
Syllogism, Syllogisms in Extension and Syllogisms in
Comprehension; and the doctrine of the Quantification
of the Predicate. To the former of these, Sir W.
Hamilton ascribed great importance. According to him,
all previous logicians, "with the doubtful exception of
"Aristotle," "have altogether overlooked the reasoning
"in Comprehension"—"have marvellously overlooked
"one, and that the simplest and most natural of these
"descriptions of reasoning,—the reasoning in the quan-
"tity of comprehension:" and he claims, in directing
attention to it, to have "relieved a radical defect and
vital inconsistency in the present logical system." *   For
the other theory, that of the Quantification of the Predicate, still loftier claims are advanced both by himself
and by others.   Mr. Baynes, with an enthusiasm natural
and not ungraceful in a pupil, concludes his Essay on
the subject (which still remains the clearest exposition
of his master's doctrine) with the following words : †

---

* Lectures, iii. 297, 304, 378.   Appendix, iv. 250.
† An Essay on the New Analytic of Logical Forms, being that which

" We cannot, however, close without expressing the true
" joy we feel (though, were the feeling less strong, we
" might shrink from the intrusion), that in our own
" country, and in our time, this discovery has been made.
" We rejoice to know that one has at length arisen, able
" to recognise and complete the plan of the mighty
" builder, Aristotle,—to lay the top stone on that fabric,
" the foundations of which were laid more than two
" thousand years ago, by the master hand of the Stagi-
" rite, which, after the labours of many generations of
" workmen, who have from time to time built up one part
" here and taken down another there—remains substan-
" tially as he left it ; but which, when finished, shall be
" seen to be an edifice of wondrous beauty, harmony,
" and completeness."

Previous to discussing these additions to the Syllogistic
Theory, it is necessary to revert to a doctrine which has
been briefly stated in a former chapter, but did not then
receive all the elucidation it requires, and which has a
most important bearing on both of Sir W. Hamilton's
supposed discoveries.   This is, that all Judgments (except where both the terms are proper names) are really
judgments in Comprehension ; though it is customary,
and the natural tendency of the mind, to express most of
them in terms of Extension.   In other words, we never
really predicate anything but attributes, though, in the
usage of language, we commonly predicate them by
means of words which are names of concrete objects.

When, for example, I say, The sky is blue ; my meaning, and my whole meaning, is that the sky has that particular colour.   I am not thinking of the class blue, as
regards extension, at all.   I am not caring, nor necessarily knowing, what blue things there are, or if there
is any blue thing except the sky.   I am thinking only
of the sensation of blue, and am judging that the sky

" gained the prize proposed by Sir William Hamilton in the year 1846 for
" the best exposition of the new Doctrine propounded in his Lectures.
" With an Historical Appendix.   By Thomas Spencer Baynes, Translator
" of the Port Royal Logic " (p. 80).

produces this sensation in my sensitive faculty; or (to express the meaning in technical language) that the quality answering to the sensation of blue, or the power of exciting the sensation of blue, is an attribute of the sky.   When again I say, All oxen ruminate, I have nothing to do with the predicate, considered in extension.   I may know, or be ignorant, that there are other ruminating animals besides oxen.   Whether I do or do not know it, it does not, unless by mere accident, pass through my mind.   In judging that oxen ruminate, I do not, unless accidentally, think under the notion ruminate (to borrow Sir W. Hamilton's phraseology) any other notion than that of an ox.   The Comprehension of the predicate—the attribute or set of attributes signified by it—are all that I have in my mind; and the relation of this attribute or these attributes to the subject is the entire matter of the judgment.

In one of the examples above given, the predicate is an adjective, and in the other a verb, which, in a logical point of view, is classed with adjectives : but its being a noun substantive makes no difference.   For reasons easily shown, a substantive is more strongly associated with the ideas of the concrete objects denoted by it, than an adjective or a verb is.   But when we predicate a substantive—when we say, Philip is a man, or, A herring is a fish—do the words man and fish signify anything to us but the bundles of attributes connoted by them?   Do the propositions mean anything except that Philip has the human attributes, and a herring the piscine ones?   Assuredly not.   Any notion of a multitude of other men, among whom Philip is ranked, or a variety of fishes besides herrings, is foreign to the proposition. The proposition does not decide whether there is this additional quantity or no.   It affirms the attributes of its own particular subject, and of no other.

Passing now from the predicate to the subject, we shall find that the subject also, if a general term or notion, is always construed in Comprehension, that is, by the attributes which constitute it, and has no other

meaning in thought. When I judge that all oxen ruminate, what do I mean by all oxen? I have no image
in my mind of all oxen. I do not, nor ever shall, know
all of them, and I am not thinking even of all those
I do know. "All oxen," in my thoughts, does not
mean particular animals—it means the objects, whatever
they may be, that have the attributes by which oxen
are recognised, and which compose the notion of an ox.
Wherever these attributes shall be found, there, as I
judge, the attribute of ruminating will be found also:
that is the entire purport of the judgment. Its meaning
is a meaning in attributes, and nothing else. It supposes
subjects, but merely as all attributes suppose them.

But there is another mode of interpreting the same
proposition, by considering it as a part of the statement
of a classification and mental co-ordination of the objects
which exist in nature. The proposition is then looked
upon as an assertion respecting given objects ; affirming
what other individual objects they are classed among by
the general scheme of human language. Thus interpreted, the proposition "all oxen ruminate" may be read
as follows : If all creatures that ruminate were collected
in a vast plain, and I were required to search the world
and point out all oxen, they would all be found among
the crowd on that plain, and none anywhere else. Moreover, this would have been the case in all past time, and
will at any future, while the present order of nature
lasts. This is the proposition "All oxen ruminate"
interpreted in Extension. Will any one say that a process of thought like this passes in the mind of whoever
makes the affirmation? It is a point of view in which the
proposition may be regarded ; it is one of the aspects of
the fact asserted in the proposition. But it is not the
aspect in which the proposition presents it to the mind.

It will, however, very naturally be objected—If the
meaning in our mind is that the bovine attributes are
always accompanied by the attribute of ruminating, why
do we, except for the purposes of abstract logic or metaphysics, never say this, but always say "All oxen rumi-

nate?" The reason is, that we have no other convenient and compact mode of speaking. Most attributes, and nearly all large "bundles of attributes," have no names of their own. We can only name them by a circumlocution. We are accustomed to speak of attributes not by names given to themselves, but by means of the names which they give to the objects they are attributes of. We do not talk of the phenomena which accompany piscinity; we talk of the phenomena of fishes. We do not frame a definition of piscinity, but a definition of a fish. The definition, however, of a fish is exactly the same which the definition of piscinity would be; it is an enumeration of the same attributes. Language is constructed upon the principle of naming concrete objects first: it does not always name abstractions at all, and when it does, the names are almost always derived from those of concrete objects. The reasons are obvious. Objects—even classes of objects—being conceivable by a much less effort of abstraction than attributes, are in the necessary order of things conceived and named earlier, and remain always more familiar to the mind: attributes, even when they come to be conceived, cannot be conceived in a detached state, but are always (as maybe said by an adaptation of the Hamiltonian phraseology) thought through objects of some sort. Consequently all familiar propositions are expressed in the language which denotes objects, and not in that which denotes attributes. Nor is this all. What is primarily important to us in our sensations and impressions, is their permanent groups. In our particular and passing sensations (unless in cases of exceptional intensity) the important thing to us is, not the sensation itself, but to what group it belongs; what concrete object, what Permanent Possibility of Sensation, it indicates the presence of. The mind consequently hurries on from the sensible impressions that proceed from an outward object, to the object itself, and its subsequent thoughts revolve round that. It is on the concrete object indicated, that the expectation of future sensations depends; and the concrete object, consequently, in most cases, exclusively engages our thoughts, and stimulates us to mark it by a name. The name, to answer its purpose, must remind ourselves, and inform others, of the sensations we or they have to expect: that is, it must connote an attribute, or set of attributes. And men did not at first name attributes in any other than this indirect manner. They gave no direct names to attributes, because they did not conceive attributes as having any separate existence. As they began by naming only concrete objects, so the first names by which they expressed even the results of abstraction, were not names of attributes in the abstract, regarded apart from their objects, but names of concrete objects signifying the presence of the attributes. Men talked of blue, or of blue things, before they talked of blueness. Even when they did talk of blueness, it was originally not as the attribute, but as an imaginary cause of the attribute, which cause they figured to themselves as itself a concrete thing, residing in the object.

It thus appears that though all judgments consist in ascribing attributes, the original and natural mode of expressing them was by general names denoting concrete objects, and only connoting attributes; and by the structure of language this remains the only concise mode, and the only one which, addressing itself to familiar associations, conveys the meaning at once, to minds not exercised in metaphysical abstraction. But this does not alter the obvious truth, that concrete objects are only known by attributes, are only distinguished by attributes, and that the concrete names by which we speak of them mean nothing but attributes, or " bundles of attributes." Our representation in thought of a concrete object is but a representation of attributes, and our concept of a class of concrete objects is but a certain portion of those attributes, not, indeed, separately conceived or imaged, but exclusively attended to. There is, therefore, nothing in our mind when we affirm a general proposition, but attributes, and their coexistence or repugnance: and the position is made out, that all judgments, expressed by means of general terms, are judgments in Comprehension, though always, unless for some special purpose, expressed in Extension.

If this be the true doctrine of Judgments, what is meant by saying that there are two sorts of Judgment, one in Extension, the other in Comprehension, and two kinds of reasoning corresponding to these, one of which, that in Comprehension, had been overlooked by all logicians, except possibly Aristotle, up to the time of Sir W. Hamilton? All our ordinary judgments are in Comprehension only, Extension not being thought of. But we may, if we please, make the Extension of our general terms an express object of thought, and this may be called thinking in Extension, though it is rather thinking about Extension. When I judge that all oxen ruminate, I have nothing in my thoughts but the attributes and their coexistence. But when, by reflection, I perceive what the proposition implies, I remark, that other things may ruminate besides oxen; and that the unknown multitude of things which ruminate form a mass, with which the unknown multitude of things having the attributes of oxen is either identical, or is wholly comprised in it. Which of these two is the truth I may not know, and if I did, took no notice of it when I assented to the proposition "all oxen ruminate." But I perceive, on consideration, that one or other of them must be true. Though I had not this in my mind when I affirmed that all oxen ruminate, I can have it now; I can make the concrete objects denoted by each of the two names an object of thought, as a collective though indefinite aggregate; in other words, I can make the Extension of the names (or notions) an object of direct consciousness. When I do this, I perceive that this operation introduces no new fact, but is only a different mode of contemplating the very fact which I had previously expressed by the words "all oxen ruminate." The fact is the same, but the mode of contemplating it is different: the mental operation, the act of thought, is not only a distinct act, but an act of a different kind.

There is thus, in all propositions (save those in which

both terms are Proper, that is, in significant, names) a judgment concerning attributes (called by Sir W. Hamilton a judgment in Comprehension), which we make as a matter of course, and a possible judgment in or concerning Extension, which we may make, and which will be true if the former is true. Nevertheless (as has just been shown), the conditions of primitive thought, and subsequent convenience, cause us generally to enunciate our propositions in terms appropriate to the derivative judgment which we seldom make, rather than to the primitive judgment which we always make. And this explains why, though the meaning of all propositions in which general terms are used is in Comprehension, writers on logic always explain the rules of the Syllogism in reference to Extension alone. It is because the framers of the rules did not concern themselves with propositions or reasonings as they exist in thought, but only as they are expressed in language. And in this they were justified. For the syllogism is not the form in which we necessarily reason, but a test of reasoning : a form into which we may translate any reasoning, with the effect of exposing all the points at which any unwarranted inference can have got in. According to this view of the Syllogism—for the justification of which I must refer to the Second Book of my System of Logic —the syllogistic theory is only concerned with providing forms suitable to test the validity of inferences : and it was not necessary that the forms in which reasoning was directed to be written, should be those in which it is carried on in thought, so long as they are practically equivalent, that is, so long as the propositions in words are always true or false according as the judgments in thought are so. The propositions in Extension, being, in this sense, exactly equivalent to the judgments in Comprehension, served quite as well to ground forms of ratiocination upon : and as the validity of the forms was more easily and conveniently shown through the concrete conception of comparing classes of objects, than through the abstract one of recognising coexistence of attributes, logicians were perfectly justified in taking the course, which, in any case, the established forms of language would doubtless have forced upon them. They are thus deserving of no blame, though their mode of proceeding has been attended with some practical mischief, by diverting the attention of thinkers from what really constitutes the meaning of Propositions. It has also been one of the causes of the prejudice so general in the last three centuries, against the syllogistic theory. For a doctrine which defined one of the two great processes of the discovery of truth as consisting in the operation of placing objects in a class and then finding them there, can never, I think, have really satisfied any competent thinker, however he may have acquiesced in it for want of a better.   There must always have been a dormant sense of discontent, an obscure feeling that this was a description of the reasoning process by one of its accidents, though an inseparable accident.*

---

* Dr. M'Cosh has some partially just observations on this subject. He admits (p. 292) that "in by far the greater number of propositions, the primary "and uppermost sense is in Comprehension." He says, however (p. 294), that in some, "the uppermost thought is in Extension. Thus, when the "young student of Natural History is told that a crocodile is a reptile, "his idea is of a class, of which he may afterwards learn the marks." And it is true that when the known purpose of the statement is to declare what place the object occupies in a classification, a fact of classification is the real meaning of the proposition. This is emphatically the exception which proves the rule. Dr. M'Cosh adds, "the mind in its discursive "operations tends to go on from Comprehension to Extension."   This I admit ; but the thought in Comprehension comes first : the thought in Extension rests on the thought in Comprehension, and follows it ; but is so closely linked with it that it can hardly help following. The circumstance, however, that the proposition is familiarly expressed in concrete language, does not prove it to be thought in Extension. The practice of so expressing it must, no doubt, as Dr. M'Cosh says, "proceed from some law of thought as applied to things ; " but the law of thought it proceeds from is merely the obvious one, that concrete language, requiring for its formation a lower degree of abstraction, was earliest formed, took possession of the field, and is still the most familiar. When Dr. M'Cosh goes on to say (p. 303) that although "so far as propositions are concerned, "spontaneous thought is chiefly in Comprehension," the case is "different "in regard to reasoning, the uppermost thought in which is always in "Extension," I cannot agree with him. If the meaning, in consciousness, of the premises when separate, is in Comprehension, it is not natural that the derivative and subordinate meaning in Extension should leap to the front as soon as the premises are brought together. But if, instead of "in reasoning," Dr. M'Cosh had said "in the artificial formula of Reasoning called Syllogism," I think he would have been right.

Sir W. Hamilton distinguishes two kinds of Syllogism, Extensive and Comprehensive. " For while * every syl-"logism infers that the part of a part is a part of the "whole, it does this either in the quantity of Extension "—the Predicate of the two notions compared in the "Question and Conclusion being the greatest whole, and "the subject the smallest part ; or in the counter quan-"tity of Comprehension, the subject of these two notions "being the greatest whole, and the Predicate the smallest "part." He acknowledges, however, that both syllogisms are identically the same argument ; " every syllogism in "the one quantity being convertible into a syllogism ab-"solutely equivalent in the other quantity." And what is the difference in form and language between the two syllogisms ? According to our author it is merely a difference in the order of the premises. The following,†

" Every morally responsible agent is a free agent ;

" Man is a morally responsible agent ;

" Therefore man is a free agent,"

is, according to him, a syllogism in Extension. Trans-pose the premises, and write it thus,‡

" Man is a responsible agent ;

" But a responsible agent is a free agent ;

" Therefore, man is a free agent,"

and we have, according to him, a syllogism in Compre-hension. Far, however, from constituting two kinds of reasoning, this does not even supply us with two different forms of it. He himself says elsewhere,§ that " the "transposition of the propositions of a syllogism affords "no modifications of form yielding more than a super-"ficial character." And even this superficial difference he with his own hands abolishes, saying,‖ that any syllo-gism whatever " can be perspicuously expressed not only "by the normal, but by any of the five consecutions of "its propositions which deviate from the regular order," and that " a syllogism in Comprehension is equally

---

* Lectures, iii. 286, 287.
† Lectures, iii. p. 270.   ‡ Ibid. p. 273.
§ Ibid. p. 399.   ‖ Ibid. pp. 397, 398.

"susceptible of a transposition of its propositions as a
" syllogism in Extension."   So that the slight distinction
of form which he seemed at first to contend for, does not
exist ; a Syllogism in Comprehension, and the corresponding Syllogism in Extension, are word for word the
same.   Instead of " every syllogism in the one quantity "
being " convertible into a syllogism absolutely equivalent
in the other quantity," every syllogism is already a
syllogism in both quantities.*

The distinction, therefore, is not between two kinds,
or even between two forms, of syllogism, but between
two modes of construing the meaning of the same syllogism.   And what are these two modes ?   Sir W. Hamilton says, that they are distinguished by a difference
in the meaning of the copula.   "In † the one process,
" that, to wit, in extension, the copula *is*, means *is con-
" tained under*, whereas in the other, it means *com-
" prehends in*.   Thus, the proposition *God is merciful*,
" viewed as in the one quantity, signifies *God is contained
" under merciful*, that is, the notion *God* is contained
" under the notion *merciful;* viewed as in the other,
" means, *God comprehends merciful*, that is, the notion
" *God comprehends in it* the notion *merciful*."

I cannot admit this to be a true analysis of the meaning
of the proposition, either in Extension or in Comprehension.   The statement that God is merciful I construe

---

* It is curious to observe with what facility Sir W. Hamilton drives two
conflicting opinions together in a team.   The passages quoted in the text
are destructive of any notion of a different order of the premises in a
Syllogism of Extension and in one of Comprehension.   Yet this notion
maintains full possession of our author's mind.   We have found him
accusing all logical writers of overlooking Reasoning in Comprehension ;
but he thinks that they exceptionally recognised it in the case of the
Sorites, and that in that case, by a contrary error, they "altogether over-
" looked the possibility of a Reasoning in Extension" (Lectures, iii. 379–384),
solely because, in the Sorites, they inverted the usual order of the premises.
On a similar foundation stands his charge against the Fourth Figure, of
being "a monster undeserving of toleration," because instead of keeping
to one of the two quantities, Extension and Comprehension, it reasons (he
says) across from one of them to the other.   This is merely because the
Fourth Figure, while it draws the same conclusion which might have been
drawn in the First, reverses the order of the premises.   (Lectures, iii.
425–428.)
    † Lectures, iii. 274.

as an affirmation not concerning the notion God, but the Being God. Interpreted in Comprehension I hold it to mean, that this Being has the attribute signified by the word merciful, or, in our author's language, comprehended in the concept. Interpreted in Extension I render it thus : the Being, God, is either the only being, or one of the beings, forming the class merciful, or, in other words, possessing the attribute mercifulness. Thus stated, who can doubt which of the two is the original and natural judgment, and which is a derivative and artificial mode of restating it? The difference between them is slight, but real, and consists in this, that the second construction introduces the idea of other possible merciful beings, an idea not suggested by the first construction. This suggestion gives rise to the idea of a *class* merciful, and of God as a member of that class : notions which are not present to the mind at all when it simply assents to the proposition that God is merciful. To make a distinction between Reasoning in Extension and in Comprehension, when the same syllogism serves for both, could only be admissible if we employed the same words having sometimes in our mind the meaning in Extension, sometimes that in Comprehension : but in reality all reasoning is thought solely in Comprehension, except when we, for a technical purpose, perform a second act of thought upon the Extension—which in general we do not, and have no need to, consider.

Nor is this the only objection to Sir W. Hamilton's doctrine. There is another, less obvious, but equally fatal. The statement in Comprehension is, that A has the attributes comprehended in B. The statement in Extension is, that A belongs to the class of things which have the attributes comprehended in B. These statements are either, as I affirm them to be, one and the same assertion in slightly different words, or they are different assertions. If they are the same assertion, there is but one judgment, which is both in Extension and in Comprehension, and but one kind of reasoning, which is in both. But, supposing them, for the sake of argument,

to be two different assertions, the judgment respecting
Extension is a corollary from that in Comprehension,
expressing an artificial point of view in which we may
regard the natural judgment. Now, on this supposition,
that the judgment respecting Extension is not the same,
but an additional judgment, it is, like all other judgments, a judgment in Comprehension. "A is part of
class B" must be interpreted thus : The phenomenon
A possesses, or the concept A comprehends, the attribute
of being included in the class B. So that, while every
judgment in Comprehension warrants, by way of immediate inference, a corresponding judgment respecting
Extension, this very judgment respecting Extension is
itself but a particular kind of judgment in Comprehension. Even, therefore, on the untenable doctrine that
there are two different judgments in the case, the distinction between judgments in Extension and judgments
in Comprehension is not sustainable ; and the supposed
addition to the theory of the Syllogism is a mere ex-
crescence and incumbrance on it.

How great the incumbrance is, all are able to judge,
who follow our author through the details of the syllogistic logic. He not only finds it necessary to expound
and demonstrate every one of the doctrines twice over,
as adapted to Extension and to Comprehension, but
struggles to express all the fundamental principles in a
manner combining both points of view ; and is thereby
compelled either to state those principles in terms too
wide and abstract for easy apprehension, in order that
what is laid down respecting wholes and their parts may
be applicable to both kinds of wholes (in Extension and in
Comprehension), or else to embarrass the learner with the
necessity of carrying on two trains of thought at once, in
the attempt to apprehend a single principle. I need not
dwell on the additional error, of considering the relation
of whole and parts as the foundation of the Syllogism in
both aspects. To the point of view of Extension that
relation is applicable. In every affirmative proposition,
if true, the object or class of objects denoted by the sub-

ject is a part (when it is not the whole) of the class of objects denoted by the predicate. But no similar relation exists between the two "bundles of attributes" comprehended in the subject and in the predicate, except in the case of Analytical Judgments, that is, of merely verbal propositions. In Synthetical Judgments, that is, in all propositions which convey information about anything except the meaning of words, the relation between the two sets of attributes is not a relation of Whole and Part, but a relation of Coexistence.

I now pass to the doctrine of the Quantification of the Predicate ; examining it by the light of the same principles which we have applied to the distinction between the supposed two kinds of Reasoning.

It will be desirable to state in Sir W. Hamilton's own words, as first published in 1846, the claims he prefers in behalf of this doctrine, and the important consequences to which he considers it to lead.*

" The self-evident truth,—That we can only ration-
" ally deal with what we already understand, determines
" the simple logical postulate,—*To state explicitly what is*
" *thought implicitly.*   From the consistent application of
" this postulate, on which Logic ever insists, but which
" Logicians have never fairly obeyed, it follows :—that,
" logically, we ought to take into account the *quantity*
" always understood in thought, but usually, and for
" manifest reasons, elided in its expression, not only of
" the *subject*, but also of the *predicate* of a judgment.
" This being done, and the necessity of doing it will be
" proved against Aristotle and his repeaters, we obtain,
" *inter alia*, the ensuing results :

" 1°. That the *preindesignate terms* of a proposition,
" whether subject or predicate, are never, on that ac-
" count, thought as *indefinite* (or indeterminate) in quan-
" tity.   The only indefinite, is *particular*, as opposed to
" *definite*, quantity ; and this last, as it is either of an
" extensive *maximum* undivided, or of an extensive
" *minimum* indivisible, constitutes quantity *universal*

* Discussions, Appendix ii. pp. 650, 651.

" (general) and quantity *singular* (individual).   In fact,
" *definite* and *indefinite* are the only quantities of which
" we ought to hear in Logic ; for it is only as indefinite
" that particular, it is only as definite that individual
" and general, quantities have any (and the same)
" logical avail.

   " 2°. The revocation of the *two terms of a Proposi-*
" *tion* to their *true relation ;* a proposition being always
" an *equation* of its subject and its predicate.

   " 3°. The consequent reduction of the *Conversion* of
" *Propositions* from three species to *one*—that of Simple
" Conversion.

   " 4°. The reduction of all the *General Laws of Cate-*
" *gorical Syllogisms* to a *Single Canon.*

   " 5°. The evolution from that *one canon* of all the
" species and varieties of Syllogism.

   " 6°. The *abrogation* of all the *Special Laws of*
" *Syllogism.*

   " 7°. A demonstration of the *exclusive Possibility of*
" *Three Syllogistic Figures ;* and (on new grounds) the
" scientific and final *abolition of the Fourth.*

   " 8°. A manifestation that *Figure* is an *unessential*
" *variation* in syllogistic form ; and the consequent
" *absurdity of Reducing* the syllogisms of the other
" figures to the first.

   " 9°. An enouncement of *one Organic Principle* for
" *each Figure.*

   " 10°. A determination of the true *number* of the
" legitimate *Moods*, with

   " 11°. Their *amplification* in number (*thirty-six*) ;

   " 12°. Their numerical *equality* under all the figures ;
" and

   " 13°. Their *relative equivalence*, or virtual identity,
" throughout every schematic difference.

   " 14°. That in the *second* and *third* figures, the ex-
" tremes holding both the same relation to the middle
" term, there *is not*, as in the first, *an opposition and*
" *subordination between a term major and a term minor*
" *mutually containing and contained, in the counter*
" *wholes of Extension and Comprehension.*

"15°. Consequently, in the *second* and *third* figures,
" there is *no determinate major and minor premise*, and
" there are *two indifferent conclusions;* whereas, in the
" *first*, the *premises* are *determinate*, and there is a *single*
" *proximate conclusion.*

" 16°. That the *third*, as the figure in which *Compre-*
hension is predominant, is more appropriate to *Induction.*

" 17°. That the *second*, as the figure in which *Exten-*
" *sion* is predominant, is more appropriate to *Deduction.*

" 18°. That the *first*, as the figure in which *Compre-*
" *hension* and *Extension* are in equilibrium, is common
" to *Induction* and *Deduction* indifferently."

The doctrine which leads to all these consequences, or
rather, which necessitates all these changes of expression
(for they are no more), is that the Predicate is always
quantified in thought; that we always think it either as
signifying the whole, or as signifying only a part, of
the objects included in its Extension. " In reality and
" in thought, every quantity is necessarily either all, or
" some, or none." * The proposition, All A is B, must
mean, in thought, either All A is all B, or All A is some
B. When I judge that all oxen ruminate, it must not
only be true, but I must mean, either that All ox is all
ruminating, or that All ox is some ruminating. Logic,
therefore, postulates to express in words what is already
in the thoughts, and to write all propositions in one
or other of these forms : which makes it necessary that
all the rules for reasoning should be altered, at least
in expression, and grounded on the relation of exact
equality between the terms.

But if, as I have endeavoured to show, the predicate
B is present in thought only in respect of its Comprehension ; if it be an error to suppose that it is thought of

---

* Discussions, Appendix ii. p. 601. But the whole meaning of this
assertion, as available for our author's purpose, is destroyed by the statement which he is presently obliged to make, that " the Indesignate is
" thought, either precisely, as whole or as part, *or vaguely, as the one or
the other, unknown which, but the worse always presumed.*" The concession, though fatal to himself, is short of the truth ; for the Indesignate is
not necessarily thought either as a whole, or as part, or as "unknown
which :" it is often not thought in any relation of quantity at all.

as an aggregate of objects at all; still less is it thought of as an aggregate with a determinate quantity, as some or all. I repeat the appeal which I have already made to every reader's consciousness: Does he, when he judges that all oxen ruminate, advert even in the minutest degree to the question, whether there is anything else which ruminates? Is this consideration at all in his thoughts, any more than any other consideration foreign to the immediate subject? One person may know that there are other ruminating animals, another may think that there are none, a third may be without any opinion on the subject: but if they all know what is meant by ruminating, they all, when they judge that every ox ruminates, mean exactly the same thing. The mental process they go through, as far as that one judgment is concerned, is precisely identical; though some of them may go on further, and add other judgments to it.*

The fact, that the proposition "Every A is B" only means every A is *some* B, far from being always present in thought, is not at first seized without some difficulty by the tyro in Logic. It requires a certain effort of thought to perceive that when we say, All As are Bs, we only identify A with a portion of the class B. When the learner is first told that the proposition All As are Bs can only be converted in the form "Some Bs are As,"

---

* Not only we do not (unless exceptionally for some special purpose) quantify the predicate in thought, but we do not even quantify the subject, in the sense which Sir W. Hamilton's theory requires. Even in an universal proposition, we do not think of the subject as an aggregate whole, but as its several parts: we do not judge that all A is B, but that all As are Bs, which is a different thing. That what is true of the whole must be true of any part, only holds good when the whole means the parts themselves, and not when it means the aggregate of them. All A, is a very different notion from Each A. What is true of A only as a whole, forms no element of a judgment concerning its parts—even concerning all its parts. Sir W. Hamilton thinks that the relation of quantity in extension which the class A bears to the class B, is always present in my thoughts when I predicate B of A. This relation of quantity, however, does not belong to individual As, but specifically and solely to A as a whole, and as a whole I am not thinking of it. When I am predicating B of all As severally, I am not adverting to any property or relation which belongs to A as their aggregate. Accordingly we do not say, all ox ruminates, but all oxen ruminate. The distinction is of little importance when A is only

I apprehend that this strikes him as a new idea; and that the truth of the statement is not quite obvious to him, until verified by a particular example in which he already knows that the simple converse would be false, such as, All men are animals, therefore all animals are men. So far is it from being true that the proposition, All As are Bs, is spontaneously quantified in thought as All A is some B.

The pretension, therefore, of the doctrine of a Quantified Predicate, to be a more correct representation and analysis of the reasoning process than the common doctrine of the syllogism, I hold to be psychologically false. And this is fatal to the doctrine, if we admit Sir W. Hamilton's theory that Logic is the science of the laws according to which we *must* think in order that our thought may be valid. But according to the very different view I myself take of Formal Logic, this doctrine might still be a valuable addition to it: since, in my view, the Syllogistic theory altogether is not an analysis of the reasoning process, but only furnishes a test of the validity of reasonings, by supplying forms of expression into which all reasonings may be translated if valid, and which, if they are invalid, will detect the hidden flaw. In this point of view it might well be, that a form which always exhibited the quantity of the predicate might be an improvement on the common form. And I am not disposed to deny that for occasional use, and for purposes of illustration, it is so. The exposition of the theory of

---

co-extensive with part of B; for if A altogether is but a part, still more must this be true of any particular A, and it is indifferent whether we say all A is some B, or each of the As is some B. But it is quite another matter when the assertion is that all A is all B. This, if true at all, is true *only* of A considered as a whole; and expresses a relation between the two classes as totals, not between either of them and its parts. Now, to affirm that when we judge every A to be a B, we always, and necessarily, recognise in thought a fact which is not true of every, or even of any A, but only of the aggregate composed of all As, seems to me as baseless a fancy as ever implanted itself in the intellect of an eminent thinker. It is, in short (as observed by one of my correspondents), a conclusive reason against the assimilation of a judgment to an equation, that in equations the terms are used collectively, and in judgments mostly distributively.

2 K

the syllogism is made clearer, by pointing out that All As
are B only implies that All A is some B, while No As
are B excludes A from the whole of B.   This, in fact,
is taught to all who learn logic in the common way, by
what is called the doctrine of Suppositio; or (in the many
books which leave this doctrine out) by the theory of
Conversion, and the syllogistic rules against Undistri-
buted Middle, and against proceeding *à non distributo
ad distributum.*   There is no harm, and some little good,
in giving to these essential doctrines the more explicit
expression demanded for them by Sir W. Hamilton.
But to obtain any advantage from it, we must be content with quantifying such propositions as, in their unquantified form, are really asserted and used.   To foist in
any others, overlays and confuses, instead of illuminating,
the theory.   " All A is some B " is inadmissible, because
it is the quantification really implied in All As are B ;
but "All A is all B " is inadmissible, because it is not the
equivalent of any single proposition capable of being
asserted in an unquantified form.   As all reasoning,
except in the process of teaching Logic, will always be
carried on in the forms which men use in real life ; and
as the only purpose of providing other forms, is to supply
a test for those which are really used ; it is essential that
the forms provided should be forms into which the propositions expressed in common language can be translated—that every proposition in logical form, should be
the exact equivalent of some proposition in the common
form.   Now, there is no proposition capable of being
expressed in the ordinary form, which is equivalent to
the proposition, All A is all B.   That form of expression combines the import of two propositions in common
language, expressive of two separate judgments, All As
are Bs, and all Bs are As.

If this had not been denied, I should have deemed it too
obvious to require either proof or illustration.   But Sir
W. Hamilton does deny it, and therefore some enforce-
ment of it is indispensable.   When we make an assertion
in the cramped and unnatural form, All man is all

rational, can anything seem more evident than that to cover the whole ground occupied by this statement, two judgments are required; namely, first, that every man has the attribute reason; and secondly, that nothing which is not man has that attribute, or (which is the same thing) that every rational creature has the attributes of man? How is it possible to make only one judgment, out of an assertion divisible into two parts, one of which may be unknown and the other known, one unthought of and the other thought of, one false and the other true? *

Unless Sir W. Hamilton was prepared to maintain that whenever the universal converse of an universal affirmative proposition would be true, we cannot know the one without knowing the other, it is in vain for him to contend that a form which asserts both of them at once is only one proposition. If in judging that " All equilateral triangles are equiangular," we judge that all equilateral triangles are all equiangular, in what condition of judgment is the mind of the tyro to whom it has just been proved that all equilateral triangles are equiangular, but who does not yet know the proof of the converse proposition that all equiangular triangles are equilateral? If " All equilateral triangles are all equiangular " is only one judgment, what is the proposition that all equilateral triangles are equiangular? Is it half a judgment? †

* The only answer I can imagine to this is, that having the two concepts Man and Rational, and being engaged in actually comparing them with each other, we *must* perceive and judge whether the one is merely a part of the other, or a whole coinciding with it. But this answer is not competent to Sir W. Hamilton, or any other Conceptualist, to make. An adversary of Sir W. Hamilton might make it. I have myself said, and have offered as a *reductio ad absurdum* of his analysis of Reasoning, that if we have two concepts and compare them, we cannot but perceive any relation of whole and part which exists between them. Sir W. Hamilton however is precluded from making this reply; for all Reasoning, even to the longest process in Mathematics, consists, according to him, in discovering this relation of whole and part by circuitous means, when direct comparison does not disclose it. From this point of view, therefore, the argument is not tenable; and from mine it has no pertinence, since I do not admit that Reasoning is a comparison of Concepts at all.

† Sir W. Hamilton goes the length of asserting (Appendix to Lectures,

This is not the only case in which Sir W. Hamilton insists upon wrapping up two different assertions in one form of words, and demands that they shall be considered one assertion.   He strenuously contends that the form "Some A is B," or (in its quantified form)

iv. 292, *et seqq.*), that to a person who knows all trilateral figures to be triangular, the proposition "all triangles are trilateral" must, if expressed as understood, be written "All triangles are all trilateral :" as if every proposition which I affirm respecting a subject, must include all I know about it.

That the proposition All A is B is not a single judgment, but compounded of two, has already been urged against Sir W. Hamilton by Mr. De Morgan, and we are in possession of Sir W. Hamilton's answer (Discussions, Appendix ii. pp. 687, 688).   Unhappily Mr. De Morgan (by an oversight not usual with that able thinker) gave Sir W. Hamilton an apparent triumph, by mistaking the two judgments which the pretended single proposition is composed of.   He appears to have said, that the proposition "All Xs are all Ys," is compounded of the propositions "All Xs are some Ys," and "Some Xs are all Ys."   Sir W. Hamilton replies, that these two propositions are (in his own peculiar language) incompossible, inasmuch as we cannot think X both as some Y, that is a part of Y, and as the whole.   The argument is little better than a quibble, because other people do not (though Sir W. Hamilton does) mean by some, *some only ;* they mean *some at least ;* and if the first of Mr. De Morgan's two propositions identifies X with only some of Y, the second superadds the remainder. But in reality the two judgments which go to the composition of "All A is all B," are not judgments with quantified predicates at all.   They are, All A is B, and all B is A.   The one ascribes the attributes of B to every A, the other the attributes of A to every B.   Judgments more distinct and independent of one another do not exist.

According to Sir W. Hamilton (Appendix to Lectures, iv. 259) "ordinary "language quantifies the Predicate as often as this determination becomes "of the smallest import."   And he cites such instances as "Virtue is the *only* nobility ;" "Of animals man alone is rational," and the like.   The truth is, that ordinary language quantifies the predicate in the rare cases in which it is quantified in thought, and in no others.   And even then the quantified proposition is an abbreviated expression of two judgments.   The German logician Schiebler, to whom our author refers in a footnote (Ibid. p. 261), could have set him right here.

"Sir W. Hamilton," says Mr. Grote (*Westminster Review*, pp. 31, 32), "insists on stating explicitly, not merely all that is thought implicitly, "but a great deal more ; adding to it something else, which may, indeed, "be thought conjointly, but which more frequently is not thought at all. "He requires us to pack two distinct judgments into one and the same "proposition : he interpolates the meaning of the Propositio Conversa "*simpliciter* into the form of the Propositio Convertenda (when an uni-"versal affirmative) and then claims it as a great advantage, that the "proposition thus interpolated admits of being converted *simpliciter*, and "not merely *per accidens.* . . . If a man is prepared to give us informa-"tion on one Quæsitum, why should he be constrained to use a mode of "speech which forces on his attention at the same time a second and dis-"tinct Quæsitum, so that he must either give us information about the two

" Some A is some B," ought in logical propriety to be
used and understood in the sense of "some and *some
only.*" * No shadow of justification is shown for thus
deviating from the practice of all writers on logic, and
of all who think and speak with any approach to precision, and adopting into logic a mere *sous-entendu* of
common conversation in its most unprecise form. If I
say to any one, "I saw some of your children to-day,"
he might be justified in inferring that I did not see
them all, not because the words mean it, but because, if
I had seen them all, it is most likely that I should have
said so : though even this cannot be presumed unless it
is presupposed that I must have known whether the
children I saw were all or not. But to carry this colloquial mode of interpreting a statement into Logic, is
something novel. If Some A is B is to be understood
of some *only*, it is a double judgment, compounded of
the propositions, Some As are Bs, and some As are not Bs.
If quantified in our author's manner, the propositions
would run thus : Some A is some B, and some (other)
A is not any B. If two statements, one of which affirms
and the other denies a different predicate of a different
subject, are not two distinct judgments, it is impossible

"at once, or confess himself ignorant respecting the second?" Mr. Grote
goes on to cite from Sir W. Hamilton's own collection of authorities, an
excellent passage from a Jewish philosopher of the fourteenth century,
Levi Ben Gerson, which exactly confutes Sir W. Hamilton's doctrine,
"The cause why the quantitative note is not usually joined with the predi-
"cate, is that there would thus be two quæsita at once ; to wit, whether the
"predicate were affirmed of the subject, and whether it were denied of
"everything beside. For when we say, All Man is all Rational, we judge
"that all man is rational, and judge likewise that rational is denied of
"everything but man. But these are, in reality, two different quæsita ;
"and therefore it has become usual to state them, not in one, but in two
"several propositions. And this is self-evident, seeing that a quæsitum
"in itself, asks only—Does or does not this inhere in that ? and not, Does
"or does not this inhere in that, and at the same time inhere in nothing
"else ?"

Propositions in Extension have absolutely no meaning but what they
derive from Comprehension. The Logic of the quantified predicate takes
the Comprehension out of them, and leaves them a *caput mortuum.*

* See, among many other places, Discussions, Appendix ii. pp. 600, 601,
where he says, "Every quantity is necessarily either *all*, or *none*, or *some* ;
of these, the third is formally *exclusive* of the other two."

to say what are so.   One of the great uses of discipline
in Formal Logic, is to make us aware when something
which claims to be a single proposition, really consists
of several, which, not being necessarily involved one in
another, require to be separated, and considered each
by itself, before we admit the compound assertion.
This separation may be called, with reason, stating
explicitly in words what is implicitly in thought.   But
it is a new postulate of Logic to state *im*plicitly in
words what is *ex*plicitly in thought, and I do not think
that Logic is at all enriched by the acquisition.

With these compound propositions falls the whole
pretension of the quantified mode of expression to yield
legitimate inferences which are not recognised by the old
Logic.   Whatever can be proved from " All A is all B,"
can be proved in the old form from one or both of its
elements, All As are Bs, and all Bs are As.   Whatever
can be proved from "Some, and only some, A is some
(or all) B," can be proved in the old form from its elements, Some As are Bs, Some As are not Bs, and (in
the case last mentioned) All Bs are As.   If we choose
to alter the forms of all our propositions, the forms of
our syllogisms naturally require alterations too ; and
there may be a greater number of forms in which quantified conclusions can be drawn from quantified premises,
than in which unquantified conclusions can be drawn
from unquantified premises.   But there is not a single
instance, nor is it possible in the nature of things that
there should be an instance, in which a conclusion that
is provable from quantified premises, could not be proved
from the same premises unquantified, if we set forth all
those which are really involved.   If there could be such
an instance, the quantified Syllogism would be a real
addition to the theory of Logic : if not, not.

As I have already once remarked, it does not follow,
because the quantified Syllogism is not a true expression
of what is in thought, that the occasional writing the
predicate with a quantification may not be a real help to
the *art* of Logic.   Though not a correct analysis of the

reasoning process, it may, in some cases, enable us more readily to see whether the conclusion really follows from the premises.   But without rejecting it as an available help for this purpose, I must observe that its use in this capacity appears to me extremely limited; for two reasons. First; the problem is, to test the validity of a reasoning as expressed in the language in which men ordinarily reason.   We do this by taking the propositions as they are, and measuring the extent of the assertions made in the two premises and in the conclusion respectively, so as to ascertain whether the former are broad enough to cover and include the latter.   This it requires some practice to do, but the task is not avoided by quantifying the predicate ; on the contrary, it must have been actually performed before the predicate can be correctly quantified; so that by quantifying it in expression, no trouble is saved.   My second reason is, that after the predicate has been quantified, it is often equally or more difficult to follow the consecution of the thought through the symbols, than as expressed in ordinary language. Take one of the common cases of invalid inference, a syllogism in the first figure with the major premise particular, such as this :

> Some Ms are Ps
> All Ss are Ms
> Therefore all Ss are Ps ;

the inference fails, because the Ms which are identified with Ss may not be the same Ms which are Ps, but other Ms.   Let us now quantify the predicates thus :

> Some Ms are some Ps
> All Ss are some Ms
> Therefore all Ss are some Ps ;

is the invalidity of the inference at all clearer? Does it require less exertion of thought to perceive that "some Ms" may not mean the same *some* in both premises, than it did to recognise the equivalent truth as to M in the minor, and "some M" in the major premise?   On the contrary, the quantified form is the more plausibly misleading of the two, since the middle term, though really ambiguous, is, in that form, verbally the same, which in the unquantified form it is not.

The general result of these considerations is, that the utility of the new forms is by no means such as to compensate for the great additional complication which they introduce into the syllogistic theory ; a complication which would make it at the same time difficult to learn or remember, and intolerably tiresome both in the learning and in the using. The sole purpose of any syllogistic forms is to afford an available test for the process of drawing inferences in the common language of life from premises in the same common language ; and the ordinary forms of Syllogism effect this purpose completely. The new forms do not, in any appreciable degree, facilitate the process, while they are chargeable, in a far greater degree than the common forms, with diverting the mind from the true meaning of propositions (the ascription of attributes to objects considered severally), and concentrating it upon the highly artificial, and generally unimportant, consideration of the relation of extent between classes of objects, considered not severally, but as collective wholes. The new forms have thus no practical advantage which can countervail the objection of their entire psychological irrelevancy ; and the invention and acquisition of them have little value, except as one among many other feats of mental gymnastic, by which students of the science may exercise and invigorate their faculties. They should, in short, be dealt with as Sir W. Hamilton deals with Mr. De Morgan's forms of " numerically definite " Syllogism, viz. " taken into account by Logic as authentic forms, " but then relegated as of little use in practice, and " cumbering the science with a superfluous mass of " words." *

---

* Appendix to Lectures, iv. 355.

CHAPTER XXIII.

OF SOME MINOR PECULIARITIES OF DOCTRINE IN SIR
WILLIAM HAMILTON'S VIEW OF FORMAL LOGIC.

THE two theories examined in the preceding chapter are
the only important novelties which Sir W. Hamilton
has introduced into the Science or Art of Logic. But he
has here and there departed from the common doctrine
of logicians on subordinate points. Some of these devia-
tions deserve notice from their connection with some
principal part of our author's doctrine, others chiefly as
throwing light on the character of his mind. The one
to which I shall first advert is of the former class.

I. Almost all writers on the Syllogistic Logic have
directed attention to the fact, that though we cannot,
while observing the forms of Logic, draw a false conclusion from true premises, we may draw a true one
from false premises : in other words, the falsity of the
premises does not prove the falsity of the conclusion ;
nor does the truth of the conclusion prove the truth of
the premises. The warning is needed ; for it is by no
means unusual to mistake a refutation of the reasons from
which a doctrine has been deduced for a disproof of the
doctrine itself ; and there is no error of thought more
common than the acceptance of premises because they
lead to a conclusion already assented to as true. Not
only is this caution useful, but it is relevant to Logic,
even in the restricted point of view of Formal Logic.
When it is affirmed that Formal Logic has nothing to
do with Material Truth, all that ought to be meant, is
that in Logic we are not to consider whether the conclusion supposed to be proved is true in fact. But we

are to consider whether it is true conditionally, true if
the premises are true: that question is the specific business of Formal Logic : if Formal Logic does not teach
us that, there is nothing for it to teach.   The theorem,
that in a valid Syllogism the falsity of the premises does
not prove the falsity of the conclusion, is as germane to
Logic as that the truth of the premises proves the truth
of the conclusion.   We have therefore reason to be
surprised at finding Sir W. Hamilton delivering himself as follows :*—

" Logic does not warrant the truth of its premises,
" except in so far as these may be the formal conclusions
" of anterior reasonings ; it only warrants (on the hypo-
" thesis that the premises are truly assumed) the truth
" of the inference.   In this view the conclusion may, as
" a separate proposition, be true ; but if this truth be not
" a necessary consequence from the premises, it is a false
" conclusion, that is, in fact, no conclusion at all.   Now
" on this point there is a doctrine prevalent among
" logicians, which is not only erroneous, but if admitted,
" is subversive of the distinction of Logic as a purely
" formal science.   The doctrine in question is in its
" result this,—that if the conclusion of a syllogism be
" true, the premises may be either true or false, but
" that if the conclusion be false, one or both of its pre-
" mises must be false : in other words, that it is possible
" to infer true from false, but not false from true.   As
" an example of this I have given the following syllo-
" gism :—

      " Aristotle is a Roman ;
      " A Roman is a European ;
      " Therefore, Aristotle is a European.
" The inference, in so far as expressed, is true; but I would
" remark, that the whole inference which the premises
" necessitate, and which the conclusion, therefore, virtu-
" ally contains, is not true,—is false.   For the premises of
" the preceding syllogism gave not only the conclusion,
" *Aristotle is a European*, but also the conclusion, *Aristotle*

" *is not a Greek;* for it not merely follows from the pre-
" mises, that Aristotle is conceived under the universal
" notion of which the concept *Roman* forms a particular
" sphere, but likewise that he is conceived as excluded
" from all the other particular spheres which are contained
" under that universal notion. The consideration of the
" truth of the premise, *Aristotle is a Roman* is, however,
" more properly to be regarded as extralogical; but if so,
" then the consideration of the conclusion, *Aristotle is a*
" *European,* on any other view than as a mere formal
" inference from certain hypothetical antecedents, is like-
" wise extralogical. Logic is only concerned with the
" formal truth,—the technical validity,—of its syllogisms,
" and anything beyond the legitimacy of the consequence
" it draws from certain hypothetical antecedents, it does
" not profess to vindicate. Logical truth and falsehood
" are thus contained in the correctness and incorrectness
" of logical inference; and it was, therefore, with no
" impropriety that we made a true or correct, and a false
" or incorrect, syllogism convertible expressions."

The statement that a true proposition may be correctly inferred from false premises, or in other words,
that a true opinion may be supported by false reasons,
is one of which we could hardly have expected to find
the truth disputed, whatever might be said of the connection of Logic with it. So unlooked-for a paradox
required to be defended by the strongest arguments :
who, then, would expect such shabby, not arguments,
but hints of arguments, as the author presents us with ?
He stops short in the middle of the first, as if afraid that
it would break down if relied upon, and hurries to the
second, which is still more incapable of bearing weight.
" The consideration of the conclusion, *Aristotle is a Euro-*
" *pean,* on any other view than as a mere formal inference
" from certain hypothetical antecedents, is extralogical."
Nobody proposes to consider it as anything but a formal
inference from certain hypothetical antecedents. The
gist of the whole question is that it is such an inference,
and consequently that a proposition really true, may be

a formal inference from premises wholly or partially false : in other words, the falsity of the conclusion does not follow from the falsity of the premises.   It is as much the business of the theory of " formal inference " to show what conclusions are not formally legitimate, as what are.   It is not the business of Formal Logic to determine what is actually true, but it is, to tell what does or does not follow from what.   In the first un-finished part of his argument, Sir W. Hamilton makes a faint attempt to show that the conclusion, Aristotle is a European, is not true.   He admits it to be true as far as expressed, but says that it virtually contains something which is false, namely, that Aristotle is not a Greek. By what analysis can he find this in the proposition, Aristotle is a European?   He does not pretend that it is in the proposition considered in itself, but only in the proposition as inferred from " Aristotle is a Roman." But it is a strange doctrine that a proposition is true or false not according to what it asserts, but according to the mode in which the belief of it has been arrived at. It is a very irrational mode of speaking to say that a proposition, besides its obvious meaning, contains a meaning which the words do not convey, which in the mouths of other people it does not bear, but which is so essential a part of it as by its falsity to make the pro-position false which otherwise would be true.   Suppose that the register of a man's birth having been destroyed, some one to whom the date is of importance, proves it by a false entry in the parish books : would that make the man not to have been born on the day he was born on ?   But let us concede this point, however unreason-able, and admit that the proposition Aristotle is a European, when inferred from the premise that he is a Roman, includes that premise as part of its own mean-ing.   Does it therefore contain an implication that he is not a Greek ?   Suppose that I have never heard of Greeks ; or that, having heard of them, I suppose a Greek to be a kind of Roman, or a Roman a kind of Greek.   Will this ignorance or misapprehension on my

part, prevent me from concluding, that if a Roman is
a European and Aristotle a Roman, Aristotle must be a
European; or will it make the inference illegitimate, or
the conclusion false? One sentence in our quotation
from Sir W. Hamilton is a singular illustration of the
length he will go to support a favourite thesis. "The
"premises," he says, "of the syllogism gave not only the
"conclusion, Aristotle is a European, but also the con-
"clusion, Aristotle is not a Greek." Let us try:—

> Aristotle is a Roman;
> A Roman is a European;
> Therefore, Aristotle is not a Greek.

This is Formal Logic. This is the philosopher who
is so rigidly bent upon excluding from Logic all consideration of what is true or false *vi materiæ*. What
shadow of connection is there, unless it be *vi materiæ*,
between this conclusion, and those premises? Nothing
can explain this aberration in a thinker of Sir W.
Hamilton's acuteness, except his dogged determination
in no shape to recognise belief as an element of judgment, or truth as in any way concerned in Pure Logic.

Sir W. Hamilton has a salvo for all this, though it is
one which would not occur to everybody. According to
him there are two kinds of truth, or rather the word
truth has two meanings, so that it is possible for a proposition to be true although it is false. There is Formal
Truth, and Real Truth.* Real Truth is "the harmony between a thought and its matter." Formal
Truth is of two kinds, Logical, and Mathematical.
Logical Truth is the "harmony or agreement of our
"thoughts with themselves as thoughts, in other words
"the correspondence of thought with the universal laws
"of thinking." And Mathematical Truth is some other
harmony of thought, in which truth of fact is equally dispensed with. In another place, he says † that if the consequent is correctly "evolved out of" the antecedent, the
conclusion out of the premises, this is "Logical or Formal
"or Subjective truth: and an inference may be sub-

* Lectures, iv. 64–68.   † Ibid. ii. 343.

"jectively or formally true, which is objectively or really
"false." To support his denial of the common doctrine,
he has to alter the meaning of words, and make false in
the new meaning what cannot be denied to be true
in the old. But I object *in toto* to such an abuse of
terms as affirming a false proposition to be true, because
it is in such a relation to another false proposition, that
if that false proposition had been true it would have been
true likewise. There is no fitness in the word truth, to
express this mere relation of consecution between false
propositions. No qualification by adjectives, whether
"logical," or "formal," or "subjective," will make this
assertion anything but a solecism in language, claiming
to be the correction of a philosophical doctrine.

The whole theory of the difference between Formal
and Real Truth is treated as it deserves, in a passage from
one of Sir W. Hamilton's favourite authorities, Esser,
which he quotes, and, strange to say, quotes with approbation.

"One party of philosophers," says Esser,* "defining
"truth in general, the absolute harmony of our thoughts
"and cognitions,—divide truth into a formal or logical,
"and into a material or metaphysical, according as that
"harmony is in consonance with the laws of formal
"thought, or over and above, with the laws of real
"knowledge. The criterion of formal truth they place
"in the principles of Contradiction and of Sufficient
"Reason, enouncing that what is non-contradictory
"and consequent is formally true. This criterion, which
"is positive and immediate of formal truth (inasmuch as
"what is non-contradictory and consequent can always
"be thought as possible), they style a negative and
"mediate criterion of material truth : as what is self-
"contradictory and logically inconsequent is in reality
"impossible ; at the same time, what is not self-contra-
"dictory and not logically inconsequent, is not, however,
"to be regarded as having an actual existence. But
"here the foundation is treacherous : the notion of truth

* Lectures, iii. 106, 107.

" is false. When we speak of truth, we are not satisfied
" with knowing that a thought harmonises with a certain
" system of thoughts and cognitions ; but, over and
" above, we require to be assured that what we think is
" real, and is as we think it to be. Are we satisfied
" on this point, we then regard our thoughts as true ;
" whereas if we are not satisfied of this, we deem them
" false, how well soever they may quadrate with any
" theory or system. It is not, therefore, in any absolute
" harmony of mere thought, that truth consists, but
" solely in the correspondence of our thoughts with their
" objects. The distinction of formal and material truth
" is thus not only unsound in itself, but opposed to the
" notion of truth universally held, and embodied in all
" languages. But if this distinction be inept, the title
" of Logic, as a positive standard of truth, must be de-
" nied ; it can only be a negative criterion, being con-
" versant with thoughts and not with things, with the
" possibility and not with the actuality of existence."

After all the experience we have had of the facility
with which Sir W. Hamilton forgets in one part of his
speculations what he has thought in another, it remains
scarcely credible that he endorses, in his third volume,
this emphatic protest against the distinction which he
draws, and the opinion which he maintains, in his
second and fourth. "Two opposite doctrines," he says,*
" have sprung up, which, on opposite sides, have over-
" looked the true relations of Logic;" and one of these is
the doctrine (the "inaccuracy" our author styles it) which
Esser, in this passage, protests against. And he there-
upon quotes Esser's condemnation of his (Sir W. Hamilton's) own doctrine. Truly, if arguments, *ad hominem*
were sufficient, a controversialist who undertakes to
refute Sir W. Hamilton would have an easy task.

II. I have already noticed one unacknowledged departure by our author from the usage of Logicians as
regards the sense of the word Disjunctive ; confining
Disjunctive judgments to those in which all the alterna-

* Lectures, iii. 106.

tive propositions have the same subject : A is either B,
or C, or D. This limitation excludes two other forms of
the assertion of an alternative ; that in which the propositions have different subjects but the same predicate,
"Either A, or B, or C, is D ; " and that in which they
have different subjects and different predicates, "Either
A is B, or C is D." The former is exemplified in such
judgments as these, Either Brown or Smith did this act ;
Either John or Thomas is dead. The latter in such as
these : Either the witness has told a falsehood, or the
prisoner has committed a murder ; Either Macbeth has
killed all Macduff's children, or Macduff has children
who were not there present. While arbitrarily excluding
both these kinds of assertion from the class and denomi-
nation in which they had always been placed, our author
does not assign to them any other ; so that the effect is
not a mere innovation in language, but a hiatus in his
logical system ; these two kinds of judgment having no
place, name, or recognition in it. I have now to point
out a second deviation from the received doctrine of
logicians in connection with the same subject. In respect
to the class of judgments to which he restricts the name
of Disjunctive, those in which two or more predicates
are disjunctively affirmed of the same subject, he takes
for granted through the whole of his exposition,* that
when we say, A is either B or C, we imply that it cannot be both ; that we may as legitimately argue, A is
either B or C, but it is B, therefore it is not C, as we
may argue, A is either B or C, but it is not B, therefore it is C. This is what enables him to affirm, as he
does, that the principle of Disjunctive Judgments is the
Law of Excluded Middle. The predicates are supposed to
be either explicitly or implicitly contradictory, so that one
or other of them must be true of the subject, but both
of them cannot. I conceive this to be both an incompleteness in his theory and a positive error in fact. An
incompleteness, because we may judge, and legitimately
judge, that a thing is either this or that, though aware

* Lectures, iii. 326, *et seqq.*

that it may possibly be both. Sir W. Hamilton is so severe on the ordinary Logic for omitting, as he thinks, some valid forms of thought, that it was peculiarly incumbent on him not to commit a similar oversight in his own exposition of the science. But Sir W. Hamilton does not merely leave unrecognised those disjunctive judgments in which the alternative predicates are mutually compatible; he assumes that the disjunctive form of assertion denies their compatibility, which it assuredly does not. If we assert that a man who has acted in some particular way, must be either a knave or a fool, we by no means assert, or intend to assert, that he cannot be both. Very important consequences may sometimes be drawn from our knowledge that one or other of two perfectly compatible suppositions must be true. Suppose such an argument as this. To make an entirely unselfish use of despotic power a man must be either a saint or a philosopher; but saints and philosophers are rare; therefore those are rare, who make an entirely unselfish use of despotic power. The conclusion follows from the premises, and is of great practical importance. But does the disjunctive premise necessarily imply, or must it be construed as supposing, that the same person cannot be both a saint and a philosopher? Such a construction would be ridiculous.*

There is a great quantity of intricate and obscure speculation, in our author's Lectures and their Appendices, relating to Disjunctive and Hypothetical Propositions. But, much as he had thought on the subject, the simple idea never seems to have occurred to him (though he might have found it in Archbishop Whately's Logic), that every disjunctive judgment is compounded of two or more Hypothetical ones. "Either A is B, or C is D," means, If A is not B, C is D; and if C is not D, A is B. This is obvious enough to most people; but if Sir W. Hamilton had thought of it, he probably would have denied it: its admission would not have been in

* Mr. Mansel does not fall into this mistake (Prolegomena Logica, p. 221).

keeping with the disposition he shows in so many places, to consider as one judgment all that it is possible to assert in one formula. Again, though he takes much pains to determine what is the real import of a Hypothetical Judgment, the thought never occurs to him that it is a judgment concerning judgments. If A is B, C is D, means, The judgment C is D follows as a consequence from the judgment A is B. Not seeing this, Sir W. Hamilton tacitly adopts the assertion of Krug, that the conversion of a hypothetical syllogism into a categorical " is not always possible." *

III. The next of Sir W. Hamilton's minor innovations in Logic has reference to the Sorites. It is scarcely necessary to say, that a Sorites is an argument in the form, A is B, B is C, C is D, D is E, therefore A is E : an abridged expression for a series of Syllogisms, but not requiring to be decomposed into them in order to make its conclusiveness visible. Sir W. Hamilton accuses all writers on Logic of having overlooked the possibility of a Sorites in the second or third Figure.† By this he does not mean, one in which the ultimate syllogism, which sums up the argument, is in the second or third figure, for this all logicians have admitted. For example, to the Sorites given above, there might be added the proposition, No F is E ; in which case, the ultimate syllogism would be, A is E, but no F is E, therefore A is not an F : a syllogism in the second figure. Or there might be added, at the opposite end of the series, A is G ; when the ultimate syllogism would be in the third figure ; A is E, but A is G, therefore some G is an E. These are real Sorites, real chain arguments, and they conclude in the second and third figures : we may call them, if we please, Sorites in the second and in the third figure, the truth being that they are Sorites in which one of the steps is in the second or third figure, all the others being in the first. And every one who understands the laws of the second and third figures (or even the general laws of the Syllogism) can see that no more

* Lectures, iii. 342.   † Ibid. Appendix to Lectures, iv. 395.

than one step in either of them is admissible in a Sorites, and that it must either be the first or the last. About this, however, Logicians have always been agreed. These are not the kinds of Sorites which Sir W. Hamilton contends for. By a Sorites in the second or third figure, he means one in which all the steps are in the second, or all in the third, figure (a thing impossible in a real Sorites) and in which, accordingly, instead of a succession of middle terms establishing a connection between the two extremes, there is but one middle term altogether. His paradigm in the second figure would be, No B is A, No C is A, No D is A, No E is A, All F is A, therefore no B, or C, or D, or E, is F. In the third figure it would be, A is B, A is C, A is D, A is E, A is F, therefore some B, and C, and D, and E, are F. One would have thought that anybody who had the smallest notion of the meaning of a Sorites, must have seen that either of these is not a Sorites at all. It is not a chain argument. It does not ascend to a conclusion by a series of steps, each introducing a new premise. It does not deduce one conclusion from a succession of premises, all necessary to its establishment. It draws as many different conclusions as there are syllogisms, each conclusion depending only on the two premises of one syllogism. That no B is F, follows from no B is A, and All F is A ; not from those premises combined with No C is A, No D is A, No E is A. That some B is F, follows from A is B and A is F ; and would be proved, though all the other premises of the pretended Sorites were rejected. If Sir W. Hamilton had found in any other writer such a misuse of logical language as he is here guilty of, he would have roundly accused him of total ignorance of logical writers. Since it cannot be imputed to any such cause in himself, I can only ascribe it to the passion which appears to have seized him, in the later years of his life, for finding more and more new discoveries to be made in Syllogistic Logic. If he had transported his ardour for originality into the other departments of the science, in which there was so great an unexhausted field for discovery, he might have enlarged the bounds of philosophy to a much greater extent than I am afraid he will now be found to have done.

IV. I next turn to a singular misapplication of logical language, in which Sir W. Hamilton departs from all good authorities, and misses one of the most important distinctions drawn by the Aristotelian logic. I refer to his use of the word Contrary. He confounds con-triariety with simple incompatibility. "Opposition of "Notions," he says,* "is twofold : 1°. *Immediate* or *Con-* "*tradictory Opposition*, called likewise *Repugnance* (τὸ "ἀντιφατικῶς ἀντικεῖσθαι, ἀντίφασις, *oppositio immediata*, "sive *contradictoria repugnantia*) ; and 2°. *Mediate* or "*Contrary Opposition* (τὸ ἐναντίως ἀντικεῖσθαι ἐναντιότης, "*oppositio media* vel *contraria*). The former emerges, "when one concept abolishes (*tollit*) directly or by "simple negation, what another establishes, *ponit* ; the "latter when one concept does this not directly or by "simple negation, but through the affirmation of some-"thing else."

The exemplification and illustration of this † is not of our author's devising, but is a citation from Krug, who had preceded him in the error. "To speak now of "the distinction of Contradictory and Contrary Opposi-"tion, or of Contradiction and Contrariety ; of these "the former, Contradiction, is exemplified in the oppo-"sites,—*yellow, not yellow; walking, not walking.* Here "each notion is directly, immediately, and absolutely, "repugnant to the other,—they are reciprocal negatives. "This opposition is, therefore, properly called that of "*Contradiction* or of *Repugnance;* and the opposing "notions themselves are *contradictory* or *repugnant* "notions, in a single word, *contradictories.* The latter, "or Contrary Opposition, is exemplified in the opposites, "*yellow, blue, red,* &c., *walking, standing, lying,* &c."

It can hardly have been imagined by Krug or Sir W. Hamilton, that this is the meaning of Contrariety in common discourse, or that any one ever speaks of yellow

* Lectures, iii. 213, 214.   † Ibid. pp. 214, 215.

or blue as the contrary of red, or even as the opposite of
it. The very phrase, "*the* contrary," testifies that a thing
cannot have more contraries than one. Black is regarded
as the contrary of white, but no other contrariety is recognised among colours at all. Sir W. Hamilton, versed
as he was in the literature of logic, can hardly have
fancied that the world of logicians, any more than the
common world, was on his side. In the language of
logicians, as in that of life, a thing has only one contrary
—its extreme opposite: the thing farthest removed from
it in the same class. Black is the contrary of white,
but neither of them is the contrary of red. Infinitely
great is the contrary of infinitely small, but is not the
contrary of finite. It is the more strange that Krug
and Sir W. Hamilton should have misunderstood or rejected this, as the definition they ignore is the foundation
of the distinction between Contradictory and Contrary
Propositions, in the famous Parallelogram of Opposition.
The contrary proposition to All A is B, is No A is B,
its extreme opposite; the assertion most widely differing
from it that can be made; denying, not it merely, but
every part of it. Its contradictory is merely, Some A
is not B. Sir W. Hamilton could not have imagined
the distinction between these negative propositions to
be, that the one denies by simple negation, the other
through the affirmation of something else.

That the teachers of the Syllogistic Logic have taken
this view, and not Sir W. Hamilton's, of the meaning of
Contrariety, might be shown by any number of quotations. I have only looked up the authorities nearest at
hand. I begin with Aristotle : Τὰ γαρ πλεῖστον ἀλλήλων
διεστηκότα τῶν ἕν τῷ αὐτῷ γένει, ἐναντία ὁρίζονται.*

Aristotle again : Τὰ γαρ ἐναντία τῶν πλεῖστον διαφερόντων
περὶ τὸ αὐτό.†

Aristotle ἐν τῷ δεκάτῳ τῆς θεολογικῆς πραγματείας, as
cited by Ammonius Hermiæ : ‡ Ἐπεὶ δὲ διαφέρειν ἐνδέχεται

* Categoriæ, cap. 6.   † Περὶ Ἑρμηνείας, cap. 14.
‡ Ammonii Hermiæ in Aristotelis de Interpretatione Librum Com-
mentarius, ed. Aldi, pp. 175, 176.

ἀλλήλων τὰ διαφέροντα πλεῖον καὶ ἔλαττον, ἐστι τίς, καὶ μεγίστη διαφορὰ, καὶ ταύτην λέγω ἐναντίωσιν.

Ammonius himself thereon: Ἡ τῶν ἐναντίων διαφορὰ μεγίστη τῶν ἄλλων, καὶ οὐδὲν ἔχουσα ἐξωτέρω αὐτῆς δυνάμενον πεσεῖν.

My next extract shall be from a well-known treatise, which Sir W. Hamilton particularly recommended to his pupils : Burgersdyk's Institutiones Logicæ.

" Oppositorum species sunt quinque : Disparata, con-
" traria, relative opposita, privative opposita, et contra-
" dictoria.

" Disparata sunt, quorum unum pluribus opponitur,
" eodem modo.   Sic homo et equus, album et cæruleum,
" sunt disparata : quia homo non equo solum, sed etiam
" cani, leoni, cæterisque bestiarum speciebus, et album,
" non solum cæruleo, sed etiam rubro, viridi, cæterisque
" coloribus mediis, opponitur *eodem modo*, hoc est, eodem
" oppositorum genere . . . .

" Contraria sunt duo absolute, quæ sub eodem genere
" plurimum distant." *

This passage informs us, not only that what Sir W. Hamilton terms Contraries were not so called by the Aristotelian logicians, but also what they were called. They were called Disparates : a term employed by Sir W. Hamilton, but in a totally different meaning.†

The next is from one of the ablest, and, though in a comparatively small compass, one of the completest in essentials, of all the expositions I have seen of Logic from the purely Aristotelian point of view : *Manuductio ad Logicam*, by the Père Du Trieu, of Douai.‡

" Contraria sunt, quæ posita sub eodem genere maxime
" a se invicem distant, eidem subjecto susceptivo vicis-
" sim insunt, a quo se mutuo expellunt, nisi alterum
" insit a natura ; ut, *album*, et *nigrum*.

" In hac definitione continentur quatuor conditiones,
" sive leges contrariorum.

" Prima, ut sint sub eodem genere. . . .

* Burgersdicii Institutiones Logicæ, lib. i. cap. 22 ; Theorema i.
† Lectures, iii. 224.   ‡ Pars Tertia, cap. iii. art. 1.

" Secunda conditio contrariorum est ut sub illo eodem
" genere maxime distent, id est *precise* repugnent. . . .
" Hinc excluduntur disparata."

The next is from Saunderson's Logicæ Artis Compendium, one of the best-known elementary treatises on
Logic by British authors.[*]

" Oppositio Contraria est inter terminos contrarios.
" Sunt autem ea contraria quæ posita sub eodem genere
" maxime inter se distant, et vim habent expellendi se
" vicissim ex eodem subjecto susceptibili."

Crackanthorp :[†] " Contraria sunt Opposita quorum
" unum alteri sic opponitur ut nulli alteri aut æque
" aut magis opponatur. Sic Albedo Nigredini, Homini
" Brutum, Rationale Irrationali contrarium est. Nam
" nihil est quod æque Albedini opponitur atque Nigredo,
" et sic in reliquis." On the other hand, " Disparata
" sunt Opposita quorum unum uni sic opponitur, ut alteri
" vel æque vel magis opponatur. Sic Liberalitas et Ava-
" ritia disparata sunt. Nam Avaritia magis opponitur
" Prodigalitati quam Liberalitati. Sic Albedo et Rubedo
" disparata sunt, quia Albedo æque opponitur Viriditati
" atque Rubedini, et magis Nigredini quam ambobus.
" Nam plus inter se semper distant extrema, quam vel
" media inter se, vel medium ab alterutro extremo."

Brerewood :[‡] " Contraria a Dialecticis ita definiri
" solent : Sunt Opposita quæ sub eodem genere posita
" maxime a se invicem distant, et eodem subjecto sus-
" ceptibili vicissim insunt, a quo se mutuo expellunt,
" nisi alterum insit a natura. . . . . Sed quoniam hæc
" definitio (quamvis sit præcipue in Dialecticorum scholis
" authoritans) laborat et tædio, et summa difficultate,
" placet ex Aristotele faciliorem adducere, et breviorem :
" *Contraria sunt quæ sub eodem genere posita, maxime*
" *distant.*"

Samuel Smith :[§] " Contraria sunt quæ sub eodem

---

[*] Pars Prima, cap. 15.   [†] Logica, cap. 20.

[‡] Tractatus Quidam Logici de Prædicabilibus et Prædicamentis. Tractatus Decimus, de Post-Prædicamentis, Sect. 5 et 6.

[§] Aditus ad Logicam, (Oxoniæ, 1656) lib. i. cap. 14.

" genere posita, maxime a se invicem distant, et eidem
" susceptibili vicissim insunt, a quo se mutuo expel-
" lunt, nisi alterum eorum insit a natura. Ad Contraria
" igitur tria requiruntur : primo ut sint sub eodem
" genere, scilicet Qualitatis : nam solarum qualitatum
" est contrarietas ; secundo, ut maxime a se invicem
" distent in natura positiva, id est, ut ambo extrema
" sint positiva."

Wallis : * " Contraria definiri solent, quæ sub eodem
" genere maxime distant. Ut calidum et frigidum, album
" et nigrum : quæ contrariæ qualitatis dici solent."

Even Aldrich, right for once, may be added to the
list of Oxford authorities.† " Contraria sub eodem
" genere maxime distant.   Non maxime distant *omnium;*
" magis enim distant quæ nec idem genus summum
" habent, magis Contradictoria : sed maxime eorum quæ
" in genere conveniunt."

Keckermann ‡ does not employ this, but another
definition of Contraries ; not, however, Sir W. Hamilton's : and all his examples of Contraries are taken
from Extreme Opposites.

Casparus Bartholinus : §   " Contraria sunt, quæ sub
" eodem genere maxime distant, eidemque subjecto sus-
" ceptibili a quo se mutuo expellunt, vicissim insunt,
" nisi alterum insit a natura."

Du Hamel : ‖ " Oppositio contraria est inter duo ex-
" trema positiva, quæ sub eodem genere posita maxime
" distant, et ab eodem subjecto sese expellunt."

Grammatica Rationis, sive Institutiones Logicæ : ¶
" Contraria adversa sunt accidentia, posita sub eodem
" genere, quæ maxime distant, et se mutuo pellunt ab
" eodem subjecto in quo vicissim insunt."

Familiar as Sir W. Hamilton was with the whole

* Institutio Logicæ, lib. i. cap. 16.
† Artis Logicæ Compendium, Quæstionum Logicarum Determinatio,
quæst. 19.
‡ Systema Logicæ.
§ Enchiridion Logicæ (Lipsiæ, 1618) lib. i. cap. 23.
‖ Philosophia vetus et nova ad usum scholæ accommodata (Amstelodami,
1700) p. 197.
¶ Oxonii, 1673.

series of writers on Logic, he cannot have overlooked, and can hardly have forgotten, such passages as these. I have not had the fortune to meet with a single passage, from a single Aristotelian writer, which can be cited in his support. I presume, therefore, that he intentionally made (or adopted from Krug) a change in the meaning of a scientific term, the inverse of that which it is the proper office and common tendency of science to make. Instead of giving a more determinate signification to a name vaguely used, by binding it down to express a precise specific distinction, he laid hold of a name which already denoted a definite species, and applied it to the entire genus, which stood in no need of a name; leaving the particular species unnamed. But if he knowingly took this very unscientific liberty with a scientific term, diverting it from both its scientific and its popular meaning,—leaving the scientific vocabulary, never too rich, with one expression the fewer, and an important scientific distinction without a name,—he at least should not have done so without informing the reader. He should not have led the unsuspecting learner to believe that this was the received use of the term. Remark, too, that he embezzles not only the English word, but its Greek and Latin equivalents, exactly as if he agreed with the writers of the Greek and Latin treatises, and was only explaining their meaning.

V. One of the charges brought by Sir W. Hamilton against the common mode of stating the doctrine of the Syllogism, is that it does not obviate the objection often made to the syllogism of being a *petitio principii*, grounded on the admitted truth, that it can assert nothing in the conclusion which has not already been asserted in the premises. This objection, our author says,[*] "stands hitherto unrefuted, if not unrefutable." But he entertains the odd idea, that it can be got rid of by merely writing the propositions in a different order, putting the conclusion first. One might almost imagine that a little irony had been intended here. Putting

---

[*] Appendix to Lectures, iv. 401, and Appendix to Discussions, p. 652.

the conclusion first, certainly makes it impossible any
longer to say that the syllogism asserts in the conclusion
what has *already* been asserted in the premises ; and if
any one is of opinion that the logical relation between
premises and a conclusion, depends on the order in which
they are pronounced, such an objector, I must allow, is
from this time silenced.   But our author can have meditated very little on the meaning of the objection of
petitio principii against the Syllogism, when he thought
that such a device as this would remove it.   The difficulty, which that objection expresses, lies in a region far
below the depth to which such logic reaches ; and he
was quite right in regarding the objection as unrefuted.
Nor is its refutation, I conceive, possible, on any theory
but that which considers the Syllogism not as a process of
Inference, but as the mere interpretation of the record of a
previous process ; the major premise as simply a formula
for making particular inferences; and the conclusions of
ratiocination as not inferences from the formula, but inferences drawn according to the formula.   This theory,
and the grounds of it, having been very fully stated in
another work, need not be further noticed here.

CHAPTER XXIV.

OF SOME NATURAL PREJUDICES COUNTENANCED BY SIR WILLIAM HAMILTON, AND SOME FALLACIES WHICH HE CONSIDERS INSOLUBLE.

WE have concluded our review of Sir W. Hamilton as a teacher of Logic; but there remain to be noticed a few points, not strictly belonging either to Logic or to Psychology, but rather to what is inappropriately termed the Philosophia Prima. It would be more properly called *ultima*, since it consists of the widest generalisations respecting the laws of Existence and Activity; generalisations which by an unfortunate, though at first inevitable mistake, men fancied that they could reach *uno saltu*, and therefore placed them at the beginning of science, though, if they were ever legitimate, they could only be so as its tardy and final result. Every physical science, up to the time of Bacon, consisted mainly of such first principles as these : The ways of Nature are perfect : Nature abhors a vacuum ; *Natura non habet saltum :* Nothing can come out of nothing : Like can only be produced by like : Things always move towards their own place : Things can only be moved by something which is itself moving ; and so forth. And the Baconian revolution was far indeed from expelling such doctrines from philosophy. On the contrary, the Cartesian movement, which went on for a full century simultaneously with the Baconian, threw up many more of these imaginary axioms concerning things in general, which took a deep root in Continental philosophy, found their way into English, and are by no means, even now, discredited as they deserve to be.

Most of these were fully believed by the philosophers who maintained them, to be intuitively evident truths—revelations of Nature in the depths of human consciousness, and recognisable by the light of reason alone: while all the time they were merely bad generalisations of the vulgarest outward experience; rough interpretations of the appearances most familiar to sense, and which therefore had grown into the strongest associations in thought; never tested by the conditions of legitimate induction, not only because those conditions were still unknown, but because these wretched first attempts at generalisation were deemed to have a higher than inductive origin, and were erected into general laws from which the order of the universe might be deduced, and to which every scientific theory for the explanation of phenomena must be required to conform. It is a material point in the estimation of a philosopher and of his doctrines, whether he has taken his side for or against this mode of philosophising; whether he has countenanced any of these spurious axioms by his adhesion. Sir W. Hamilton cannot be acquitted of having done so, in more than one instance.

In treating of the problem of Causality, Sir W. Hamilton had occasion to argue, that we ought not to postulate a special mental law in order to explain the belief that everything must have a cause, since that belief is sufficiently accounted for by the "Law of the Conditioned," which makes it impossible for us to conceive an absolute commencement of anything. I do not mean to return to the discussion of this theory of Causality; but let us ask ourselves why we are interdicted from assuming a special law, in order to account for that which is already sufficiently accounted for by a general one. The real ground of the prohibition is what our author terms the Law of Parsimony; a principle identical with the famous maxim of the Nominalists, known as Occam's Razor—*Entia non sunt multiplicanda prœter necessitatem;* understanding by Entia, not merely substances but also Powers. Sir W. Hamilton, instead of resting it on this logical injunction, grounds it on an ontological theory. His reason is, "Nature never works "by more and more complex instruments than are neces-"sary.* He cites,† with approbation, the maxims of Aristotle, "that God and Nature never operate without "effect (οὐδὲν μάτην, οὐδὲν ἐλλειπῶς, ποιοῦσι); they never "operate superfluously (μηδὲν περίεργον—περιττῶς— "ἀργῶς); but always through one rather than through a "plurality of means (καθ᾽ ἕν, μᾶλλον ἢ κατὰ πολλὰ):" thus borrowing a general theory of the very kind which Bacon exploded, to support a rule which can stand perfectly well without it. Have *we* authority to declare that there is anything which God and Nature never do? Do we know all Nature's combinations? Were we called into counsel in fixing its limits? By what canons of induction has this theory ever been tried? By what observations has it been verified? We know well that Nature, in many of its operations, works by means which are of a complexity so extreme, as to be an almost insuperable obstacle to our investigations. On what evidence do we presume to say that this complexity was necessary, and that the effect could not have been produced in a simpler manner? If we look into the meaning of words, of what kind is the necessity which is supposed to be binding on God and Nature—the pressure they are unable to escape from? Is there any necessity in Nature which Nature did not make? or if not, what did? What is this power superior to Nature and its author, and to which Nature is compelled to adapt itself?

There is one supposition under which this doctrine has an intelligible meaning—the hypothesis of the Two Principles. If the universe was moulded into its present form by a Being who did not make it wholly, and who was impeded by an obstacle which he could only partially overcome—whether that obstacle was a rival intelligence, or, as Plato thought, an inherent incapacity in Matter; it is on that supposition admissible, that the Demiourgos may have always worked by the simplest

---

* Appendix to Discussions, p. 622.   † Ibid. p. 629.

possible means; the simplest, namely, which were permitted by the opposition of the conflicting Power, or
the intractableness of the material. This is, in fact, the
doctrine of Leibnitz's Théodicée; his famous theory that
a world, made by God, must be the best of all possible
worlds, that is, the best world which could be made
under the conditions by which, as it would appear, Providence was restricted. This doctrine, commonly called
Optimism, is really Manicheism, or, to call it by its more
proper name, Sabæism. The word " possible " assumes
the existence of hindrances insurmountable by the divine
power, and Leibnitz was only wrong in calling a power
limited by obstacles by the name Omnipotence: for it is
almost too obvious to be worth stating, that real Omnipotence could have effected its ends totally without
means, or could have made any means sufficient. This
Sabæan theory is the only one by which the assertion,
that Nature always works by the simplest means, can be
made consistent with known fact. Even so, it remains
wholly unproved; and, were it proved, would be but a
speculative truth of Theology, incapable of affording
any practical guidance. We could never be justified in
rejecting an hypothesis for being too complicated; it
being beyond our power to set limits to the complication
of the means that might possibly be necessary, to evade
the obstacles which Ahriman or Matter may have per-
versely thrown in the Creator's way.

The "Law of Parsimony" needs no such support; it
rests on no assumption respecting the ways or proceedings of Nature. It is a purely logical precept; a case of
the broad practical principle, not to believe anything of
which there is no evidence. When we have no direct
knowledge of the matter of fact, and no reason for believing it except that it would account for another matter
of fact, all reason for admitting it is at an end when the
fact requiring explanation can be explained from known
causes. The assumption of a superfluous cause, is a
belief without evidence; as if we were to suppose that
a man who was killed by falling over a precipice, must

have taken poison as well.   The same principle which forbids the assumption of a superfluous fact, forbids that of a superfluous law.   When Newton had shown that the same theorem would express the conditions of the planetary motions and the conditions of the fall of bodies to the earth, it would have been illogical to recognise two distinct laws of nature, one for heavenly and the other for earthly attraction ; since both these laws, when stripped of the circumstances ascertained to be irrelevant to the effect, would have had to be expressed in the very same words.   The reduction of each of the two generalisations to the expression of only those circumstances which influence the result, reduces both of them to the same proposition ; and to decline to do so, would be to make an assumption of difference between the cases, for which none of the observations afforded the smallest ground.   The rule of Parsimony, therefore, whether applied to facts or to theories, implies no theory concerning the propensities or proceedings of Nature.   If Nature's ways and inclinations were the reverse of what they are supposed to be, it would have been as illegitimate as it is now, to assume a fact of Nature without any evidence for it, or to consider the same property as two different properties, because found in two different kinds of objects.

In another place,* Sir W. Hamilton says that the Law of Parsimony, which he terms " the most impor- " tant maxim in regulation of philosophical procedure " when it is necessary to resort to an hypothesis, has " never, perhaps, been adequately expressed ; " and he proposes the following expression for it : " Neither *more* " nor *more onerous* causes are to be assumed, than are " necessary to account for the phenomena." This conception of some causes as " more onerous " to the general scheme of things than others, is a distinction greatly requiring what our author says it has never yet had— to be " articulately expressed." He does not, however, articulate it in general terms, but only in its application

* Appendix to Discussions, pp. 628, 631.

to the particular question of Causality. From this we may collect,—1st. That a "positive power" is a more onerous hypothesis than a "negative impotence." 2nd. That a special hypothesis, which serves to explain only one phenomenon, is more onerous than a general one which will explain many. 3rd. That the explanation of an effect by cause of which the very existence is hypothetical, is more onerous than its hypothetical explanation by a cause otherwise known to exist. The last two of these three canons are but particular cases of the general rule, that we should not assume an hypothetical cause of a phenomenon which admits of being accounted for by a cause of which there is other evidence.* The remaining canon, that we should prefer the hypothesis of an incapacity to that of a power, is, I apprehend, only valid when its infringement would be a violation of one of the other two rules.

The time-honoured, but gratuitous, assumption, respecting Nature, on which I have now commented, is not the only generality of the pre-Baconian type which Sir W. Hamilton has countenanced. He gives his sanction to the old doctrine that "a thing can act only where it is." The dictum appears in this direct form in one of the very latest of his writings, the notes for an intended memoir of Professor Dugald Stewart.† He has so much faith in it as to make it the foundation of two of his favourite theories. One is, that ‡ "the thing perceived, "and the percipient organ, must meet in place, must "be contiguous. The consequence of this doctrine is a "complete simplification of the theory of perception, and "a return to the most ancient speculation on the point.

---

* This is what Newton meant by a *vera causa*, in his celebrated maxim, "Causas rerum naturalium non plures admitti debere quam quæ *et veræ* "*sint*, et earum phænomenis explicandis sufficiant." It is singular that Sir W. Hamilton does not seem to have understood, that by *veræ causæ* Newton meant agencies the existence of which was otherwise authenticated : for he says (footnote to Reid, p. 236), "In their plain meaning, "the words et *veræ sint* are redundant ; or what follows is redundant, and "the whole rule a barren truism." [But in the Appendix to the Discussions (p. 631) Sir W. Hamilton puts the right interpretation on Newton's maxim.]

† Appendix to Lectures, ii. 522.   ‡ Ibid.

" All sensible cognition is, in a certain acceptation, re-
" duced to Touch, and this is the very conclusion main-
" tained by the venerable authority of Democritus. "Ac-
" cording to this doctrine, it is erroneous to affirm that
" we are percipient of distant objects." Conformably
to this, we have seen him not only maintaining, in
opposition to Reid, that we do not see the sun—that
we see only an image of it in our eye—but also, that we
directly perceive Extension, whether by sight or touch,
only in our own bodily organs : thus preferring the *à
priori* axiom, that a thing can only act where it is, to
the authority of those "natural beliefs" which he, in
other cases, so strenuously asserts against impugners,
and so often affirms that we ought either to accept as a
whole, or never appeal to at all.

The other theory which our author maintains on the
authority of the same dictum, is that the mind acts
directly throughout the whole body, and not through
the brain only.   "There is * no good ground to suppose
" that the mind is situate solely in the brain, or ex-
" clusively in any part of the body.   On the contrary,
" the supposition that it is really present wherever we
" are conscious that it acts,—in a word, the Peripatetic
" aphorism, The soul is all in the whole, and all in
" every part,—is more philosophical, and consequently,
" more probable than any other opinion. . . . . . Even if
" we admit that the nervous system is the part to which
" it is proximately united, still the nervous system is
" itself universally ramified throughout the body ; and
" we have no more right to deny that the mind feels
" at the finger-points, as consciousness assures us, than
" to assert that it thinks exclusively in the brain."   Sir
W. Hamilton should at least have shown how this
hypothesis can be reconciled with the fact, that a slight
pressure on the nerve at a place intermediate between
the finger and the brain, takes away the mind's power of
feeling in the finger, while at any point above the liga-
ture the feeling is the same as before.   If he object that

* Lectures, ii. 127, 128.

2 M

the mode in which the pressure impedes sensation need
not be by interrupting the communication between the
finger and the brain, but may be by disturbing the
functions of the nerve itself, we may ask, why is this
disturbance confined to the part of the nerve which is
below the point of pressure, while above that point the
functions remain unimpaired?   Many other objections
might be brought against Sir W. Hamilton's theory, if
my object were to discuss the physiological question; but
my object is only to show the amount of evidence which
Sir W. Hamilton will disregard, rather than admit that
one thing can act directly upon another without immediate contact.*   What he would have thought of the
application of his doctrine to the solar system, he has not
told us (the recent developments of the doctrine of the
Unity of Force being posterior to his time): but it com-
mits him to the opinion, that gravitation acts through
an intervening medium, which he must postulate, first
as existing, and secondly, as possessed of inscrutable
properties; in palpable repugnance to his own Law of
Parsimony, and to all the canons grounded thereon.
Descartes postulated his vortices in obedience to the
same axiom.

What, however, is the worth of this doctrine, that
things can only act upon one another by direct contact?
Mr. Carlyle says, "a thing can only act where it is;
with all my heart; only where is it?"   In one sense of
the word, a thing *is* wherever its action is: its power is
there, though not its corporeal presence.   But to say
that a thing can only act where its power is, would be
the idlest of mere identical propositions.   And where is
the warrant for asserting that a thing cannot act when
it is not locally contiguous to the thing it acts upon?
Shall we be told that such action is inconceivable?   Even
if it was, this, according to Sir W. Hamilton's philosophy, is no evidence of impossibility.   But that it is

* In the Lectures, I mean: for, in the Dissertations on Reid (p. 861),
the doctrine, that we feel in the toe, and not in a *sensorium commune*, is at
least so far retracted, that the possibility of the opposite theory is explicitly acknowledged.

conceivable, is shown by every fairy tale, as well as by every religion. Then, again, what is the meaning of contiguity? According to the best physical knowledge we possess, things are never actually contiguous: what we term contact between particles, only means that they are in the degree of proximity at which their mutual repulsions are in equilibrium with their attractions. If so, instead of never, things always act on one another at some, though it may be a very small distance. The belief that a thing can only act where it is, is a common case of inseparable, though not ultimately indissoluble, association. It is an unconscious generalisation, of the roughest possible description, from the most familiar cases of the mutual action of bodies, superficially considered. The temporary difficulty found in apprehending any action of body upon body unlike what people were accustomed to, created a Natural Prejudice, which was long a serious impediment to the reception of the Newtonian theory : but it was hoped that the final triumph of that theory had extinguished it; that all educated persons were now aware that action at a distance is intrinsically quite as credible as action in contact, and that there is no reason, apart from specific experience, to regard the one as in any respect less probable than the other. That Sir W. Hamilton should be an instance to the contrary, is an example of the obstinate vitality of these *idola tribûs*, and shows that we are never safe against the rejuvenescence of the most superannuated error, if in throwing it off we have not reformed the bad habit of thought, the wrong and unscientific tendency of the intellect, from which the error took its rise.*

---

* In the course of his speculations our author comes across a fact which is positively irreconcileable with his axiom ; the fact of repulsion. This brings him to a dead stand. He knows not whether to advance or recede. Repulsion, he says (Dissertations on Reid, p. 852), "remains, as apparently an *actio in distans*, even when forced upon us as a fact, still "inconceivable as a possibility." He is soon afterwards obliged to confess that the same is true of attraction: "As attraction and repulsion seem " equally *actiones in distans*, it is not more difficult to realise to ourselves "the action of the one, than the action of the other." Action from a distance being "a fact," though inconceivable, this fact would seem to

Though but remotely connected with the preceding considerations, yet as belonging in common with them to the subject of Fallacies, I will notice in this place the curious partiality which our author shows to a particular group of sophisms, the Eleatic arguments for the impossibility of motion.   He deemed these arguments, though leading to a false conclusion, to be irrefutable; as Brown thought concerning Berkeley's argument against the existence of matter—that as a mere play of reasoning it was unanswerable, while it was impossible for the human mind to admit the conclusion; forgetting that if this were so it would be a *reductio ad absurdum* of the reasoning faculty.   There is no philosopher to whom, I imagine, Sir W. Hamilton would have less liked to be assimilated, than Brown; and he would probably have defended himself against the imputation, by saying that the Eleatic arguments do not prove motion to be impossible, but only to be inconceivable by us.   Yet if a fact which we see and feel every minute of our lives, is not conceivable by us, what is?   Our author does not enter at any length into the question, but expresses his opinion on several occasions incidentally.   "It is," he says,* "on the inability of the mind to conceive either the "ultimate indivisibility, or the endless divisibility of "space and time, that the arguments of the Eleatic "Zeno against the possibility of motion are founded; "arguments which at least show, that motion, however "certain as a fact, cannot be conceived possible, as it "involves a contradiction."   We have been told in very emphatic terms by Sir W. Hamilton, that the Law of Contradiction is binding not on our conceptions merely, but on Things.   If, then, motion involves a contradiction, how is it possible? and if it is possible, and a fact, as we know it to be, how can it involve a contradiction?

---

require of him the retractation of his axiom: yet he does not retract it. I need hardly remark that attraction and repulsion are not inconceivable; except indeed in another of the numerous senses of that equivocal word; that in which it is used when our author tells us that all ultimate facts are inconceivable, meaning only that they are inexplicable.

    * Lectures, ii. 373.   To the same effect, iv. 71.

The appearance of contradiction must necessarily be fallacious, even were we unable to point out the fallacy. Our author, apparently, has attempted to resolve it, and failed.   He calls the argument * "an exposition of the contradictions involved in our notion of motion," and says that its "fallacy has not yet been detected."   And, again,† "The Eleatic Zeno's demonstration of the impos- "sibility of motion is not more insoluble than could be "framed a proof that the present has no reality : for "however certain we may be of both, we can positively "think neither."   It must, one would suppose, be a great difficulty, which could appear insoluble to Sir W. Hamilton.   The "demonstration," at all events, cannot yet have been refuted, and superhuman ingenuity must be needed to refute it.   Yet the fallacy in it has been pointed out again and again ; and the contradictions which Sir W. Hamilton regards it as an exposure of, do not exist.

Zeno's reasonings against motion, as handed down by Aristotle, consist of four arguments, which are stated and criticised with considerable prolixity by Bayle. Several of these are substantially the same argument in different forms, and if we examine the two most plausible of them it will suffice.   The first is the ingenious fallacy of Achilles and the Tortoise.   If Achilles starts a thousand yards behind the tortoise, and runs a hundred times as fast ; still, while Achilles runs those thousand yards, the tortoise will have got on ten ; while Achilles runs those ten, the tortoise will have run a tenth of a yard ; and as this process may be continued to infinity, Achilles will never overtake the tortoise.   In our author's opinion, this argument is logically correct, and evolves a contradiction in our idea of motion.   But it is neither logically correct, nor evolves a contradiction in anything. It assumes, of course, the infinite divisibility of space. But we have no need to entangle ourselves in the meta-physical discussion whether this assumption is warrant-able.   Let it be granted or not, the argument always

* Foot-note to Reid, p. 102.   † Appendix to Discussions, p. 606.

remains fallacious.   The fallacy lies in the assertion that
" this process may be continued to infinity."   Infinity
is here ambiguous.   The conclusion drawn is that the
process may be continued for an *infinite duration* of time.
But the premise is only true in the sense, that it may be
continued for an *infinite number of divisions* of time.
The argument confounds infinity and infinite divisibility.
It assumes that to pass through an infinitely divisible
space, requires an infinite time.   But the infinite divisibility of space means the infinite divisibility of *finite*
space : and it is only infinite space which cannot be
passed over in less than infinite time.   What the argument proves is, that to pass over the infinitely divisible
space, requires an infinitely divisible time : but an infinitely divisible time may itself be finite ; the smallest
finite time is infinitely divisible; the argument, therefore,
is consistent with the tortoise's being overtaken in the
smallest finite time.   It is a sophism of the type Ignoratio Elenchi, or, as Archbishop Whately terms it, Irrelevant Conclusion; an argument which proves a different
proposition from that which it pretends to prove, the
difference of meaning being disguised by an ambiguity
of language.

The other plausible form of Zeno's argument is at
first sight more favourable to Sir W. Hamilton's theory,
being a real attempt to prove that the fact of motion
involves impossible conditions.   The usual mode of
stating it is this.   If a body moves, it must move either
in the place where it is, or in the place where it is not :
but either of these is impossible : therefore it cannot
move.   First of all, this argument, even if we were
unable to refute it, does not exhibit any contradiction
in our " notion " of motion.   We do not conceive a
body as moving either in the place where it is, or in the
place where it is not, but from the former to the latter :
in other words, we conceive the body as in the one place
and in the other at successive instants.   Where is the
" contradiction " between being in one place at this
moment, and in another at the next ?   As for the fallacy

itself, it is strange that when everybody sees the answer
to it, a practised logician should have any difficulty in
putting that answer into logical forms. It is not necessary that motion should be *in* a place. A body must
be in a place ; but motion is not a body—it is a change :
and that a change of place should be either in the old
place or in the new, is a real contradiction in terms. To
put the thing in another way ; Place may be understood
in two senses : it may either be a divisible, or an indivisible part of space. If it be a divisible part, as a room,
or a street, it is true that in that sense, every motion
is in a place, that is within a limited portion of space :
but in this meaning of the term the dilemma breaks
down, for the body really moves in the place where it
is ; the room, the field, or the house. If, on the contrary, we are to understand by Place an indivisible
minimum of space, the proposition that motion must be
in a place is evidently false ; for motion cannot be *in*
that which has no parts ; it can only be *to* or *from* it.

A parallel sophism might easily be invented, turning
upon Time instead of Space. It might be said that sunset is impossible, since if it be possible, it must take place
either while the sun is still up, or after it is down. The
answer is obvious : it is just the change from one to the
other which is sunset. And so it is the change from
one position in space to another which is motion. The
parallelism between the two cases was evidently seen
by Sir W. Hamilton, and the sophism was too hard for
him in both : and this is what he must have meant by
saying that we cannot " positively think " the Present.
That he should have missed the solution of the fallacy
is strange enough : but, as a matter of fact, the assertion that we have no positive perception, on the one
hand of Motion, on the other, of present time, deserves
notice as one of the most curious deliverances of so
earnest an asserter of " our natural beliefs."

These paralogisms are only part of a long list of
puzzles concerning infinity, which, though by no means
hard to clear up, appear to our author insoluble. I

append in a note the entire list.* Many of them are
resolved by the observations already made, their difficulty
being merely that of separating the two ideas of Infinite
and Infinitely Divisible. To our author's thinking, infinite divisibility and the Finite contradict one another.
But even allowing (which, as was seen in a former
chapter, I do not) that infinite divisibility is inconceivable, it does not therefore involve a contradiction. The
remaining puzzles mostly result from inability to conceive that one infinity can be greater or less than another;
a conception familiar to all mathematicians. Our author
refuses to consider that a space or a time which is infinite
in one direction and bounded in another, is necessarily
less than a space or a time which is infinite in every
direction. The space between two parallels, or between
two diverging lines or surfaces, extends to infinity, but
it is necessarily less than entire space, being a part
of it. Not only is one infinity greater than another,
but one infinity may be infinitely greater than another.

* " Contradictions proving the Psychological Theory of the Conditioned.
  "1. Finite cannot comprehend, contain, the Infinite.—Yet an inch or
"minute, say, are finites, and are divisible *ad infinitum*, that is, their ter-
"minated division incogitable.
  "2. Infinite cannot be terminated or begun.—Yet eternity *ab ante* ends
"*now;* and eternity *a post* begins now. So apply to Space.
  "3. There cannot be two infinite maxima.—Yet eternity *ab ante* and *a*
"*post* are two infinite maxima of time.
  "4. Infinite maximum if cut in two, the halves cannot be each infinite,
"for nothing can be greater than infinite, and thus they could not be
"parts; nor finite, for thus two finite halves would make an infinite
"whole.
  "5. What contains infinite quantities (extensions, protensions, inten-
"sions) cannot be passed through,—come to an end. An inch, a minute,
"a degree contains these: *ergo*, &c. Take a minute. This contains an
"infinitude of protended quantities, which must follow one after another;
"but an infinite series of successive protensions can, *ex termino*, never be
"ended; *ergo*, &c.
  "6. An infinite maximum cannot but be all-inclusive. Time *ab ante*
"and *a post* infinite and exclusive of each other; *ergo*, &c.
  "7. An infinite number of quantities must make up either an infinite or
"a finite whole. I. The former.—But an inch, a minute, a degree, contain
"each an infinite number of quantities; therefore an inch, a minute, a
"degree, are each infinite wholes; which is absurd. II. The latter.—An
"infinite number of quantities would thus make up a finite quantity, which
"is equally absurd.
  "8. If we take a finite quantity (as an inch, a minute, a degree), it would

Mathematicians habitually assume this, and reason from it; and the result always coming out true, the assumption is justified. But mathematicians, I must admit, seldom know exactly what they are about when they do this. As the results always prove right, they know empirically that the process cannot be wrong—that the premises must be true in a sense; but in what sense, it is beyond the ingenuity of most of them to understand. The doctrine long remained a part of that mathematical mysticism, so mercilessly shown up by Berkeley in his " Analyst," and " Defence of Freethinking in Mathematics." To clear it up required a philosophical mathematician—one who should be both a mathematician and a metaphysician: and it found one. To complete Sir W. Hamilton's discomfiture, this philosophic mathematician is his old antagonist Mr. De Morgan, whom he described as too much of a mathematician to be anything of a philosopher.* Mr. De Morgan, however, has proved himself, as far as this subject is concerned, a far better

"appear equally that there are, and that there are not, an equal number "of quantities between these and a greatest, and between these and a "least.

"9. An absolutely quickest motion is that which passes from one point "to another in space in a minimum of time. But a quickest motion from "one point to another, say a mile distance, and from one to another, say a "million million of miles, is thought the same: which is absurd.

"10. A wheel turned with quickest motion; if a spoke be prolonged, "it will, therefore, be moved by a motion quicker than the quickest. The "same may be shown using the rim and the nave.

"11. Contradictory are Boscovich Points, which occupy space, and are "unextended. Dynamism, therefore, inconceivable. *E contra.*

"12. Atomism also inconceivable; for this supposes atoms,—minima "extended but indivisible.

"13. A quantity, say a foot, has an infinity of parts. Any part of this "quantity, say an inch, has also an infinity. But one infinity is not larger "than another. Therefore an inch is equal to a foot.

"14. If two divaricating lines are produced *ad infinitum* from a point "where they form an acute angle, like a pyramid, the base will be infinite, "and, at the same time, not infinite; 1°. Because terminated by two points; "and, 2°. Because shorter than the sides; 3°. Base could not be drawn, "because sides infinitely long.

"15. An atom, as existent, must be able to be turned round. But if "turned round, it must have a right and left hand, &c., and these its signs " [sides ?] "must change their place: therefore, be extended." (Appendix to Lectures, ii. 527–529.)

* Appendix to Discussions, p. 707.

metaphysician than Sir W. Hamilton. He has let the light of reason into all the logical obscurities and paradoxes of the infinitesimal calculus. By merely following out, more thoroughly than had been done before, the rational conception of infinitesimal division, as synonymous with division into as many and as small parts as we choose, without any limit, Mr. De Morgan, in his Algebra, has fully explained and justified the conception of successive orders of differentials, each of them infinitely less than the differential of the preceding, and infinitely greater than that of the succeeding order. Whoever is acquainted with this masterly specimen of analysis, will find his way through Sir W. Hamilton's series of riddles respecting Infinity, without ever being at a loss for their solution. I shall therefore trouble the reader no further with them in this place.

CHAPTER XXV.

SIR WILLIAM HAMILTON'S THEORY OF PLEASURE AND PAIN.

I HAVE now concluded my remarks on the principal department of Sir W. Hamilton's psychology, that which relates to the Cognitive Faculties. The remaining two of the three portions into which he divides the subject, are the Feelings, and what he terms the Conative Faculties, meaning those which tend to Action. On the Conative Faculties, however, he barely touches, in the concluding part of his last lecture; and of the Feelings he does not treat at any length. What he propounds on the subject, chiefly consists of a general theory of Pleasure and Pain. Not a theory of what they are in themselves, for he is not so much the dupe of words as to suppose that they are anything but what we feel them to be. The speculation with which he has presented us, does not relate to their essence, but to the causes they depend on; " the * general conditions which determine " the existence of Pleasure and Pain . . . . the funda-" mental law by which these phenomena are governed " in all their manifestations."

The inquiry is scientifically legitimate, and of great interest; but we must not be very confident that it is a practicable one, or can lead to any positive result. It is quite possible that in seeking for the law of pleasure and pain, like Bacon in seeking for the laws of the sensible properties of bodies, we may be looking for unity of cause, where there is a plurality, perhaps a multitude, of different causes. Such attempts, however, even if unsuccessful, are far from being entirely useless. They

---

* Lectures, ii. 434.

often lead to a more careful study of the phenomenon
in some of its aspects, and to the discovery of relations
between them, not previously understood, which though
not adequate to the formation of an universal theory of
the phenomenon, afford a clearer insight into some of its
forms and varieties. This merit must be allowed to Sir
W. Hamilton's theory, in common with several others
which preceded it on the same subject. But, regarded as
a theorem of the universal conditions which are present
whenever pleasure (or pain) is present, and absent whenever it is absent, the doctrine will hardly bear investigation. The simplest and most familiar cases are exactly
those which obstinately refuse to be reduced within it.

I shall, as usual, state Sir W. Hamilton's theory in his
own words, though in the present case it is a questionable advantage, the terms being so general and abstract
that they are scarcely capable of being understood, apart
from the illustrations. "Pleasure," he says,* " is a
"reflex of the spontaneous and unimpeded exertion of
"a power, of whose energy we are conscious. Pain, a
"reflex of the overstrained or repressed exertion of such
"a power." By a "reflex" he has shortly before said
that † he means merely a "concomitant;" but I think
it will appear that he means at least an effect. At
all events, these are what he regards as the ultimate
conditions of pleasure and pain; the most general
expression of the circumstances in which they occur.

This theory was of course suggested by the pleasures
and pains of intellectual or physical exertion, or, as it is
otherwise termed, exercise. These are the phenomena
which principally afford to it such foundation of fact,
and such plausibility in speculation, as it possesses. As
we all know, moderate exertion, either of body or mind,
is pleasurable ; a greater amount is painful, except when
set in motion by an impulse which renders it, in our
author's meaning of the word, "spontaneous:" and a felt
impediment to any kind of active exertion, when there is
an impulse towards it, is painful. It at first appears as

* Lectures, ii. 440.   † Ibid. p. 436.

if Sir W. Hamilton had overlooked the pains and pleasures in which the mind and body are passive, as in most of the organic, and a large proportion of the emotional pleasures and pains. He claims, however, to include all these in his formula. The " powers " and " energies " whose free action he holds to be the condition of pleasure, and their impeded or overstrained action, of pain, include our passive susceptibilities as well as our active energies. Accordingly he suggests a correction of his own language, saying that " occupation " or " exercise " would perhaps be fitter expressions than " energy." *
" The term *energy*,† which is equivalent to *act, activity*, " or *operation*, is here used to comprehend also all the " mixed states of action and passion of which we are " conscious; for, inasmuch as we are conscious of any " modification of mind, there is necessarily more than " a mere passivity of the subject; consciousness itself " implying at least a reaction " (what has become of his doctrine that to be conscious of a feeling is only another phrase for having the feeling?) " Be this, however, as " it may, the nouns *energy, act, activity, operation*, with " the correspondent verbs, are to be understood to denote, " indifferently and in general, all the processes of our " higher and our lower life of which we are conscious."

Understanding the theory in this enlarged sense, let us test it by application to one of the simplest of our organic feelings, the pleasure of a sweet taste. This pleasure, according to the theory, arises from the free exercise, without either restraint or excess, of one of our powers or capacities : what capacity shall we call it? That of tasting sweetness? This will not do ; for if the capacity of having the sensation of sweet is called into play in any degree, great or small, the effect is a sweet taste, which is a pleasure. Besides, instead of a sweet taste, let us suppose an acrid taste. In this taste the capacity exercised is that of tasting acridity. But the result of the exercise of this capacity, neither repressed nor overstrained, which therefore, according to the

* Lectures, ii. note to p. 435, and p. 466.　　† Ibid. p. 435.

theory, should be a pleasure, is an acrid taste, which is
a pain.   It must, therefore, be meant that the capacity
which when freely exercised causes pleasure, and when
repressed or overstrained, pain, is some more general
capacity than that of sweet or acrid taste—say the
power of taste in the abstract: that the power of taste,
the organic action of the gustatory nerves, by its spontaneous exercise, yields pleasure, and by its repression,
or its strained exercise, produces pain.   The theory
thus entirely turns upon what is meant by spontaneous;
as is shown still more clearly by our author's comments.
" It has been stated," he observes in a recapitulation of
his doctrine,* " that a feeling of pleasure is experienced,
" when any power is consciously exercised in a suitable
" manner; that is, when we are neither, on the one hand,
" conscious of any restraint upon the energy which it is
" disposed spontaneously to put forth, nor on the other,
" conscious of any effort in it to put forth an amount of
" energy greater either in degree or in continuance, than
" what it is disposed freely to exert.   In other words, we
" feel positive pleasure, in proportion as our powers are
" exercised, but not over-exercised; we feel positive
" pain, in proportion as they are compelled either not
" to operate, or to operate too much.   All pleasure,
" thus, arises from the free play of our faculties and
" capacities; all pain from their compulsory repression
" or compulsory activity."

All, therefore, depends upon what is meant by " free "
or " spontaneous," and what by " compulsory" activity.
The difference cannot be that which the words suggest,
the presence or absence of will.   It cannot be meant,
that pleasure accompanies the process when wholly
involuntary, and that pain begins when a voluntary element enters into the exercise of the sensitive faculty.
There is nothing voluntary in the agonies of the rack,
or of an excruciating bodily disease: while, in the case
of a pleasure, the exercise of will, in the only mode
in which it can be exercised on a feeling, namely, by

* Lectures, ii. 477.

voluntarily attending to it, instead of converting it from a pleasure into a pain, often greatly heightens the pleasure. This doctrine, therefore, would be absurd, nor is Sir W. Hamilton chargeable with it. What he means by "spontaneous" as applied to the exercise of our capacities of feeling, we gather from the following passage,[*] and others similar to it.

"Every power, all conditions being supplied, and all "impediments being removed, tends, of its proper nature "and without effort, to put forth a certain determinate "maximum, intensive and protensive, of free energy. "This determinate maximum of free energy, it, there- "fore, exerts spontaneously : if a less amount than this "be actually put forth, a certain quantity of tendency "has been forcibly repressed : whereas, if a greater than "this has been actually exerted, a certain amount of "nisus has been forcibly stimulated in the power. The "term *spontaneously*, therefore, provides that the exer- "tion of the power has not been constrained beyond the "proper limit,—the natural maximum, to which, if left "to itself, it freely springs.—Again, in regard to the "term *unimpeded*,—this stipulates that the conditions "requisite to allow this spring have been supplied, and "that all impediments to it have been removed. This "postulates, of course, the presence of an object."

The spontaneous and unimpeded exercise of a capacity means, therefore, it would appear, the exercise which takes place when "all conditions" are "supplied," and "all impediments removed." Let us apply this to a particular case. I taste, at different instants, two different objects ; an orange, and rhubarb. In both cases, all conditions are supplied ; the object is present and in contact with my organs ; and in both cases, all impediments are removed to the unstrained and natural action of the object upon my gustatory organs. Yet the result is in one case a pleasure, in the other a sensation of nauseousness. On Sir W. Hamilton's theory, it ought, in both cases, to have been pleasure : for in neither does

* Lectures, ii. 441.

anything interfere with the free action of my sense of taste.

Sir W. Hamilton can scarcely have overlooked this objection, and the answer which he may be supposed to make, is that in the case of the rhubarb, the object itself was of a nature to disturb the gustative faculty, and exact from it a greater degree of action (or a less, for I would not undertake to say which) than is exacted by the orange. But where is the proof of this? and what, even, does the assertion mean? A greater degree of what action? Of the action of tasting? If so, a pain should differ from a pleasure only by being more (or perhaps less) intense. Is the action that is meant, some occult process in the organ? But what ground is there for affirming that there is more action of any kind, on the part of the organ or the sense of taste, in a disagreeable savour than in an agreeable one? It is perhaps true that more than a certain quantity of action is always painful: every sensation intensified beyond a certain degree may become a pain. But the converse proposition, that wherever there is a pain there is an excess of action (or a deficiency, for we are offered that alternative), I know of no reason for believing. Moreover, if admitted, it would seem to involve the consequence, that in every case of pain, a less or a greater degree of the cause which produces it is pleasurable, which is certainly not true, however true it may be that in many cases of organic pleasure (especially tastes and smells) a less or a greater quantity of the substance which produces the pleasure is either insipid or positively disagreeable.

Our author is more than half aware that his theory breaks down when applied to pleasures or pains that are heterogeneous to one another; for he says,* "When it "is required of us to explain particularly and in detail, "why the rose, for example, produces this sensation of "smell, assafœtida that other, and so forth, and to say "in what peculiar action does the perfect or pleasurable,

* Lectures, ii. 495.

"and the imperfect or painful, activity of an organ
"consist, we must at once profess our ignorance." He
lays the responsibility of the failure, not upon his
theory, but upon the general inexplicability of ultimate facts. "But it is the same with all our attempts
"at explaining any of the ultimate phenomena of crea-
"tion. In general, we may account for much; in
"detail, we can rarely account for anything: for we
"soon remount to facts which lie beyond our powers
"of analysis and observation."

This appears to me a great misconception, on our
author's part, of what may rightfully be demanded from
a theorist. He is not entitled to frame a theory from
one class of phenomena, extend it to another class
which it does not fit, and excuse himself by saying
that if we cannot make it fit, it is because ultimate
facts are inexplicable. Newton did not proceed in this
manner with the theory of gravitation. He made it
an absolute condition of adopting the theory, that it
should fit; and when, owing to incorrect data, he could
not make it fit perfectly, he abandoned the speculation
for many years. If the smell of a rose and the smell
of assafœtida are ultimate facts, be it so: but in that
case, it is useless setting up a theory to explain them.
If we do propound a theory, we are bound to prove all
it asserts: and this, in the present case, is, that in
smelling a rose the organ is in "perfect" activity, but
when smelling assafœtida, in "imperfect," which is
either greater or less than perfect. It is not philosophical to assert this, and fall back upon the incomprehensibility of the subject as a dispensation from
proving it. What is a hindrance to proving a theory,
ought to be a hindrance to affirming it.

What meaning, in fact, can be attached to perfect
and imperfect activity, as the phrases are here used?
Perfection or imperfection is treated as a question of
quantity; activity is called perfect when there is exactly
the right quantity, imperfect when there is either more
or less. But what is the test of right or wrong quantity,

2 N

except the pleasure or pain attending it? The theory
amounts to this, that pleasure or pain is felt, according
as the activity is of the amount fitted to produce the one
or the other. In this futile mode of explaining the phenomena our author had been preceded by Aristotle, one
of the greatest of recorded thinkers, but who must have
been more than human if, in the state of knowledge and
scientific cultivation in his time, he had avoided slips
which hardly any one, even now, is able completely to
guard against. Aristotle's theory, which, as understood
by our author, differs little from his own, is presented by
Sir W. Hamilton in the following words : * " When a
" sense, for example, is in perfect health, and it is pre-
" sented with a suitable object of the most perfect kind,
" there is elicited the most perfect energy, which, at
" every instant of its continuance, is accompanied with
" pleasure. The same holds good with the function of
" Imagination, Thought, &c. Pleasure is the concomi-
" tant in every case where powers and objects are in
" themselves perfect, and between which there subsists
" a suitable relation." The conditions whereon, upon
this showing, pleasure depends, are the healthiness of
the sense, and the perfection of the object presented to
it. This is simply making the fact its own theory. When
is a sense in perfect health, and its object perfect? The
function of a sense is twofold ; as a source of cognition,
and of feeling. If the perfection meant be in the function
of cognition, the doctrine that pleasure depends on this
is manifestly erroneous : according to Sir W. Hamilton,
it is even the reverse of the truth, for he holds that the
knowledge given by an act of sense, and the feeling
accompanying it, are in an inverse proportion to one
another. There remains the supposition that the perfection, of which Aristotle spoke, was perfection not in
respect of cognition but of feeling. It cannot, however,
consist in acuteness of feeling, for our acutest feelings are
pains. What then constitutes it? Pleasurableness of
feeling : and the theory only tells us, that pleasure is the

* Lectures, ii. 452.

result of a pleasurable state of the sense, and a pleasure-giving quality in the object presented to it. Aristotle and Sir W. Hamilton did not, certainly, state the doctrine to themselves in this manner; but they reduced it to this, by affirming pleasure or pain to depend on the perfect or imperfect action of the sense, when there was no criterion of imperfect or perfect action except that it produced pain or pleasure.

The theory of our author, considered as a *résumé* of the universal conditions of pleasure and pain, being so manifestly inadequate, this is not the place for sifting out the detached fragments of valuable thought which are disseminated through it. Such stray truths may be gleaned from every excursion through the phenomena of human nature by a person of ability. What Sir W. Hamilton says of the different classes of mental pleasures and pains, though brief, is very suggestive of thought. To make a proper use of the hints he throws out towards an explanation of the pleasures derived from sublimity and beauty, would require much study, and a wide survey of the subject, as well as of the speculations of other thinkers regarding it. The question has no direct connection with any other of those discussed in the present volume, and but a slight one with Sir W. Hamilton's merits as a philosopher; since the brevity with which he treats it, gives ground for believing that he had not bestowed on it the amount of thought which would enable his opinion to claim the rank of a philosophic theory.

CHAPTER XXVI.

ON THE FREEDOM OF THE WILL.

THE last of the three classes of mental phenomena, that of Conation, in other words, of Desire and Will, is barely commenced upon in the last pages of Sir W. Hamilton's last lecture: whether it be that in the many years during which he taught the class, he never got beyond this point, or that his teaching in the concluding part of the course was purely oral, and has not been preserved. Nor has he, in any of his writings, treated *ex professo* of this subject; though doubtless he would have done so, had his health permitted him to complete the Dissertations on Reid. We consequently know little of what his sentiments were on any of the topics comprised in this branch of Psychology, except the *vexata quæstio* of the Freedom of the Will; on which he could not help giving indications, in various parts of his works, both of his opinion and of the reasons on which he grounded it. The doctrine of Free-will was indeed so fundamental with him, that it may be regarded as the central idea of his system —the determining cause of most of his philosophical opinions; and, in a peculiar manner, of the two which are most completely emanations from his own mind, the Law of the Conditioned, and his singular theory of Causation. He breaks ground on the subject at the very opening of his Lectures, in his introductory remarks on the utility of the study of Metaphysics. He puts in a claim for metaphysics, grounded on the free-will doctrine, of being the only medium " through which our " unassisted reason can ascend to the knowledge of a

"God." * He supports this position by a line of argument which, I think, must be startling to the majority of believers.

"The Deity," he says, "is not an object of imme
"diate contemplation ; as existing and in himself, he is
"beyond our reach ; we can know him only mediately
"through his works, and are only warranted in assuming
"his existence as a certain kind of cause necessary to
"account for a certain state of things, of whose reality
"our faculties are supposed to inform us. The affirma
"tion of a God being thus a regressive inference, from
"the existence of a special class of effects to the exist
"ence of a special character of cause, it is evident that
"the whole argument hinges on the fact,—Does a state
"of things really exist, such as is only possible through
"the agency of a Divine Cause? For if it can be shown
"that such a state of things does not really exist, then,
"our inference to the kind of cause requisite to account
"for it, is necessarily null.

"This being understood, I now proceed to show you
"that the class of phenomena which requires that kind
"of cause we denominate a Deity, is exclusively given
"in the phenomena of mind,—that the phenomena of
"matter, taken by themselves (you will observe the
"qualification, taken by themselves) so far from warrant
"ing any inference to the existence of a God, would, on
"the contrary, ground even an argument to his negation ;
"that the study of the external world, taken with, and
"in subordination to, that of the internal, not only loses
"its atheistic tendency, but, under such subservience,
"may be rendered conducive to the great conclusion
"from which, if left to itself, it would dissuade us."

The reasoning by which he thinks that he establishes this position runs as follows. A God is only an inference from Nature ; a cause assumed, as necessary to account for phenomena. Now, fate or necessity, without a God, might account for the phenomena of matter. It is only as man is a free intelligence, that to account for his

* Lectures, i. 25, *et seqq.*

existence requires the hypothesis of a Creator who is a free intelligence. If our feeling of liberty is an illusion ; if our intelligence is only a result of material organisation ; we are entitled to conclude that in the universe also, the phenomena of intelligence and design are, in the last analysis, the products of brute necessity. Existence in itself being unknown to us, we can only infer its character from the particular order presented to us within the sphere of our experience, which in the case under consideration means observation of our own minds. If, therefore, our intelligence is produced and bounded by a blind fate, the like may be concluded to be true of the Divine Intelligence. If, on the contrary, intelligence in man is a free power, independent of matter, we may legitimately conclude the same thing of the intelligence manifested in the universe. Again, there is properly no God at all unless there is a moral Governor of the world. "Now,* it is self-evident, in the first "place, that if there be no moral world, there can be no "moral governor of such a world ; and in the second, that "we have, and can have, no ground on which to believe "in the reality of a moral world, except in so far as we "ourselves are moral agents. . . . But in what does "the character of man as a moral agent consist? Man "is a moral agent only as he is accountable for his "actions,—in other words, as he is the object of praise or "blame ; and this he is, only inasmuch as he has pre-"scribed to him a rule of duty, and as he is able to act, "or not to act, in conformity with its precepts. The "possibility of morality thus depends on the possibility "of liberty ; for if man be not a free agent, he is not the "author of his actions, and has, therefore, no responsi-"bility, no moral personality at all." †

Fully to develop all the just criticisms which might be made on this single thesis, would require a long chapter. In the first place, the practice of bribing the

* Lectures, i. 32, 33.
† See also a passage in the essay on the Study of Mathematics, Discussions, pp. 307, 308.

pupil to accept a metaphysical dogma, by the promise
or threat that it affords the only valid argument for a
foregone conclusion—however transcendently important that conclusion may be thought to be—is not only
repugnant to all the rules of philosophising, but a grave
offence against the morality of philosophic enquiry.   The
eager attempts of almost every metaphysical writer to
create a religious prejudice in favour of the theory he
patronises, are a very serious grievance in philosophy.
If I could permit myself, even by way of retort, to
follow so bad· an example, I might warn the defenders
of religion, of the danger of sacrificing, in turn, every
one of its evidences to some other.   It has been remarked, with truth, that there is not one of the received
arguments in support either of natural religion or of
revelation, a formal condemnation of which might not
be extracted from the writings of sincerely religious
thinkers.   I am far from imputing this to them as
matter of blame : the rejection of what they deem bad
arguments in a good cause must always be honourable to
them, when led to it by honestly following the prompt-
ings of their reason, and not by an egotistic preference
for their own special modes of proof.   But, looking at
the question as one of prudence, it would be wise in
them, whatever else they give up, not to part company with the Design argument.   For, in the first place,
it is the best ; and besides, it is by far the most per-
suasive.   It would be difficult to find a stronger argument in favour of Theism, than that the eye must have
been made by one who sees, and the ear by one who
hears.   If, after this, it pleases Sir W. Hamilton or any
other person to say that unless we believe in free will,
the Being who by hypothesis made the ear and the eye
is no God ; or that to regard the goodness of God as
the result of a necessity, which, from the very meaning
of a First Cause, can only be a necessity of his own
nature, a love of Good which is part of himself and
inseparable from him, is denying him to be a moral
being ; there is really nothing left for us but, with

equal positiveness, to aver the contrary : for the two parties will never be able to agree about the meaning of terms.

This is but one specimen among many of the bad logic which pervades Sir W. Hamilton's attempt to show that Theism depends on the reception of his favourite doctrine. He proceeds, throughout, on the assumption that the falsely called Doctrine of Necessity * is the same thing with Materialism. He treats those opinions as precisely equivalent.† Yet no two doctrines can be more distinct. Reid, an enemy of both, affirms that Necessity, " far from being a direct inference," " can receive no support from" Materialism.‡ It may be true, nevertheless, that Materialists are always or generally Necessitarians ; and it is not denied that many Necessitarians are Materialists : but nearly all the theologians of the Reformation, beginning with Luther, and the entire series of Calvinistic divines represented by Jonathan Edwards, are proofs that the most sincere Spiritualists may consistently hold the doctrine of so-called Necessity. Of such Spiritualists there is an illustrious example in Leibnitz, to say nothing of Condillac § or Brown. They believe man to be a spiritual being, not dependent on Matter, but yet, in respect of his actions as in all other respects, subject to the law of Causation : his volitions not being self-caused, but determined by spiritual antecedents (*e.g.* desires, associations of ideas, &c., all of

---

* Both Sir W. Hamilton and Mr. Mansel sometimes call it by the fairer name of Determinism. But both of them, when they come to close quarters with the doctrine, in general call it either Necessity, or, less excusably, Fatalism. The truth is, that the assailants of the doctrine cannot do without the associations engendered by the double meaning of the word Necessity, which, in this application, signifies only invariability, but in its common employment, compulsion. *Vide* System of Logic, Book vi. chap. 2.

† " The atheist who holds *matter or necessity* to be the original principle " of all that is." (Lectures i. 26, 37.) " Those who do not allow that mind " is matter—who hold that there is in man a principle of action superior " to the determinations of a physical necessity, a brute or blind fate." (Ibid. p. 133.) And the entire argument in page 31 of the same volume.

‡ Reid's Works, Hamilton's edition, p. 635.

§ That Condillac was a Spiritualist, is shown by the chapter on the Soul, which stands as the first chapter of his Art de Penser.

which are spiritual if the mind is spiritual) in such sort that when the antecedents are the same, the volitions will always be the same. But to confound necessity with Materialism, though an historical and psychological error, is indispensable to Sir W. Hamilton's argument, which depends for all its plausibility on the picture he draws of a God subject to a "brute necessity" of a purely material character. For if the necessity predicated of human actions is not a material, but a spiritual necessity; if the assertion that the virtuous man is virtuous necessarily, only means that he is so because he dreads a departure from virtue more than he dreads any personal consequence; there is nothing absurd or invidious in taking a similar view of the Deity, and believing that he is necessitated to will what is good, by the love of good and detestation of evil which are in his own nature.

There is also at the root of our author's argument another logical error—that of inferring that whatever is given by observation and analysis as a law of human intelligence, must be supposed to be an absolute law extending to the Divine. He says, truly, that the Divine Intelligence is but an assumption, to account for the phenomena of the universe; and that we can only be warranted in referring the origin of those phenomena to an Intelligence, by analogy to the effects of human intellect. But can this analogy be carried up to complete identity in conditions and modes of action between the human and the Divine intelligence? Does Sir W. Hamilton draw this inference in any other case? On the contrary, he holds us bound to believe that the Deity, whether as Will or as Intelligence, is Absolute—unrestricted by any conditions; though, as such, neither knowable nor conceivable by us. And though I do not acknowledge the obligation of believing what can neither be known nor conceived, as little can it be admitted, that the Divine Will cannot be free unless ours is so; any more than that the Divine Intelligence cannot know the truths of geometry by direct intuition, because we are obliged to mount laboriously up to them through the twelve books of Euclid.

So much for Sir W. Hamilton's attempt to prove that one who disbelieves free-will, has no business to believe in a God.   Let us now consider his view of the doctrine itself, and of the evidence for it.

His view of the controversy is peculiar, but harmonises with his Philosophy of the Conditioned, which seems indeed to have been principally suggested to him by the supposed requirements of this question.   He is of opinion that Free-will and Necessity are both inconceivable.   Free-will, because it supposes volitions to originate without cause ; * because it affirms an absolute commencement, which, as we are aware, our author deems it impossible for the human mind to conceive.   On the other hand, the mind is equally unable to conceive an infinite regress ; a chain of causation going back to all eternity.   Both the one and the other theory thus involve difficulties insurmountable by the human faculties.   But, as Sir W. Hamilton has so often told us, the inconceivability of a thing by us, is no proof that it is objectively impossible by the laws of the universe ; on the contrary, it often happens that both sides of an alternative are alike incomprehensible to us, while from their nature we are certain that the one or the other must be true.   Such an alternative, according to Sir W. Hamilton, exists between the conflicting doctrines of Free-will

---

* Sir W. Hamilton thinks it a fair statement of the Free-will doctrine, that it supposes our volitions to be uncaused.   But the " Inquirer " (p. 45) considers this a misstatement, and thinks the real free-will doctrine to be that " I " am the cause.   I prefer the other language, as being more consistent with the use of the word cause in other cases.   If we take the word, we must take the acknowledged Law of Causation along with it, viz., that a cause which is the same in every respect, is always followed by the same effects.   But on the free-will theory, the " I " is the same, and all the other conditions the same, and yet the effect may not only be different, but contrary.   For instead of saying that " I " am the cause, the " Inquirer " should at least say, some state or mode of me, which is different when the effect is different : though what state or mode this could be, unless it were a will to will (the notion so justly ridiculed by Hobbes), it is difficult to imagine.   I persist, therefore, in saying, with Sir W. Hamilton, that, on the free-will doctrine, volitions are emancipated from causation altogether.

and Necessity. By the law of Excluded Middle, one or other of them must be true ; and inconceivability, as common to both, not operating more against one than against the other, does not operate against either. The balance, therefore, must turn in favour of the side for which there is positive evidence. In favour of Free-will we have the distinct testimony of consciousness; perhaps directly, though of this he speaks with some appearance of doubt ; * but at all events, indirectly, freedom being implied in the consciousness of moral responsibility. As there is no corresponding evidence in favour of the other theory, the Free-will doctrine must prevail. " How †
" the will can possibly be free must remain to us, under
" the present limitation of our faculties, wholly incom-
" prehensible. We cannot conceive absolute commence-
" ment ; we cannot, therefore, conceive a free volition.
" But as little can we conceive the alternative on which
" liberty is denied, on which necessity is affirmed. And
" in favour of our moral nature, the fact that we are free
" is given us in the consciousness of an uncompromising
" law of Duty, in the consciousness of our moral account-
" ability ; and this fact of liberty cannot be redargued
" on the ground that it is incomprehensible, for the
" doctrine of the Conditioned proves, against the neces-
" sitarian, that something may, nay must, be true, of
" which the mind is wholly unable to construe to itself
" the possibility, whilst it shows that the objection of
" incomprehensibility applies no less to the doctrine of
" fatalism than to the doctrine of moral freedom."
The inconceivability of the Free-will doctrine is main- tained by our author, not only on the general ground just stated, of our incapacity to conceive an absolute commencement, but on the further and special ground, that the will is determined by motives. In rewriting the preceding passage for the Appendix to his " Discus- sions," he made the following addition to it : ‡ " A de- " termination by motives cannot, to our understanding,

* Foot-notes to Reid, pp. 599, 602, 624.
† Lectures, ii. 412, 413.   ‡ Appendix to Discussions, pp. 624, 625.

THE FREEDOM OF THE WILL.

572

"escape from necessitation.   Nay, were we even to
"admit as true, what we cannot think as possible,
"still the doctrine of a motiveless volition would be
"only casualism; and the free acts of an indifferent,
"are, morally and rationally, as worthless as the pre-
"ordered passions of a determined will.*   *How*, there-
"fore, I repeat, moral liberty is possible in man or God,
"we are utterly unable speculatively to understand.
"But . . . the scheme of freedom is not more inconceiv-
"able than the scheme of necessity.   For whilst fatalism
"is a recoil from the more obtrusive inconceivability of
"an *absolute* commencement, on the fact of which com-
"mencement the doctrine of liberty proceeds; the fatalist
"is shown to overlook the equal, but less obtrusive, in-
"conceivability of an *infinite* non-commencement, on the
"assertion of which non-commencement his own doc-
"trine of necessity must ultimately rest."   It rests on
no such thing, if he believes in a First Cause, which a
Necessitarian may.   What is more, even if he does not
believe in a First Cause, he makes no "assertion of non-
commencement;" he only declines to make an assertion
of commencement; and, therefore, is not in the position
of asserting what is inconceivable : which, however, as
Sir W. Hamilton is perpetually declaring, is a position
perfectly tenable, and the position he avowedly chooses
for himself on this very subject.   But to resume the
quotation : "As equally unthinkable, the two counter,
"the two one-sided, schemes are thus theoretically
"balanced.   But, practically, our consciousness of the
"moral law, which, without a moral liberty in man,
"would be a mendacious imperative, gives a decisive

* To the same effect in another passage : "That, though inconceivable,
"a motiveless volition would, if conceived, be conceived as morally worth-
"less, only shows our impotence more clearly."   (Appendix to Discussions,
pp. 614, 615.)   And in a foot-note to Reid (p. 602), "Is the person an
"*original undetermined* cause of the determination of his will?   If he be
"not, then he is not a *free agent*, and the scheme of Necessity is admitted.
"If he be, in the first place, it is impossible to *conceive* the possibility of
"this ; and, in the second, if the fact, though inconceivable, be allowed, it
"is impossible to see how a cause, undetermined by any motive, can be a
"rational, moral, and accountable cause."

" preponderance to the doctrine of freedom over the doc-
" trine of fate.   We are free in act, if we are account-
" able for our actions."

Sir W. Hamilton is of opinion that both sides are
alike unsuccessful in repelling each other's attacks. The
arguments against both are, he thinks, to the human
faculties, irrefutable. " The champions * of the opposite
" doctrines are at once resistless in assault and impotent
" in defence. Each is hewn down, and appears to die
" under the home thrusts of his adversary; but each again
" recovers life from the very death of his antagonist, and,
" to borrow a simile, both are like the heroes in Valhalla,
" ready in a moment to amuse themselves anew in the
" same bloodless and interminable conflict. The doctrine
" of Moral Liberty cannot be made conceivable, for we
" can only conceive the determined and the relative. As
" already stated, all that can be done is to show, 1°. That,
" for the *fact* of Liberty, we have immediately or mediately,
" the evidence of Consciousness ; and 2°. That there are
" among the phenomena of mind, many facts which we
" *must* admit as actual, but of whose possibility we are
" wholly unable to form any notion. I may merely
" observe that the fact of *Motion* can be shown to be
" impossible, on grounds not less strong than those on
" which it is attempted to disprove the fact of Liberty."
These " grounds no less strong" are the mere paralogisms
which we examined in a recent chapter, and with regard
to which our author showed so surprising a deficiency
in the acuteness and subtlety to be expected from the
general quality of his mind.

Conformably to these views, Sir W. Hamilton, in his
foot-notes on Reid, promptly puts an extinguisher on
several of that philosopher's arguments against the doctrine of so-called Necessity. When Reid affirms that
Motives are not causes—that they may influence to action,
but do not act, Sir W. Hamilton observes : † " If Motives
" influence to action, they must co-operate in producing a

---

* Foot-note on Reid, p. 602.   † Ibid. p. 608.

" certain effect upon the agent ; and the determination to
" act, and to act in a certain manner, is that effect. They
" are thus, on Reid's own view, in this relation, *causes*, and
" *efficient* causes. It is of no consequence in the argument
" whether motives be said to determine a man to act, or
" to influence (that is, to determine) him to determine
" himself to act." * This is one of the neatest specimens
in our author's writings of a fallacy cut clean through
by a single stroke.

Again, when Reid says that acts are often done without
any motive, or when there is no motive for preferring the
means used, rather than others by which the same end
might have been attained, Sir W. Hamilton asks,† " Can
" we conceive any act of which there was not a sufficient
" cause or concourse of causes why the man performed
" it and no other? If not, call this cause, or these
" concauses, the *motive*, and there is no longer a
" dispute."

Reid asks, "Is there no such thing as wilfulness,
caprice, or obstinacy among mankind?" Sir W. Hamilton, *e contra:* ‡ " But are not these all tendencies, and
" fatal tendencies, to act or not to act? By contradistin-
" guishing such tendencies from motives strictly so called,
" or rational impulses, we do not advance a single step
" towards rendering liberty comprehensible."

According to Reid, the determination is made by the
man, and not by the motive. "But," asks Sir W.
Hamilton,§ " was the *man* determined by no motive to
" that determination? Was his specific volition to this
" or to that without a cause? On the supposition that
" the sum of influences (motives, dispositions, and ten-
" dencies) to volition A, is equal to 12, and the sum of
" influences to counter-volition B equal to 8—can we
" conceive that the determination of volition A should
" not be necessary?—We can only conceive the volition
" B to be determined by supposing that the man *creates*

* To the same effect see Discussions, Appendix on Causality, p. 614.
† Footnote to Reid, p. 609.
‡ Ibid. p. 610.   § Ibid. p. 611.

" (calls from non-existence into existence) a certain sup-
" plement of influences. But this creation as actual, or
" in itself, is inconceivable, and even to conceive the
" possibility of this inconceivable act, we must sup-
" pose some cause by which the man is determined to
" exert it. We thus, in *thought*, never escape determina-
" tion and necessity. It will be observed that I do not
" consider this inability to the *notion*, any disproof of
" the *fact* of Free-will." Nor is it: but if, as our
author so strongly inculcates, " every * effort to bring
" the fact of liberty within the compass of our concep-
" tions only results in the substitution in its place of
" some more or less disguised form of necessity," it is a
strong indication that some form of necessity is the
opinion naturally suggested by our collective experience
of life.†

Sir W. Hamilton having thus, as is often the case
(and it is one of the best things he does), saved his opponents the trouble of answering his friends, his doctrine
is left resting exclusively on the supports which he has
himself provided for it. In examining them, let us place
ourselves, in the first instance, completely at his point of
view, and concede to him the coequal inconceivability
of the conflicting hypotheses, an uncaused commencement, and an infinite egress. But this choice of inconceivabilities is not offered to us in the case of volitions
only. We are held, as he not only admits but contends,
to the same alternative in all cases of causation whatsoever. But we find our way out of the difficulty, in
other cases, in quite a different manner. In the case of
every other kind of fact, we do not elect the hypothesis
that the event took place without a cause : we accept

---

* Lectures, i. 34.
† So difficult is it to escape from this fact, that Sir W. Hamilton himself
says (Lectures, i. 188), " Voluntary conation is a faculty which can only
" be determined to energy through a pain or pleasure—through an estimate
" of the relative worth of objects." If I am determined to prefer innocence to the satisfaction of a particular desire, through an estimate of the
relative worth of innocence and of the gratification, can this estimate,
while unchanged, leave me at liberty to choose the gratification in preference to innocence ?

the other supposition, that of a regress, not indeed to
infinity, but either generally into the region of the Unknowable, or back to an Universal Cause, regarding
which, as we are only concerned with it in respect of
attributes bearing relation to what it preceded, and not
as itself preceded by anything, we can afford to consider
this reference as ultimate.

Now, what is the reason, which, in the case of all
things within the range of our knowledge except volitions, makes us choose this side of the alternative?
Why do we, without scruple, register all of them as
depending on causes, by which (to use our author's language) they are determined necessarily, though, in believing this, we, according to Sir W. Hamilton, believe as
utter an inconceivability as if we supposed them to take
place without a cause? Apparently it is because the
causation hypothesis, inconceivable as he may think it,
possesses the advantage of having experience on its side.
And how or by what evidence does experience testify to
it? Not by disclosing any *nexus* between the cause and
the effect, any Sufficient Reason in the cause itself why
the effect should follow it. No philosopher now makes
this supposition, and Sir W. Hamilton positively disclaims it. What experience makes known, is the fact of
an invariable sequence between every event and some
special combination of antecedent conditions, in such
sort that wherever and whenever that union of antecedents exists, the event does not fail to occur. Any *must*
in the case, any necessity, other than the unconditional
universality of the fact, we know nothing of. Still,
this *à posteriori* " does," though not confirmed by an *à
priori* "must," decides our choice between the two inconceivables, and leads us to the belief that every event
within the phenomenal universe, except human volitions, is determined to take place by a cause. Now, the
so-called Necessitarians demand the application of the
same rule of judgment to our volitions. They maintain
that there is the same evidence for it. They affirm, as
a truth of experience, that volitions do, in point of fact,

follow determinate moral antecedents with the same uniformity, and (when we have sufficient knowledge of the circumstances) with the same certainty, as physical effects follow their physical causes. These moral antecedents are desires, aversions, habits, and dispositions, combined with outward circumstances suited to call those internal incentives into action. All these again are effects of causes, those of them which are mental being consequences of education, and of other moral and physical influences. This is what Necessitarians affirm; and they court every possible mode in which its truth can be verified. They test it by each person's observation of his own volitions. They test it by each person's observation of the voluntary actions of those with whom he comes into contact; and by the power which every one has of foreseeing actions, with a degree of exactness proportioned to his previous experience and knowledge of the agents, and with a certainty often quite equal to that with which we predict the commonest physical events. They test it further, by the statistical results of the observation of human beings acting in numbers sufficient to eliminate the influences which operate only on a few, and which on a large scale neutralise one another, leaving the total result about the same as if the volitions of the whole mass had been affected by such only of the determining causes as were common to them all. In cases of this description the results are as uniform, and may be as accurately foretold, as in any physical inquiries in which the effect depends upon a multiplicity of causes. The cases in which volitions seem too uncertain to admit of being confidently predicted, are those in which our knowledge of the influences antecedently in operation is so incomplete, that with equally imperfect data there would be the same uncertainty in the predictions of the astronomer and the chemist. On these grounds it is contended that our choice between the conflicting inconceivables should be the same in the case of volitions as of all other phenomena; we must reject equally in both cases the hypothesis of spontaneousness, and con-

578 THE FREEDOM OF THE WILL.

sider them all as caused. A volition is a moral effect,
which follows the corresponding moral causes as certainly and invariably as physical effects follow their physical causes. Whether it *must* do so, I acknowledge
myself to be entirely ignorant, be the phenomenon
moral or physical; and I condemn, accordingly, the
word Necessity as applied to either case. All I know
is, that it always *does.* [*]

This argument from experience Sir W. Hamilton
passes unnoticed, but urges, on the opposite side of the
question, the argument from Consciousness. We are
conscious, he affirms, either of our freedom, or at all
events (it is odd that, on his theory, there should be any
doubt) of something which implies freedom. If this is
true, our internal consciousness tells us that we have a
power, which the whole outward experience of the human
race tells us that we never use. This is surely a very
unfortunate predicament we are in, and a sore trial to
the puzzled metaphysician. Philosophy is far from
having so easy a business before her as our author
thinks: the arbiter Consciousness is by no means
invoked to turn the scale between two equally balanced
difficulties; on the contrary, she has to sit in judgment
between herself and a complete induction from experience. Consciousness, it will probably be said, is the
best evidence; and so it would be, if we were always
certain what is Consciousness. But while there are
so many varying testimonies respecting this; when Sir
W. Hamilton can himself say, [†] "many philosophers

* The "Inquirer" accuses this argument (p. 45) of "gratuitously assuming that free-will is inconsistent with foreknowledge." This is a
misapprehension. That vexed question is not even approached in the text.
All that is maintained is that the possibility to human intelligence, of
predicting human actions, implies a constancy of observed sequence between the same antecedents and the same consequents, which, in the case
of all events except volitions, is deemed to justify the assertion of a law
of nature (called in the language of the free-will philosophers Necessity).
This constancy of sequence between motives, mental dispositions, and
actions, is a strong reason against admitting free-will as a fact; but I
have not meddled, and do not intend to meddle, with the metaphysical
question whether a contingent event can be foreknown.
† Dissertations on Reid, p. 749.

"have attempted to establish, on the principles of
"common sense, propositions which are not original
"data of consciousness, while the original data of con-
"sciousness from which these propositions were derived,
"and to which they owed all their necessity and truth,
"these same philosophers were (strange to say) not
"disposed to admit;" when M. Cousin and nearly all
Germany find the Infinite and the Absolute in Consciousness, Sir W. Hamilton thinking them utterly repugnant
to it; when philosophers, for many generations, fancied
that they had Abstract Ideas—that they could conceive
a triangle which was neither equilateral, isosceles, nor
scalene,* which Sir W. Hamilton and all other people
now consider to be simply absurd; with all these conflicting opinions respecting the things to which Consciousness testifies, what is the perplexed inquirer to
think? Does all philosophy end, as in our author's
opinion Hume believed it to do, in a persistent contradiction between one of our mental faculties and another?
We shall find, there is a solution, which relieves the
human mind from this embarrassment: namely, that the
question to which experience says yes, and that to which
consciousness says no, are different questions.

Let us cross-examine the alleged testimony of consciousness. And, first, it is left in some uncertainty by
Sir W. Hamilton whether Consciousness makes only
one deliverance on the subject, or two: whether we are
conscious only of moral responsibility, in which free-will

* "Does it not require," says Locke (Essay on the Human Understanding, Book iv. chap. 7, sect. 9), "some pains and skill to form the
"general idea of a triangle (which yet is none of the most abstract, com-
"prehensive and difficult?) for it must be neither oblique nor rectangle,
"neither equilateral, equicrural, nor scalene; but all and none of these at
"once. In effect, it is something imperfect, that cannot exist; an idea
"wherein some parts of several different and inconsistent ideas are put
"together." Yet this union of contradictory elements such a philosopher
as Locke was able to fancy that he conceived. I scarcely know a more
striking example of the tendency of the human mind to believe that things
can exist separately because they can be separately named; a tendency
strong enough, in this case, to make a mind like Locke's believe itself
to be conscious of that which by the laws of mind cannot be a subject of
consciousness to any one.

is implied, or are directly conscious of free-will. In his Lectures, Sir W. Hamilton speaks only of the first. In the notes on Reid, which were written subsequently, he seems to affirm both, but the latter of the two in a doubtful and hesitating manner : so difficult, in reality, does he find it to ascertain with certainty what it is that Consciousness certifies. But as there are many who maintain with a confidence far greater than his, that we are directly conscious of free-will,* it is necessary to examine that question.

To be conscious of free-will, must mean, to be conscious, before I have decided, that I am able to decide either way. Exception may be taken *in limine* to the use of the word consciousness in such an application. Consciousness tells me what I do or feel. But what I am *able* to do, is not a subject of consciousness. Consciousness is not prophetic ; we are conscious of what is, not of what will or can be. We never know that we are able to do a thing, except from having done it, or something equal and similar to it. We should not know that we were capable of action at all, if we had never acted. Having acted, we know, as far as that experience reaches, how we are able to act ; and this knowledge, when it has become familiar, is often confounded with, and called by the name of, consciousness. But it does not derive any increase of authority from being misnamed ; its truth is not supreme over, but depends on, experience. If our so-called consciousness of what we are able to do is not borne out by experience, it is a

---

* Mr. Mansel, among others, makes the assertion in the broadest form it is capable of, saying, " In every act of volition, I am fully conscious " that I can at this moment act in either of two ways, and that, all the " antecedent phenomena being precisely the same, I may determine one " way to-day and another way to-morrow." (Prolegomena Logica, p. 152.) Yes, though the antecedent phenomena remain the same : but not if my judgment of the antecedent phenomena remains the same. If my conduct changes, either the external inducements or my estimate of them must have changed.

Mr. Mansel (as I have already observed) goes so far as to maintain that our immediate intuition of Power is given us by the ego producing its own volitions, not by its volitions producing bodily movements (pp. 139–140, and 151).

delusion. It has no title to credence but as an interpretation of experience, and if it is a false interpretation,
it must give way.*

But this conviction, whether termed consciousness or
only belief, that our will is free—what is it? Of what
are we convinced? I am told that whether I decide to
do or to abstain, I feel that I could have decided the

---

* In answer to the statement that what I am *able* to do is not a subject
of consciousness, Mr. Alexander says (pp. 22 *et seqq.*), "Perhaps it is not;
"but what I *feel* I am able to do is surely a subject of consciousness. . . .
"As to 'consciousness is not prophetic, we are conscious of what is, not
"of what will or can be,' it seems enough to say that if we are conscious
"of a free force of volition continuously inherent in us, we are conscious of
"what *is.*" If we can be conscious of a force, and can feel an ability, independently of any present or past exercise thereof, the fact has nothing
similar or analogous in all the rest of our nature. We are not conscious
of a muscular force continuously inherent in us. If we were born with a
cataract, we are not conscious, previous to being couched, of our ability to
see. We should not feel able to walk if we had never walked, nor to think
if we had never thought. Ability and force are not real entities, which
can be felt as present when no effect follows; they are abstract names for
the happening of the effect on the occurrence of the needful conditions, or
for our expectation of its happening. It is of course possible that this
may be all wrong, and that there may be a concrete real thing called ability,
of which consciousness discloses to us the positive existence in this one
case, though there is no evidence of it in any other. But it is surely, to
say the least, much more probable that we mistake for consciousness our
habitual affirmation to ourselves of an acquired knowledge or belief. This
very common mistake may have escaped the notice of Mr. Alexander, who
(p. 23) considers knowledge to be the same thing as direct consciousness!
but it is a possibility which it will not do to overlook, when one takes for
one's standard (p. 25) the "general consciousness of the race;" especially if, with Mr. Alexander, one restricts "the race" to those who are not
philosophers, on the ground that no philosopher "unless he be one of a
thousand," can see or feel anything that is inconsistent with his precon-
ceived opinion. If this be the normal effect of philosophy on the human
mind; if, nine hundred and ninety-nine times against one, the effect of
cultivating our power of mental discrimination is to pervert it; let us close
our books, and accept Hodge as a better authority in metaphysics than
Locke or Kant, and, I suppose, in astronomy than Newton. An appeal
to consciousness, however, to be of any value, must be to those who have
formed a habit of sifting their consciousness, and distinguishing what
they perceive or feel from what they infer; to those who can be made to
understand that they do not see the sun move: and, to have attained this
power of criticising their own consciousness on metaphysical subjects,
they must have reflected on those subjects, in a manner and degree which
quite entitle any one to the name of a philosopher.

Mr. Alexander denies that the belief that I was free to act can possibly
be tested by experience *à posteriori*, since experience only tells me the way
in which I did act, and says nothing about my having been able to act
otherwise. Mr. Alexander's idea of the conditions of proof by experience

other way. I ask my consciousness what I do feel, and
I find, indeed, that I feel (or am convinced) that I could,
and even should, have chosen the other course if I had
preferred it, that is, if I had liked it better; but not
that I could have chosen one course while I preferred
the other. When I say preferred, I of course include
with the thing itself, all that accompanies it. I know
that I can, because I know that I often do, elect to do
one thing, when I should have preferred another in itself,
apart from its consequences, or from a moral law which
it violates. And this preference for a thing in itself,
abstractedly from its accompaniments, is often loosely
described as preference for the thing. It is this unprecise mode of speech which makes it not seem absurd to
say that I act in opposition to my preference; that I do
one thing when I would rather do another; that my

is not a very enlarged one. Suppose that my experience of myself afforded
two undeniable cases, alike in all the mental and physical antecedents, in
one of which cases I acted in one way, and in the other in the direct
opposite: there would then be proof by experience that I had been able
to act either in the one way or in the other. It is by experience of this
sort I learn that I can act at all, viz., by finding that an event takes place
or not, according as (other circumstances being the same) a volition of
mine does or does not take place. But when this power of my volitions
over my actions has become a familiar fact, the knowledge of it is so constantly present to my mind as to be popularly called, and habitually confounded with, consciousness. And the supposed power of myself over my
volitions, which is termed Free-will, though it cannot be a fact of consciousness, yet if true, or even if believed, would similarly work itself into
our inmost knowledge of ourselves, in such a manner as to be mistaken
for consciousness.

It would hardly be worth while to notice a pretended inconsistency discovered by Mr. Alexander between what is here said, and my recognition
in a former work of a "practical feeling of Free Will"—"a feeling of Moral
Freedom which we are conscious of," if Mr. Alexander had not inferred
from it that I "was at one time conscious" of what I now, for the convenience of my argument, deny to be a subject of consciousness. Mr.
Alexander himself quotes the words in which I spoke of this practical
feeling of free-will as not one of free-will at all, in a sense implying the
theory; and took pains to describe what it really is, expressly declaring
our feeling of moral freedom to be a feeling of our being able to modify
our own character *if we wish*. When I applied the words feeling and
consciousness to this acquired knowledge, I did not use those terms in
their strict psychological meaning, there being no necessity for doing so
in that place; but, agreeably to popular usage, extended them to (what
there is no appropriate scientific name for) the whole of our familiar and
intimate knowledge concerning ourselves.

conscience prevails over my desires—as if conscience were not itself a desire—the desire to do right. Take any alternative: say to murder or not to murder. I am told, that if I elect to murder, I am conscious that I could have elected to abstain: but am I conscious that I could have abstained if my aversion to the crime, and my dread of its consequences, had been weaker than the temptation? If I elect to abstain: in what sense am I conscious that I could have elected to commit the crime? Only if I had desired to commit it with a desire stronger than my horror of murder; not with one less strong. When we think of ourselves hypothetically as having acted otherwise than we did, we always suppose a difference in the antecedents: we picture ourselves as having known something that we did not know, or not known something that we did know; which is a difference in the external inducements; or as having desired something, or disliked something, more or less than we did; which is a difference in the internal inducements.*

In refutation of this it is said, that in resisting a desire, I am conscious of making an effort; that after I have resisted, I have the remembrance of having made an effort; that "if the temptation was long continued, "or if I have been resisting the strong will of another, "I am as sensibly exhausted by that effort, as after any

---

* Preferring, as he says, a homely instance, Mr. Alexander supposes (p. 29), that a man puts his finger to his nose, and asks, "Is not he con-"scious of being able to touch at will either the right side of his nose or "the left? Having touched, let us say, the left side, is he not conscious "he could have touched the right side had he so willed it, and conscious "that he *could* have so willed, chosen, or preferred?" Mr. Alexander's *naïf* expectation that his opponent's answer will be different because of the futility of the example, reminds one of the *asinus Buridani*. I should, on the supposition which he makes, be aware (I will not say conscious) that I could have touched the right side had I so willed it; and aware that I could, and even should, have so willed, chosen, and preferred, if there had existed a sufficient inducement to make me do so, and not otherwise. If any one's consciousness tells him that he could have done so without an inducement, or in opposition to a stronger inducement, I venture to express my opinion, in words borrowed from Mr. Alexander, that it is not his "veritable consciousness." I will not imitate Mr. Alexander in calling it a "fraudulent substitute palmed upon him" by his philosophical system.

" physical exertion I ever made : " and it is added, " If
" my volition is wholly determined by the strongest
" present desire, it will be decided without any effort.
" . . . When the greater weight goes down, and the
" lesser up, no effort is needed on the part of the scale." *
It is implied in this argument, that in a battle between
contrary impulses, the victory must always be decided in
a moment ; that the force which is really the strongest,
and prevails ultimately, must prevail instantaneously.
The fact is not quite thus even in inanimate nature :
the hurricane does not level the house or blow down the
tree without resistance ; even the balance trembles, and
the scales oscillate for a short time, when the difference
of the weights is not considerable. Far less does victory
come without a contest to the strongest of two moral,
or even two vital forces, whose nature it is to be never
fixed, but always flowing, quantities. In a struggle
between passion, there is not a single instant in which
there does not pass across the mind some thought, which
adds strength to, or takes it from, one or the other of
the contending powers. Unless one of them was, from
the beginning, out of all proportion stronger than the
other, some time must elapse before the balance adjusts
itself between forces neither of which is for any two
successive instants the same. During that interval the
agent is in the peculiar mental and physical state which
we call a conflict of feelings : and we all know that a
conflict between strong feelings *is*, in an extraordinary
degree, exhaustive of the nervous energies.† The consciousness of effort, which we are told of, is this state
of conflict. The author I am quoting considers what
he calls, I think improperly, an effort, to be only on one

* The Battle of the Two Philosophies, pp. 13, 14.
† The writer I quote says, "Balancing one motive against another is
not willing but judging." The state of mind I am speaking of is by no
means a state of judging. It is an emotional, not an intellectual state,
and the judging may be finished before it commences. If there were any
indispensable act of judging in this stage, it could only be judging which
of the two pains or pleasures was the greatest : and to regard this as the
operative force would be conceding the point in favour of Necessi-
tarianism.

side, because he represents to himself the conflict as taking place between me and some foreign power, which I conquer, or by which I am overcome. But it is obvious that "I" am both parties in the contest; the conflict is between me and myself; between (for instance) me desiring a pleasure, and me dreading self-reproach. What causes Me, or, if you please, my Will, to be identified with one side rather than with the other, is that one of the Me's represents a more permanent state of my feelings than the other does. After the temptation has been yielded to, the desiring "I" will come to an end, but the conscience-stricken "I" may endure to the end of life.

I therefore dispute altogether that we are conscious of being able to act in opposition to the strongest present desire or aversion. The difference between a bad and a good man is not that the latter acts in opposition to his strongest desires; it is that his desire to do right, and his aversion to doing wrong, are strong enough to overcome, and in the case of perfect virtue, to silence, any other desire or aversion which may conflict with them. It is because this state of mind is possible to human nature, that human beings are capable of moral government: and moral education consists in subjecting them to the discipline which has most tendency to bring them into this state. The object of moral education is to educate the will: but the will can only be educated through the desires and aversions; by eradicating or weakening such of them as are likeliest to lead to evil; exalting to the highest pitch the desire of right conduct and the aversion to wrong; cultivating all other desires and aversions of which the ordinary operation is auxiliary to right, while discountenancing so immoderate an indulgence of them, as might render them too powerful to be overcome by the moral sentiment, when they chance to be in opposition to it. The other requisites are, a clear intellectual standard of right and wrong, that moral desire and aversion may act in the proper places, and such general mental habits as shall prevent moral considerations from being forgotten or overlooked, in cases to which they are rightly applicable.

Rejecting, then, the figment of a direct consciousness of the freedom of the will, in other words, our ability to will in opposition to our strongest preference; it remains to consider whether, as affirmed by Sir W. Hamilton, a freedom of this kind is implied in what is called our consciousness of moral responsibility. There must be something very plausible in this opinion, since it is shared even by Necessitarians. Many of these—in particular Mr. Owen and his followers—from a recognition of the fact that volitions are effects of causes, have been led to deny human responsibility. I do not mean that they denied moral distinctions. Few persons have had a stronger sense of right and wrong, or been more devoted to the things they deemed right. What they denied was the rightfulness of inflicting punishment. A man's actions, they said, are the result of his character, and he is not the author of his own character. It is made *for* him, not *by* him. There is no justice in punishing him for what he cannot help. We should try to convince or persuade him that he had better act in a different manner; and should educate all, especially the young, in the habits and dispositions which lead to well-doing : though how this is to be effected without any use whatever of punishment as a means of education, is a question they have failed to resolve. The confusion of ideas, which makes the subjection of human volitions to the law of Causation seem inconsistent with accountability, must thus be very natural to the human mind ; but this may be said of a thousand errors, and even of some merely verbal fallacies. In the present case there is more than a verbal fallacy, but verbal fallacies also contribute their part.

What is meant by moral responsibility? Responsibility means punishment. When we are said to have the feeling of being morally responsible for our actions, the idea of being punished for them is uppermost in the speaker's mind. But the feeling of liability to punishment is of two kinds. It may mean, expectation that if we act in a certain manner, punishment will actually be inflicted upon us, by our fellow creatures or by a Supreme Power. Or it may only mean, knowing that we shall deserve that infliction.

The first of these cannot, in any correct meaning of the term, be designated as a consciousness. If we believe that we shall be punished for doing wrong, it is because the belief has been taught to us by our parents and tutors, or by our religion, or is generally held by those who surround us, or because we have ourselves come to the conclusion, by reasoning, or from the experience of life. This is not Consciousness. And, by whatever name it is called, its evidence is not dependent on any theory of the spontaneousness of volition. The punishment of guilt in another world is believed with undoubting conviction by Turkish fatalists, and by professed Christians who are not only Necessitarians, but believe that the majority of mankind were divinely predestined from all eternity to sin and to be punished for sinning. It is not, therefore, the belief that we shall be *made* accountable, which can be deemed to require or presuppose the free-will hypothesis; it is the belief that we ought so to be; that we are justly accountable; that guilt deserves punishment. It here that issue is joined between the two opinions.

In discussing it, there is no need to postulate any theory respecting the nature or criterion of moral distinctions. It matters not, for this purpose, whether the right and wrong of actions depends on the consequences they tend to produce, or on an inherent quality of the actions themselves. It is indifferent whether we are utilitarians or anti-utilitarians; whether our ethics rest on intuition or on experience. It is sufficient if we believe that there is a difference between right and wrong, and a natural reason for preferring the former; that people in general, unless when they expect personal benefit from a wrong, naturally and usually prefer what they think to be right: whether because we are all dependent for what makes existence tolerable, upon the right conduct of other people, while their wrong conduct is a standing menace to our security, or for some more mystical and transcendental reason. Whatever be the cause, we are entitled to assume the fact: and its consequence is, that whoever cultivates a disposition to wrong, places his mind out of sympathy with the rest of his fellow creatures, and if they are aware of his disposition, becomes a natural object of their active dislike. He not only forfeits the pleasure of their good will, and the benefit of their good offices, except when compassion for the human being is stronger than distaste towards the wrongdoer; but he also renders himself liable to whatever they may think it necessary to do in order to protect themselves against him; which may probably include punishment, as such, and will certainly involve much that is equivalent in its operation on himself. In this way he is certain to be made accountable, at least to his fellow creatures, through the normal action of their natural sentiments. And it is well worth consideration, whether the practical expectation of being thus called to account, has not a great deal to do with the internal feeling of being accountable; a feeling, assuredly, which is seldom found existing in any strength in the absence of that practical expectation. It is not usually found that Oriental despots, who cannot be called to account by anybody, have much consciousness of being morally accountable. And (what is still more significant) in societies in which caste or class distinctions are really strong—a state so strange to us now, that we seldom realise it in its full force—it is a matter of daily experience that persons may show the strongest sense of moral accountability as regards their equals, who can make them accountable, and not the smallest vestige of a similar feeling towards their inferiors who cannot.

This does not imply that the feeling of accountability, even when proportioned very exactly to the chance of being called to account, is a mere interested calculation, having nothing more in it than an expectation and dread of external punishment. When pain has long been thought of as a consequence of a given fact, the fact becomes wrapt up in associations which make it painful in itself, and cause the mind to shrink from it even when, in the particular case, no painful consequences are apprehended : just as the dislike to spending money, which grows up while money can ill be spared, may be an absorbing passion after the possessor has grown so rich that the expenditure would not really cause him the most trifling inconvenience. On this familiar principle of association it is abundantly certain that even if wrong meant merely what is forbidden, a disinterested detestation of doing wrong would naturally grow up, and might become, in its strength and promptitude, and in the immediateness of its action, without reflection or ulterior purpose, undistinguishable from any of our instincts or natural passions.

Another fact, which it is of importance to keep in view, is, that the highest and strongest sense of the worth of goodness, and the odiousness of its opposite, is perfectly compatible with even the most exaggerated form of Fatalism. Suppose that there were two peculiar breeds of human beings,—one of them so constituted from the beginning, that however educated or treated, nothing could prevent them from always feeling and acting so as to be a blessing to all whom they approached ; another, of such original perversity of nature that neither education nor punishment could inspire them with a feeling of duty, or prevent them from being active in evil doing. Neither of these races of human beings would have free-will ; yet the former would be honoured as demigods, while the latter would be regarded and treated as noxious beasts : not punished perhaps, since punishment would have no effect on them, and it might be thought wrong to indulge the mere instinct of vengeance : but kept carefully at a distance, and killed like other dangerous creatures when there was no other convenient way of being rid of them. We thus see that even under the utmost possible exaggeration of the doctrine of Neces-

sity, the distinction between moral good and evil in conduct would not only subsist, but would stand out in a
more marked manner than now, when the good and the
wicked, however unlike, are still regarded as of one
common nature.

An opponent may say, this is not a distinction between
moral good and evil ; and I am far from intending to beg
the question against him.   But neither can he be permitted to beg the question, by assuming that the distinction is not moral because it does not imply free-will.
The reality of moral distinctions, and the freedom of our
volitions, are questions independent of one another.
My position is, that a human being who loves, disinte-
restedly and consistently, his fellow creatures and
whatever tends to their good, who hates with a vigorous
hatred what causes them evil, and whose actions correspond in character with these feelings, is naturally,
necessarily, and reasonably an object to be loved, admired,
sympathised with, and in all ways cherished and en-
couraged by mankind ; while a person who has none of
these qualities, or so little, that his actions continually
jar and conflict with the good of others, and that for
purposes of his own he is ready to inflict on them a
great amount of evil, is a natural and legitimate object
of their fixed aversion, and of conduct conformable
thereto : and this whether the will be free or not, and
even independently of any theory of the difference between right and wrong ; whether right means productive
of happiness, and wrong productive of misery, or right
and wrong are intrinsic qualities of the actions themselves, provided only we recognise that there is a difference, and that the difference is highly important.   What
I maintain is, that this is a sufficient distinction between
moral good and evil : sufficient for the ends of society
and sufficient for the individual conscience : that we need
no other distinction ; that if there be any other distinction, we can dispense with it ; and that, supposing acts in
themselves good or evil to be as unconditionally determined from the beginning of things as if they were

phenomena of dead matter, still, if the determination from the beginning of things has been that they shall take place through my love of good and hatred of evil, I am a proper object of esteem and affection, and if that they shall take place through my love of self and indifference to good, I am a fit object of aversion which may rise to abhorrence. And no competently informed person will deny that, as a matter of fact, those who have held this creed have had as strong a feeling, both emotional and practical, of moral distinctions, as any other people.*

But these considerations, however pertinent to the subject, do not touch the root of the difficulty. The real question is one of justice—the legitimacy of retribution, or punishment. On the theory of Necessity (we are told) a man cannot help acting as he does; and it cannot be just that he should be punished for what he cannot help.

Not if the expectation of punishment enables him to help it, and is the only means by which he can be enabled to help it?

To say that he cannot help it, is true or false, according to the qualification with which the assertion is accompanied. Supposing him to be of a vicious disposition,

---

* Mr. Alexander draws a woeful picture of the pass which mankind would come to, if belief in so-called Necessity became general. All "our current moralities" would come to be regarded "as a form of superstition," all "moral ideas as illusions," by which "it is plain we get rid of them as "motives:" consequently the internal sanction of conscience would no longer exist. "The external sanctions remain, but not quite as they were. "That important section of them which rests on the *moral* approval or "disapproval of our fellow-men has, of course, evaporated:" and "in "virtue of a deadly moral indifference," the remaining external sanctions "might come to be much more languidly enforced than as now they are," and the progressive degradation would in a sufficient time "succeed in re- "producing the real original gorilla," (pp 118–121). A formidable prospect: but Mr. Alexander must not suppose that other people's feelings, about the matters of highest importance to them, are bound up with a certain speculative dogma, and even a certain form of words, because, it seems, his are. As long as guilt is thoroughly regarded as an evil, it would be quite safe even to hold with Plato, that it is the mental equivalent of bodily disease : people would be none the less anxious to avoid it for themselves, and to cure it in others. Whatever else may be an illusion, it is no illusion that some types of conduct and character are salutary, and others pernicious, to the race and to each of its members ; and there is no

he cannot help doing the criminal act, if he is allowed to believe that he will be able to commit it unpunished. If, on the contrary, the impression is strong in his mind that a heavy punishment will follow, he can, and in most cases does, help it.

The question deemed to be so puzzling is, how punishment can be justified, if men's actions are determined by motives, among which motives punishment is one. A more difficult question would be, how it can be justified if they are not so determined. Punishment proceeds on the assumption that the will is governed by motives. If punishment had no power of acting on the will, it would be illegitimate, however natural might be the inclination to inflict it. Just so far as the will is supposed free, that is, capable of acting *against* motives, punishment is disappointed of its object, and deprived of its justification.

There are two ends which, on the Necessitarian theory, are sufficient to justify punishment : the benefit of the offender himself, and the protection of others. The first justifies it, because to benefit a person cannot be to do him an injury. To punish him for his own good, provided the inflictor has any proper title to constitute himself a judge, is no more unjust than to administer

fear that mankind will not retain the property of their nature by which they prefer what is salutary to what is pernicious, and proclaim and act upon the preference. It is no illusion that human beings are objects of sympathy or of antipathy as they belong to the one type or to the other, and that the sympathies and antipathies excited in us by others react on ourselves. The qualities which each man feels to be odious in others, are odious, without illusion, in himself. The basis of Mr. Alexander's gloomy prophecy thus fails him. I might add, that even if his groundless anticipations came to pass in some other manner, and disinterested love of virtue and hatred of guilt faded away from the earth ; though the human race, thus degenerated, would be little worth preserving, it would probably find the means of preserving itself notwithstanding. The external sanctions, instead of being more languidly, would probably be far more rigidly enforced than at present ; for more rigorous penalties would be necessary when there was less inward sentiment to aid them : and however destitute of pure virtuous feeling mankind might be, each one of them would be far too well aware of the importance of other people's conduct to his own interest, not to exact those penalties without stint, and without any of the scruples which at present make conscientious men afraid of carrying repression too far.

medicine. As far, indeed, as respects the criminal himself, the theory of punishment is, that by counterbalancing the influence of present temptations, or acquired bad habits, it restores the mind to that normal preponderance of the love of right, which many moralists and theologians consider to constitute the true definition of our freedom.* In its other aspect, punishment is a

* " La liberté, complète, réelle, de l'homme, est la perfection humaine, " le but à atteindre." From a paper by M. Albert Réville, in the *Revue Germanique* for September, 1863, in which the question of free-will is discussed (though only parenthetically) with a good sense and philosophy seldom found in recent writings on that subject.

The "Inquirer" accuses me (pp. 49–51) of throwing aside a "well con-"sidered and deliberate opinion, because it refuses to fit in with a foregone "conclusion on another subject," when I affirm that the good of the person punished can ever be one of the ends of punishment ; and he quotes, on that subject, my essay on Liberty. I am responsible for the Essay, but not for this absurd perversion of its doctrines. Does it anywhere assert that children ought not to be punished for their own good ? that parents, and even the magistrate, when dealing with that class of delinquents, are not entitled to constitute themselves judges of the delinquent's good, and even bound to make it the principal consideration ? Did I not expressly leave open, as similar to the case of children, that of adult communities which are still in the infantine stage of development ? And did I say, or did any one ever say, that when, for the protection of society, we punish those who have done injury to society, the reformation of the offenders is not one of the ends to be aimed at, in the kind and mode, at least, of the punishment ?

The "Inquirer" adds (p. 49), "If I deserve punishment, only because "my love of right is too weak, and my desire for wrong pleasures is too "strong, and therefore punishment will help me to dislike the latter the "most, then I equally deserve rewards ; 'by counterbalancing the in-"fluence of present temptation or bad habits,' rewards 'restore the mind "to the normal preponderance of the love of right.' . . . And the more "wicked I am, the greater reward I deserve. . . . . For children, and for "all so far as their own improvement is concerned, rewards for evil-doers "must be more moral than punishments, as tending directly to diminish "misery, and increase the sum of human happiness."

Supposing even that the matter of reward were sufficiently plentiful to allow of compensating everybody for every temptation he foregoes, I submit that this plan would scarcely fulfil the other, and still more important end of punishment, the discouragment of future offenders. And even in the case of children, whose own improvement, as long as their education lasts, is the main end to be considered, every one knows, though he may forget it in confuting an adversary, that pain is a stronger thing than pleasure, and punishment vastly more efficacious than reward. Punishment, too, can alone produce the associations which make the conduct that incurs it, ultimately hateful in itself, and which by rendering that which is injurious to society, sincerely distasteful to its individual members, produces the fellowship of feeling which gives them a sense of common interest, and enables them to sympathise and co-operate as creatures of

2 P

precaution taken by society in self-defence. To make this just, the only condition required is, that the end which society is attempting to enforce by punishment, should be a just one. Used as a means of aggression by society on the just rights of the individual, punishment is unjust. Used to protect the just rights of others against unjust aggression by the offender, it is just. If it is possible to have just rights (which is the same thing as to have rights at all), it cannot be unjust to defend them. Free-will or no free-will, it is just to punish so far as is necessary for this purpose, as it is just to put a wild beast to death (without unnecessary suffering) for the same object.

Now, the primitive consciousness we are said to have, that we are accountable for our actions, and that if we violate the rule of right we shall deserve punishment, I contend is nothing else than our knowledge that punishment will be just: that by such conduct we shall place ourselves in the position in which our fellow creatures,

---

one kin. Thus much to show (if it needs showing) that the preference of punishment to reward as a protection against violations of right, is no inconsistency in the conception of social justice laid down in the text. If the objector now asks—But, supposing this were not so, and that rewarding an offender were as effectual a means of improving his own character and protecting society as punishing him, would it equally commend itself to our feeling of desert? I answer, no. It would conflict with that natural, and even animal, desire of retaliation—of hurting those who have hurt us, either in ourselves or in anything we care for—which, as I have elsewhere maintained, is the root of all that distinguishes our feeling of justice from our ordinary sense of expediency. This natural feeling, whether instinctive or acquired, though in itself it has nothing moral in it, yet when moralised by being allied with, and limited by, regard for the general welfare, becomes, in my view of the matter, our moral sentiment of justice. And this sentiment is necessarily offended by rewarding delinquents, and gratified by their punishment. The sentiment is entitled to consideration in a world like ours, in which punishment is really necessary: but granting the absurd supposition of a state of human affairs in which rewarding offenders would really be more expedient than punishing them, there would be no need of this particular moral sentiment, and, like other sentiments the use of which is superseded by changes in the circumstances of mankind, it might, and probably would, die away.

The chapter in which I have discussed this question (*Utilitarianism*, chap. v.) is quite familiar to Mr. Alexander; who shows himself extremely well acquainted with all parts of it, except those which tell against his own side. Even when he accomplishes (pp. 52 and 59) the great feat of finding in it the two statements, that justice, in the general mind, has a

or the Deity, or both, will naturally, and may justly, inflict punishment upon us. By using the word *justly*, I
am not assuming, in the explanation, the thing I profess
to explain. As before observed, I am entitled to postulate the reality, and the knowledge and feeling, of moral
distinctions. These, it is both evident metaphysically
and notorious historically, are independent of any theory
concerning the will. We are supposed capable of understanding that other people have rights, and all that follows from this. The mind which possesses this idea, if
capable of placing itself at the point of view of another
person, must recognise it as not unjust that others should
protect themselves against any disposition on his part to
infringe their rights ; and he will do so the more readily,
because he also has rights, and his rights continually require the same protection. This, I maintain, is our feeling of accountability, in so far as it can be separated
from the associations engendered by the prospect of being
actually called to account. No one who understands the
power of the principle of association, can doubt its suffi-

great deal to do with the notion of desert, and that justice is not synonymous with expediency, no one who reads him would suspect that I had
explained in the same chapter what, in my view, the notion of desert is,
and what there is in our idea of justice besides expediency. Mr. Alexander's perpetual insinuations, and more than insinuations, of bad faith,
since he makes a kind of retraction of their grossest meaning in one line
of his essay, I pardon, as one of the incidents of his rollicking style; but
it is well that he should be aware how easy, if any one were disposed, it
would be to retaliate them.

How far Mr. Alexander understands the first elements of the ethical
system which he denounces, is shown by one of his arguments, which he
is so fond of that he repeats it several times ; that if the protection of
society is a sufficient reason for hanging any one, it holds good for hanging an innocent person, or a madman (pp. 36, 37, 65, 89). He repeatedly
says, that this has just as deterring an effect as hanging a real criminal ;
being of opinion, apparently, that hanging a person who is not guilty
gives people a motive to abstain from being guilty. As to the madman
he asks (p. 65), "How should the state of mind of the maniac, as unamen-
"able to motive, any way affect the efficacy of our hanging him for mur-
"der, as a means to deter others from murder?" Mr. Alexander really
has no claim to be answered, until he has got a step or two beyond this.
Perhaps, however, he may be able to see, that all the deterring effect
which hanging can produce on men who are amenable to motive, is produced by hanging men who are amenable to motive. Hanging, in addition, those who are not amenable to motive, adds nothing to the deterring
effect, and is therefore a gratuitous brutality.

ciency to create out of these elements the whole of the feeling of which we are conscious. To rebut this view of the case would require positive evidence; as, for example, if it could be proved that the feeling of accountability precedes, in the order of development, all experience of punishment. No such evidence has been produced, or is producible. Owing to the limited accessibility to observation of the mental processes of infancy, direct proof can as little be produced on the other side : but if there is any validity in Sir W. Hamilton's Law of Parsimony, we ought not to assume any mental phenomenon as an ultimate fact, which can be accounted for by other known properties of our mental nature.

I ask any one who thinks that the justice of punishment is not sufficiently vindicated by its being for the protection of just rights, how he reconciles his sense of justice to the punishment of crimes committed in obedience to a perverted conscience? Ravaillac, and Balthasar Gérard, did not regard themselves as criminals, but as heroic martyrs. If they were justly put to death, the justice of punishment has nothing to do with the state of mind of the offender, further than as this may affect the efficacy of punishment as a means to its end. It is impossible to assert the justice of punishment for crimes of fanaticism, on any other ground than its necessity for the attainment of a just end. If that is not a justification, there is no justification. All other imaginary justifications break down in their application to this case.*

* The force of this argument is attested by the straits to which my most persevering assailant, Mr. Alexander, is reduced by it (pp. 63, 64). He finds himself obliged to say that " could we have positive assurance," in the case of such people, "that their outrage of the obligation to respect "life was solely an act of self-sacrifice to what they considered a higher "and more sacred one, we should be obliged to admit that their doom was "not just in the particular instance." This is very well, but we want practice as well as theory. Would you hang them? Mr. Alexander makes a halting half-admission that he would. "A dubious point of jus- "tice—dubious, because the true motive of the act must always remain "obscure—may here be allowed to be overridden by a plain and potent "mandate of expediency." Mr. Alexander therefore would hang men when it is doubtful whether they deserve it ; would hang them for what " may really have been an act of sublime virtue." But what is the amount

If, indeed, punishment is inflicted for any other reason than in order to operate on the will; if its purpose be other than that of improving the culprit himself, or securing the just rights of others against unjust violation, then, I admit, the case is totally altered. If any one thinks that there is justice in the infliction of purposeless suffering; that there is a natural affinity between the two ideas of guilt and punishment, which makes it intrinsically fitting that wherever there has been guilt, pain should be inflicted by way of retribution; I acknowledge that I can find no argument to justify punishment inflicted on this principle. As a legitimate satisfaction to feelings of indignation and resentment which are on the whole salutary and worthy of cultivation, I can in certain cases admit it; but here it is still a means to an end. The merely retributive view of punishment derives no justification from the doctrine I support. But it derives quite as little from the free-will doctrine. Suppose it true that the will of a malefactor, when he committed an offence, was free, or in other words, that he acted badly, not because he was of a bad disposition, but from no cause in particular: it is not easy to deduce from this the conclusion that it is just to punish him. That his acts were beyond the command of motives might be a good reason for keeping out of his way, or placing him under bodily

of real dubiousness in cases like these? Of all acts that a man can do, those by which he knowingly sacrifices his life, sometimes with the addition of horrible torments, are the clearest from suspicion of any motives but honest ones. Mr. Alexander talks of Brutus and Charlotte Corday, but I am content with Ravaillac. Is there the smallest reason to doubt that Ravaillac's "outrage of the obligation to respect life" was "an act of self-sacrifice" to what, in his opinion, was "a higher and more sacred one"? What motive had Ravaillac for his abominable action except a supposed duty to God, and did he not deem this his highest and most sacred duty? As for Mr. Alexander's hint that such a man, if not culpable in the act, was "culpable in the perversion of his conscience which led to it," it is the old odious assumption of persecutors, that acts which they cannot show to have been wicked in intention, must have originated in previous wickedness. The act of Ravaillac simply originated in false teaching, coming to him from the same quarter from which had come most of the good teaching which he had received during life. It came from the fountain of goodness, not of wickedness.

restraint; but no reason for inflicting pain upon him, when that pain, by supposition, could not operate as a deterring motive.*

While the doctrine I advocate does not support the idea that punishment in mere retaliation is justifiable, it at the same time fully accounts for the general and natural sentiment of its being so. From our earliest childhood, the idea of doing wrong (that is, of doing what is forbidden, or what is injurious to others) and the idea of punishment are presented to our mind together, and the intense character of the impressions causes the association between them to attain the highest degree of closeness and intimacy. Is it strange, or unlike the usual processes of the human mind, that in these circumstances we should retain the feeling, and forget the reason on which it is grounded? But why do I speak of forgetting? In most cases the reason has never, in our early education, been presented to the mind. The only ideas presented have been those of wrong and punishment, and an inseparable association has been

---

* Several of Sir W. Hamilton's admissions are strong arguments against the alleged self-evident connection between free-will and accountability. We have found him affirming that a volition not determined by motives " would, if conceived, be conceived as morally worthless;" that "the free " acts of an indifferent, are, morally and rationally, as worthless as the " preordained passions of a determined will;" and that "it is impossible " to see how a cause, undetermined by any motive, can be a rational, moral, " and accountable cause." If all this be so, there can be no intuitive perception of a necessary connection between free-will and morality; it would appear, on the contrary, that we are naturally unable to recognise an act as moral, if it is, in the sense of the theory, free.

[Mr. Alexander (p. 80) actually thinks that in these passages, Sir W. Hamilton is "asserting the determination of the will by motives;" and cannot believe that he intended "to assert an absolute commencement as " the mode under which Freedom, though inconceivable, has yet to be " believed;" since this " would have been to rush with his eyes open on " the staring contradictory, of a thing at once caused and uncaused." Yet, presently after, he himself charges Sir W. Hamilton's doctrine with requiring belief in two contrary inconceivables. In the present case it only requires a belief in one of them, an absolute, or uncaused, commencement. Mr. Alexander does not lay claim to much knowledge of Sir W. Hamilton; and certainly no one who understood what that philosopher, and most others who discuss this question, mean by "to determine," could fail to see that with him the determination of the will by motives means Determinism, or as it is commonly called, Necessity.]

created between these directly, without the help of any intervening idea. This is quite enough to make the spontaneous feelings of mankind regard punishment and a wrongdoer as naturally fitted to each other—as a conjunction appropriate in itself, independently of any consequences. Even Sir W. Hamilton recognises as one of the common sources of error, that " the associations of thought are mistaken for the connections of existence." * If this is true anywhere, it is truest of all in the associations into which emotions enter. A strong feeling, directly excited by an object, is felt (except when contradicted by the feelings of other people) as its own sufficient justification—no more requiring the support of a reason than the fact that ginger is hot in the mouth: and it almost requires a philosopher to recognise the need of a reason for his feelings, unless he has been under the practical necessity of justifying them to persons by whom they are not shared.

That a person holding what is called the Necessitarian doctrine should on that account *feel* that it would be unjust to punish him for his wrong actions, seems to me the veriest of chimeras. Yes, if he really "could not help" acting as he did, that is, if it did not depend on his will; if he was under physical constraint, or even if he was under the action of such a violent motive that no fear of punishment could have any effect; which, if capable of being ascertained, is a just ground of exemption, and is the reason why by the laws of most countries people are not punished for what they were compelled to do by immediate danger of death. But if the criminal was in a state capable of being operated upon by the fear of punishment, no metaphysical objection, I believe, will make him feel his punishment unjust. Neither will he feel that because his act was the consequence of motives, operating upon a certain mental disposition, it was not his own fault. For, first, it was at all events his own defect or infirmity, for which the expectation of punishment is the appropriate cure. And secondly, the word

* Lectures, iii. 47.

fault, so far from being inapplicable, is the specific name
for the kind of defect or infirmity which he has displayed—insufficient love of good and aversion to evil.
The weakness of these feelings or their strength is in
every one's mind the standard of fault or merit, of
degrees of fault and degrees of merit.   Whether we are
judging of particular actions, or of the character of a
person, we are wholly guided by the indications afforded
of the energy of these influences.   If the desire of right
and aversion to wrong have yielded to a small temptation, we judge them to be weak, and our disapprobation
is strong.   If the temptation to which they have yielded
is so great that even strong feelings of virtue might have
succumbed to it, our moral reprobation is less intense.
If, again, the moral desires and aversions have prevailed,
but not over a very strong force, we hold that the action
was good, but that there was little merit in it; and our
estimate of the merit rises, in exact proportion to the
greatness of the obstacle which the moral feeling proved
strong enough to overcome.

Mr. Mansel[*] has furnished what he thinks a refutation
of the Necessitarian argument, of which it is well to
take notice, the more so, perhaps, as it is directed against
some remarks on the subject by the present writer in a
former work :[†] remarks which were not intended as an
argument for so-called Necessity, but only to place the
nature and meaning of that ill-understood doctrine in a
truer light.   With this purpose in view, it was remarked that " by saying that a man's actions necessarily
" follow from his character, all that is really meant (for
" no more is meant in any case whatever of causation) is
" that he invariably does act in conformity to his char-
" acter, and that any one who thoroughly knew his
" character, could certainly predict how he would act in
" any supposable case.   No more than this is contended
" for by any one but an Asiatic fatalist."   " And no more

* Prolegomena Logica, Note C at the end.
† System of Logic, Book vi. ch. 2.

"than this," observes Mr. Mansel, "is needed to con-
"struct a system of fatalism as rigid as any Asiatic can
"desire."

Mr. Mansel is mistaken in thinking that the doctrine
of the causation of human actions is fatalism at all, or resembles fatalism in any of its moral or intellectual effects.
To call it by that name is to break down a fundamental
distinction. Real fatalism is of two kinds. Pure, or
Asiatic fatalism,—the fatalism of the Œdipus,—holds
that our actions do not depend upon our desires. Whatever our wishes may be, a superior power, or an abstract
destiny, will overrule them, and compel us to act, not as
we desire, but in the manner predestined. Our love of
good and hatred of evil are of no efficacy, and though in
themselves they may be virtuous, as far as conduct is
concerned it is unavailing to cultivate them. The other
kind, Modified Fatalism I will call it, holds that our
actions are determined by our will, our will by our
desires, and our desires by the joint influence of the
motives presented to us and of our individual character;
but that, our character having been made for us and not
by us, we are not responsible for it, nor for the actions it
leads to, and should in vain attempt to alter them. The
true doctrine of the Causation of human actions maintains, in opposition to both, that not only our conduct,
but our character, is in part amenable to our will; that
we can, by employing the proper means, improve our
character; and that if our character is such that while
it remains what it is, it necessitates us to do wrong, it
will be just to apply motives which will necessitate us to
strive for its improvement, and so emancipate ourselves
from the other necessity. In other words, we are under a
moral obligation to seek the improvement of our moral
character. We shall not indeed do so unless we desire
our improvement, and desire it more than we dislike the
means which must be employed for the purpose. But
does Mr. Mansel, or any other of the free-will philosophers, think that we can will the means if we do not

desire the end, or if our desire of the end is weaker than our aversion to the means ? *

Mr. Mansel is more rigid in his ideas of what the free-will theory requires, than one of the most eminent of the thinkers who have adopted it. According to Mr. Mansel, the belief that whoever knew perfectly our character and our circumstances could predict our actions, amounts to Asiatic fatalism. According to Kant, in his Metaphysics of Ethics, such capability of prediction is quite compatible with the freedom of the will. This seems, at first sight, to be an admission of everything which the rational supporters of the opposite theory could desire. But Kant avoids this consequence, by changing (as lawyers would say) the *venue* of free-will, from our actions generally, to the formation of our character. It is in that, he thinks, we are free, and he is almost willing to admit that while our character is what it is, our actions are necessitated by it. In drawing this distinction, the philosopher of Königsberg saves inconvenient facts at the expense of the consistency of his theory. There cannot be one theory for one kind of voluntary actions, and another theory for the other

* This vital truth in moral psychology, that we can improve our character if we will, is a great stumbling block both to the "Inquirer" and to Mr. Alexander. They maintain that this fact makes no difference at all, and that the Causation of human actions is exactly the same thing with Modified Fatalism. That the "Inquirer" cannot see any difference, excites no surprise, since he professes himself (p. 46) unable to understand "how our conduct is amenable to our will if it is wholly caused by our "character and circumstances." Is not the very doctrine he is contending against, that our character and circumstances cause it *through* our will? Both he and Mr. Alexander protest vehemently, and Mr. Alexander at much length, that the Causation doctrine is as incompatible with Free-will as Fatalism is. As if anybody had denied that. In the very next paragraph, when arguing against Kant, I expressly affirmed it. But, if it is not too much to ask, let them try to put their own opinion in abeyance, and condescend for a few moments to look at the question from mine. Suppose (I have as much right to make the supposition as they have) that a person dislikes some part of his own character, and would be glad to change it. He cannot, as he well knows, change it by a mere act of volition. He must use the means which nature gives to ourselves, as she gave to our parents and teachers, of influencing our character by appropriate circumstances. If he is a Modified Fatalist, he will not use those means, for he will not believe in their efficacy ; but will remain passively discontented with himself, or what is worse, will learn to be contented,

kinds. When we voluntarily exert ourselves, as it is our duty to do, for the improvement of our character, or when we act in a manner which (either consciously on our part or unconsciously) deteriorates it, these, like all other voluntary acts, presuppose that there was already something in our character, or in that combined with our circumstances, which led us to do so, and accounts for our doing so. The person, therefore, who is supposed able to predict our actions from our character as it now is, would, under the same conditions of perfect knowledge, be equally able to predict what we should do to change our character: and if this be the meaning of necessity, that part of our conduct is as necessary as all the rest. If necessity means more than this abstract possibility of being foreseen; if it means any mysterious compulsion, apart from simple invariability of sequence, I deny it as strenuously as any one in the case of human volitions, but I deny just as much of all other phenomena. To enforce this distinction was the principal object of the remarks which Mr. Mansel has criticised. If an unessential distinction from Mr. Mansel's point of view, it is essential from mine, and of supreme importance in a practical aspect.

thinking that his character has been made for him, and that he cannot make it over again, however willing. If, on the contrary, he is a Moral Causationist, he will know that the work is not finally and irrevocably done; that the improvement of his character is still possible by the proper means, the only needful condition being that he should desire, what by the supposition he does desire: consequently if the desire is stronger than the means are disagreeable, he will set about doing that which, if done, will improve his character. I cannot suppose my critics capable of maintaining that such a difference as this, between the two theories, is of no practical importance; and I must, with all courtesy, decline to recognise as entitled to any voice in the question, whoever is not able to seize a distinction so broad and obvious.

Mr. Alexander's curious dictum (pp. 18–20) that a motive is itself an act, can only have a true meaning, or any meaning at all, if understood of this indirect influence of our voluntary acts over our mental dispositions. That a person can, by an act of will, either give to himself, or take away from himself, a desire or an aversion, I suppose even Mr. Alexander will hardly affirm: but we can, by a course of self-culture, finally modify, to a greater or less extent, our desires and aversions; which is the doctrine of Moral Causation, as distinguished from Modified Fatalism.

The free-will metaphysicians have made little endeavour to prove that we can will in opposition to our
strongest desire, but have strenuously maintained that
we can will when we have no strongest desire. With
this view Dr. Reid formerly, and Mr. Mansel now, have
thrown in the teeth of Necessitarians the famous *asinus
Buridani*. If, say they, the will were solely determined
by motives, the ass, between two bundles of hay, exactly
alike, and equally distant from him, would remain undecided until he died of hunger. From Sir W. Hamilton's notes on this chapter of Reid,* I infer that he did
not countenance this argument; and it is surprising
that writers of talent should have seen anything in it.
I waive the objection that if it applies at all, it proves that
the ass also has free-will; for perhaps he has. But the
ass, it is affirmed, would starve before he decided. Yes,
possibly, if he remained all the time in a fixed attitude of deliberation; if he never for an instant ceased to
balance one against another the rival attractions, and if
they really were so exactly equal that no dwelling on
them could detect any difference. But this is not the
way in which things take place on our planet. From
mere lassitude, if from no other cause, he would intermit
the process, and cease thinking of the rival objects at
all: until a moment arrived when he would be seeing or
thinking of one only, and that fact, combined with the
sensation of hunger, would determine him to a decision.
But the argument on which Mr. Mansel lays most stress
(it is also one of Reid's) is the following. Necessitarians
say that the will is governed by the strongest motive:
" but I only know the strength of motives in relation to
" the will by the test of ultimate prevalence; so that
" this means no more than that the prevailing motive
" prevails." I have heretofore complimented Mr. Mansel
on seeing farther, in some things, than his master. In
the present instance I am compelled to remark, that he
has not seen so far. Sir W. Hamilton was not the man
to neglect an argument like this, had there been no

* Pp. 609–611.

flaw in it. The fact is that there are two. First, those who say that the will follows the strongest motive, do not mean the motive which is strongest in relation to the will, or in other words, that the will follows what it does follow. They mean the motive which is strongest in relation to pain and pleasure ; since a motive, being a desire or aversion, is proportional to the pleasantness, as conceived by us, of the thing desired, or the painfulness of the thing shunned. And when what was at first a direct impulse towards pleasure, or recoil from pain, has passed into a habit or a fixed purpose, then the strength of the motive means the completeness and promptitude of the association which has been formed between an idea and an outward act. This is the first answer to Mr. Mansel. The second is, that even supposing there were no test of the strength of motives but their effect on the will, the proposition that the will follows the strongest motive would not, as Mr. Mansel supposes, be identical and unmeaning. We say, without absurdity, that if two weights are placed in opposite scales, the heavier will lift the other up ; yet we mean nothing by the heavier, except the weight which will lift up the other. The proposition, nevertheless, is not unmeaning, for it signifies that in many or most cases there *is* a heavier, and that this is always the same one, not one or the other as it may happen. In like manner, even if the strongest motive meant only the motive which prevails, yet if there is a prevailing motive—if, all other antecedents being the same, the motive which prevails to-day will prevail to-morrow and every subsequent day—Sir W. Hamilton was acute enough to see that the free-will theory is not saved. I regret that I cannot, in this instance, credit Mr. Mansel with the same acuteness.

Before leaving the subject, it is worth while to remark, that not only the doctrine of Necessity, but Predestination in its coarsest form—the belief that all our actions are divinely preordained—though, in my view, inconsistent with ascribing any moral attributes whatever to

THE FREEDOM OF THE WILL.

the Deity, yet if combined with the belief that God works according to general laws, which have to be learnt from experience, has no tendency to make us act in any respect otherwise than we should do if we thought our actions really contingent. For if God acts according to general laws, then, whatever he may have preordained, he has preordained that it shall take place through the causes on which experience shows it to be consequent: and if he has predestined that I shall attain my ends, he has predestined that I shall do so by studying and putting in practice the means which lead to their attainment. When the belief in predestination has a paralysing effect on conduct, as is sometimes the case with Mahomedans, it is because they fancy they can infer what God has predestined, without waiting for the result. They think that either by particular signs of some sort, or from the general aspect of things, they can perceive the issue towards which God is working, and having discovered this, naturally deem useless any attempt to defeat it. Because something will certainly happen if nothing is done to prevent it, they think it will certainly happen whatever may be done to prevent it; in a word, they believe in Necessity in the only proper meaning of the term—an issue unalterable by human efforts or desires.

CHAPTER XXVII.

SIR WILLIAM HAMILTON'S OPINIONS ON THE STUDY OF MATHEMATICS.

No account of Sir W. Hamilton's philosophy could be complete, which omitted to notice his famous attack on the tendency of mathematical studies : for though there is no direct connection between this and his metaphysical opinions, it affords the most express evidence we have of those fatal *lacunæ* in the circle of his knowledge, which unfitted him for taking a comprehensive or even an accurate view of the processes of the human mind in the establishment of truth. If there is any pre-requisite which all must see to be indispensable in one who attempts to give laws to human intellect, it is a thorough acquaintance with the modes by which human intellect has proceeded, in the cases where, by universal acknowledgment, grounded on subsequent direct verification, it has succeeded in ascertaining the greatest number of important and recondite truths.   This requisite Sir W. Hamilton had not, in any tolerable degree, fulfilled. Even of pure mathematics he apparently knew little but the rudiments. Of mathematics as applied to investigating the laws of physical nature; of the mode in which the properties of number, extension, and figure, are made instrumental to the ascertainment of truths other than arithmetical or geometrical—it is too much to say that he had even a superficial knowledge : there is not a line in his works which shows him to have had any knowledge at all. He had no conception of what the process is.   In this he differed greatly and disadvantageously from his immediate predecessor in the same school of

metaphysical thought, Professor Dugald Stewart; whose
works derive a great part of their value from the foundation of sound and accurate scientific knowledge laid
by his mathematical and physical studies, and which
his subsequent metaphysical pursuits enabled him,
quite successfully to the length of his tether, to clarify
and reduce to principles.

If Sir W. Hamilton had contented himself with saying of mathematics, that it is not, of itself alone, a sufficient education of the intellectual faculties; that it
cultivates the mind only partially; that there are important kinds of intellectual cultivation and discipline
which it does not give, and to which, therefore, if pursued to the exclusion of the studies which do give them,
it is unfavourable; he would have said something, not
new indeed, but true, not of mathematics alone, but of
every limited and special employment of the mental
faculties; of every study in which the human mind can
engage, except the two or three highest, most difficult,
and most imperfect, which, requiring all the faculties
in their greatest attainable perfection, can never be recommended or thought of as preparatory discipline, but
are themselves the chief purpose for which such preparation is required. Sir W. Hamilton, however, has asserted much more than this. He undertakes to show that
the study of mathematics is not an useful intellectual
discipline at all, except in one comparatively humble particular, which it has in common with some of the most
despised pursuits; and that, if prosecuted far, it positively unfits the mind for the useful employment of its
faculties on any other object. As might be expected
from an attempt to maintain such a thesis by one who,
however acute on other matters, had no sufficient knowledge of the subject he was writing about, this celebrated
dissertation is one of the weakest parts of his works.
He ignores not only the whole of his adversary's case, but
the most important part of his own; and has made a far
less powerful attack on the tendencies of mathematical
studies, than could easily be made by one who under-

stood the subject. He has, in fact, missed the most considerable of the evil effects to the production of which those studies have contributed; and has thrown no light on the intellectual shortcomings of the common run of mathematicians, so signally displayed in their wretched treatment of the generalities of their own science. He finds hardly anything to say to their disadvantage but things so trite and obvious, that the greatest zealot for mathematics could afford to pass them by, insisting only on the inestimable benefits which are to be set against them, and which alone are really to the purpose; for it is no objection to a harrow that it is not a plough, nor to a saw that it is not a chisel.

For instance, are we much the wiser for being once more told, at great length, and with a cloud of witnesses brought to back the assertion, that mathematics, being concerned only with demonstrative evidence, does not teach us, either by theory or practice, to estimate probabilities? Did any mathematician, or eulogist of mathematics, ever pretend that it did? Does the science to which Sir W. Hamilton assigns a place above all others as an intellectual discipline—does Metaphysics enable us to judge of probable evidence? If such a claim has ever been made in its behalf, I am not aware of it; Sir W. Hamilton, certainly, was too well acquainted with the subject to make any such pretension. Metaphysics, like Mathematics, and all the rest of the fundamental sciences, demands, not probable, but certain evidence. The province of Probabilities in science is not the abstract, but what M. Comte terms the concrete sciences; those which treat of the combinations actually realised in Nature, as distinguished from the general laws which would equally govern any other combinations of the same elements: zoology and botany, for example, as contrasted with physiology; geology, as opposed to thermology and chemistry. In an abstract science a probability is of no account; it is but a momentary halt on the road to certainty, and a hint for fresh experiments.

Inasmuch as abstract science in general, and mathe-

matics in particular, afford no practice in the estimation
of conflicting probabilities, which is the kind of sagacity
most required in the conduct of practical affairs, it follows that, when made so exclusive an occupation as to
prevent the mind from obtaining enough of this necessary
practice in other ways, it does worse than not cultivate the
faculty—it prevents it from being acquired, and *pro tanto*
unfits the person for the general business of life. It is natural that people who are bad judges of probability, should
be, according to their temperament, unduly credulous or
unreasonably sceptical; both which charges our author,
with great earnestness and a heavy artillery of authorities, drives home against the mathematicians. But he
would have made little progress towards proving his
case, even by a much more complete catalogue of the
intellectual defects of a mathematician who is nothing
but a mathematician. A person may be keenly alive to
these, and may hate them, as M. Comte did, with a perfect hatred, while upholding mathematical instruction
as not only an useful but the indispensable first stage of
all scientific education worthy of the name.* Nor can
any reasonable view of the subject refuse to recognise,
in the very faults which our author imputes to mathematicians, the excesses of a most valuable quality. Let
us be assured that for the formation of a well-trained
intellect, it is no slight recommendation of a study, that
it is the means by which the mind is earliest and most
easily brought to maintain within itself a standard of

* I do not know that the logical value of mathematics has ever been
more finely and discriminatingly appreciated than by M. Comte in his latest
work, "*Synthèse Subjective*," (p. 98). "Bornée à son vrai domaine, la raison
"mathématique y peut admirablement remplir l'office universel de la saine
"logique : induire pour déduire, afin de construire. Renonçant à de vaines
"prétentions, elle sent que ses meilleurs succès restent toujours incapables
"de nous faire, partout ailleurs, induire, ou même déduire, et surtout
"construire. Elle se contente de fournir, dans le domaine le plus favor-
"able, un type de clarté, de précision, et de consistance, dont la contem-
"plation familière peut seule disposer l'esprit à rendre les autres concep-
"tions aussi parfaites que le comporte leur nature. Sa réaction générale,
"plus négative que positive, doit surtout consister à nous inspirer partout
"une invincible répugnance pour le vague, l'incohérence, et l'obscurité, que
"nous pouvons réellement éviter envers des pensées quelconques, si nous
"y faisons assez d'efforts."

complete proof. A mind thus furnished, and not duly instructed on other subjects, may commit the error of expecting in all proof too close an adherence to the type with which it is familiar. That type may and ought to be widened by greater variety of culture; but he who has never acquired it, has no just sense of the difference between what is proved and what is not proved: the first foundation of the scientific habit of mind has not been laid. It has long been a complaint against mathematicians that they are hard to convince: but it is a far greater disqualification both for philosophy, and for the affairs of life, to be too easily convinced; to have too low a standard of proof. The only sound intellects are those which, in the first instance, set their standard of proof high. Practice in concrete affairs soon teaches them to make the necessary abatement: but they retain the consciousness, without which there is no sound practical reasoning, that in accepting inferior evidence because there is none better to be had, they do not by that acceptance raise it to completeness. They remain aware of what is wanting to it.

Besides accustoming the student to demand complete proof, and to know when he has not obtained it, mathematical studies are of immense benefit to his education by habituating him to precision. It is one of the peculiar excellences of mathematical discipline, that the mathematician is never satisfied with an *à peu près*. He requires the *exact* truth. Hardly any of the non-mathematical sciences, except chemistry, has this advantage. One of the commonest modes of loose thought, and sources of error both in opinion and in practice, is to overlook the importance of quantities. Mathematicians and chemists are taught by the whole course of their studies, that the most fundamental differences of quality depend on some very slight difference in proportional quantity; and that from the qualities of the influencing elements, without careful attention to their quantities, false expectations would constantly be formed as to the very nature and essential character of the result pro-

duced.   If Sir W. Hamilton's mind had undergone this
improving discipline, we should not have found him
employing the most precise mathematical terms with
the laxity which is habitual in his writings.   For instance; whenever he means that one of two things
diminishes while another increases, he says that they
are in the inverse ratio of one another.   He affirms
this of the Extension and Comprehension of a general
notion; * of the number of objects among which our
attention is divided, and the intensity with which it is
applied to each ;† of the knowledge-giving and the
sensation-giving properties of an impression of sense ; ‡
and of the intensity and the prolongation of an energy.§
That an inverse ratio is the name of a definite relation
between quantities, seems never to have occurred to
him.

Neither is it a small advantage of mathematical
studies, even in their poorest and most meagre form, that
they at least habituate the mind to resolve a train of
reasoning into steps, and make sure of each step before
advancing to another.   If the practice of mathematical
reasoning gives nothing else, it gives wariness of mind ;
it accustoms us to demand a sure footing ; and though it
leaves us no better judges of ultimate premises than it
found us (which is no more than may be said of almost
all metaphysics) at least it does not suffer us to let in, at
any of the joints in the reasoning, any assumption which
we have not previously faced in the shape of an axiom,
postulate, or definition.   This is a merit which it has in
common with Formal Logic, and is the chief ground on
which some have thought that it could perform the functions and supply the place of that science ; an opinion in
which I by no means agree.

That mathematics "do not cultivate the power of
generalisation," ‖ which to our author appears so obvious
a truth that he need not give himself the trouble of

---

* See, among other passages, Lectures, iii. 146, 147.
† Ibid. i. 246.   ‡ Ibid. ii. 98.
§ Ibid. p. 439.   ‖ Discussions, p. 282.

proving it, will be admitted by no person of competent knowledge, except in a very qualified sense. The generalisations of mathematics, are, no doubt, a different thing from the generalisations of physical science; but in the difficulty of seizing them, and the mental tension they require, they are no contemptible preparation for the most arduous efforts of the scientific mind. Even the undamental notions of the higher mathematics, from those of the differential calculus upwards, are products of a very high abstraction. Merely to master the idea of centrifugal force, or of the centre of gravity, are efforts of mental analysis surpassed by few in our author's metaphysics. To perceive the mathematical law common to the results of many mathematical operations, even in so simple a case as that of the binomial theorem, involves a vigorous exercise of the same faculty which gave us Kepler's laws, and rose through those laws to the theory of universal gravitation. Every process of what has been called Universal Geometry—that great creation of Descartes and his successors, in which a single train of reasoning solves whole classes of problems at once, and demonstrates properties common to all curves or surfaces, and others common to large groups of them—is a practical lesson in the management of wide generalisations, and abstraction of the points of agreement from those of difference among objects of great and confusing diversity, to which the most purely inductive science cannot furnish many superior. Even so elementary an operation as that of abstracting from the particular configuration of the triangles or other figures, and the relative situation of the particular lines or points, in the diagram which aids the apprehension of a common geometrical demonstration, is a very useful, and far from being always an easy, exercise of the faculty of generalisation so strangely imagined to have no place or part in the processes of mathematics.

Sir W. Hamilton allows no efficacy to mathematical studies in the cultivation of any valuable intellectual habit, except the single one of continuous attention.

"Are mathematics then," he asks,* "of no value as an
"instrument of mental culture? Nay, do they exercise
"only to distort the mind? To this we answer: That
"their study, if pursued in moderation and efficiently
"counteracted, may be beneficial in the correction of a
"certain vice, and in the formation of its corresponding
"virtue. The vice is the habit of mental distraction;
"the virtue the habit of continuous attention. This is
"the single benefit, to which the study of mathematics
"can justly pretend, in the cultivation of the mind."
He adds, truly enough,† "But mathematics are not the
"only study which cultivates the attention: neither is
"the kind and degree of attention which they tend to
"induce, the kind and degree of attention which our
"other and higher speculations require and exercise."
So that, according to him, there is no purpose answered
by mathematics in general education, but one which
would be better fulfilled by something else.

Without stopping to express my amazement at the
assertion that the student of mathematics exercises no
mental faculty but that of continuous attention, I will
avail myself of an admission which Sir W. Hamilton
cannot help making, but the full force of which he
does not perceive. "We are far," he says,‡ "from
"meaning hereby to disparage the mathematical genius
"which *invents* new methods and formulæ, or new and
"felicitous applications of the old. . . . . Unlike their
"divergent studies, the inventive talents of the mathe-
"matician and philosopher in fact approximate." Was,
then, Sir W. Hamilton so ill-acquainted with everything
deserving the name of mathematical tuition as to suppose
that the inventive powers which, in their higher degree,
constitute mathematical genius, are not called forth and
fostered in the process of teaching mathematics to the
merest tyro? What sort of mathematical instruction is
it of which solving problems forms no part? We come,
within a page afterwards, to the following almost incre-

* Discussions, pp. 313, 314.   † Ibid. p. 322.
‡ Ibid. p. 290.

dible announcement : * " Mathematical demonstration is
" solely occupied in deducing conclusions ; probable
" reasoning, principally concerned in looking out for
" premises."   Sir W. Hamilton thinks he can never be
severe enough upon Cambridge for laying any stress on
mathematics as an instrument of mental instruction.
Did he ever turn over, I do not say a volume of Cambridge
Problems, for these, it may be said, test the knowledge
of the pupil rather than his inventive powers, and may
be an exercise chiefly of memory : but did he ever see
two such volumes as Bland's Algebraical and Geometrical
Problems ?   Did he really imagine that working these
was not " looking out for premises " ? He seems actually
to have thought that learning mathematics meant
cramming it ; and apparently believed that a mathematical tutor resolves all the equations himself, and merely
asks his pupil to follow the solutions.   For in every
problem which the pupil himself solves, or theorem which
he demonstrates, not having previously seen it solved or
demonstrated, the same faculties are exercised which, in
their higher degrees, produced the greatest discoveries
in geometry.   Mathematical teaching, therefore, even as
now carried on, trains the mind to capacities, which, by
our author's admission, are of the closest kin to those of
the greatest metaphysician and philosopher.   There is
some colour of truth for the opposite doctrine in the
case of elementary algebra.   The resolution of a common
equation can be reduced to almost as mechanical a process
as the working of a sum in arithmetic.   The reduction
of the question to an equation, however, is no mechanical
operation, but one which, according to the degree of
its difficulty, requires nearly every possible grade of
ingenuity : not to speak of the new, and in the present
state of science insoluble, equations, which start up at
every fresh step attempted in the application of mathematics to other branches of knowledge.   On all this, Sir
W. Hamilton never bestows a thought.   It is hardly
necessary to point out that any other study, pursued in

* Discussions, p. 291.

the manner in which he supposes mathematics to be, would as little exercise any other faculty than that of " continuous attention" as mathematics would.   Next to metaphysics, the study he most patronises is that of languages ; of which he has so lofty an opinion, as to say * that " to master, for example, the Minerva of " Sanctius with its commentators, is, I conceive, a far " more profitable exercise of mind than to conquer the " Principia of Newton : " we may at least say that he was a better judge of the profit that might be derived from it.   I, also, rate very highly the value, as a discipline to the mind, of the thorough grammatical study of any of the more logically constructed languages : but if the study consisted in learning the Minerva of Sanctius, or its commentators either, by rote, I believe the benefit derived would be about the same with that which Sir W. Hamilton considered to result from the exercise of " continuous attention " in mathematics.

It is a characteristic fact, that when the paper " on the Study of Mathematics " originally appeared as an article in the *Edinburgh Review,* no mention was made in it of Mixed or Applied Mathematics : the little which now appears on that subject being a subsequent addition, called forth by Dr. Whewell's reply.   Dr. Whewell must have looked down from a considerable height upon an assault on the utility of Mathematics, in which the part of it that, in the opinion of its rational defenders, consti- tutes three-fourths of its utility, was silently overlooked. When Sir W. Hamilton's attention was called to what he had previously omitted to think of, this is the way in which he disposes of it : †   " Mathematics can be applied " to objects of experience only in so far as these are " measurable ; that is, in so far as they come, or are " supposed to come, under the categories of extension " and number.   Applied mathematics are, therefore, " equally limited and equally unimproving as pure.   The " sciences, indeed, with which mathematics are thus as- " sociated, may afford a more profitable exercise of mind ;

* Discussions, note to p. 268.   † Ibid. pp. 334, 335.

"but this is only in so far as they supply the matter
"of observation, and of probable reasoning, and there-
"fore *before* this matter is hypothetically subjected to
"mathematical demonstration or calculus."

This passage amounts to proof that the writer simply
did not know what applied mathematics mean. The
words are those of a person who had heard that there
was such a thing, but knew absolutely nothing about
what it was.

Applied mathematics is not the measurement of
extension and number. It is the measurement *by
means* of extension and number, of other quantities
which extension and number are marks of; and the
ascertainment by means of quantities of all sorts, of
those qualities of things which quantities are marks of.

For the information of readers who are no better informed than Sir W. Hamilton, and the reminding of
those who are, I will illustrate this general statement by
bringing it down to particulars; which a person, himself
of very slender mathematical acquirements, can do, provided he has studied the science as every philosophical
student ought to study it, but as Sir W. Hamilton has
not done, with especial reference to its Methods.

The first, and typical example of the application of
mathematics to the indirect investigation of truth, is
within the limits of the pure science itself; the application of algebra to geometry; the introduction of which,
far more than any of his metaphysical speculations, has
immortalised the name of Descartes, and constitutes the
greatest single step ever made in the progress of the
exact sciences. Its rationale is simple. It is grounded
on the general truth, that the position of every point,
the direction of every line, and consequently the shape
and magnitude of every enclosed space, may be fixed by
the length of perpendiculars thrown down upon two
straight lines, or (when the third dimension of space is
taken into account) upon three plane surfaces, meeting
one another at right angles in the same point. A consequence, or rather a part, of this general truth, is that

curve lines and surfaces may be determined by their *equations*. If from any number of points in a curve line or surface, perpendiculars are drawn to two rectangular axes, or to three rectangular planes, there exists between the lengths of these perpendiculars a relation of quantity, which is always the same for the same curve, or surface, and is expressed by an equation in which these variable are combined with certain constant qualities. From this relation, every other property of the curve or surface may always be deduced. In this way, numbers become the means of ascertaining truths not numerical. The periphery of an ellipse is not a number; but a certain numerical relation between straight lines is a mark of an ellipse, being proved to be an inseparable accompaniment of it. The equation which expresses this characteristic mark of any curve, may be handed over to algebraists, to deduce from it, through the properties of numbers, any other numerical relation which depends on it; with the certainty that when the conclusion is translated back again from symbols into words, it will come out a real, and perhaps previously unknown, geometrical property of the curve.

In such an example as this, the application of algebra to geometry appears only in its most elementary form; but its extent is indefinite, and its flights almost beyond the reach of measurement. Its general scheme may be thus stated: In order to resolve any question, either of quality or quantity, concerning a line or space, find something whose magnitude, if known, would give the solution required, and which stands in some known relation to the rectangular co-ordinates (for instance, in the problem of Tangents, the length of the subtangent). Express this known relation in an equation: if the equation can be resolved, we have solved the geometrical problem. Or if the question be the converse one—not what are the properties of a given line or space, but what line or space is indicated by a given property; find what relation between rectangular co-ordinates that property requires: express it in an equation, and this equation, or some other deducible from it, will be the equation of the curve or surface sought. If it be a known curve or surface, this process will point it out: if not, we shall have obtained the necessary starting point for its study.

This application of one branch of mathematics to another branch, ranks as the first step in applied Mathematics. The second is the application to Mechanics. The object-matter of Mechanics is the general laws, or theory, of Force in the abstract, that is, of forces, considered independently of their origin. As an extension is not a number, though a numerical fact may be a mark of an extension; so a force is neither a number nor an extension. But a force is only cognisable through its effects, and the effects by which forces are best known are effects in extension. The measure of a force, is the space through which it will carry a body of given magnitude in a given time. Quantities of force are thus ascertained, through marks which are quantities of extension. The other properties of forces are, their direction (a question of extension, which has already been reduced to a numerical relation between co-ordinates), and the nature of the motion which they generate, either singly or in combination; which is a mixed question of direction and of magnitude in extension. All questions of Force, therefore, can be reduced to questions of direction and of magnitude: and as all questions of direction or magnitude are capable of being reduced to equations between numbers, every question which can be raised respecting Force abstractedly from its origin, can be resolved if the corresponding algebraical equation can.

While the laws of Number thus underlie the laws of Extension, and these two underlie the laws of Force, so do the laws of Force underlie all the other laws of the material universe. Nature, as it falls within our ken, is composed of a multitude of forces, of which the origin (at least the immediate origin) is different, and the effects of which on our senses are extremely various. But all these forces agree in producing motions in space; and even those of their effects which are not actual motions, nevertheless travel; are propagated through spaces, in determinate times: they are all, therefore, amenable to, and conform to, the laws of extension and number. Often, indeed, we have no means of measuring these spaces and times; nor, if we could, are the resources of mathematics sufficient to enable us, in cases of great complexity, to arrive at the quantities of things we cannot directly measure, through those which we can. Fortunately, however, we can do this, sufficiently for all practical purposes, in the case of the great cosmic forces, gravitation and light, and to a less but still a considerable extent, heat and electricity. And here the domain of Applied Mathematics, for the present, ends. To it we are indebted, not only for all we know of the laws of these great and universal agencies, considered as connected bodies of truth, but also for the one complete type and model of the investigation of Nature by deductive reasoning; the ascertainment of the special laws of nature by means of the general. I will not offer to the understanding of any one who knows what this operation is, the affront of asking him if it is all performed "before" the matter is "hypothetically subjected to mathematical demonstration or calculus."

In being the great instrument of Deductive investigation, applied mathematics comes to be also the source of our principal inductions, which invariably depend on previous deductions. For where the inaccessibility or unmanageableness of the phenomena precludes the necessary experiments, mathematical deduction often supplies their place, by making us acquainted with points of resemblance which could not have been reached by direct observation. Phenomena apparently very remote from one another, are found, in the mode of their accomplishment, to follow the same or very similar numerical laws; and the mind, grasping up seemingly heterogeneous natural agencies which have the same equation, and classing them together, often lays a ground for the recognition of them as having either a common, or an analogous, origin. What were previously thought to be distinct

powers in Nature, are identified with each other, by ascertaining that they produce similar effects according to
the same mathematical laws. It was thus that the force
which governs the planetary motions was shown to be
identical with that by which bodies fall to the ground.
Sir W. Hamilton would probably have admitted that the
original discovery of this truth required as great a reach
of intellect as has ever yet been displayed in abstract
speculation. But is no exercise of intellect needed to
apprehend the proof? Is it like an experiment in
chemistry or an observation in anatomy, which may require mind for its origination, but to recognise which,
when once made, requires only eyesight? Is "continuous attention" the only mental capacity required here?
To think so would require an ignorance of the subject
greater than can be imputed to any educated mind, not
to speak of a philosopher.

In the achievements which still remain to be effected
in the way of scientific generalisation, it is not probable
that the direct employment of mathematics will be to
any great extent available : the nature of the phenomena precludes such an employment for a long time to
come—perhaps for ever. But the process itself—the
deductive investigation of Nature ; the application of
elementary laws, generalised from the more simple cases,
to disentangle the phenomena of complex cases—explaining as much of them as can be so explained, and
putting in evidence the nature and limits of the irre-
ducible residuum, so as to suggest fresh observations
preparatory to recommencing the same process with
additional data : *this* is common to all science, moral and
metaphysical included ; and the greater the difficulty,
the more needful is it that the inquirer should come
prepared with an exact understanding of the requisites
of this mode of investigation, and a mental type of its
perfect realisation. In the great problems of physical
generalisation now occupying the higher scientific minds,
chemistry seems destined to an important and conspicuous participation, by supplying, as mathematics did

in the cosmic phenomena, many of the premises of the deduction, as well as part of the preparatory discipline. But this use of chemistry is as yet only in its dawn ; while, as a training in the deductive art, its utmost capacity can never approach to that of mathematics: and in the great inquiries of the moral and social sciences, to which neither of the two is directly applicable, mathematics (I always mean Applied Mathematics) affords the only sufficiently perfect type.   Up to this time, I may venture to say that no one ever knew what deduction is, as a means of investigating the laws of nature, who had not learnt it from mathematics ; nor can any one hope to understand it thoroughly, who has not, at some time of his life, known enough of mathematics to be familiar with the instrument at work.   Had Sir W. Hamilton been so, he would probably have cancelled the two volumes of his Lectures on Logic, and begun again on a different system, in which we should have heard less about Concepts and more about Things, less about Forms of Thought, and more about grounds of Knowledge.

Nor is even this the whole of what the inquirer loses, who knows not scientific Deduction in this its most perfect form.   To have an inadequate conception of one of the two instruments by which we acquire our knowledge of nature, and consequently an imperfect comprehension even of the other in its higher forms, is not all.   He is almost necessarily without any sufficient conception of human knowledge itself as an organic whole.   He can have no clear perception of science as a system of truths flowing out of, and confirming and corroborating, one another ; in which one truth sums up a multitude of others, and explains them, special truths being merely general ones modified by specialities of circumstance. He can but imperfectly understand the absorption of concrete truths into abstract, and the additional certainty given to theorems drawn from specific experience, when they can be affiliated as corollaries on general laws of nature—a certainty more entire than any direct observation can give.   Neither, therefore, can he perceive how the larger inductions reflect an increase of certainty even upon those narrower ones from which they were themselves generalised, by reconciling superficial inconsistencies, and converting apparent exceptions into real confirmations.* To see these things requires more than a mere mathematician; but the ablest mind which has never gone through a course of mathematics has small chance of ever perceiving them.

In the face of such considerations, it is a very small achievement to fill thirty octavo pages with the ill-natured things which persons of the most miscellaneous character, through a series of ages, have said about mathematicians, from a sneer of the Cynic Diogenes to a sarcasm of Gibbon, or a colloquial platitude of Horace Walpole; without any discrimination as to how many of the persons quoted were entitled to any opinion at all on such a subject; and with such entire disregard of all that gives weight to authority, as to include men who lived and died before algebra was invented, before the conic sections had been defined and studied by the mathematicians of Alexandria, or the first lines of the theory of statics had been traced by the genius of Archimedes; men whose whole mathematical knowledge consisted of a clumsy arithmetic, and the mere elements of geometry. Had there been twenty times as many of these testimonies, what proportion of them would have been of any value? Until quite recently, the professors of the different arts and sciences have made it a conside-

* Ignorance of this important principle of the logic of induction, or want of familiarity with it, continually leads to gross misapplications, even by able writers, of the logic of ratiocination. For instance, we are constantly told that the uniformity of the course of nature cannot be itself an induction, since every inductive reasoning assumes it, and the premise must have been known before the conclusion. Those who argue in this manner can never have directed their attention to the continual process of giving and taking, in respect of certainty, which reciprocally goes on between this great premise and all the narrower truths of experience; the effect of which is, that, though originally a generalisation from the more obvious of the narrower truths, it ends by having a fulness of certainty which overflows upon these, and raises the proof of them to a higher level; so that its relation to them is reversed, and instead of an inference from them, it becomes a principle from which any one of them may be deduced.

rable part of their occupation to cry down one another's
pursuits; and men of the world and *littérateurs* have
been, in all ages, ready and eager to join with every set
of them against the rest: the man who dares to know
what they neither know nor care for, and to value himself on the knowledge, having always and everywhere
been regarded as the common enemy. Did Sir W.
Hamilton suppose that a person of half his reading
would have any difficulty in furnishing at a few hours'
notice, an equally long list of amenities on the subject
of grammarians or of metaphysicians? When our
author does get hold of a witness who has a claim to a
hearing, the witness is pressed into the service without
any sifting of what he really says; it makes no difference whether he asserts that the study of mathematics
does harm, or only that it does not simply suffice for all
possible good. One of the authorities on whom most
stress is laid is that of Descartes. I extract the important part of the quotation as our author gives it, partly
from Descartes himself and partly from Baillet, his bio-
grapher.* The italics are Sir W. Hamilton's. "It was
"now a long time, says Baillet, since he had been con-
"vinced of the *small utility* of the *mathematics*, especially
"when studied on their own account, and not applied to
"other things. There was nothing, in truth, which ap-
"peared to him *more futile* than to occupy ourselves with
"simple numbers and imaginary figures, as if it were
"proper to confine ourselves to these *trifles* (bagatelles)
"without carrying our view beyond. There even seemed
"to him in this something *worse than useless.* His maxim
"was that *such application insensibly disaccustomed*
"*us to the use of our reason*, and made us run the danger
"of losing the path which it traces. The words them-
"selves of Descartes deserve quotation; Revera nihil
"*inanius* est, quam circa nudos numeros figurasque ima-
"ginarias ita versari, ut velle videamur in talium *nuga-*
"*rum* cognitione conquiescere, atque superficiariis istis
"demonstrationibus, quæ casu sæpius quam arte inveni-

* Discussions, pp. 277, 278.

"unter, et magis ad oculos et *imaginationem* pertinent,
"quam ad intellectum, sic incubare, ut quodammodo
"*ipsa ratione uti desuescamus;* simulque nihil intrica-
"tius, quam tali probandi modo, novas difficultates con-
"fusis numeris involutas expedire.". . . Baillet goes
on : "In a letter to Mersenne, written in 1630, M. Des-
"cartes recalled to him that *he had renounced the study*
"*of mathematics for many years: and that he was*
"*anxious not to lose any more of his time in the barren*
"*operations of geometry and arithmetic, studies which*
"*never lead to anything important.*" Finally, speaking
of the general character of the philosopher, Baillet adds :
—"In regard to the rest of mathematics" (he had
"just spoken of astronomy—which Descartes thought,
"*though he dreamt in it himself, only a loss of time*")
"in regard to the rest of mathematics, those who know
"the rank which he held above all mathematicians,
"ancient and modern, will agree that he was the man
"in the world best qualified to judge them. We have
"observed that, after having studied these sciences to
"the bottom, *he had renounced them as of no use for*
"*the conduct of life and solace of mankind.*"

Whoever reads this passage as if it were all printed
in Roman characters, and declines to submit his understanding to the italics which Sir W. Hamilton has introduced, will perceive the following three things. First,
that Descartes was not speaking of the study of mathematics, but of its exclusive study. His objection is to
stopping there, without proceeding to anything ulterior:
conquiescere, incubare. Secondly, that he was speaking only of pure mathematics, as distinguished from
its applications, and under the belief, how prodigiously
erroneous we now know, that it did not admit of applications of any importance. Finally, that his disparage-
ment of the pursuit, even as thus limited—his representation of it as "*nugæ,*" as "a loss of time," rested
mainly on a ground which Sir W. Hamilton gave up,
the unimportance of its object-matter. It was a repetition of the objection of Socrates, whom also our author

thinks it worth while to cite as an authority on such a question, and who "did * not perceive of what utility "they" (mathematical studies) "could be, calculated as "they were to consume the life of a man, and to turn "him away from many other and important acquire- "ments." Such an opinion, in the days of Socrates, and from one whose glorious business it was to recall the minds of speculative men to dialectics and morals, reflects no discredit on his great mind. But the objection is one which Sir W. Hamilton, with every thinker of the last two centuries, disclaims. "The question," he expressly says,† "does not regard the value of mathematical *science*, "considered in itself, or in its objective results, but "the utility of mathematical *study*, that is, in its sub- "jective effect, as an exercise of mind." All that Des- cartes said against it in this aspect (at least in the passage quoted, which we may suppose to be one of the strongest) is, that by affording other objects of thought, it diverts the mind from the use of *ipsa ratio*, that is, from the study of pure mental abstractions; which Descartes, to the great detriment of his philosophy, regarded as of much superior value to the employment of the thoughts upon objects of sense, "quæ magis ad "oculos et imaginationem pertinent."

It was by his example, rather than by his precepts, that Descartes was destined to illustrate the unfavour- able side of the intellectual influence of mathematical studies; and he must have been a still more extraor- dinary man than he was, could he have really under- stood a kind of mental perversions of which he is himself, in the history of philosophy, the most prominent example. Descartes is the completest type which history presents of the purely mathematical type of mind—that in which the tendencies produced by mathematical cultivation reign unbalanced and supreme. This is visible not only in the abuse of Deduction, which he carried to a greater length than any distinguished thinker known to us, not excepting the schoolmen; but even more so in the char-

* Discussions, p. 323.   † Ibid. p. 266.

acter of the premises from which his deductions set out
And here we come upon the one really grave charge
which rests on the mathematical spirit, in respect of the
influence it exercises on pursuits other than mathematical.
It leads men to place their ideal of Science in deriving
all knowledge from a small number of axiomatic premises,
accepted as self-evident, and taken for immediate intuitions of reason. This is what Descartes attempted to
do, and inculcated as the thing to be done: and as he
shares with only one other name the honour of having
given his impress to the whole character of the modern
speculative movement, the consequences of his error
have been most calamitous. Nearly everything that is
objectionable, along with much of what is admirable,
in the character of French thought, whether on metaphysics, ethics, or politics, is directly traceable to the
fact that French speculation descends from Descartes
instead of from Bacon.* All reflecting persons in England, and many in France, perceive that the chief
infirmities of French thinking arise from its geometrical
spirit; its determination to evolve its conclusions, even
on the most practical subjects, by mere deduction from
some single accepted generalisation: the generalisation,
too, being frequently not even a theorem, but a practical
rule, supposed to be obtained directly from the fountains
of reason: a mode of thinking which erects one-sidedness
into a principle, under the misapplied name of Logic, and
makes the popular political reasoning in France resemble
that of a theologian arguing from a text, or a lawyer
from a maxim of law. If this be the case even in France,

---

* It is but just to add, that the English mode of thought has suffered
in a different, but almost equally injurious manner, by its exclusive
following of what it imagined to be the teaching of Bacon, being in reality
a slovenly misconception of him, leaving on one side the whole spirit and
scope of his speculations. The philosopher who laboured to construct a
canon of scientific Induction, by which the observations of mankind, instead of remaining empirical, might be so combined and marshalled as to
be made the foundation of safe general theories, little expected that his
name would become the stock authority for disclaiming generalisation, and
enthroning empiricism, under the name of experience, as the only solid
foundation of practice.

it is still worse in Germany, the whole of whose speculative philosophy is an emanation from Descartes, and to
most of whose thinkers the Baconian point of view is
still below the horizon.   Through Spinoza, who gave to
his system the very forms as well as the entire spirit of
geometry; through the mathematician Leibnitz, who
reigned supreme over the German speculative mind for
above a generation; with its spirit temporarily modified
by the powerful intellectual individuality of Kant, but
flying back after him to its uncorrected tendencies, the
geometrical spirit went on from bad to worse, until in
Schelling and Hegel the laws even of physical nature
were deduced by ratiocination from subjective deliverances of the mind.   The whole of German philosophical
speculation has run from the beginning in this wrong
groove, and having only recently become aware of the
fact, is at present making convulsive efforts to get out
of it.*   All these mistakes, and this deplorable waste of
time and intellectual power by some of the most gifted
and cultivated portions of the human race, are effects of
the too unqualified predominance of the mental habits
and tendencies engendered by elementary mathematics.
Applied mathematics in its post-Newtonian development does nothing to strengthen, and very much to correct, these errors, provided the applications are studied in
such a manner that the intellect is aware of what it is
about, and does not go to sleep over algebraical symbols;
a didactic improvement which Dr. Whewell, to his honour
be it said, was earnestly and successfully labouring to
introduce, thus practically correcting the real defects of
mathematics, as a branch of general education, at the
very time when Sir W. Hamilton, who had not the
smallest insight into those defects, selected him for the

* The character here drawn of German thought is, I hardly need say,
not intended to apply to such a man as Goethe, or to those who received
their intellectual impulse from him.   In him, indeed, not to speak of his
almost universal culture, the intellectual operations were always guided
by an intense spirit of observation and experiment, and a constant reference to the exigencies, outward and inward, of practical human life.   Such
criticism as can justly be made on Goethe as a thinker, rests on entirely
different grounds.

immediate recipient of an attack on mathematics, which as it only included what Sir W. Hamilton knew of the subject, left out everything which was much worth saying.

It is not solely to Mathematical studies that Sir W. Hamilton professes and shows hostility. Physical investigations generally, apart from their material fruits, he holds but in low estimation. We have seen in a former chapter how singularly unaware he is of the power and exertion of intellect which they often require. Touching their effect on the mind, he makes two serious complaints, which come out at the very commencement of his Lectures on Metaphysics.* The first is, that the study of Physics indisposes persons to believe in Freewill. To this accusation it must plead guilty: physical science undoubtedly has that tendency. But I maintain that this is only because physical science teaches people to judge of evidence. If the free-will doctrine could be proved, there is nothing in the habits of thought engendered by physical science that would indispose any one to yield to the evidence. A person who knows only one physical science, may be unable to feel the force of a kind of proof different from that which is customary in his department; but any one who is generally versed in physical science is accustomed to so many different modes of investigation, that he is well prepared to feel the force of whatever is really proof. Metaphysicians of Sir W. Hamilton's school, who pursue their investigations without regard to the cautions suggested by physical science, are equally catholic and comprehensive in the wrong way; they can mistake for proof anything or everything which is not so, provided it tends to form an association of ideas in their own minds.

The other objection of Sir W. Hamilton to the scientific study of the laws of Matter, is one which we should scarcely have expected from him, namely, that it annihilates Wonder.

"Wonder,† says Aristotle, is the first cause of philo-
"sophy; but in the discovery that all existence is but

* Lectures, i. 35, 42.   † Ibid. p. 37.

" mechanism, the consummation of science would be an
" extinction of the very interest from which it originally
" sprang. 'Even the gorgeous majesty of the heavens,'
" says a great religious philosopher,* 'the object of a
" kneeling adoration to an infant world,' subdues no more
" the mind of him who comprehends the one mechanical
" law by which the planetary systems move, maintain
" their motion, and even originally form themselves.
" He no longer wonders at the object, infinite as it
" always is, but at the human intellect alone which in a
" Copernicus, Kepler, Gassendi, Newton, and Laplace,
" was able to transcend the object, by science to ter-
" minate the miracle, to reave the heaven of its divinities,
" and to exorcise the universe. But even this, the only
" admiration of which our intelligent faculties are now
" capable, would vanish, were a future Hartley, Darwin,
" Condillac, or Bonnet, to succeed in displaying to us a
" mechanical system of the human mind, as compre-
" hensive, intelligible, and satisfactory as the Newtonian
" mechanism of the heavens." We may be well assured
that no Hartley, Darwin, or Condillac will obtain a hearing, if the " great religious philosopher" can prevent it.

I shall not enter into all the topics suggested by this
remarkable argument. I shall not ask whether, after all,
it is better to be " subdued " than instructed ; or whether
human nature would suffer a great loss in losing wonder,
if love and admiration remained; for admiration, *pace
tantorum virorum*, is a different thing from wonder, and
is often at its greatest height when the strangeness,
which is a necessary condition of wonder, has died away.
But I do wonder at the barrenness of imagination of a
man who can see nothing wonderful in the material universe, since Newton, in an evil hour, partially unravelled
a limited portion of it. If ignorance is with him a necessary condition of wonder, can he find nothing to wonder
at in the *origin* of the system of which Newton discovered
the laws ? nothing in the probable former extension of
the solar substance beyond the orbit of Neptune? nothing

* F. H. Jacobi. The entire passage is in Discussions, p. 312.

in the starry heavens, which, with a full knowledge of what Newton taught, Kant, in the famous passage which Sir W. Hamilton is so fond of quoting (and quotes in this very lecture), placed on the same level of sublimity with the moral law? If ignorance is the cause of wonder, it is downright impossible that scientific explanation can ever take it away, since all which explanation does, in the final resort, is to refer us back to a prior inexplicable. Were the catastrophe to arrive which is to expel Wonder from the universe—were it conclusively shown that the mental operations are dependent upon organic agency—would wonder be at an end because the fact, at which we should then have to wonder, would be that an arrangement of material particles could produce thought and feeling? Jacobi and Sir W. Hamilton might have put their minds at ease. It is not understanding that destroys wonder, it is familiarity. To a person whose feelings have depth enough to withstand that, no insight which can ever be attained into natural phenomena will make Nature less wonderful. And as for those whose sensibilities are shallow, did Jacobi suppose that *they* wondered one iota the more at the planetary motions, when astronomers imagined them to take place by the complicated evolutions of "cycle on epicycle, orb on orb"? A spectacle which they saw every day, had, we may rely upon it, as little effect in kindling their imaginations then, as now. Hear the opinion of a great poet:* not speaking particularly of wonder, but of the emotions generally which the spectacle of nature excites, and in words which apply to that emotion equally with the rest.

" Some are of opinion that the habit of analysing, de-
" composing, and anatomising, is inevitably unfavourable
" to the perception of beauty. People are led into this
" mistake by overlooking the fact that such processes
" being to a certain extent within the reach of a limited
" intellect, we are apt to ascribe to them that insensibility
" of which they are, in truth, the effect, and not the cause.

* Wordsworth, in the Biography by his nephew, ii. 159.

" Admiration and love, to which all knowledge truly vital
" must tend, are felt by men of real genius in proportion
" as their discoveries in natural philosophy are enlarged ;
" and the beauty, in form, of a plant or an animal, is not
" made less but more apparent, as a whole, by more accu-
" rate insight into its constituent properties and powers."

Hear next one of the most illustrious discoverers in
physical science.   Instead of regarding understanding
as antithetical to wonder, Dr. Faraday complains that
people do not wonder sufficiently at the material universe, because they do not sufficiently understand it.

" Let us now consider, for a little while, how wonder-
" fully we stand upon this world.   Here it is we are
" born, bred, and live, and yet we view these things with
" an almost entire absence of wonder to ourselves re-
" specting the way in which all this happens.   So small,
" indeed, is our wonder, that we are never taken by sur-
" prise ; and I do think that, to a young person of ten,
" fifteen, or twenty years of age, perhaps the first sight
" of a cataract or a mountain would occasion him more
" surprise than he had ever felt concerning the means of
" his own existence ; how he came here ; how he lives ;
" by what means he stands upright ; and through what
" means he moves about from place to place.   Hence,
" we come into this world, we live, and depart from it,
" without our thoughts being called specifically to con-
" sider how all this takes place ; and were it not for the
" exertions of some few inquiring minds who have looked
" into these things, and ascertained the very beautiful
" laws and conditions by which we *do* live and stand
" upon the earth, we should hardly be aware that there
" was anything wonderful in it." *

If any additional authority be desired, the greatest
poet of modern Germany was also the keenest scientific
naturalist in it.

* Lectures on the Forces of Matter, pp. 2, 3.   The philosophy of this
is well given by Mr. Lewes in his valuable work on Aristotle (p. 212).
"Surprise starts from a background of knowledge, or fixed belief.   Nothing
"is surprising to ignorance, because the mind in that state has no precon-
"ceptions to be contradicted."

CHAPTER XXVIII.

CONCLUDING REMARKS.

IN the examination which I have now concluded of Sir W. Hamilton's philosophical achievements, I have unavoidably laid stress on points of difference from him rather than on those of agreement; the reason being, that I differ from almost everything in his philosophy on which he particularly valued himself, or which is specially his own. His merits, which, though I do not rate them so high, I feel and admire as sincerely as his most enthusiastic disciples, are rather diffused through his speculations generally, than concentrated on any particular point. They chiefly consist in his clear and distinct mode of bringing before the reader many of the fundamental questions of metaphysics; some good specimens of psychological analysis on a small scale; and the many detached logical and psychological truths which he has separately seized, and which are scattered through his writings, mostly applied to resolve some special difficulty and again lost sight of. I can hardly point to anything he has done towards helping the more thorough understanding of the greater mental phenomena, unless it be his theory of Attention (including Abstraction), which seems to me the most perfect we have.* The facts and speculations on Sleep and Dream-

---

* Even on this subject he has not been able to avoid some fallacies in reasoning. Thus, in maintaining against Stewart and Brown that we can attend to more than one object at once, he defends this true doctrine by some very bad arguments. He says (Lectures, i. 252), that if the mind could "attend to, or be conscious of, only a single object at a time," the conclusion would be involved, "that all comparison and discrimination are impossible." This assumes that we cannot compare and discriminate any impressions but those which are exactly simultaneous. May not the con-

ing in his Seventeenth Lecture on Metaphysics, have
been credited to him as an acquisition to philosophy,
and are a good specimen of inductive enquiry; but
their principal merit, both in point of observation and
of thought, is avowedly Jouffroy's.[*]

dition of discrimination be consciousness not at the same, but at immediately successive instants? May not discrimination depend on *change*
of consciousness; the transition from one state to another? This is a
tenable opinion; it was actually maintained by the philosophers against
whom our author was arguing; and if he thought it erroneous, he should
have disproved it. Unless he did, he was not entitled to treat a doctrine
shown to involve this consequence, as reduced to absurdity. Another of
his proofs of our ability to attend to a plurality of things at once, is our
perception of harmony between sounds. He argues (Lectures, i. 244), that
to perceive a relation between two sounds implies a comparison, and that
if this comparison is not between the sounds themselves, simultaneously
attended to, it must be a comparison of "past sound as retained in memory,
with the present as actually perceived;" which still implies attending to
two objects at once. His opponents however might say, that if there be a
comparison, it is not between two simultaneous impressions, either sensations or memories, but between two successive sounds in the instant of
transition. They might add, that the perception of harmony does not
necessarily involve comparison. When a number of sounds in perfect
harmony strike the ear simultaneously, we have but a single impression;
we perceive but one mass of sound. Analysing this into its component
parts is an act of intelligence, not of direct perception, and is performed
by fixing our attention first on the whole, and then on the separate elements, not all at once, but one after another. These objections to his
doctrine our author seems not to have thought of, because those of Stewart,
whom as an opponent he principally had in view, were different (Lectures,
ii. 145). But they ought to have occurred to him without prompting,
being in complete unison with his doctrine that consciousness of wholes
usually precedes that of their parts; that "instead of commencing with
minima, perception commences with masses." (Lectures, ii. 327, and many
similar passages.)

Sir W. Hamilton is also inconsistent in affirming (Lectures, i. 237) that
attention is "an act of will or desire," and afterwards (247, 248) that it is
in some cases automatic, "a mere vital and irresistible act." This, however, is only a verbal inaccuracy. He doubtless meant that attention is
generally voluntary, but occasionally automatic.

[*] I see with regret that what I have said above, or rather perhaps what
I have omitted to say, has given an impression even to friendly critics
that I think considerably less highly of Sir W. Hamilton's intellectual
calibre, and of his general services to mankind, than I do. My business
in this work was to estimate not the man, but the permanent additions
made by him to the sum of speculative philosophy. These I cannot rate
very high, but I join sincerely and heartily in the tribute to his merits, so
justly paid by Mr. Grote in the Westminster Review (pp. 2, 3).

"He kept up the idea of philosophy as a subject to be studied from its
"own points of view: a dignity which in earlier times it enjoyed, perhaps
"to mischievous excess, but from which in recent times it has far too much
"receded, especially in England. He performed the great service of

With regard to the causes which prevented a thinker of such abundant acuteness, and more than abundant industry, from accomplishing the great things at which he aimed, it would ill become me to speak dogmatically. It would be a very unwarrantable assumption of superiority over a mind like Sir W. Hamilton's, if I attempted

" labouring strenuously to piece together the past traditions of philosophy, " to rediscover those which had been allowed to drop into oblivion, and to "make out the genealogy of opinions as far as negligent predecessors had " still left the possibility of doing so. We recognise also in Sir W. Hamil- "ton an amount of intellectual independence which seldom accompanies "such vast erudition. He recites many different opinions, but he judges "them all for himself; and, what is of still greater moment, he constantly "gives the reasons for his judgments. To us these reasons are always of "more or less value, whether we admit them to be valid or not. . . . . . "To those who dissent from him, as well as to those who agree with him, "his reasonings are highly instructive : while the full citations from so "many other writers contribute materially not only to elucidate the "points directly approached, but also to enlarge our knowledge of philo- "sophy generally."

And in the emphatic words of Professor Masson (pp. 308, 309): "Try " him even in respect of the importance of his effects on the national "thought. Whether from his learning or by reason of his independent "thinkings, was it not he that hurled into the midst of us the very ques- "tions of metaphysics, and the very forms of those questions, that have "become the academic theses everywhere in this British age for real "metaphysical discussion ? . . . Let it be said of Sir W. Hamilton that, " simply and by whatever means, he did more than any other man to re- "instate the worship of Difficulty in the higher mind of Great Britain."

Moreover, as Mr. Grote further observes, "in a subject so abstract, ob- " scure, and generally unpalatable, as Logic and Metaphysics, the difficulty "which the teacher finds in inspiring interest is extreme. That Sir W. "Hamilton overcame such difficulty with remarkable success is the affir- "mation of his two editors," and is proved by the profound impression left by the teacher and his teaching on the intellects and feelings of his pupils. The "Inquirer" (p. 6) charges me with ignoring "that which " formed the greater part of his work—the living teaching he gave to living "men—whereby he has raised up for our age and nation that which we "most needed, a school of men who can and do think." It would be very unworthy to ignore so important an item in his services to mankind. I acknowledge it with a feeling, in which I am surpassed by none, of the inestimable worth of all such services. But if I had been attempting a summary of the benefits which the world owes to Sir W. Hamilton, neither could I have ignored his articles on Education, and especially those on the English Universities, to which it is impossible not to attribute a great in- fluence in shaming those bodies out of their long-continued selfish betrayal of their national trust, and putting the new life into them which they have since manifested and are manifesting, with so much advantage to the spirit of the time and to the national culture.

Even in the character of a speculative thinker, my estimate of Sir W. Hamilton is prodigiously misjudged by those who have made themselves, to gauge and measure his faculties, or give a complete theory of his successes and failures. The utmost I venture on, is to suggest, as simple possibilities, some of the causes which may have partly contributed to his shortcomings as a philosopher. One of those causes is so common as to be the next thing to universal, but requires all the more to be signalised for its unfortunate consequences :

as they had good right to do, the champions of his philosophic reputation. I cannot sufficiently protest against such assertions as that of Mr. Mansel (p. 181), to which there are several equivalent by the "Inquirer," that, if all is true which I have alleged, "Sir W. Hamilton, instead of being a "great philosopher, is the veriest blunderer that ever put pen to paper." Such exaggerations are intelligible in those by whose own estimate he stands almost at the summit of existing philosophy, and who having climbed, as they think, by his assistance, to the same pinnacle, think an inferior eminence unworthy to be counted for anything at all. But some of the most conspicuous figures in the history of philosophy, distinguished no less by the power of their intellect than by the greatness of their influence on subsequent thought, have not, at least in my judgment, left behind them even so much of positive addition to philosophic truth as Sir W. Hamilton. Kant, for example, of whose mental powers no one who is not a disciple probably forms a higher estimate than I do, and who holds so essential a place in the development of philosophic thought, that until somebody had done what Kant did, metaphysics according to our present conception of it could not have been constituted—Kant, probably, will be finally judged to have left no noticeable contribution to philosophy which was both new and true, except some of his refutations of predecessors. Kant, it is true, was a more consecutive, and therefore a more consistent thinker than Sir W. Hamilton, and it is chiefly by that quality that he has become one of the turning points in the history of philosophy, which Sir W. Hamilton has no claim to be : but in ability to discern psychological truths uncoloured by a theory, he seems to me inferior to Sir W. Hamilton. Perhaps, though of a very different character of mind, the nearest parallel in philosophic merit to Sir W. Hamilton (apart from erudition, in which he has probably no parallel among philosophers), was Professor Dugald Stewart. Neither of them can be numbered among the great original thinkers who have carried philosophy into one of its indispensable phases, as did Locke, Descartes, Hume, Kant, and with all his shortcomings, even Reid. Neither of them saw into the heart of great psychological questions which had never been fathomed before, like Berkeley, Hartley, Brown, or James Mill. Both of them have thrown considerable light on minor questions : both have gathered, and more or less perfectly assimilated, truths from very opposite quarters : both have committed great oversights, though Sir W. Hamilton, coming last, and having the benefit of the Kantian movement, stood on a considerably higher platform of metaphysical thought. Both had some, though but moderate, powers of analysis ; their philosophic style, though extremely unlike, was, in both, excellent : both gave an important stimulus to the national intellect by their extraordinary power as public teachers ; and both will be remembered as meritoriously handing on the torch of philosophy, but neither of them, I venture to say, as among those who have much brightened or fed its flame.

over-anxiety to make safe a foregone conclusion. The whole philosophy of Sir W. Hamilton seems to have had its character determined by the requirements of the doctrine of Free-will ; and to that doctrine he clung, because he had persuaded himself that it afforded the only premises from which human reason could deduce the doctrines of natural religion. I believe that in this persuasion he was thoroughly his own dupe, and that his speculations have weakened the philosophical foundation of religion fully as much as they have confirmed it.

A second cause which may help to account for his not having effected more in philosophy, is the enormous amount of time and mental vigour which he expended on mere philosophical erudition, leaving, it may be said, only the remains of his mind for the real business of thinking. While he seems to have known, almost by heart, the voluminous Greek commentators on Aristotle, and to have read all that the most obscure schoolman or fifth-rate German transcendentalist had written on the subjects with which he occupied himself; while, not content with a general knowledge of these authors, he could tell with the greatest precision what each of them thought on any given topic, and in what each differed from every other ; while expending his time and energy on all this, he had not enough of them left to complete his Lectures. Those on Metaphysics, as already remarked, stopped short on the threshold of what was, especially in his own opinion, the most important part of it, and never reached even the threshold of the third and last of the parts into which, in an early lecture, he divided his subject.* Those on Logic he left dependent, for most of the subordinate developments, on extracts strung together from German writers, chiefly Krug and Esser; often not destitute of merit, but generally so vague

---

* Lectures, i. 123-125. This third part is "Ontology, or Metaphysics Proper ; " "the science conversant about inferences of unknown being from its known manifestations ; " things not manifested in consciousness, but legitimately inferrible from those which are.

as to make all those parts of his exposition in which they predominate, unsatisfactory ; * sometimes written from points of view different from Sir W. Hamilton's own, but which he never found time or took the trouble to re-express in adaptation to his own mode of thought.† In the whole circle of psychological and logical speculation, it is astonishing how few are the topics into which he has thrown any of the powers of his own intellect ; and on how small a proportion even of these he has pushed his investigations beyond what seemed necessary for the purposes of some particular controversy.   In consequence, philosophical doctrines are taken up, and again laid down, with perfect unconsciousness, and his philosophy seems made up of scraps from several conflicting metaphysical systems.   The Relativity of human knowledge is made a great deal of in opposition to Schelling and Cousin, but drops out or dwindles into nothing in Sir W. Hamilton's own psychology.   The validity of our natural beliefs, and the doctrine that the incogitable is not therefore impossible, are strenuously asserted in this place and disregarded in that, according to the question in hand.   On the subject of General Notions he ·is avowedly a Nominalist, but teaches the whole of Logic as if he had never heard of any doctrine but the Conceptualist ; what he presents as a reconcilement of the two being never adverted to afterwards, and serving only as an excuse to himself for accepting the one doctrine and invariably using the language of the other. Arriving at his doctrines almost always under the

---

* This is strikingly the case, among many others, with the Lectures on Definition and Division. On those subjects our author lets Krug and Esser think for him. Those authors stand to him instead, not merely of finding a fit expression for his thoughts, but apparently of having any thoughts at all.

† I have already given an example of this from the Lectures, iii, 159-162. His own idea of Clearness as a property of concepts, is that "a con-"cept is said to be clear when the degree of consciousness is such as to "enable us to distinguish it" (the concept) "as a whole from others :" but this idea is expounded by a passage from Esser, in which it is not the concept, but the objects thought through the concept, which, if sufficiently distinguished from all others, constitute the concept a clear one.   I confess that Esser has here greatly the advantage over Sir W. Hamilton, who might have usefully corrected his own theory from the borrowed commentary on it.

stimulus of some special dispute, he never knows how far to press them : consequently there is a region of haze round the place where opinions of different origin meet. I formerly quoted from him a felicitous illustration drawn from the mechanical operation of tunnelling ; that process affords another, justly applicable to himself. The reader must have heard of that gigantic enterprise of the Italian Government, the tunnel through Mont Cenis. This great work is carried on simultaneously from both ends, in well-grounded confidence (such is now the minute accuracy of engineering operations) that the two parties of workmen will correctly meet in the middle. Were they to disappoint this expectation, and work past one another in the dark, they would afford a likeness of Sir W. Hamilton's mode of tunnelling the human mind.

This failure to think out subjects until they had been thoroughly mastered, or until consistency had been attained between the different views which the author took of them from different points of observation, may, like the unfinished state of the Lectures, be with great probability ascribed to the excessive absorption of his time and energies by the study of old writers. That absorption did worse ; for it left him with neither leisure nor vigour for what was far more important in every sense, and an entirely indispensable qualification for a master in philosophy—the systematic study of the sciences. Except physiology, on some parts of which his mental powers were really employed, he may be said to have known nothing of any physical science. I do not mean that he was ignorant of familiar facts, or that he may not, in the course of his education, have gone through the curriculum. But it must have been as Gibbon did, who says, in his autobiography, " I was content to re-" ceive the passive impressions of my professor's lectures, " without any active exercise of my own powers." For any trace the study had left in Sir W. Hamilton's mind, he might as well never have heard of it.*

* The signs of Sir W. Hamilton's want of familiarity with the physical sciences meet us in every corner of his works. One, which I have not

It is much to be regretted that Sir W. Hamilton did
not write the history of philosophy, instead of choosing,
as the direct object of his intellectual exertions, philosophy itself. He possessed a knowledge of the materials
such as no one, probably, for many generations, will take
the trouble of acquiring again ; and the erudition of philosophy is emphatically one of the things which it is
good that a few should acquire for the benefit of the
rest. Independently of the great interest and value
attaching to a knowledge of the historical development on speculation, there is much in the old writers on
philosophy, even those of the middle ages, really worth
preserving for its scientific value.* But this should be

hitherto found a convenient place for noticing, is the singular view he
takes of analysis and synthesis. He imagines that synthesis always presupposes analysis, and that unless grounded on a previous analysis, synthesis can afford no knowledge. "Synthesis without a previous analysis
"is baseless ; for synthesis receives from analysis the elements which it
"recomposes" (Lectures, i. 98). "Synthesis without analysis is a false
"knowledge, that is, no knowledge at all. . . . A synthesis without a
"previous analysis is radically and *ab initio* null" (Ibid. 99). This
affirmation is the more surprising, as the example he himself selects to
illustrate analysis and synthesis is a case of chemical composition ; a
neutral salt, compounded of an acid and an alkali. Did he suppose that
when a chemist succeeds in forming a salt by synthesis merely, putting
together two substances never actually found in combination, he does not
make exactly the same addition to chemical science as if he had met with
the compound first, and analysed it into its elements afterwards? Did
Sir W. Hamilton ever read a memoir by a chemist on a newly-discovered
elementary substance? If so, did he not find that the discoverer invariably proceeds to ascertain by synthesis what combinations the new element
will form with all other elements for which it has any affinity? Sir W.
Hamilton, though he drew his example from physics, forgot all that
related to the example, and thought only of psychological investigation,
in which it does commonly happen that the compound fact is presented
to us first, and we have to begin by analysing it ; our synthesis, if practical at all, taking place afterwards, and serving only to verify the
analysis. Therefore, in spite of his own example, Sir W. Hamilton
defines synthesis as being always a recomposition and "reconstruction"
(Lectures, i. 98). Could any one who had the smallest familiarity with
physical science have committed this strange oversight?
    Another example, to which I shall content myself with referring, is
the incapacity of understanding an argument respecting a principle of
Mechanics, shown in his controversy with Dr. Whewell respecting the
law that the pressure of a lever on the fulcrum, when the weights
balance one another, is equal to the sum of the two weights (Discussions,
pp. 338, 339).
    * "We set particular value upon this preservation of the traditions of
"philosophy, and upon this maintenance of a known perpetual succes-

extracted, and rendered into the phraseology of modern thought, by persons as familiar with that as with the ancient, and possessing a command of its language ; a combination never yet so perfectly realised as in Sir W. Hamilton. It is waste of time for a mere student of philosophy, to have to learn the familiar use of fifty philosophic phraseologies, all greatly inferior to that of his own time ; and if this were required from all thinkers, there would be very little time left for thought. A man who had done it so thoroughly as Sir W. Hamilton, should have made his cotemporaries and successors, once for all, partakers of the benefit ; and rendered it unnecessary for any one to do it again, except for verifying and correcting his representations. This, which no one but himself could have done, he has left undone ; and has given us, instead, a contribution to mental philosophy which has been more than equalled by many not superior to him in powers, and wholly destitute of erudition. Of all persons, in modern times, entitled to the name of philosophers, the two, probably, whose reading on their own subjects was the scantiest, in proportion to their intellectual capacity, were Dr. Thomas Brown and Archbishop Whately : accordingly they are the only two of whom Sir W. Hamilton, though acknowledging their abilities, habitually speaks with a certain tinge of superciliousness. It cannot be denied that both Dr. Brown and Archbishop Whately would have thought and written better than they did, if they had been better read in the writings of previous thinkers : but I am not afraid that

"sion among the speculative minds of humanity, with proper comparisons "and contrasts. We have found among the names quoted by Sir W. "Hamilton, and thanks to his care, several authors hardly at all known "to us, and opinions cited from them not less instructive than curious. "He deserves the more gratitude, because he departs herein from received "usage since Bacon and Descartes. The example set by these great men "was admirable, so far as it went to throw off the authority of prede-"cessors ; but pernicious so far as it banished those predecessors out of "knowledge, like mere magazines of immaturity and error. Throughout "the eighteenth century, all study of the earlier modes of philosophising "was, for the most part, neglected. Of such neglect, remarkable ing "stances are pointed out by Sir W. Hamilton."—Mr. Grote, in *Westminster Review*, p. 2.

posterity will contradict me when I say, that either of them
has done greater service to the world, in the origination
and diffusion of important thought, than Sir W. Hamilton
with all his learning : because, though indolent readers,
they were, both of them, active and fertile thinkers.*

It is not that Sir W. Hamilton's erudition is not
frequently of real use to him on particular questions of
philosophy. It does him one valuable service : it enables him to know all the various opinions which can be
held on the questions he discusses, and to conceive and
express them clearly, leaving none of them out. This it
does, though even this not always ; but it does little
else, even of what might be expected from erudition
when enlightened by philosophy. He knew, with extraordinary accuracy, the ὅτι of every philosopher's doctrine, but gave himself little trouble about the διότι.
With one exception, I find no remarks bearing upon
that point in any part of his writings.† I imagine he

---

* Mr. Grote, agreeing with me as to Brown, demurs to this judgment
as regards Archbishop Whately ; of which latter comparison Professor
Masson, still more naturally, complains. Our difference, I suspect, is not
that I value Sir W. Hamilton less, but Archbishop Whately more. The
result of my reading of many of his multifarious writings is a much higher
estimation than Mr. Grote's seems to be, both of his originality and of
his services to thought. As a metaphysician proper, no one would compare him with Sir W. Hamilton : but I am speaking of him in the more
general character of a thinker, and in respect of the number of true and
valuable thoughts on many various subjects, metaphysics being one, which
he brought into the general stock, and threw into circulation

Let me add that in speaking of Brown and Whately as active and fertile thinkers, I had no idea that I should be considered as refusing those
attributes to Sir W. Hamilton.

† This solitary exception relates to Hume. Respecting the general
scope and purpose, the pervading spirit, of Hume's speculations, Sir W.
Hamilton does give an opinion, and, I venture to think, a wrong one. He
regards Hume's philosophy as scepticism in its legitimate sense. Hume's
object, he thinks, was to prove the uncertainty of all knowledge. With
this intent he represents him as reasoning from premises " not established
by himself," but " accepted only as principles universally conceded in the
previous schools of philosophy." These premises Hume showed (according to Sir W. Hamilton) to lead to conclusions which contradicted the
evidence of consciousness ; thus proving, not that consciousness deceives,
but that the premises generally accepted on the authority of philosophers,
and leading to these conclusions, must be false. (*Discussions*, pp. 87, 88,
and elsewhere.)

This is certainly the use which has been made of Hume's arguments, by

would have been much at a loss if he had been required
to draw up a philosophical estimate of the mind of any
great thinker.   He rarely seems to look at any opinion
of a philosopher in connection with the same philosopher's other opinions.   Accordingly, he is weak as to
the mutual relations of philosophical doctrines.   He
seldom knows any of the corollaries from a thinker's
opinions, unless the thinker has himself drawn them;
and even then he knows them, not as corollaries, but only
as opinions.   One of the most striking examples he affords
of this inability is in the case of Leibnitz; and it is
worth while to analyse this instance, because nothing

Reid and many other of his opponents.   Admitting their validity as arguments, Reid considered them, not as proving Hume's conclusions, but as
a *reductio ad absurdum* of his premises.   That Hume however had any
foresight of their being put to this use, either for a dogmatical or a
purely sceptical purpose, appears to me supremely improbable.   If we
form our opinion by reading the series of Hume's metaphysical essays
straight through, instead of judging from a few detached expressions in a
single essay (that "on the Academical or Sceptical Philosophy,") I think
our judgment will be that Hume sincerely accepted both the premises
and the conclusions.   It would be difficult, no doubt, to prove this by conclusive evidence, nor would I venture absolutely to affirm it.   In the case
of the freethinking philosophers of the last century, it is often impossible
to be quite certain what their opinions really were; how far the reserva-
tions they made, expressed real convictions, or were concessions to supposed necessities of position.   Hume, it is certain, made such concessions
largely : insincere they can hardly be called, being so evidently intended
to be φωνήεντα, at least συνετοῖσι.   I have a strong impression that Hume's
scepticism, or rather his professed admiration of scepticism, was a disguise of this description, intended rather to avoid offence than to conceal his
opinion ; that he preferred to be called a sceptic, rather than by a more
odious name ; and having to promulgate conclusions which he knew would
be regarded as contradicting, on one hand the evidence of common sense,
on the other the doctrines of religion, did not like to declare them as
positive convictions, but thought it more judicious to exhibit them as the
results we *might* come to, if we put complete confidence in the trustworthiness of our rational faculty.   I have little doubt that he himself
did feel this confidence, and wished it to be felt by his readers.   There is
certainly no trace of a different feeling in his speculations on any of the
other important subjects treated in his works; and even on this subject,
the general tenor of what he wrote pointing one way, and only single
passages the other, it is most reasonable to interpret the latter in the
mode which will least contradict the expression of his habitual state of
mind in the former.

   I cannot but believe, therefore, that Sir W. Hamilton has misunderstood the essential character of Hume's mind : but his hearty admiration and honest vindication of him as a thinker are highly honourable to
Sir W. Hamilton, both as a philosopher and as a man.

can more conclusively show, how little capable he was of entering into the spirit of a system unlike his own.

If there ever was a thinker whose system of thought could without difficulty be conceived as a connected whole, it was Leibnitz. Hardly any philosopher has taken so much pains to explain the filiation of all his main conceptions, in a manner at once satisfactory to his own mind and intelligible to the world. And there is hardly any one in whom the filiation is more complete, these various conceptions being all applications of one common principle. Yet Sir W. Hamilton understands them so ill, as to be able to say, after giving an account of the Pre-established Harmony, that "its author him-"self probably regarded it more as a specimen of inge-"nuity than as a serious doctrine." * And again : "It "is a disputed point whether Leibnitz was serious in "his monadology and pre-established harmony." † To say nothing of the injustice done, by this surmise, to the deep sincerity and high philosophic earnestness of that most eminent man ; it is obvious to those who study opinions in their relation to the mind entertaining them, that a person, who could thus think concerning the Pre-established Harmony and the Monadology, however correctly he may have seized many particular opinions of Leibnitz, had never taken into his mind a conception of Leibnitz himself as a philosopher. These theories were necessitated by Leibnitz's other opinions. They were the only outlet from the difficulties of the fundamental doctrine of his philosophy, the Principle of Sufficient Reason.

All who know anything of Leibnitz, are aware that he affirmed it to be a principle of the universe, that nothing exists which has not an antecedent ground in reason, and cognisable by reason; a ground which, when known, gives all the properties of the thing by natural and necessary consequence. This Sufficient Reason might be some abstract property of the thing, serving as the pattern on which it was constructed, and being the key

---

* Lectures, i. 304.   † Foot-note to Reid, p. 309.

to all its other attributes. Such, for example, is the property by which mathematicians define the circle or the triangle, and from which, by mere reasoning, the remaining properties of those figures are deducible. In other cases, the Sufficient Reason of a phenomenon is found in its physical cause. But the mere existence of the cause as an invariable antecedent, does not constitute it the Sufficient Reason of the effect. There must be something in the nature of the cause itself, something capable of being detected in it, which, once known, accounts for its being followed by that particular effect; something which explains the character of the effect, and, had it been known beforehand, would have enabled us to foretell the precise effect that would be produced. To so great a length did Leibnitz carry this doctrine, as to affirm that God (saving actual miracle, which as a highly exceptional fact he was willing to admit) could not, in the exercise of his ordinary providence, conduct the government of the world except *par la nature des créatures;* through second causes, each containing, in its own properties, wherewithal to furnish a complete explanation of the phenomena to which it gives rise.

Setting out with this *à priori* conception of the order of the universe, Leibnitz found Mind apparently acting upon Matter and Matter upon Mind, and was utterly unable to discover in the nature and attributes of either, any Sufficient Reason for this action. The two substances seemed wholly disparate : there was nothing in them from which action of any kind upon one another could have been presumed to be so much as possible. He saw in this one case, what is true, though he did not see it, in all cases whatever—that there is no *nexus*, no natural link, between agent and patient, between cause and effect, and that all we know or can know of their relation is, that the one always follows the other. But to accept the mere fact as ultimate, without craving for a demonstration, could not enter into Leibnitz's geometrical mind; and was positively forbidden by his Principle of Sufficient Reason. Here was a dilemma !

Happily, however, the difficulty of admitting that Mind could act upon Matter, disappeared in the case of an Infinite Mind. In the Omnipotence of the Deity there lay a Sufficient Reason for the possibility of anything which the Deity might be pleased to do. It must be God, therefore, and no subordinate agency, that directly produces the effects on Matter which seem owing to Mind, and the effects on Mind which seem owing to Matter. This being admitted, there were only two possible theories to choose from. Either God, from the beginning, wound up Mind and Matter to go together like two clocks, though without any connection with one another; and I see an object, not because the object is before my eyes, but because it was prearranged from eternity that the presence of the object and the fact of my seeing should occur at the same instant; or else, at the moment when the object appears, God intervenes, and gives me the perception of sight, exactly as if the object had caused it. The former theory is the Pre-established Harmony; the latter is the doctrine of Occasional Causes, to which, as rather the less grotesque supposition of the two, the Cartesians had been driven by the pressure of the same difficulty. But this hypothesis, as it supposed nothing less than a standing miracle, was wholly inadmissible by Leibnitz. It was inconsistent with the idea which he had formed to himself of the perfections of the Deity. He considered it as assimilating Providence to a bad workman, whose engines will not work unless he himself stands by, and gives them a helping hand; "a watchmaker, who, having constructed "a timepiece, would still be obliged himself to turn the "hands, to make it mark the hours."* Leibnitz could not find, in the idea of God, any Sufficient Reason why so roundabout a mode of governing the universe should have been chosen by him. He was thus thrown upon the hypothesis of a Pre-established Harmony, as his only refuge; and there can be no doubt that he accepted it, with the full conviction of an intellect accustomed to

* Quoted from Leibnitz by Sir W. Hamilton, Lectures, i. 303.

pursue given premises to their consequences with all the rigour of geometrical demonstration.

The doctrine of Monads was as necessary a corollary from Leibnitz's first principle as the Pre-established Harmony. Everything, whether physical or spiritual, which has an individual existence, is a compound of innumerable attributes, between many of which we cannot seize any connection, but on Leibnitz's theory it was not admissible to suppose that no connection exists. There must be something, somewhere, which contains in its own nature the complete theory and explanation of the combination of attributes, and is the reason of its being that combination and no other : and what could this be unless a sort of kernel of the entire Being—the Soul in the case of a spiritual being, a kind of Essence of the Individual in that of a merely physical object ? The Monads of Leibnitz do not really differ from the imaginary Essences of the schoolmen, except in not being abstractions, but objective realities in the completest meaning of the word ; which, indeed, the Substantiæ Secundæ of the Realists already were, only that they were essences of classes, and were conceived as inhering simultaneously in numerous individuals, while the Monads of Leibnitz were lively little beings, the principles of animation and activity, each of them the real agent or Force at the bottom of one individual. All this may seem poor stuff, and a melancholy exhibition of a great intellect. But as there is nothing in experience which directly disproves these theories, they are not really more absurd than many a one which has not so quaint an appearance : and it is the strength, not the weakness of a systematic intellect, that it does not shrink from conclusions because they have an absurd look, when they are necessary corollaries from premises which the thinker, and probably most of those who criticise him, have not ceased to regard as true. Leibnitz was led to the Monads and the Pre-established Harmony by the same logical necessity, which made Descartes, far more absurdly, affirm the automatism of animals ; and we might as reasonably doubt the seriousness of the latter opinion, as of the former. The same logical consistency made him a Necessitarian, and an Optimist; since the doctrine of Sufficient Reason made God the author of all that happens, consequently of all human actions; and God's attributes could not be a Sufficient Reason for any world but the best possible.

Other examples may be given, though none greater than this, of Sir W. Hamilton's inability to enter into the very mind of another thinker. Is it not, for instance, a surprising thing, that one who knew Socrates, Plato, and Aristotle so well, should attribute * to all of them his own opinion that (at least in the case of speculative knowledge) not truth but the search for truth is the important matter, and that the pursuit of it is not for the sake of the attainment, but of the mental activity and energy developed in the search? † If there have been three men since speculation began who would have vehemently rejected such a doctrine, they are the three who are here placed at the head of the authorities in its support. Our author arrives at this strange misunderstanding, by giving a meaning to single expressions, derived from his own mode of thought and not from theirs. In Aristotle's case the assertion rests on a mistake of the meaning of the Aristotelian word ἐνέργεια, which did not signify energy, but fact as opposed to possibility, *actus* to *potentia*.‡ One hardly knows what to say to a writer who understands Τέλος οὐ γνῶσις ἀλλὰ πρᾶξις, to mean, "The intellect is perfected not by knowledge but by activity." §

---

* Lectures, i. 11, 12.

† "Speculative truth is only pursued and held of value for the sake of intellectual activity" (Lectures, i. 7), and again (at p. 13) "speculative truth" is said to be "only valuable as a mean of intellectual activity."

‡ The very passage quoted from Aristotle by the editors in support of this representation of him, shows that he was using the word in his own and not in Sir W. Hamilton's sense. Τέλος δ' ἡ ἐνέργεια, καὶ τούτου χάριν ἡ δύναμις λαμβάνεται . . . . καὶ τὴν θεωρητικὴν (ἔχουσιν) ἵνα θεωρῶσιν· ἀλλ' οὐ θεωρῶσιν ἵνα θεωρητικὴν ἔχωσιν.

§ Professor Veitch, in the third appendix to his Memoir of Sir W. Hamilton, points out that in this last sentence I have done Sir W. Hamilton an injustice. The passage, Τέλος οὐ γνῶσις ἀλλὰ πρᾶξις, was not quoted

We see, from such instances, how much even Sir W. Hamilton's erudition wanted of what we have a right to expect from erudition in a superior mind—that it should enter into the general spirit of the things it knows, not know them merely in their details. Sir W. Hamilton studied the eminent thinkers of old, only from the outside. He did not throw his own mind into their manner of thought; he did not survey the field of philosophic speculation from their standing point, and see each object as it would be seen with their lights, and with their modes of looking. The opinion of an author stands an isolated fact in Sir W. Hamilton's pages, without foundation in the author's individuality, or connection with his other doctrines. For want of this elucidation one by another, even the opinions themselves are, as in the case last cited, very liable to be misunderstood. A history of philosophy from his hand, unless proposing to himself a new object had altered his point of view, could not have been final; it would not have been a philosophical history of philosophy; but it would have stood in the same relation to such a work, in which accurate and complete annals stand to political history: it would have been an invaluable protection against the mistakes of subsequent historians, and would have prodigiously abridged their labours. Such, therefore, as his expositions of the opinions of philosophers are, it is greatly to be regretted that we have not more of them; and that his unrivalled knowledge of all the antecedents of Philosophy has enriched the world with nothing but a few selections of passages on topics on which circumstances had led Sir W. Hamilton to write. He is known to have left copious common-place books, without which indeed it would have been hardly possible that such stores of knowledge could be kept within easy reference. Let us hope that they are carefully preserved; that they will, in some form or

---

by himself, but by his editors, as the nearest they had found to a justification of the statement that Aristotle held the opinion attributed to him in the text. They would have done more wisely by making no reference, than one which so totally fails to support the inference drawn from it.

other, be made accessible to students, and will yet do good service to the future historian of philosophy. Should this hope be fulfilled, future ages will have greater cause than, I think, Sir W. Hamilton's published philosophical speculations will ever give them, to rejoice in the fruits of his labours, and to celebrate his name.

THE END.

PRINTED BY BALLANTYNE, HANSON AND CO.
EDINBURGH AND LONDON.

A Catalogue of Works

IN

GENERAL LITERATURE

PUBLISHED BY

MESSRS. LONGMANS, GREEN, & CO.

39 PATERNOSTER ROW, LONDON, E.C.

MESSRS. LONGMANS, GREEN, & CO.

Issue the undermentioned Lists of their Publications, which may be had post free on application :—

1. MONTHLY LIST OF NEW WORKS AND NEW EDITIONS.

2. QUARTERLY LIST OF ANNOUNCEMENTS AND NEW WORKS.

3. NOTES ON BOOKS ; BEING AN ANALYSIS OF THE WORKS PUBLISHED DURING EACH QUARTER.

4. CATALOGUE OF SCIENTIFIC WORKS.

5. CATALOGUE OF MEDICAL AND SURGICAL WORKS.

6. CATALOGUE OF SCHOOL BOOKS AND EDUCATIONAL WORKS.

7. CATALOGUE OF BOOKS FOR ELEMENTARY SCHOOLS AND PUPIL TEACHERS.

8. CATALOGUE OF THEOLOGICAL WORKS BY DIVINES AND MEMBERS OF THE CHURCH OF ENGLAND.

9. CATALOGUE OF WORKS IN GENERAL LITERATURE.

ABBEY and OVERTON.—The English Church in the Eighteenth Century. By CHARLES J. ABBEY and JOHN H. OVERTON. Cr. 8vo. 7s. 6d.

ABBOTT.—Hellenica. A Collection of Essays on Greek Poetry, Philosophy, History, and Religion. Edited by EVELYN ABBOTT, M.A. LL.D. Fellow and Tutor of Balliol College, Oxford. 8vo. 16s.

ABBOTT (Evelyn, M.A. LL.D.)— Works by.

A Skeleton Outline of Greek History. Chronologically Arranged. Crown 8vo. 2s. 6d.

A History of Greece. In Two Parts.
Part I.—From the Earliest Times to the Ionian Revolt. Crown 8vo. 10s. 6d.
Part II. Vol. I.—500-445 B.C. [*In the press.*
Vol. II.—[*In preparation.*]

ACLAND and RANSOME.—A Handbook in Outline of the Political History of England to 1887. Chronologically Arranged. By A. H. DYKE ACLAND, M.P. and CYRIL RANSOME, M.A. Crown 8vo. 6s.

ACTON.—Modern Cookery. By ELIZA ACTON. With 150 Woodcuts. Fcp. 8vo. 4s. 6d.

A. K. H. B.—The Essays and Contributions of. Cr. 8vo.

Autumn Holidays of a Country Parson. 3s. 6d.
Changed Aspects of Unchanged Truths. 3s. 6d.
Commonplace Philosopher. 3s. 6d.
Counsel and Comfort from a City Pulpit. 3s. 6d.
Critical Essays of a Country Parson. 3s. 6d.
East Coast Days and Memories. 3s. 6d.
[*Continued on next page.*

A

A. K. H. B.—The Essays and Contributions of—*continued.*
Graver Thoughts of a Country Parson. Three Series. 3*s.* 6*d.* each.
Landscapes, Churches, and Moralities. 3*s.*6*d.*
Leisure Hours in Town. 3*s.* 6*d.*
Lessons of Middle Age. 3*s.* 6*d.*
Our Little Life. Two Series. 3*s.* 6*d.* each.
Our Homely Comedy and Tragedy. 3*s.* 6*d.*
Present Day Thoughts. 3*s.* 6*d.*
Recreations of a Country Parson. Three Series. 3*s.* 6*d.* each.
Seaside Musings. 3*s.* 6*d.*
Sunday Afternoons in the Parish Church of a Scottish University City. 3*s.* 6*d.*
'To Meet the Day' through the Christian Year: being a Text of Scripture, with an Original Meditation and a Short Selection in Verse for Every Day. 4*s.* 6*d.*

American Whist, Illustrated: containing the Laws and Principles of the Game, the Analysis of the New Play and American Leads, and a Series of Hands in Diagram, and combining Whist Universal and American Whist. By G. W. P. Fcp. 8vo. 6*s.* 6*d.*

AMOS.—A Primer of the English Constitution and Government. By SHELDON AMOS. Crown 8vo. 6*s.*

Annual Register (The). A Review of Public Events at Home and Abroad, for the year 1889. 8vo. 18*s.*
*** Volumes of the 'Annual Register' for the years 1863–1888 can still be had.

ANSTEY.—Works by F. Anstey, Author of 'Vice Versâ.'
The Black Poodle, and other Stories. Crown 8vo. 2*s.* bds.; 2*s.* 6*d.* cl.
Voces Populi. Reprinted from *Punch.* With 20 Illustrations by J. BERNARD PARTRIDGE. Fcp. 4to. 5*s.*

ARISTOTLE.—The Works of.
The Politics, G. Bekker's Greek Text of Books I. III. IV. (VII.) with an English Translation by W. E. BOLLAND, M.A.; and short Introductory Essays by A. LANG, M.A. Cr. 8vo. 7*s.*6*d.*
The Politics: Introductory Essays. By ANDREW LANG. (From Bolland and Lang's 'Politics.') Crown 8vo. 2*s.* 6*d.*
The Ethics; Greek Text, illustrated with Essays and Notes. By Sir ALEXANDER GRANT, Bart. M.A. LL.D. 2 vols. 8vo. 32*s.*
The Nicomachean Ethics, Newly Translated into English. By ROBERT WILLIAMS, Barrister-at-Law. Crown 8vo. 7*s.* 6*d.*

ARMSTRONG (G. F. SAVAGE-) — Works by.
Poems: Lyrical and Dramatic. Fcp. 8vo. 6*s.*
King Saul. (The Tragedy of Israel, Part I.) Fcp. 8vo. 5*s.*
King David. (The Tragedy of Israel, Part II.) Fcp. 8vo. 6*s.*
King Solomon. (The Tragedy of Israel, Part III.) Fcp. 8vo. 6*s.*
Ugone: A Tragedy. Fcp. 8vo. 6*s.*
A Garland from Greece; Poems. Fcp. 8vo. 9*s.*
Stories of Wicklow; Poems. Fcp. 8vo. 9*s.*
Victoria Regina et Imperatrix: a Jubilee Song from Ireland, 1887. 4to. 2*s.* 6*d.*
Mephistopheles in Broadcloth: a Satire. Fcp. 8vo. 4*s.*
The Life and Letters of Edmund J. Armstrong. Fcp. 8vo. 7*s.* 6*d.*

ARMSTRONG (E. J.)—Works by.
Poetical Works. Fcp. 8vo. 5*s.*
Essays and Sketches. Fcp. 8vo. 5*s.*

ARNOLD. — The Light of the World; or, the Great Consummation. A Poem. By Sir EDWIN ARNOLD, K.C.I.E. Crown 8vo. 7*s.* 6*d.* net.

ARNOLD (Dr. T.)—Works by.
Introductory Lectures on Modern History. 8vo. 7*s.* 6*d.*
Sermons Preached mostly in the Chapel of Rugby School. 6 vols. crown 8vo. 30*s.* or separately, 5*s.* ea.
Miscellaneous Works. 8vo. 7*s.* 6*d.*

ASHLEY.—English Economic History and Theory. By W. J. ASHLEY, M.A. Professor of Political Economy in the University of Toronto.
Part I.—The Middle Ages. 5*s.*

Atelier (The) du Lys; or, an Art Student in the Reign of Terror. By the Author of 'Mademoiselle Mori.' Crown 8vo. 2*s.* 6*d.*
BY THE SAME AUTHOR.
Mademoiselle Mori: a Tale of Modern Rome. Crown 8vo. 2*s.* 6*d.*
That Child. Illustrated by GORDON BROWNE. Crown 8vo. 2*s.* 6*d.*

Atelier (The) du Lys—Works by the Author of—*continued.*

Under a Cloud. Crown 8vo. 2s. 6d.

The Fiddler of Lugau. With Illustrations by W. RALSTON. Crown 8vo. 2s. 6d.

A Child of the Revolution. With Illustrations by C. J. STANILAND. Crown 8vo. 2s. 6d.

Hester's Venture : a Novel. Crown 8vo. 2s. 6d.

In the Olden Time : a Tale of the Peasant War in Germany. Crown. 8vo. 2s. 6d.

BACON.—The Works and Life of.

Complete Works. Edited by R. L. ELLIS, J. SPEDDING, and D. D. HEATH. 7 vols. 8vo. £3. 13s. 6d.

Letters and Life, including all his Occasional Works. Edited by J. SPEDDING. 7 vols. 8vo. £4. 4s.

The Essays; with Annotations. By RICHARD WHATELY, D.D., 8vo. 10s. 6d.

The Essays; with Introduction, Notes, and Index. By E. A. ABBOTT, D.D. 2 vols. fcp. 8vo. price 6s. Text and Index only, without Introduction and Notes, in 1 vol. fcp. 8vo. 2s. 6d.

The BADMINTON LIBRARY, edited by the DUKE OF BEAUFORT, K.G. assisted by ALFRED E. T. WATSON.

Hunting. By the DUKE OF BEAUFORT, K.G. and MOWBRAY MORRIS. With 53 Illus. by J. Sturgess, J. Charlton, and A. M. Biddulph. Crown 8vo. 10s. 6d.

Fishing. By H. CHOLMONDELEY-PENNELL.
Vol. I. Salmon, Trout, and Grayling. With 158 Illustrations. Cr. 8vo. 10s. 6d.
Vol. II. Pike and other Coarse Fish. With 132 Illustrations. Cr. 8vo. 10s. 6d.

Racing and Steeplechasing. By the EARL OF SUFFOLK AND BERKSHIRE, W. G. CRAVEN, &c. With 56 Illustrations by J. Sturgess. Cr. 8vo. 10s. 6d.

Shooting. By Lord WALSINGHAM and Sir RALPH PAYNE-GALLWEY, Bart.
Vol. I. Field and Covert. With 105 Illustrations. Cr. 8vo. 10s. 6d.
Vol. II. Moor and Marsh. With 65 Illustrations. Cr. 8vo. 10s. 6d.

The BADMINTON LIBRARY —*continued.*

Cycling. By VISCOUNT BURY, K.C.M.G. and G. LACY HILLIER. With 19 Plates and 70 Woodcuts by Viscount Bury, Joseph Pennell, &c. Cr. 8vo. 10s. 6d.

Athletics and Football. By MONTAGUE SHEARMAN. With 6 full-page Illustrations and 45 Woodcuts by Stanley Berkeley, and from Photographs by G. Mitchell. Cr. 8vo. 10s. 6d.

Boating. By W. B. WOODGATE. With 10 full-page Illustrations and 39 Woodcuts in the Text. Cr. 8vo. 10s. 6d.

Cricket. By A. G. STEEL and the Hon. R. H. LYTTELTON. With 11 full-page Illustrations and 52 Woodcuts in the Text, by Lucien Davis. Cr. 8vo. 10s. 6d.

Driving. By the DUKE OF BEAUFORT. With 11 Plates and 54 Woodcuts by J. Sturgess and G. D. Giles. Cr. 8vo. 10s. 6d.

Fencing, Boxing, and Wrestling. By WALTER H. POLLOCK, F. C. GROVE, C. PREVOST, E. B. MICHELL, and WALTER ARMSTRONG. With 18 Plates and 24 Woodcuts. Crown 8vo. 10s. 6d.

Golf. By HORACE HUTCHINSON, the Rt. Hon. A. J. BALFOUR, M.P. ANDREW LANG, Sir W. G. SIMPSON, Bart. &c. With 19 Plates and 69 Woodcuts. Crown 8vo. 10s. 6d.

Tennis, Lawn Tennis, Rackets, and Fives. By J. M. and C. G. HEATHCOTE, E. O. PLEYDELL-BOUVERIE, and A. C. AINGER. With 12 Plates and 67 Woodcuts, &c. Crown 8vo. 10s. 6d.

BAGEHOT (Walter)—Works by.

Biographical Studies. 8vo. 12s.

Economic Studies. 8vo. 10s. 6d.

Literary Studies. 2 vols. 8vo. 28s.

The Postulates of English Political Economy. Cr. 8vo. 2s. 6d.

A Practical Plan for Assimilating the English and American Money as a Step towards a Universal Money. Cr. 8vo. 2s. 6d.

BAGWELL. — Ireland under the Tudors, with a Succinct Account of the Earlier History. By RICHARD BAGWELL, M.A. (3 vols.) Vols. I. and II. From the first invasion of the Northmen to the year 1578. 8vo. 32s. Vol. III. 1578–1603. 8vo. 18s.

A 2

BAIN (Alexander)—Works by.

Mental and Moral Science.
Crown 8vo. 10s. 6d.

Senses and the Intellect. 8vo. 15s.

Emotions and the Will. 8vo. 15s.

Logic, Deductive and Inductive.
PART I. *Deduction*, 4s. PART II. *Induction*, 6s. 6d.

Practical Essays. Cr. 8vo. 2s.

BAKER.—**By the Western Sea :**
a Summer Idyll. By JAMES BAKER, F.R.G.S. Author of 'John Westacott.' Cr. 8vo. 6s.

BAKER (Sir S. W.)—Works by.

Eight Years in Ceylon. With 6 Illustrations. Crown 8vo. 3s. 6d.

The Rifle and the Hound in Ceylon. With 6 Illustrations. Crown 8vo. 3s. 6d.

BALL (The Rt. Hon. J. T.)—Works by.

The Reformed Church of Ireland (1537–1889). 8vo. 7s. 6d.

Historical Review of the Legislative Systems Operative in Ireland, from the Invasion of Henry the Second to the Union (1172–1800). 8vo. 6s.

BEACONSFIELD (The Earl of) — Works by.

Novels and Tales. The Hughenden Edition. With 2 Portraits and 11 Vignettes. 11 vols. Crown 8vo. 42s.

Endymion.	Henrietta Temple.
Lothair.	Contarini Fleming, &c.
Coningsby.	Alroy, Ixion, &c.
Tancred. Sybil.	The Young Duke, &c.
Venetia.	Vivian Grey.

Novels and Tales. Cheap Edition. complete in 11 vols. Crown 8vo. 1s. each, boards ; 1s. 6d. each, cloth.

BECKER (Professor)—Works by.

Gallus ; or, Roman Scenes in the Time of Augustus. Post 8vo. 7s. 6d.

Charicles ; or, Illustrations of the Private Life of the Ancient Greeks. Post 8vo. 7s. 6d.

BELL (Mrs. Hugh).—Works by.

Will o' the Wisp : a Story. Illustrated by E. L. SHUTE. Crown 8vo. 3s. 6d.

Chamber Comedies : a Collection of Plays and Monologues for the Drawing Room. Crown 8vo. 6s.

BLAKE.—**Tables for the Conversion of 5 per Cent. Interest from $\frac{1}{16}$ to 7 per Cent.** By J. BLAKE, of the London Joint Stock Bank, Limited. 8vo. 12s. 6d.

Book (The) of Wedding Days.
Arranged on the Plan of a Birthday Book. With 96 Illustrated Borders, Frontispiece, and Title-page by WALTER CRANE ; and Quotations for each Day. Compiled and Arranged by K. E. J. REID, MAY ROSS, and MABEL BAMFIELD. 4to. 21s.

BRASSEY (Lady)—Works by.

A Voyage in the 'Sunbeam,' our Home on the Ocean for Eleven Months.

Library Edition. With 8 Maps and Charts, and 118 Illustrations, 8vo. 21s.

Cabinet Edition. With Map and 66 Illustrations, crown 8vo. 7s. 6d.

School Edition. With 37 Illustrations, fcp. 2s. cloth, or 3s. white parchment.

Popular Edition. With 60 Illustrations, 4to. 6d. sewed, 1s. cloth.

Sunshine and Storm in the East.

Library Edition. With 2 Maps and 114 Illustrations, 8vo. 21s.

Cabinet Edition. With 2 Maps and 114 Illustrations, crown 8vo. 7s. 6d.

Popular Edition. With 103 Illustrations, 4to. 6d. sewed, 1s. cloth.

In the Trades, the Tropics, and the 'Roaring Forties.'

Cabinet Edition. With Map and 220 Illustrations, crown 8vo. 7s. 6d.

Popular Edition. With 183 Illustrations, 4to. 6d. sewed, 1s. cloth.

BRASSEY (Lady) — Works by — *continued.*

The Last Voyage to India and Australia in the 'Sunbeam.' With Charts and Maps, and 40 Illustrations in Monotone (20 full-page), and nearly 200 Illustrations in the Text from Drawings by R. T. PRITCHETT. 8vo. 21*s.*

Three Voyages in the 'Sunbeam.' Popular Edition. With 346 Illustrations, 4to. 2*s.* 6*d.*

BRAY.—The Philosophy of Necessity ; or, Law in Mind as in Matter. By CHARLES BRAY. Crown 8vo. 5*s.*

BRIGHT.—A History of England. By the Rev. J. FRANCK BRIGHT, D.D. Master of University College, Oxford. 4 vols. crown 8vo.

Period I.—Mediæval Monarchy : The Departure of the Romans to Richard III. From A.D. 449 to 1485. 4*s.* 6*d.*
Period II.—Personal Monarchy : Henry VII. to James II. From 1485 to 1688. 5*s.*
Period III.—Constitutional Monarchy : William and Mary to William IV. From 1689 to 1837. 7*s.* 6*d.*
Period IV.—The Growth of Democracy : Victoria. From 1837 to 1880. 6*s.*

BRYDEN. — Kloof and Karroo : Sport, Legend, and Natural History in Cape Colony. By H. A. BRYDEN. With 17 Illustrations. 8vo. 10*s.* 6*d.*

BUCKLE. — History of Civilisation in England and France, Spain and Scotland. By HENRY THOMAS BUCKLE. 3 vols. cr. 8vo. 24*s.*

BUCKTON (Mrs. C. M.)—Works by.

Food and Home Cookery. With 11 Woodcuts. Crown 8vo. 2*s.* 6*d.*

Health in the House. With 41 Woodcuts and Diagrams. Crown 8vo. 2*s.*

BULL (Thomas)—Works by.

Hints to Mothers on the Management of their Health during the Period of Pregnancy. Fcp. 8vo. 1*s.* 6*d.*

The Maternal Management of Children in Health and Disease. Fcp. 8vo. 1*s.* 6*d.*

BUTLER (Samuel)—Works by.

Op. 1. Erewhon. Cr. 8vo. 5*s.*

Op. 2. The Fair Haven. A Work in Defence of the Miraculous Element in our Lord's Ministry. Cr. 8vo. 7*s.* 6*d.*

Op. 3. Life and Habit. An Essay after a Completer View of Evolution. Cr. 8vo. 7*s.* 6*d.*

Op. 4. Evolution, Old and New. Cr. 8vo. 10*s.* 6*d.*

Op. 5. Unconscious Memory. Cr. 8vo. 7*s.* 6*d.*

Op. 6. Alps and Sanctuaries of Piedmont and the Canton Ticino. Illustrated. Pott 4to. 10*s.* 6*d.*

Op. 7. Selections from Ops. 1–6. With Remarks on Mr. G. J. ROMANES' 'Mental Evolution in Animals.' Cr. 8vo. 7*s.* 6*d.*

Op. 8. Luck, or Cunning, as the Main Means of Organic Modification ? Cr. 8vo. 7*s.* 6*d.*

Op. 9. Ex Voto. An Account of the Sacro Monte or New Jerusalem at Varallo-Sesia. 10*s.* 6*d.*

Holbein's 'La Dansé.' A Note on a Drawing called 'La Danse.' 3*s.*

CARLYLE. — Thomas Carlyle: a History of his Life. By J. A. FROUDE. 1795–1835, 2 vols. crown 8vo. 7*s.* 1834–1881, 2 vols. crown 8vo. 7*s.*

CASE. — Physical Realism : being an Analytical Philosophy from the Physical Objects of Science to the Physical Data of Sense. By THOMAS CASE, M.A. Fellow and Senior Tutor C.C.C. 8vo. 15*s.*

CHETWYND. — Racing Reminiscences and Experiences of the Turf. By Sir GEORGE CHETWYND, Bart. 2 vols. 8vo. 21*s.*

CHILD. — Church and State under the Tudors. By GILBERT W. CHILD, M.A. Exeter College, Oxford. 8vo. 15*s.*

CHISHOLM.—Handbook of Commercial Geography. By G. G. CHISHOLM, B.Sc. With 29 Maps. 8vo. 16*s.*

CHURCH.—Sir Richard Church, C.B. G.C.H. Commander-in-Chief of the Greeks in the War of Independence: a Memoir. By STANLEY LANE-POOLE, Author of 'The Life of Viscount Stratford de Redcliffe.' With 2 Plans. 8vo. 5*s.*

CLARK-KENNEDY.—Pictures in Rhyme. By ARTHUR CLARK-KENNEDY. With Illustrations by MAURICE GREIFFENHAGEN. Cr. 8vo.

CLIVE.—Poems. By V. (Mrs. ARCHER CLIVE), Author of 'Paul Ferroll.' Including the IX. Poems. New Edition. Fcp. 8vo. 6*s.*

CLODD.—The Story of Creation: a Plain Account of Evolution. By EDWARD CLODD. With 77 Illustrations. Crown 8vo. 3*s. 6d.*

CLUTTERBUCK.—The Skipper in Arctic Seas. By W. J. CLUTTERBUCK, one of the Authors of 'Three in Norway.' With 39 Illustrations. Cr. 8vo. 10*s. 6d.*

COLENSO.—The Pentateuch and Book of Joshua Critically Examined. By J. W. COLENSO, D.D. late Bishop of Natal. Crown 8vo. 6*s.*

COLMORE.—A Living Epitaph. By G. COLMORE, Author of 'A Conspiracy of Silence' &c. Crown 8vo. 6*s.*

COMYN.—Atherstone Priory: a Tale. By L. N. COMYN. Cr. 8vo. 2*s. 6d.*

CONINGTON (John)—Works by.

The Æneid of Virgil. Translated into English Verse. Crown 8vo. 6*s.*

The Poems of Virgil. Translated into English Prose. Crown 8vo. 6*s.*

COX.—A General History of Greece, from the Earliest Period to the Death of Alexander the Great; with a sketch of the subsequent History to the Present Time. By the Rev. Sir G. W. COX, Bart. M.A. With 11 Maps and Plans. Crown 8vo. 7*s. 6d.*

CRAKE.—Historical Tales. By A. D. CRAKE, B.A. Author of 'History of the Church under the Roman Empire,' &c. &c. Crown 8vo. 5 vols. 3*s. 6d.* each. Sold separately.

Edwy the Fair; or, The First Chronicle of Æscendune.

Alfgar the Dane; or, The Second Chronicle of Æscendune.

The Rival Heirs: being the Third and Last Chronicle of Æscendune.

The House of Walderne. A Tale of the Cloister and the Forest in the Days of the Barons' Wars.

Brian Fitz-Count. A Story of Wallingford Castle and Dorchester Abbey.

CRAKE.—History of the Church under the Roman Empire, A.D. 30-476. By the Rev. A. D. CRAKE, B.A. late Vicar of Cholsey, Berks. Crown 8vo. 7*s. 6d.*

CREIGHTON.—History of the Papacy During the Reformation. By MANDELL CREIGHTON, D.D. LL.D. Bishop of Peterborough. 8vo. Vols. I. and II. 1378-1464, 32*s.*; Vols. III. and IV. 1464-1518, 24*s.*

CRUMP (A.)—Works by.

A Short Enquiry into the Formation of Political Opinion, from the Reign of the Great Families to the Advent of Democracy. 8vo. 7*s. 6d.*

An Investigation into the Causes of the Great Fall in Prices which took place coincidently with the Demonetisation of Silver by Germany. 8vo. 6*s.*

CURZON.—Russia in Central Asia in 1889 and the Anglo-Russian Question. By the Hon. GEORGE N. CURZON, M.P. 8vo. 21*s.*

DANTE.—La Commedia di Dante. A New Text, carefully Revised with the aid of the most recent Editions and Collations. Small 8vo. 6*s.*
*** Fifty Copies (of which Forty-five are for Sale) have been printed on Japanese paper, £1. 1*s.* net.

DAVIDSON (W. L.)—Works by.

The Logic of Definition Explained and Applied. Cr. 8vo. 6s.

Leading and Important English Words Explained and Exemplified. Fcp. 8vo. 3s. 6d.

DELAND (Mrs.)—Works by.

John Ward, Preacher: a Story. Crown 8vo. 2s. boards, 2s. 6d. cloth.

Sidney: a Novel. Crown 8vo. 6s.

The Old Garden, and other Verses. Fcp. 8vo. 5s.

Florida Days. With 12 Full-page Plates (2 Etched and 4 in Colours), and about 50 Illustrations in the Text, by LOUIS K. HARLOW. 8vo. 21s.

DE LA SAUSSAYE.—A Manual of the Science of Religion. By Professor CHANTEPIE DE LA SAUSSAYE. Translated by Mrs. COLYER FERGUSSON (*née* MAX MÜLLER). Revised by the Author.

DE REDCLIFFE.—The Life of the Right Hon. Stratford Canning: Viscount Stratford De Redcliffe. By STANLEY LANE-POOLE.

Cabinet Edition, abridged, with 3 Portraits, 1 vol. crown 8vo. 7s. 6d.

DE SALIS (Mrs.)—Works by.

Savouries à la Mode. Fcp. 8vo. 1s. 6d. boards.

Entrées à la Mode. Fcp. 8vo. 1s. 6d. boards.

Soups and Dressed Fish à la Mode. Fcp. 8vo. 1s. 6d. boards.

Oysters à la Mode. Fcp. 8vo. 1s. 6d. boards.

Sweets and Supper Dishes à la Mode. Fcp. 8vo. 1s. 6d. boards.

Dressed Vegetables à la Mode. Fcp. 8vo. 1s. 6d. boards.

Dressed Game and Poultry à la Mode. Fcp. 8vo. 1s. 6d. boards.

Puddings and Pastry à la Mode. Fcp. 8vo. 1s. 6d. boards.

DE SALIS (Mrs.)—Works by—*cont.*

Cakes and Confections à la Mode. Fcp. 8vo. 1s. 6d. boards.

Tempting Dishes for Small Incomes. Fcp. 8vo. 1s. 6d.

Wrinkles and Notions for every Household. Crown 8vo. 2s. 6d.

DE TOCQUEVILLE.—Democracy in America. By ALEXIS DE TOCQUEVILLE. Translated by HENRY REEVE, C.B. 2 vols. crown 8vo. 16s.

DOWELL.—A History of Taxation and Taxes in England from the Earliest Times to the Year 1885. By STEPHEN DOWELL. (4 vols. 8vo.) Vols. I. and II. The History of Taxation, 21s. Vols. III. and IV. The History of Taxes, 21s.

DOYLE (A. Conan)—Works by.

Micah Clarke: his Statement as made to his three Grandchildren, Joseph, Gervas, and Reuben, during the hard Winter of 1734. With Frontispiece and Vignette. Crown 8vo. 3s. 6d.

The Captain of the Polestar; and other Tales. Crown 8vo. 6s.

Dublin University Press Series (The): a Series of Works undertaken by the Provost and Senior Fellows of Trinity College, Dublin.

Abbott's (T. K.) Codex Rescriptus Dublinensis of St. Matthew. 4to. 21s.

———————— Evangeliorum Versio Antehieronymiana ex Codice Usseriano (Dublinensi). 2 vols. crown 8vo. 21s.

Allman's (G. J.) Greek Geometry from Thales to Euclid. 8vo. 10s. 6d.

Burnside (W. S.) and Panton's (A. W.) Theory of Equations. 8vo. 12s. 6d.

Casey's (John) Sequel to Euclid's Elements. Crown 8vo. 3s. 6d.

———————— Analytical Geometry of the Conic Sections. Crown 8vo. 7s. 6d.

Davies' (J. F.) Eumenides of Æschylus. With Metrical English Translation. 8vo. 7s.

Dublin Translations into Greek and Latin Verse. Edited by R. Y. Tyrrell. 8vo. 6s.

[*Continued on next page.*]

Dublin University Press Series (The)—*continued.*

Graves' (R. P.) Life of Sir William Hamilton. 3 vols. 15*s.* each.

Griffin (R. W.) on Parabola, Ellipse, and Hyperbola. Crown 8vo. 6*s.*

Hobart's (W. K.) Medical Language of St. Luke. 8vo. 16*s.*

Leslie's (T. E. Cliffe) Essays in Political Economy. 8vo. 10*s.* 6*d.*

Macalister's (A.) Zoology and Morphology of Vertebrata. 8vo. 10*s.* 6*d.*

MacCullagh's (James) Mathematical and other Tracts. 8vo. 15*s.*

Maguire's (T.) Parmenides of Plato, Text with Introduction, Analysis, &c. 8vo. 7*s.* 6*d.*

Monck's (W. H. S.) Introduction to Logic. Crown 8vo. 5*s.*

Roberts' (R. A.) Examples in the Analytic 5*s.*

Southey's (R.) Correspondence with Caroline Bowles. Edited by E. Dowden. 8vo. 14*s.*

Stubbs' (J. W.) History of the University of Dublin, from its Foundation to the End of the Eighteenth Century. 8vo. 12*s.* 6*d.*

Thornhill's (W. J.) The Æneid of Virgil, freely translated into English Blank Verse. Crown 8vo. 7*s.* 6*d.*

Tyrrell's (R. Y.) Cicero's Correspondence. Vols. I. II. and III. 8vo. each 12*s.*

———————— The Acharnians of Aristophanes, translated into English Verse. Crown 8vo. 1*s.*

Webb's (T. E.) Goethe's Faust, Translation and Notes. 8vo. 12*s.* 6*d.*

———————— The Veil of Isis : a Series of Essays on Idealism. 8vo. 10*s.* 6*d.*

Wilkins' (G.) The Growth of the Homeric Poems. 8vo. 6*s.*

Epochs of Modern History.

Edited by C. Colbeck, M.A. 19 vols. fcp. 8vo. with Maps, 2*s.* 6*d.* each.

Church's (Very Rev. R. W.) The Beginning of the Middle Ages. With 3 Maps.

Johnson's (Rev. A. H.) The Normans in Europe. With 3 Maps.

Cox's (Rev. Sir G. W.) The Crusades. With a Map.

Stubbs's (Right Rev. W.) The Early Plantagenets. With 2 Maps.

Warburton's (Rev. W.) Edward the Third. With 3 Maps and 3 Genealogical Tables.

Epochs of Modern History—*continued.*

Gairdner's (J.) The Houses of Lancaster and York ; with the Conquest and Loss of France. With 5 Maps.

Moberly's (Rev. C. E.) The Early Tudors.

Seebohm's (F.) The Era of the Protestant Revolution. With 4 Maps and 12 Diagrams.

Creighton's (Rev. M.) The Age of Elizabeth. With 5 Maps and 4 Genealogical Tables.

Gardiner's (S. R.) The First Two Stuarts and the Puritan Revolution (1603–1660). With 4 Maps.

Gardiner's (S. R.) The Thirty Years' War (1618–1648). With a Map.

Airy's (O.) The English Restoration and Louis XIV. (1648–1678).

Hale's (Rev. E.) The Fall of the Stuarts ; and Western Europe (1678–1697). With 11 Maps and Plans.

Morris's (E. E.) The Age of Anne. With 7 Maps and Plans.

Morris's (E. E.) The Early Hanoverians. With 9 Maps and Plans.

Longman's (F. W.) Frederick the Great and the Seven Years' War. With 2 Maps.

Ludlow's (J. M.) The War of American Independence (1775–1783). With 4 Maps.

Gardiner's (Mrs. S. R.) The French Revolution (1789–1795). With 7 Maps.

McCarthy's (Justin) The Epoch of Reform (1830–1850).

Epochs of Church History.

Edited by Mandell Creighton, D.D. Bishop of Peterborough. Fcp. 8vo. 2*s.* 6*d.* each.

Tucker's (Rev. H. W.) The English Church in other Lands.

Perry's (Rev. G. G.) The History of the Reformation in England.

Brodrick's (Hon. G. C.) A History of the University of Oxford.

Mullinger's (J. B.) A History of the University of Cambridge.

Plummer's (A.) The Church of the Early Fathers.

Carr's (Rev. A.) The Church and the Roman Empire.

Wakeman's (H. O.) The Church and the Puritans (1570–1660).

Overton's (Rev. J. H.) The Evangelical Revival in the Eighteenth Century.

Tozer's (Rev. H. F.) The Church and the Eastern Empire.

Epochs of Church History—
continued.

Stephens's (Rev. W. R. W.) Hildebrand and his Times.

Hunt's (Rev. W.) The English Church in the Middle Ages.

Balzani's (U.) The Popes and the Hohenstaufen.

Gwatkin's (H. M.) The Arian Controversy.

Ward's (A. W.) The Counter-Reformation.

Poole's (R. L.) Wycliffe and Early Movements of Reform.

Epochs of Ancient History. Edited by the Rev. Sir G. W. Cox, Bart. M.A. and by C. Sankey, M.A. 10 volumes, fcp. 8vo. with Maps, 2s. 6d. each.

Beesly's (A. H.) The Gracchi, Marius, and Sulla. With 2 Maps.

Capes's (Rev. W. W.) The Early Roman Empire. From the Assassination of Julius Cæsar to the Assassination of Domitian. With 2 Maps.

———————— The Roman Empire of the Second Century, or the Age of the Antonines. With 2 Maps.

Cox's (Rev. Sir G. W.) The Athenian Empire from the Flight of Xerxes to the Fall of Athens. With 5 Maps.

———————— The Greeks and the Persians. With 4 Maps.

Curteis's (A. M.) The Rise of the Macedonian Empire. With 8 Maps.

Ihne's (W.) Rome to its Capture by the Gauls. With a Map.

Merivale's (Very Rev. C.) The Roman Triumvirates. With a Map.

Sankey's (C.) The Spartan and Theban Supremacies. With 5 Maps.

Smith's (R. B.) Rome and Carthage, the Punic Wars. With 9 Maps and Plans.

Epochs of American History. Edited by Dr. Albert Bushnell Hart, Assistant Professor of History in Harvard College.

Thwaites's (R. G.) The Colonies (1492–1763). Fcp. 8vo. 3s. 6d. [*Ready.*

Hart's (A. B.) Formation of the Union (1763-1829). Fcp. 8vo. [*In preparation.*

Wilson's (W.) Division and Re-union (1829-1889). Fcp. 8vo. [*In preparation.*

Epochs of English History. Complete in One Volume, with 27 Tables and Pedigrees, and 23 Maps. Fcp. 8vo. 5s.

*** For details of Parts *see* Longmans & Co.'s Catalogue of School Books.

EWALD (Heinrich)—Works by.

The Antiquities of Israel. Translated from the German by H. S. Solly, M.A. 8vo. 12s. 6d.

The History of Israel. Translated from the German. 8 vols. 8vo. Vols. I. and II. 24s. Vols. III. and IV. 21s. Vol. V. 18s. Vol. VI. 16s. Vol. VII. 21s. Vol. VIII. with Index to the Complete Work. 18s.

FARNELL.—The Greek Lyric Poets. Edited, with Introductions and Notes, by G. S. Farnell, M.A. 8vo.

FARRAR.—Language and Languages. A Revised Edition of *Chapters on Language and Families of Speech.* By F. W. Farrar, D.D. Crown 8vo. 6s.

FIRTH.—Nation Making: a Story of New Zealand Savageism and Civilisation. By J. C. Firth, Author of 'Luck' and 'Our Kin across the Sea.' Crown 8vo. 6s.

FITZWYGRAM. — Horses and Stables. By Major-General Sir F. Fitzwygram, Bart. With 19 pages of Illustrations. 8vo. 5s.

FORD.—The Theory and Practice of Archery. By the late Horace Ford. New Edition, thoroughly Revised and Re-written by W. Butt, M.A. With a Preface by C. J. Longman, M.A. F.S.A. 8vo. 14s.

FOUARD.—The Christ the Son of God: a Life of our Lord and Saviour Jesus Christ. By the Abbé Constant Fouard. Translated from the Fifth Edition, with the Author's sanction, by George F. X. Griffith. With an Introduction by Cardinal Manning. 2 vols. crown 8vo. 14s.

FOX.—The Early History of Charles James Fox. By the Right Hon. Sir G. O. Trevelyan, Bart. Library Edition, 8vo. 18s. Cabinet Edition, cr. 8vo. 6s.

FRANCIS—A Book on Angling; or, Treatise on the Art of Fishing in every branch; including full Illustrated List of Salmon Flies. By Francis Francis. Post 8vo. Portrait and Plates, 15s.

FREEMAN.—The Historical Geography of Europe. By E. A. Freeman. With 65 Maps. 2 vols. 8vo. 31s. 6d.

A 3

FROUDE (James A.)—Works by.

The History of England, from the Fall of Wolsey to the Defeat of the Spanish Armada. 12 vols. crown 8vo. £2. 2s.

Short Studies on Great Subjects. Cabinet Edition, 4 vols. crown 8vo. 24s. Cheap Edition, 4 vols. crown 8vo. 3s. 6d. each.

Cæsar : a Sketch. Crown 8vo. 3s. 6d.

The English in Ireland in the Eighteenth Century. 3 vols. crown 8vo. 18s.

Oceana ; or, England and Her Colonies. With 9 Illustrations. Crown 8vo. 2s. boards, 2s. 6d. cloth.

The English in the West Indies; or, the Bow of Ulysses. With 9 Illustrations. Crown 8vo. 2s. boards, 2s. 6d. cloth.

The Two Chiefs of Dunboy; an Irish Romance of the Last Century. Crown 8vo. 6s.

Thomas Carlyle, a History of his Life. 1795 to 1835. 2 vols. crown 8vo. 7s. 1834 to 1881. 2 vols. crown 8vo. 7s.

GALLWEY.—Letters to Young Shooters. (First Series.) On the Choice and Use of a Gun. By Sir RALPH PAYNE-GALLWEY, Bart. With Illustrations. Crown 8vo. 7s. 6d.

GARDINER (Samuel Rawson)— Works by.

History of England, from the Accession of James I. to the Outbreak of the Civil War, 1603–1642. 10 vols. crown 8vo. price 6s. each.

A History of the Great Civil War, 1642–1649. (3 vols.) Vol. I. 1642–1644. With 24 Maps. 8vo. 21s. (*out of print*). Vol. II. 1644–1647. With 21 Maps. 8vo. 24s.

The Student's History of England. Illustrated under the superintendence of Mr. ST. JOHN HOPE, Secretary to the Society of Antiquaries. Vol. I. B.C. 55—A.D. 1509, with 173 Illustrations, crown 8vo. 4s. Vol. II. 1509–1689, with 96 Illustrations. Crown 8vo. 4s.

The work will be published in Three Volumes, and also in One Volume complete.

GIBERNE—Works by.

Ralph Hardcastle's Will. By AGNES GIBERNE. With Frontispiece. Crown 8vo. 5s.

Nigel Browning. Crown 8vo. 5s.

GOETHE.—Faust. A New Translation chiefly in Blank Verse ; with Introduction and Notes. By JAMES ADEY BIRDS. Crown 8vo. 6s.

Faust. The Second Part. A New Translation in Verse. By JAMES ADEY BIRDS. Crown 8vo. 6s.

GREEN.—The Works of Thomas Hill Green. Edited by R. L. NETTLESHIP (3 vols.) Vols. I. and II.— Philosophical Works. 8vo. 16s. each. Vol. III.—Miscellanies. With Index to the three Volumes and Memoir. 8vo. 21s.

The Witness of God and Faith : Two Lay Sermons. By T. H. GREEN. Fcp. 8vo. 2s.

GREVILLE.—A Journal of the Reigns of King George IV. King William IV. and Queen Victoria. By C. C. F. GREVILLE. Edited by H. REEVE. 8 vols. Cr. 8vo. 6s. ea.

GREY.—Last Words to Girls. On Life in School and after School. By Mrs. WILLIAM GREY. Cr 8vo. 3s. 6d.

GWILT. — An Encyclopædia of Architecture. By JOSEPH GWILT, F.S.A. Illustrated with more than 1,700 Engravings on Wood. 8vo. 52s. 6d.

HAGGARD.—Life and its Author : an Essay in Verse. By ELLA HAGGARD. With a Memoir by H. RIDER HAGGARD, and Portrait. Fcp. 8vo. 3s. 6d.

HAGGARD (H. Rider)—Works by.

She. With 32 Illustrations by M. GREIFFENHAGEN and C. H. M. KERR. Crown 8vo. 3s. 6d.

Allan Quatermain. With 31 Illustrations by C. H. M. KERR. Crown 8vo. 3s. 6d.

Maiwa's Revenge ; or, the War of the Little Hand. Crown 8vo 2s. boards ; 2s. 6d. cloth.

Colonel Quaritch, V.C. A Novel. Crown 8vo. 3s. 6d.

HAGGARD (H. Rider)—Works by—
continued.

Cleopatra : being an Account of the Fall and Vengeance of Harmachis, the Royal Egyptian. With 29 Full-page Illustrations by M. Greiffenhagen and R. Caton Woodville. Crown 8vo. 3s. 6d.

Beatrice. A Novel. Cr. 8vo. 6s.

HAGGARD and LANG.—The World's Desire. By H. RIDER HAGGARD and ANDREW LANG. Crown 8vo. 6s.

HARRISON.—Myths of the Odyssey in Art and Literature. Illustrated with Outline Drawings. By JANE E. HARRISON. 8vo. 18s.

HARRISON.—The Contemporary History of the French Revolution, compiled from the 'Annual Register.' By F. BAYFORD HARRISON. Crown 8vo. 3s. 6d.

HARTE (Bret)—Works by.

In the Carquinez Woods. Fcp. 8vo. 1s. boards ; 1s. 6d. cloth.

On the Frontier. 16mo. 1s.

By Shore and Sedge. 16mo. 1s.

HARTWIG (Dr.)—Works by.

The Sea and its Living Wonders. With 12 Plates and 303 Woodcuts. 8vo. 10s. 6d.

The Tropical World. With 8 Plates, and 172 Woodcuts. 8vo. 10s. 6d.

The Polar World. With 3 Maps, 8 Plates, and 85 Woodcuts. 8vo. 10s. 6d.

The Subterranean World. With 3 Maps and 80 Woodcuts. 8vo. 10s. 6d.

The Aerial World. With Map, 8 Plates, and 60 Woodcuts. 8vo. 10s. 6d.

The following books are extracted from the foregoing works by Dr. HARTWIG :—

Heroes of the Arctic Regions. With 19 Illustrations. Crown 8vo. 2s.

Wonders of the Tropical Forests. With 40 Illustrations. Crown 8vo. 2s.

Workers Under the Ground. or, Mines and Mining. With 29 Illustrations. Crown 8vo. 2s.

Marvels Over Our Heads. With 29 Illustrations. Crown 8vo. 2s.

Marvels Under Our Feet. With 22 Illustrations. Crown 8vo. 2s.

HARTWIG (Dr.)—Works by—*cont.*

Dwellers in the Arctic Regions. With 29 Illustrations. Crown 8vo. 2s. 6d.

Winged Life in the Tropics. With 55 Illustrations. Crown 8vo. 2s. 6d.

Volcanoes and Earthquakes. With 30 Illustrations. Crown 8vo. 2s. 6d.

Wild Animals of the Tropics. With 66 Illustrations. Crown 8vo. 3s. 6d.

Sea Monsters and Sea Birds. With 75 Illustrations. Crown 8vo. 2s. 6d.

Denizens of the Deep. With 117 Illustrations. Crown 8vo. 2s. 6d.

HAVELOCK. — Memoirs of Sir Henry Havelock, K.C.B. By JOHN CLARK MARSHMAN. Cr. 8vo. 3s. 6d.

HEARN (W. Edward)—Works by.

The Government of England ; its Structure and its Development. 8vo. 16s.

The Aryan Household : its Structure and its Development. An Introduction to Comparative Jurisprudence. 8vo. 16s.

HISTORIC TOWNS. Edited by E. A. FREEMAN, D.C.L. and Rev. WILLIAM HUNT, M.A. With Maps and Plans. Crown 8vo. 3s. 6d. each.

Bristol. By Rev. W. HUNT.

Carlisle. By Rev. MANDELL CREIGHTON.

Cinque Ports. By MONTAGU BURROWS.

Colchester. By Rev. E. L. CUTTS.

Exeter. By E. A. FREEMAN.

London. By Rev. W. J. LOFTIE.

Oxford. By Rev. C. W. BOASE.

Winchester. By Rev. G. W. KITCHIN, D.D.

New York. By THEODORE ROOSEVELT.

Boston (U.S.) By HENRY CABOT LODGE. *[In the press.*

York. By Rev. JAMES RAINE. *[In preparation.*

HODGSON (Shadworth H.)—Works by.

Time and Space : a Metaphysical Essay. 8vo. 16s.

The Theory of Practice: an Ethical Enquiry. 2 vols. 8vo. 24s.

The Philosophy of Reflection : 2 vols. 8vo. 21s.

[Continued on next page.

HODGSON (Shadworth H.)—Works by—*continued.*

Outcast Essays and Verse Translations. Essays: The Genius of De Quincey—De Quincey as Political Economist—The Supernatural in English Poetry; with Note on the True Symbol of Christian Union — English Verse. Verse Translations : Nineteen Passages from Lucretius, Horace, Homer, &c. Crown 8vo. 8*s.* 6*d.*

HOWITT.—Visits to Remarkable Places, Old Halls, Battle-Fields, Scenes illustrative of Striking Passages in English History and Poetry. By WILLIAM HOWITT. 80 Illustrations. Cr. 8vo. 3*s.* 6*d.*

HULLAH (John)—Works by.

Course of Lectures on the History of Modern Music. 8vo. 8*s.* 6*d.*

Course of Lectures on the Transition Period of Musical History. 8vo. 10*s.* 6*d.*

HUME.—The Philosophical Works of David Hume. Edited by T. H. GREEN and T. H. GROSE. 4 vols. 8vo. 56*s.* Or separately, Essays, 2 vols. 28*s.* Treatise of Human Nature. 2 vols. 28*s.*

HUTCHINSON (Horace)—Works by.

Cricketing Saws and Stories. By HORACE HUTCHINSON. With rectilinear Illustrations by the Author. 16mo. 1*s.*

Some Great Golf Links. Edited by HORACE HUTCHINSON. With Illustrations.
This book is mainly a reprint of articles that have recently appeared in the *Saturday Review.*

HUTH.—The Marriage of Near Kin, considered with respect to the Law of Nations, the Result of Experience, and the Teachings of Biology. By ALFRED H. HUTH. Royal 8vo. 21*s.*

INGELOW (Jean)—Works by.

Poetical Works. Vols. I. and II. Fcp. 8vo. 12*s.* Vol. III. Fcp. 8vo. 5*s.*

Lyrical and Other Poems. Selected from the Writings of JEAN INGELOW. Fcp. 8vo. 2*s.* 6*d.* cloth plain ; 3*s.* cloth gilt.

Very Young and Quite Another Story : Two Stories. Crown 8vo. 6*s.*

JAMES.—The Long White Mountain ; or, a Journey in Manchuria, with an Account of the History, Administration, and Religion of that Province. By H. E. JAMES. With Illustrations. 8vo. 24*s.*

JAMESON (Mrs.)—Works by.

Legends of the Saints and Martyrs. With 19 Etchings and 187 Woodcuts. 2 vols. 8vo. 20*s.* *net.*

Legends of the Madonna, the Virgin Mary as represented in Sacred and Legendary Art. With 27 Etchings and 165 Woodcuts. 1 vol. 8vo. 10*s.* *net.*

Legends of the Monastic Orders. With 11 Etchings and 88 Woodcuts. 1 vol. 8vo. 10*s.* *net.*

History of Our Lord, His Types and Precursors. Completed by Lady EASTLAKE. With 31 Etchings and 281 Woodcuts. 2 vols. 8vo. 20*s.* *net.*

JEFFERIES.—Field and Hedgerow : last Essays of RICHARD JEFFERIES. Crown 8vo. 3*s.* 6*d.*

JENNINGS.—Ecclesia Anglicana. A History of the Church of Christ in England, from the Earliest to the Present Times. By the Rev. ARTHUR CHARLES JENNINGS, M.A. Crown 8vo. 7*s.* 6*d.*

JESSOP (G. H.)—Works by.

Judge Lynch : a Tale of the California Vineyards. Crown 8vo. 6*s.*

Gerald Ffrench's Friends. Cr. 8vo. 6*s.* A collection of Irish-American character stories.

JOHNSON. — The Patentee's Manual ; a Treatise on the Law and Practice of Letters Patent. By J. JOHNSON and J. H. JOHNSON. 8vo. 10*s.* 6*d.*

JORDAN (William Leighton) — The Standard of Value. By WILLIAM LEIGHTON JORDAN. 8vo. 6*s.*

JUSTINIAN. — The Institutes of Justinian ; Latin Text, chiefly that of Huschke, with English Introduction. Translation, Notes, and Summary. By THOMAS C. SANDARS, M.A. 8vo. 18*s.*

KALISCH (M. M.)—Works by.

Bible Studies. Part I. The Prophecies of Balaam. 8vo. 10*s.* 6*d.* Part II. The Book of Jonah. 8vo 10*s.* 6*d.*

KALISCH (M. M.)—Works by—*contd.*

Commentary on the Old Testament; with a New Translation. Vol. I. Genesis, 8vo. 18*s.* or adapted for the General Reader, 12*s.* Vol. II. Exodus, 15*s.* or adapted for the General Reader, 12*s.* Vol. III. Leviticus, Part I. 15*s.* or adapted for the General Reader, 8*s.* Vol. IV. Leviticus, Part II. 15*s.* or adapted for the General Reader, 8*s.*

Hebrew Grammar. With Exercises. Part I. 8vo. 12*s.* 6*d.* Key, 5*s.* Part II. 12*s.* 6*d.*

KANT (Immanuel)—Works by.

Critique of Practical Reason, and other Works on the Theory of Ethics. Translated by T. K. Abbott, B.D. With Memoir. 8vo. 12*s.* 6*d.*

Introduction to Logic, and his Essay on the Mistaken Subtilty of the Four Figures. Translated by T. K. Abbott. Notes by S. T. Coleridge. 8vo. 6*s.*

KENDALL (May)—Works by.

From a Garrett. Crown 8vo. 6*s.*

Dreams to Sell; Poems. Fcp. 8vo. 6*s.*

'Such is Life': a Novel. Crown 8vo. 6*s.*

KILLICK. — Handbook to Mill's System of Logic. By the Rev. A. H. Killick, M.A. Crown 8vo. 3*s.* 6*d.*

KNIGHT. — The Cruise of the 'Alerte': the Narrative of a Search for Treasure on the Desert Island of Trinidad. By E. F. Knight, Author of 'The Cruise of the "Falcon."' With 2 Maps and 23 Illustrations. Crown 8vo. 10*s.* 6*d.*

LADD (George T.)—Works by.

Elements of Physiological Psychology. 8vo. 21*s.*

Outlines of Physiological Psychology. A Text-Book of Mental Science for Academies and Colleges. 8vo. 12*s.*

LANG (Andrew)—Works by.

Custom and Myth: Studies of Early Usage and Belief. With 15 Illustrations. Crown 8vo. 7*s.* 6*d.*

Books and Bookmen. With 2 Coloured Plates and 17 Illustrations. Cr. 8vo. 6*s.* 6*d.*

LANG (Andrew)—Works by—*contd.*

Grass of Parnassus. A Volume of Selected Verses. Fcp. 8vo. 6*s.*

Letters on Literature. Crown 8vo. 6*s.* 6*d.*

Old Friends: Essays in Epistolary Parody. 6*s.* 6*d.*

Ballads of Books. Edited by Andrew Lang. Fcp. 8vo. 6*s.*

The Blue Fairy Book. Edited by Andrew Lang. With 8 Plates and 130 Illustrations in the Text by H. J. Ford and G. P. Jacomb Hood. Crown 8vo. 6*s.*

The Red Fairy Book. Edited by Andrew Lang. With 4 Plates and 96 Illustrations in the Text by H. J. Ford and Lancelot Speed. Crown 8vo. 6*s.*

LAVIGERIE.—Cardinal Lavigerie and the African Slave Trade. 1 vol. 8vo. 14*s.*

LAYARD.—Poems. By Nina F Layard. Crown 8vo. 6*s.*

LECKY (W. E. H.)—Works by.

History of England in the Eighteenth Century. 8vo. Vols. I. & II. 1700–1760. 36*s.* Vols. III. & IV. 1760–1784. 36*s.* Vols. V. & VI. 1784–1793. 36*s.* Vols. VII. & VIII. 1793–1800. 36*s.*

The History of European Morals from Augustus to Charlemagne. 2 vols. crown 8vo. 16*s.*

History of the Rise and Influence of the Spirit of Rationalism in Europe. 2 vols. crown 8vo. 16*s.*

LEES and CLUTTERBUCK. — B. C. 1887, A Ramble in British Columbia. By J. A. Lees and W. J. Clutterbuck. With Map and 75 Illustrations. Crown 8vo. 6*s.*

LEGER.—A History of Austro-Hungary. From the Earliest Time to the year 1889. By Louis Leger. Translated from the French by Mrs. Birkbeck Hill. With a Preface by E. A. Freeman, D.C.L. Crown 8vo. 10*s.* 6*d.*

LEWES.—The History of Philosophy, from Thales to Comte. By George Henry Lewes. 2 vols. 8vo. 32*s.*

LIDDELL.—Memoirs of the Tenth Royal Hussars : Historical and Social. By Colonel LIDDELL. With Portraits and Coloured Illustration. 2 vols. Imperial 8vo.

LLOYD.—The Science of Agriculture. By F. J. LLOYD. 8vo. 12s.

LONGMAN (Frederick W.)—Works by.

Chess Openings. Fcp. 8vo. 2s. 6d.

Frederick the Great and the Seven Years' War. Fcp. 8vo. 2s. 6d.

Longman's Magazine. Published Monthly. Price Sixpence.
Vols. 1-16, 8vo. price 5s. each.

Longmans' New Atlas. Political and Physical. For the Use of Schools and Private Persons. Consisting of 40 Quarto and 16 Octavo Maps and Diagrams, and 16 Plates of Views. Edited by GEO. G. CHISHOLM, M.A. B.Sc. Imp. 4to. or imp. 8vo. 12s. 6d.

LOUDON (J. C.)—Works by.

Encyclopædia of Gardening. With 1,000 Woodcuts. 8vo. 21s.

Encyclopædia of Agriculture ; the Laying-out, Improvement, and Management of Landed Property. With 1,100 Woodcuts. 8vo. 21s.

Encyclopædia of Plants ; the Specific Character, &c. of all Plants found in Great Britain. With 12,000 Woodcuts. 8vo. 42s.

LUBBOCK.—The Origin of Civilisation and the Primitive Condition of Man. By Sir J. LUBBOCK, Bart. M.P. With 5 Plates and 20 Illustrations in the text. 8vo. 18s.

LYALL.—The Autobiography of a Slander. By EDNA LYALL, Author of 'Donovan,' &c. Fcp. 8vo. 1s. sewed.

LYDE.—An Introduction to Ancient History : being a Sketch of the History of Egypt, Mesopotamia, Greece, and Rome. With a Chapter on the Development of the Roman Empire into the Powers of Modern Europe. By LIONEL W. LYDE, M.A. With 3 Coloured Maps. Crown 8vo. 3s.

MACAULAY (Lord).—Works of.

Complete Works of Lord Macaulay.
Library Edition, 8 vols. 8vo. £5. 5s.
Cabinet Edition, 16 vols. post 8vo. £4. 16s.

History of England from the Accession of James the Second.
Popular Edition, 2 vols. crown 8vo. 5s.
Student's Edition, 2 vols. crown 8vo. 12s.
People's Edition, 4 vols. crown 8vo. 16s.
Cabinet Edition, 8 vols. post 8vo. 48s.
Library Edition, 5 vols. 8vo. £4.

Critical and Historical Essays, with Lays of Ancient Rome, in 1 volume :
Popular Edition, crown 8vo. 2s. 6d.
Authorised Edition, crown 8vo. 2s. 6d. or 3s. 6d. gilt edges.

Critical and Historical Essays :
Student's Edition, 1 vol. crown 8vo. 6s.
People's Edition, 2 vols. crown 8vo. 8s.
Trevelyan Edition, 2 vols. crown 8vo. 9s.
Cabinet Edition, 4 vols. post 8vo. 24s.
Library Edition, 3 vols. 8vo. 36s.

Essays which may be had separately price 6d. each sewed, 1s. each cloth :
Addison and Walpole.
Frederick the Great.
Croker's Boswell's Johnson.
Hallam's Constitutional History.
Warren Hastings. (3d. sewed, 6d. cloth.)
The Earl of Chatham (Two Essays).
Ranke and Gladstone.
Milton and Machiavelli.
Lord Bacon.
Lord Clive.
Lord Byron, and The Comic Dramatists of the Restoration.

The Essay on Warren Hastings annotated by S. HALES, 1s. 6d.
The Essay on Lord Clive annotated by H. COURTHOPE BOWEN, M.A. 2s. 6d.

Speeches :
People's Edition, crown 8vo. 3s. 6d.

Lays of Ancient Rome, &c.
Illustrated by G. Scharf, fcp. 4to. 10s. 6d.
——————— Bijou Edition, 18mo. 2s. 6d. gilt top.
——————— Popular Edition, fcp. 4to. 6d. sewed, 1s. cloth.
Illustrated by J. R. Weguelin, crown 8vo. 3s. 6d. cloth extra, gilt edges.
Cabinet Edition, post 8vo. 3s. 6d.
Annotated Edit. fcp. 8vo. 1s. sewed, 1s. 6d. cl.

MACAULAY (Lord)—Works of —
continued.

Miscellaneous Writings:
People's Edition, 1 vol. crown 8vo. 4*s.* 6*d.*
Library Edition, 2 vols. 8vo. 21*s.*

Miscellaneous Writings and Speeches:
Popular edition, 1 vol. crown 8vo. 2*s.* 6*d.*
Student's Edition, in 1 vol. crown 8vo. 6*s.*
Cabinet Edition, including Indian Penal Code, Lays of Ancient Rome, and Miscellaneous Poems, 4 vols. post 8vo. 24*s.*

Selections from the Writings of Lord Macaulay. Edited, with Occasional Notes, by the Right Hon. Sir G. O. TREVELYAN, Bart. Crown 8vo. 6*s.*

The Life and Letters of Lord Macaulay. By the Right Hon. Sir G. O. TREVELYAN, Bart.
Popular Edition, 1 vol. crown 8vo. 2*s.* 6*d.*
Student's Edition, 1 vol. crown 8vo. 6*s.* .
Cabinet Edition, 2 vols. post 8vo. 12*s.*
Library Edition, 2 vols. 8vo. 36*s.*

MACDONALD (Geo.)—Works by.

Unspoken Sermons. Three Series. Crown 8vo. 3*s.* 6*d.* each.

The Miracles of Our Lord. Crown 8vo. 3*s.* 6*d.*

A Book of Strife, in the Form of the Diary of an Old Soul: Poems. 12mo. 6*s.*

MACFARREN—Lectures on Harmony. By Sir G. A. MACFARREN. 8vo. 12*s.*

MACKAIL.—Select Epigrams from the Greek Anthology. Edited, with a Revised Text, Introduction, Translation, and Notes, by J. W. MACKAIL, M.A. Fellow of Balliol College, Oxford. 8vo. 16*s.*

MACLEOD (Henry D.)—Works by.

The Elements of Banking. Crown 8vo. 5*s.*

The Theory and Practice of Banking. Vol. I. 8vo. 12*s.* Vol. II. 14*s.*

The Theory of Credit. 8vo. Vol. I. 7*s.* 6*d.* ; Vol. II. Part I. 4*s.* 6*d.* ; Vol. II. Part II. 10*s.* 6*d.*

McCULLOCH—The Dictionary of Commerce and Commercial Navigation of the late J. R. McCULLOCH. 8vo. with 11 Maps and 30 Charts, 63*s.*

MALMESBURY.— Memoirs of an Ex-Minister. By the Earl of MALMESBURY. Crown 8vo. 7*s.* 6*d.*

MANUALS OF CATHOLIC PHILOSOPHY (*Stonyhurst Series*):

Logic. By RICHARD F. CLARKE, S.J. Crown 8vo. 5*s.*

First Principles of Knowledge. By JOHN RICKABY, S.J. Crown 8vo. 5*s.*

Moral Philosophy (Ethics and Natural Law). By JOSEPH RICKABY, S.J. Crown 8vo. 5*s.*

General Metaphysics. By JOHN RICKABY, S.J. Crown 8vo. 5*s.*

Psychology. By MICHAEL MAHER, S.J. Crown 8vo. 6*s.* 6*d.*

Natural Theology. By BERNARD BOEDDER, S.J. Crown 8vo. 6*s.* 6*d.*
[*Nearly ready.*

A Manual of Political Economy. By C. S. DEVAS, Esq. M.A. Examiner in Political Economy in the Royal University of Ireland. 6*s.* 6*d.* [*In preparation.*

MARTINEAU (James)—Works by.

Hours of Thought on Sacred Things. Two Volumes of Sermons. 2 vols. crown 8vo. 7*s.* 6*d.* each.

Endeavours after the Christian Life. Discourses. Crown 8vo. 7*s.* 6*d.*

The Seat of Authority in Religion. 8vo. 14*s.*

Essays, Reviews and Addresses. 4 vols. crown 8vo. 7*s.* 6*d.* each.
I. Personal: Political.	III. Theological: Philosophical.
II. Ecclesiastical : Historical.	IV. Academical : Religious.

[*In course of publication.*

MASON.—The Steps of the Sun: Daily Readings of Prose. Selected by AGNES MASON. 16mo. 3*s.* 6*d.*

MAUNDER'S TREASURIES.

Biographical Treasury. With Supplement brought down to 1889, by Rev. JAS. WOOD. Fcp. 8vo. 6*s.*

Treasury of Natural History; or, Popular Dictionary of Zoology. Fcp. 8vo. with 900 Woodcuts, 6*s.*

Treasury of Geography, Physical, Historical, Descriptive, and Political. With 7 Maps and 16 Plates. Fcp. 8vo. 9*s.*

[*Continued on next page.*

MAUNDER'S TREASURIES
—continued.

Scientific and Literary Treasury. Fcp. 8vo. 6s.

Historical Treasury: Outlines of Universal History, Separate Histories of all Nations. Fcp. 8vo. 6s.

Treasury of Knowledge and Library of Reference. Comprising an English Dictionary and Grammar, Universal Gazetteer, Classical Dictionary, Chronology, Law Dictionary, &c. Fcp. 8vo. 6s.

The Treasury of Bible Knowledge. By the Rev. J. AYRE, M.A. With 5 Maps, 15 Plates, and 300 Woodcuts. Fcp. 8vo. 6s.

The Treasury of Botany. Edited by J. LINDLEY, F.R.S. and T. MOORE, F.L.S.. With 274 Woodcuts and 20 Steel Plates. 2 vols. fcp. 8vo. 12s.

MAX MÜLLER (F.)—Works by.

Selected Essays on Language, Mythology and Religion. 2 vols. crown 8vo. 16s.

Lectures on the Science of Language. 2 vols. crown 8vo. 16s.

Hibbert Lectures on the Origin and Growth of Religion, as illustrated by the Religions of India. Crown 8vo. 7s. 6d.

Introduction to the Science of Religion; Four Lectures delivered at the Royal Institution. Crown 8vo. 7s. 6d.

Natural Religion. The Gifford Lectures, delivered before the University of Glasgow in 1888. Crown 8vo. 10s. 6d.

Physical Religion. The Gifford Lectures, delivered before the University of Glasgow in 1890. Crown 8vo. 10s. 6d.

The Science of Thought. 8vo. 21s.

Three Introductory Lectures on the Science of Thought. 8vo. 2s. 6d.

Biographies of Words, and the Home of the Aryas. Cr 8vo. 7s.6d

A Sanskrit Grammar for Beginners. New and Abridged Edition. By A. A. MACDONELL. Crown 8vo. 6s.

MAY.—The Constitutional History of England since the Accession of George III. 1760-1870. By the Right Hon. Sir THOMAS ERSKINE MAY, K.C.B. 3 vols. crown 8vo. 18s.

MEADE (L. T.)—Works by.

The O'Donnells of Inchfawn. With Frontispiece by A. CHASEMORE. Crown 8vo. 6s.

Daddy's Boy. With Illustrations. Crown 8vo. 5s.

Deb and the Duchess. With Illustrations by M. E. EDWARDS. Crown 8vo. 5s.

House of Surprises. With Illustrations by EDITH M. SCANNELL. Crown 8vo. 3s. 6d.

The Beresford Prize. With Illustrations by M. E. EDWARDS. Crown 8vo. 5s.

MEATH (The Earl of)—Works by.

Social Arrows: Reprinted Articles on various Social Subjects. Cr. 8vo. 5s.

Prosperity or Pauperism? Physical, Industrial, and Technical Training. (Edited by the EARL OF MEATH). 8vo. 5s.

MELVILLE (G. J. Whyte)—Novels by. Crown 8vo. 1s. each, boards; 1s. 6d. each, cloth.

The Gladiators.	Holmby House.
The Interpreter.	Kate Coventry.
Good for Nothing.	Digby Grand.
The Queen's Maries.	General Bounce.

MENDELSSOHN.—The Letters of Felix Mendelssohn. Translated by Lady WALLACE. 2 vols. cr. 8vo. 10s.

MERIVALE (The Very Rev. Chas.)—Works by.

History of the Romans under the Empire. Cabinet Edition, 8 vols. crown 8vo. 48s.
Popular Edition, 8 vols. crown 8vo. 3s. 6d. each.

The Fall of the Roman Republic: a Short History of the Last Century of the Commonwealth. 12mo. 7s. 6d.

General History of Rome from B.C. 753 to A.D. 476. Cr. 8vo. 7s. 6d.

MERIVALE (The Very Rev. Chas.)—
Works by—*continued.*

The Roman Triumvirates. With
Maps. Fcp. 8vo. 2*s.* 6*d.*

MILES.—The Correspondence
of William Augustus Miles
on the French Revolution,
1789-1817. Edited by the Rev.
CHARLES POPHAM MILES, M.A. F.L.S.
Honorary Canon of Durham, Membre
de la Société d'Histoire Diplomatique.
2 vols. 8vo. 32*s.*

MILL.—Analysis of the Phenomena of the Human Mind.
By JAMES MILL. 2 vols. 8vo. 28*s.*

MILL (John Stuart)—Works by.

Principles of Political Economy.
Library Edition, 2 vols. 8vo. 30*s.*
People's Edition, 1 vol. crown 8vo. 5*s.*

A System of Logic. Cr. 8vo. 5*s.*

On Liberty. Crown 8vo. 1*s.* 4*d.*

On Representative Government.
Crown 8vo. 2*s.*

Utilitarianism. 8vo. 5*s.*

Examination of Sir William
Hamilton's Philosophy. 8vo. 16*s.*

Nature, the Utility of Religion,
and Theism. Three Essays. 8vo. 5*s.*

MOLESWORTH (Mrs.)—Works by.

Marrying and Giving in Marriage : a Novel. By Mrs. MOLES-
WORTH. Fcp. 8vo. 2*s.* 6*d.*

Silverthorns. With Illustrations by
F. NOEL PATON. Crown 8vo. 5*s.*

The Palace in the Garden. With
Illustrations by HARRIET M. BENNETT.
Crown 8vo. 5*s.*

The Third Miss St. Quentin.
Crown 8vo. 6*s.*

Neighbours. With Illustrations by
M. ELLEN EDWARDS. Crown 8vo. 6*s.*

The Story of a Spring Morning,
&c. With Illustrations by M. ELLEN
EDWARDS. Crown 8vo. 5*s.*

MOON (G. Washington)—Works by.

The King's English. Fcp. 8vo.
3*s.* 6*d.*

The Soul's Inquiries Answered
in the Words of Scripture.
A Year-Book of Scripture Texts.
Pocket Edition. Royal 32mo. 2*s.* 6*d.*
Common Edition. Royal 32mo. 8*d.* limp;
1*s.* 6*d.* cloth.

The Soul's Desires Breathed to
God in the Words of Scrip-
ture : being Prayers, and a Treatise on
Prayer in the Language of the Bible.
Royal 32mo. 2*s.* 6*d.*

MOORE.—Dante and his Early
Biographers. By EDWARD MOORE,
D.D. Principal of St. Edmund Hall,
Oxford. Crown 8vo. 4*s.* 6*d.*

MULHALL.— History of Prices
since the Year 1850. By MICHAEL
G. MULHALL. Crown 8vo. 6*s.*

MURDOCK.—The Reconstruction
of Europe : a Sketch of the Diplo-
matic and Military History of Continental Europe, from the Rise to the
Fall of the Second French Empire. By
HENRY MURDOCK. Crown 8vo. 9*s.*

MURRAY.—A Dangerous Cats-
paw : a Story. By DAVID CHRISTIE
MURRAY and HENRY MURRAY. Cr. 8vo.
2*s.* 6*d.*

MURRAY and HERMAN. — Wild
Darrie : a Story. By CHRISTIE MURRAY
and HENRY HERMAN. Crown 8vo. 2*s.*
boards ; 2*s.* 6*d.* cloth.

NANSEN.—The First Crossing of
Greenland. By Dr. FRIDTJOF
NANSEN. With 5 Maps, 12 Plates, and
150 Illustrations in the Text. 2 vols.
8vo. 36*s.*

NAPIER.—The Life of Sir Joseph
Napier, Bart. Ex-Lord Chancellor of Ireland. By ALEX.
CHARLES EWALD, F.S.A. With Portrait.
8vo. 15*s.*

NAPIER.—The Lectures, Essays,
and Letters of the Right Hon.
Sir Joseph Napier, Bart. late
Lord Chancellor of Ireland. 8vo. 12*s.* 6*d.*

NESBIT—Leaves of Life: Verses.
By E. NESBIT.   Crown 8vo. 5s.

NEWMAN.—The Letters and Correspondence of John Henry
Newman during his Life in the
English Church. With a brief Autobio-
graphical Memoir. Arranged and Edited,
at Cardinal Newman's request, by Miss
ANNE MOZLEY, Editor of the 'Letters
of the Rev. J. B. Mozley, D.D.' With
Portraits, 2 vols. 8vo. 30s. net.

NEWMAN (Cardinal)—Works by.

Apologia pro Vitâ Sua.   Cabinet
Edition, cr. 8vo. 6s.   Cheap Edition, 3s. 6d.

Sermons to Mixed Congrega-
tions.   Crown 8vo. 6s.

Occasional Sermons.   Crown 8vo.
6s.

The Idea of a University defined
and illustrated.   Crown 8vo. 7s.

Historical Sketches.   3 vols.
crown 8vo. 6s. each.

The Arians of the Fourth Century.   Cabinet Edition, crown 8vo. 6s.
Cheap Edition, crown 8vo. 3s. 6d.

Select Treatises of St. Athan-
asius in Controversy with the Arians.
Freely Translated.   2 vols. cr. 8vo. 15s.

Discussions and Arguments on
Various Subjects. Cabinet Edition,
crown 8vo. 6s.   Cheap Edition, crown
8vo. 3s. 6d.

An Essay on the Development
of Christian Doctrine.   Cabinet
Edition, crown 8vo. 6s.   Cheap Edition,
crown 8vo. 3s. 6d.

Certain Difficulties felt by
Anglicans in Catholic Teaching Considered.   Vol. 1, crown
8vo. 7s. 6d.; Vol. 2, crown 8vo. 5s. 6d.

The Via Media of the Anglican
Church, illustrated in Lectures, &c.
2 vols. crown 8vo. 6s. each.

Essays, Critical and Historical.
Cabinet Edition, 2 vols. crown 8vo. 12s.
Cheap Edition, 2 vols. crown 8vo. 7s.

Essays on Biblical and on Ecclesiastical Miracles.   Cabinet
Edition, crown 8vo. 6s.   Cheap Edition,
crown 8vo. 3s. 6d.   •

NEWMAN (Cardinal)—Works by—
continued.

Tracts.   1. Dissertatiunculæ. 2. On
the Text of the Seven Epistles of St.
Ignatius. 3. Doctrinal Causes of Arian-
ism. 4. Apollinarianism. 5. St. Cyril's
Formula. 6. Ordo de Tempore. 7.
Douay Version of Scripture.   Crown 8vo.
8s.

An Essay in Aid of a Grammar
of Assent.   Cabinet Edition, crown
8vo. 7s. 6d.   Cheap Edition, crown 8vo.
3s. 6d.

Present Position of Catholics in
England.   Crown 8vo. 7s. 6d.

Callista : a Tale of the Third Century.   Cabinet Edition, crown 8vo. 6s.
Cheap Edition, crown 8vo. 3s. 6d.

Loss and Gain: a Tale.   Crown
8vo. 6s.

The Dream of Gerontius.   16mo.
6d. sewed, 1s. cloth.

Verses on Various Occasions.
Cabinet Edition, crown 8vo. 6s.   Cheap
Edition, crown 8vo. 3s. 6d.

** For Cardinal Newman's other Works
see Messrs. Longmans & Co.'s Catalogue
of Theological Works.

NORRIS.—Mrs. Fenton: a Sketch.
By W. E. NORRIS.   Crown 8vo. 6s.

NORTON (Charles L.)—Works by.

Political Americanisms : a Glos-
sary of Terms and Phrases Current at
Different Periods in American Politics.

A Handbook of Florida.   With
49 Maps and Plans.   Fcp. 8vo. 5s.

NORTHCOTT.—Lathes and Turning, Simple, Mechanical, and Orna-
mental.   By W. H. NORTHCOTT.   With
338 Illustrations.   8vo. 18s.

O'BRIEN.—When we were Boys :
a Novel.   By WILLIAM O'BRIEN, M.P.
Cabinet Edition, crown 8vo. 6s.   Cheap
Edition, crown 8vo. 2s. 6d.

OLIPHANT (Mrs.)—Novels by.

Madam.   Cr. 8vo. 1s. bds.; 1s. 6d. cl.

In Trust.   Cr. 8vo. 1s. bds.; 1s. 6d. cl.

Lady Car : the Sequel of a Life.
Crown 8vo. 2s. 6d.

OMAN.—A History of Greece from the Earliest Times to the Macedonian Conquest. By C. W. C. OMAN, M.A. F.S.A. Fellow of All Souls College, and Lecturer at New College, Oxford. With Maps and Plans. Crown 8vo. 4s. 6d.

O'REILLY.—Hurstleigh Dene : a Tale. By Mrs. O'REILLY. Illustrated by M. ELLEN EDWARDS. Crown 8vo. 5s.

PAYN (James)—Novels by.

The Luck of the Darrells. Cr. 8vo. 1s. boards; 1s. 6d. cloth.

Thicker than Water. Crown 8vo. 1s. boards; 1s. 6d. cloth.

PERRING (Sir PHILIP)—Works by.

Hard Knots in Shakespeare. 8vo. 7s. 6d.

The 'Works and Days' of Moses. Crown 8vo. 3s. 6d.

PHILLIPPS-WOLLEY.—Snap: a Legend of the Lone Mountain. By C. PHILLIPPS-WOLLEY, Author of 'Sport in the Crimea and Caucasus' &c. With 13 Illustrations by H. G. WILLINK. Crown 8vo. 6s.

POLE.—The Theory of the Modern Scientific Game of Whist. By W. POLE, F.R.S. Fcp. 8vo. 2s. 6d.

POLLOCK.—The Seal of Fate: a Novel. By W. H. POLLOCK and Lady POLLOCK. Crown 8vo.

PRENDERGAST.—Ireland, from the Restoration to the Revolution, 1660-1690. By JOHN P. PRENDERGAST. 8vo. 5s.

PRINSEP.—Virginie: a Tale of One Hundred Years Ago. By VAL PRINSEP, A.R.A. 3 vols. crown 8vo. 25s. 6d.

PROCTOR (R. A.)—Works by.

Old and New Astronomy. 12 Parts, 2s. 6d. each. Supplementary Section, 1s. Complete in 1 vol. 4to. 36s. [*In course of publication.*

The Orbs Around Us ; a Series of Essays on the Moon and Planets, Meteors and Comets. With Chart and Diagrams. Crown 8vo. 5s.

PROCTOR (R. A.)—Works by—*cont.*

Other Worlds than Ours; The Plurality of Worlds Studied under the Light of Recent Scientific Researches. With 14 Illustrations. Crown 8vo. 5s.

The Moon ; her Motions, Aspects, Scenery, and Physical Condition. With Plates, Charts, Woodcuts, &c. Cr. 8vo. 5s.

Universe of Stars ; Presenting Researches into and New Views respecting the Constitution of the Heavens. With 22 Charts and 22 Diagrams. 8vo. 10s. 6d.

Larger Star Atlas for the Library, in 12 Circular Maps, with Introduction and 2 Index Pages. Folio, 15s. or Maps only, 12s. 6d.

The Student's Atlas. In Twelve Circular Maps on a Uniform Projection and one Scale. 8vo. 5s.

New Star Atlas for the Library, the School, and the Observatory, in 12 Circular Maps. Crown 8vo. 5s.

Light Science for Leisure Hours; Familiar Essays on Scientific Subjects. 3 vols. crown 8vo. 5s. each.

Chance and Luck ; a Discussion of the Laws of Luck, Coincidences, Wagers, Lotteries, and the Fallacies of Gambling &c. Crown 8vo. 2s. boards ; 2s. 6d. cloth.

Studies of Venus-Transits. With 7 Diagrams and 10 Plates. 8vo. 5s.

How to Play Whist : with the Laws and Etiquette of Whist. Crown 8vo. 3s. 6d.

ome Whist: an Easy Guide to Correct Play. 16mo 1s.

The Stars in their Seasons. An Easy Guide to a Knowledge of the Star Groups, in 12 Maps. Roy. 8vo. 5s.

Star Primer. Showing the Starry Sky Week by Week, in 24 Hourly Maps. Crown 4to. 2s. 6d.

The Seasons Pictured in 48 Sun-Views of the Earth, and 24 Zodiacal Maps, &c. Demy 4to. 5s.

Strength and Happiness. With 9 Illustrations. Crown 8vo. 5s. [*Continued on next page.*

PROCTOR (R. A.)—Works by—*cont.*

Strength : How to get Strong and keep Strong, with Chapters on Rowing and Swimming, Fat, Age, and the Waist. With 9 Illustrations. Crown 8vo. 2s.

Rough Ways Made Smooth. Familiar Essays on Scientific Subjects. Crown 8vo. 5s.

Our Place Among Infinities. A Series of Essays contrasting our Little Abode in Space and Time with the Infinities Around us. Crown 8vo. 5s.

The Expanse of Heaven. Essays on the Wonders of the Firmament. Crown 8vo. 5s.

The Great Pyramid, Observatory, Tomb, and Temple. With Illustrations. Crown 8vo. 5s.

Pleasant Ways in Science. Crown 8vo. 5s.

Myths and Marvels of Astronomy. Crown 8vo. 5s.

Nature Studies. By Grant Allen, A. Wilson, T. Foster, E. Clodd, and R. A. Proctor. Crown 8vo. 5s.

Leisure Readings. By E. Clodd, A. Wilson, T. Foster, A. C. Ranyard, and R. A. Proctor. Crown 8vo. 5s.

PRYCE.—The Ancient British Church : an Historical Essay. By John Pryce, M.A. Crown 8vo. 6s.

RANSOME.—The Rise of Constitutional Government in England : being a Series of Twenty Lectures on the History of the English Constitution delivered to a Popular Audience. By Cyril Ransome, M.A. Crown 8vo. 6s.

RAWLINSON.— The History of Phœnicia. By George Rawlinson, M.A. Canon of Canterbury, &c. With numerous Illustrations. 8vo. 24s.

READER.—Echoes of Thought : a Medley of Verse. By Emily E. Reader. Fcp. 8vo. 5s. cloth, gilt top.

RENDLE and NORMAN.—The Inns of Old Southwark, and their Associations. By William Rendle, F.R.C.S. and Philip Norman, F.S.A. With numerous Illustrations. Roy.8vo.28s.

RIBOT.—The Psychology of Attention. By Th. Ribot. Crown 8vo. 3s.

RICH.—A Dictionary of Roman and Greek Antiquities. With 2,000 Woodcuts. By A. Rich. Cr. 8vo. 7s. 6d.

RICHARDSON.—National Health. Abridged from 'The Health of Nations.' A Review of the Works of Sir Edwin Chadwick, K.C.B. By Dr. B. W. Richardson. Crown, 4s. 6d.

RILEY.—Athos ; or, the Mountain of the Monks. By Athelstan Riley, M.A. F.R.G.S. With Map and 29 Illustrations. 8vo. 21s.

RIVERS. — The Miniature Fruit Garden ; or, the Culture of Pyramidal and Bush Fruit Trees. By Thomas Rivers. With 32 Illustrations. Fcp. 8vo. 4s.

ROBERTS.—Greek the Language of Christ and His Apostles. By Alexander Roberts, D.D. 8vo. 18s.

ROGET.—A History of the 'Old Water-Colour' Society (now the Royal Society of Painters in Water-Colours). With Biographical Notices of its Older and all its *Deceased* Members and Associates. Preceded by an Account of English Water-Colour Art and Artists in the Eighteenth Century. By John Lewis Roget, M.A. Barrister-at-Law. 2 vols. royal 8vo.

ROGET.—Thesaurus of English Words and Phrases. Classified and Arranged so as to facilitate the Expression of Ideas. By Peter M. Roget. Crown 8vo. 10s. 6d

RONALDS.—The Fly-Fisher's Entomology. By Alfred Ronalds. With 20 Coloured Plates. 8vo. 14s.

ROSSETTI.—A Shadow of Dante : being an Essay towards studying Himself, his World, and his Pilgrimage. By MARIA FRANCESCA ROSSETTI. With Illustrations. Crown 8vo. 10s. 6d.

RUSSELL.—A Life of Lord John Russell (Earl Russell, K.G.). By SPENCER WALPOLE. With 2 Portraits. 2 vols. 8vo. 36s. Cabinet Edition, 2 vols. crown 8vo. 12s.

SEEBOHM (Frederic)—Works by.

The Oxford Reformers—John Colet, Erasmus, and Thomas More ; a History of their Fellow-Work. 8vo. 14s.

The Era of the Protestant Revolution. With Map. Fcp. 8vo. 2s. 6d.

The English Village Community Examined in its Relations to the Manorial and Tribal Systems, &c, 13 Maps and Plates. 8vo. 16s.

SEWELL.—Stories and Tales. By ELIZABETH M. SEWELL. Crown 8vo. 1s. 6d. each, cloth plain ; 2s. 6d. each, cloth extra, gilt edges :—

Amy Herbert.	Laneton Parsonage.
The Earl's Daughter.	Ursula.
The Experience of Life.	Gertrude.
A Glimpse of the World.	Ivors.
Cleve Hall.	Home Life.
Katharine Ashton.	After Life.
Margaret Percival.	

SHAKESPEARE.—Bowdler's Family Shakespeare. 1 vol. 8vo. With 36 Woodcuts, 14s. or in 6 vols. fcp. 8vo. 21s.

Outlines of the Life of Shakespeare. By J. O. HALLIWELL-PHILLIPPS. 2 vols. Royal 8vo. £1. 1s.

Shakespeare's True Life. By JAMES WALTER. With 500 Illustrations. Imp. 8vo. 21s.

The Shakespeare Birthday Book. By MARY F. DUNBAR. 32mo. 1s. 6d. cloth. With Photographs, 32mo. 5s. Drawing-Room Edition, with Photographs, fcp. 8vo. 10s. 6d.

SHORT.—Sketch of the History of the Church of England to the Revolution of 1688. By T. V. SHORT, D.D. Crown 8vo. 7s. 6d.

SMITH (Gregory).—Fra Angelico, and other Short Poems. By GREGORY SMITH. Crown 8vo. 4s. 6d.

SMITH (R. Bosworth).—Carthage and the Carthagenians. By R. BOSWORTH SMITH, M.A. Maps, Plans, &c. Crown 8vo. 6s.

Sophocles. Translated into English Verse. By ROBERT WHITELAW, M.A. Assistant-Master in Rugby School ; late Fellow of Trinity College, Cambridge. Crown 8vo. 8s. 6d.

STANLEY.—A Familiar History of Birds. By E. STANLEY, D.D. With 160 Woodcuts. Crown 8vo. 3s. 6d.

STEEL (J. H.)—Works by.

A Treatise on the Diseases of the Dog ; being a Manual of Canine Pathology. Especially adapted for the Use of Veterinary Practitioners and Students. 88 Illustrations. 8vo. 10s. 6d.

A Treatise on the Diseases of the Ox ; being a Manual of Bovine Pathology specially adapted for the use of Veterinary Practitioners and Students. 2 Plates and 117 Woodcuts. 8vo. 15s.

A Treatise on the Diseases of the Sheep : being a Manual of Ovine Pathology. Especially adapted for the use of Veterinary Practitioners and Students. With Coloured Plate and 99 Woodcuts. 8vo. 12s.

STEPHEN. — Essays in Ecclesiastical Biography. By the Right Hon. Sir J. STEPHEN. Cr. 8vo. 7s. 6d.

STEPHENS.—A History of the French Revolution. By H. MORSE STEPHENS, Balliol College, Oxford. 3 vols. 8vo. Vol. I. 18s. *Ready. Vol. II. in the press.*

STEVENSON (Robt. Louis) —Works by.

A Child's Garden of Verses. Small fcp. 8vo. 5s.

The Dynamiter. Fcp. 8vo. 1s. swd. 1s. 6d. cloth.

Strange Case of Dr. Jekyll and Mr. Hyde. Fcp. 8vo. 1s. swd.; 1s. 6d. cloth.

STEVENSON and OSBOURNE.—The Wrong Box. By ROBERT LOUIS STEVENSON and LLOYD OSBOURNE. Crown 8vo. 5s.

STOCK.—Deductive Logic. By ST. GEORGE STOCK. Fcp. 8vo. 3s. 6d.

'STONEHENGE.'—The Dog in Health and Disease. By 'STONEHENGE.' With 84 Wood Engravings. Square crown 8vo. 7s. 6d.

STRONG and LOGEMAN.—Introduction to the Study of the History of Language. By HERBERT A. STRONG, M.A. LL.D.; WILLEM S. LOGEMAN; and BENJAMIN IDE WHEELER. 8vo. 10s. 6d.

SULLY (James)—Works by.

Outlines of Psychology, with Special Reference to the Theory of Education. 8vo. 12s. 6d.

The Teacher's Handbook of Psychology, on the Basis of 'Outlines of Psychology.' Cr. 8vo. 6s. 6d.

Supernatural Religion; an Inquiry into the Reality of Divine Revelation. 3 vols. 8vo. 36s.

Reply (A) to Dr. Lightfoot's Essays. By the Author of 'Supernatural Religion.' 1 vol. 8vo. 6s.

SWINBURNE.—Picture Logic; an Attempt to Popularise the Science of Reasoning. By A. J. SWINBURNE, B.A. Post 8vo. 5s.

SYMES.—Prelude to Modern History: being a Brief Sketch of the World's History from the Third to the Ninth Century. By J. E. SYMES, M.A. University College, Nottingham. With 5 Maps. Crown 8vo. 2s. 6d.

TAYLOR.—A Student's Manual of the History of India, from the Earliest Period to the Present Time. By Colonel MEADOWS TAYLOR, C.S.I. &c. Crown 8vo. 7s. 6d.

THOMPSON (D. Greenleaf)—Works by.

The Problem of Evil: an Introduction to the Practical Sciences. 8vo. 10s. 6d.

THOMPSON (D. Greenleaf)—Works by—continued.

A System of Psychology. 2 vols. 8vo. 36s.

The Religious Sentiments of the Human Mind. 8vo. 7s. 6d.

Social Progress: an Essay. 8vo. 7s. 6d.

The Philosophy of Fiction in Literature: an Essay. Cr. 8vo. 6s.

Three in Norway. By Two of THEM. With a Map and 59 Illustrations. Cr. 8vo. 2s. boards; 2s. 6d. cloth.

TOYNBEE.—Lectures on the Industrial Revolution of the 18th Century in England. By the late ARNOLD TOYNBEE, Tutor of Balliol College, Oxford. Together with a Short Memoir by B. JOWETT, Master of Balliol College, Oxford. 8vo. 10s. 6d.

TREVELYAN (Sir G. O. Bart.)—Works by.

The Life and Letters of Lord Macaulay.

POPULAR EDITION, 1 vol. cr. 8vo. 2s. 6d.
STUDENT'S EDITION, 1 vol. cr. 8vo. 6s.
CABINET EDITION, 2 vols. cr. 8vo. 12s.
LIBRARY EDITION, 2 vols. 8vo. 36s.

The Early History of Charles James Fox. Library Edition, 8vo. 18s. Cabinet Edition, crown 8vo. 6s.

TROLLOPE (Anthony).—Novels by.

The Warden. Crown 8vo. 1s. boards; 1s. 6d. cloth.

Barchester Towers. Crown 8vo. 1s. boards; 1s. 6d. cloth.

VILLE.—On Artificial Manures, their Chemical Selection and Scientific Application to Agriculture. By GEORGES VILLE. Translated and edited by W. CROOKES. With 31 Plates. 8vo. 21s.

VIRGIL.—Publi Vergili Maronis Bucolica, Georgica, Æneis; the Works of VIRGIL, Latin Text, with English Commentary and Index. By B. H. KENNEDY, D.D. Cr. 8vo. 10s. 6d.

The Æneid of Virgil. Translated into English Verse. By JOHN CONINGTON, M.A. Crown 8vo. 6s.

The Poems of Virgil. Translated into English Prose. By JOHN CONINGTON, M.A. Crown 8vo. 6s.

The Eclogues and Georgics of Virgil. Translated from the Latin by J. W. MACKAIL, M.A. Fellow of Balliol College, Oxford. Printed on Dutch Hand-made Paper. Royal 16mo. 5s.

WAKEMAN and HASSALL.—Essays Introductory to the Study of English Constitutional History. By Resident Members of the University of Oxford. Edited by HENRY OFFLEY WAKEMAN, M.A. Fellow of All Souls College, and ARTHUR HASSALL, M.A. Student of Christ Church. Crown 8vo. 6s.

WALKER.—The Correct Card; or How to Play at Whist; a Whist Catechism. By Major A. CAMPBELL-WALKER, F.R.G.S. Fcp. 8vo. 2s. 6d.

WALPOLE.—History of England from the Conclusion of the Great War in 1815 to 1858. By SPENCER WALPOLE. Library Edition. 5 vols. 8vo. £4. 10s. Cabinet Edition. 6 vols. crown 8vo. 6s. each.

WELLINGTON.—Life of the Duke of Wellington. By the Rev. G. R. GLEIG, M.A. Crown 8vo. 3s. 6d.

WELLS.—Recent Economic Changes and their Effect on the Production and Distribution of Wealth and the Well-being of Society. By DAVID A. WELLS, LL.D. D.C.L. late United States Special Commissioner of Revenue, &c. Crown 8vo. 10s. 6d.

WENDT.—Papers on Maritime Legislation, with a Translation of the German Mercantile Laws relating to Maritime Commerce. By ERNEST EMIL WENDT, D.C.L. Royal 8vo. £1. 11s. 6d.

WEST.—Lectures on the Diseases of Infancy and Childhood. By CHARLES WEST, M.D. 8vo. 18s.

WEYMAN.—The House of the Wolf: a Romance. By STANLEY J. WEYMAN. Crown 8vo. 6s.

WHATELY (E. Jane)—Works by.

English Synonyms. Edited by R. WHATELY, D.D. Fcp. 8vo. 3s.

Life and Correspondence of Richard Whately, D.D. late Archbishop of Dublin. With Portrait. Crown 8vo. 10s. 6d.

WHATELY (Archbishop)—Works by.

Elements of Logic. Cr. 8vo. 4s. 6d.

Elements of Rhetoric. Crown 8vo. 4s. 6d.

Lessons on Reasoning. Fcp. 8vo. 1s. 6d.

Bacon's Essays, with Annotations. 8vo. 10s. 6d.

WILCOCKS.—The Sea Fisherman. Comprising the Chief Methods of Hook and Line Fishing in the British and other Seas, and Remarks on Nets, Boats, and Boating. By J. C. WILCOCKS. Profusely Illustrated. Crown 8vo. 6s.

WILLICH.—Popular Tables for giving Information for ascertaining the value of Lifehold, Leasehold, and Church Property, the Public Funds, &c. By CHARLES M. WILLICH. Edited by H. BENCE JONES. Crown 8vo. 10s. 6d.

WILLOUGHBY.—East Africa and its Big Game. The Narrative of a Sporting Trip from Zanzibar to the Borders of the Masai. By Capt. Sir JOHN C. WILLOUGHBY, Bart. Illustrated by G. D. Giles and Mrs. Gordon Hake. Royal 8vo. 21s.

WITT (Prof.)—Works by. Translated by FRANCES YOUNGHUSBAND.

The Trojan War. Crown 8vo. 2s.

Myths of Hellas; or, Greek Tales. Crown 8vo. 3s. 6d.

WITT (Prof.)—Works by—*cont.*

The Wanderings of Ulysses. Crown 8vo. 3*s.* 6*d.*

The Retreat of the Ten Thousand; being the Story of Xenophon's 'Anabasis.' With Illustrations.

WOLFF.—Rambles in the Black Forest. By HENRY W. WOLFF. Crown 8vo. 7*s.* 6*d.*

WOOD (Rev. J. G.)—Works by.

Homes Without Hands; a Description of the Habitations of Animals, classed according to the Principle of Construction. With 140 Illustrations. 8vo. 10*s.* 6*d.*

Insects at Home; a Popular Account of British Insects, their Structure, Habits, and Transformations. With 700 Illustrations. 8vo. 10*s.* 6*d.*

Insects Abroad; a Popular Account of Foreign Insects, their Structure, Habits, and Transformations. With 600 Illustrations. 8vo. 10*s.* 6*d.*

Bible Animals; a Description of every Living Creature mentioned in the Scriptures. With 112 Illustrations. 8vo. 10*s.* 6*d.*

Strange Dwellings; a Description of the Habitations of Animals, abridged from 'Homes without Hands.' With 60 Illustrations. Crown 8vo. 3*s.* 6*d.*

Out of Doors; a Selection of Original Articles on Practical Natural History. With 11 Illustrations. Crown 8vo. 3*s.* 6*d.*

Petland Revisited. With 33 Illustrations. Crown 8vo. 3*s.* 6*d.*

The following books are extracted from the foregoing works by the Rev. J. G. WOOD :

Social Habitations and Parasitic Nests. With 18 Illustrations. Crown 8vo. 2*s.*

The Branch Builders. With 28 Illustrations. Crown 8vo. 2*s.* 6*d.*

Wild Animals of the Bible. With 29 Illustrations. Crown 8vo. 3*s.* 6*d.*

Domestic Animals of the Bible. With 23 Illustrations. Crown 8vo. 3*s.* 6*d.*

WOOD (Rev. J. G.)—Works by—*cont.*

Bird-Life of the Bible. With 32 Illustrations. Crown 8vo. 3*s.* 6*d.*

Wonderful Nests. With 30 Illustrations. Crown 8vo. 3*s.* 6*d.*

Homes under the Ground. With 28 Illustrations. Crown 8vo. 3*s.* 6*d.*

YOUATT (William)—Works by.

The Horse. Revised and enlarged. 8vo. Woodcuts, 7*s.* 6*d.*

The Dog. Revised and enlarged. 8vo. Woodcuts. 6*s.*

YOUNGHUSBAND (Frances)—Works by.

The Story of our Lord, told in Simple Language for Children. With 25 Illustrations on Wood from Pictures by the Old Masters. Crown 8vo. 2*s.* 6*d.*

The Story of Genesis. Crown 8vo. 2*s.* 6*d.*

ZELLER (Dr. E.)—Works by.

History of Eclecticism in Greek Philosophy. Translated by SARAH F. ALLEYNE. Crown 8vo. 10*s.* 6*d.*

The Stoics, Epicureans, and Sceptics. Translated by the Rev. O. J. REICHEL, M.A. Crown 8vo. 15*s.*

Socrates and the Socratic Schools. Translated by the Rev. O. J. REICHEL, M.A. Crown 8vo. 10*s.* 6*d.*

Plato and the Older Academy. Translated by SARAH F. ALLEYNE and ALFRED GOODWIN, B.A. Crown 8vo. 18*s.*

The Pre-Socratic Schools: a History of Greek Philosophy from the Earliest Period to the time of Socrates. Translated by SARAH F. ALLEYNE. 2 vols. crown 8vo. 30*s.*

Outlines of the History of Greek Philosophy. Translated by SARAH F. ALLEYNE and EVELYN ABBOTT. Crown 8vo. 10*s.* 6*d.*

1077724